DATE DUE

GAYLORD			PRINTED IN U.S.A.

DEVELOPMENTS IN SEMANTICS

EDITORS

ALEX ORENSTEIN   **RAPHAEL STERN**

Haven Publications, Inc.

Developments in Semantics
Eds. Orenstein and Stern
Vol 2 in the series
LANGUAGE AND LOGIC AND LINGUISTICS
Copyright © 1983 by Haven Publications.
Published in 1983.
Printed in the United States of America. All rights reserved.
Published by Haven Publishing Corporation.
G. P. O. Box 2046
New York, N. Y.

ISBN # 0-930586-13-1

Dedicated to
Henry Hiż

TABLE OF CONTENTS

Preface

I. Dispensing With Domains

II. Montague Frameworks

Several assumptions have been challenged in recent work on language. Some of these developments present alternatives to more standard, or classical, semantical systems. While the adjective "classical" has, of course, different senses, the classical approach to semantics, in the sense of philosophers and logicians, is derived from the work of Alfred Tarski. Tarski confined his attention to the artificial languages of logic, mathematics and to reconstructions of the exact sciences. More recently attempts have been made to adapt Tarski's semantics to the study of natural languages. Many of the essays in this collection question the Tarskian approach to the study of language. These challenges are quite diverse. Some non-classical approaches such as Henry Hiz's aletheic semantic theory and the substitutional approach to quantification dispense with the domains that are a central component of Tarskian semantics. Montague semanticists like Barbara Hall Partee revise the classical framework by appealing to multiple domains in the sense of possible worlds. The essays on conceptual role semantics are, to some extent, divided as to how to modify the Tarskian framework. The alternatives are either to supplement certain referential features of Tarskian semantics or to supplant reference with an account of role in a conceptual scheme. An even more basic Tarskian assumption is challenged by Hartry Field's paper where he provides a semantics that dispenses with the concept of truth and uses, instead, the subjective probability theorist's concept of certainty. In the section on computer models of language use Roger Schank, Wendy Lehnert and John Moyne question whether either Tarskian approaches or those of transformational grammarians are suitable for the study of certain features of language that concern them, and for which they propose computer models. In the remaining sections of the volume, other classical or standard theses about language are investigated. P. Stanley Peters and R. W. Ritchie raise a problem for certain "classical" Chomskian transformational theories. And in the last section Robert Fiengo and Thomas Sebeok assess recent evidence from the field of animal species communicate, and do so in some very subtle ways, only the human species has *language.*

Many of the papers in this volume were given at a conference, *Language and Psychotherapy,* held at Wagner College in April, 1977. The conference was sponsored by the Association for Philosophy of Science, Psychotherapy and Ethics. The intention of the conference was to study, as a preliminary step, grammatical and semantical properties of natural and formal languages and then use these findings to study linguistic aspects of psychotherapeutic theory and practice. The studies in this volume emphasize, on the whole, the grammatical and semantical properties of natural and formal languages. In planning the book the conference papers were supplemented by invited papers and section introductions.

We wish to thank Dr. John Satterfeld, the President of Wagner College, for his encouragement, his support to the Association, and his enlightened goodwill. Thanks are also due to Hugues Leblanc for suggestions and encouragement, to Raymond Gumb and K. D. Irani for several themes appearing in essays in the volume, to members of the Association who contributed essays and, often, considerable time, and the Graduate Center of the City University for help and encouragement.

PART I

DISPENSING WITH DOMAINS

INTRODUCTION

Our problem is to show just why we use truth and why we prefer denoting accounts of truth. Suppose, then, a language, L', and a method for providing a denoting account of truth. Let us call any function mapping the sentences of L' to (t, f) and assigning each sentence either a t or an f, an "evaluation function." One can define an evaluation function only once we have some way of defining truth. Add to the pot a set of stories about entities in the domain. Once we add the set of stories we can get a choice function on the set J of possible evaluation functions for, originally, if the language admitted sentence operators on the atomic sentences and if all we have is the capacity to define truth, then we could supply any number of evaluation functions, g_i, each providing a mapping from L' to (t, f). The stories about the domain cut down the number of plausible evaluation functions (for some purposes). A two-tuple (DEN, S) with *DEN* some denoting account of truth and *S* a set of stories, might provide a single evaluation function and this, in turn, enables us to order sentences.

Why can we order sentences? Suppose L' = (s, s'), suppose a definition of truth and a set of stories. We then determine a preferred evaluation function, g, such that $g(s) = t$ and $g(s') = f$, and suppose our arithmetic is such that we indicate we prefer t to f. This in turn, will allow us to say—s' $<$ s—with "$<$" reading "is weaker than."

But why do we want orderings of this sort? A language involves a set of sentences, true enough, but it is not merely an unordered heap of sentences; it also involves relations between sentences. What an account of truth plus our stories enable us to do is provide an ordering on the sentences.

But why, you ask, use a denoting account of truth? Would not another account do as well? It all depends. But with a denoting account we feel a bit reassured because an account of this sort enables us to justify the orderings. We feel it is not quite so arbitrary when we assign t to the sentence "John is near Mary" if we find that "John" denotes John, "Mary" denotes Mary and that they are indeed near one another. An account in terms of subjective probability functions cannot provide this kind of explanation, this sort of reassurance then. (I would also argue that, re. explanations of this sort, a denoting account is the sort of account we cannot duplicate using other notions.) Now if all of the above were the case, and there is some very good reason for assuming it is the case, we would have a strong reason for preferring denoting accounts of truth.

Granted that we would *like* to use denoting accounts of truth where do our problems enter? The class of stories and theories, and the denoting account itself, all give rise to paradoxes. These are the paradoxes of recursivity and the Lowenheim-Skolem paradox.

So on the one hand we would like to enjoy the benefits of an account of truth and on the other we are compelled to recognize the dangers. Theorists have had a number of misgivings about this sort of thing. They have proposed theories to cope with at least some of the difficulties and still retain the concept *truth* in some form. On occasion the argument is about the form in which truth is to be retained (Hiż and Martin argue about this). Hiż prefers truth, he just does not define it in order to avoid paradox and philosophical commitments which he assumes a denoting account of truth engender. Martin insists that the notion of truth that Hiż uses can be duplicated in non-translational systems that he, Martin, had constructed, and that Hiż's notion of truth is far too weak for constructing a semantical theory. Hiż replies that Martin's mistake has been to assume all along that there is just one sort of theory that qualifies as a semantic theory; Hiż feels there are many different sorts of theories. In his article here he reminds us that he developed a number of different theories, some stronger than others. Both Hiż and Martin seem to agree on minimizing ontic commitment but Hiż prefers to avoid reference to individuals entirely whereas Martin wishes to retain individuals but restrict their number (he wants to avoid non-denumerable domains).

This rather rough history accounts for a period stretching to about 1970. Around this time Hiż began, given the work of Smaby, to recognize shortcomings in his own work, in particular his theory of cross-reference. Thus at about this time Smaby began to articulate the formal machinery needed to develop a richer aletheic theory.

As we turn to the mid-1970's we find another development in semantics. Probabilistic semantics becomes more than just a faint hope. At this point Hartry Field suggests a form of weak-semantics that involves conditional probability functions on, for example, pairs of sentences. This would, assuming it works, give substance to Harman's notion that we need a theory of conceptual role. But Field does not stop here. He suggests that the structure of earlier semantical theories of natural languages were too simple. Rather than admitting just one theory (either weak- or strong-semantics) Field wants to combine a denoting semantics *and* a conceptual role semantics. With Field the structure of a semantical theory has become far more complex than earlier theorists anticipated.

Hiż, however, remained unconvinced that we needed a denoting account at all. In later discussions and seminars still other workers began to feel that the proper road to a modified aletheism (a semantics taking truth as a primitive) might involve some adaptation of Leblanc's formalisms to Hiż's earlier work (now used as model enabling us to select and adjust our formalisms in ways more responsive to the semantical requirements of a natural language.) In an essay in this section Stern espouses a semantical theory that contains three semantical subtheories. At the same time he suggests that the proper form of an aletheic theory would be far more complex than either Hiż, Martin or Field anticipate, necessitating a topological base, both truth and preference models in the weak-semantical part, and still other constructions involving insights from Field, Hiż and Leblanc. Thus pressure to retain truth and to avoid the paradoxes seems to force us to acknowledge a more complex semantical theory and a more complex form of aletheism.

Another instance of doing without denoting in semantics is provided in Orenstein's essay where he examines the role of referring accounts of truth in providing different interpretations of quantification. He raises questions about the place of referring relations in the substitutional interpretation of quantification and where they are present what types of word-object relations are involved.

There is another problem posed in essays in this section that ties in with questions raised by Partee, Bach and Teller in the section on Montague, and by Munz in the section on Field. This is the problem of whether accounts of the semantics of a natural language are symmetric with accounts of the grammar. Note that the Montague tradition demands a 1:1 relation between grammatical and semantical rules. Also notice Partee's description of the Montague position on grammar: The aim is to find a finitary device. This turns out to be an extended axiomatic system. When she turns to semantics we find a kind of isomorphism with the grammar (in part). There too we find an axiomatic structure. However, in the same section Teller raises questions about whether, in fact, there is a symmetry of the sort followers of Montague require and in this section Hiż suggests that one may give quite varied semantical accounts, *some* of which will by no means exhibit structures that are in any way (apparently) symmetric with those of the grammar. In the section on Field's work, James Munz holds that there is no clear data for attesting to one sort of logical structure on a language rather than another, and that the data that may be relevant and sufficient for entertaining one rather than another grammatical hypothesis is not sufficient for supporting one rather than another semantic hypothesis. Indeed asymmetries abound in Munz's account. In another passage he remarks that the structure of the grammar varies with the *intent* of the grammarian and that the amount and kind of meaning the grammar can attribute seems to vary so remorselessly that one can only conclude from this account that the grammar and semantics are *not* symmetric.

Whether explicitly or tacitly this problem (symmetry) crops up throughout the volume. On one side there is an enormous temptation, I suppose, to reason as follows: If we are constructing devices to generate all and only English sentences, and if persons are thought to generate sentences, the devices we propose should describe some sort of 'internal' mechanism available to persons (this frequently issues in a kind of developmental rationalism positing innate mechanisms and a search for comparable descriptive analogues in semantics). On the other side, however, one can question the grammarians assumption that he is doing a kind of psychology. Why not, then, merely assume one is providing a device for generating sentences? Why assume that the device must also, in some sense, provide an account of how persons operate when they produce sentences?

There are, then, at least two bents in the literature. One emphasizes the virtue of empiricizing the field and developing formal techniques which 'describe' reality or are close to the world. This is the realist side represented by Partee, Bach, Chomsky, and others. The nominalist prefers rather more abstract devices and constructions and where the devices are the same, a different attitude toward them, and divorces linguistics and semantics (in particular) from *strong* postulates to the effect that the devices describe the world. (We find, for example that the Montague semanticist typically adopts a very special kind of realist semantics with possible worlds taken quite literally. There is a symmetry in their treatment of grammar and semantics, whereas the nominalist thinks these are *just* devices without descriptive efficacy.) Thus there is no clear reason, some think, to assume that a semantics using possible "worlds" need, as well, utilize extralinguistic entities in the model (Hiż and Stern, for example, make no such assumption and yet a system of truth models should be able to give the very same account of modal expressions).

There is as much (current) evidence for the claim that semantics and grammar are asymmetric as there is for the claim that they are symmetric. On the assumption that they are asymmetric one would not use the Montague approach, at least in the form described. Whatever the outcome of this controversy, though, it is useful to see that, apart from the issue of classical vs. nonclassical, the realist/nominalist issue, prompted by symmetry postulates, is the single most "vocal" one in the collection. Virtually half the essayists are affected by it and take sides one way or another.

The hint above concerning possible world semantics using items of the world (a realist's approach) vs. that using linguistic entities, is rather interesting and suggests another characterization of the issue. Throughout one senses one possibility—that the linquist who has come of late to Montague semantics assumes that what *might* be construed as (simply) a computing device is *also* a potent tool for describing reality. Thus the Montaguist in this tradition tends to interpret possible worlds in a somewhat straightforward way in terms of entities, rather than, say, in terms of points on which we impose structures generating the models we need to do semantics. And the linguist qua Montaguist tends as well to interpret doing grammar very much as if he or she were doing psychology. Notice however that by extension of Hiż's views here, the nominalist using possible worlds would operate (in some fashion) with sufficient generality so that he or she is not committed to individuals (he might think of points and relations on points instead, but his apparatus would take on a more abstract cast). We might, then, put the problem about asymmetry in a rather different way so that the dispute between logicians (on the whole) doing semantics (those nominalists) and linguists (on the whole) doing semantics (the realists) is one between the level of abstraction and generality at which each finds it suitable and appropriate to operate. One, the nominalist, would prefer straightforward topological constructions for the semantics (talk of points and relations on points), and the linguist would prefer individuals and the whole baggage appropriate to giving him an empirical theory describing how persons operate. (Notice, in this respect, that Bach, when he claims that the linguist is not doing semantics when he maps languages onto languages, is firmly in the realist camp whereas Munz is ambiguous in this respect, on occasion showing nominalist sympathies, on occasion realist as when he wishes the linguist would swear off semantics because he is not doing the sort of thing the logician is doing and because when he *is* doing something it is so confusingly portrayed that it hardly seems worth the game.)

The difference, then, is in the level of abstraction one agrees to work at. The nominalist prefers a different, "higher" level of abstraction (talk of points rather than individuals in worlds). As a result his strategies for doing semantics and, in particular, science, are rather different. The nominalist's theories tend to involve constructions that are some "distance away" from the world, his theory is less "exposed" to the world. The realist, on the other hand, creates theories that are more exposed—realists tend to be a bit more empirically minded, more intent on constructing a science with a theory "touching" the world at more points.

There are virtues to both ways of proceeding. One wonders, however, where future researchers will place their faith, for each approach is different, representing bifurcations in the fundamental research tradition they share.

Raphael Stern

Henry Hiż

ALETHEIC SEMANTIC THEORY

The purpose of this paper is to outline the main points of a theory of semantics of natural languages which may prove useful in the study of the semantics of a particular natural language or of a part, a sublanguage, of a natural language. The envisaged theory is to explain the general methods and concepts which should be applicable in the semantics of various languages. The fundamentals of model theory for formalized languages, as it is known in mathematical logic, will be a particular case of the sketched semantic theory. The theory is rather simple, maybe even simple-minded. It minimizes philosophical involvement; its content is more neutral philosophically than is the case in other semantic theories. By this and, perhaps, by some other properties the presented theory should be more useful in establishing a scientific study of semantics and in discovering some non-trivial facts about the semantics of languages. It contrasts sharply with all attempts at semantics which use as fundamental the naming relation or denotation. Consequently, any "platonic" suggestion of a similarity between the structure of the world and the structure of the language will be avoided. More specifically, it does not try to construct semantical categories. (A semantical category is a relation between a syntactical category and an ontological category under which every member of the ontologicial category is referred to, or is named, or otherwise is mapped into by a member of the syntactical category.)

Such a similarity between a model and a formalized language is, as a rule, accepted by model theory (Robinson, 1963, pp. 9-11; Lyndon, 1966, pp. 13-15). In fact, the models are constructed so as to reflect the structure of the language. For a variable, one may substitute any phrase of the same grammatical category as the grammatical category of the variable and the range of the variable consists exactly of entities from the model which are named by phrases of that grammatical category. Thus, in

$$\Lambda f \Lambda x \Lambda y [f(xy) \supset Vg[g(yx)]]$$

for 'f' a two-place relation symbol can be substituted, e.g., '$<$' which names the relation of being smaller than and for 'x' and 'y' numerals are substitutable which are names of numbers if the considered model is a structure of natural numbers and their relations. To the syntactical category of numerals corresponds the category of natural numbers (constant numerals name natural numbers) and to the syntactical category of two-place relation symbols—the model category of binary relations. A model is a structure composed of a set and relations between the members of the set, unary, binary, ternary, etc., relations as well as, perhaps, relations between those relations, etc. Philosophically, those structures may be put in doubt, the traditional doubt about the supposed nature of mathematical entities. But they have proved to be a very successful instrument of study. The crucial theorems of the semantics of mathematics are stated and proved by referring to such structures, e.g., the famous Malcev-Gödel-Henkin theorem that every consistent set of sentences has a model, or the Lövenheim-Skolem theorem that if a set of sentences has a model, it has a model in natural numbers, or the Vaught-Łos' theorem that a consistent system which has no finite models and is categorical in an infinite power, is complete.

There are many intrinsic reasons why the study of the semantics of a natural language cannot take a course similar to the semantics of formalized languages. The construction of models needed here will be much more involved. The subtle classification of phrases would have to be reflected in a similar classification of entities. We would multiply the kinds of entities in the model much beyond the transparency of models considered by a mathematical logician. There is no reason at all to think that structures based on a single set of objects will suffice. On the contrary there are serious indications that the grammar of a language cannot be reduced to a single category of entity-phrases and relational phrases among them. Moreover, there seems to be no reason to think that a good account of grammar can be given just by assigning to consecutive phrases of a sentence grammatical categories. This would correspond to a phrase structure grammar and much has been said recently about short-comings of such grammars. Again, the grammatical distinctions are often semantically artificial or relics of views on ontology from previous times. The distinction between verbs of different conjugations in Latin does not seem to have any semantic ontological ground. That the distinction between the so-called animate and inanimate nouns in Slavic languages corresponds to a distinction between natural classes in the world is hard to uphold (*mushroom, dollar, gingerbread* and *cadaver* are animate). These distinctions, required by grammar, are not felt by the native speaker as semantically significant. There seems to be no reason to suppose that there is a parallelism between the syntactical and the semantical distinctive features. Also, the distinctions which different languages make are so apart from each other that it does not seem reasonable to present a unified treatment of all of them.

Instead of making structures and taking them as models, one may start with sets of sentences considered to be true. Those sets may be inconsistent with each other but each must be consistent internally; no two contradictory sentences should belong to the same set. The sets are called 'truth models'. Some truth models may be maximally consistent sets of sentences, i.e., such sets which cannot be augmented without rendering them inconsistent. A truth model may be thought of as a set of sentences one believes to be true, or a set of sentences, each two of which are paraphrases of each other, or a set of sentences which must be accepted as the content of a mythology. (E.g., in Greek mythology *Zeus was often angry* is generally accepted.) Or a truth model may be an infinite set of sentences of a book. This set is infinite, for it is composed of sentences actually printed and sentences "read between lines," tacit assumptions, consequences, paraphrases of the text, all the sentences needed to understand the text. It may be that sometimes it is more convenient to take as truth models sets not of sentences but also of longer texts, i.e., strings of sentences. The essential point here is that a member of a truth model should be in principle true or false, should be evaluable with respect to truth. Some declarative sentences are not true or false when taken alone, out of their context. *The second person was late* is an English sentence but one cannot reasonably ask about its truth or falsity. The sentence contains a referential *the second person,* "un renvoi" to a previous sentence and before the reference is resolved it is not proper to ask whether the sentence *The second person was late* is true or not. What kind of sentences or strings of sentences may be members of truth models should, of course, be discussed with greater care.

Somebody might try to allow only simple sentences as members of truth models, sentences which are either sentences of the kernel of the language or are based on a single kernel sentence augmented by modifiers which themselves do not come from other sentences. If Harris' program of developing all sentences of a language from such simple sentences via transformations is plausible, one might then say that some simple sentences are in a truth model Γ, other simple sentences are not in Γ, and then one could state that if a sentence α is obtained by a paraphrastic transformation from a sentence β, then α is in the truth extension, ext (Γ), if β is in ext (Γ) provided that Γ is included in ext (Γ). If, on the other hand, α is obtained from β and γ by a non-paraphrastic, binary transformation, one has to state under what conditions on β and on γ α is in ext (Γ). For instance if α is: nominalization (β) *prevents* nominalization (γ) (as in *John's illness prevents my vacation*), then α is in ext (Γ) if and only if not both β and γ are in ext (Γ).

Whether such a program is really sound and plausible is doubtful or, to say the least, is unknown with our present state of knowledge about natural languages. This problem for a natural language is substantially different from the same method applied to the languages of mathematics. For the languages of mathematics the sentential connectives were chosen in such a way that the truth value of their result depended on truth values of their components. But for a natural language it is rarely so. For instance, the above example with *prevents* seems for that reason to be wrong. It is not correct that if not both β and γ are true, then nominalization (β) *prevents* nominalization (γ) is true. Only the converse seems correct: if nominalization (β) *prevents* nominalization (γ) is true, then not both β and γ are true. For these and other reasons I will not pursue the reductionist line, though in some future stage of the development of grammar we may be ready to return to this tempting idea.

To state the starting point of the semantic theory in all generality, consider that there is a language M. M does not have to be the language L which is under study. M may be a sublanguage of L (as in the Harris-like attempt in the preceding paragraph) or it may be a completely different language. A set Γ_i of sentences or texts (i.e., strings of sentences) in M is a truth model in M if and only if there is an operation 0_i on sentences of M and resulting in sentences of M (or from texts in M to texts in M) such that for every α in Γ_i, $0_i(\alpha)$ is in M or $\alpha = 0_i(\beta)$ where β is in M and for no α both α and $0_i(\alpha)$ are in Γ_i.

Thus 0_i is a sort of negation, a negation appropriate to this particular Γ_i. Γ_i is a set consistent with respect to the negation 0_i. We can take different operations 0_i and 0_j for the different Γ_i and Γ_j. A negation *by no means* is usable for some subsets of English but not for all kinds of English. It may happen that we will find one negation for all sublanguages of M. Of course it is not excluded that we will form one operation of negation which takes different forms when applied to different kinds of sentences. (In English *He did not open the door* is the flat negation of *He opened the door,* as well as *The way he opened the door was not sudden* is the flat negation of *He opened the door suddenly.* We can treat those sentences as related by the same flat negation, though realized in each case differently. Whether we find an ingenious common formula or define the flat negation by cases, or even not define it at all, does not matter for our considerations here, provided that we assume that for each truth model there is a proper negation having the stated properties and that, presumably, for many truth models there is a similar negation.) The properties we require from a negation are that the truth model be consistent with respect to that negation and that, for each sentence (or for each reading of an ambiguous sentence) in the truth model, either its negation or its affirmation be present in the language M. About the negation, we do not assume that it is iterative. English distinguishes sharply between affirmative and negative sentences and does not allow negation to be reapplied. (Again, as before, we can use a more general concept of negation according to which the negation of a negative sentence is its affirmative.)

In order for the semantic theory to apply to natural languages some linguistic universals must hold. In any language there should be sentences. There should be also true sentences. And there should be an operation of negation. These linguistic universals are much more plausible than those which would be required had we followed construction of models out of individual objects rather than construction of truth models by sentences.

The concept of truth which is here fundamental receives a twist which may look "relativistic." There are many truth models, and a sentence may be a member of one and not of another of them; another truth model may contain its negation. This is a very natural schema for the study of a natural language in which the "truth" of a fairy tale must be taken equally seriously as a report of a chemistry laboratory. The set of all true sentences of a language is neither very natural, therefore, nor desirable. It is not desirable (Tarski 1956) because it may lead to well-known semantic antinomies.[1]

A truth model may be finite, may be denumerably infinite, may be empty. Consideration of non-denumerably infinite truth models may be introduced but it does not seem necessary. If M is the language of atomic sentences of the kind considered in the first order functional calculus and of their negations and L the language of all sentences composed from M by logical constants and quantifiers, then a standard model theory could proceed smoothly from this point on without asking why the atomic sentences are true. The only difficulty which might arise could be in trying to deal with non-denumerably infinite models, like a model based on real numbers while there is only denumerably many sentences.

Truth being the basic primitive term of the semantic theory, the spirit with which the theory is built may be called *aletheism* from $\alpha'\lambda\eta\theta\epsilon\iota\alpha$, truth. Aletheism may be also a philosophical point of view, according to which we know first of all that some sentences are true or we know the content of some true sentences; the knowledge of objects, relations, properties is a secondary construction on the bases of known true sentences. And aletheic philosophy may be an epistemic hypothesis or may be a methodological device of organization of our knowledge.

Now we can introduce some further semantical concepts, first the concept of interpretation. A phrase α interprets in the truth model Γ_i a phrase γ in a sentence (or a text) β if and only if replacement of γ by α in β results in a sentence which is in Γ_i. We also will say that α interprets β at the place γ. Thus the phrase *Isaac Newton* interprets in the truth model of ordinary high school history the phrase *John* in *John never married* because the sentence *Isaac Newton never married* appears in high school history. The definition will be presently slightly generalized but first a restriction must be added. The sentence *Granite is a rock and no rock is an animal* is true and *A horse is an animal* is a sentence. The definition as stated would allow us to conclude that the phrase *Granite is a rock and no rock* interprets the phrase *a horse* in the sentence *A horse is an animal*. But this would go too far. It would allow interpretation to destroy completely grammatical structures. Such a loose concept would presumably be useless. We want the interpreting phrase and the phrase being interpreted to be of the same grammatical category (abbreviated 'g.c.'). If $\beta_1 \, \alpha \, \beta_2$ is the interpretation, i.e., the result of α interpreting γ in $\beta_1 \, \gamma \, \beta_2$, then β_1 is supposed to be in the same g.c. in both sentences. And so is β_2. Then α must be of the same g.c. in $\beta_1 \, \alpha \, \beta_2$ as γ in $\beta_1 \, \gamma \, \beta_2$.

We will also say that a sequence of phrases interprets a sentence, so that we can say that the sequence *Isaac Newton, married* interprets *John never flunked an examination*. For that purpose we assign the segmentation *(John) never (flunked an examination)* and attribute—which is most natural—the same g.c. to *John* as to *Isaac Newton,* namely the category of names and the same category to *flunked an examination* as to *married*, namely the category of verb phrases. The relation of interpretation occurs between sequences of phrases and sentences segmented and with grammatical categories assigned to the segments.

Here are a few examples of sequences which interpret sentences. We mark by γ_1, γ_2, ..., γ_n the places at which we will interpret a sentence and by $\beta_1, \beta_2, ..., \beta_{n+1}$ the places which are not changed by the interpretation. The sequence (which single term) $<$ *the Odyssey* $>$ interprets the sentence $\underbrace{Homer\ composed}_{\beta_1}$

$\underbrace{the\ Iliad}_{\gamma_1}$ since the result of replacing *the Iliad* by *the Odyssey* is a true sentence, and the g.c.s. of the replaced and replacing phrases are identical. The sequence $<$*Homer, composed, the Odyssey*$>$ does not interpret $\underbrace{Homer}_{\beta_1}\ \underbrace{wrote}_{\gamma_1}\ \underbrace{Hamlet}_{\gamma_2}$ since we want

the substitution to be such that the first term in the sequence of the proper g.c. replaces each term given by a γ_i in the representation. Thus we would have $\underbrace{Homer}_{\beta_1}\ \underbrace{composed}_{\alpha_2}\ \underbrace{Homer}_{\alpha_1}$ which is

presumably false. However $<$*Homer, composed, the Odyssey*$>$ does interpret $\underbrace{Homer}_{\gamma_1}\ \underbrace{wrote}_{\gamma_2}\ \underbrace{Hamlet}_{\gamma_3}$ with a different assignment

of the γ_i to the sentence. This gives $\underbrace{Homer}_{\alpha_1}\ \underbrace{composed}_{\alpha_2}\ \underbrace{the\ Odyssey}_{\alpha_3}$

which is according to our stipulation that different γ_i's of the same g.c. be replaced by different α_j with the first appropriate α_j in $<\alpha_1, \alpha_2, \ldots>$ being chosen.

Next we give a formal definition of the notion of interpretation.

An infinite sequence $\sigma = <\alpha_1, \alpha_2, \ldots>$ of phrases interprets in Γ_k the sentence δ which has the grouping $\delta = \beta_1 \gamma_1 \beta_2 \gamma_2 \ldots \beta_n \gamma_n \beta_{n+1}$ if and only if there is a ψ in Γ_k which is like δ except for having some members of σ in place of $\gamma_1, \ldots, \gamma_n$ under some assignment A which assigns phrases from σ to occurrences $\gamma_1, \ldots, \gamma_n$ in δ in such a way that if $\alpha_j = A(\gamma_i)$, then the g.c. of α_j in ψ is the same as the g.c. of γ_i in δ, and if γ_k and γ_m are two occurrences of the same phrase and of the same g.c. in α, then $A(\gamma_k) = A(\gamma_m)$. In other words, if the assignment A replaces some phrases of a sentence by other phrases preserving g.c.s and if result is true, then a sequence containing the other phrases at their respective places interprets the sentence. The formal definition must deal with the bookkeeping of the assignment A.

An infinite sequence σ of phrases jointly interprets in Γ_k a set Δ of sentences of L if and only if σ interprets in Γ_k each sentence of Δ under the same assignment A.

Though interpretation is a semantical concept, as it uses truth in its definiens, it is a relation between sequences of phrases and sentences. This contrasts with the concept of satisfaction which Tarski introduced and which is a relation between a sequence of objects and a sentential function. Interpretation has on both sides linguistic entities, sequences of phrases and their grammatical specifications. Satisfaction has as its first argument a sequence of non-linguistic entities. So that, e.g., a sequence that starts with Isaac Newton (not with 'Isaac Newton') satisfies the function 'x was a bachelor' but a sequence that starts with 'Isaac Newton' (not with Isaac Newton himself) interprets the sentence 'John is a bachelor'.

Where there is no danger of confusion, one can say that a phrase or a pair of phrases (a triple of phrases, etc.) interprets in Γ_k a sentence at a particular place (or places) instead of saying that an infinite sequence with these phrases at proper positions interprets in Γ_k the sentence with a given segmentation. E.g., one can simply say, as I did before introducing the formal definition, that *the Odyssey* interprets in the history of literature *Homer composed the Iliad* at the occurrence of *the Iliad*.

It was said above that the aletheic semantics based on truth models can be applied to the standard treatments of model theory in the foundations of mathematics, so that most of the standard model theory becomes, *mutatis mutandis,* a particular case of the aletheic semantic theory. To show how to overcome the difficulty with non-denumerable models (say a model with real numbers) consider a sentence 'a $<$ 5' which is interpretable by '$\sqrt{2}$' in place of 'a'.

We will use the main idea of a Dedekind cut and express it in terms of interpretations. The fundamental change is that instead of speaking of a sequence interpreting a sentence we will speak, more generally, about a set of sequences interpreting a sentence (or jointly interpreting a set of sentences). Now, instead of saying that '$\sqrt{2}$' interprets in the theory of real numbers the sentence 'a $<$ 5', we will say that a set of rational numerals (more exactly a set of sequences of rational numerals) interprets in the arithmetic of rationals the sentence 'a $<$ 5' at the occurrence of 'a'. Thus, we may, first, define the set of rational numerals which is a suitable synonym for the real numeral '$\sqrt{2}$':

A phrase α is in the set $\Delta_{\sqrt{2}}$ of rational numerals if and only if α interprets in the arithmetic of rationals the sentence 'b^2 $<$ 2' at the occurrence of 'b'.

Now $\Delta_{\sqrt{2}}$ interprets in the arithmetic of rationals the sentence 'a $<$ 5' at the place of 'a', if and only if every phrase in $\Delta_{\sqrt{2}}$ interprets in the arithmetic of rationals this sentence at this place.

Returning now to the discussion of the general case including natural languages let us consider those truth models which contain with every sentence (or text) all its paraphrases. These are truth models closed with respect to paraphrase (concerning paraphrase see Bellert and Hiż, 1965; also Hiż, 1964).

Whether two texts are in the relation of paraphrase to each other is to some extent empirically testable. If a truth model Γ_k is maximal (maximally consistent with respect to the chosen negation), then we will mark it: Γ_k^{max}. If, in addition, it is closed with respect to paraphrase we will mark it: $\Gamma_k^{par,\,max}$.

The concept of paraphrase could perhaps be defined by the concept of consequence. Namely, paraphrase is consequence both ways; two texts are paraphrases of each other just when either of them is a consequence of the other. It is generally accepted, after Tarski, that α is a consequence of β if and only if every model of α is also a model of β. Therefore, α is a paraphrase of β if and only if, for every Γ_k^{max}, α is in Γ_k^{max} if and only if β is in Γ_k^{max}. It is much easier to test empirically paraphrases than consequences. Linguists often hesitate to enter work on consequences. But it seems that one can attempt also to define the concept of consequence by means of the concept of paraphrase. At least for English the following is a fair hypothesis that relates the concept of consequence to that of paraphrase.

α *is a consequence of* β *if and only if either* α *is a paraphrase of* β *or else there is a* γ *such that* $\alpha \cdot \gamma$ *is a paraphrase of* β.

Here '$\cdot$' is a period between sentences (or an intonational pattern associated with it). *John arrived* is a consequence of *I was surprised that John arrived*. Now *I was surprised that John arrived* is a paraphrase of *John arrived. I was surprised by that.* Therefore *John arrived* is a consequence of *I was surprised that John arrived*. Similarly, *The train ran fast* has as its consequence the sentence *The train ran* because it has as its paraphrase the text *The train ran. It ran fast.* There are, however, some cases in English which speak against the suggested hypothesis. For instance, cases where α in $\alpha \cdot \gamma$ contains an epiphoric (anticipatory) referential to an occurrence of a phrase in γ. Examples are: *Here is what John did* where *here* refers to the succeeding text. Similarly, *The following was what happened*. The text *Here is what John did. He broke the window* is a paraphrase of *John broke the window*. But *Here is what John did* is not a consequence of anything. So we should require that α in our hypothesis should not contain epiphoric referentials which refer to referends outside α itself, or that all the referentials in α be to referends within α (Hiż 1968, 1969).

It is natural to consider in practice only truth models which are closed with respect to paraphrase. For we want to say that either all paraphrases are true together or all are false together, so either all or none should occur in a truth model. Indeed, paraphrases within Γ_k are sentences (or texts) that are interpreted in Γ_k by exactly the same sequences of phrases. Now if a truth model Γ_k is closed with respect to the rule $\alpha \cdot \beta \rightarrow \alpha$, i.e., any time it contains $\alpha \cdot \beta$, then it contains α, provided that α does not have referentials to referends inside β; then we say that Γ_k is closed with respect to consequence, symbolically: Γ_k^{con}.

The following theorem of semantics is fundamental:

If a maximally consistent truth model $\Gamma_k^{par, \, con, \, max}$ is closed with respect to paraphrase and with respect to consequence, then α is a consequence of γ if and only if every sequence which interprets in $\Gamma_k^{par, \, con, max}$ the text γ interprets the text α in the same truth model under the same assignment A.

We can define the meaning of a phrase in a way which leads to desirable conclusions. One of the useful features of the definition will be that the meaning of a sentence or of a text will be defined in the same way as the meaning of any shorter phrase (of some g.c.). Next, the meaning of a sentence or of a text will be the set of its consequences. Furthermore, the meaning of $\alpha \, \beta$ will be a product (in a natural sense explained below) of the meaning of α and the meaning of β. Also, synonymity will be the equality of meanings. These are suitable criteria for an intuitively adequate definition of meaning.

The definition of the meaning of a phrase will be relativized to a truth model. Had we not made this restriction we could easily reconstruct some semantical antinomies, e.g., the Richard's antinomy. The meaning in $\Gamma_k^{par, \, con, \, max}$ of a phrase α as it appears in the text $\beta = \gamma \alpha \delta$ is the set $\Delta_k^{par, \, con}$ which has exactly all the texts $\vartheta \alpha \eta$ of $\Gamma_k^{par, \, con, \, max}$ in which α occurs in the same g.c. as in β and ϑ and η occur in the same g.c.s as γ and δ respectively in β, and such that $\Delta_k^{par, con}$ is closed with respect to paraphase and consequence (γ or δ may be empty). Thus, in a maximal truth model closed with respect to paraphrase and with respect to consequence, the meaning of an occurrence of a phrase in a text is the subset of the model which is the set of texts in which that phrase occurs in the same g.c. and in the environments of the same g.c.s as in the text, provided that the subset is closed with respect to paraphrase and consequence. A moment's reflection suffices to see that the stated criteria for adequacy of the definition of meaning are satisfied by the proposed definition. If α is a sentence, take γ and δ to be empty and the meaning of α coincides with the set of all consequences (including paraphrases) of α which are in Γ. If Δ is the meaning of α as it appears in β and Δ' is the meaning of γ as it appears in β and Δ'' is the meaning of $\alpha \gamma$ as it appears in β, then every member of Δ' is of the form $\delta \alpha \gamma \vartheta$ where δ occurs to the left of α in a member of Δ and ϑ occurs to the right of γ in the same text as a member of Δ'. Thus $\Delta'' =$ the common part of Δ and Δ'. As to synonyms, it is better to consider them relative to a set consisting of a paraphrase set and its consequences rather than absolutely to the entire language. Whether two phrases are mutually replaceable anywhere in the language is very hard to test. Moreover, we do want to say that *bachelor* and *unmarried man* are synonyms within some large paraphrastic set but not for a text in which *bachelor of arts* occurs. To ask for unrestricted synonymy is to make the concept of synonymy useless. Two phrases are synonymous within a set if either of them can be replaced by the other with the result being still in the set. So the meanings of two synonyms will be here exactly the same. The meaning in Γ of a phrase α as it occurs in β is a set Δ of sentences. If in a member γ of Δ one replaces α by its synonym δ, one obtains a paraphrase of γ. But Δ is closed with respect to paraphrase so the paraphrase of γ is still in Δ. Thus the meanings relative to Γ of the synonyms are the same.

Members of a paraphrase set are different wordings of the same meaning. However, each wording of the same meaning gives to the meaning a different slant. The distinction between the meaning of a text and a slant of the meaning of the text consists in that the meaning is a set of texts, an unordered, an unstructured set of texts, while a slant of the meaning is a highly structured set of the same texts. The slant of the meaning of a text starts with that text and lists other wordings of the same meaning and their consequences and states how they are formally related to the starting text. They are related by various rules of paraphrase and rules of consequence. A slant of the meaning is a class of derivations of the members of the meaning, each one with rules by which it is derived from a particular wording.

Newton wrote Principia and *It was Newton who wrote Principia* are paraphrases of each other and therefore have the same meaning. In the meaning of each of them is the other, as well as, e.g., *Principia was what Newton wrote*. Now the slant of the meaning given by *Newton wrote Principia* can be shown in the following sketchy way:

1. *Newton wrote Principia*
   From 1, by *it* extraposition from the subject:
2. *It was Newton who wrote Principia*

From 1, by extraposition of the object:

3. *Principia was what Newton wrote*

   From 2, by permutation with a classifier instead of *it:*

4. *Newton was the man who wrote Principia*

   etc.

A slant given to a meaning by a particular wording of that meaning is an alternating sequence. The first entry of the sequence is that wording and any odd entry is a text. Any even entry is a statement of how to use a rule of paraphrase or of consequence to obtain the next text from previous ones.

a1. *It was Newton who wrote Principia*

   From a1, by resettlement of the subject:

a2. *Newton wrote Principia*

   From a1, by permutation with a classifier instead of *it:*

a3. *Newton was the man who wrote Principia*

   From a2, by extraposition from the object:

a4. *Principia was what Newton wrote*

   From a2, by *it* extraposition from the object:

a5. *It was Principia that Newton wrote*

   From a2, by referential division:

a6. *Newton wrote something. It was Principia*

   From a6, by the rule of consequence $\alpha \cdot \beta \to \alpha$:

a7. *Newton wrote something.*

It is actually the slants given to a meaning by a text which are one of the main centers of interest of many grammarians. One may ask many intriguing questions about slants of meanings. First, some derivations differ only in a nonessential way. For instance in the derivation from 1 we could have first derived 4 and later 3. Or in the derivation from a1 we could have derived a6 just after a2. Some derivations, and therefore some slants of meanings, are therefore equivalent and could be identified with each other. This identification may go further than such change of relative positions of independent parts of the derivations. For instance, one may derive a6, not from a2 by the referential division, but from a5 by a rule which allows in such cases permutation with an insertion of an indefinite pronoun. Which derivations are better, more elegant, shorter, simpler, which way of deriving will require fewer rules for the grammar or fewer grammatical rules of a particular kind? E.g., is the rule $\alpha \cdot \beta \to \alpha$ sufficient as the only rule of consequence which is not paraphrastic? Can there be a standard direction of deriving the first few steps in the slant so as to obtain a "decomposition" of the text which will completely determine all further derivations? In such a case there would be no point in making those further derivations and the slant of a meaning can be identified with the decomposition. Finally, could we find a general measure of kinds of differences between slants of meanings? Is the difference of slant given by a1 and that given by 1 to the same meaning completely exhibited by the derivation of a2 from a1 and the fact that a2=1?

We may be tempted to say that the difference between slants given to a meaning by two different wordings is the sequence of statements of how to apply rules to derive one wording from the other.

1. Note that Tarski suggested the possibility of a system of semantics to be based on truth as a primitive concept.

REFERENCES

Bellert, I. and Hiż, H. 1965. Paraphrastic sets and grammatical analysis. In *Transformations and discourse analysis papers #59*: Philadelphia.

Hiż, H. 1964. The role of paraphrase in grammar. *Monograph series on language and linguistics #17*.

. . . . .1968. Referentials. *Transformations and discourse analysis papers #76*. Philadelphia.

. . . . .1969. Referentials. *Semiotica* 1.

Lyndon, R. 1966. *Notes on logic:* Princeton.

Robinson, A. 1963. *Introduction to model theory and to the metamathematics of algebra*. Amsterdam: North Holland.

Tarski, A. 1956. *Logic, semantics, metamathematics*. Oxford: Clarendon.

NON-STANDARD SEMANTICS: TWO ESSAYS
BY RICHARD MARTIN*

Richard Martin

Non-Standard Semantics**

ON HIZ'S ALETHIC SEMANTICS AND NON-TRANSLATIONALITY

Most semantical metalanguages contain the object language as a part, either directly or at least in translation. Hence metalanguages of this kind can be conveniently referred to as *translational.* The Tarski metalanguages, those of Carnap, those of model theorists, and those of the foregoing essays, all share this one crucial feature. In a paper presented at the International Congress in 1953, and later incorporated and expanded in *Truth and Denotation* (Chapters 8, 9 and 13), a sketch of a semantical metalanguage was presented that lacked this crucial feature. Such metalanguages are *non-translational.* In non-translational semantics something is sacrificed no doubt, but much less than might appear. Non-translational semantics can be made surprisingly powerful and in fact can do pretty much everything one wants a semantics to do.

In an important recent paper Hiż has sketched what he calls an "aletheic semantic theory" that is non-translational in character (Hiż 1969). Hiż develops the theory as primarily applicable to natural languages as object languages whereas the object languages of the 1953 paper were applied first-order language systems. The core semantical primitive for Hiż is presumably the semantical truth predicate itself applicable to

---

*The following two essays are reprinted from Events, Reference and Logical Form, published by the Catholic University Press. Copyright for these articles belongs to the Catholic University Press and we are grateful to them for permission rights

**Martin's papers are consecutive chapters in a single work and constitute a unified body of criticism.

sentences, whereas that of the 1953 paper was a relational predicate for *comprehension* as a relation between one-place predicate constants. Finally, Hiż assumes by way of logical substructure all manner of sets, classes, and relations as provided by a suitable set or type theory, whereas the semantics of the 1953 paper was itself formalized as a first-order system without using such powerful additional devices.

The point of the present paper is to show that what Hiż purports to achieve in his aletheic theory can apparently be achieved equally well in the much simpler kind of theory of the 1953 paper. In addition some philosophical comments are given concerning both the details and general character of Hiż's semantics.

"Truth [or rather, a predicate for it (?)] being the basic primitive term of the semantic theory, the spirit with which the theory is built may be called *aletheism* from $\alpha\lambda\acute{\eta}\theta\epsilon\iota\alpha$, truth," Hiż notes (p. 443). More particularly, of course, his is a nontranslational aletheic theory. Translational metalanguages may also be aletheic. There is nothing sacrosanct about taking the truth predicate as a primitive, however, the crucial feature of Hiż's, theory being its non-translationality. The predicate for truth is easily definable in terms of 'Cmprh' for comprehension, and conversely. And there are of course other possible primitives to consider here also.

In taking a truth-predicate as a primitive one must have tagging along with it the notion of being a *sentence* of the object language, the truth predicate being applicable to sentences and sentences only. Thus Hiż's theory is syntactically very strong. Let "Sent a" as above express that a is a sentence of the object language, which for Hiż is a natural language. "Sent" or some equivalent must then be taken as a primitive, no satisfactory definition of it for a natural language having ever been given. In fact, much of linguistics may be described as being devoted to gaining a satisfactory definition of this notion for given languages. Hiż's employment of "Sent" as a primitive is thus very bold, a kind of theft, as it were.

If "Cmprh" for comprehension is taken as a primitive in place of the truth predicate, no theft is required. "Cmprh" has as its arguments one-place predicates and only such, and hence the notion 'Sent' need not be presupposed. Thus 'Cmprh' actually seems more appropriate than the truth predicate when the object language is a natural language, provided one has available for it a general notion of *one-place predicate*. But such a notion is much simpler than that of being a sentence and presumably more readily available for natural languages.

Hiż makes much of the notion of a *truth model.* "A truth model may be thought of as a set of sentences one believes to be true, or a set of sentences each two of which are paraphrases of each other, or a set of sentences which must be accepted as the content of a mythology. . . . Or a truth model may be an infinite set of sentences of a book." In any case "no two contradictory sentences should belong to the same set." The notion of a truth model is thus relative to a notion of *negation* in terms of which 'contradictory' is to be construed.

More precisely, Hiż states that a "set Γ_i of sentences . . .in [language or sub-language] M is a truth model in M if and only if there is an operation O_i on sentences of M and resulting in sentences of M. . . such that for every α in Γ_i, $O_i(\alpha)$ is in M or $\alpha = O_i(\beta)$ where β is in M, and for no α both α and $O_i(\alpha)$ are in Γ_i;" the O_i being "the sort of negation appropriate to this particular Γ_i." Is this sentence intended to provide a definition of "truth model in M [relative to O_i]"? It seems so. Yet note that the truth predicate does not occur explicitly in the definiens. The notion of a truth model seems, as thus defined, quite independent of the semantical notion of truth. The notion of a truth model, as thus defined, is in fact merely a notion of syntax.

"The concept of truth which is here fundamental receives a twist which may look 'relativistic,'" Hiż writes, "There are many truth models, and a sentence may be a member of one and not of another of them; another truth model may contain its negation." The question arises as to what notion of truth is being referred to here. If none is referred to in the definiens of the definition of "truth model," it is not clear that any concept of truth at all is being employed, whether as "fundamental" or "derivative," "relativistic" or not.

It might be replied that a semantic notion of truth is needed to characterize the negation O_i. "The essential point . . . is that a member of a truth model should be in principle true or false, should be evaluable with respect to truth." Hiz does not explain, however, how negation is supposed to be related to truth and falsehood. Is any O_i such that, for any α, either α is true or $O_i(\alpha)$ is true? Also, for any O_i and any α, it is not the case that both α and $O_i(\alpha)$ are true? In any event, Hiż's definition of "truth model" as it stands seems inadequate and needs supplementation. There may be many truth models, but a sentence α cannot, it would seem, be a member of one Γ_i and $O_i(\alpha)$ a member of another Γ_j. Of course $O_j(\alpha)$ might be a member of Γ_j, but this is a very different matter.

Another point is that a given set of sentences Γ_i might be inconsistent even if no sentence together with its negation occurs therein explicitly. Thus much spelling out of the theory of negation and of contradiction seems needed for Hiż's account to work.

Further, it is by no means clear that the notion of a truth model should be relative only to negation. How about conjunction, disjunction, and so on, to say nothing of the quantifiers? If a truth model contains a conjunctive sentence, this conjunction must presumably have the property of being true if and only if both conjuncts are. Hence the truth model Γ_i should be relative to a conjunction operator C_i having suitable properties.

Actually Hiż needs as a primitive not a one-place predicate for truth, but a two-place *relational* predicate in accord with which one can say that a sentence α is *true in* a given set of sentences Γ_i. Only in terms of such a two-place predicate, it would seem, can the theory accomplish what it is intended to. To the definiens of the definition of 'Γ_i is a truth model in M (relative to O_i)' above one would add a conjunct to the effect that *every member of Γ_i is true in Γ_i.*

Incidentally it may be noticed that this reconstituted definition can be given within the first-order version, that essentially of the 1953 paper, by speaking of Γ_i as a virtual class of sentences and construing 'Cmprh' as a triadic relation with Γ_i as another argument. Thus a one-place predicate may be said to comprehend another in a given virtual class of sentences Γ_i. For this "relativistic" notion, of course, the notion of being a sentence is presupposed. Alternatively, one could perhaps take Γ_i as merely a virtual class of *expressions,* but choose it always in such a fashion that in fact all its members are sentences. (Perhaps Hiż could avoid using the notion of sentence in full generality in a similar way. But see below for a more pragmatical account.)

Hiż goes on to define a number of interesting notions concerned with *interpretation in a truth model under a given assignment.* "Though interpretation is a semantical concept, as it uses truth in its definiens, it is a relation between sequences of phrases and sentences," Hiż notes. The definition embodies an adaptation of Tarski's use of infinite sequences. It is not clear, however, how "it uses truth in its definiens." In an assignment some phrases are replaced by others in the same "grammatical category." Here, too, it would seem, a crucial clause concerning being true in a given set of sentences Γ_i is left out.

Especially interesting, Hiż thinks, are truth models closed with respect to paraphrase. The relation of *being a paraphrase of* is not defined, however. Perhaps "paraphrase is [logical] consequence both ways; two texts are paraphrases of each other just when either of them is a consequence of the other." Hiż notes, however, that "it is much easier to test empirically paraphrases than consequences. Linguists often hesitate to enter work on consequences." Thus apparently a symbol for paraphrase is taken as an additional primitive.

If paraphrase is taken as mutual consequence, it is of course a notion quite different from synonymy. Paraphrase is presumably a necessary condition for synonymy but not a sufficient one. Mutual consequence or L-equivalence is surely a most significant semantical relation, but for paraphrase some deeper structural similarity seems needed. Thus sentence α is a paraphrase of a sentence β if and only if α and β are mutual consequences of each other and α and β are structurally interrelated in a very intimate way (Martin). Unfortunately Hiż tells us little about the inner structure of paraphrase, so to speak, either here or elsewhere. It is difficult to see how by means of this notion there is much advance over earlier discussions of synonymy and the like.

Note that for Hiż paraphrase is a semantical relation, not a pragmatical one. For some purposes, however, it might be of interest to regard it as the latter. It is persons who paraphrase, and different persons in quite different ways. And even one and the same person, quite differently at different times. The important notion here would perhaps best be expressed by "person p paraphrases sentence (or phrase) α as sentence (or phrase) β at time t." Here is a suitable locution with which to capture the "empirical" character of paraphrase. The results of all empirical tests concerning paraphrase could no doubt be couched in terms of it.

The only point at which Hiż needs set theory, more particularly, a quantifier over a set of sentences, is in his reference to essentially Tarski's definition "that α is a consequence of β if and only if every model of β is also a model of α. Therefore, α is a paraphrase of β if and only if, for every Γ_k (maximally consistent with respect to O_k), α is in Γ_k if and only if β is in Γ_k." This definition, however, Hiż does not adopt, the notion of paraphrase embodied in the definiendum being, according to him, not sufficiently testable empirically. All other uses of sets or quantifiers over them in Hiż's paper can easily be accommodated in terms of virtual classes. Accordingly the set theory may be dropped.

The point is an important one. In some circles it is thought that model theory provides the logic needed for all philosophic, linguistic, and methodological problems. Its adherents claim this with an almost fanatical enthusiasm. The fact is, however, that model theory is primarily of mathematical interest and its use elsewhere has not served to illuminate where simpler methods fail to do so. Surely in linguistics there is no evidence that model-theoretic methods are needed, all the results of hard empirical and theoretical toil being expressible in a more restricted vocabulary.

As an aside, Hiż comments "that the alethetic semantics based on truth models can be applied to the standard treatments of model theory in the foundations of mathematics, so that most of the standard model theory becomes, *mutatis mutandis,* a particular case of the aletheic semantic theory." The resulting model theory is of course a non-translational one. The lack of a translation of the object language is in effect compensated for by variables and quantifiers over all manner of sets. This is not very surprising. Given any individuals or *Urelemente,* if a vast domain of sets, of sets of sets, and so on, is admitted with sufficiently strong axioms, one can of course easily develop mathematics. The linguistic expressions of the object language can be regarded as the *Urelemente.* Hiż seems to think that there is a "difficulty with non-denumerable models (say a model with real numbers)." But real numbers can easily be constructed in the usual way in aletheic semantics based on set theory. In a first-order aletheic theory, however, the matter is quite different. There, Hiż's suggestion of expressing a Dedekind cut in terms of interpretations is of interest. The details may be omitted. Hiż says that he defines "the set of rational numerals which is a suitable synonym for the real numeral '$\sqrt{2}$'," but he actually defines only "a phrase α is in the set $\Delta_{\sqrt{2}}$ of rational numerals," a very different matter. A similar restriction occurs in most attempts to build up the reals from the integers with variables and quantifiers only over the latter. It is very doubtful that Hiż can provide in this way very much of the full arithmetic of real numbers.

What now is to be made of Hiż's relativism? He tells us that "in Greek mythology *Zeus was often angry* is generally accepted" and hence may be regarded as true in a suitable truth model for Greek mythology. But it would be false in a model for atomic physics or Greek history. All manner of sentences can be "believed to be true" or "accepted as the content of a mythology" or taken as paraphrases of each other, without thereby being true. The kind of relativity Hiż has in mind has less to do with truth than with belief, acceptance, paraphrase (in the pragmatic sense suggested above), and the like. With only slight changes in wording Hiż's entire theory could thus be restated in pragmatical terms. In place of "true in a set (or virtual class) Γ_i," one could read "accepted at time t and in Γ_i," or "believed at time t and in Γ_i," or something of the sort. That Hiż has these pragmatical notions in mind anyhow is evident from the informal explanations. The empirical character of Hiż's theory is thus accommodated, but no longer as merely a semantics.

What happens then to truth? Is it no longer needed? Does it play no role in linguistics? None in the philosophy of science? What role should "true," as opposed to "accepted at t and in Γ_i," play in linguistics and elsewhere? There is no doubt but that a great deal can be done with only the latter and without the former. Hiż's paper attests to this. Nonetheless something seems left out. One can never say in Hiż's theory that a sentence is true *simpliciter,* true in our world, true once and for all *sans phrase.* No, instead, one must always specify the set of sentences *in* which it is true. Truths of logic itself seem as relative as any other. A tautology "Jones is tall if and only if Jones is tall" may be true in some Γ_i, but nothing seems to prevent its being false in some other Γ_k. One could not even say thus that this tautology is true in *all* Γ_i, for it might well not be accepted or believed to be true by everyone. And similarly for the presumed "truths" of mathematics, sciences, and daily life. Something very significant has been left out in Hiż's semantics. Some one truth model must be picked out as standard or paradigmatic in some fashion to capture the notion of *true in this world* or simply *true actually.* Hiż's theory does not account for this and, as he notes, apparently cannot be extended to include it lest semantical antinomies result. "The set of all true sentences of a language is neither very natural... nor desirable," he notes. "It is not desirable because it may lead to well-known semantic antinomies." Yet without an account of *true actually* one cannot give a deep structure for many English sentences containing "true" nor can one provide for the key paradigmatic use of it that has been of such interest to philosophers since at least the time of Aristotle. Hiż's aletheic semantics is, in fact, like a performance of "Hamlet" without the key character.

The mention of Aristotle leads at once to the Aristotle-Tarski "paradigm"

(A) To say of what is that it is or of what is not that it is not is true, or, in more modern terms and somewhat more generally, essentially as in III above,

(T)   Tr $a \equiv$ _____,

where in place of "_____" a sentence is inserted and in place of "a" its shape or structural descriptive name. That (T) holds for all sentences of the language is essential for adequacy.

In Hiż's semantics, not only can (T) not be stated, it does not even hold. What condition of adequacy is there for his 'true in Γ_i'? None is given. Yet some condition here is surely essential if Hiż's 'true in Γ_i' is even remotely to capture some of what is contained in 'true'. Note that in the non-translational semantics of the 1953 paper although (T) cannot be stated, the theory is clearly constructed in accord with it. A semantics which accords with (T) may be said to be *genuine,* for within such a semantics the real content of 'true' is captured.

Hiż no doubt thinks it is a merit of his theory that within it the barriers between syntax and semantics, and between semantics and pragmatics, are ostensibly broken down. Non-translational semantics, of whatever kind, can be viewed as a kind of extended syntax, only linguistic expressions being values for variables. If his 'true in Γ_i' is taken as primitive, no genuine semantics results, as noted. If in place of 'true in Γ_i' the locution 'believed at t and in Γ_i' or 'accepted at t and in Γ_i' is used, no genuine semantics emerges, but rather something that borders on a pragmatics. Only if variables over *users* of the language are brought in do we have a genuine pragmatics. It seems then that Hiż has not succeeded in breaking down these barriers but has rather trespassed upon them illicitly. Let us be clear about our boundaries, and let us bring to light explicitly the character of each theory being dealt with. If pragmatic or epistemic notions such as *accepts* or *believes* are used, let us bring them out clearly and with the "natural" arguments they take. *Human beings* accept or believe, and thus they are taken as natural values for variables in pragmatics.

If Hiż's theory is reconstructed by using a pragmatical 'accepts' in place of 'true in Γ_i', the notions of sentence and of paraphrase should perhaps be pragmatized as well. Thus the full notion of being a sentence in the natural language is dropped in favor of α's being *taken as a sentence* by person X at time t, where α is in Γ_i. And similarly, in place of the notion of paraphrase, one would now use the locution 'person X paraphrases α as β at t, where both α and β are in Γ_i'.

Semantics is a normative discipline, to some extent anyhow, whereas Hiż has tried to turn it into an empirical one. A theory built upon 'person X accepts α at t where α is in Γ_i', 'person X takes α as a sentence at t where α is in Γ_i', and 'person X paraphrases α as β at t, where α and β are both in Γ_i' would be properly empirical and "testable" and would enable us to achieve non-translationally, and on the basis of a first-order logic only, everything that Hiż attempts to do. Perhaps in fact these are the very notions he has in mind. In any case, no harm can arise from bringing in the additional arguments or factors, for they can always be handled as parameters if not needed in a given context.

Even if it could be worked out successfully, however, it is doubtful that Hiż's aletheic semantics or the reconstruction of it just suggested can accomplish for linguistics all that is expected of it. It is remarkable and interesting that so much can be done non-translationally in connection with natural language. However, this approach neglects the key topic of logical form. It is this that has interested logicians of language since the time of Mill, Peirce, and Frege. Presumably the deep structure of a sentence is its logical form, as suggested above, or at any event is to be gotten at by means of it. How does Hiż's semantics help in the study of logical form? How does it help in constructing a viable theory of the parts of speech? How does it help in formulating rules concerning how the parts of speech are combinable into longer locutions? How does it help to gain an adequate theory of adverbs, or of adjectives for that matter, or of prepositions? For answers to these and similar questions one must presumably build an object language L of very great expressive power and then study how words, phrases, and sentences of a natural language can best be correlated with corresponding expressions of L. This is a task of enormous difficulty that aletheic semantics merely tries to avoid.

Such an object language is of course of philosophic interest also, throwing light on fundamental problems of ontology, of how our natural language is related to the world, of the logical structure of fundamental epistemic notions such as 'believes', 'knows', and so on, and of their interrelations. It paves the way for analyses of the deontic notions, for handling values, human acts, and the like. And so on. Hiż's semantics, on the other hand, is of little interest in connection with any of these topics. It merely takes language as it finds it and leaves it there. The alternative approach suggested also takes language as it finds it, does not "regiment" it or make it behave in any other way than is customary, but seeks to give as exact an account as possible of all relevant logical forms. In short, logical form is the fundamental notion that we should seek to explicate, every English sentence being, in the phrase of Mill, "a lesson in logic."

Hiż's paper is obviously an important one. It is interesting that in dealing with natural language a non-translational semantics may be helpful. Hiż's specific suggestions concerning 'synonymy' and 'meaning' are of interest, although given 'true' and 'logically true' or 'analytically true' it is no longer surprising that suitable definitions of these notions are forthcoming. And, above all, the use of modern semantics or pragmatics in the study of natural language is to be welcomed most warmly, scarcely anything really serious along this line having yet been achieved, in spite of valuable steps forward here and there. Hiż's paper is thus the kind of paper that one must agree with and do likewise, or disagree with and not. The various points raised above give grounds for the disagreement and, in part, for the not.

Richard Martin

ON CARNAP'S SEMANTICS, HIZ'S NOTION
OF CONSEQUENCE, AND DEEP STRUCTURE

I come to praise Carnap and not to bury him. He was one of the first—along with Frege and Tarski—to have recognized the very central role that semantical considerations must play in analytical philosophy, particularly in the methodology of science and the philosophy of language. He was one of the first to realize that these disciplines must themselves become increasingly scientific and that the philosophy of the future will make more and more use, in the phrase of Peirce, of an "immense technical vocabulary."

Let us recall first the remarkable passage in *The Logical Syntax of Language* (Carnap 1934) to the effect that logical syntax–which even then Carnap treated so widely that it embraced a good deal of what later came to be called "semantics"–will help in "the analysis of the incredibly complicated word-languages. The direct analysis of these, which has been prevalent hitherto"–and is still prevalent in such remote places as the Massachusetts Institute of Technology–" must inevitably fail, just as a physicist would be frustrated were he from the outset to attempt to relate his laws to natural things–trees, stones, and so on. In the first place, the physicist relates his laws to the simplest of constructed forms, to a thin straight lever, to a simple pendulum, to punctiform masses, etc. Then, with the help of the laws relating to these constructed forms, he is later in a position to analyze into suitable elements the complicated behavior of real bodies, and thus to control them. One more comparison: The complicated configurations of mountain chains, rivers, frontiers, and the like are most easily represented and investigated by the help of geographical coordinates–or, in other words, by constructed lines not given in nature. In the same way, the syntactical (and semantical) properties of a particular word-language, such as English, ..., are best represented and investigated by comparison with such a constructed language which serves as a frame of reference."

To be sure, this famous passage has been criticized by certain linguists who, it seems, have failed to understand the aims and methods of logical syntax and so could not succeed in using those methods in any effective way in linguistics. Now, 40 years after it was written, this passage may be assessed anew. First, let us reflect a little upon logical syntax and semantics, which help to make possible a theory of deep structure sufficiently broad to be linguistically interesting.

Carnap learned much from his study of Tarski's *Der Wahrheitsbegriff in den formalisierten Sprachen* (1956) and was always most generous in acknowledging his indebtedness to it. In fact, he was the first to recognize the significance for philosophy of Tarski's work. However, Carnap went about building up semantics in quite a different way by attaching primary importance to semantical relations of *designation* (Carnap 1942).

There is not just one relation of designation, there are several. If the object language is first-order with some primitive non-logical individual and predicate constants, it is appropriate to consider separately the designation of individuals, the designation of classes or properties or attributes, the designation of relations, and perhaps even the designation of propositions. Carnap first uses "designation" in a technically self-conscious way, in his monograph *Foundations of Logic and Mathematics* in the *Encyclopedia of Unified Science* (1939). There, in effect, he gave the first systematic definition of "true" in terms of "designation" taken as a semantical primitive. The definition, however, is far from being technically correct and leaves much to be desired. Nor is the matter ever put to rights later. In *Introduction to Semantics* (1942) the definitions are for the most part informal and the systems considered extremely weak. However, these matters may be remedied and a technically correct and materially adequate definition of "true" in terms of "designation may be given if a higher-order logic in the metalanguage is presupposed.

The most controversial of Carnap's relations of designation is DesProp, that of propositions regarded as extra-linguistic intensional entities of some kind or another. Carnap thought "there is no danger in speaking of propositions and classes of propositions provided it is done in a cautious way .... However, there are advantages to avoiding propositions altogether and instead speaking about the sentences or classes of sentences expressing them, whenever this is possible. First, we avoid a discussion of the controversial question whether the use of the concept *proposition* would involve us in a kind of Platonic metaphysics and would violate the principles of empiricism. Second, there is the technical advantage that for this method a metalanguage of simpler structure suffices" (Carnap 1950). Although Carnap vacillated on this point, there is no need to review the various issues involved. Even so, he is one of the first to have emphasized the significance for semantics of purely extensionalist procedures and their philosophical advantages. This does not require that intensionalist procedures be eschewed, but that they should be shown to be forthcoming by definition from an extensionalist or at least "neutral" base (Carnap 1956).

Designation of individuals, already mentioned, and of classes and relations remain, it seems, as important relations, providing in fact some of the semantical roots of reference. Another is denotation, also mentioned above, in the sense in which a one-place predicate applies severally to the individuals that fall under it. If 'denotes' is taken as fundamental, the various relations of designation are forthcoming by definition (Martin 1958).

Tarski emphasized rather a very complex relation of *satisfaction,* in accord with which an infinite sequence of objects is said to satisfy a sentential function containing any arbitrary number of free variables. A *sentence,* that is, sentential function containing no free variables, is then shown to be satisfied either by all sequences or by none. A *true* sentence is one by definition satisfied by all sequences, a false sentence by none. To achieve the effect of this definition, however, one may equally well use only finite sequences, as noted by Popper. And, in fact, one can go still further, and use a much simpler satisfaction relation in accord with which an object is said to satisfy a sentential function of just one variable. A suitable definition of truth, both technically correct and materially adequate, is forthcoming on the basis of such a relation.

Another interesting semantical relation, first studied by Carnap, is that of *determination,* a relation between a sentential function of one variable and a class. Thus, for example, the sentential function '*x* is red and *x* is a rose' may be said to determine the class of red roses. Determination may be taken as a basis for semantics and, of course, these relations (designation, denotation, satisfaction, and determination) are, under appropriate circumstances, interdefinable.

Carnap was also one of the first to call attention to the usefulness of introducing into semantics a parameter for the human user of language, in other words, of introducing pragmatics. "There is an urgent need for a system of theoretical pragmatics." he wrote in 1955, "not only for psychology *and linguistics* (italics added), but also for analytic philosophy" (Carnap 1956). The extent to which pragmatics is needed in methodological and linguistic discussions is controversial, but Carnap was clear that the adjunction of pragmatics to semantics might prove to be helpful in all manner of ways.

Carnap's semantical writings did not meet with much approval in the philosophic world. In fact they were greeted by many with open hostility, especially in reviews by Nagel and Ryle (1942, 1949). In spite of these infelicitous reviews, however, Carnap's technical semantics lives on to bury its undertakers. If the real roots of reference are to be found in semantics, as it seems they should be, then the subject might be approached somewhat *de novo* as follows. Let

(Ref)   '*p* Ref *a, x, b*'

Express that person *p* uses the sign event *a* (as occurring in the sentence *b*) to refer to the entity *x*. In terms of "Ref' taken as a primitive, it will be recalled that 'truth' as applicable to occasion sentences—in Quine's sense—may be defined. Thus, for example, "He opened the door" is a true occasion sentence if the predicate "opened the door" denotes or is true of the person referred to by the speaker.

To illustrate further, consider an example like those of Hiż of a supposedly valid inference in natural language involving an occasion sentence (Hiż 1973).

(1) John went home.
(2) He opened the door.
(3) John opened the door.

Hiż would contend that the inference from (1) and (2) to (3) is valid in natural language. But is it? If the "He" of (2) is taken to refer to John, then presumably yes, although *the exact form of the inference must be spelled out.* But we are not compelled to regard the "He" of (2) as referential of John. Suppose John and his pet retriever are side by side. Wherever John goes his pet retriever is sure to follow. In the context John is referred to by his name, but his pet retriever is referred to by a low-keyed, prolonged, tremulous "He-e-e." Then it by no means follows from "John went home" and "He-e-e- opened the door," that John opened the door. Still more clearly, interchange the order of (1) and (2). From "He opened the door" and "John went home" it by no means follows logically that John opened the door. The point is obvious enough, namely, that a good deal must be spelled out concerning the reference of "He" in (2) before the validity of the inference from (1) and (2) (or from (2) and (1)) to (3) may be established. It is far from clear that this can be done without bringing in a parameter for the speaker or user of language. Of this, more in a moment.

Carnap suggested, it will be recalled, that it would be useful for linguistics to introduce the speaker explicitly. Hiż denies this. "The relation between premisses and consequence is an objective fact," Hiż writes "if $\ulcorner\alpha\supset\beta\urcorner$ and α are true sentences, so is β. It is misleading to formulate *modus ponens* or any other rule of consequence (or any other rule of language (?)), by saying that if you (or one) has accepted $\ulcorner(\alpha\supset\beta)\urcorner$ and α, you (or he) may accept β. If such a reading is taken seriously, metalogic (and grammar) would be a peculiar theory about (or about somebody) asserting your (his) possibilities of action. But neither metalogic nor grammar are about you. They are about sentences and their semantic relations .... Anyone may choose to use metalogic or grammar, just as he may choose to use physics. A grammatical or metalogical rule is not to be read as an instruction or program. It is rather an assertion that a sentence is true if another sentence is true. It is perhaps better not to use the term *rule.* For, misreading what rules say, some people may conclude, as it were, that man is a rule-obeying animal when using language and not when falling off the roof. The rules of grammar are essentially not different from the rules of physics. As man obeys the rules of grammar in speaking, so an electron obeys the rules of mechanics in circling the nucleus."

Several comments are in order, in defense of Carnap's position as over and against Hiż's. In the first place "modus ponens" is a highly ambiguous phrase, standing *inter alia* now for a logical law of the object language,

'$(x) (y) ((Px \cdot (Px \supset Qy)) \supset Qy)$',

now for a law of syntax,

'$(a) (b) ((\text{Thm } a \cdot \text{Thm } (a \, hrsh \, b)) \supset \text{Thm } b)$',

now for a law of semantics,

'$(a) (b) ((\text{Tr } a \cdot \text{Tr } (a \, hrsh \, b)) \supset \text{Tr } b)$',

and now for a statement in the pragmatics of acceptance,

'$(p) (a) (b) ((p \text{ Acpt } a \cdot p \text{ Acpt } (a \, hrsh \, b)) \supset p \text{ Acpt } b)$',

and so on.[1] No one formulation is any more "misleading" than any other. They are merely different, but closely interrelated laws. Surely the pragmatical forms are to be taken "seriously," but pragmatics need not therewith become a "peculiar theory about you" or me, but a theory nonetheless. Such a theory is needed, as already suggested, to accommodate Hiż's validation of the inference from (1) and (2) to (3).

"Anyone may choose to use metalogic or grammar, just as he may choose to use physics," he writes, but the intent of this contention is not too clear. The use of "use" here is vague. Clearly one has no choice—if he wishes to speak correctly—when it comes to obeying the rules of the grammar of the language he uses, nor of course does he have any choice in obeying the laws of physics. But there is an important difference nonetheless. The study of language is human oriented in a way in which physics is not. The language of physics contains no special names or variables for human beings—except perhaps in the case of reference to the observer in realtivity theory. Reference to the speaker, especially the fluent or native speaker, is essential in some areas at least of linguistics. You and I are no doubt flattered in being values for the physicists' variables too, but along with much else. In linguistics the only values for variables are (presumably) human persons together with those of his artifacts that constitute items of language. To leave out the human person would be like leaving out the nucleus in quantum mechanics. One could not formulate laws concerning circling the nucleus unless "circling" and "nucleus" were words of the language. Hiż, however, would have us formulate all rules of grammar for speaking, and indeed for the whole of linguistics, but never admit the word "speaking" itself nor any reference to who is speaking.

Hiż attaches more importance to reference than most current linguists, and in this respect is a follower of Carnap. He does not admit a form such as (Ref) above, however, but rather uses what is essentially Jespersen's notion of a *referential*.

Hiż uses "referential" in such a way that "if α is a referential for β, then α and β are occurrences of phrases in the text" (Hiż 1969). Evidently then "referential" is a word within a non-translational semantics. The semantics employed, moreover (Referentials 1969, p. 147), "is based on paraphrase and consequence as primitives, and those in turn can be reduced to truth. Truth is a property of sentences, and more generally, of texts." If definitions of "consequence" and "paraphrase" were to be given in terms of "truth" it is natural to think that a higher-order logic or set theory would be presupposed. Hiż gives no such definitions, however, and we may thus take him at his word that 'paraphrase' and 'consequence' are the primitive semantical notions, and that we are presumably free to employ wherever needed or desired notions of a higher-order logic or set theory. To employ such, however, is suspect if the semantics be non-translational. There is not much point of insisting upon non-translationality if the ontological economy thereof is tossed to the winds in admitting as values for variables all manner of sets of, and relations between or among, the basic linguistic expressions.

Note that if α is a referential for β, both α and β are for Hiż *occurrences* of phrases, occurrences being taken as inscriptions (sign events) rather than shapes (sign designs). An inscriptional syntax is thus apparently presupposed. The language of the "text" is a fragment of natural language. In addition to structural-descriptive predicates for the letters of the alphabet of the language of the text, a predicate for a *pause* or *caesura* is presumably needed as well as predicates for the various punctuation marks, comma, period, semicolon, and so on. Only thus could the structural description of an entire text be given. No doubt all of this can easily be characterized by a straightforward extension of known syntactical axioms for concatenation as applied to inscriptions.

Concerning 'consequence' and 'paraphrase' certain rules must be presumed given in the metalanguage. (Note that rules of consequence and of paraphrase are thus themselves metalinguistic statements, a point that will be significant in a moment). We can imagine what these rules would be like—Hiż does not state them—by reflection upon the rules of truth needed within an inscriptional, non-translational semantics. The key theoretical innovation of Hiż's paper (*Referentials,* p. 145) is the purported definition (4.14) of "an occurrence α_1 of a phrase α (in a text β) is a referential for an occurrence γ_1 of a phrase γ. . . with respect to a rule R." The definiens uses in effect the locution "rule R is applied to the text β in a way preserving the occurrence α_1 in β" in a most fundamental way. This locution is defined in turn by (4.13), in the definiens of which we find as one clause "R is stated in such a way that it speaks about a string. . . ." This latter clause is surely clear enough. The difficulty is that it is *not a clause in the metalanguage*. It concerns the way in which a metalinguistic sentence R is formulated, and all such discussion must, in the context at hand, be metametalinguistic. Definitions (4.13) and (4.14) are thus, as they stand, not definitions within Hiż's semantics but within its (syntactical or semantical (?)) metalanguage, a significant lapse of rigor and contrary no doubt to the intention.

Hiż speaks of
$$(4.2)\ S_1 \cdot S_2 \rightarrow S_2$$
as a "rule of consequence" in accord with which (3) is correctly inferred from (1) and (2). Presumably, then, we are to construe (4.2) as
$$(4.2')\{S_1, S_2\} \rightarrow S_2$$
where "$\rightarrow$" is a metalinguistic sign read 'has a logical consequence'. (1) and (2) consist of two sentences, not one, and thus the rule should concern $\{S_1, S_2\}$ not the conjunctive sentence $\ulcorner(S_1 \cdot S_2)\urcorner$. The difference may seem unimportant. Hiż has equated the '·' of conjunction with the caesura, or rather with the period followed by the caesura, of (1) and (2) taken together. Often this equating can be made but not always. Nor do all English uses of "or" go over into "v", of "not" into "~", and so on. To equate these too readily is the source of much confusion in the study of the exact relations between constructed logical systems and natural languages.

However, this may be, a notion closely akin to the Jespersen-Hiż notion of a *referential*, or *cross*-referential, with the user explicitly brought in, may be defined in terms of 'Ref' as follows.

(Def.) '*p* CoRefntl *a, b, c, d' abbreviates* '(Sent *b* · Sent *d* · *a* Occ *b* · *c* Occ *d* · (Ex) (*p* Ref *a, x, b* · *p* Ref *c, x, d*))'.

In terms of 'Ref', let us explore a little more deeply now the inference of (3) from (1) and (2). This is to be done by "representing"—the word is Carnap's, recall, and it is interesting to note that it is creeping back in the technical literature on deep structure—these sentences within a constructed system as a frame of comparison. Let (1) and (2) be represented by
$$(1')\ \text{'Wjh'}$$
and
$$(2')\ \text{'O}hed\text{'}.$$
Then
$$(3')\ \text{'Ojd'}$$
represents (3). Let '*sp*' refer to the speaker, or whatever. Let e be the inscription of (2') and ei of (3') uttered by the speaker. And

let e_1 be the inscription of '*he*' occurring in e and e_2 of 'j' in e'. Consider now the following pertinent statements or principles.

(4) '$(sp$ Utt e $\cdot$ 'O*hed*' e $\cdot$ '*he*' e_1 $\cdot$ e_1 Occ e $\cdot sp$ Utt e' $\cdot$ 'Ojd' e' $\cdot$ 'j' e_2 $\cdot$ e_2 Occ e')',

(5) 'sp Ref e_1, j, e',

(6) '$(sp$ Ref e_1, j, e $\cdot sp$ Utt e) $\supset$ TrOcsnSent e, j, sp',

(7) '(TrOcsnSent e, j, sp $\cdot sp$ Ref e_1, j, e $\cdot sp$ Ref e_2, j, e') $\supset$ TrEtSent e',

(8) 'sp Ref e_1, j, e',

(9) 'TrEtSent e' $\equiv$ Ojd'.

From (4), (5), and (6)

(10) 'TrOcsnSent e, j, sp'

follows. And from (11) and (9), (3') itself follows.

Of these principles (4) and (5) are empirical assumptions or boundary conditions. (6) follows from (2') using the definition of 'TrOcsnSent'. (7) is an instance of a general principle connecting reference with truth. (8) is a principle of reference—recall *RefR3* of III—and (9) is an instance of the Tarski paradigm or Adequacy Condition for the truth of eternal sentences within inscriptional semantics.

Can we conclude now that (3) is a logical consequence of (1)? Certainly not. First, it should be observed that at best the inference is enthymematic. Statements (4) through (9) are required to carry out the inference. And secondly, (1)-(3) are sentences of English, whereas (1')-(3'), and (4)-(11), are formulae within a formalized theory of reference. The only meaning for 'logical consequence of' admitted here is the standard one for logical systems of first order. What then does 'logical consequence of' in English mean? Clearly we should say that sentence α is a logical consequence in English of sentences β and γ if and only if the (or a) deep-structure representative of α is a logical consequence of the (or a) deep-structural representatives of β and γ. In this sense of course, (3) may be regarded as an enthymematic consequence of (1) and (2) in English.

Note incidentally that in the derivation of (3') from (1') and (2') via (4)-(11), no use was made of (1'). In fact (3') was obtained from (2') alone. This might be thought a defect of the foregoing. To rectify this the supposition (5) may be replaced by the following, where e'' is the relevant inscription of (1') and e_3 the inscription of 'j' occuring in e''.

(5') '$(sp$ Ref e_3, j, e'' $\cdot$ 'Wjh'e'' $\circ$ 'j'e_3 $\circ$ e_3 Occ e'')',

(5'') 'sp CoRefntl e_3, e'', e_1, e'.

From these, however, (5) itself is forthcoming using the principle of reference that

(12) '$(sp$ Ref e_3,j,e'' $\circ sp$ Ref e_3,x,e'') $\supset$ j = x'.

Putting the assumptions (5') and (5'') here in place of (5) is no doubt the better procedure. Even so, it is interesting to note that (1′) need not be regarded as asserted. It may be commanded, questioned, or exclaimed, or whatever. Nor need it even be uttered, which is more surprizing yet. It may merely hover vaguely in the speaker's consciousness. Its role in the inference here is merely to supply a basis for the cross-referentiality.

It is by no means clear now Hiż can justify the inference of (3) from (1) and (2), however, even non-enthymematically. Nor does there seem to be any way for Hiż to supply the missing premisses within the semantics he allows himself. He lacks any way of speaking of the objects to which expressions are supposed to refer, in view of non-translationality. So even if he were to allow the premiss (5″), it is not clear what he could do with it. Further, of course, Hiż has no way of establishing (9), an instance of the Adequacy Condition for 'Tr'. The reason, again, is his use of a non-translational truth predicate.

In the foregoing, there has been no discussion of tense nor of the descriptive phrases 'home' and 'the door', which are irrelevant for present considerations. However, these should be looked at separately, for they raise interesting problems on their own.

Hiż is concerned with the "rules of consequence" for a natural language. Strictly, however, if the foregoing is correct, there are no such rules. There are rules of consequence for logical systems in which sentences of natural language may be "represented," but this is something quite different. In seeking to enunciate rules of consequence for natural language, Hiż seems to be using the direct approach disparaged by Carnap.

Incidentally, Hiż is not friendly to deep-structure linguists. "I suspect the hypothesis of deep structure to be implausible," he writes ("Rules of Consequence," p. 320, footnote 4), "at least if the structures allowed are of the sort used by Chomsky and others in practice and if the structures are assigned to sentences only, and not to longer utterances." Quite. The real defect of the M.I.T. deep structures is that they are not very deep after all, and that the "theory" governing them is far from being anything of the kind that a logician would be willing to call 'a theory'. Referential considerations such as those above must be brought in explicitly, it would seem, as well as various notions from event logic and the theory of intentionality.

Notes

1. 'Thm a' here expresses that a is a theorem, 'Tr a' that a is true, 'p Acpt a' that person p accepts a, and '$hrsh$' is the structural-descriptive

name of ' ' within non-inscriptional syntax. Cf. *Truth and Denotation,* Chapter III. In some subsequent papers also, a non-inscriptional or classical semantics will occasionally be used or mentioned.

References

Carnap, R. 1934. *Logical syntax of language.* London: Routledge and Kegan Paul.

_____ 1939. *Foundations of logic and mathematics.* In *Encyclopedia of unified science.* Chicago: Univ. of Chicago Press.

_____ 1942. *Introduction to semantics.* Cambridge: Harvard Univ. Press.

_____ 1950. *Logical foundations of probability.* Chicago: Univ. of Chicago Press.

_____ 1956. *Meaning and necessity.* Chicago: Univ. of Chicago Press. Hiż, H. 1969. Referentials. *Semiotica.*

_____ 1973. On the rules of consequence for a natural language. *The Monist:*57.

Martin, R. 1958. *Truth and denotation.* Chicago: Univ. of Chicago Press.

_____ 1972. On some criticisms of Carnap's early semantics: Nagle and Ryle. *Philosophia:*2.

Nagel, E. 1942. Review of Carnap. *The Journal of Philosophy:*39.

Ryle, G. 1947. Review of Carnap. *Philosophy:*24.

Tarski, A. 1956. *Logic, semantics, metamathematics.* Oxford: Clarendon Press.

Henry Hiż

REBUTTER WITH AMPLIFICATIONS

In a series of papers and in oral admonitions, Richard Martin has carefully examined some of my semantic opinions (Martin 1979a, 1979b, forthcoming Reidel; I will refer to the 1979a paper as HASNT, the 1979b paper as CSHNCDS and the forthcoming as SHH). The examination is critical and pointed, though never acrimonious; and it is all to the good. Reading it I realized many times that I have to rethink a problem, find better arguments, reword my statements, or give up a point or two. I feel much affinity with my distinguished critic. We have some common "ancestors"; Russell, Tarski, Carnap. He understands quite well where I depart from the "line". He calls my views "heretical", and in that he is correct. Only people with a common background can make such accusations with authority; only they are sensitive to deviations and revisionism. But let us be aware that every heretic can point out a verse in the scripture in his favor.

Translation and non-translational semantics

For some time it has been customary to include truth among the concepts studied by semantics. There are, however, differences among semantical theories in the extent to which truth is studied. For not all considerations about truth are equally easily accommodated in a theory. That Jean knows the truth of 'The valency of carbon is 1' and that Frank does not know it are facts about truth. Only a pragmatics which distinguishes between Frank and Jean can deal with this. Semantics done by a linguist or by a philosopher cannot record such a distinction. Then, some semantic theories will actually recognize some studied (object-language) sentences as true while other theories try to deal with the concept of truth more abstractly, without specifying which sentences are actually true. In a similar way, I may know what algebraic numbers are, without being able to specify which real numbers are algebraic, or even whether a particular real number is algebraic. Thus we have a variety of semantic theories, some answering more concrete questions about truth than others. To follow the algebraic example, from the definition

x is an algebraic number if and only if x is a root
of an equation with integers as coefficients

no test follows for deciding the algebraity of a real number. One may develop a theory of algebraic numbers without developing such a test. This is a useful enterprise. In such a theory we may take a case or two of real numbers known not to be algebraic (π, e) and dwell upon them. This is a middle course; without a machinery for producing non-algebraic (transcendental) numbers, one uses some known cases. Similarly there are semantic theories which, without saying whether any given sentence is true, assert— perhaps hypothetically—the truth or the falsehood of some particular sentences.

Furthermore, a semantic theory may use a stronger or a weaker language. Some semantic theories may choose to speak about anything: Houses, cities, antagonisms between people, and what not. Other theories may be restricted to a more natural semantical field and speak about linguistic utterances. Some may consider speakers (like our Jean and Frank), others only typical speakers (a normal Englishman, an average Frenchman) or exclude even that kind of pragmatics.

There may be reasons for doing this or another semantics; and all, or most, can flourish side by side. In part, I differ with Martin in what each of us is trying to do. Such differences are harmless provided that each side explains exactly what it plans to do. Even this is not always easy and the confrontation may help us to formulate our respective programs.

The language of semantics which Tarski used in his book on the concept of truth (Tarski 1956) has the property that every sentence of the studied language can be stated, either directly or under a suitable translation in the language of the semantic theory, the language called the 'metalanguage'. This assures that the metalanguage is at least as rich in what can be said in it as the studied language, the object language. Translatability is used in the condition which Tarski states for the adequacy of any definition of truth. This condition, called 'condition (T)', requires that every sentence of the form

α is true if and only if p

follows from the definition of truth and from the principles of semantics, where 'α' is a name of a studied-language sentence of which 'p' is a translation into the metalanguage. If the metalanguage is the same as the object language, then 'α' is a name of 'p'. If French is the object of our study and English the language in which we carry out our investigation, i.e., if English is our metalanguage for French, then the sentence 'The sentence *Lyon est plus petit que Paris* is true if and only if Lyons is smaller than Paris' should be a theorem of the semantic theory. If the condition (T) is to be satisfied then the concept of truth is applicable, in a semantic theory, only to sentences which have translations into the metalanguage. Note that the condition (T) requires more than the existence of a translation of α into the metalanguage. For the truth of *Lyon est plus petit que Paris* it is required that the city of Lyons be smaller than the city of Paris. The condition is on the cities and their respective sizes, not on any sentence. This is so even though the condition is formulated in an English (in this case metalinguistic) sentence. To say that *Lyon est plus petit que Paris* is translatable into *Lyon is smaller than Paris,* or to say that one is true if and only if the other is, is not enough for Tarski's theory. What is required is not only translation of a French sentence into an English sentence, but the assertion of a fact by the English sentence (the fact asserted in the French sentence). A theory which can do this is called *translational* by Martin. Twenty five years ago Martin showed that there may be semantic theories which do not satisfy this condition and, therefore, which can be labelled *non-translational.* Martin was the first to examine some of them systematically (Martin 1958). Now he claims that the theory I sketched (Hiż: 1969a, 1969b, 1973, 1976, 1979) is non-translational. And he says that it is equivalent to a theory he developed which is based on the concept of comprehension. I will take these two claims in turn.

An aletheic semantic theory is a semantics which studies the concept of truth independently of the problem of its definability. It is like the theory of real numbers which tries to establish the fundamental laws of real numbers and their functions. Real numbers are definable, for instance, by means of Dedekind's cuts within rational numbers. But a theory of real numbers can proceed, and often does proceed, without starting with that definition. Rational numbers do not have to be regarded as more "fundamental" or "prior"; they can be rightfully treated as particular cases of real numbers. Similarly, syntactic regularities, instead of being the bases to which semantics is to be reduced, can be rightfully treated as particular cases of semantic regularities. (Note that only those syntactic facts which have semantic import are worth recording in a theory; that two phrases have the same length or that they start by the same phoneme are not important.) The definition of real numbers by cuts within rationals connects two different theories. Similarly semantics, or a large part of it, can be syntactized—expressed by syntactic means—and in this way two linguistic sciences can be related.

preserves truth, that a set of true sentences is consistent but not

Whether or not truth can be defined, there are many facts about truth to be established, for instance, that consequence every consistent set of sentences contains only true sentences, that the set S of all sentences is not included in the set T of all true sentences, that T is maximally consistent, i.e., that if $\alpha \in S$ and not ($\alpha \in T$), then $Cn(T \cup \{\alpha\}) = S$, that the meaning of a phrase is determined by its occurrences in true sentences, etc. Any adequate aletheic semantics has to establish these (or similar) general facts. There are, also, more specific studies of true sentences. Some sentences are true due entirely to the fact that they contain words from arithmetic. Thus, 'Two piglets and three piglets make five piglets' is true independently of whether it is about piglets, or acts of Congress. The sentence is "arithmetically true" if it remains true in all interpretations which do not change the interpretation of arithmetical words. Logicians are familiar with a similar method as applied to the concept of logical truth. Such interpretations can be called *biased interpretations* and the corresponding notions of truth *biased truth,* e.g., arithmetical truth (AT), logical truth (TL), physical truth (PT), chemical truth (CT). Biased truth plays an important role in the study of the semantics of a natural language as well as in the semantics of the languages of science. It is because we decide not to change the interpretation of the arithmetical words that the sentence *Tom has three sisters,* does not change the meaning of the word *three* when Tom's third sister is born. When talking about family life we assume arithmetic is not changed by the facts. Similarly physics assumes mathematics, geology assumes both of them. I will return to this point when speaking about assumptions.

An aletheic theory may be translational or may be non-translational. All Tarski's semantic theories are aletheic in the broad sense that truth plays an important part in the development of the theory. All his semantical theories are translational. Translationality is a necessary condition for the definability of truth as shown by condition (T). Avoiding the attempt to define truth opens up the possibility of constructing a more general theory which will be non-translational and which, then, will not have cities, their relative sizes, and everything else as its subject matter—a theory which does not attempt to be omniscient.

A non-translational semantic theory can be extended to a translational one. We can add as new axioms all the cases of condition (T). Tarski showed that if a semantic theory is consistent then it remains consistent after adding all such sentences as new axioms. In such an extended theory, truth will still be undefined; it will be treated only axiomatically. But the theory will be translational. In our illustrative case one can state the following rule for that purpose, the Translational Rule:

> *If a French sentence α is translatable into an English sentence β, then one can accept as a theorem of the semantic theory the sentence 'α is true if and only if p', where for 'p' one puts β.*

The use of the Translational Rule requires that the concept of truth for French sentences already be introduced into the theory and that the concept of translation between French and English sentences be presented by the theory. In cases in which we cannot translate sentence by sentence, or in important cases where the concept of truth does not apply to a sentence (cases about which Martin writes, see section *Sentences and their strings* in the present paper) the Translational Rule has to be adjusted and rephrased.

There may be also semantic theories which are essentially weaker than an aletheic semantics. Instead of speaking about the truth of sentences, one may limit himself to speaking about simultaneity of truth of sets of sentences. In the same vein, instead of speaking about the meaning, one may speak about equality of meaning, instead of the message of a sentence, about paraphrase. To my knowledge the first explicit way of doing weak semantics in that sense is in a paper by Jerzy Kreczmar in 1934. I followed this style in my 1964 paper. A still weaker theory, with a minimum of semantics, was presented in my 1961 paper. A particularly attractive choice of a weak semantics involves using the consequence relation between a set of sentences and a sentence. This allows us to treat many problems which cannot be stated in a paraphrase grammar.

The problem of equivalence between my aletheic semantics and Martin's non-translational semantics as presented, e.g., in his book *Truth and Denotation* (1958), calls for some comment. Trivially, the systems are not equivalent because Martin's theory is a first-order theory and mine, if formalized in a more explicit way than I have done so far in my publications is not a first-order theory. I allow sets, relations of anything including sets of sets and sets of relations and I quantify over them. My logic is Leśniewski's, Martin's logic is a part of that. Those differences may be motivated by differences in our respective philosophies of logic, by different ways of understanding what sentences of logic assert, and also by our differences in "metaphysics" or "ontology". Martin's use of first-order logic is in harmony with his acceptance of individuals, for instance in Chapter III of his book (1978e). I look at the concept of individuals with suspicion (Hiż 1971). Given my "philosophical" inclinations I would prefer not to use the relation of denotation because of my skepticism not only about individuals but also about all sorts of entities. And it does not seem to me that the concept of denotation is definable in the aletheic theory outlined in my 1969a paper and in later papers.

In some of Martin's formulations the relation of comprehension is used as primitive. It can be defined as a relation between two predicate constants α and β such that every individual denoted by β is also denoted by α (Martin 1958). It seems that a concept closely resembling Martin's comprehension can be defined in the semantics containing the concept of consequence. Namely

(1) α comprehends β relative to A if and only if for every $\gamma_1, \dots, \gamma_n, \alpha(\gamma_1, \dots, \gamma_n) \in Cn((\beta(\alpha_1, \dots, \alpha_n))$ where A is a set of sentences (assumed sentences) and, for every i, $(1 \leqslant i \leqslant n)$, α_i in $\alpha(\gamma_1, \dots, \gamma_n)$ is of the same grammatical category as γ_i in $\beta(\gamma_1, \dots, \gamma_n)$. The concept defined in (1) is more general than that used by Martin in that it applies to many different grammatical categories whereas Martin's applies to phrases of one category only—to phrases of the grammatical category (s;n). Whether the concept of comprehension, even in the extended sense of (1), can be taken as the primitive for the aletheic semantics or for my consequence grammar (Hiż 1979) is far from clear.[1] In particular, the concept of consequence seems to elude a definition by comprehension unless some other semantical concepts are available.

About my aletheic semantics Martin writes, "In taking a truth-predicate as a primitive one must have tagging along with it the notion of being a sentence of the object language, the truth predicate being applicable to sentences and sentences only .... Hiż's employment of (sentence) as primitive is thus very bold, a kind of theft, as it were" (HASNT). If it is a theft I am ready, and forced, to perpetrate it, and in my opinion everybody thinking about those problems perpetrates it also, knowingly or not. Note that comprehension requires the concept of one-place predicate, or (s;n) in the same sense in which truth "tags along" with the notion of sentence. Martin thinks that the concept of one-place predicate "is much simpler than that of being a sentence and presumably more readily available for natural languages". I doubt that the concept of a one-place predicate is "much simpler" or "more readily available" than that of a sentence. A one-place predicate is a phrase of the grammatical category (s;a), i.e., of the grammatical category of a function which, together with one argument of the grammatical category a, forms a sentence. Thus this concept presupposes or has the concept of a sentence "tagging along with it". Moreover, to say that a phrase plays the role of a predicate in a sentence is to assign to the sentence structure, whereas to say that something is a sentence does not go into its structure. Martin would replace the variable category a in (s;a) by a nominal grammatical category or perhaps by a category of proper names of individuals. But I doubt that there is such a grammatical category; whether *Zeus* is a name of an individual is not a matter of grammar. That *Zeus* is a name is a matter of grammar; it may be an empty name. It is prudent to take sentences as an ab *initio* grammatical category. Leśniewski also took nouns as an *ab initio* grammatical category and treated other categories as relations between previously introduced categories (Hiż 1960). Whether or not the choice of other *ab initio* categories is justified and sufficient for a natural language, the choice of sentence in that role is sound. The choice of other categories should depend on what the actual sentences met in the language are and how speakers operate on them. If the speakers of the linguistic community reason from a sentence by changing the position of a fragment, then one may begin to develop the grammar of the language by the starting assignment of say a to that fragment and the category to the remaining part of the sentence (s;a). In principle, this was the procedure followed by Leśniewski; he did not assign a category to a phrase which did not play a role in the derivation of theorems.

A translational semantics requires that a proper rendering of the studied language sentences be possible in the metalanguage—i.e., that there be a translation into the metalanguage of every sentence of the studied language. But what does it mean to admit that there is such a translation? In the case when the metalanguage is the same as the object language, the problem is simple; translation is an identity mapping. Where the two languages differ, the problem is more complicated. What is preserved under translation? A natural and common answer is that meaning is preserved under translation. As we are not concerned here with translation of words but with translation of texts or of sentences, we do not have to consider the meaning of words, which would complicate our problem. By the meaning of a sentence I understand, roughly, the set of sentences which are consequences of that sentence but which were not known without this sentence. More precisely, the meaning of a sentence α, relative to assumptions A, is the set of consequences of the set $A \cup \{\alpha\}$ minus the consequences of A itself (Hiż 1979). But conclusions are in a language, normally in the language of the premises. To consider conclusions in a different language than the premises would be to consider again the problem of translation which would beg the question.

The meaning of the French sentence *Lyon est plus petit que Paris* considered together with our normal geographic knowledge and with our knowledge about the relation of being smaller than is the set of French sentences which a French speaking person, with average knowledge, would conclude from it. It contains *Paris est plus grand que Lyon, Paris et Lyon ne sons pas de même grandeur, Paris est plus grand qu'une autre ville,* etc. If one says that the meaning is preserved by the above translation, and intuitively it certainly is, we must understand by preservation of meaning something different from identity of meaning under translation. For those French sentences are not consequences of the English sentence *Lyons is smaller than Paris.* It may be that it is one thing to assert that the meaning of the two sentences, under some assumptions, are the same, and something else to assert that meaning is preserved under translation. Translation is a semantic relation. It is a homomorphism H such that for every French sentence α there is an English sentence $H(\alpha)$ such that if a French sentence β is a consequence of α, relative to some assumptions, then $H(\beta)$ is a consequence of $H(\alpha)$, relative to assumptions which are also H images of the French assumptions. It is rather doubtful whether there is such a homomorphism and, even if there is one, it is also doubtful whether it is computable—whether we can effectively find out whether two sentences, one French the other English, are in that relation. The actual practice of translating does not go sentence by sentence. The tacit assumptions in a French society differ, not only in wording but also in content, from the assumptions in an English speaking group. If the homomorphism H is not decidable, then the Translational Rule is ineffective; we never can be sure when to apply it, for we do not have a procedure to check whether the premiss holds.

One more topic must be mentioned before we leave the problems of translationality. Tarski's condition (T), or the Translational Rule, requires a translation of a sentence of the object language into a sentence of the metalanguage. But it is not clear what can count as a metalanguage. The oft-heard statement that a natural language contains its metalanguage is misleading. A natural language contains a metalanguage of itself but, of course, it does not contain all of its possible metalanguages.

There is another translation of a sentence, namely translation of a sentence into a phrase of another grammatical category than a sentence. For instance the "content" of a sentence can be expressed by a phrase of the grammatical category of negation. Consider the definition

$$\Lambda p \Lambda q \ulcorner \text{assert} \langle p \rangle (q) \equiv (p \ \& \ (q \equiv q)) \urcorner$$

'assert' is a functor which with one sentential argument, namely 'p', forms a functor, 'assert ⟨p⟩', which, in turn, with one sentential argument, 'q', forms a sentence. The sentence 'assert ⟨She is nice⟩ (q)' is equivalent to 'She is nice and (q ≡ q)' which, in turn, is equivalent to 'She is nice'. Now, 'assert ⟨She is nice⟩' and 'She is nice' say the same thing but are in different grammatical categories. The second is a sentence, the first is not. 'assert ⟨she is nice⟩' can be read in English *She is nice no matter whether* or *She is nice even if.* The point here is that translation does not have to preserve grammatical categories, or other features of the structure. There may be a translation homomorphism which leads from sentences to non-sentences and the Translational Rule would have to be abandoned or adjusted in such a way that not only sentences could be true.

The concept of translationality requires further explanation. If the metalanguage uses higher grammatical categories and renders sentences of the object language into sentences involving those higher categories, as in the above example, is the semantic theory coined in that metalanguage translational? Let me develop an example. A particularly interesting case of a mapping of a sentence into another grammatical category is to form a nominalization of the sentence. Thus *She is innocent* is nominalized into *Her innocence, Snow is white* into *The whiteness of snow, They divorced* into *Their divorce.* The nominalized sentences (and not the names of the sentences) can take such predicates as *is a fact, took place, occurred, happened.*[2] When used with nominalized sentences these predicates form sentences which are not only equivalent but which are paraphrases of the sentences with *is true* predicated about the name of the sentences. Thus *'She is innocent' is true* says the same thing as *Her innocence is a fact, 'Snow is white' is true* the same thing as *The whiteness of snow is a fact. 'They divorced' is true* the same thing as *Their divorce took place, 'The second sentence on the fifth page of this book' is true* says the same thing as *What is said in the second sentence on the fifth page of this book is so* (Hiż 1973, Kahn 1973).[3] Is a semantics that admits these paraphrases translational in the sense intended by Martin? If it is, that fact has some theoretical consequences. First of all, the language that contains those nominalizations and their predicates is not a first-order language. It seems that Martin requires not only the studied language but also the metalanguage to be first-order and therefore the topic I am now speaking about is not formulatable in his theory. In the second place, here translationality does not eliminate the predicate *true*. In the above examples we have some other metapredicates to the same effect: *is a fact, took place,* etc. Another nominalization of a sentence, namely preceeding the sentence by *that,* allows the predicate *true* to remain. We say *That she is innocent is true, That snow is white is true, That they divorced is true.* Here, *That she is innocent* is not a sentence but its rendering in another category. If these phrases are taken to be metalinguistic renderings of the elementary sentences, then the condition of translationality does not suffice for eliminability of the predicate *true.*

All this may not disturb Martin and is said here by way of showing that translationality is a concept which needs further explanation.

Let me recall different senses of the terms *aletheic* and *aletheism.* 1. An aletheic semantics accepts truth as a primitive. In our present state of knowledge this is a convenient starting point but there is nothing necessary about it. 2. Truth is undefinable by extra-semantic means (except for degenerate cases), in particular by syntactic or by pragmatic means. There are indications that aletheism in this sense is correct. 3. Truth is a main subject of semantic studies. This is only a question of habitual boundaries of sciences. 4. Truth is necessary for defining meaning. Aletheism in this sense is a substantial claim: In order to know what a phrase means one has to know many sentences containing that phrase to be true. Dictionaries are collections of abbreviated sentences; they are in large part encyclopedias. This view of explaining meaning applies to truth itself; to understand the word *true* one has to know important sentences with that word. To understand a sentence one has to know what sentences must be true, if this one were true. 5. Truth is necessary for defining grammaticality, sentencehood, linguistic acceptability. In particular, co-occurrence restrictions on words, or selectional restrictions, are explicable and justifiable from knowledge about the truth of simple sentences with those words. I will not go further with this claim here, but aletheism in this sense is a serious hypothesis. 6. Finally, aletheism is an epistemological attitude. To know is to know that some sentences are true. We do not know objects, people, events, numbers, relations, etc., but by knowing the truth of some sentences. The aletheic reformulation of epistemic problems seems a simple requirement of rigor; otherwise one uses the verb *to know* in different and confusing ways.

In summary, aletheic theories are not inherently non-translational. The decision to do translational or non-translational semantics may be determined by other considerations or goals. Alternatively, the translational or non-translational character of a semantic theory may be a relatively inconsequential feature of the theory. My formulation of aletheic semantics is non-translational; yet its equivalence to Martin's non-translational semantics is moot. Clearly, one reason to do non-translational semantics is the desire to avoid the oft-overlooked problems with the relation of being a translation of. What is more important is the variety of claims that count as aletheic and the motivation they provide for doing aletheic semantics whether translational or non-translational.

Sentences and their strings

As in most linguistic and philosophico-linguistic discussions, so in my exchange with Martin there are many senses in which each of us uses the term *sentence*. For instance, we confuse a sentence with its readings. When, a moment ago, I said that to know is to know the truth of some sentences, I should be reminded that most sentences are ambiguous and that the slogan should read rather that to know is to know the truth of some sentences, each in a reading. Martin makes exactly the same inaccuracy when, in his book *Semiotics and Linguistic Structure* (p. 121), he asserts that paraphrase is transitive: If p paraphrases a as b, and if p paraphrases b as c, then p paraphrases a as c. But this can be true only if a, b, and c are taken not as sentences but as particular readings of sentences. The sentences themselves may be ambiguous and a sentence may have a common reading with another one, and the second a common reading with a third, but there may be no common reading between the first and the third sentences. Therefore, Martin is speaking about readings, or meanings, or otherwise disambiguated sentences. Then the person p uses not sentences themselves but some abstractions from the sentences. This is not merely a simplication of a minor anomaly; ambiguity is an ever present phenomenon in language and linguists spend a lot of effort describing it.

To constantly make the distinction between a sentence and its reading may be pedantry because from the context it is clear what is intended. Similarly the distinction between a sentence and its occurrences are easily recognized. This distinction is often confused, however, with the distinction between type and token. An occurrence of a word in a sentence is not a token, for a sentence is not a token. In this respect Martin is always correct.

One may have more essential doubts about the concept of a sentence in a natural language. It may be that the concept of a sentence, just as other grammatical categories, is an artifact of grammarians. Language is not composed of sentences but of utterances, of texts, of sayings. In linguistic and in philosophical literature there are two main groups of senses of the term *sentence*. The first deals with intonation. Roughly, an intonational sentence is a fragment of an utterance which has the intonation which can be the intonation of an entire utterance. There may be many refinements of this idea but we do not have to go into them here. The second group deals with logical values. A sentence is a fragment of an utterance which is true or false. In both groups one may take a sentence to be a minimal fragment with the given property, when minimality is understood in such a way that the utterance is divided into non-overlapping sentences. The second group contains several semantic senses of the term *sentence*. Besides the concept of a sentence as a stretch which is true or false one may speak about fragments which are like sentences in that sense, except for containing cross-referential (anaphoric or epiphoric) phrases, such that, after replacing the cross-referentials by (grammatically adjusted) referends (i.e., phrases to which the cross-reference was made) one obtains a true or a false sentence.[4] Sentences with cross-referentials are in many ways like sentential functions (matrices) with free variables which are well known to logicians. Both sentences which are true or false and sentential functions are, in Leśniewski's theory, of the grammatical category of a sentence.[5] In another sense a sentence is a phrase that can be a consequence of a set. (In particular, a consequence of a set is also a consequence of a set containing that phrase only. Thus a sentence in this sense is, also, a phrase which has consequences.) Sentential functions, or sentences with cross-referentials, do have that property. From *Her brother is at school* one concludes, from understanding English sentences, the sentence *She has a brother*. It is not clear which concept of a sentence the generative grammars are trying to enumerate recursively. It seems that a crucial problem of linguistics is, or should be, the relation between the intonational concept of a sentence and various semantical concepts of a sentence.

Martin shows some examples of alleged reasonings from sentences with typical cross-referential phrases. He writes: "Consider an example like those of Hiż of a supposedly valid inference in natural language involving an occasion sentence.

(1) John went home.
(2) He opened the door.
(3) John opened the door.

Hiż would contend that the inference from (1) and (2) to (3) is valid in natural language" (CSHNCDS, p. 161). And, of course, he shows that such inferences do not hold. I never intended to claim anything of the sort. What I was suggesting is that from the text 'John went home. He opened the door' the sentence 'John opened the door' follows. And in one reading of the premiss the conclusion holds. To consider sentences (1) and (2) as separate premisses is a different matter than to consider one premiss with a particular connective between them, the connective marked by a period. It is also essential that the intonation of this joined premiss be "normal", that the word *he* be not stressed. One may state other relevant conditions on the premiss and on the context in which it occurs. Even then what I am claiming is that English speaking people do reason that way, that if somebody thinks such reasons are invalid he does not understand English. But of course the premiss may be understood in such a way that the reasoning is not valid. There may, for example, be in the context a sentence preceding the premiss and another following it which will practically exclude the conclusion. For example, 'Frank always opens the door when he learns that somebody is coming home. John went home. He opened the door. But John did not arrive'. Here *he* is a cross-referential to the occurrence of *Frank*. It is the business of a grammar to describe the conditions under which an occurrence of a phrase is a cross-referential to an occurrence of another phrase. This means describing the conditions under which the inference of replacing the first by the second is valid. This is a difficult task but we know more about it than we did a few years ago. Many linguists are studying such cases intensely. I can also add that if from the text 'John went home. He opened the door' somebody concludes 'John opened the door', then he is forced by the customs governing reasoning in English to accept another conclusion—'John went home and opened the door'. The deletion of the second subject and the cross-referentiality go together. Many of these "second-order" rules are important for grammar. The "first-order" rules are the ways people reason. In particular, when one draws conclusions from an utterance, he tells us how he understands the utterance. The utterance *He gave me a book. It was most amusing* has as its consequence either *The book he gave me was most amusing* or *That he gave me a book was most amusing* but not both. But from *He gave me a book and a newspaper. It was most amusing* the sentence *The book he gave me was most amusing* does not follow. Anybody who makes such inferences will violate the grammar of English. *It* in the last example cannot be a cross-referential to *book* though perhaps it can be a cross-referential to *newspaper*. We assign logical structures to utterances according to what is concluded from them. The way I am treating the relation between the consequences and the structure of utterances leads to *consequence grammar*.

The cases cited contain cross-sentential cross-referentials. It may facilitate the study of such cases to realize that often when we hear only the first part of a longer utterance we learned part of what was said. This means that in such cases any initial starting string of sentences of a string is a consequence of the utterance. Generally, if $S_1 . S_2 . ...S_n$ gives as its consequences S_1, and $S_1 . S_2$, and $S_1 . S_2 . ...S_m$ for every $m \leqslant n$, then we call the utterance a "file of sentences". On the other hand, if the utterance $S_1 . S_2 . ...S_n$ gives as its consequences S_n, and $S_n . S_{n-1}$, and $S_n . S_{n-1} . ...S_{n-k}$ for every $k < n$, we call the utterance a reverse file of sentences. If there are no epiphoras, the utterance may be a file of sentences. If there are no anaphoras, the utterance may be a reverse file of sentences. But the ways anaphoras and epiphoras work may be hidden. For example, *Suppose Bill knows algebra. He will solve the equation* contains not only an anaphoric *he,* but the first sentence contains a condition under which the second is asserted, a prolepsis. It is indicated here by an imperative which in this case does not play the role of a command.

A file of sentences may be considered a sentence, in one of the listed senses, as it has consequences. It has some important semantic properties. Thus each step in a file leads us from an information state to a new information state. This is a function which changes the set of consequences by adding to it new consequences. This function may be taken to be the meaning of a sentence in a file. A given sentence changes the set of consequences in a specific way, no matter what the file so far developed. This concept of meaning, introduced by Smaby, is perhaps closer to the intuitive concept of meaning. But it is limited to files.

Logic

Martin urges the study of simple, constructed languages before we engage in a description of a natural language. This advice is proper but belated. We are all familiar with the work of Frege, Tarski, Carnap, Post, and, above all, Leśniewski, concerning constructed languages and we profit from these works all the time. There would be no Chomskyian grammar without Post production rules. We would not have Harris-transformations without algebraic transformations in group theory. There would be no Montague grammar without Leśniewski's and Tarski's studies of the structure of non-homogeneous languages. Harris' operator grammar of recent years is an application of Leśniewski's theory of semantic categories. The theory of recursive functions is the mathematics of most generative grammars. Without the great advances of logic and algebra in the first half of the century there would be no modern linguistics as we know it. Even historical linguistics uses graph theory. Grammarians, on the whole, follow another piece of Carnap's and Martin's methodological advice. They really do not study the speech of this or another person on this or another occasion. They study language as an instrument of communication, abstracting from peculiarities of its use. An utterance is not a speech act. It is, rather, an invariant of speech acts, an invariant under repetition, abstracting from who speaks and when, abstracting from peculiarities of an act.

But Martin would not only use in linguistics concepts and methods coined and forged by logic; he wants to reduce linguistics to logic. He thinks that every sentence of a natural language can be rendered into its logical form. The logical form consists of logical constants, some extralogical constants and one kind of variable, the individual variables. To the logical forms, and only to them, one applies normal rules of the first-order functional calculus and obtains all the consequences of the sentence one started with. Thus we have, say, the English sentence, its logical form, the purely logical consequence of the logical form, and rendering the consequence which is in logical form into an English sentence. The logical form of a sentence is uniquely (up to ambiguities) determined by the sentence. Transformations (presumably reversible) lead from a sentence to its logical form and from a logical form to a sentence. For the deduction of consequences one uses meaning postulates which regulate the use of extra-logical constants. The procedure seems as follows: From an English sentence to its logical form, by transformations; from the logical form and meaning postulates concerning the extralinguistic constants in it to the consequence by rules of elementary logic; from that consequence to the English sentence of which this consequence is the logical structure, by transformations. This procedure seems to me both roundabout and insufficient. It is roundabout because the final test of the entire procedure rests with whether the resulting sentence is a (linguistic, not logical) consequence of the English sentence which was the premiss. Therefore, why not work directly on the natural language consequence relation, without translating the language into the logical formulae and logical formulae back to sentences of the language. The opinion that the "underlying logical substructure is thought to be the same for all languages", that it provides a "universal logic" is a logician's dream (and not a well-founded one either). In Martin's scheme, and for that matter in the scheme of Carnap, the meaning postulates and their actual use are not clear. And it would be important to make them explicit. But it is difficult to make them explicit as they appear on the level of an abstract sublanguage, rather than in English.

The roundabout way Martin treats the consequence seems also insufficient to describe and explain some facts of semantic relations between sentences of a language. I see no chance of logic, the first-order quantification theory, or any stronger logic, theory of types, or set theory, telling us that *I gave Mary flowers* has as a consequence *I gave flowers to Mary.* We, of course, may decide to fix the "logical structure" of each of these sentences in the same way, but this is not taught by logic but by our knowledge of English. Knowledge of English consists partly in knowing such facts. Such facts may be called facts about the "logic" of English. But this is not the sense of logic Martin is using. What is, then, the relation between the logic in the standard, academic sense and the logical relations between English sentences? I think logic in the academic sense is a part of the logic of English. It speaks about consequences based on the standard, chosen, particular meanings of *if, not, every,* whereas the logic of English is based on other constants as well. And on other meanings of the same constants perhaps.

But I do not intend to criticise (or even to characterize) Martin's original work. I am only contrasting his attempt with mine, to explain mine, not to undermine his. The concept of consequence that I think is central for grammar is a generalization of the concept of consequence used in logic. It is a generalization in this simple sense: A consequence of a set of sentences is any sentence (in any appropriate sense) which remains true in any interpretation in which the sentences of the set are true, without reinterpreting the fundamental constants. Martin wants to keep as fundamental constants only a few logical words. I am allowing a host of grammatical constants not to be reinterpreted for the sake of grammatical consequence. This is the crux of our difference.

Consequences, logical or otherwise, are often drawn from sets containing more than one sentence—not all necessarily stated explicitly. In our reasonings we use anything we know and often, hypothetically, many things we do not know. It seems that we always have at our disposal a large set of sentences called *knowledge.* This set varies in time and there is, at a particular time, a knowledge common to a linguistic community. At least it is useful to postulate such knowledge. All our reasoning are relative to that set. It plays in grammar, as I see grammar, a somewhat analogous role to the meaning postulates of Carnap and Martin. But the membership in this set is testable. And the use of its members explicit. As a matter of fact so explicit that we often neglect to mention it. *The heart beats, Gloves, not socks are worn on hands, The weather changes, A father is a male older than his child*—all belong to this set (the set consisting of the common knowledge of English speaking people). To recite such sentences in our utterances would be a pedantic nuisance. They are used enthymematically.

Sometimes, in our reasoning, we assume an entire science. I spoke about those situations before. Now, among the assumptions of a reasoning can figure every theorem of that science, or more generally every true sentence of that science. Morever, we can not reinterpret the constants of that science for the sake of our consequences. And what goes for an assumed science can go for an assumed field of knowledge or fiction. We always work under assumptions and we are not able to question all of them all the time. My concept of consequence and my handling of the concept of truth meets a severe comment from Martin.

"When all is said and done Hiz's semantics is really nothing but syntax with all the limitations thereunto appertaining. The concept of truth is handled merely as a predicate of sentences, the only connection with actual truth being that "we form sets of sentences which are supposed to be true for a given kind of discourse. Truth may vary depending on the disciplines we talk about." But this is precisely what truth does not do. Hiz is merely using here one of the illicit surrogates for truth. His rules of consequence likewise are essentially syntactical. And also for him the notions of sentence, string, and meaning. The essential semantic properties of these notions are not provided for" (SHH).

A sweeping accusation. I hope at best partially true. I may have given reason for some of it by my work, especially by my comments about truth models. The work is a reconstruction of model theory for aletheic semantics and I think, in its essentials, it is correct. My comments in the paper "Aletheic Semantic Theory" may have given an impression that truth models are all that the theory needs, that there is no truth but membership in one or another truth models. This was not, and is not, intended. However, there is still a matter of assumptions. We reason from assumptions. If they are true, in the same sense of *true* intended by Martin and all the prophets, then the consequence is true. In my explicit use of assumptions, in my assuming that there are assumptions which are not necessarily true but are only assumed to be true for that discourse, I am adopting a kind of relativism. But this relativism is of a methodological kind. We never explain the meaning of all the words *ab initio*. Such a task is hopeless. We explain the meaning of words relative to the meaning of some other words which are assumed to be known. We always start in the middle.

Once I am allowed to make conclusions using assumptions which are not known to be true, I have opened the door for fictitious assumptions and for the study of meaning based on fiction. This may be a fault of the theory. But it may be viewed as its merit. For sentences in a mythology are not deprived of meaning and reasoning in mythology can also be valid or not. A speaker of the language in which the mythology is told can, as such, judge the correctness of the reasoning and grasp the meaning of the sentences.

Martin claims, in the passage quoted, that my rules of consequence are essentially syntactical. Usually rules of consequence are stated syntactically—referring to the shape and arrangement of phrases. But the message may be semantical. I intend it to be so. *Modus ponens* is indeed often a syntactic rule which asserts that if a conditional is a theorem and its antecedent is a theorem, then its consequence can be taken as (or *is*) a theorem. But with the soundness theorem asserting that all theorems are true, one may prove *modus ponens* as a semantic rule asserting that if a conditional and its antecedent are true, so is its consequent.

I will refer, once more, to the principle which in my paper *On Some General Principles of Semantics of a Natural Language* is called the Axiom of Consequence and which asserts that $\alpha \in Cn(X)$ if and only if, for all f, if f is an interpretation of X, then f is an interpretation of α. In that principle interpretation is used in such a way that f is an interpretation of X if and only if X is a set of sentences and f is the replacement of occurrences of a phrase by another in every sentence of X which results in a true sentence. I may add that this principle is not accepted as a definition of consequence only because the replacement f is supposed to preserve grammatical categories. In a language for which we do not have pre-established grammatical categories and in a methodology which considers grammatical categories to be roles in consequence rules, to accept this principle as a definition of consequence would be circular.

In summary, Martin's position is that there is a universal logic which is to say a logic that is not language specific. The sentences of any natural language have essentially unique logical forms (for each of their readings) in the logic. Martin's position is fairly traditional.

On my view speakers' practice of drawing consequences in a natural language is fundamental to any conception of logic and grammar. From the point of view of actual, legitimate drawing of consequences in a natural language there is no clear demarcation between Martin's universal logic and other kinds of consequence-drawing behavior. For the same reason there is no set of logical constants which is clearly defined for a natural language. My linguistic goal is the study of the totality of consequence relations in a natural language.

When we accept the goal of a realistic, uncompromising account of the consequence relation in a natural language, then the inclusion of assumptions and the apparent relativism of allowing them to change are unavoidable. This deviation from Martin neither indicates nor implies a different or non-semantic sense of truth.

Primitive terms

In his book on the concept of truth Tarski considers two different possibilities. Either we try to define the concept of truth by allowed means, or we may state some axioms in which the term *true* appears as primitive. There are some situations, described in the book, in which the first avenue is open. There are other cases, depending on the structure of the language used, in which the definition is impossible, and only the second way is available. About that possibility there are some important theorems in Tarski's book, for instance, that if a metatheory is consistent, then this metatheory remains consistent after adding to it the new primitive term 'true', and adding as new axioms all the cases of the schema

α is true if and only if p

where "p" is a metalinguistic rendering of the sentence α (Tarski 1956, p. 256 Theorem III). But Tarski, on several occasions, had misgivings about the axiomatic approach to introducing semantic primitives. Four misgivings are stated by Tarski (1956, 405-6) and I will now discuss them briefly. First, "the choice of axioms always has a rather accidental character, depending on inessential factors (such as e.g. the actual state of knowledge)." Although Tarski does not elaborate, I assume that the point is the same as my contention that the semantic concepts, and especially those of truth and of meaning, depend on a set of assumptions which are supposed, or known, to be true. I do not see it as a fault of the theory that it considers the semantic notions relative to the assumptions rather than in some absolute way. The meaning of sentences depends on the sentences that are assumed in a given linguistic group to be true. With a change of assumptions, with a change in the "actual state of knowledge" the content of semantic concepts may change. This seems to me plausible rather than undesirable. Second, the question of consistency of an axiomatic semantic theory is particularly difficult in view of the semantic antinomies. In this respect Tarski's theorem, which I just cited, concerning relative consistency is important. Moreover, some semantic antinomies are supposedly reconstructable in a natural language, if the metalanguage is the same as the object language. Instead of the distinction between a language and its metalanguage as a remedy for semantic antinomies, one may attempt to rule out, as ill-formed, some sentences which lead to the antinomies. I suggest that at least some of the antinomies can be resolved in principle by observing that they result from self-referentiality. If we exclude from the language all pseudo-sentences which contain a cross-referential with the referend in which this cross-referential occurs, we will eliminate the semantic antinomies in their usual formulations. There may be still some formulations of the antinomies which require further refinements on the conditions on sentencehood. A more penetrating analysis may reveal that some of the antinomies are related to the connection between cross-referentiality and the deictic expressions (*it, he, this* play both roles). If the deictic expressions are reduced to cross-referentials, the stated condition excluding self-referentiality may suffice. Third, "a method of constructing a theory does not seem to be very natural from the psychological point of view if in this method the role of primitive concepts—thus of concepts whose meaning should appear evident—is played by concepts which have led to various misunderstandings in the past". But to me it seems a vain and misplaced hope to expect the meaning of primitive terms to be evident. Such an expectation may be connected with a special sense of the expression *primitive term*—a sense listed below as the fourth sense. The meaning of any term is given by the true sentences in which it appears and by nothing else. Sometimes definitions are tools of obtaining such sentences, and are themselves some of the true sentences in which the term occurs. If the meaning of a term is not evident, it is not clear what sentences are to be proven containing that term. One may propose several sets of such sentences, sets only partially over-laping, that is, several different concepts. Fourth, Tarski thinks, or at least thought forty odd years ago, that if the axiomatic method in semantics is not replaced by definitions of semantical concepts using non-semantical ones, it would be difficult to bring semantics into harmony with the postulates of the unity of science, "since the concepts of semantics would be neither logical nor physical concepts". Today the unity of science is a long abandoned goal in view of diversity of scientific concepts which are hardly reducible to a small subset of them, let alone to physical or logical concepts only. But it may be added that grammatical constants of a natural language are like logical constants of a mathematical language; their meaning may be given not by true sentences in which they occur, but by valid rules of inference concerning them. Even so, it is an open question whether all semantical concepts for a natural (and for a mathematical) language can be defined by extra-semantical terms, in particular by syntactic terms. So far I do not see much evidence for such a claim. And if it is the case that semantical concepts are irreducible to syntactical ones, then the axiomatic method in semantics is the only one open to us at present.

Tarski's definition of truth for languages of finite order is not necessarily an exception to that suspicion. It is defined by the concept of satisfaction and the concept of satisfaction of a sentential function by an infinite sequence of entities is defined *ab initio* from cases like:

(4) the sequence 3, 5 satisfies 'x + 2 = y' if and only
if 3 + 2 = 5

For non-elementary sentences one is to proceed inductively following the process of constructing the molecular sentences. There are many reasons, not all equally important, why this procedure is neither free from semantics nor applicable to a natural language. Here are some of the most important points.

The assumption, made by Tarski, that molecular sentences are always obtainable from elementary sentences by an inductive process is far from established for natural languages. One may doubt that this can be done without using some semantic properties.

A natural language does not contain variables. Of course, we can introduce variables into an artificial extension of the natural language. But then we have to know which variable ranges over what entities which are named by expressions of the language. This in turn requires that the entities be organized into ontological categories and expressions into semantic or grammatical categories and that we assume a correspondence between the two organizations. This however is a strong metaphysical, syntactical and semantical assumption.

The formula (4) conveys what it is to convey only if the relation $+ 2 =$ is named by the expression ' $+ 2 =$ ' but this is a semantic assumption.

Tarski's construction assumes that the ontological categories correspond to grammatical or semantical categories in such a way that for the variables of a grammatical category one can substitute any and only terms that are names of corresponding ontological categories. Again this is a semantical technique.

The inductive process of defining sentencehood and of defining satisfaction is based on the assumption that there are individuals, the most elementary objects and that there are individual names that name them. All further ontology and all further syntax is constructed from them respectively. In a natural language it is doubtful whether the reduction to names of individuals, to proper names can be performed. In English mass nouns (*water, flesh, wood*) and abstract nouns (*vision, perspective, distance, melody*) are not reducible to proper names or to verbs or predicates of proper names. The structure used as a model for a language of mathematics is not applicable to a natural language.

Those are some of the reasons for trying to build semantic theory axiomatically. For each axiomatization some semantic terms are to be accepted as primitive. Martin thinks that the notion of logical consequence, along with truth, sentencehood and paraphrase appear as primitive in my aletheic semantic theory and that "no attempt is made to analyze any of them *au fond.*" The last comment may be unfortunately correct and I can only promise more attempts to this end; that means to find more and more important true sentences in which those concepts appear. Concerning these four notions Martin adds: "Whether they are the kind of notions that should be taken as primitives, however, may be doubted". He wants to find "the real internal constitution of the notions of truth and logical consequence in terms of other notions regarded as prior or more fundamental. Analysis of 'true' in terms of prior notions of satisfaction, denotation, designation, or determination are cases in point" (SHH).

It may be useful to recall that there are, at least, four senses of primitive term (*concept, notion, term* are used in this discussion interchangeably even though the last one is referring to some expressions and the former two to the meaning of the expressions; this harmless practice is fairly common): 1) a concept that is not defined, 2) a concept that appears in the axioms, 3) a concept used in the formulation of the (primitive) rules of inference; 4) a concept that is more fundamental or basic or evident than others. It seems that Martin uses this term in the fourth sense. But this sense is far from clear. Sometimes it is motivated by a specific philosophy, as for Tarski and neo-positivists the logical and physical concepts are primitive. I will not use the term in this sense. In any of the first three senses of primitiveness, no concept which is used as primitive must be used as primitive (except for degenerate, artificial cases). Just as no axiom is necessary, so no primitive concept is necessary. If a set is recursively enumerable, the enumeration can be performed in many, usually infinitely many, different ways. Axiomatization is a recursive enumeration of theorems. A chain of definitions is a recursive enumeration of the set of concepts appearing in a theory. Of course, a term may be primitive in one of the three senses without being primitive in the remaining two.

An especially important case occurs when the theory in question is not axiomatizable. Then there are no primitive terms in the second sense. There may be many, may be infinitely many, primitive terms in the first sense, even if there are infinitely many defined terms. There may be still rules of inference valid for such a system and therefore primitive terms in the third sense; such rules lead from some sets of sentences to sentences, even if there is no finite subset of theorems from which all theorems are obtainable. Also, for a natural language there are rules of inference which we use any time we hear utterances with understanding, as understanding consists on drawing consequences. But for the natural language there is no system, no axioms. There may be some common assumptions, the common knowledge of the linguistic group but the rest of the sentences come and go with a conversation, they are considered only momentarily, with a variety of degree of persuasiveness, but still with the rules of inference valid for the language as a whole. Those rules refer to grammatical constants and thus the grammatical constants are the primitive terms in the third sense. Most of them do not seem to be definable by means of others. Those constants constitute a special case of primitive terms in the third sense; they appear not only in the rules of the language, but also in the language itself. For instance in

(5) If α and β are sentences, then, except in certain specifiable cases, from the sentence α and β the sentence α follows.

the word *and* is a word from the studied language referred to by the meta-rule. But the words *sentence* or *follows* do not have to appear in the studied language. If we translate (5) into French, the word *sentence* becomes *phrase* and the word *follows* becomes *suit.* The word *and* in its second occurrence remains *and.* In that special sense *and* is a primitive term of English in the usual formulations of the grammar. In other places I refer to such words (or morphemes) as grammatical constants.

In summary, a large number of semantic properties have been described. The relations between concepts—for instances their interdefinability—have been given considerable attention, but very many questions remain to be answered. Martin correctly observes that there are many which I have not addressed.

If in asking whether some semantic concept is primitive with respect to another, we are asking whether the second is definable from the first, we are asking a question which is clear, significant and difficult. But if by primitiveness we mean, as Martin seems to, some sort of epistemic priority, then the question is not clear and will not be so until some precise sense is given to priority. It may be that the differences here between Martin and myself are just aesthetic.

Pragmatics

Following Morris and Carnap, Martin champions the role of pragmatics in linguistics and in analytical philosophy. Pragmatics, as conceived by its classics, was based on syntax and semantics and asked not only what is said and what does it mean but also who said it. One can also imagine pragmatics without semantics or even without much of syntax. That somebody made some sound is a pragmatical statement. There is much confusion about what pragmatics is to be, what questions and what terminology is to be typically pragmatic. In recent years pragmatics has entered linguistic literature. Some of the problems put under that heading are discourse analytical, some are psychological, some are socio-linguistic. Many of the problems discussed as pragmatics are sound problems and some of the answers are penetrating. But the field of pragmatics is not yet established as a coherent domain of specific studies.

Introducing the pragmatical concepts, Martin avails himself not only of terminology describing a speaker uttering a string of words but also of terminology which tells what was the intention of the speaker in uttering it. He employs not only purely pragmatic phrases like

x uses α

but also, and mainly, intentional pragmatic phrases like

x uses α to ...

where the preposition *to* indicates the purpose, the intent of the speaker in using α. Typically, after the occurrence of this preposition *to,* Martin puts a verb which characterizes the attitude of the speaker to the phrase α. For instance, Martin employs the phrase

x uses α to refer to the entity y

Uses by itself is a behavioral term while *uses to refer to* is not. Linguistics in a way uses *uses,* if usually tacitly. Perhaps it is present in any statement about a language. For any such statement asserts that a group (or more precisely the members of the group) typically uses some locutions. A socio-linguist may add that some members of the group use a locution whereas other members do not. He differentiates the group into subgroups. Linguists, of course, not only state that some people use a locution but that they operate with it in a standard way, in particular, that they draw conclusions from it, that they deny it in such and such fashion, that it is used in particular contexts and not in some other environments, etc. All these are statements about the use of the phrase but not about the intention of its use. At least not explicitly. Perhaps a locution is used with a given intention exactly when it occurs in particular surroundings, when it has some typical consequences or has some other syntactical or semantical properties. But this doubtful hypothesis is not at issue here. The hypothesis itself would be a pragmatic hypothesis, belonging to that extended pragmatics of Martin which includes the purpose of the speaker. There is virtue in keeping different kinds of problems apart. In particular, it is of interest to keep the behavioral concepts apart from non-behavioral. The concept of purpose is a non-behavioral one; people may tell us what is their purpose in saying something, but they may be wrong. For a long time linguistics used some semantical concepts, explicitly or implicitly, in all linguistic sciences. The concepts of repetition or of contrast, the concept of cognate words are basic in phonology and in historical linguistics. One may suspect that the generative grammars cannot avoid some similar semantic concepts. I think that a consequence grammar can describe systematically all the important facts a generative grammar of this or another style tries to describe. And, I think, no less will do; no grammar without the consequence relation can be an adequate grammar for a "conversational" language. But it would be a different thing to try to persuade linguists that they tacitly used in their theories the concept of intention. Strawson tried to argue for a claim like that, but his is not a convincing argument. Martin never claims intention is necessary for semantics as Strawson does. But he does not make the distinction between those concepts which enter a grammar (in essentially traditional sense though with modern explicit formalization) and those which are outside of the purely grammatical domain. It may be that the distinction is not exactly between behavioral and non-behavioral concepts, but it is clear that post-Saussurian linguistics is trying to avoid intention. Martin advocates the study of language in the broadest possible way. He writes (SHH):

> An important omission in Hiż's outlook is that no provision is made for contexts other than linguistic ones. It is insisted upon that sentences should not be considered in isolation, but rather as ingredients in strings. It is often only the whole string that has meaning. Indeed, even sentencehood may depend upon location within a string, much depending upon what precedes and what follows in the string. This is a point well worth emphasizing, and harks back to the early work of Harris. But no provision is made for non-linguistic contexts—states of body, states of mind of speaker and hearer, the social and personal relations between them, situation within a social group, grimaces, gestures, purposes, intentions, and so on and on. Such factors are often essential in communication, meaning, and paraphrase, influencing them in fundamental ways.... The study of language should be allowed to overflow in all directions, into bio-, psycho-, socio-linguistics, into cultural and historical studies, and the like. Hiż's conception seems too narrow for this. In any case, no explicit provision is made for it, for which a very extensive pragmatical vocabulary is needed.

I have no qualms about the study of language from all those, and other points of view—or with the reasonable study of any reasonable question. But just as the scarcity of a metal does not belong to chemistry, nor the market value of a painting to esthetics, so a grammarian may not consider in his work the intention of the speaker nor the personal relations between him and the hearer. Perhaps it is not a matter of principle; it is a matter of sharpening the problems and limiting the theories properly. Of course the limits of theories are set partly arbitrarily, but not observing them leads to a mental chaos. We do not want to be reminded every time we discover that a root of a polynomial is 5 that it is exactly how many children a friend has or, even, that it is the limit of 4.999(9). The problem of grammar is what is sayable and for that purpose some study of what is said is necessary (but not from all points of view, even if they are otherwise interesting). I am astonished to read that I do not "provide" for the study of non-linguistic context, for the state of mind of the speaker or of the hearer, for the purposes, intentions, and for many other things connected with language. I have nothing against somebody adding to the semantics as I narrowly outlined it. I *do not know what I* would have to provide for that purpose. The extensions of the aletheic semantics should be consistent with it. In addition, I would prefer if denotation or reference are not added, as I consider them misleading. Any extending of semantics should be judged by its own clarity. Somebody may add an aesthetic predicate and proclaim some locution elegant and some other clumsy. But a semanticist as such has nothing to "provide" for it. It is only in the unlikely case when somebody shows that an aletheic semantics cannot be developed without some aesthetic concepts that a semanticist must "provide" for aesthetics of language.

In one way a small part of pragmatics is involved in any linguistic research. To say that *A jay is a bird* is an English sentence or that *jay* and *bird* are English words is to say that some people use or may use them, that those words are used habitually by a large group of people and that those people are able to use the sentence *A jay is a bird* in their reasonings. These are pragmatic statements but not about this or another person as distinct from others; rather about anybody who conforms to the custom of the group. As with all other language facts, consequence, and therefore paraphrase, is a custom of a linguistic group. A necessary condition for a sentence to be a consequence of a set of sentences is that it customarily be used in such a role or that it customarily be used as a consequence of a subset of the set. But linguistic customs are not capricious. I postulate that if α is a consequence of A in linguistic custom, then α is true in all interpretations in which all sentences of A are true. Interpretation consists in replacing phrases by other phrases of the same grammatical category. The postulate says that speakers, when they are drawing consequences according to the custom, are in principle logically correct.

Notes

1. A consequence grammar imposes a structure on sentences by examining the facts of consequence in which the sentences take part.
2. This idea is from Zellig Harris.
3. About the veridical uses of *so* see my paper from *The Monist* and Charles H. Kahn.
4. The exact analysis of cross-reference is a complicated matter. I refer here to my paper "Referentials", but this paper is out of date. For

cross-reference within a single sentence, see several recent works of Noam Chomsky, e.g., in his *Essays on Form and Interpretation*. The extension of the concept of a sentence with cross-referential may partly coincide with what Martin, following Quine (and a long tradition, see, e.g., T. Kotarbinski, *Gnoseology,* Pergamon, originally published in 1929) calls *occasion sentences*. But Martin's characterization is pragmatical. I prefer to avoid this characterization not only because of my scepticism about pragmatics but mainly because cross-reference plays an essential role in the grammatical structure of sentences; cross-references within a sentence are an element in the syntax of that sentence; cross-references outside of a sentence contribute substantially to the fact that, as Martin well described it, "the sentences of a text "interanimate" each other in most intimate ways, and this interanimation must be made explicit in the sequence of forms by suitable cross-referential devices". (See my "On Logic-Linguistics: Structure, Transformation, and Paraphrase".)

5. In the same manner, generally, a phrase which is like a phrase α of a grammatical category but contains a free variable (or, in a natural language, a cross-referential) is of the same grammatical category as α. For instance, *her father* in *Peter is afraid of her father* is a noun phrase.

References

Chomsky, N. 1977. *Essays on form and interpretation*. North Holland: Amsterdam.

Hiż, H. 1960. The intuitions of grammatical categories. *Methods* 12, pp. 1-9.

_____ 1961. Congrammaticality, batteries of transformations and grammatical categories. In *Proceedings of symposia in applied mathematics,* 12, Structure of language and its mathematical aspects: American Math. Soc.

_____ 1964. The role of paraphrase in grammar. In *Monograph series on languages and linguistics* 17: Georgetown Univ.

_____ 1969a. Aletheic semantic theory. *The Philosophic Forum* 1, pp. 438-451.

_____ 1969b. Referentials. *Semiotica* 1, pp. 136-166.

_____ 1971. On the abstractness of individuals. In *Identity and individuation,* ed. Munitz, M. New York Univ. Press.

_____ 1973. On the rules of consequence for a natural language. *The Monist* 57, pp. 312-327.

_____ 1976. On some general principles of semantics of a natural language. *Philosophica* 18, pp. 129-138.

_____ 1979a. *Syntax and semantics*. Vol. 10. Academic Press: New York.

_____ 1979b. On logic-linguistics: structure, transformation, and paraphrase. In *Sixth international congress for logic, methodology and philosophy of science:* Hanover.

Kahn, C. 1973. *The verb 'be' in Ancient Greek*. Reidel: Dordrecht.

Kotarbinski, T. 1966. *Gnoseology*. Pergamon Press: New York.

Martin, R. 1953. On non-translational semantics. In *Proceedings of the XIth international congress of philosophy,* Vol. V: Amsterdam.

_____ 1958. *Truth and denotation:* a study in semantic theory. Chicago: Univ. of Chicago Press.

_____ 1978a. On Hiż's aletheic semantics and non-translationality. In *Events, reference and logical form,* pp. 145-155. Catholic Univ. of America Press: Wash., D. C.

_____ 1978b. On Carnap's semantics, Hiż's notion of consequence, and deep structure. In *Events, reference and logical form,* pp. 157-169. Catholic Univ. of America Press: Wash., D. C.

_____ 1978c. *Semiotics and linguistic structure.* SUNY Press: Albany.

_____ 1979. Some Hiżean heresies. In *Pragmatics, truth and language,* pp. 257-270. Reidel: Dordrecht.

Tarski, A. 1956. *Logic, semantics, metamathematics.* trans. Woodger, J. Oxford.

Richard M. Smaby

INFORMING WITH PRONOUNS
Extending Truth-Semantics

There is a growing interest in the semantics of natural languages. Some of the work in semantics takes the form of classical distributional analysis: What words can co-occur with what other words? How can we systematize these co-occurrence relations? Other work in semantics focuses on explicating formally the meaning of syntactic constructions and the meaning of a few constants, such as tense, negative particles, quantifiers, or pronouns.

Formalized semantics can be very consuming, making one lose sight of the goals of language description. What I will propose to you is a way of studying the semantics of natural languages that always tries to keep the roles of language in view. It may even shed some light on some pre-theoretical questions about language.

Let me focus on one use of language. We can use our language to inform, or to transmit information, to whatever use that information may be put. I remember my first course as a student of linguistics: In the first meeting the teacher drew a diagram on the board showing an information source or sender, with an encoding device, an information receiver, with a decoding device, and a transmission channel.

Unfortunately, that nice diagram was soon forgotten in the progress of the lectures of that course, and in most of my study and research since that time. I suppose that each of us who studies language scientifically thinks we are studying some small part of this information transmission system. I would like to suggest that we take this diagram seriously. In the last couple of years I have been trying to do that in the areas of syntax and semantics. But to do so requires something more than a diagram. It requires a cleanly articulated formal system. I would like to exhibit one attempt at such a formal system and persuade you that it helps us understand certain linguistic phenomena, in particular how pronouns function in the transmission of information.

1. Informing

Let me offer, then, a fairly simple but, hopefully, useful account of informing. A sentence of a language is uttered for the purpose of altering information. I prefer, in the first instance, to think of the purpose as a cooperative effort: The participants in a conversation are engaged in constructing a common information base, for some desired purpose. In the simplest case, one of the participants utters a sentence in order to add to the information content of the common information base.

The first idea to clarify is that of "information content." One should not be dogmatic here: There are a number of options. One approach is to let our common information consist of a set of sentences in some language particularly well-suited for storing information; the sentences in this set are simply the sentences we have agreed to take as true. Another approach is to use "models" or "state-descriptions." A state-description is simply a complete description of the world. Our own information about the world is never complete, and so our limited common information is consonant with a whole set of complete state-descriptions, each of which is an extension of our own partial information. On the state-description approach information content is simply a set of state-descriptions. Each approach has its advantages. Rather than argue for one position over another, let me simply take information content as given and operate with the concept informally, with the understanding that we can formalize it.

I said *operate* with them and, indeed, we must. But, in order to do so, we have to become clear about relations among information contents. The most basic relation is that of *having more information*. Given two information contents k_1 and k_2, one, say k_2, may have at least as much information as, if not more information than, the other, k_1. We can express this relation as in diagram 1, by connecting k_1 to k_2 by an upward tending line. For example, at a certain point in our conversation the common information content may be k_1. Then I utter the sentence:

(1) *John tickled Bill.*

and you accept it, at least for the sake of argument. So the new

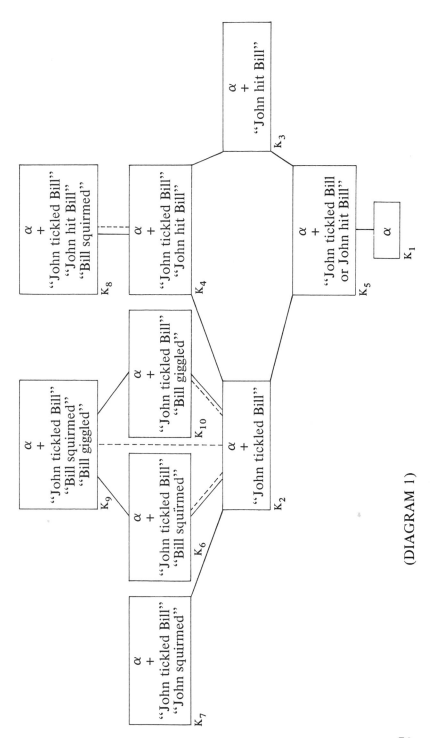

(DIAGRAM 1)

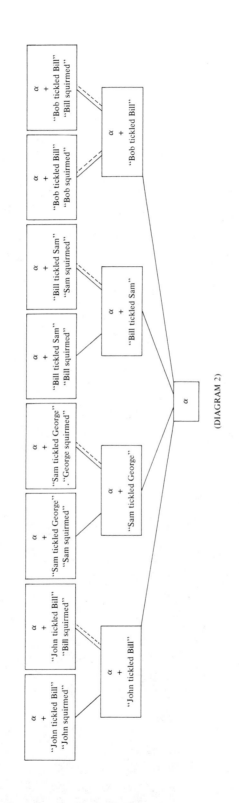

(DIAGRAM 2)

74

information content, k_2, is k_1 + "John tickled Bill," where the sentence in quotes indicates that, according to whatever formal mechanism has been adopted, the information that John tickled Bill has been added to k_1. Of course, k_2 has at least as much information as k_1. Instead of saying *John tickled Bill* I could have said

(2) *John hit Bill,*

which would have extended k_1 to k_3 on the diagram 1. K_3 has at least as much information as k_1. However, there is not necessarily any relation between k_2 and k_3. In fact, the global structure of the set of information contents is probably a lattice: Which is to say that the relation of having at least as much information is

    (i) reflexive, i.e., any content has at least as much information as itself,

    (ii) antisymmetric, i.e., if two contents each have as much information as the other, they are really the same content,

    (iii) transitive, i.e., if k_3 has at least as much information as k_2, and k_2 at least as much as k_1, then k_3 has at least as much information as k_1,

    (iv) given two information contents, there is a third content which is precisely the sum of the information of the two,

    (v) given two information contents there is a third which is precisely the information common to the two.

The first three conditions seem rather obvious; the last two come from simply reflecting on sentences like

(3) *John tickled Bill and John hit Bill.*

and

(4) *John tickled Bill or John hit Bill.*

When uttered at k_1, these sentences provide information contents k_4 and k_5 respectively fleshing out the relationships among contents. One may want to add more structure to the set of information contents; indeed, in a few minutes I will suggest more structure.

2. Pronouns

Now let me turn to pronouns. Pronouns are very interesting, even third-person pronouns. They are so interesting that they will require augmenting the concept of information content to that of information state, of which information content is only a part.

Pronouns have been studied in some detail. I am particularly interested in the coreference patterns of pronouns with other forms.

The advantage of adding pronouns to a language is nowhere clearly demonstrated (though it perhaps could be). There may be some truth in the claims that they are a device of economy. It remains, of course, to spell out what sort of economy. One could guess that the process of semantic interpretation of a phrase like *the boy who lost his toothbrush* is more energy-consuming than that of *he*, but is it so clear that *he* is more efficient than a proper name, for example, *John?* I can't be precise about these questions now. I will simply assume that pronouns have a reason for being, and see how they function semantically.

What I am going to say now will be reminiscent of the old prescriptive grammars or style manuals. Remember statements like: "The antecedent of the pronoun should be the closest full noun in the preceding text of the corresponding gender." Such statements were not really so bad, except that they were false. The rule does hold up in the example:

(5) *John arrived at 10. Bill arrived at 11. He drove.*

But not in

(6) *John outweighs Bill. He's 160.*

where the antecedent of he is *John*, nor in

(7) *John arrived after Bill left. He was looking for George.*

(8) *Bill left before John arrived. He was looking for George.*

However, let me suggest that some such rule is in order: The syntactic structure of the context does contribute to the interpretation of a pronoun. Let me make this more specific: The syntactic structure of the context provides a surface topic structure, ranking the individuals in the domain of discourse in preparation for continuing the discourse. In particular, the subject of the main clause of the most recent sentence is the highest in the topic ranking; then come other elements of its main clause, then elements of its subordinate clause, if any, and then elements of previous sentences according to the same pattern, as indicated in (9)

DIAGRAM (9) FOLLOWS ON NEXT PAGE

If there is textual material within the sentence in which the pronoun occurs, topic ranking is provided as in (10)

DIAGRAM (10) FOLLOWS ON NEXT PAGE

That is, for a pronoun in a subordinate clause, the subject of the main clause has the highest rank, next the object of that main clause, and then the ranking as in (9).

I will make the following strong claim: The syntactically preferred interpretations of a pronoun are those individuals higher on the topic ranking provided by the syntactic structure of the context. Or, somewhat anthropomorphically: "The pronoun wants the topic to stay the same."

(9)

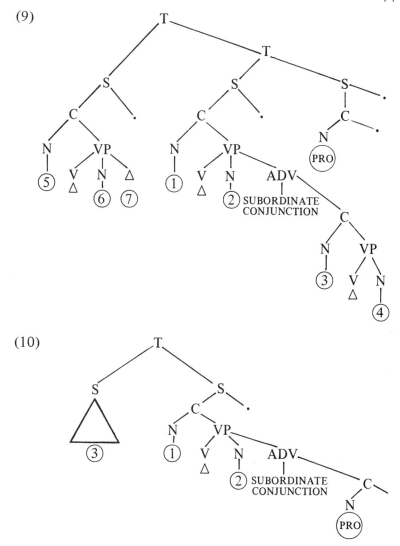

(10)

It might appear that counter-examples abound. For example, in

(11) *John tickled Bill. He squirmed.*

we seem to be following what makes sense for the pronoun, rather than the topic ranking of the preceding context.

Well, now what? Let me remind you that I said things like the topic structure of the context *contributes* to the interpretation of the pronoun; the higher ranked interpretations are *syntactically preferred*; the pronoun *wants* the topic to stay the same. Well, the pronoun doesn't always get what it wants. You say that sounds like downright obfuscation. And I agree, unless I can spell out more precisely just how the topic ranking contributes to the interpretation of the pronoun.

3. Relevance

To do this I will have recourse to the notion of information content I discussed earlier. At any given point in a discourse, there is a syntactic topic ranking, but there is also a predisposition toward some later information contents over others. For example, after learning that John tickled Bill, we anticipate further discourse by immediately wondering whether Bill squirmed or not, what the speaker's evaluation of John is, whether Bill tickled John back or not. One thing we don't generally consider is whether John squirmed or not. The term I will use for this anticipation is "relevance." Referring to diagram 1, information content k_6 is relevant to k_2, but k_7 is not. Thus, we want to add to the basic lattice structure a relevance relation R. We can indicate R pictorially by dotted connections on the lattice, as in diagram 1. Of course, the relation between tickling and squirming was not a peculiar property of John and Bill, but should hold for any tickler and ticklee. So we impose a general condition on the relation R that whenever k_i contains, for any x and y, information that x tickled y, then the state k_j obtained by adding the information that y squirmed is relevant to k_i. So we have the situation as in diagram 2. Note that once Bill's squirming becomes relevant to an information content, it remains relevant to all greater information contents. For example, k_8 is relevant to k_4 in diagram 1. This property of relevance seems correct, if we consider a text like

(12) *John tickled and hit Bill. He squirmed.*

We may want to add general structural conditions on R. Perhaps the sum of two relevant information contents should be relevant. This condition would account for

(13) *John tickled Bill. He giggled and squirmed.*

Thus, in diagram 1, k_9 is relevant to k_2, because k_6 and k_{10} are, and k_9 is the sum of k_6 and k_{10}. Perhaps R should be reflexive; that is, to repeat oneself may be awkward, but is nevertheless relevant, for example,

(14) *John tickled Bill. He tickled him.*

Note that stating R to account for the general relation between tickling and squirming, we should not prohibit the tickler from squirming. Indeed, there may be an individual, call him Bob, who has the strange trait of squirming when he tickles other people. Then we would have the situation at the right of diagram 2. Furthermore, besides tickling and squirming there are many other associated activities and properties: hitting and crying, shooting and dying, hitting and regretting, etc. We let the lack of any requirement of relevance provide the necessary negative information. For example, k_7 will fail to be relevant to k_2, since there are no associated activities to make it relevant.

   Keep in mind that to say one information content fails to be relevant to another does not mean it cannot be reached from that other. We can get to k_7 from k_2, as in the text

(15) *John tickled Bill. John squirmed.*

Relevance is used to resolve ambiguities, not as a barrier to more explicit informing.

4. Information states and informing with pronouns

   Now how does the relevance relation help with the interpretation of pronouns? The relevance relation is really the final arbiter, but it works in conjunction with the topic ranking discussed earlier. At a given point in the discourse a topic ranking is provided; then the relevance relation is invoked to pick the top item on the ranking which, when taken as the interpretation of the pronoun, results in an information content which is relevant. For example, the text (11) *John tickled Bill. He squirmed* informs as follows. First, *John tickled Bill* informs at k_1, yielding information content k_2, but also providing the topic ranking in (16)

(16)

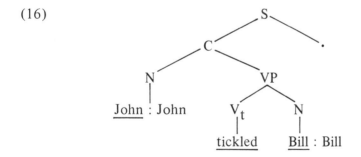

which is recorded, along with the information content, as part of the information state. That is, I am now saying that informing consists in moving from information state to information state, where each information state consists of recorded information content and recorded topic structure. It is convenient to record the latter in terms of syntactic analysis trees. Now, *He squirmed* informs at k_2 and the topic structure indicated in (16). The manner in which it informs is to work down the topic ranking until an item is found which will result in a relevant information content. So, it first attempts to inform with *he* interpreted as the first item in the topic ranking, namely John. The result is k_7, which is not relevant to k_2; so the interpretation of *he* as John fails. The next item on the topic ranking, namely Bill, is tried as the interpretation of *he*. The result is k_6 which is relevant to k_2.

80

So the search ends and *he* is interpreted as Bill. The result of informing with *He squirmed* is, thus, information content k_6 and the topic ranking in (17)

(17)

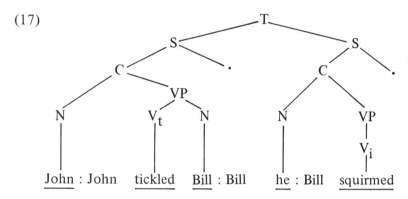

John : John   tickled   Bill : Bill   he : Bill   squirmed

5. Naming function

Before proceeding to indicate how to formalize these ideas, there is a classical fact of the coreference patterns of pronouns of English that I must integrate into this presentation. It is the fact that a subject pronoun cannot be coreferential with a following full-form. For example, in

(18) *He left after Bill ate.*

Bill and *he* cannot be coreferential; it is not a matter of a preferred interpretation. It was originally taken as a grammatical phenomenon that *he* and *Bill* could not be coreferential in such a frame. I will take it rather as a semantic phenomenon. The informal idea behind the present account is that an individual in the domain of discourse has a unique proper name in a given context. So, I may be called "Rich" by my wife, and "Dick" by my parents, but it will not do for me to have more than one proper name. For example,

(19) *Rich left after Dick ate.*

must be talking about two different people, if it is to be understood at all.

Let me suggest that it is this having one proper name in a given context that accounts for the restriction of non-coreference of *he* and *Bill* in (18). Using the name *he* for an individual in the subject of the sentence makes *he* the proper name of that individual for the rest of that sentence. So, attempting to use a full proper name like *Bill* for the same individual results in not being able to find a referent for *Bill*, or finding a different referent for *Bill*, a different Bill.

So let us assume that there is a naming function ν which assigns each individual a single name, and which will change with the context.

We will also need a denotation function δ which assigns each proper name an individual, if there is an individual for it. δ can best be thought of as an inverse to ν.

6. Formalizing informing with pronouns

This may be suggestive but it won't suffice. Let us discuss how to formalize a semantics of informing such as that suggested above.

I assume that we have a context-free grammar of English, which will provide analyses of phrases of the language. Thus, we can write the semantics making use of analyzability in a fashion similar to transformations in a transformational grammar.

By now we have agreed at least for the sake of argument that an information state consists of a number of things:
–information content
–topic ranking (in the form of syntactic trees)
–naming function

It is convenient to represent these components (and a couple more yet to come) in the pictorial form.

(20)

$$\alpha$$
$$|$$
$$(K)\ [\beta\ ]$$
$$\nu$$

The interpretation of the picture is that the phrase β is informing at the location indicated on the tree α, on information content K, with naming function ν.

We will take verbs as the atomic units of informing. However, in English, verbs by themselves don't inform. They are typically accompanied by subjects and possibly objects. But subjects and objects serve merely to specify the arguments of the verb. So, as long as we specify the arguments of the verb, we can inform with the verb.

This can be accomplished with semantic rules like (21):

(21)

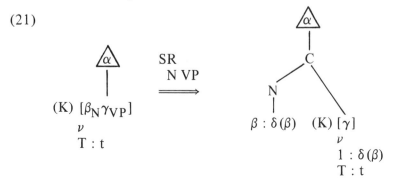

82

The rule (21) is to be read as follows, from left to right. Given an information state consisting of information content K, a naming function ν, and a topic-structure syntactic tree α, if we inform at the indicated location on α with a string analyzable as a noun followed by a verb phrase, we change the information state by constructing on α some additions, namely a subject sub-tree: A node labelled N dominating a node labelled with a pair consisting of the linguistic form β which was the subject and the denotation of that form $\delta(\beta)$, and informing now with the verb-phrase γ in the new context composed of the additions to the tree just described, the same content K and naming function ν, but with the first argument of the verb specified to be $\delta(\beta)$, the denotation of β, which is indicated by the new subscript on the square brackets $1:\delta(\beta)$.

For example, informing with *Bill squirmed* is indicated in (22)

(22)

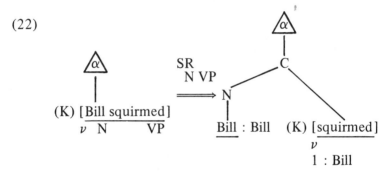

The original node of the informing is labelled C. On the left that node dominates a node labelled N which in turn dominates a node labelled with the pair consisting of the word *Bill* and Bill himself. On the right it dominates the node at which informing with the verb-phrase *squirmed* takes place with its first argument specified as Bill.

Next, we must specify how an intransitive verb informs:

(23)

Looking at (23), informing with an intransitive verb takes place at a location on a tree and information content K, with first argument specified. Informing results in adding to the tree the label

V_i at the node of original informing and a node dominated by that node, which is labelled with the verb β. It also produces addition to the information content K that d β's. For example, to continue informing as in the above example, see figure (24), in which the verb *squirmed* is added to the tree and the content K is augmented by the information that Bill squirmed.

(24)

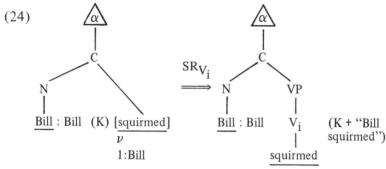

We need to go one step further with transitive verb phrases. Referring to figure (25), we see that the object of a transitive verb is added to the tree together with its denotation, and its denotation is specified as the second argument of the verb, by means of the subscript 2: $\delta(\beta)$. Then according to (26), informing with a transitive verb consists in adding the verb to the tree and adding the information that the two arguments are in the relation corresponding to the verb.

(25)

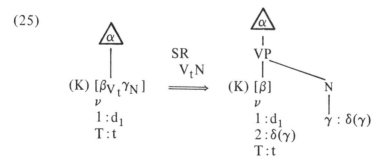

(26)

A text is analyzed as a sentence followed by a text:

(27)

$$\text{(K) } [\beta_S \gamma_T] \quad \overset{SR}{\underset{ST}{\Longrightarrow}} \quad \text{(K) } [\beta][\gamma]$$

The concept behind the notation (K) $[\beta]$ $[\gamma]$ is that you first inform with β on K at the location on the tree indicated and then inform with γ at the resulting information content, at the location indicated. The naming function distributes unaltered across the composition of informing.

A sentence consists of a clause plus sentence boundary—say, the period in written English. Informing with a sentence is the same as informing with a clause, but with an indication of sentence boundary, a feature important to topic ranking in a text:

(28)

$$\text{(K) } [\beta_C \cdot] \quad \overset{SR}{\underset{C \cdot}{\Longrightarrow}} \quad \text{(K) } [\beta]$$

Now we can give an extended text example:

DIAGRAM (29) FOLLOWS ON NEXT PAGE

Informing with the text
   John tickled Bill. Bill squirmed.
consists in first informing with the sentence
   John tickled Bill.
and on the result of that, informing with the sentence
   Bill squirmed.
After informing with
   John tickled Bill ,
its syntactic structure is recorded, as well as its information content. Then on that structured context and information content, the sentence
   Bill squirmed.
informs, yielding the structured text and information content indicated at the end of (29).

Now consider the case of a subject pronoun. Referring to

(29)

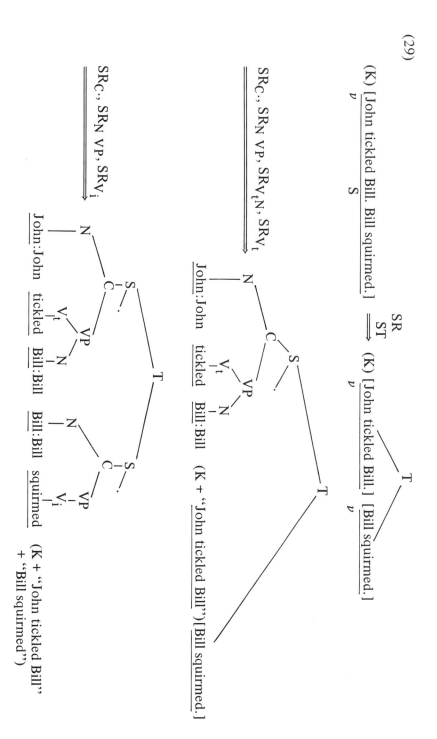

(K) [John tickled Bill. Bill squirmed.]
$$\underset{v}{\quad} \underset{S}{\quad} \overset{SR}{\underset{ST}{\Longrightarrow}} \text{(K) } [\underline{\text{John tickled Bill.}}] \; [\underline{\text{Bill squirmed.}}]$$

SR$_{C.}$, SR$_{N}$ VP, SR$_{V_tN}$, SR$_{V_t}$
$$\Longrightarrow$$

SR$_{C.}$, SR$_{N}$ VP, SR$_{V_i}$
$$\Longrightarrow$$

John:John   tickled   Bill:Bill
(K + ''John tickled Bill'')[Bill squirmed.]

Bill:Bill   squirmed
(K + ''John tickled Bill''
 + ''Bill squirmed'')

85

(30), we see that informing with a subject pronoun is very much like informing with a subject proper noun, the primary difference being in the choice of the referent for the pronoun. The referent of the pronoun is the first individual of the appropriate gender on the topic ranking such that informing with it as the interpretation of the pronoun yields an information content relevant to the input content k.

(30)

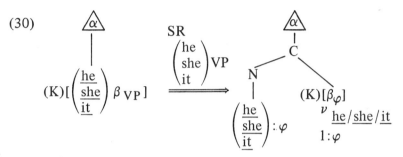

where φ is the first individual of
$\begin{pmatrix} \text{masculine} \\ \text{feminine} \\ \text{neuter} \end{pmatrix}$ gender in the topic ranking such that informing with it as indicated yields an information content relevant to K.

The notation $\nu\ {}^{\varphi}_{\text{he/she/it}}$ indicates that φ's name is now he, she, or it, respectively. The selection of φ can be formalized. The most difficult part of that task is the formalization of the topic ranking.

    Take the example

(11) *John tickled Bill. He squirmed.*

We will need to refer to the relevance structure in diagram 1.

DIAGRAM (31) FOLLOWS ON NEXT PAGE

Informing with this text proceeds the same as in the previous example until we get to the pronoun subject of the second sentence. Looking now at (31), there are two routes the informing could take. One, the one preferred by the syntactic topic ranking, is by interpreting *he* as John; and the other, second in the syntactic topic ranking, by interpreting *he* as Bill. The two routes are indicated in the braces of (31), with the higher one syntactically preferred over the lower one. But even though interpreting *he* as John is syntactically preferred, if we consult the relevance structure of diagram 1, we see that John's squirm-

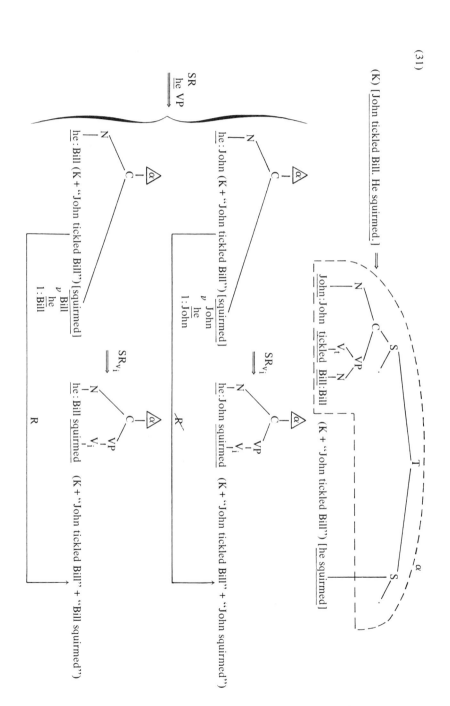

(31)

(K) [John tickled Bill. He squirmed.] ⟹

ing is not relevant information, given only that John tickled Bill. Thus, the syntactically preferred route fails to provide a relevant result, and the next route is considered. Since Bill's squirming upon being tickled is relevant, that route is successful and the result of informing with the text is the structured text with *he* interpreted as Bill and content that John tickled Bill and Bill squirmed.

Now you have the key idea of how syntax and semantics interact in the transmission of information to resolve the reference of pronouns.

Alex Orenstein

TOWARDS A PHILOSOPHICAL
CLASSIFICATION OF QUANTIFIERS

For philosophical conceptions which vary by a hair's breadth from those for which suitable terms exist, . . . invent terms with a due regard for the usages of philosophical terminology and those of the English language . . . Before proposing a term, notation, or other symbol, consider maturely whether it perfectly suits the conception and will lend itself to every occasion, whether it interferes with any existing term, and whether it may not create an inconvenience by interfering with the expression of some conception that may hereafter be introduced into philosophy.
C. S. Peirce "The Ethics of Terminology"
(Peirce 1931-1935, Vol. II p. 133)

There are several confusions in the literature concerning substitutional quantification. Dunn and Belnap, in their admirable paper "The Substitution Interpretation of the Quantifiers" (1968), have taken steps toward removing a number of these confusions. Kripke's excellent "Is There a Problem about Substitutional Quantification?" (1976) serves this purpose as well. In this paper, I would like to examine one such confusion and, after reflecting on it, propose a classification of the leading approaches to quantifiers. The paper offers no new technical insights but, rather, some needed philosophical clarification.

It was Quine who introduced the terms "substitutional" and "referential" or "objectual" to mark a distinction of different kinds of interpretations of the quantifiers. The use of this terminology and the classification it represents is widespread. I shall argue that this way of making the distinction can be seriously misleading. The paper is divided into three parts. In the first I provide an informal introduction to the issues. In the second part I propose a revision of the accepted classification of the quantifiers. In the last portion I illustrate the utility of the new classification for critically evaluating the views of historical figures such as Ramsey and Lesniewski as well as contemporary writers such as Hintikka, Leblanc, Barcan-Marcus, and others.

I. The Confusion

Quine has used the terms "substitutional" and "referential" (or "objectual") quantification (1969; pp. 64, 105). By "referential"–"objectual" he means reference to a referent, i.e., usually a non-linguistic object, and not reference to a referend, i.e., a linguistic entity. Though this terminology and the classification it represents are widely accepted, I want to put the reader on guard that I shall argue that Quine's terminology can be misleading. Adopting for the moment Quine's terminology, one way to understand the difference between the substitutional and referential–objectual views would be to construct a paradigm to contrast them. Consider the sentence "All humans are mortal," which is almost always symbolized as "$(x)(Hx \supset Mx)$". On the substitutional view, we are concerned with the individual variable and its substituends. Here the substituends would most likely be individual constants. The truth of the universal conditional would be a matter of the truth of every one of its substitution instances. Another way of putting the matter is to consider the expansion for this sentence, e.g., "$(Ha \supset Ma)$ & $(Hb \supset Mb)$ & $(Hc \supset Mc)$ & . . . etc." For the finite case, a universal conditional is true if and only if its expansion is also true. On the referential view "All humans are mortal" is true when all the objects ranged over by "x" are such that if any one is a human then it is mortal. Here we are concerned with all the values of the variable, while on the substitutional view we are concerned with all the substituends. In a domain containing only Alfred, Betty, and Charles these three objects would, as human and mortal, suffice for the truth of the referential reading. By contrast the names "Alfred," "Betty," and "Charles," substituted for "x" in "$Hx \supset Mx$," and each time yielding a true sentence, would suffice for the truth of the substitutional reading.

What is misleading about Quine's classification is that it suggests that the two kinds of quantification are mutually exclusive. As a case in point of how one can be misled consider Quine's own views over the years on Lesniewskian quantification. In Quine's earlier work (i.e., before his debates with Ruth Barcan-Marcus in the 1960's) he regarded all quantification as being what he now calls referential. In his forthcoming intellectual autobiography, for a volume in the Schillp Library of Living Philosophers series, Quine recalls his arguments with Lesniewski in the 1930's, that the latter's quantification with regard to diverse grammatical categories results in enormous ontological commitments.

> With Lesniewski I would argue far into the night, trying to convince him that his quantification over all syntactic categories carried ontological commitment.

According to Quine's views at the time, Lesniewski's system of protothetic (an expanded propositional logic) which requires quantifying into sentence positions, e.g., $(p)(p \supset p)$ and truth-functional connective positions, e.g., $(\exists f)(pfp)$, requires special objects reckoned among one's ontology as the values of such variables.

Another of Lesniewski's systems, one called "Ontology," bothered Quine too and for analogous reasons. Ontology is a sort of calculus of nouns which includes common nouns as well as proper nouns. Now while quantification into proper noun positions is the staple of the first-order canonic notation favored by Quinians, quantification into noun positions as such (be the nouns common, proper, universal, or vacuous) is something Quine regarded with concern, a concern which he expressed to Lesniewski, and his concern persisted over the years. As late as 1951, when he reviewed Ajdukiewicz's paper "On the Notion of Existence" which appeared in *The Journal of Symbolic Logic,* Quine expressed similar misgivings. In his paper Ajdukiewicz had been, to a large extent, merely employing the definition of existence found in Lesniewski's system of Ontology. The definition:

$$b \text{ exists} \equiv (\exists a)(a \in b)$$

requires quantifying into noun positions, i.e., the variables "a" and "b" are, so to speak, *noun variables.* Quine (1951, p. 141) wrote:

> Then, where 'a' and 'b' are thought of as general terms, 'a ε b' is construed as true if and only if 'a' is true of one and only one object and 'b' is true of that object. Leśniewski, and others who have found this part of his logic useful (Kotarbiński, Ajdukiewicz), have entertained an amiable distaste for abstract entities and hence have liked to appeal to general terms, more or less as above, rather than to classes. Too little significance, however, has been attached to the fact that the variables which have been said to stand in places appropriate to general terms are subjected in Lesniewski's theory to quantification. Such quantification surely commits Leśniewski to a realm of values of his variables of quantification; and all his would-be general terms must be viewed as naming these values singly. If quantification as Leśniewski used it did not commit him squarely to a theory of classes as abstract entities, then the present reviewer is at a loss to imagine wherein such commitment even on the part of a professing Platonist can consist.

In the course of his interchanges with Barcan-Marcus, Quine became aware of the ontologically neutral possibilities of substitutional quantification. The most publicized of these discussions occurred when he commented on a paper of hers at a meeting of the Boston Colloquium for the Philosophy of Science in 1962. Quine spoke of the substitutional view as "deviating" from his own standard referential account and in later works he spoke of it as comprising a "deviant logic" (Quine 1966, p. 181). He commented that:

> Quantification ordinarily so-called is purely and simply the logical idiom of objective reference. When we reconstrue it in terms of substituted expressions rather than real values, we waive reference. We preserve distinctions between the true and false, as in truth-function logic itself, but we cease to depict the referential dimension.

Speaking thus of substitutional quantification as "waiving matters of reference," and hence of issues of ontological import, Quine took a different attitude towards Lesniewskian quantification. Now Quine construed Lesniewski's quantifiers for diverse grammatical categories as being substitutional and thereby not involving any questions of reference and the attendant additional ontological commitments. In *Ontological Relativity* he wrote:

Such is the course that has been favored by Leśniewski and by Ruth Marcus. Its nonreferential orientation is seen in the fact that it makes no essential use of namehood. That is, additional quantifications could be explained whose variables are place-holders for words of any syntactical category. Substitutional quantification, as I call it, thus brings no way of distinguishing names from other vocabulary, nor any way of distinguishing between genuinely referential or value-taking variables and other place-holders. Ontology is thus meaningless for a theory whose only quantification is substitutionally construed; meaningless, that is, insofar as the theory is considered in and of itself. The question of its ontology makes sense only relative to some translation of the theory into a background theory in which we use referential quantification (Quine 1969, pp. 63-64).

Quine's conclusion that Lesniewskian quantifications, especially those that are part of a system carefully named "Ontology," should have no bearing on issues of reference and ontology must strike one, at the very least, as unusual. It was to refute this Quinian interpretation that lead Küng and Canty to reply in their paper "Substitutional Quantification and Lesniewskian Quantifiers" (1970). In that paper they rejected Quine's classification in the application to Lesniewski's quantifiers. The alternative classifications that I present in this paper allow for a more natural understanding of Lesniewski's systems of logic.

As we have seen, Quine's terms "referential" and "substitutional" quantification can mislead us into thinking that the two are mutually exclusive. In the referential case when we quantify, we refer to objects. As is well known, this reference is the basis for connecting the particular quantifier with existence claims and for ontological commitment being a matter of values of variables. Implicit in this classification is the suggestion that with substitutional quantification there are no questions of reference, but merely of substituends, constants, or, put slightly differently, merely questions of substitution instances. Going along with this suggestion is the view that substitutional quantification has nothing to do with questions of ontology and that the particular quantifier substitutionally construed cannot be used to express existence claims.

However, the distinction made in the preceding paragraph is faulty. Contrary to the suggestion above, substitutional quantifications can be referential, can have existential import, and can be a vehicle for ontological commitments. To illustrate this point, let us consider again the sentence: All humans are mortal, i.e., $(x)(Hx \supset Mx)$. On the substitutional construal a universal sentence is true if every instance is true. Thus this sentence's being true requires that "If Alfred is human then Alfred is mortal," "If Betty is human then Betty is mortal," and so on would all have to be true. Now there is no reason why the substituends (the singular terms) in these instances "Alfred," "Betty," etc., cannot be taken as referring to precisely the objects Alfred, Betty, etc., that are referred to on a non-substitutional reading. The quantification is *per se* substitutional because the quantifier is explained in terms of substituends and instances, but it is also *per accidens* referential because the substituends refer. In cases of this sort where the substituends refer to the same objects that are appealed to on a non-substitutional referential reading (as would be the case in explaining "All humans are mortal" as true without appealing to substitution instances, e.g., as true when all the objects "x" ranges over are such that if any are human they are mortal), then the two accounts of the quantifiers coincide. Tarski's account of the quantifiers provides a paradigm of such non-substitutional quantification.

As Kripke (using Quine's terminology though innocently only to distinguish substitutional from Tarskian quantifiers) puts it in his recent paper (1976, p. 351) on substitutional quantification:

> *So, in the special case where (a) and (b) are postulated in the metatheory*, there is indeed little difference between a substitutional quantifier and a referential quantifier ranging over the set of denotata.*
>
> **(a) a totally defined denotation function is given for all the terms of L and (b) all formulae in L are transparent.*

In a similar spirit "Some humans are mortal, " i.e., $(\exists x)(Hx \& Mx)$, can be construed substitutionally and referentially. The truth of the instance, "Alfred is human and Alfred is mortal," suffices for the truth of the substitutional generalization. If the singular term "Alfred" is used to refer and if our referents are limited to existents, then this substitutional account coincides with the referential one. In this way, substitutional quantification can be adapted to express existence claims and to record ontological commitments. (As this essay was going to press I received a letter from Professor Quine in which he clarifies his position:

> *You write that "Quine's introduction of the terms "referential" and "substitutional" quantification suggests that the two kinds are mutually exclusive." It*

shouldn't suggest that. They overlap. Quantification in elementary number theory is referential and substitutional; there is no difference when everything quantified over has a designator. See Roots of Reference, page 114, lines 21-24; Ways of Paradox, enlarged edition, pages 318-320; Philosophy of Logic, page 92, fourth line from bottom. Actually my view is the one you propose toward the bottom of page 39. (Quine is referring to the combination of the substitutional and referential views for first-order cases discussed in the preceding paragraph and again later in this essay.)

Had time permitted I would have rewritten material to stress that though Quine's terminology has been the occasion for some to view the two kinds of quantification as being exclusive, he himself does not hold this view.)

A proper understanding of the substitutional—nonsubstitutional distinction requires seeing that the distinction essentially marks different kinds of truth conditions for general sentences, and that in the substitutional case, this distinction leaves open the question of how to formulate the truth conditions for the instances. When the truth conditions for the instances involve reference, e.g., "Alfred is human" is true if "Alfred" refers to one of the objects "is human" applies to, the substitutional quantification inherits the referential force of its instances. (Substitutional quantification ceases to be referential when the truth of the instances is not a matter of reference. I provide examples of such cases later.)

To reinforce the central point that substitutional generalizations can inherit referential force from their instances, consider certain analogies between the quantifiers and truth functional connectives. Just as the generalizations

$(x)(Hx \supset Mx)$ and $(\exists x)(Hx \mathbin{\&} Mx)$

can be understood in terms of their respective substitution instances

$(Ha \supset Ma)$, $(Hb \supset Mb)$, etc.,

and

$(Ha \mathbin{\&} Ma)$, $(Hb \mathbin{\&} Mb)$, etc.,

so are the truth conditions for truth functional complex sentences such as the above conditionals and conjunctions construed in terms of their constituents. Thus the constituents of the above conjunctions that need be taken account of are:

Ha, Ma, Hb, Mb, etc.

The explanation of the truth conditions for the instances and those for the atomic constituents can be independent of the exact formulation of the conditions for the generalizations and the conjunctions. A universal generalization is true if all its instances are and nothing need be said here as to how the instances acquire their truth value. Similarly, a conjunction is true when both conjuncts are, and nothing need be said at this point as to how the conjuncts acquire their truth value. To maintain that substitutionally construed quantifications are not referential would be like saying that the truth of the conjunctive claim that Socrates is human and Plato is human, as it is ordinarily understood, has no referential force because it suffices for the truth of the conjunction merely that both conjuncts be true. The conjunction, though, has referential force, i.e., those who make this claim refer to Socrates and Plato. The conjunction is a referential vehicle, not because of the truth conditions for the conjunction per se, but because of the reference that is part of the ordinary truth conditions for the conjuncts.

The convergence of substitutional quantification and reference, as well as with the existential reading of the particular quantifier, has many precedents. To begin with this unification provides a more generous way of understanding Russell's assimilation of the expression "sometimes true" and the "there exists" locutions in his early writings.

Somewhat more surprising is that it furnishes a way of interpreting some of Quine's early remarks. In fact these remarks provide a fine account of how the substitutional treatment of quantifiers and the referential treatment of instances can be put in the service of expressing existence claims by the use of the particular quantifier (Quine 1939, pp. 49-50).

> Instead of describing names as expressions with respect to which existential generalization is valid, we might equivalently omit express mention of existential generalization and describe names simply as those constant expressions which replace variables and are replaced by variables according to the usual logical laws of quantification.
>
> Here, then, are five ways of saying the same thing: "There is such a thing as appendicitis"; "The word 'appendicitis' designates"; "The word 'appendicitis' is a name"; "The word 'appendicitis' is a substituend for a variable"; "The disease appendicitis is a value of a variable." The universe of entities is the range of values of variables. To be is to be the value of a variable.

I have distinguished substitutional from non-substitutional quantification, in that the former appeals to the notion of instances and the latter does not. But we should be aware that there are different variants of substitutional quantification . So far, I have emphasized a variant which is referential. The convergence of substitutional quantification and "referential" is most functional when the substituends are straightforwardly referential. This occurs in the case of the non-vacuous names, etc., that serve as substitutends for the variables of extensional first-order logic. Substitutional quantification and "referential" quantification may diverge where the substituends are not clearly referential. Cases of this sort are more likely to occur when the substituends are vacuous names, or names embedded in intensional contexts, or not names at all, e.g., predicate constants, sentences, or sentence connectives. Substitutional quantification for vacuous terms, intensional contexts and non-nominal positions appears, at first glance, as if it can profitably be treated in a non-referential fashion. It is here that the substitutional reading of the particular quantifier seems to have less connection with existence and ontological commitment.

II. The Classification

The idea behind the classification I propose is rather simple. Let us call an analysis of quantification "substitutional" when the analysans segment of the truth conditions for the quantifier makes essential use of the notion of a substitution instance but not necessarily of notions such as that of a domain, values of variables, or sequences of objects satisfying an open sentence. If substitutional quantification is so construed, then non-substitutional quantification can be distinguished from it as not involving the concepts of a substitution instance in accounting for the truth of a generalization. Tarski's account remains the paradigm for non-substitutional quantification. He takes sequences as the objects satisfying a sentential function, and says that a sequence satisfies an open sentence of the form of a universal quantification if and only if, no matter how we vary the sequence with repect to the variable bound by the quantifier, the open sentence is still satisfied. To repeat, the major difference between substitutional and non-substitutional quantification as presently explicated is that the former makes essential reference to substitution instances and the latter does not.

Another point made earlier was that the matter of how the instances of substitutional quantifications are themselves made true is independent of (and need not be given in) the analysans of the quantificational sentences. Consider the following truth condition intended to explicate substitutional quantification for a standard first-order language:

The valuation of $((x)A) = T$ iff the valuation of $((t/x)A) = T$, for all singular expressions t.

Such a condition for a quantification is independent of the truth conditions for its instances, the "$((t/x)A)$," in the above. (The point is the simple one mentioned earlier that is analogous to the case of truth conditions for truth functional sentences like conjunction. These truth conditions do not mention how the conjuncts get their truth values.)

To further illustrate the point that a generalization can be *per se* substitutional, i.e., its truth condition involves the concept of instances, and *per accidens*, either referential, i.e., the truth conditions for these instances involves the concept of reference, or non-referential, i.e., the truth conditions for the instances don't involve the concept of reference, let us contrast the views of two substitutional theorists. Our first theorist assigns truth values to instances in the usual way, e.g., "Socrates is human" is true if and only if "Socrates" refers to (is assigned) an individual that is also referred to by (is a member of the set assigned to) "is human." The resulting particular generalization "$(\exists x)(x$ is human)," (though explained substitutionally) does derivatively have a referential effect. For the second theorist, the situation is quite different. She regards the instance "Pegasus is a flying horse" as true even though no referents are assigned to its parts. The resulting generalization "$(\exists x)(x$ is a flying horse)," taken substitutionally, is true but need not have any referential or ontological force.

The present recommendation for the use of the locutions "substitutional" and "referential" quantification helps us to see that a generalization can be substitutional as well as referential (our first theorist), or substitutional but not referential (our second theorist), or non-substitutional (Tarski and following him Quine). Quine's opposition of substitutional and referential quantification has led many astray. A quantification is interpreted substitutionally when its truth conditions essentially involve the notion of an instance but this does not preclude the possibility that the truth conditions for these instances secure the reference in question.

My informal way of discussing substitutional quantification coincides with Kripke's much more adequate account. Kripke provides a restricted language L_0 and at first assumes that the truth conditions for its sentences have been given (later in his essay he provides these conditions using a new and rather unique semantical primitive). Probably the most familiar sentences that could be included in L_0 are the atomic sentences. L_0 is extended to the Language L by syntactical rules which introduce negations, conjunctions, and quantifications on the sentences of L_0. The truth conditions for negations and conjunctions are the usual ones and the conditions for quantification are substitutional.

While L_o provides the substituends for the substitutional quantifiers of L the question of whether these substituends designate/refer is left open. If the sentences of L_o are atomic sentences the individual constants need not be assigned objects. Moreover the sentences of L_o need not be our atomic sentences and the substituends from L_o may be predicate constants or sentences, and these presumably need not be assigned objects. L_o may even contain opaque constructions. It may also contain negations, conjunctions and quantifications so long as we distinguish these from the negations, conjunctions and quantifications of L. By setting up and separating L_o and L in this way, Kripke is able to establish results for substitutional quantification in all its varied uses, referentially and non-referentially, in opaque and in transparent constructions, and quantifying over non-nominal positions.

In this paper I have maintained that substitutional quantification pertains to how generalizations are true (truth in all or in some instances) and that the way in which instances acquire their truth value is left open. Kripke has much more adequately made the same point about the independence of the truth conditions for quantifiers in sentences of the language L, and truth conditions for the sentences of the language L_o. This relation of Kripke's approach to the one I have adopted is as follows:

Truth Conditions for

| | L_o | | | Atomic Sentences |
| L | $\begin{cases} \text{Negations} \\ \text{Conjunctions} \\ \text{Quantifications} \end{cases}$ | | Instances | $\begin{cases} \text{Negations} \\ \text{Conjunctions} \\ \text{Quantifications} \end{cases}$ |

Kripke in fact notes that L_o need not be taken as containing only atomic sentences, but could contain conjunctions, negations etc. (and thereby be very much more like my instances). He does not actually use this broader L_o because metalogical results are not as readily provable   with it as a basis.

While Kripke's essay provides the firmest foundations to date for substitutional quantification, I would like to take exception on two minor points. The first is that he continues to use Quine's terminology of "substitutional" versus "referential-objectual" quantification (though he himself uses the terms harmlessly for the legitimate substitutional versus Tarskian distinction). The second is his suggestion for a more perspicuous treatment of these two types of quantification by using a different notation for each; "(x)" and "$(\exists x)$" as the referential idiom and "(πx)" and "$(\exists x)$" as the substitutional notation.

Where these different notations add clarity as shorthand for the Tarskian and non-Tarskian (substitutional) distinction, e.g., in Kripke's metalogical queries, I see no problem. Difficulties might arise, however, if the signs are taken to reflect the philosophical positions associated with the misleading substitutional-referential distinction. This would be unfortunate, for as I mentioned earlier, "$(\exists x)$" and "(Σx)" could be used both to have the same referential force and to express the same concept of existence. If we wanted different notations to record philosophically interpretations of quantifiers, it might be more perspicuous to use subscripts and to have many, and not just two, new locutions, e.g., "$(\exists x)_t$" for the Tarskian, "$(\exists x)_{sr}$" for the substitutional and referential, "$(\exists x)_t$" for the Tarskian and existential, "$(\exists x)_{tm}$" for the Tarskian and Meinongian, "$(\exists x)_{sre}$" for the substitutional, referential and existential, etc.

One line of argumentation for the classification I have proposed consists of looking at alternatives. Let us examine the consequences of saying a quantifier is interpreted referentially if there is mention of reference (objects) in the truth conditions or their instances, and substitutionally otherwise. Such a view is implicit in a recent paper by Baldwin (1979; pp. 232-233). There are good reasons for rejecting such a classification. The first that I give is mainly polemical but helps us to see the extreme consequences of this view. On such a classification substitutional quantification would almost amount to a straw man for it is not easy to see many interesting applications of substitutional quantification where the instances are not explained in terms of reference or any word-object relation. A second and more important point is that this classification, unlike the one offered in this paper, does not rely on an essential feature of the interpretation of the quantifiers, but mentions the truth conditions for the instances as well. In so doing it involves a decided disanalogy with the classifications of other diverging interpretations of logical constants, e.g., intuitionist versus classical negation. Moreover, the classification would ignore the similarity between two cases where the quantifiers are both explained in terms of instances, but diverge over whether to explain the instances in terms of reference. As a last consideration, it will not have escaped the reader's attention that whatever needs such a classification might have could be as readily accomplished by using our substitutional versus non-substitutional distinction and thereby focusing on the substitutional-referential variant.

Guido Kung and John Canty have suggested abandoning Quine's substitutional-referential distinction when the word-object relation involved in the instances is not a singular term one-to-one (naming) relation to an object. Their classification is somewhat *ad hoc* (substitutional, referential and Lesniewskian quantification), in being designed for their special purpose of clarifying Lesniewski's views. All but the first of the critical remarks made of the classification considered in the preceding paragraph can be brought to bear here. In addition, in the next part of this paper, I will argue for the utility of our classification in understanding Lesniewski's views.

III. Applying the Revised Classification

In discussing applications of this classification I will somewhat artifically arrange the material according to the areas where substitutional quantification appears most plausibly to be non-referential, i.e., quantification with respect to (a) diverse grammatical categories, (b) vacuous terms and (c) intensional contexts.

A. Diverse Grammatical Categories

"Stanislaus Lesniewski's system of formal logic is as far as we know the only generally known system in which quantifiers are uniformly applied to variables belonging to every syntactical category." (Kotarbinski 1957; p. 152).

As mentioned earlier, Quine has stated that Lesniewskian quantification is substitutional and not referential. Quine's reason for saying this is that Lesniewski has quantification for diverse grammatical categories, e.g., for sentences and connectives in protothetic and, of special interest to us here, for nouns in elementary ontology. And yet a philosopher-logician of a nominalist cast of mind, such as Quine presumes Lesniewski to be, would not want to be committed to the existence of abstract objects like the sets nouns might name. Although not mentioned by Quine, another reason for this conjecture is that for Lesniewski, the particular quantifier does not have the force of existence. For example, reflect on how the sentence 'Something doesn't exist' fares in the Lesniewskian and Quinean traditions. For Lesniewski it is rendered as "$(\exists a) \sim (ex\ a)$", i.e., "$(\exists a) \sim (a\ exists)$" and is a contingent truth, i.e., some object a doesn't exist, given the truth of substitution instances such as "Unicorns don't exist," or Pegasus doesn't exist." It is hard to see how a Quinian would render the above as a contingent truth.[1]

In opposition to Quine, Küng and Canty (1970, p. 179) have argued that Lesniewski did not interpret quantification substitutionally (nor, for that matter, referentially, if "reference" is understood narrowly in terms of the relation of singular denotation, i.e., naming). Chief among their reasons for denying that Lesniewskian quantification is substitutional is that an adequate account of his quantification in ontology must take account of the "extensions" nouns can have, not merely the possible substituends for noun variables.

Of course, if there are n objects in the domain of discourse, there are 2^n extensions to be assigned to names. And if the universe of discourse is infinite (and Lesniewskian logic does not rule out this possibility), then there are more than denumerably many extensions. Now in this last case, there can be no system which contains or will contain constants for all the extensions, because any given system can contain only at most denumerably many definitions and axioms. We must distinguish between the false claim that more than denumerably many different constants can be introduced into the system and the true claim that each of the denumerably many constants which can be introduced can have any one of the more than denumerably many possible extensions.

To answer the question of whether Lesniewskian quantification is substitutional, we must clarify exactly what is and what is not involved in the substitutional interpretation. On the classification we gave above, the account of a particular generalization is that the quantification is true if at least one of its substitution instances is true. (A universal generalization is true if every instance is true.) We noted that the analysans segment of such a truth condition makes essential use of the notion of a substitution instance and not primarily of notions such as that of a domain, values of variables, or sequences of objects satisfying an open sentence. The major difference between substitutional and non-substitutional quantification as presently explicated is that the former makes essential reference to substitution instances and the latter does not. Another point we noted was that the matter of how the instances of substitutional quantifications are themselves made true is independent of (and need not be given in) the analysans of the quantificational sentences.

Now if we take seriously the independence of spelling out the truth conditions for instances from those for quantifications, Lesniewski's systems lend themselves very nicely to being interpreted as uniformly having substitutional truth conditions for quantifying with regard to diverse grammatical categories. That is to say, a universal generalization is true if all the instances are, where the instances are constructed by putting the appropriate substituends, sentences, sentence connectives, nouns, etc., for the appropriate variables. Of special importance for elementary ontology are nouns as substituends, e.g., as in the definition of 'exists'

$$(b)[\text{ex } b \leftrightarrow (\exists a)(a \text{ est } b)]$$

This leaves open, as it should, the question of how the instances become true. Lesniewski has answered this. The substituends for variables like 'a' and 'b' are nouns which, depending on whether they are proper nouns, common nouns, empty nouns, or universal nouns, are assigned one object as a referent, several or no objects as referents, or every object. The truth condition for crucial instances of the form "−est−" is that the subject noun be a proper noun and its referent be identical with a referent of the predicate noun. This account has been compared with William of Ockham's remarks on what is requisite for the truth of a singular sentence (Boehner, 1964, pp. 83–85). If viewed in this way Lesniewskian generalizations of the above sort, e.g., the definition of existence, are both substitutional and referential. A generalization such as "$(\exists b)$ (Socrates ϵ b)" is true if it has at least one true substitution instance. Furthermore, it is because of the referential character of the truth of such an instance that the generalization succeeds in referring.

Küng and Canty say that Lesniewskian quantification in ontology is not referential because they accept aspects of Quine's account of reference and quantification, viz., that substituends always be of the category of names and that naming or its surrogate (being the value of a variable of the grammatical category of names) is the only means for achieving reference. (Kung and Canty 1970, pp. 170 and 178). Quine's view of variables as being only of the category of singular terms is questionable, but will not be dealt with here. More relevant is the terminological point that 'refers' can unquestionably be used equally well for all nouns and not just proper nouns (singular terms). If our terminology is correct, then we are justified in calling some Lesniewskian quantifications, such as those in elementary ontology, "referential." Just how well the above reconstruction of parts of elementary ontology fits with what we know of Lesniewski is partly a historical question. It seems to be indirectly confirmed by looking at remarks by Kotarbinski and Ajdukiewicz, who were writing at the time. (Orenstein 1978, pp. 28–30).

A large question remains outstanding, however, whether Lesniewskian quantification for other grammatical categories like those found in protothetic or higher order ontology is referential (in the above sense) as well as substitutional. That is, granted, for instance, that the sentential and connective variables of protothetic have sentences and connectives as substituends, do these sentences and/or connectives, as such, refer? Similarly, are the functor predicates of ontology, e.g., 'ex', which can serve as substituends referring expressions? It is unfortunate that Küng and Canty have not discussed this matter in their paper.

The issue is the following. If the term "referential" applies to quantifications either because of variables having values in a Quinian-Tarskian fashion or because substituends are referring expressions, then it is incumbent upon us to decide for the latter case whether substituends can be vehicles of reference.

I shall not be able to answer this question definitively. There are, however, two answers which I would like to put aside. The first is Carnap's view that it is merely a matter of convention precisely which expressions are designators (Carnap 1956; pp. 6–7). Aside from the arbitrariness involved in this line and its clashes with our intuitions as to which expressions refer (e.g., names do refer but parentheses do not), mere conventional stipulation sheds no light on the ontological issues surrounding the referents involved. Given Carnap's views on the triviality or cognitive meaninglessness of ontological questions the latter issue may be of little consequence to a Carnapian. Others such as the present author see this as a hindrance.

Fortunately few philosophers are inclined to take Carnap's views on stipulation as determining the bearers of reference seriously. Unfortunately the second view I wish to put aside is in good repute. This view, shared by many philosophers (including Quinians) is that singular terms are the sole vehicles of reference. Singular terms are taken to be names, definite descriptions, or the variables of first order logic that take names as their substituends. While there is no question that singular terms—at the very least names—are paradigmatic cases of referring expressions, I wish to resist the temptation to regiment, explicate, or partially stipulate that forms such as "—refers" can take only singular terms as their arguments. Instead, let us examine in a liberal spirit how we actually use the term "refers," and more importantly see what, if anything, is common to these uses.

Our question is what categories of expressions shall be considered referring ones. Proper nouns obviously qualify. Thus the sentence: The words "Socrates" and "the teacher of Plato" are used to refer to the same object" is faultless. It appears equally compelling to me that common nouns are also referring expressions. Thus: "The word "man" refers to a certain kind of mammal" is also above reproach. But, what of predicates, e.g., "is human," (in the Fregean sense of the term), granting that they are not proper nouns (or even common ones), do we speak of them as referring? To my ear the following sounds strange: "The expression 'is human' is used to refer to a certain kind of mammal," or, at least not as good as "The expression 'is human' applies to (or is true of) a certain kind of mammal." Next, consider sentences. One can say: "The sentence 'Socrates drank the hemlock' refers to a state of affairs that actually obtained," though many philosophers would prefer saying instead that the sentence "Socrates drank the hemlock" refers to something that happened provided the sentence in question is true, (where "is true" conforms to Tarski's convention T). Last of all consider sentence connectives. Can one say: "The sentence connective "and" is used to refer to a special operation for forming truth functionally complex sentences"?

The existence of such cases makes me loath to restrict the first term of the referring relation to some one grammatical category of names or even nouns. Perhaps we can sidestep the unimportant and in a pejorative sense "merely terminological" side of our question by focusing on what these cases have in common. All of them express a relation of words to objects. Philosophically entrenched ways   (or perhaps merely more philosophically regimented ways) putting each of these relations is to say that proper nouns name or denote singularly, common nouns denote multiply, predicates are true of or apply to, and sentences are satisfied by or correspond to. While there is the pressure of conforming to good philosophical usage to explicate "refers" so as to restrict it to singular terms, one might equally well note that "refers" functions in English (and would have philosophical value) as a generic term for all these different ways of words relating to objects. It is this common feature that is important and not so much whether all the above are considered referring expressions. It is also in this vein that we can answer the question posed earlier—as to how much of Lesniewskian quantification is referential. The answer is: To precisely the exent that the substituends in question are referential, i.e., explained in terms of relations between words and objects.

Perhaps Quine's locution "objectual" can be adapted to these cases. It appears to be less controversial than the term "referential". Part of the reason for Quine's choice of the locution "objectual quantification" must have been the word versus object distinction, i.e., linguistic object versus non-linguistic object distinction, implicit in the title of one of his books (Quine 1973; p. xi). One might in a non-Quinian fashion use "objectual quantification" as a more generic category, one species of which is "referential quantification". The latter could apply to nouns of all sorts, whereas a case could be made for the former applying to predicates, sentences and perhaps even connectives when these involve a word-object relation. If one adopted this terminology it would be important to note that substitutional quantification could be in this new sense "objectual" as well, viz., when the substituends are explained by appeal to non-linguistic objects.

At this juncture, let us digress for a moment and consider the two conditions in Quine's account of quantification. He requires

(1) values for variables, e.g., predicate variables if admitted require sets or properties

and (2) that the values of the variables be *named* by the substituends for the variable e.g. 'is human' names the set of humans.

It is this second requirement that I wish to subject to scrutiny. For even where substituends appeal to objects, these substituends need not be names. For "objectual" quantification as I have in the preceding paragraph construed the term, all that is required is that the substituend be explained by appeal to objects. Nothing further need be said about those objects, whether they are assumed *sui generis,* e.g., as states of affairs for sentences might be assumed or reduced to less questionable objects. Quine's slogan "to be is to be the value of a variable" is simplistic, applying only where his two conditions are met. Indeed the second condition bears a striking resemblance to a mistake made by parties to debates on the traditional problem of universals. An unreal ontological problem was generated in connection with the problem of universals by assuming that all nouns (especially common nouns) name some one thing, i.e., function as proper nouns. Quine adheres to the view that "referential"or "objectual quantification" in his use of these terms requires that all substituends are names. A consequence of treating non-names as names is that one generates rather bizarre nominata as part of one's ontology.

The issue of the referential character of non-nominal categories is not of concern solely to Lesniewskians. Ramsey and Russell furnish two more historical examples of the utility of quantifying into non-nominal positions. It is a commonplace in discussions of Ramsey's approach to theoretical sentences to assume a Quinian stance. Recall Ramsey's suggestion that theoretical predicates be eliminated by forming particular generalizations in which the function of the theoretical predicate was accomplished by a predicate variable existentially generalized upon.

Thus on one account, assuming "was a U.S. president" is a theoretical predicate, the theoretical sentence:

(2) $(\exists x)(x$ was a U. S. President and x slept here) is eliminated in favor of

(3) $(\exists \phi)(\exists x)(\phi x$ & x slept here).

Scheffler, whose account we are following, comments in the following Quinian vein.

> *Whereas the existential quantifier of (2) may therefore be read straightforwardly 'There is some individual object x, such that . . .', we cannot thus read the first existential quantifier of (3). We need, in fact, to determine some reading for the latter which will make clear what sort of entity is here said to exist. Further, we need to specify a way of construing 'ϕx'. Two possibilities suggest themselves: We may read the quantifier, 'There is some property ϕ etc.' and construe 'ϕx' as 'x has the property ϕ'. Alternatively, we may read the quantifier, 'There is some class ϕ, etc.' construing 'ϕx' as 'x is a member of the class ϕ'. In either case (3) makes (despite its indefiniteness) a stronger ontological claim than (2), asserting not only the existence of some individual but also the existence of some non-individual—property or class.*
>
> *The latter consequence is clearly objectionable to nominalists, but even those who are generally prepared to admit the existence of properties or classes may wish to minimize the scope of their non-nominalistic commitments. (Scheffler 1963; pp. 205–206)*

Such introductory remarks on Ramsey sentences are often repeated in the literature. From what we have said earlier, it should be obvious that it is theoretically possible to treat quantification into predicate positions substitutionally. One such alternative would be to do so in a non-referential and possibly even a non-objectual fashion, and thus avoid any question of ontological increase. Another possibility would be to treat Ramseyan predicate quantifications substitutionally and objectually. In this case there need be no obvious appeal to properties or sets as the values of Ramseyan variables or as named by the predicate constants that are substituends for those variables. It is somehow ironic that the suggestion to treat second order quantifications substitutionally is to be found in Ramsey himself (Orenstein 1978: fn. 15 pp. 53–54).

Without going into the details, Russell described a procedure, which he called his "no class theory," for eliminating class expressions in favour of quantification with regard to predicate positions. However, Quine construes such non-nominal quantification according to his earlier views on quantification and so sees no philosophical advantage in Russell's purported reduction. Thus Quine often argues as follows:

> Russell ([2], [3], Principia) had a no-class theory. Notations purporting to refer to classes were so defined, in context, that all such references would disappear on expansion. This result was hailed by some, notably Hans Hahn, as freeing mathematics from platonism, as reconciling mathematics with an exclusively concrete ontology. But this interpretation is wrong. Russell's method eliminates 'classes, but only by appeal to another realm of equally abstract or universal entities—so-called propositional functions. The phrase 'propositional function' is used ambiguously in Principia Mathematica; sometimes it means an open sentence and sometimes it means an attribute. Russell's no-class theory uses propositional functions in this second sense as values of bound variables; so nothing can be claimed for the theory beyond a reduction of certain universals to others, classes to attributes. Such reduction comes to seem pretty idle when we reflect that the underlying theory of attributes itself might better have been interpreted as a theory of classes all along, in conformity with the policy of identifying indiscernibles. (Quine 1963; pp. 122-123)

Once again, it is ironic that Russell's no class theory should be so misinterpreted. Ironic, because there is so much evidence that he held a substitutional view of quantifiers which, while straightforwardly referential for his first order quantifiers, might be construed as not appealing to either sets or properties for the second order quantifications required by his no class theory.

Vacuous Terms and Free Logic

A second area where the classification I have been preposing may shed some light involves singular sentences and particularly those where the subject term might be vacuous.

Let me begin by once again contrasting the approaches of two substitutional theorists on the example "Pegasus is a flying horse." The first approach is found in LeBlanc and is also implict in the early Quine. (Quine 1939). LeBlanc in a number of his papers as well as his recent book *Truth Value Semantics* propounds a substitutional interpretation of the quantifiers. (LeBlanc 1971; p. 154 and 1976; pp. 134-136). However, on singular terms he holds a referential view that is in effect very much like that of Quine. Singular sentences such as the above are true only if the subject designates an existent object. A particular generalization derived from such a sentence is hence true only if something exists, so that LeBlanc's substitutionally construed first order particular quantifier has the same existential force Quine and Russell would accord it. In contrast to LeBlanc, consider Ruth Barcan-Marcus' position in her 1962 paper, "Interpreting Quantification" (pp. 256–257. There she considered the Pegasus sentence as true, presumably by divorcing its truth from any questions of reference. She sanctioned the particular generalization from that Pegasus sentence to the substitutionally construed: "There is a true substitution instance of 'x is a winged horse.' " The generalization is considered true in virtue of the truth of its instance and unlike the LeBlanc substitutional generalization has no existential force.

With these two cases as a guide let us turn to examine Hintikka's views on singular sentences and existential generalization. Quine and Follesdal have claimed that Hintikka's quantification is substitutional while Hintikka maintains that it is not (Follesdal 1967; pp. 278-280 and Hintikka 1970; p. 415 and 1973; pp. 103-104).

One of the topics that interests Hintikka is the type of inference to an existential conclusion found in Moore's argument for the existence of material objects and Descartes: *Cogito* (Hintikka, 1967 pp. 111-119 and 1973 pp 71-73). Hintikka wants to show that Moore's "This is a hand" and Descartes' "I think," even if true, do not by themselves entail the existential conclusions that hands and thinkers exist. For Hintikka an additional premise of the form "This exists" and "I exist" is required to validly infer the existential conclusions. The semantics Hintikka provides gives an account of the truth of singular sentences as instances without appealing to the notion of reference, and an account of the truth of substitutional generalizations that are true only on the condition that the substituend in question designates an existing individual. Singular sentences are accommodated by being members of model sets, i.e., are consistent with a set of other sentences. Membership in a model set need make no appeal to the notion of reference. The condition for an existential generalization holding is that some instance is in the model set and the substituend in question in the instance, e.g., "This" or "I" refers to an existing object, i.e., $(\exists x) (x = this)$ or $(\exists x) (x = I)$. On the classification I have proposed, Hintikka's account is both substitutional, referential, and the particular quantifier, given his usage expresses existence claims. Hintikka's position is like Barcan-Marcus'in that "Pegasus is a flying horse" could obtain via membership in a model set even though Pegasus doesn't exist. His position is like that of LeBlanc and Quine insofar as the existential generalization would be false.

A topic frequently discussed in the literature in question in connection with vacuous singular terms is the concept of a free logic. Lambert introduced the term and intended by it two things: (1) logic should allow for any individual constants, vacuous or otherwise, and (2) that there should be no existence theorems in a free logic. It is to this second sense of free logic that I would like to bring to bear the classification proposed above. Consider the following remarks by Susan Haack in her book *Deviant Logic:*

> *Classical logic—as I observed with what may have seemed to be excessive caution—appears to be committed to some existential assumptions. It appears to be committed to these assumptions because it has certain theorems, which, if the existential quantifier is read, as it generally is read, 'there is (at least one) object such that . . .' explicitly make existence claims.'*
>
> *This reading of the quantifier, which Quine calls the 'objectual' interpretation, is standard. But there is an alternative, the 'substitutional' interpretation. On this interpretation*
> $(\exists x)Fx$
> *is to be read: some substitution instance of 'Fx' is true, and*
> $(x)Fx$
> *is to be read: all substitution instances of 'Fx' are true. It is clear that if the 'troublesome theorems' are interpreted in this way, they cease to be troublesome; and so there no longer appears to be a need for modification of logic to avoid them. (Haack 1974; pp. 142-143)*

Let us consider Professor Haack's claim that particular generalizations can be viewed as logical truths when they are interpreted substitutionally, for three different cases.

1) Substitutionally interpreted quantifiers, where the instances generalized on are interpreted as referring to existents, e.g., LeBlanc and Quine;

2) Substitutionally interpreted quantifiers, where the instances generalized upon are interpreted as referring to Meinongian beings as well as existents;

3) Substitutionally interpreted quantifers, where the instances generalized on are not construed referentially, e.g., the early Barcan-Marcus.

That substitutional quantification can have referential force and that as a consequence of this the particular quantifier substitutionally construed can express existence claims has by now been fairly well documented. One of Professor Haack's errors, the most obvious one, is to think that the substitutional interpretation has no place in expressing existence claims by the use of the particular quantifier.

A second error consists in construing the term "free logic" rather narrowly. This narrow view is suggested by focusing on the most popular and somewhat superficial account of a free logic as having no existence theorems. The deeper point behind the no-existence theorems phrase is that the theorems of logic should be true on every interpretation ("in every possible world") including the empty domain. Inspection of the truth conditions for the universal and particular quantifiers, whether these conditions are substitutional or not, reveals that for the empty domain (or empty range of substituends) universal generalizations are true, but particular generalizations not. Thus it is not a question of whether the particular quantifier is read existentially as Prof. Haack seems to think. One could arrange for a reading of the particular quantifier that is somewhat Meinongian, where "($\exists$x)" would be read as "There is an x" and be construed as broader than "There exists an x." This Meinongian reading could be sanctioned by a non-substitutional Tarskian approach where the domain of objects—sequences satisfying sentential functions are non-existent beings as well as actual ones. A similar Meinongian effect would be achieved by adopting a substitutional account of the quantifiers and letting substituends refer to objects that are Meinongian as well as the more familiar ones (Orenstein 1978; pp. 50-51 and 76-77). A full sense of the term "free logic" prohibits particular generalizations as theorems even if such sentences required only the assumption that every domain is populated by at least one being and that being need not actually exist.

The last case to be examined is whether we should require that logic be free of particular generalizations as theorems where these are construed substitutionally and have no referential or objectual force. The answer is dictated by the substitutional truth conditions in these cases. As in the truth conditions for the above two cases, 1 and 2, the universal generalization will remain true where there are no true substitution instances and the particular generalization, false.

An Intensional Context

As a last area of application I turn briefly to intensional contexts. Ruth Barcan-Marcus has championed the substitutional interpretation and especially its use in modal contexts. Let us examine some of her views.

To begin with consider the controversial Barcan formula:

$$\Diamond \, (\exists x) \, Fx \supset (\exists x) \, \Diamond \, Fx$$

Early critics of this formula noted that it is possible that F's exist, and it not be the case that there exist an x that is possibly an F. In reply to this line of criticism Barcan-Marcus in her 1962 paper invoked the following reading of her formula: If it is logically possible that a substitution instance of $(\exists x) \, Fx$ is true, then it is true that a substitution instance of $(\exists x) \, Fx$ is logically possible (Barcan-Marus 1962; pp. 257-258). Read in this non-existential fashion it is not as apparent that the formula could be false. Professor Barcan-Marcus at the time intended the formula to be read substitutionally and (judging by other remarks in her paper above) non-referentially as well. This may have had the unfortunate consequence that many philosophers came to associate substitutional quantifiers with their non-referential use.

There is a parallel between this intensional case and Haack's claim. The problems associated with the Barcan formula are not resolved by merely switching to a substitutional reading. Professor Marcus has more recently interpreted this formula in a new way—by adopting a referential and existential treatment of her substitutional quantifiers for one domain (the actual world) and by treating quantification in to modal contexts as involving non-referential substitutional quantification. But this is only one part of her new defense of the formula (Barcan Marcus 1975, pp. 22-38). Here it is taken as the sole basis, it would be inadequate. The problem with the Barcan formula as a truth of logic is the same as that of so regarding particular generalizations. For both cases the truth conditions for the quantifiers and modal operators indicate that there are interpretations for which the formulas are false.

With regard to the Barcan formula, Kripke showed this for referential (even if) substitutional interpretations of the quantifiers; more recently LeBlanc and Dunn have extended his results for substitutional and non-referential interpretations (Dunn 1973, pp. 87-100 and LeBlanc 1976, pp. 232-233). Where the truth conditions for interpretations of quantifiers parallel each other it is unlikely that switching interpretations will make for a difference in logical truths.

In this paper I have discussed the terminology introduced by Quine which has misled several philosophers. In this last section I have been trying to illustrate the impression some have that merely adopting a substitutional approach to quantification serves as a panacea for a number of ontological ills. The moral I wish to draw is that substitutional quantification has its legitimate uses, even in areas with disputes over ontology, but that some of the claims made for it prove on closer inspection to be unwarranted.

NOTES

1. Quine appears to regard "everything exists" as a "conceptual" truth of some sort. In *Mathematical Logic* he says "To say that *something* does not *exist,* or that there *is* something which *is not,* is clearly a contradiction in terms; hence '(x)(x exists)' must be true." (1951, p. 150)

   The famous opening of "On What There Is" expresses the same sentiments. "A curious thing about the ontological problem is its simplicity. It can be put in three Anglo-Saxon monosyllables: 'What is there?' It can be answered, moreover, in a word—'Everything'—and everyone will accept this answer as true." (1963, p. 1)
2. All the relevant nuances of the word-object distinction should be made apparent as Nelson Goodman humorously attempted to do so in his introduction to Quine's Carus lectures:

REFERENCES

Baldwin, Thomas. "Interpretations of Quantifiers," *Mind* (350) 1979, 215-240.

Boehner, Philotheus. *Philosophical Writings: William of Ockham.* Indianapolis: Bobbs Merrill Co., 1964.

Carnap, Rudolf. *Meaning and Necessity.* Chicago: University of Chicago Press, 2nd ed., 1956.

Dunn, J. Michael. "A Truth Value Semantics for Modal Systems" in Truth, Value Semantics for Modal Systems" in *Truth, Syntax and Modality* ed. H. LeBlanc, (Amsterdam: North Holland, 1973).

Dunn, Michael and Noel D. Belnap, Jr., "The Substitution Interpretation of the Quantifiers," *Nous* (2) (1968), 177-185.

English, Jane. "Underdetermination: Craig and Ramsey," *The Journal of Philosophy.* (14), 1973, 453-462.

Follesdal. Dagfinn. "Interpretations of Quantifiers." *Logic, Methodology and Philosophy of Science, Proceedings of the 1967 International Congress.* Edited by B. van Rootselaar and J. F. Staal. Amsterdam: North Holland Publishing Co., 1968.

Haack, Susan. *Deviant Logic.* London: Cambridge University Press, 1974.

Hintikka, Jaako. "Cogito, Ergo Sum: Inference or Performance? in *Descartes* ed. W. Doney. Garden City: Doubleday & Co., 1967.

---. "The Semantics of Modal Notions and the Indeterminacy of Ontology," *Synthese,* 21 (1970), 408-424.

---. *Logic, Language-Games and Information.* Oxford: The Clarendon Press, 1973.

Kotarbinski, Thadeus. *Lectures on the History of Logic.* Lodz: Lodz Scientific Society, 1957.

Kripke, Saul. "Is There a Problem about Substitutional Quantification?" *Truth and Meaning.* Edited by G. Evans and J. McDowell. Oxford: Oxford University Press, 1976.

Kung, Guido and John T. Canty. "Substitutional Quantification and Lesniewskian quantifiers," *Theoria* (36), 1970, 165-182.

LeBlanc, H. *Truth-Value Semantics.* Amsterdam: North Holland Publishing Co., 1976.

---. "Truth-value Semantics for a Logic of Existence," *Notre Dame Journal of Formal Logic,* 12 (April, 1971).

Marcus, Ruth Barcan. "Interpreting Quantification," *Inquiry,* 5 (1962), 252-259.

---. "Dispensing with Possibilia," *Proceedings and Addresses of the American Philosophical Association.* Vol. XLIX, Nov. 1976. University of Delaware, Newark: The American Philosophical Association, 1976.

Martin, Richard M. "On Theoretical Constructs and Ramsey Constants" *Philosophy of Science* (33), 1966, 1-13.

Orenstein, Alex. *Existence and the Particular Quantifier.* Philadelphia: Temple University Press, 1978.

Peirce, Charles Saunders. *Collected Papers.* Edited by C. Hartshorne and P. Weiss, Cambridge: Harvard University Press, 1931-1935.

Quine, Willard Van Orman. *Mathematical Logic.* Rev. ed. New York Harper Torchbooks, 1951.

---. *From a Logical Point of View.* New York: Harper Torchbooks, 1963.

---. *Word and Object.* New York: Wiley and Sons, 1960.

---. *The Ways of Paradox and Other Essays.* New York: Random House, 1966.

---. *Ontological Relativity and Other Essays.* New York: Columbia University Press, 1969.

---. *The Roots of Reference.* La Salle: Open Court, 1973.

---. "Designation and Existence," *Journal of Philosophy,* 36 (1939), 701-709. (Reprinted in Readings in Philosophical Analysis. Edited by H. Feigl and W. Sellars. New York: Appleton-Century-Crofts, 1949.)

---. "Review of K. Ajdukiewicz, On the Notion of Existence," *Studia Philosophica,* 4 (1951), 7-22; in Journal of Symbolic Logic, 17 (1952), 141-142.

Scheffler, Israel. *The Anatomy of Inquiry.* New York: Knopf, 1963.

Raphael Stern

RELATIONAL MODEL SYSTEMS

I intend to present a novel semantical device. These systems are similar to those developed by Hintikka, to some discussed by Leblanc and to others devised by Henry Hiz. I think the systems I envision here are, though, a bit richer than the others which they model to some degree. I think the systems introduced here are well-suited to semantic analyses of the languages of science and of sublanguages of a natural language.

INTRODUCTION

What are relational model systems?

A relational model system is used to do semantics. These systems are particularly responsive to the requirements of sublanguages of natural languages. They can, however, be used to provide a semantics for many different sorts of languages. To construct such a system we proceed as follows: we suppose a language, L, in whose semantic properties we are interested; we assume L has the following properties—there are infinitely many sentences of L, there are connectives, and there are basic or atomic sentences of L; we then take the power set of the set of basic sentences; suppose we call the set of basic sentences, "AT," and the power set of AT, "PA"; we then devise rules of construction or constraints for extending or enlarging the sets in PA; these rules enable one to go from the atomic wffs and build more and more complex wffs; the result of this is a relational model system; this consists of a non-denumerable family of sets of wffs which obey certain rules, namely rules of construction; it is on this family of sets that we can then specify various relations and define various functions including valuation functions. There is still another way of illustrating this. Suppose the set, PC, of all wffs of the propositional calculus. A *relational model system on PC* is a family of subsets, non-denumerably large, which obeys a set of constraints or rules which we lay down. These constraints determine the content of the sets.

Are relational models like Hintikka model sets?

The relational models are very much like Hintikka model sets. The rules of construction or constraints and the content are different. There are other differences. Hintikka thinks of the elements in his model sets as true. There are, however, no value term ideologies that reign over relational models. We might think of one system all of whose wffs—those in the sets in the model system, as true, but we could, equally, introduce another system where the wffs are all *preferred*. There are many types of relational model systems and the types vary as follows—in virtue of the sorts of relations specified over the family of sets, in virtue of the value terms predicated of the wffs in the relational model sets, and in virtue of the sorts of relations used in devising rules of construction. I have constructed five types of relational model systems. I illustrate two here: I introduce type 1 systems, and these are either truth relational models or preference relational models. A set of families of relational model systems can be constructed so that each system in the set takes different value terms and relations. Our task in constructing a set of families of sets—the different types of relational model systems— is to see just how to best distribute value terms and relations over the systems so that our set of families of sets works best to analyze semantic properties of sublanguages of a natural language and so that the systems we create serve, best, as symbols (not in the sense that they refer to entities, but in the sense that a symbol "looks beyond" itself to other systems, and connects up with and resonates with these other systems). We introduce one system that takes truth as the value term, and another that takes preference as the value notion, because there are sublanguages of a natural language that contain sentences that are either true or false and there are others that do not, and we are obliged to analyze both sorts.[1]

Truth relational models

These are very simple devices. We construct a family of sets. The family of sets is non-denumerable. Each set is denumerably infinite. All sets but one contain atomic wffs. There are rules of construction telling us what can and what cannot get into a set. All wffs in a set are true with respect to *that* set but possibly false with respect to other sets. We then define valuation functions and other semantical notions.

Preference relational models

These devices are not quite so simple. For one thing we use a number of preference relations. For another we abandon truth entirely. If a wff is in a preference model we say it is preferred, not true, relative to *that* model. Wffs get into models in virtue of rules which say such things as—if X and Y are equally preferred, then X belongs to the set, M, and so does Y. In short, our relations play a distinctive part in the rules of construction.

And we rule-bind all of the preference relations. We do exhibit, however, various ways in which one might set up rules—some rather "minimalist" and making use of very little, others far more radical. And then we devise different valuation functions, each distinct function depending, if you will, on a distinct set of rules.

All of the models here assume a standard grammar for PC that generates the set, WFF, of all wffs of PC. The symbol "AT" refers to the set of atomic wffs of the propositional calculus.

Given this we can now introduce Type-1 systems.

TYPE-1 RELATIONAL MODELS—TRUTH MODELS

Recall that relational models exhibit two features: there are sets that we construct using rules, and there are relations imposed on sets in one fashion or another. The rules of construction and relations are used to impose a structure, T, on a language, L. T is a non-denumerable family of sets of wffs. The sets and the wffs therein are governed by rules, values, and relations. In effect, the rules "tell us" how to get wffs into the Tms (the truth models) and which wffs go where. From these constructions we then go on to develop valuational functions and a semantic vocabulary. What follows are the type-1 systems with valuation terms and rules. These are useful for one of two types of sublanguages—relatively unproblematic ones that take truth and falsity as values, or those for which the significant term is *prefer*. (There are, after all, type-1 truth relational models and type-1 preference relational models.)

RULES OF CONSTRUCTION

1. There is one Tm in T with no atomic wffs.
2. There is one Tm in T such that $AT \subset Tm$.
3. Every other Tm contains a proper subset, J, of AT, such that J is not empty, and J contains just one atomic wff, or just two atomic wffs, or just three atomic wffs, and so on.
3.1. No two Tms that are not identical contain the same set of atomic wffs.
4. Every $X \in Tm_i$, for $Tm_i \in T$, is true relative to Tm_i, or true in Tm_i; we think of a truth model and its wffs as follows—wffs in a Tm_i are true relative to that model in which they appear.
5. Either $X \in Tm$ or $-X \in Tm$ but not both X and $-X$ are in one and the same Tm.
6. $(X, Y \in Tm_i)$ v $(Y \in Tm_i)$ v $(-X, -Y, \in Tm_i)$ iff $(X \supset Y \in Tm_i)$

These rules determine the structure of the Tm_i and so of the family, T, of sets. Using the sets we can now define a valuation function, V, such that V maps a wff belonging to a Tm to either T or F. The valuation function will, in turn, enable us to define a semantic vocabulary and ultimately, consequence pairs.

$V(W, Tm_i) = T$ iff $W \in Tm_i$; otherwise $V(W, Tm_i) = F$

$V(-X, Tm_i) = T$ iff $X \notin Tm_i$; otherwise $V(-X, Tm_i) = F$

$V(X \supset Y, Tm_i) = T$ iff either $Y \in Tm_i$ or X, $Y \in Tm_i$ or $-X$, $-Y \in Tm_i$; otherwise $V(X \supset Y, Tm_i) = F$

OTHER SEMANTIC DEFINITIONS

X is $Valid_1$ in T iff $V(X, Tm_i) = T$ for every $i \in I$ (with I the index set ordering the sets in T)

X is Logically False in T iff $V(X, Tm_i) = F$ for every $i \in I$

X is Satisfiable in T iff $V(X, Tm_i) = T$ for some $i \in I$

X is Satisfiable at Tm_i iff X is Satisfiable in T & $V(X, Tm_i) = T$

X is as Satisfiable as Y in Tm_i iff $V(X, Tm_i) = T$ & $V(Y, Tm_i) = T$

X is $Valid_2$ iff X is Satisfiable at Tm_i for all $i \in I$

X is as Satisfiable as Y in T iff X is as Satisfiable as Y in Tm_i for all $i \in I$

X is $Valid_3$ iff X is as Satisfiable as X in T

Theorem 1

$X \supset Y$ is $VALID_1$ iff X is as SATISFIABLE as Y in T

Suppose, now, we take advantage of our construction and begin introducing more and more relations on T. For example, we can define an accessibility relation, R', on T such that R' = T X T. If we do this we can admit that

X is $VALID_4$ in T iff

(i) $V(X, Tm_i) = T$ for some $i \in I$, and,

(ii) $V(X, Tm_j) = T$ for all $j \in I$ such that $R' (Tm_i, Tm_j)$

Theorem 2

X is $VALID_1$ iff X is $VALID_2$ iff X is $VALID_3$ iff X is $VALID_4$

COMMENTS

We do assume in all of this a set theory but in spite of this our ontology is very "thin." Indeed, we adopt a comparatively small ontology. Furthermore, as opposed to other non-standard approaches, this one does not significantly rely (for its *raison d'etre*) on arguments or sentiments concerning the desirability of reducing the ontic commitment of one's universe. For example, this is one thing Leblanc and other worker's in truth value semantics and later in probabilistic semantics tend to think of as a virtue of the new systems with which they work. The universe to which one's logic commits one in the case of standard model theory, for example, is far too large according to these workers. And so, they say, we have good reason to take a look at new logical devices and, indeed, they propose some for our consideration. The relational model theory I propose does involve an ontic reduction but this is not the be and end all of our interest. In fact, it turns out to weigh rather lightly in decisions about whether or not to use these devices. I tend to think that, on the whole, ontic claims of the sort other logicians have proposed are not *very* persuasive; they smack of aesthetic considerations, of a preference for a modest, tidier universe than some logics allow. I prefer a far more systematic concern when we are worrying about admitting new logics, one where we are looking at the role of theorizing, the ties to other theories, etc. As a matter of fact, large vs. small universes register, for us, very dimly. Thus, if one had a choice of two theories, equal in most respects, one would, presumably, choose the one with the smaller universe on the grounds of simplicity. Occamist considerations, however, are not operative in our account, indeed we usually prefer the more complex theory on the grounds that it holds out far more hope for an account of rationality. Consequently, considerations of size and complexity are no longer of great moment here. What I am suggesting is that if we are to take a more systematic view of these matters then we ought to look askance at aesthetic considerations of the sort that have weighed so heavily with others.[2]

PREFERENCE MODELS

Suppose we look, for a time, informally at our preference notions. We shall use several of them. We use "P_1" as a two-place valuational predicate embedding "prefer." This is predicated of wffs in a Pm (= preference model). Any wff in Pm_i is *preferred* (or is P_1) in Pm_i. In the same way any wff in Pm_j, for i ≠ j, is P_1 in Pm_j. If X is in Pm_i and if X is not in Pm_j then X is P_1 in Pm_i and X is not P_1 in Pm_j. If X ≠ Y and Y belongs to Pm_j and X does not belong to Pm_j then Y is P_1 in Pm_j but X is not P_1 in Pm_j.

P_1 relativizes preference. It relativizes it to a Pm. There is still another relation, a three-place predicate. This is "P_2." This reads—"___ is preferred over ___ in ___." P_2 is related to P_1 in the following way—If X P_1 in Pm_i and Y P_1 in Pm_j and Y ∉ Pm_i and i ≠ j, then X is P2 Y in Pm_i. Something is preferred over something else relative to a Pm_i only when they are in different Pm_i.

In addition we admit "P_3" which reads—"___is preferred over ___in P." These are all valuational uses of 'prefer'. Also we admit "Eq-P_1" as a three-place predicate—it means that two wffs can be equally preferred in a Pm.

Suppose, now, we introduce the first set of rules regulating these predicates.

A–Rule

(i) If $X \in Pm_i$ then $X\, P_1\, Pm_i$

If $X\, P_1\, Pm_i$ then $X \in Pm_i$

(ii) $X\, P_2\, Y$ in Pm_i iff $X \in Pm_i$ & $Y \notin Pm_i$

(iii) $X \in Pm_i$ & $Y \in Pm_i$ iff $-(X\, P_2\, Y$ in $Pm_i)$ & $X \in Pm_i$

(iv) $X\, P_2\, Y$ in Pm_i iff $X\, P_1\, Pm_i$ & $-(Y\, P_1\, Pm_i)$

(v) $-(X\, P_2\, Y$ in $Pm_i)$ & $-(Y\, P_2\, X$ in $Pm_i)$ & $X\, P_1\, Pm_i$ iff $EqP_1\, (X, Y, Pm_i)$

(vi) $EqP_1(X, X, Pm_i)$

(vii) $EqP_1(X, Y, Pm_i)$ iff $EqP_1(Y, X, Pm_i)$

(viii) $-(X\, P_2\, X$ in $Pm_i)$

(ix) $X\, P_2\, -X$ in Pm_i or $-X\, P_2\, X$ in Pm_i

B-Rule

(i) If $W_i, W_j \in Pm_i$ & $W_i \supset W_j \in Pm_i$ & $W_k, W_1 \in Pm_i$ then $Eq\text{-}P_1$ $(W_i \supset W_j,\ W_k \supset W_1, Pm_i)$ with $i \leqslant j, k \leqslant 1$

(2) If $W_i, W_j, X, Y \in Pm_i$ and $W_i \supset W_j \in Pm_i$ then $Eq\text{-}P_1$ $(W_i \supset W_j, X \supset Y, Pm_i)$

(iii) If $Eq\text{-}P_1 (X \supset Y, X, Pm_i)$ then $Eq\text{-}P_1 (X \supset Y, Y, Pm_i)$

C-Rule

(i) $(X, Y, P)Eq\text{-}P_2$ iff $Eq\text{-}P_1 (X, Y, Pm_i)$ for all i in I

(ii) $(X, Y, P) Eq\text{-}P_2$ & $Eq\text{-}P_1 (X, Z, Pm)$ then $Eq\text{-}P_1 (Z, Y, Pm)$

Notice that from B-axioms one can derive rules of substitution and modus ponens as constraints on Pms.

THEOREM 1 $(X, Y, P) Eq\text{-}P_2$ iff $X\, P_1$ in Pm_i & $Y\, P_1$ in Pm_i for all i in I

With these rules we should not turn to rules of construction. There are, obviously, alternative ways to set up the rules. We can use one or more of the relations introduced above. We can, then, introduce a "modest" construal of the rules or a more complicated one. Each set of rules will define the set, P, of preference models. I shall illustrate, below, with different constructions.

RULES: Straightforward Membership Method

1. There is one Pm_i such that $Pm_i \cap AT = \emptyset$
2. There is one Pm_i such that $AT \subset Pm_i$
3. Infinitely many of the Pm_i each contain but one atomic wff
3.1. Infinitely many of the Pm_i each contain two and only two atomic wffs
3.2. Infinitely many of the Pm_i each contains three and only three atomic wffs
3.3 and so on

4.   No two Pms contain exactly the same atomic wffs.

4.1.   Either X or $-$X belongs to Pm_i, for all $i \in I$

4.2.   Not both X and $-$X in Pm_i for all $i \in I$

5.   Either X, Y $\in Pm_i$ or Y $\in Pm_i$ or $-$X, $-$Y $\in Pm_i$ iff X $\supset$ Y $\in Pm_i$

RULES: *Equally Prefer*

1–4   (same as above)

5. $-Eq\text{-}P_1$ (X, $-$X, Pm_i) for all $i \in I$; either $Eq\text{-}P_1$ (X, X, Pm_i) or $Eq\text{-}P_1$ ($-$X, $-$X, Pm_i) for all $i \in I$

6.   Either $Eq\text{-}P_1$ (X, Y, Pm_i) or $Eq\text{-}P_1$ (Y, Y, Pm_i) or $Eq\text{-}P_1$ ($-$X, $-$Y, Pm_i) iff $Eq\text{-}P_1$ (X $\supset$ Y, X $\supset$ Y, Pm_i)

Given the rules we can also set up valuation functions which differ from one set of rules to another. The valuation function, then, is relative to the set of rules used.

V' *Straightforward Membership Operator*

1) V' (W, Pm) = P_1 iff W $\in$ Pm; otherwise V' (W, Pm) = $\not{P}_1$

2) V' ($-$X, Pm) = P_1 iff X $\notin$ Pm; otherwise V' ($-$X, Pm) = $\not{P}_1$

3) V' (X $\supset$ Y, Pm) = P_1 iff X, Y, $\in$ Pm or Y $\in$ Pm or $-$X, $-$Y $\in$ Pm; otherwise V' (X $\supset$ Y, Pm) = $\not{P}_1$

V'' *Preference Operator*

1) V'' (W, Pm) = P_1 iff W $\in$ Pm; otherwise V'' (W, Pm) = $\not{P}_1$

2) V'' ($-$X, Pm) = P_1 iff $-Eq\text{-}P_1$ (X, X, Pm); otherwise V'' ($-$X, Pm) = $\not{P}_1$

3) V'' (X $\supset$ Y, Pm) = P_1 iff $Eq\text{-}P_1$ (X, Y, Pm) or $Eq\text{-}P_1$ (Y, Y, Pm) or $Eq\text{-}P_1$ ($-$X, $-$Y, Pm) otherwise V'' (X $\supset$ Y, Pm) = $\not{P}_1$

A type 1 logical device is defined by a three-tuple (R, V, R$'$) with R$'$ a set of relations, R a set of rules of construction and V a valuation function. We take it that the axioms for relations are important when we talk about R—the axioms and relations provide the "backing" for R. Evidently the second set of rules of construction will provide the wherewithal for a different valuation function. In the case of the first set of rules and the corresponding valuation function, we exercise an option to use the relations and axioms minimally to help characterize P_1 and we go no further with them. In the case of the second we exercise an option to use them more fully but we choose one rather than another relation for defining the valuation function. We now use still another relation to define *still another* valuation function, V_a, below.

Suppose we take a look at a second valuation function defined relative to the second set of rules.

V_a *Another Preference Operator*

1) V_a(W, Pm) = P_1 iff W $\in$ Pm; otherwise V_a (W, Pm) = $\not{P}_1$

2) V_a($-$X, Pm) = P_1 iff $-$X P_2 X in Pm; otherwise V_a($-$X, Pm) = $\not{P}_1$

3) $V_a(X \supset Y, Pm) = P_1$ iff either $X\, P_2\, -Y$ in Pm or $Y\, P_2\, X$ in Pm or $(-X\, P_2\, X$ in Pm & $-Y\, P_2\, Y$ in Pm); otherwise $V_a\ (X \supset Y, Pm) = P_1$

It should be evident that both rules of construction (and we shall refrain from boring you with still another set of such rules) and valuation functions can use quite varied combinations of these relations. Let me give one brief sample of this by using a mixed set of relations to construct a valuation function.

V_b *Still Another Preference Operator*

1) $V_b(W, Pm) = P_1$ iff $Eq\text{-}P_1\ (W, W, Pm)$; otherwise $V_b(W, Pm) = P_1$

2) $V_b\ (-X, Pm) = P_1$ iff $-X\, P_2\, X$ in Pm; otherwise $V_b\ (-X, Pm) = P_1$

3) $V_b\ (X \supset Y, Pm) = P_1$ iff either $X\, P_2\, -Y$ in Pm or $Y\, P_2\, X$ in Pm or $Eq\text{-}P_1\ (-X, -Y, Pm)$; otherwise $V_b\ (X \supset Y, Pm) = P_1$

Once this much is clear, once we see that we can use several relations, then it becomes apparent just how we can use theories symbolically. If we are, for example, looking for hints, models, and constructions, which foster an account of rational belief, we might want to seed our theory in crucial ways with epistemic notions, and we might want to tie these to preference notions. Let's try this out to get a feel for how we quite willingly complicate theories with relations such as (formal) epistemic ones, given which we can then go on to provide useful non-formal models. All other things about P_1, $Eq\text{-}P_1$, $Eq\text{-}P_2$, etc. remaining the same, let me introduce the four-place relation, C, as—

. . . C in . . . from . . . in . . .

where this reads—"a wff X is clear in Pm_i from a wff Y in Pm_j," where i may or may not be equal to j. I gather the gist of this is patent by now—we tend to think that one thing is clear relative to something else, and here we mock up this instinct, technically, by admitting a relation on wffs and sets. Our expectation is that from a wff, X, in one Pm we can *see* other wffs clearly in the same or other Pms. We have not, for now, said anything about the conditions that would obtain. Once we do impose constraints in the axioms for C, then we tie C to the preference relations. Suppose we lay down a set of axioms, and then once this is done introduce still another valuation function.

D-Axioms

1) C is reflexive
2) $X \in Pm_i$ & $Y \in Pm_i$ iff $X\, C$ in Pm_i from Y in Pm_i
3) If $X, Y \in Pm_j$ & $Y \in Pm_k$, for $j \neq k$, then $Y\, C$ in Pm_k from X in Pm_j

Theorems

Theorem X C in Pm_i from Y in Pm_i iff X P_1 Pm_i & Y P_1 Pm_i

Theorem X C in Pm_i from Y in Pm_i iff Eq-P_1 (X, Y, Pm_i)

Theorem If X, Y $\in$ Pm_i & X P_2 Y in Pm_j, with i $\neq$ j, then Y C in Pm_j from X in Pm_i

Theorem If Eq-P_2 (X, Y, P) then there exists a Pm_i such that X $\in$ Pm_i and such that X C in Pm_j from X in Pm_i, for all j $\in$ I

With this we grant still another valuation function and here it is instructive to see that, whether we make this a matter of truth or of preference (whether we map a wff to T or to P_1), epistemic considerations *can* be prior to valuation ones, and can be conditions for stating valuational ones. (We are reminded of Ellis's worries about values being prior in accounts of rationality; this is a comparable consideration for we reflect, all along, that, somehow, on one tradition an account of knowing is arrived at only after we introduce a well-defined notion of truth; this is not the case here and it seems that whether or not truth is prior is a function of the tradition within which one works and the size of the theory onc is after.)

V_c Epistemic Evaluations

1) V_c(W, Pm) = P_1 iff W C in Pm from W in Pm; otherwise, V_c (W, Pm) = $P̸_1$

2) V_c(-X, Pm) = P_1 iff Eq-P_1 (-X, -X, Pm); otherwise, V_c (-X, Pm) = $P̸_1$

3) V_c(X $\supset$ Y, Pm) = P iff either X C in Pm from Y in Pm, or, -X C in Pm from -Y in Pm, or, Y P_2 X in Pm; otherwise, V_c (X $\supset$ Y, Pm) = $P̸_1$

Theorem V_c (p $\supset$ p, Pm_i) = P_1 for all i $\in$ I

Theorem If V_c (X $\supset$ Y, Pm_i) = P_1 & V_c (-Y, Pm_i) = P_1 then V_c (-X, Pm_i) = P_1 for all i $\in$ I

Theorem (X $\supset$ Y) C in Pm_i from X in Pm_i iff Eq-P_1 (X, Y, Pm_i), for all i $\in$ I

Theorem X C in Pm_i from X in Pm_i for all i $\in$ I

Theorem If (X $\supset$ Y) C in Pm_i from (Y $\supset$ Z) in Pm_i then (X $\supset$ Z) C in Pm_i from (X $\supset$ Y) in Pm_i

(An aside. We might refer to the alternative tradition for doing logic as "minimalist" for it invariably uses the smallest number of assumptions and constructions and pretends that the devices constructed either have no or little practical bearing. The work here is far from minimalist; it is a very different approach based on a different view of theory and of rational choice.)

Theorem$_9$ (p $\supset$ q) $\supset$ (-q $\supset$ -p) P_1 in Pm_i for all i $\in$ I

Theorem$_{10}$ (p $\supset$ (q $\supset$ r)) $\supset$ ((p $\supset$ q) $\supset$ (p $\supset$ r)) P_1 in Pm_i for all i $\in$ I

Def: X is everywhere preferred in P iff X $\in$ Pm_i for all i $\in$ I

Def: X is VALID$_i$ iff X is everywhere preferred in P

Theorem$_1$ If X, Y are both everywhere preferred in P then X ⊃ Y is everywhere preferred in P

Comments

Every Type 1 relational model system builds in the computational devices needed to do semantics. But it does more as well. We don't *simply* confine logic to computational routines or, rather, whether one does or not is a function of a point of view and tradition. Here we radicalize our logics a bit. We construct an elaborate theoretical system, TH, in which logics are embedded. Logics are designed to optimize the theory by optimizing the mathematical structures we can impose on languages and also by optimizing value term distribution as well. We do this relative to a set of criteria: that theories should be symbolic, that we aim at a modest account of rationality as well as getting out standard semantic insights. If our point of view and criteria were different, we would consider fewer structures an optimization. What is considered optimal is a function of ones aims—it is simply that our aims have shifted. We invoke logics on behalf of TH because, in a way, we must do so. What logic *is* and *does* emerges in the context of sizeable theories, such as TH, constructed from certain points of view. What is preserved over points of view is computational efficacy. (TH is a theory of meaning, elaborated elsewhere.)

BELIEF

If we operate with larger theoretical aims and if an account of rationality is one of our aims, then how we talk about belief becomes crucial.

Let me get to the second point I want to recommend here, the description of the two views. I shall introduce it all a bit longwindedly by first talking about belief. I tend to think that actions people perform can be viewed as altering or shaping or adding to belief systems. We can, then, view actions as if they were *operators* on beliefs (emotions and other belief systems function in comparable ways), as if they were mappings from belief subsystems to other belief subsystems. Now we can go on and abstract a bit and view a set of beliefs as a set of points and then abstract still more, in the light of what we have just said, and talk about points *and* operators as the technical counterparts to the less formal way of thinking about belief just described. When we do think in this way then a dynamics of belief emerges, so that technically we can interpret the dynamics of belief in terms of continuous functions on topological spaces. Now we can state the two points of view about logic. Since the first is rather old-hat and has the longer history, I shall refer to this as "view$_a$" and also as the "conservative" view about belief. The second I simply call "view$_b$".

VIEW$_a$

On this view logics "recommend" what to believe in the sense that, if in constructing our logics we find a wff, X, is a tautology, then we constrain belief systems in such a way that one ought to believe X, among other things one believes of course. In this way we look to logics to recommend what to believe and, more technically, logics provide constraints on the sorts of properties we give to continuous functions mapping belief subsystems to other belief subsystems. In the same spirit, if we tend to look at complex belief systems as embodying the capacity for thinking in certain ways which have certain mathematical properties, then we can, as well, look at belief systems as embodying the capacity for using a family of computational devices. Now obviously we have just got through saying that logics engender computational devices, and so we can talk of the relation of logic to belief systems as follows—logics, viewed as constraints on proper computational devices, can be thought of as providing constraints on the sorts of belief subsystems one can adopt, and hence on the sorts of changes in belief subsystems that one can make, and so on the family of operators that map belief subsystems to other belief subsystems, and so on the sorts of spaces we construct and on the subspace to subspace relations. From this point of view logics provide insights into topologies by providing clues about the sorts of spaces that are acceptable. View$_b$ is very different.

VIEW$_b$

View$_b$ reverses the relation of logic to belief systems, very much in the spirit recommended by Ellis. In this case beliefs are viewed, again, in terms of operators and spaces and continuous functions on subspaces to subspaces but on View$_b$ *beliefs constrain logics*. So, on this view, once we set up the formal language for talking about belief, in terms of operators and spaces, then logics emerge as a *result* of these spaces in the sense that logics emerge only when and if the class of continuous functions, J, that map belief subspaces to other subspaces, has a certain set, K, of properties. Logics emerge, then, as properties of classes of functions on belief subspaces.

NOTES

1. I have always thought cross reference central to natural languages. I had suspected for some time that a proof could be given of the nonrecursivity of the set of all cross reference pairs that one could form over the sen-

tences of a natural language. I think I have managed that proof here by using cross reference pairings to "mock up" the word problem for semi-Thue systems. Given this, and the centrality of cross reference, we find a kind of "Domino effect" with repercussions for paraphrase, consequence, for hypotheses about logics and natural language, about thinking, knowing, belief, thought and about meaning and truth. In what follows we first give the proof of the nonrecursivity of cross reference and then suggest what are the consequences of this.

The results derived from these proofs determined the methodology of the paper: not to search for a semantics for *all* sentences of a natural language, to deal with sublanguages, to find value terms suitable for these sublanguages, and, consequently, to introduce the preference logics.

CROSS REFERENCE

1. We assume the natural language English; we assume that it contains noun phrases and operations on noun phrases which pair a noun phrase such as "John" with a noun phrase such as "the father of John."
2. We assume a set of grammatical constants such as the set, N = {someone, something, he, she it, etc.}
3. We assume that there exists a set, A, of noun phrases that is countably infinite.
4. We assume an operation on any sentence with a noun phrase, such as "John is tall," which substitutes a grammatical constant for the noun phrase and would give "Someone is tall" as a consequence, and "Someone is tall; it is John" as a paraphrase.
5. We assume that for each sentence of this sort (with one of the countably many noun phrases) for which we can perform a substitution and find a substitution pair, we can extract a set of cross reference pairs, such as ⟨someone, John⟩ and in other cases, ⟨John, he⟩ or ⟨Sarah, she⟩. We assume that there are countably many cross reference pairs, and that they are a subset of $A \times A$.
6. We regard A as our alphabet or vocabulary. We assume, given A, once and for all, a fixed, countable vocabulary. We assume that we can select from A subsets J and with regard to each subset we can perform the following constructions—

   we can define a U-system as follows—select any element, z, from J, with z a fixed, initial word; select a finite set, K, of ordered pairs on J, namely, ⟨x, y⟩ and regard these as productions. Thus, given these productions we assume the pair can link the initial word to a theorem and the initial word or axiom and the theorem constitute or purport to constitute a cross reference pair. That is, given z and ⟨x, y⟩ one can "produce" what purports to be a legitimate cross-reference pair in virtue of the production pairing z and a theorem derived from the production "operating" on z.
7. Now we produce the following set, W—

   What we want is a large set with all sorts of U-systems in it.
   (i)   Take any subset, J, of A
   (ii) For each set J selected, use each member of J as an initial word for a different set of U-systems. With each word z chosen as an initial word, we can have a set of U-systems depending on how we choose the productions. With each word z, we get a set of U-systems; for each subset, J, we get a family, Ka of sets of U-systems

(iii) Now for each U-system in each set in each family of sets, Ka_i, we form the pair, $\langle U_i, y \rangle$, and we think of such a pair as implying that in system U_i, relative to initial word, z, $\langle z, y \rangle$ is purportedly a legitimate production. Now we form the set M of all such pairs.

(iv) We assume a preferred set, B, a subset of M, of pairs, such that it really is the case that for each pair, b in B if b = $\langle U, y \rangle$ and z is the initial word in U, then $\langle z, y \rangle$ is a legitimate production. (In effect this is to claim that (z, y) is a legitimate cross reference pair.)

But this is just an analogue, exactly similar in all details, of the word problem for semi-Thue Systems. But the decision problem for this is unsolvable. But this is to say that the decision problem for the analogue is also unsolvable. But since the analogue "says" something about cross reference, indeed deals with cross reference pairs, if CR is taken as the set of cross reference pairs that are legitimate and formed on English, and if q is its characteristic function, and if CR is recursive iff q is recursive iff q is Turing decidable, we find that q is Turing decidable only if the problem for the analogue of the word problem for semi-Thue systems is solvable. Since the latter is not solvable, we find that q is not recursive, and so neither is CR.

We do need for a good deal of what follows to tie cross reference results to paraphrase and consequence. Suppose PAR the set of pairs consisting of a sentence x and a paraphrase of x, for all sentences x of the English language. Thus, each pair in PAR consists of a sentence and its paraphrase. Suppose CON is a set of pairs with each pair consisting of a sentence x and one of its consequences. CON would be the set of all consequence pairs specifiable on sentences of English.

We find that for any sentence x, the paraphrases of x are a subset of the consequences of x, so that PAR is a proper subset of CON. In this discussion we let "P(x)" sometimes stand for all the paraphrases of x, sometimes for just one paraphrase.

A subset of the paraphrases of x are formed as follows:
1. take x as a paraphrase of x
2. let $- - x$ be a paraphrase of x
3. form a set of grammatical constants, G, with G = {he, she, it, anyone, anything, anywhere, someone, somewhere, something, they, etc.}
4. sentences to be paraphrased are divided into grammatical categories
5. form the set, A, of cross reference pairs, by pairing substrings of sentences in certain grammatical categories with constants—thus $\langle John, he \rangle$ is a pair under the rule that we may pair names with he or she or it.
6. Lay down a set of substitution rules for substituting constants for nouns, verbs, etc., and put substitution pairs in PAR. One such substitution pair might be—from x = John ate fish, given the pair $\langle someone, John \rangle$ we get the paraphrase, P(x) = Someone ate fish; it was John. (P(x) would also be a consequence of x; so would "Someone ate fish" be a consequence of x.)

One can specify pairings of constants with substrings of sentences of L so that every substring of L that is a noun, or a noun phrase, or a verb or a verb phrase and so on (that is at least one substring per sentence) is paired with one or more constants. There is no English sentence that does not have a paraphrase and a cross-reference pair associated with it. Thus for any English sentence we can construct a paraphrase where the central focus of the paraphrase pair is cross reference. The decision on paraphrase is a function of making the right sorts of decisions about cross-reference. CON is recursive only if paraphrase is recursive, hence only if PAR is recursive, and PAR is recursive only if CR is recursive. CR is not recursive, consequently neither PAR nor CON are recursive.

The recursive properties of paraphrase and consequence will prove to be an extremely useful analytic tool. There is a related and slightly different side to this conceptual coin. It turns out that there is a rather useful mathematical system which can be constructed whenever we have paraphrase and consequence relations defined on a natural language. These systems are called "axiom systems" and they turn out to exhibit very elegant and very useful recursive and nonrecursive features as well. Indeed because of the "logification" of our thinking recently especially in the area of studies of language and thought, attending to axiom systems turns out to be extremely important. As an example of this we might take a moment and reflect on Chomsky's grammatical devices; these are extended axiom systems. Chomsky proposes that the set, AG, of pairs ⟨A, I⟩, with A an extended axiom system or device that a child may choose when the child selects the grammar appropriate to his community, and I the linguistic inputs to the child, is a recursive set. And from Chomsky's position, a number of hypotheses, also involving recursivity, about our knowledge capabilities have been generated. It behooves us, then, to study axiom systems and so, at least, the axiom system counterpart of our work with paraphrase and consequence. We shall do so, for a time, below.

For each sentences x of English for which we can form a set, P(x) of paraphrases, we can also using the sentence x and P(x) construct an axiom system. How is this possible? We use x as the axiom, we use each y in P(x) as a theorem, and we use the pairs ⟨x, y⟩ for each y in P(x) as the production rules of the axiom system. Let AX stand for the set of all axiom systems that can be defined given the sets of paraphrases of all English sentences. AX is infinitely large. Let AW be another set of systems. Thus for each sentence x and its paraphrases, P(x), let Pa be P(x) x P(x), and let the systems be constructed as follows: let x be the axiom, let the elements of P(x) be the theorems, and let a subset of Pa be a set of production rules and allow as many axiom systems to be defined on x and P(x) as there are subsets of Pa. Do the same thing for every other English sentence and its paraphrases. Take the set of all such systems, and let "AW" stand for this set. For any arbitrary pair in AW we want to know whether or not this pair belongs to AX. This is the problem of the recursivity of AX.

Now since the production rules of systems in AX are essentially paraphrase pairs, the question of whether some member of AW belongs to AX or not is a question about what constitutes a correct paraphrase for all sentences of English. But whether PAR is recursive is a function of whether CR is recursive; consequently, AX is recursive only if PAR is recursive only if CR is recursive. Since CR is not recursive, it then follows that neither PAR nor AX are recursive either.

We can construct still other sets of axiom systems. Suppose we let LAX be the set of all axiom systems defineable on a natural language such as English in virtue of its paraphrase and consequence relations. (Each pairing of a sentence x and its set of consequences also allows us to construct an axiom system.) And suppose we let TAX stand for the set of all axiom systems whatsoever. Then since AX is a proper subset both of LAX and of TAX then LAX and TAX are recursive only if AX is recursive. Since AX is not recursive then neither are TAX or LAX recursive.

Let CAX stand for the set of all axiom systems formed by taking an English sentence as an axiom, a sentence z of the set of consequences of x as a theorem and the pair ⟨x, y⟩ as a production rule. Also form the superset of CAX, CAX' as follows—

Suppose x and the set of its consequences, C(x). Let F = C(x) x C(x). Let X be an axiom, let the theorems be the sentences in C(x) and take a subset of F as the production rules. Construct as many systems as there are subsets of F. Do the same for every English sentence. Let CAX' be the set of all such systems. Can we tell when any arbitrary J in CAX' belongs to CAX or not?

This is a question about the recursivity of CAX. CAX is recursive only if CON is recursive and CON is recursive only if CR is; since CR is not recursive then neither is CON and so then CAX is not recursive.

Now given these results there are an extraordinary number of things we can say about logics, the relation of logics to natural languages, theories of truth and about denoting.

A. Logics
What is expected when we design a logic?

We specify an alphabet A (usually a countable one) of symbols. We also specify a set of rules (a grammar) which defines a class B of appropriate structures (relations) on subsets of the set A (having a grammar entails that out of all possible juxtapositions of symbols of A only some are appropriate). Having a grammar here also presupposes that we can assign all symbols and all combinations of symbols that are well-formed, grammatical categories (occasionally abbreviated as "g.c."). Then we adopt a second set of relations (inference rules) to define a second set of structures on elements of B. (This is a topological view of logic. In exploring the structures defined when we define a logic over an alphabet we may treat the alphabet as points and study the topological properties and constraints involved in introducing these structures and in theorem-proving.) From all possible n-tuples on B our rules pick out the preferred ones.

A logic exists then if we can impose at least two sets of structures, one on A and then one on B. Assuming traditional uses of a logic, such as theorem proving, there is one more set of structures involved: as a result of pairings of all elements of A with two elements, we can then assign various orderings on elements of B; this is a semantical approach; the sorts of orderings used and the apparatus used to define orderings will determine the character of the semantics.

In formulating a logic we assume that the relation, R', is recursive, with R' = _____ is in the same g.c. as _____.

B. How are relations of a logic, L, to other languages, in particular to a natural language, Lo, established? One defines appropriate mappings between sets of symbols of L and of Lo and also between operations of both languages. The logic, under a suitable function, may then be thought to "pick out" appropriate structures on Lo (whether or not these are appropriate for Lo is moot; this would need investigation). From one point of view what the logic can be thought of as "doing" is introducing a set, HYP, of hypotheses about Lo to the effect that certain orderings of wffs (the structures on Lo) are appropriate and to the effect that the logic isolates all and only the significant consequence structures. We might then find out whether these hypotheses are true, in some cases by reflection, in others by asking native speakers or by observing their habits. On occasion the logic will be found to be correct, on occasion it will be found to be wrong. No one today thinks that this sort of thing constitutes the sole task of a logic any more than they think that a logic is supposed to investigate how we think (as its sole task). Nonetheless this is one of the things it is plausible to allow that logics "do"–they can "pick out" a set, STR, of (appropriate) structures over a language, Lo. Suppose K = the set Lo x Lo. We might ask whether we can, for any arbitrary pair in K, say whether or not this pair is in STR. This is the problem of the recursivity of STR.

If we think of a logic as defining structures over *all* sentences of Lo and if we require, as I think we should, a recursive specification of the g.c.'s of Lo (else how are we to pair off the right substrings of L with substrings of Lo and the right operations with one another), then we might find that

STR is recursive only if R″ is recursive, where, R″ = . . . is in the same g.c. as . . . in Lo.

And since we are talking about structures which are supposed to capture consequence and paraphrase structures on Lo, then we should add that

STR is recursive only if CON is recursive, and, STR is recursive only if PAR is recursive.

Suppose we take a closer look at this.

C. To repeat, when relations between a logic and a natural language are established it is often assumed that there is a recursive specification of the grammatical categories of the natural language and that the logic is defining structures over the set of *all* sentences of the natural language. (This is not invariably assumed but this is very frequently assumed.) Suppose we devise a test for sameness of grammatical category. We shall illustrate with noun phrases but this would apply across the board. Take two putative nouns. Are they nouns or not? How would we devise a test for items like "Joan" and "Sheila"? One test of sameness of grammatical category for a noun is that, for example, for two putative nouns, N and N′, N and N′ are both in the same grammatical category only if there exists at least one grammatical constant, C, (it, she, he, thing, someone, etc., are among the grammatical constants) with C appropriate for cross referring to nouns like these, such that for any environment, E, if C cross refers to N in E, then if N′ is substituted for N in E, C will cross refer to N′ in E as well without loss of grammaticality.

But this method of deciding whether two items are in the same grammatical category presupposes that CR is recursive. Thus for R″ to be recursive, so must CR be recursive. But Cr is not recursive, therefore R″ is not recursive either. Consequently the set of grammatical categories of English is not recursive. There are a number of consequences of this.

(a) It is implausible to assume that there exists an *Aspects* style grammar for *all* English sentences for this presupposes that there exists a device on an alphabet which produces all and only English sentences and assigns to each of the sentences a structural description, and this presupposes a recursive enumeration of the grammatical categories and this is impossible.

(a.1.) It is implausible to assume that the class SENTENCE of all legitimate English sentences is recursive for one test of a proper sentence is proper cross referencing and part and parcel of being able to make a decision of this sort entails the ability to tell, for any pair of substrings, whether they cross refer. Consequently, SENTENCE is recursive only if CR is recursive and since CR is not recursive neither is SENTENCE.

(b) It is implausible, on the same grounds, to assume that there exists a single logic for all English sentences. This too would depend upon a recursive specification of grammatical categories of English substrings and so depends upon whether R″ is recursive. (This does not mean that some logics will not work for some sublanguages.) Furthermore this position assumes that CON and PAR are recursive and they are not.

(c) It is implausible to assume (as van Fraassen, for example, seems to do on occasion) that if we cannot find just the *one* logic for English that perhaps we can find a set of logics which will do the trick. One logic failing, several are then thought to be relevant, each to some part or sublanguage for which some other fails. One logic would then be appropriate for *this* sublanguage, another for *that* sublanguage and so on till we have exhausted all of the sublanguages of Lo. This is implausible because this presupposes that if AX is the set of axiom systems and SUB is the class of sublanguages of English, and then if we take AX x SUB and let this be W, then we can decide for any arbitrary pair in W whether Z is an appropriate logic for the language with which it is paired. This would be the problem of finding a subset, W', of W that is recursive, contains pairs each of which provide a suitable logic for the paired sublanguage, and of making sure that all pairs in W' are such that the union over all second members of each pair is the set of English sentences. But this is merely the problem all over again of finding a suitable logic and here too we must assume, if this is to go through, that R″ and CON and PAR and CR are all recursive. Since none are, this gambit fails as well.

We are not assuming here that it is impossible for someone to study this sublanguage and find a logic for it, and then study that sublanguage and do the same, and so on. We are treating a different hypothesis, namely that it is the case that there is a logical structure to English *in the sense that* for each and every sublanguage we can pair that sublanguage with an appropriate logic. (We are not claiming that one cannot go on doing logic, nor that the results are not applicable on occasion to English.)

D. There are still other difficulties. Recall the denoting paradoxes. In my introduction I suggested that we should like to provide a denoting account of truth if we could avoid paradox. We should like to do so because, as we saw in my introduction to this section, denoting accounts enable us to justify orderings on n-tuples of sentences of languages for which the account is provided, and they also enable us to explain just why such orderings seem plausible.

It is assumed by some that we can use a denoting account and get around the paradoxes by the device of creating a hierarchy of metalanguages. This presupposes, though, that for English we can define, recursively, the following classes: names, names of names, names of names of names, sentence, nouns, names of nouns, and so on, in short, the class of grammatical categories. But we can't provide a recursive specification of grammatical categories. Consequently the metalanguage solution won't do and we seem stuck with the paradoxes. Hiz's solution is no better. He proposes that we ought to just rule out certain sentences, such as 'This sentence is true' (let "T" stand for this sentence) as improper. But on what grounds? On the grounds one would hope that there are proper environments for T and improper ones, and that the proper environments provide the right sorts of cross referential connexions and the wrong environments do not. It is not that T is improper, it is merely that T is ungrammatical in certain environments given the failure of "this" to cross refer properly in such environments.

Since T can cross refer to every English sentence in some environment or other, a proper determination about T entails a recursive specification of SENTENCE, and since SENTENCE is not recursive Hiz's solution will not work. But we do like the explanatory virtues of a denoting account in spite of its other shortcomings, so if we do design a semantics and if we avoid denoting accounts, then we must be sure to provide the sort of theory which will make up for the explanatory losses we find as a result of giving up denoting accounts.

E. We are forced by this to consider a different methodology for studying natural languages. We should turn to systems that use truth but that also use, as well, different value terms, for without the denoting approach to truth the virtues of truth in semantics are purely computational and other systems using other value terms would do this sort of computational work as well. Denoting accounts of truth *added* to the virtue of semantical systems using truth, for the denoting accounts provided, in addition to the computational side of a semantics, explanations. This was their main virtue apart from their computational side. We can now, in the light of this, free ourselves from bondage to truth (it does not define work in semantics, it is not even needed in semantical work) and we can construct other systems (see my essay) using truth but also using other value terms as well. These are the computational equivalents of accounts using non-denoting versions of truth. Should we do so? Well, yes, we should do so with regard to some sublanguages of English because these sublanguages do not require truth, indeed they "implacably refuse" truth—the value term "true" is inappropriate to these sublanguages whereas other values terms are more appropriate. On occasion a sublanguage does not specifically "demand" or "call out for" any particular value term and so we are free to choose one and we may choose a value term for many reasons—computational reasons, symbolic reasons, because this rather than that term relative to this sublanguage provides greater unity over some domain, etc.

And we are also compelled to find a semantic theory that makes up the explanatory deficits we introduce once we refuse a denoting account. As Field suggests we need a more complex semantic theory to make up these explanatory deficits but we need not as Field does, indeed should not, turn to denoting accounts. I suggest, instead, topological logics (see the notes in this essay and my book on topological logics, forthcoming).

There is one further point. In some cases there are strong claims about meaning and truth and so truth is thought relevant to all sentences of the natural language. On this strong thesis about truth it is clear that the results above apply. But in some cases it is thought that truth applies to a denumerable *subset* of the sentences of the natural language. However, this weaker thesis still calls for a recursive enumeration of grammatical categories, and so the same results obtain on the stronger and on the weaker thesis. (This is again not to say that one cannot define truth for this or that sublanguage—it is just when we are concerned with *all* sentences of the natural language that these results ensue.)

F. Suppose a denoting theory. It uses, most assume, a two-place denoting function, D, to define truth. A characteristic function, g, on D would assign a 1 when the denoting pair is proper and 0 when it is not. All theorists such as Davidson and Field who sanction denoting accounts assume that D is recursive. Obviously when we try to decide whether some substring denotes or not we need to study all of its cross references and whether or not it cross refers will affect our decision about denoting. So any sort of decision about denoting must take cross reference into account. Consequently D is recursive only if g is recursive and g is recursive only if CR is recursive. But CR is not recursive so we cannot provide a recursive denoting function to define truth. But if we cannot achieve this, we cannot provide the sort of account of truth and so of meaning that Davidson and Field assume we can for natural languages. Indeed if TRUTH stands for the set of truth conditions for a natural language, TRUTH is recursive only if D is recursive and we find that D is not recursive.

2. A number of philosophers have held that the meaning of a sentence is its set of consequences. They also hold, however, that they are concerned only with a set, or unordered heap, on which there are no relations. This is an unusual view of consequence sets; one would think, instead, that a great deal of structure could be imposed on the set of consequences of a sentence x, and that this would be quite revealing about the meaning of x.

I hold there is a good deal of structure one can impose on $C(x)$, the set of consequences of x; others seem to hold that the set of consequences, naked and without structure on it, will do. There is here the sense that in studying the meaning of sentences we are going to talk about structure and debate how much structure to impose and compare the amount of structure on $C(x)$ that seems relevant to eliciting the meaning of x properly. And we seem to be saying that we can compare structures introduced by a semantic apparatus designed to study meaning and that implicit in a good deal of our talk about meaning and the systems used to study them is a lot of talk about structure and a lot of comparisons made about the structures imposed by different systems.

Now a number of other people have made comparable claims—claims about truth, meaning and structure. Martin in his criticisms of Hiz thinks that his (Martin's) systems are clearer, stronger, and more adequate, and often the judgment of adequacy is based on the fact that Martin assumes that his systems impose more structure, or more of the more appropriate sorts of structures, or more of the right structures for defining meaning.

Hiz's reply to Martin explicitly sings the virtues of fewer structures for some systems and so holds out hope for weak semantic systems which introduce fewer structures on the languages he studies.

Martin himself does a domain semantics which he labels "first-order denumerabilism" because of the cardinality constraints it imposes on the domain, and so he sings the virtue of less structure as well but less than others of *his* peers who acknowledge no cardinality restrictions.

All of this tends to call, more and more, for some more determinate talk about structure and about comparing structures and amounts of structure introduced by semantic and other systems. In particular the growth of mathematical means of studying language systems and the assumptions listed below, contribute to this, for if one feels, as many do, that mathematics involves generating new structures to study old ones, and if language is regarded, at least in part, as a system, and so as structured, however slightly, one would import mathematical systems to study structures evinced by languages and then be prone to all of this "structure talk" and to comparisons of systems in virtue of the number and kinds of structures they impose. We shall first list the assumptions about language that contribute to this and then go on to introduce some relations that would facilitate talk about structure and also enable us to study some of the properties of this talk.

In a preliminary kind of way we should note some of the things that are assumed, all *too* often one might say from a sceptical point of view, about studies in language, and about language as a system with orderings defined on it. What follows below cries out for a mathematical study of language and that would, of course, engender a lot of crosstalk about structure. The assumptions are—

(a) a language is a system

(b) for any such system, Z, we wish to know, when characterizing it, just how much structure to impose, or, if we may put it badly, just how much structure does the system "have",

(c) what structures should we impose if we are fairly representing the system,

(d) what devices or systems should be constructed to take care of imposing the structures we wish to see imposed if we are fairly characterizing the language system.

Nothing could be more structure-nagging than the above questions and what is implicit in them.

We should now get on to talk more systematically about structure and consequently introduce the relations we have promised which facilitate comparisons of structures. Wherever possible, to motivate the study, we should attempt to introduce relations that provide the formal counterpart to assumptions or presuppositions made by philosophers or linguists, or, if this is not feasible, then the starred positions will represent what I assume is fairly close to what someone has said or what someone presupposes, or what is *suggested* by what someone says or presupposes, or what it is *reasonable to hold* given what some people actually hold and given certain other things it seems warranted to assume or hold but which no one may *actually* have held.

Those using logics to study natural languages have, on occasion, assumed that there exists a single logic that can be of use in studying a natural language and that this logic is capable of "picking out" and examining structures on the language and that it picks out the maximum number of structures—this logic picks out only and all those structures which the speakers of the natural language would acknowledge were the significant consequence relations, if asked.

Indeed from this point of view, and in comparison with the basic or preferred logic, there are axiom systems that *seem* to deal with fewer structures than the preferred logic and one could easily construct a denumerable set, CA, of axioms systems, a good many of which do seem weaker than the usual logic proposed (the quantificational logic).

This should not be difficult. An axiom system is a 3-tuple involving an axiom(s), theorems (one or more) and production rules. The simplest, formed on English, would consist of one sentence, S, as an axiom, one sentence S' as the theorem, and the pair (S, S') as the production rule. This sort of system could be repeated infinitely many times. It is evidently weak. However, we could put others into CA, some stronger, some very strong, so that it would not be evident in every case just which systems are obviously weaker than the preferred logic and which are just purportedly weaker. In any case, CA is a set of axiom systems formed on English. Now we need some way of talking about the capacity of a logic, L, to do more than an axiom system. Suppose to accomplish this we introduce the relation, Ra. Ra stands for—logic . . . imposes a greater number of structures on the language . . . than logic . . .

R1 is the restriction of Ra to L and members of CA. Consider the set Rj of all pairs (L, M_i) with M_i a member of CA and all pairs (M_i, L). R1 is a subset of Rj and R1 consists of the ordered pair (L, M_i) *or* the pair (M_i, L) depending upon which logic imposes more structure.

Along similar lines one would presumably wish to be able to compare the efficacy of two logics. It may be that of two logics one is better than another in some fashion. Suppose we let Rm stand for

logic . . . imposes more structure on the natural language, English, than logic . . .

And suppose we let Rn mean

logic . . . imposes the same amount of structure on the natural language, English, than does logic . . .

In the light of our contentions about structure suppose, now, we cite several positions that are held by others, *and* analogues of positions held by philosophers or linguists (the analogues are similar to real positions though to my knowledge they have never been held by anyone). I cite these positions to motivate the construction of several relations which are structure-comparing and structure-assessing. I will then show, briefly, how these relations might figure in contemporary positions and then make an effort to decide whether some of them are recursive or not.

Let us consider, first, the following position about meaning. If the meaning of a sentence of a natural language is simply its set of consequences, and if one believes that one can find the meaning of each and every sentence of a natural language, then for each and every sentence, x, of the natural language, Lo, Say Lo is English, we should be able to pair x with one and only one set, S, of its consequences. Suppose we do this. Let Ro stand for the set of pairs of a sentence of a natural language such as English with its set of consequences. (On occasion, both Tarski and Hiz seem to talk this way; on many an occasion Tarski seems to deny that he ever said anything of the kind; Hiz, however, remains steadfast and does seem, on more than one occasion, to hold some such view.)

Suppose we consider still another position. Many people have held this one. They have contended that language expresses thought, that natural languages are most suitable for expressing thought, and that for any thought one might have there exists at least one sentence of a natural language which can express that thought. There are potentially infinitely many thoughts; for each thought we can find one natural language sentence, say of English, to pair with a thought. We should then be able to form the set, Rp, of pairs of thoughts with English sentences. Rp should be denumerably infinite.

The next position is an analogue of one that Chomsky held in Aspects.* It is not necessarily, to my mind, a position that anyone has ever actually held. Chomsky held that of an infinite set of potential grammatical devices that one might entertain and with finite inputs from his linguistic community, a young child will be able to select that device which will generate (or recognize) all and only sentences of his language community. Along the very same lines, let's create an analogous hypothesis, namely that a child learns to impose logical structures over sets of sentences heard or uttered and to recognize logical connections. Suppose that of an infinite set, T, of devices that he could adopt, he selects one, again with limited inputs from his linguistic community. Suppose Lx the set of all natural languages. Suppose T x Lx the set of all possible pairings of devices with languages. Now let Rq be a subset of T x Lx, namely that subset which contains the correct pairings of devices with languages. (The language is paired with the logic most suitable to it and most efficacious in discovering logical connections.) What is assumed here is that the device enables the child to recognize what follows from x so that if Lo is the natural language then from the set Lo x Lo the child can find the correct pairs, or all and only pairs of Rs, with Rs a subset of Lo x Lo that contains all and only the correct consequence pairs.

Let me summarize the relations introduced so far and then motivate the study a bit by showing how the relations figure into various positions.

relation	*explanation*
Rl	L or M_i is assumed the most suitable logic for a natural language such as English; this is a two-place relation ... imposes more structure on Lo than ..., with the last dots filled by L or by members of CA, a set of axiom systems, and the first by the special logic L or a member of CA.
Rm	Logic ... imposes more structure on the natural language, English, than logic ...
Rn	Logic ... imposes the same amount of structure on the natural language English as does logic ...
Ro	This is the set of pairs of a sentence of a natural language such as English with its set of consequences, for all sentences of English
Rp	This is the set of pairs consisting of a thought with the sentence that expresses it, for all thoughts that a speaker of a natural language such as English might have
Rq	This is a set of pairs, the correct pairing of a natural language with a logical device
Rs	This is the set of all consequence pairs on English—the set of all correct pairings
Ra	This is the relation—logic ... imposes a greater number of structures on the language ... than logic. ... It talks about all languages and all logics.

Let me illustrate further, before going on, and suggest just where and how and into what positions these relations and their recursive properties, or nonrecursive properties for that matter, might figure. If one thinks as Hiz does, one would assume that the set of consequences of the sentences of a natural language provide an account of the meaning of the sentences of that language. (This is perhaps Hiz_1 the Hiz who seems very clear that this is so, and not the Doppleganger Hiz who demurs when this position is advanced, or who would qualify it as being too simple.) In this case one would presuppose that Ro is recursive.

Suppose, as philosophers as varied in their dispositions as Bouchenski and Jerrold Katz have held, one thinks that a natural language is ineffable, intending by this that the language is capable of expressing anything one might think. This would entail holding that Rp is recursive, if one holds that sentences express all that we can think.

If one also holds, besides the above thesis, that it is theoretically possible to understand all that someone thinks, if one can first find a verbal expression and then find the meaning of the verbal expression through the set of consequences associated with the sentence uttered, then one holds that Ro is recursive *and* that Rp is recursive. Sometimes philosophers hold modified versions of the ineffability thesis, contending that a natural language can express all that can be expressed by any language whatsoever. Since there are nondenumerably many languages, a translation function from all of these languages to the natural language, such as English, would be nonrecursive. It is fairly easy to see that a number of views, those held by linguists and others held by philosophers and psychologists, entail theses about the recursivity of certain relations. It is important then to study these relations.

Thus it follows from what we have suggested so far that whether these relations are recursive or not is of great moment. A number of the positions stated and a sizable number of other positions presuppose some claim about these relations or about still other relations, with some positions presupposing that the relations implicated are recursive. It behooves us, then, to see which are recursive. Indeed apart from being aware of which are recursive, it is even more important to see if we can determine which are not recursive, which might be recursive, and to isolate those for which some proof seems plausible and those for which we have no hope whatsoever of providing a proof of nonrecursivity.

Suppose we turn to a few of the relations listed. Suppose we turn to Ra. Ra consists of triples, comparisons as to relative strength (insofar as they impose more or fewer structures) of pairs of logics relative to some language, L. In this case L can be any language whatsoever. Since there are nondenumerably many languages, Ra is nonrecursive.

Suppose we turn to Rl. If Rl is recursive then surely CR must also be recursive. Since CR is not recursive then neither is Rl. (The structures we are considering re. Rl are consequence ones. Rl contains pairs and in each pair a logic, L, which pretends to provide all and only appropriate consequence pairings for English. In this respect L may or may not do so; we are in the dark, and within Rl each pair compares the efficacy of L to another logic from CA. But L itself presupposes that we can re. English say for any pair of sentences (x, y) whether y is a consequence of x, or not. But since consequence, or as we have put it, the set CON is recursive only if the set CR is, then CON is not recursive, but then neither is Rl.) It strikes me further that from the vantage point already developed the other relations in the list stand a fair chance of being proven nonrecursive.

These relations and their properties have enormous consequences for us. For example, on one view of what it means to know something, knowing something is believing something which is true (plus some additional conditions, such as, for example, justified belief in some cases). But this view presupposes *something of which* we can predicate truth and falsity. Suppose we hold, as for example some philosophers did, that sentences and only sentences are true or false. Defining knowing in this way then entails that we can, in principle, say of any English sentence that it is either true or false. Suppose we let TR be the set of all English sentences that are either true or false. TR is recursive only if the set of grammatical categories of English are recursive, and since they are not recursive, neither is TR. It is then not clear what we would mean by *knowing* for this particular sense of *knowing*.

But suppose we turn to beliefs then as the vehicle for predications of truth. Suppose knowing is entertaining true beliefs. How is it possible to talk about belief and true belief? Some philosophers entertain the view that one must be able to talk sensibly about the propositional content of a belief and to do so one relies on sentences. The class of true beliefs would then lean upon the class of sentences, TR; we should, in principle, wish to say that we could tell what it means to talk about true belief, and it would seem to me that if BELIEF is the class of *true beliefs,* we would want BELIEF to be recursive, but this is recursive only if TR is, and since TR is not, neither is BELIEF. But then we doubly wonder how to characterize *knowing*.

There are still other difficulties. If we assume a recursive device, D, that generates all and only English sentences, then we can potentially utter any sentence generable by D. Now we are at a loss as to how to characterize the meaning of such sentences for any combination of paraphrase, or consequence, or denoting accounts of truth, or probabilistic semantics fail to provide a recursive specification of meaning. But lacking this we can say that we can utter sentences whose meaning we cannot provide. That is, it is not the case that for any arbitrary sentence that we can utter that we can provide the meaning of such a sentence.

Difficulties mount as we consider more and more hypotheses. The only thing that seems clear is that these relations and their recursive properties constitute a powerful analytic tool.

PART II

MONTAGUE FRAMEWORKS

INTRODUCTION

A common strand in the essays in this section is that they touch on Montague Grammars. The first two essays, by Partee and Bach, make a case for the virtues of a Montague approach, while the last essay by Teller and Bachenko casts a critical shadow on it. Following Partee and Bach, a Montague Grammar can be summarized as providing rules for translating natural language sentences into sentences of a logical language, that is an intensional logic, and then providing an account of the truth conditions for this intensional logic in terms of possible worlds semantics. There are a number of ways in which this approach differs from more classical ones. To begin with, the use of possible worlds to supply truth conditions is a deviation from the classical Tarskian semantics that many philosophers and logicians use in setting down truth conditions. In Tarskian semantics, truth conditions depend upon assignments of extensions to expressions in only one domain, usually taken to be the actual world. The Montague approach is a species of semantics, dubbed "possible worlds semantics," in that truth conditions for sentences depend on assignments of extensions in more than one domain, i.e., in possible worlds, and not just in the actual world. But the appeal to possible worlds—multiple domains—is only one way in which Montague Grammars differ from standard philosophical and logical approaches. Another deviation is in the account of the logical form of various expressions of natural language as opposed to that found in the works of more orthodox figures such as Russell, Quine, Davidson, etc. To illustrate this difference, we could compare Montague's suggestion for treating quantifier phrases with the one found in almost all contemporary logic text books. In this sense, the classical or standard description of the logical form of quantifiers is that they are operations on propositional functions (open sentences) to form propositions (closed sentences or statements). Russell and many others believe this to be an important insight and argue that alternative treatment of quantifiers such as forming noun phrases, leads to various excesses. Recall the standard remarks that treating quantifier phrases as constitutents of nouns yields such oddities as Heidegger's "Nothing nothings," and the remark of Alice's respondent who upon being informed by her that she saw no one on the road congratulated her for her eyesight on being able to see no one. In direct contrast to these widely accepted views is one of Montague's most important suggestions, namely that we treat quantifiers as noun-forming. A further area of divergence discussed in some of the essays in this section is with more classical, i.e., more standard, transformational theory. Examples of these are Partee's Montague-inspired suggestions for dealing with relative clauses, the attributive-predicative distinction, pseudo-cleft sentences, etc.

In her essay, Barbara Hall Partee addresses the question of the suitability of Montague's philosophical and hence very general conception of language to the more specialized interests of linguists and psychologists. As a philosopher and logician, Montague was interested in a grammar suitable to very abstract concepts of a language—to languages *per se*—e.g., artificial ones such as those of modern logic, and not merely natural languages such as English. Of course, the linguist is interested primarily in natural language, so part of Partee's purpose is to show how a Montague framework can be adapted to serve the linguist's needs. Similarly, psychologists interested in language as a crucial part of man's cognitive equipment ("language as a window to the mind") have a more specialized interest in studying language than does the philosopher-logician.

As an illustration of Partee's endeavor consider the "possible worlds semantics" component of Montague Grammars as applied to three different concepts of entailment. The three concepts are those of the logician—logical entailment, of the linguist (and general cognitive psychologist)—"natural language" entailments, and of the psychologist's—certain personal patterns of inference. The very general, philosophical-logical concept of possible worlds will explain why the sentence "Snow is white and grass is green" formally or strictly logically entails the sentence "Snow is white" by appealing to the fact that there is no possible world where the first sentence is true and the second is not. However, this purely logical sort of entailment does not capture other entailments that interest linguists. (Entailments like: that John is a brother entails that John is male.) To capture such entailments which are not strictly logical further constraints must be placed on possible worlds. Instead of considering all purely or arbitrary logically possible worlds we restrict ourselves to those in which brothers are males. The above "natural language" entailment is readily accounted for in relation to these possible worlds. As a final example, note that there are inferences of interest to a psychologist (or perhaps a psychotherapist) that are not accounted for in terms of the restricted possible worlds which will do for "natural language" entailments. To adapt one of Partee's examples, a couple could agree on the remark that she always gets angry at his not shutting the dresser drawers, but might make different inferences (have different but correct entailment patterns relative to what each takes to be possible). Thus, given his idea of what is possible he infers that he could leave a drawer open and she would not get angry. Given her idea of what is possible she infers that he could always shut the dresser drawers. Placing different restrictions on the possible worlds compatible with his or her other beliefs accounts for his or her entailment patterns.

In her essay Partee also discusses several other areas where Montague's abstract frameworks can be made to serve the purposes of linguists and psychologists.

Emmon Bach's essay illustrates one of the above-mentioned central themes in Partee's essay—the utility of the Montague framework to the interests of the linguist. Bach's proposal in this direction is to reconcile Montague Grammar with an early pre-*Aspects* Chomskyan transformational approach (1955, 1957). This transformational theory of syntax abides by the classical-Fregean thesis of compositionality which can be adapted to Montague's semantic compositionality thesis. Thus Bach weds some of Montague's ideas from "The Proper Treatment of Quantification in Ordinary English" to the early Chomskyan transformational account. The word "nonclassical" has been used in many senses in this section to describe how Montague's approach diverges from the more orthodox ones. However, Bach proposes in his essay to show how Montague's grammars are in a sense very classical—the compositional quality of syntactical and semantic theory—and in that sense that they are reconcilable with an early transformational account.

One very valuable idea in Bach's essay is the sharp distinction he makes between the concept of semantics of the philosopher-logician and that of the linguist. Following Tarski and Carnap, philosopher-logicians speak of semantics as the assigning of truth values to the well-formed formulas generated by the syntax. In effect, then, this concept of semantics is the laying down of truth conditions. This is accomplished (the most classical version) in a Tarskian way by assigning extensions to expressions. (It is this concept of semantics which is most often referred to by the editors of this volume in their introductory material.) Bach wisely suggests that the concept of semantics used by the linguist might better be called "rules of translation." They are rules for mapping some syntactical objects onto others, e.g., to speak of "brother" having among its semantic markers "male." Bach also notes that linguists tend to provide these rules of translation without supplying the associated assignments that comprise a philosopher-logician's concept of semantics. In fact, the question of whether truth conditions should be added to rules of translation is debatable. Some linguists refrain from this additional step. Others, like Partee (Hiz, Field, etc.) give truth conditions in a non-Tarskian fashion.

The paper by Teller and Bachenko is more marginally related to Montague Grammar than are those of Partee and Bach. The purpose of Teller and Bachenko is to discuss three views of the relation of syntax to semantics (semantics in the linguist's sense of rules of translation, possibly supplemented by se-mantics—truth conditions—in the logician's sense). The first of the three views of the relation of syntax to semantics they deal with is a Semantic Hypothesis found in Kiparsky and Kiparsky, and both criticized but also subscribed to partly by R. Lakoff. The hypothesis is that semantic factors determine syntactic ones. The second view of the relation of syntax to semantics is the Laxicalist's Hypothesis, found in Chomsky amongst others. The Lexicalist's thesis leaves open the question of whether semantics affects syntax. The third view is the Montague approach as found in Partee, in which there is a close correspondence between syntactical and semantical rules.

Teller and Bachenko somewhat guardedly adjudicate between these three different views. They cite evidence such as factivity that works in favor of the Lexicalist's Hypothesis and against the Semantic Hypothesis, and other evidence concerning relative clauses and pseudo-cleft sentences that works in favor of the Lexicalist's Hypothesis and against the Montague approach.

Alex Orenstein

Barbara H. Partee

MONTAGUE GRAMMAR AND ISSUES OF
PSYCHOLOGICAL REALITY*

I. *Introduction*

Philosophers, linguists, and psychologists all share an interest in the semantics of ordinary language, but the same facts which account for the relevance of natural language semantics to such a wide range of fields also lead to frequent disagreement as to what the central questions of semantics are and as to the criteria by which semantic descriptions and semantic theories should be judged. Without trying to be prescriptive, I will begin by indicating three kinds of central problems which I believe are potentially of common concern in all of these approaches to semantics; then I will suggest some ways in which reasonable differences as to goals and criteria of adequacy may be reflected in different idealizations that are invoked by investigators in different fields.

The first problem can be put as follows: Each natural language has infinitely many sentences, and native speakers can produce and understand indefinitely many sentences they have never heard or uttered before. The semantic side of this ability is the ability to associate meanings, whatever meanings may be, with each of the infinite set of sentences of the language. The task for a semantic theory then is to specify how this can be done in a finite way, presumably via a system involving a direct specification of the meanings of some finite set of primitive elements and a finite set of rules capable of associating meanings with all of the remaining, non-primitive expressions. The second and third questions relate to narrowing down somewhat the vague concept of meaning. The second is how to appropriately capture entailment relations between sentences within a semantic description; this assumes that part of what is to be understood by the meaning of a sentence is that by virtue of which certain sentences can be said to follow from other sentences. The psychologist may be interested primarily in the inferences people actually draw, and the philosopher primarily in characterizing inferences which are logically valid, but I believe such differences can be expressed mainly as differences in criteria for the correctness of competing answers to the same question, namely how to characterize entailment relations between sentences. The third question, which is the least universally accepted of the three, is how to characterize the truth-conditions for sentences of a natural language. The importance of this question rests on the idea that a fundamental part of knowing the meaning of a sentence is knowing something like under what conditions it would be true, coupled with the observation that even the most complete specification of entailment relations among sentences will not tie the meanings of any of the sentences down to anything outside of language but only to other sentences of the same language. I will return below to some of the difficulties involved in taking the search for truth-conditions as one of the central problems of semantics, but at the outset I will simply accept it, since it has been taken as fundamental in the kind of semantic theory I want to discuss.

Now let us elaborate briefly on the suggestion above that the different interests in such questions from the perspectives of different fields may lead to different criteria of adequacy and, in turn, to different idealizations. Richard Montague, who should be regarded as relatively extreme in this respect even for a philosopher, was interested in a very general conception of possible languages, one at least broad enough to cover both natural languages and the artificial languages constructed by logicians; he had no interest in delimiting the class of possible human languages, which is the central concern of linguists. Hence where the linguist idealizes to an ideally competent speaker-hearer in a homogeneous speech community, and asks about the internalized systems of rules and representations that such a language user must have "in his head," so to speak, Montague idealized still farther, and did not talk of speaker-hearers at all. Much as a mathematician can study alternative systems of geometry without being concerned either about which geometry fits physical space or about how people form conceptions or intuitions about geometrical objects, Montague studied languages as formal objects, consisting of pairings between forms and meanings, where the meaning of a sentence is taken to be a structural specification of the conditions under which it would be true in any possible state of affairs, or possible world, to use the favored expression. A psychologist interested in general human cognition and language might accept the linguist's idealizations as a starting point, but a psychologist interested in individual differences among people might not want to accept the assumption of the homogeneous speech community, particularly if he wanted to explore the extent to which individual differences in knowledge, beliefs, and attitudes may be reflected in individual differences in language use within what may otherwise be reasonably regarded as a homogeneous speech community.

If we try to impose the talk of speaker-hearers on Montague, we have to assume a speaker who knows his language perfectly, is ideally rational, and is, furthermore, capable of conceptualizing a complete description of every possible world, e.g., God; the linguist is inclined to assume something like complete knowledge of the language and idealized if not perfect rationality but not complete knowledge of what all the possible worlds are like (but rather some internalized model corresponding to conceptual possibility, or what Chomsky[1] has called 'common-sense understanding'); and the psychologist interested in individual differences probably wants to weaken the idealizations still further in various directions. The question of whether an approach to semantics developed with one set of idealizations can be relevant to an inquiry with a different set is a serious one, and of course one which cannot be answered *a priori* in a general way. My goal in this paper is to suggest that Montague's framework can be of relevance to linguistic and psychological concerns as well as philosophical ones, and that one can profitably attempt to develop linguistic and psychological theories of semantics by a combination of extensions and restrictions on various components of a Montague-like general theory.

In section 2, below, I will describe Montague's framework briefly, and sketch some of the kinds of restrictions that a linguist might incorporate to try to characterize a theory of possible human languages as a subtheory of Montague's general theory. In section 3 I will suggest that the underlying models of Montague's model-theoretic semantics might be interpreted in various ways that could be relevant to a consideration of individual differences in beliefs and conceptions of reality, although I believe this will require extensions as well as restrictions on the class of models allowed by the theory. The purpose of the discussion is not to argue that linguists, philosophers, and psychologists should all tackle semantic issues by "doing" Montague grammar, but rather to suggest that if this way of looking at things is coherent and fruitful, it could help to facilitate discussion of theoretical issues involving quite different-looking theories.

2. *Montague grammar and transformational modifications*
2.1 *Syntax and semantics*

The version of Montague's framework that I will outline here, which comes from Montague (1973), gives a description of a natural language in three parts: A set of syntactic formation rules for the set of well-formed expressions of the language; a corresponding set of translation rules translating the set of natural language expressions into a language of intensional logic; and a model-theoretic semantics for the intensional logic, which gives for each sentence of the intensional logic a specification of the conditions under which it would be true with respect to any given possible world. Truth conditions for English sentences are obtained via the truth conditions for their translations, and entailment relations are definable in terms of the truth conditions. I will say more about the intensional models in section 2.3 below; here I will concentrate on the basic form of the syntactic rules and their relation to the translation rules.

The syntactic rules in a Montague grammar specify how to build up complex expressions of all of the categories of a given language, starting from a specification of the lexical items and their assignment to syntactic categories. Each rule specifies a way in which expressions of some given categories can be combined, and specifies the category of the resulting combination. The form of a syntactic rule can be represented as in (1) below:[2]

(1) If α is of category C_1 and β is of category C_2, then γ is of category C_3, where $\gamma = F_i(\alpha, \beta)$.

The syntactic details of how α and β are combined to give a new phrase γ are all contained in the function F_i; the syntactic operations may be as simple as concatenation or as complex as a transformational operation. To a linguist familiar with transformational grammar, Montague's syntax gives the appearance of a bottom-up derivation, with phrase-structure-like rules and transformation-like rules freely interspersed in building up complex expressions from their constituents.

A main source of interest in Montague's system is the basic constraint he imposes on the relation between syntax and semantics. For each syntactic rule which combines expressions α and β to form a new expression γ, there must be a corresponding semantic rule[3] which gives the interpretation of the complex expression γ as a function of the interpretations of the constituent expressions α and β. We can represent the form of a semantic rule as in (2) below:

(2) If α translates into α' and β translates into β', then $F_i(\alpha, \beta)$ translates into $G_k(\alpha', \beta')$.

Here α' and β' are expressions in the intensional logic, and the function G_k will yield a new expression of the logic having α' and β' as subparts. One could think of the grammar then as a set of ordered pairs ⟨syntactic rule$_i$, semantic rule$_i$⟩; the syntactic rule will give the syntax-specific details of how the component phrases are to be combined, and the semantic rule will give the semantics-specific details of how the meaning of the whole is determined from the meanings of the parts.

Let me illustrate both the rules and the constraint with a pair of examples. The first concerns noun phrases containing restrictive relative clauses, as in example (3).

(3) *The dress which Mary bought* is blue.

Syntactically, linguists have debated about the following two possible structures for the noun phrase (ignoring for the moment the question of the underlying source of the relative pronoun *which*):

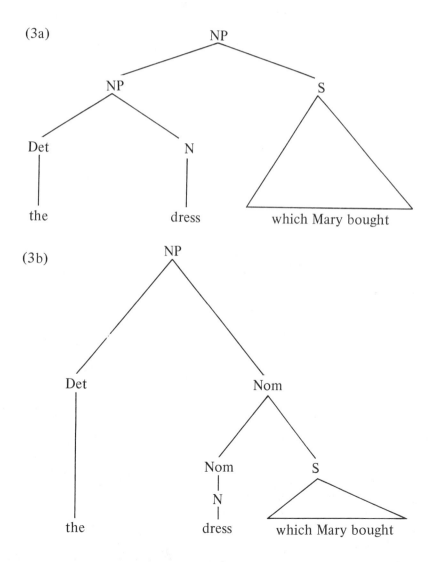

I have argued elsewhere[4] that Montague's constraint forces the choice of the second structure, with the relative clause modifying the common noun, if we wish to be able to give a uniform account of the semantics of *the* and other determiner and quantifier words. A first approximation to the semantics of *the* in singular noun phrases involves the condition that there is one and only one something-or-other in the given universe of discourse; (3) does not imply that there is only one dress, but that there is only one thing which both is a dress and is something Mary bought. Thus the relative clause should be part of the structure to which the determiner applies as it is in (3b) but is not in (3a). The structure diagrammed in (3b) can be represented in terms of Montague grammar by a pair of rules: One rule which combines a common noun phrase (NOM) with an open sentence to make a new common noun phrase, and another which combines a determiner with a common noun phrase (NOM) to make a term phrase(NP). Omitting details, the first of these can be written as follows:

(4) If α is of category NOM and φ is of category S,
then γ is of category NOM, where $\gamma = F_3(\alpha, \varphi)$, and
$F_3(\alpha, \gamma)$ is ....

The specification of F_3 spells out the operations involved in relative clause formation, by which an input sentence φ of the form "Mary bought x_1" is converted into the relative clause "which Mary bought," and the result is concatenated with the head NOM.

The corresponding semantic interpretation rule is basically just a conjunction of predicates, the two relevant predicates in this case amounting to (i) being a dress and (ii) being an x_i such that Mary bought x_1. The rule can be stated formally[5] as follows:

(5) If α translates into α' and φ translates into φ',
then $F_3(\alpha, \varphi)$ translates into $\lambda x_i(\alpha'(x_i) \& \varphi')$

For this example, the interpretation of 'dress which Mary bought' would come out essentially as follows:

(6) $\lambda x_1(\text{dress}'(x_1) \& \text{Past}(\text{buy}'(\text{Mary}', x_1)))$

The lambda operator turns a sentence into a predicate; the resulting predicate in (6) can be thought of as expressing 'the property of being an x_1 such that x_1 is a dress and Mary bought x_1'.

The details of the example are not of great interest *per se* to the issues at hand; I have included some of the details here in order to illustrate the force of the requirement that each syntactic formation rule be given a uniform semantic interpretation, and also to illustrate how having an explicit formalism for the semantic interpretation rules makes it quite explicit whether a proposed grammar meets that requirement. In my opinion, one of the big methodological advances made possible by Montague's work is to put semantics on as rigorous and explicit a footing as was done for syntax by Chomsky.

The second example concerns the distinction between predicative and attributive adjectives,[6] which can be illustrated by the difference in validity of the inferences in (7) and (8).

(7) (a) *Susan is a red-haired doctor.*
    (b) *Susan is a violinist.*
    (c) *Therefore Susan is a red-haired violinist.*
        [VALID]

(8) (a) *Susan is a skillful doctor.*
    (b) *Susan is a violinist.*
    (c) *Therefore Susan is a skillful violinist.* *[IN-VALID]*

"Red-haired", a predicative adjective, simply picks out a set of individuals; the inference in (7) is valid, since (7a) involves simply the conjunction of the properties of being red-haired and being a doctor. "Skillful," an attributive adjective, does not simply express a property of individuals, however, as the invalidity of the inference in (8) shows. Parsons (1970) and others have proposed an elegant treatment of the semantics of attributive adjectives that represents them as functions which apply to the meanings or intensions of the common nouns with which they are in construction; informally, what it means to be a skillful doctor depends on what it means to be a doctor, and similarly for other nouns. (One corollary observation with potential practical utility for therapy is that any sentence which uses an attributive adjective alone in predicate position is semantically incomplete; a sentence like "Susan is skillful" or "I'm not successful" must be interpreted with respect to a further predicate to which "skillful" or "successful" can apply, and the choice of predicate may or may not be determinable from the context.)

This distinction between predicative and attributive adjectives can be captured in a Montague framework by providing two distinct syntactic derivations, each with its own semantic interpretation. Predicative adjectives start out in predicate positions, as in (9), and get into prenominal position by way of relative clauses, as in (10).

(9) *This block is cylindrical.*
(10) (a) *Every block which is cylindrical is yellow.*
     (b) *Every cylindrical block is yellow.*

Such a derivation corresponds to the standard transformational treatment of all adjectives. For attributive adjectives, however, their semantic properties together with Montague's constraint rule out such a derivation. Those adjectives are best treated as combining directly with a common noun to form a new common noun phrase, semantically interpreted as a function applied to its argument. Many adjectives are ambiguous as between a predicative and attributive use, as is illustrated by sentence (11)[7], for which both derivations are possible.

(11) Marya is a beautiful dancer.

Siegel (1976b) shows that there is a great deal of syntactic evidence in both Russian and English to support the double derivation of adjective-noun constructions and hence indirectly to support the requirement that each syntactic rule have a uniform semantic interpretation. It is this requirement, which is by no means uncontroversial, that accounts for a great deal of the current interest in Montague grammar; if it is borne out, it implies a strong connection between form and meaning in natural language; if it fails, it will be interesting to examine why and where syntax and semantics must diverge.

2.2. *Adding further constraints for natural languages.*

So far I have emphasized the constraint Montague's framework imposes on the relation between syntax and semantics. Now I must turn to some of the ways in which Montague's theory is much too unconstrained with respect to the interests of linguists. The syntactic and semantic rule forms given in (1) and (2) above involve syntactic operations F_i and semantic operations G_k, and Montague put essentially no constraints whatever on the form of these operations. If one is interested in characterizing the class of all and only possible human languages, it is imperative to look for constraints on the form of the operations allowed, and some of the recent linguistic work in the Montague framework is aimed at just that goal.[8] I will not go into specifics here, but mention only that in this respect it seems reasonably natural to try to formulate a theory of possible grammars of natural languages as a restricted subtheory of Montague's more general theory, making use of the kinds of constraints on rules that have been formulated for transformational grammars.

A quite different sort of constraint which is to some extent implicit in Montague's own work is what I call the "well-formedness constraint."[9] Since a Montague grammar works "bottom-up", constructing complex expressions from simpler ones, it is quite natural to impose the constraint that each expression built up in the course of a derivation be itself a well-formed expression of its respective syntactic category. This contrasts with the practice common in transformational grammar of positing underlying or intermediate stages in derivations which are not themselves well-formed expressions, but which are transformed into well-formed expressions by obligatory rules. To give just one illustration of the effect of this constraint, let us consider attributive adjectives again.

If all prenominal adjectives are derived from relative clauses, the postulated underlying sources are sometimes ungrammatical, as in a transformational derivation of (12b) from (12a).

(12a) *the owner $\begin{Bmatrix} who \\ which \end{Bmatrix}$ is rightful

(12b) the rightful owner

Since all of the cases in which the relative clause source is ungrammatical are also cases where the adjective is semantically attributive, the analysis which generates attributive adjectives directly in prenominal position avoids positing ill-formed underlying forms. Thus the well-formedness constraint in this case provides independent syntactic motivation for choosing the same analysis that is required by the constraint on the relation between syntactic and semantic rules.

The well-formedness constraint does not eliminate abstractness in syntax, but it essentially limits it to the operation of the rules which combine expressions to form new ones. By limiting the class of syntactic derivations, it limits the class of grammars compatible with the surface data of a given language, and thereby provides a potentially important restriction on the range of hypotheses a child might have to (unconsciously) consider in the process of mastering the adult language.

There are other kinds of constraints that could be sought within a Montague framework; for example, one might try to find correlations between the form of a given syntactic rule and the form of the corresponding semantic interpretation rule so as to strengthen still further the constraint on the relation between syntax and semantics. A great deal more descriptive analysis of particular constructions is required, however, since arguments about the correctness of various proposed constraints are invariably intertwined with arguments about the best analysis of particular constructions. But from the fragmentary evidence available so far, one can at least say that there appears to be no obstacle to pursuing the goal of characterizing the syntax and semantics of possible human language as a subtheory of Montague's theory by adding certain constraints motivated by empirical criteria of adequacy, criteria which may be of little interest to a philosopher or logician but of central concern to the linguist.

2.3. *Model-theoretic semantics with possible-worlds models.*

As I indicated earlier, semantic interpretation in the framework of Montague (1973) proceeds in two stages. The first stage, illustrated above, is a rule-by-rule translation of expressions of the natural language into expressions in a language of intensional logic; the second stage involves a model-theoretic interpretation of the intensional logic. It is at the second stage that the notion of possible worlds plays a critical role, and I want to try to sketch, non-technically, enough of what is involved in this second stage to raise certain issues about psychological reality.

The intensional logic has primitive *constants* of various types, such as names of individuals, one-place predicates, operators on predicates, etc., as well as *variables* of all these same types; the logic also contains various recursive means for forming complex expressions of all the different types. An *intensional model* provides a domain of things outside of language for the expressions of the logic to refer to or be true of and a means of associating the expressions of the logic with particular entities or states-of-affairs in the model, so as to tie down the truth-conditions of the sentences of the logic and the references of the terms to appropriate non-linguistic anchors. The aspect of the models that I want to focus on is their inclusion of a set of non-actual possible worlds, treated as primitive (i.e., not defined or derived) within the theory. The motivation for the possible worlds part of possible worlds semantics has been its fruitfulness in providing an adequate account of the truth conditions in the actual world for sentences involving such "intensional" notions as logical possibility and necessity, contrary-to-fact conditionals, and psychological attitudes such as beliefs, hopes, and wishes, just to mention a small sample.

Let me illustrate the key notions of *extension* and *intension* and the role possible worlds play in their explication with some examples. Consider first the following inference:

(13) (a) *Alice wants to marry the richest man in town.*

(b) *The richest man in town is the stingiest man in town.*

(c) *Alice wants to marry the stingiest man in town.*

The first and third sentences above are actually ambiguous; if we understand them as asserting of a particular individual that Alice wants to marry him, the inference is legitimate. But the reading I am interested in is one that could be brought out more sharply by appending "whoever he may be" to the final noun phrases of (13) (a) and (13) (c); on this reading, the inference is clearly invalid. The second premise asserts that the two descriptive noun phrases in fact pick out the same individual; this is what is meant by saying that the two expressions have the same extension in the actual world. The invalidity of the inference shows that the semantic contribution of the noun phrase to the truth-conditions of a sentence involving an intensional construction like "wants to" must involve more than just the extension of the noun phrase in the actual world. If we go further and consider how the same noun phrase, say "the richest man in town," would pick out different individuals in different possible states of affairs, or possible worlds, we recognize that "the richest man in town" would not always pick out the same individual as "the stingiest man in town." The function which picks out the appropriate individual or extension in *each* possible world is the *intension* of the term; in an intensional context such as the "wants to" construction, it is the intension and not the extension of the terms that is crucial for the truth-conditions of the sentence.[10] Substituting in (13) (a) another term with the same *intension*, e.g. "the man in town who has the most money" would preserve the truth-conditions of the sentence, but substituting a term with merely the same extension does not.

The attributive adjective plus common noun construction discussed above can also be seen to be intensional in many cases. First we must consider what extension and intension amount to for common nouns: The simplest treatment is to take the extension of a common noun like *doctor* to be a set of individuals: the extension of *doctor* in the actual world is the set of individuals who are doctors in that world. The intension of *doctor* is the function which picks out the extension, i.e. the appropriate set of individuals, in each possible world. Now consider the attributive adjective construction *good doctor.* Let us suppose, just for the sake of examining our intuitions, that in fact all and only doctors were violinists. It would clearly not follow that the good doctors were the good violinists or conversely. Why? Because an attributive adjective like *good* operates on the *intension*, not the extension, of the common noun it is in construction with; its interpretation is a function which applies to a function to produce a new function.

Now perhaps we are in a position to say a little more formally what an intensional model looks like. In Montague's system, an intensional model is a quadruple $\eta = \langle A, I, J, F \rangle$, where A is a set of individuals, I is a set of possible worlds, J is an ordered set of moments of time, and F is an interpretation function which assigns to each constant of the intensional logic an appropriate intension in the model. The extension of an individual constant in a given world will be some individual in the set A; the intension will be a function from worlds to individuals. The extension of a predicate constant, like *Man* or *Runs,* in a given world, will be a set of individuals, and the intension will be a function from possible worlds to such sets of individuals. The function F which assigns an intension to the primitive constants of the logic thus determines for each constant its extension in each possible world. The rest of the model-theoretic semantics involves specifying the interpretation of the complex expressions of the logic; for example, one interpretation rule will say that a conjunction $[\varphi \,\&\, \Psi]$ is true in a given world if and only if each of the conjuncts is true in that world. The rule for sentences of the form $\Box\,\varphi$ ("necessarily φ") says that $\Box\,\varphi$ is true in a given world w if and only if φ is true in *every* possible world.

It is impossible to convey an adequate picture of the workings of possible worlds semantics with such a brief and fragmentary sketch. One of its chief benefits has been in providing an account that is both rigorous and intuitive of semantic differences between sentences which superficially appear to be of the same grammatical and logical form. As a final example before turning to psychological issues, consider the following pair of inferences, one involving the intensional transitive verb *look for* and the other the extensional transitive verb *talk to*:

(14) (a) *Sam is looking for the president of the bank.*
    (b) *The president of the bank is the leader of the spy ring.*
    (c) *Sam is looking for the leader of the spy ring.*
(15) (a) *Sam is talking to the president of the bank.*
    (b) *The president of the bank is the leader of the spy ring.*
    (c) *Sam is talking to the leader of the spy ring.*

The distinction between the extension and the intension of expressions such as "the president of the bank" or "the leader of the spy ring", which is formally captured by considering what such phrases would refer to in alternative possible worlds, makes it possible to explain neatly why the inference in (14) is invalid while that in (15) is valid.

3. Abstract models and speakers' models.

3.1. Logically possible worlds.

As I indicated in the last section, an intensional model is a quadruple $\eta = \langle A, I, J, F \rangle$, with A a set of individuals, I a set of possible worlds, J a set of moments of time, and F an interpretation function. For the purposes of model theoretic semantics, which is centrally concerned with characterizing valid inferences, it is sufficient to consider such models abstractly, and one generally introduces a model by saying "Let A, I, and J be arbitrary non-empty sets, ..." Certain constraints on the possible models may be imposed by adding *meaning postulates* to the system; one can require, for example, that a proper name pick out the same individual in every possible world, or that the interpretations assigned by F to the predicates[11] *bachelor* and *male* be such that the extension of *bachelor* is always a subset of the extensions of *male*. But the set of intensional models which count as potential interpretations of the intensional logic and hence indirectly of English is still very large, so there is a sense in which one has not by this means been given *the* interpretation of English. That does not matter for the task of characterizing valid inferences; a formula φ *logically entails* a formula Ψ of the intensional logic if the conditional $[\varphi \rightarrow \Psi]$ is true in every intensional model consistent with the meaning postulates, with respect to all worlds and moments of time in that model.

But not only is it unnecessary and inappropriate to the logician's task to try to present particular intensional models in any concrete or explicit form, it is clearly impossible to do so with the resources of language. With the most conservative assumptions, the number of logically possible worlds in any realistic model must be at least non-denumerably infinite, which means that there is no way they could be listed or enumerated by a finite description or set or rules. By the same token, the interpretation function F must also be given abstractly: One simply stipulates that to each constant of the logic there is assigned an intension of the appropriate type, i.e. a function from each possible world to an extension in that world. We can describe these functions by saying, e.g., that the intension assigned to the constant *bachelor* is the function which picks out in each world the set of individuals who are bachelors in that world. But we certainly cannot specify such a function by considering the possible worlds one by one and saying what the extension of *bachelor* is in each, since we cannot specify all the possible worlds individually. If we try to describe the intension assigned by F to some constant at all, we *must* do so by considering how the function applies to arbitrary possible worlds. To say that we must consider all possible worlds and cannot consider each possible world one by one is not as paradoxical as it may sound; we do the same when we consider functions defined on the real numbers, which are also a non-denumerably infinite set. But the nature of the psychological processes underlying such abstract reasoning ability is, I believe, a large and unexplored problem, and one to which I will return briefly below.

For the moment, however, I want to stay away from the psychological questions and consider further the logical models. The real work of the intensional model is performed not by the stipulation of the basic elements of the model, which is done in the abstract manner described above, but by the rules which define on the basis of the model how the interpretation of a complex expression is determined on the basis of the interpretation of its parts. In assessing the adequacy of a proposed semantics for English, say, we assume that we have a model in which the lexical elements have their intended interpretations, and we then judge the adequacy of the interpretations assigned to sentences by checking them against our intuitions about their truth conditions and entailment relations. It is easy to bring empirical evidence to bear on proposed semantic analyses at this level; the earlier-cited argument against the treatment of all adjectives as simple predicates is a case in point. The model may not specify anything about the difference between the intension of *red-haired* and that of *blonde,* nor about the difference between *good* and *competent,* but the difference in logical type between the two pairs has a great deal of explanatory force in accounting for the syntax and semantics of adjective constructions.

So let us assume we simply take as given a set of possible worlds. A sentence of the form $'\Diamond \varphi'$, where the diamond is the symbol for logical possibility, is interpreted as true in a given model if the sentence φ is true in the model at some possible world at some time. A model gives a 'correct' account of logical possibility if its possible worlds and the rest of the interpretation are such that each sentence that is in fact logically possible does come out true at some world and time in that model. But the attempt to determine which model or models are 'correct' in this sense is part of the enterprise of metaphysics, not of semantics. Similarly, we can characterize other notions of possibility, such as physical possibility, or possibility with respect to alternative future courses of events starting from the actual present. We can say, for instance, that 'Physically-possible φ' is true in the actual world if φ is true in some logically possible world in which all the physical laws of the actual world hold; in this case, it is a matter for physics to give a characterization of the relevant class of possible worlds. Similarly, we can say that 'Future-possible φ' is true at a given world and time if φ is true at some later time in some possible world which coincides with the given world up until the given time. There are many areas where the tools of possible worlds semantics can offer fruitful analysis of such modal constructions without giving more than an abstract specification of the relevant set of possible worlds.

3.4. *Human conceptions of possibility.*

At this point, I want to turn away from the logician's conception of language as a formal system and back to the linguist's or psychologist's concern with the variously idealized competent speaker-hearer. Suppose we ask what it would take for a person to know a language as described in a Montague framework. Looking at the syntax, we find a finite number of primitive lexical items and a finite number of syntactic formation rules,[12] so there is no obstacle in principle to a speaker knowing that part. Similarly for the rules for translating the natural language into the language of intensional logic.[13] But when we get to the models as described above, which form the basis of the interpretation of the intensional logic, we face some interesting problems. Let me focus on the possible worlds part of the model, since the sorts of problems I have in mind can all be illustrated there, although they arise for other parts of the model as well.

The first problem concerns finite representability. Suppose we accept the claim[14] that any model adequate for getting the semantics of English right must have a non-denumerably infinite set of possible worlds. Then a human cannot have a finite representation of each of them any more than the logician can give a finite description of each of them. But it doesn't follow that we cannot have some internalized conception of 'all possible worlds', only that such a conception cannot consist of an itemized enumeration. It seems to me that we certainly do have conceptions of non-actual possible states of affairs, but not in the form of complete specifications of possible worlds. Among the clearest examples of conceptions of possibility are 'local' variations on actuality, as expressed in the sentences of (16), or the constructions of fantasy, which involve highly incomplete specifications of alternative possible worlds, as in (17).

(16) (a) *Shirley could have been a linguist.*
    (b) *If John had gotten home on time, ...*
    (c) *Sam wishes that he had a son.*

(17) (a) *Suppose people walked on their heads and had eyes in their toes.*
    (b) *Superman was born on the planet Krypton, where . . .*

We do not know all the facts about the actual world, but we presumably all share the notion that there *is* one, and from that basis we can generate partial specifications of many alternative possible worlds by the sorts of local variation illustrated in (16); we could think of these representations as generated by a formula like that of (18);

(18) *'like the actual world except that . . . .'*

Such specifications will be only partial, since a given change will usually entail that certain other things change as well, generally with considerable indeterminancy. (E.g. if we say "like the actual world except that Shirley becomes a linguist," we haven't specified whether Shirley goes to a different school, reads different books, meets different people, or who had the job Shirley now has, etc.)

The conceptual abilities involved in considering even these partial specifications of 'local' alternative worlds seem complex and powerful and worth a great deal of serious investigation; but especially interesting is the way in which we seem to be able to generate higher-order abstract possibilities. For instance, here is one simple way to arrive at a non-denumerably infinite subset of the set of possible worlds:

(19) *Consider some actual couple, say the Smiths, and consider some children they might have, and their children's possible children, and so on ad infinitum. For simplicity, fix the number of offspring of each couple and attach names to the individuals by generation and order of birth. This gives an infinite domain A of possible individuals (incompletely specified.) Now suppose we conceive that the property of having blue eyes may be distributed in any way among these individuals, so that for any subset of A, it could be the case that all and only the individuals in that subset have blue eyes.*

The description in (19) is finite, but it is already enough to provide for the existence of a conception of non-denumerably many distinct possible worlds; all we need for that are the notion of an infinite set and the notion of subset.

So it seems to me that the problem of finite representability is potentially solvable; we can arrive by finite means at a conception of possible worlds such that there must be non-denumerably many of them, without anything like particular descriptions of each one, and in fact without having complete descriptions of any of them, and without having to have any explicit concept of non-denumerability.

But there are other interesting problems to consider as well. There are undoubtedly general limits imposed by our cognitive capacity on the kinds of alternative possible worlds we can consider. And since we are not able to process all the logical entailments of a given proposition, we are prone to fall into inconsistency both in our beliefs about the actual world and in our considerations of alternative possible worlds. Hence if we wanted to construct a theory of 'conceptually possible models,' we would probably need to allow for some sort of 'impossible worlds' as well as possible worlds, as Hintikka has urged for the semantics of *belief*-sentences.[15]

If we think about human conceptions of physical possibility or future possibility, we see that there are limitations imposed by our ignorance of facts as well as by our general cognitive apparatus. We may well have some notion of alternative possible worlds or states of affairs subject to the actual physical laws, but we clearly don't know enough facts to know what the physical laws are. And with respect to conceptions of alternative ways the future might turn out, we are limited not only in the foregoing ways but also by our ignorance of many present actual particular facts which could have a causal bearing on future events.

What I want to suggest is that the kind of model posited by possible worlds semantics may well have a kind of psychological reality, but where the logician simply stipulates the model in a highly abstract way, the psychologist and perhaps the linguist could profitably investigate the ways in which the individual's internalized model of both the actual world and of possible worlds is built up through the interaction of mind and reality. Different individuals' models undoubtedly share some properties and differ in others. What is shared presumably reflects properties of the human perceptual and cognitive apparatus plus the most universal features of human experience. Individual differences presumably result in part from differences in experience, which lead in many case to differences in inductive generalizations and consequent differences in conceptions of what is possible, and probably in part from differential application of the cognitive apparatus (e.g., the creative imagination of great poets).

General cognitive psychologists, like most linguists, would presumably be more interested in the common part, raising questions of how our cognitive and perceptual apparatus operates on experience to generate conceptions of non-actual possibilities. The prelinguistic infant clearly has some notions of non-actual possibilities, as demonstrated by surprise reactions (presumably evinced by non-conformity of some actual state of affairs to some alternative expected state of affairs) and nonverbal expressions of wants (e.g. carrying a cup to an adult to ask for a drink). One might attempt a kind of generative model of conceptions of possibilities to try to show how conceptions of novel possibilities could be derived by basic cognitive operations applied to the objects of perception plus whatever innate non-perceptual ideas we may start out with. The nature of inductive generalization as a psychological process might be a central object of investigation. These suggestions are quite speculative and tentative, and I should apologize immediately for my lack of familiarity with most of the psychological literature; perhaps what I am suggesting is already underway.[16]

For the psychologist interested in individual differences, including those concerned with therapy, the relevant questions would presumably be how individual differences in internalized models arise, and how models can be changed. Perhaps a prior practical question to consider is how individual differences in models can be detected; here the notion of "language as a window on the mind" might take on a new importance. When two individuals have different models of what is possible—logically possible, physically possible, humanly possible, or whatever—they could utter the same sentence, and with the same meaning in one sense, and yet their conceptions of the truth conditions and entailments of that sentence could differ markedly. A typical case might be one in which a couple agree on the statement that she always gets angry at certain things he does; in his model of alternative possible worlds there are none in which he stops doing whatever it is (it's 'part of his nature') but there are worlds in which she doesn't get angry at it, while in her model of alternative possible worlds there are none in which that behavior of his fails to provoke anger (it's an 'involuntary reaction') but some in which he stops doing it. For some reason that therapists have probably figured out, the biggest holes in our conceptions of possibilities often seem to be in imagining ways we could ourselves change; we seem to have much less difficulty in imagining changes in others.

For the linguist or philosopher of language, a closely related issue is the question of how a public language is possible if all that speakers have to operate with are their internalized models.[17] Perhaps the use of demonstratives is crucial here, as a link between language and reality that bypasses the need for descriptive accuracy.[18] But that issue would take us too far afield here.

In conclusion, what I hope to have accomplished here is to describe enough of the framework of Montague grammar to show something of its suitability for describing the syntax and semantics of natural languages, and to show how issues that arise in considering the potential psychological reality of the possible worlds models that lie at its base may open up new areas for profitable joint exploration by philosophers, linguists, and psychologists.

NOTES

*I am grateful to Emmon Bach for much helpful discussion and support, to students and faculty at UC Berkeley and at Stanford University for opportunities to present and discuss early stages of my thoughts on this topic, particularly Julius Moravcsik, Patrick Suppes, Herbert Clark, Eve Clark, Jaakko Hintikka, and Alice ter Meulen. I am also grateful to the Center for Advanced Study in the Behavioral Sciences for the fellowship which made the preparation of this paper possible; part of the funds for the Center fellowship came from the National Science Foundation and the Andrew W. Mellon Foundation. I also wish to express my gratitude to Raphael Stern for inviting me to participate in the conference for which the paper was prepared. (Prepared for the conference on Language and Psychotherapy held April, 1977; final version July, 1977.)

1. See Chomsky (1975), p. 4 and pp. 42-51.
2. For expository simplicity I am considering only binary constructions, but in fact the syntactic rules can combine any finite number of constituent expressions.
3. The rules I am here for simplicity calling 'semantic rules' are just the first stage of the two-stage semantics described above; their function is to provide the translation from English into the language of intensional logic.
4. Partee (1973); but see Bach and Cooper (forthcoming) for an argument that shows that a structure like (3a) is tenable if *the* is allowed to have more than one interpretation.
5. The formulations in (4) and (5) omit the important technical detail that both the syntactic and semantic rules in this case are actually schemata; F_3 is actually an infinite set of functions $F_{3,i}$ one for each choice of variable to relativize over syntactically and perform lambda abstraction on semantically.
6. This discussion of adjectives draws heavily on the work of Terence Parsons (1970) and Muffy Siegel (1976a,b).
7. The example is from Siegel (1976b).
8. See Partee (forthcoming) for a discussion and some proposals.
9. See Partee (forthcoming).
10. Hintikka (1969) has interesting suggestions for not always considering the extension in *all* possible worlds, but rather in an example such as this one considering the extension in the set of all worlds compatible with Alice's wants. In this discussion I am ignoring the disputes and problems that still remain in the area of "propositional attitudes," and concentrating on the arguments for showing that something at *least* as powerful as the extension/intension distinction is needed.

164

11. More precisely, the predicate constants in the intensional logic into which the English words *bachelor* and *male* are translated.
12. In one sense, the schemata mentioned in footnote 5 result in there being an infinite number of syntactic formation rules, but since the schemata are finitely expressible, the distinction is not important here.
13. The same remarks apply here as in footnote 12.
14. See David Lewis (1973), p. 90, footnote. The chapter of which that is part is also an excellent statement of the "realist" position on possible worlds.
15. See Hintikka (1970a), (1970b), (1975).
16. Since the rest of this was written, I have become aware that there is indeed some apparent progress in this direction in cognitive psychology and artificial intelligence, including in particular a growing concern with the nature of mental representations and their acquisition. See, for example, Anderson and Bower (1973), Klahr and Wallace (1976), Miller and Johnson-Laird (1976), Kintsch (1974), Piaget (1970), Fodor (1975). I am grateful to Lauren Resnick for bringing several of these works to my attention.
17. In this connection, Hilary Putnam's ideas about the social division of linguistic labor and about the extent to which the nature of real-world paradigms determines the extension of our terms are of great potential interest. See Putnam (1975).
18. See Putnam (1975), Kripke (1972), Kaplan (1977).

REFERENCES

Anderson, R. and Bower, G. 1973. *Human associative memory.* Washington, D.C.: V.H. Winston and Sons.

Bach, E. 1968. Nouns and Noun phrases. In *Universal in linguistic theory,* eds. Bach, E. and Harms, R. New York.

Bach, E. and Cooper, R. The NP—S analysis of relative clauses and compositional semantics. Forthcoming, *Linguistics and philosophy.*

Bandler, R. and Grinder, J. 1975. *The structure of magic: a book about language and therapy.* Palo Alto: Science and Behavior Books.

Chomsky, N. 1975. *Reflections on language.* New York: Pantheon Books.

Fodor, J. 1975. *The language of thought.* New York: Thomas Y. Crowell Co.

Hintikka, J. 1969. *Models for modalities: selected essays.* Dordrecht: Reidel. _____. 1970a. Knowledge, belief, and logical consequence. *Ajatus* 32, pp. 32-47.

_____. 1970b. Surface information and depth information. In *Information and inference,* eds. Hintikka, J. and Suppes, P. Dordrecht: Reidel.

_____. 1975. Impossible possible worlds vindicated, *Journal of Philosophical Logic* 4, pp. 475-484.

Kaplan, D. 1977. Demonstratives: an essay on the semantics, logic, metaphysics and epistemology and demonstrates and other indexicals. Pacific Division, APA.

Kintsch, W. 1974. *The representation of meaning in memory.* New Jersey: Lawrence Erlbaum Assoc.

Klahr, D. and Wallace, J. 1976. *Cognitive development: an information processing view.* New Jersey: Lawrence Erlbaum Assoc.

Kripke, S. 1972. Naming and necessity. *In Semantics of natural languages,* eds. Davidson, D. and Harman, G. Dordrecht: Reidel

Lewis, D. 1973. *Counterfactuals.* Cambridge: Harvard.

Miller, G. and Philip, N. 1976. *Language and perception.* Cambridge: Belknap Press.

Montague, R. 1973. The proper treatment of quantification in ordinary English. In Formal philosophy: selected papers of Richard Montague, 1974.

_____. 1974. *Formal philosophy: selected papers of Richard Montague,* ed. Thomason, R. New Haven: Yale University Press.

Parsons, T. 1970. Some problems concerning the logic of grammatical modifiers. *Synthese* 21, pp. 320-334.

Partee, B. 1973. Some transformational extensions of Montague grammar. *Journal of Philosophical Logic* 2, pp. 509-534.

_____ 1975. Montague grammar and transformational grammar. *Linguistic Inquiry* 6, pp. 203-300.

_____. 1976. In *Montague grammar.* New York: Academic Press

_____. Forthcoming. Montague grammar and the well-formedness constraint. In a collection of papers from the Third Groningen Round Table of 1976, eds. Heny, F. and Schnelle, H.

Piaget, J. 1970. *Genetic epistemology.* New York; Columbia University Press.

Putnam, H. 1975. The meaning of "meaning". In *Language, mind and knowledge,* ed. Gunderson, K. Minneapolis: Minnesota Studies.

Seigel, M. 1976.a. Capturing the Russian adjective, In *Montague grammar* ed. Partee, B. New York: Academic Press.

_____. 1976.b. Capturing the adjective. Unpublished PhD. dissertation, Univ. of Mass., Amherst.

Emmon Bach

A FRAMEWORK FOR SYNTAX AND SEMANTICS

I accept the idea that the proper way to come to understand the
working of a language is to give an explicit account of the syntax,
semantics, and pragmatics of increasingly rich fragments of
natural languages. This aim is shared by Montague and workers in
his tradition, and by generative transformational grammarians
taking their inspiration from Chomsky (see the remarks in the
first paragraph of Montague, 1970). I also accept the idea that
the goal of such study for a linguist *qua* general linguist is to discover the necessary and sufficient properties of natural languages.
A logician or philosopher is free to create artificial systems and
study their properties, and he is free to treat natural language in
any way he wishes. A linguist is not. Thus, a linguist can view the
results of philosophers in a number of different ways. First off,
in what they say about their languages philosophers are inform-
ants; their theories and their claims about language deserve careful study in the same way that we study both what our inform-
ants say in some language new to us and what they say about
what they say. Further, just as prescriptive grammarians offer
valuable evidence about what people do say and think, when
they tell them not to think or talk that way, prescriptive meta-
physicians offer valuable evidence about what the person on the
street actually thinks he is saying when he says something. Second, I can treat the products of the philosopher in much the
same way as the physicist treats the products of the pure mathematician. The most familiar example of the value of such work
is the use to which Einstein put the purely mathematical work
of Reimann and others. Here philosophy and logic are a kind of
poetry of ideas.

The third way to view the work of philosophers is when they
put on the hat of the linguist and make empirical claims about a

language or Language. Here we are entitled to judge their work in the way we judge any linguistic work: Are their grammars descriptively adequate? That is, are the factual predictions made by particular fragments correct? How well do their general theories perform when viewed as answers to the question: What are natural languages like? I believe Montague was interested in the empirical adequacy of his fragments, but as has often been remarked he was completely uninterested in the second, *meta-question* as to the empirical adequacy of his general theory of language. "Universal grammar" (1970) was really meant to be universal in some such sense as "logically possible." The theory was broad enough to express whatever could be said about any language one would be willing to call a language. Here, linguists who follow Montague are likely to want to ask about how one might pare down the general theory so as to come a little closer to catching natural languages ([Partee, 1976b, forthcoming] has done most to urge this aim on her colleagues in the Montague tradition and to begin the actual work of stating and motivating constraints).

I believe that the most promising approach to a theory of semantics for natural languages is to be found in the work of Montague and his followers. What I find most attractive about the work is the requirement that the theory give explicit rules both for syntax and for semantics and tie down their relationship precisely. But to say this is just to say that the theorists follow the methodological program of the first sentence above. Montague has been widely criticised for his indifference to syntax except as a framework for doing semantics. Just as justly I think one can criticise generative transformational grammarians for their indifference to semantics except as a kind of wastebasket for what they don't want to treat in their syntax. Surely, we would all agree that we can't seriously compare competing theories about the relationships between form and meaning for given languages (or language in general) without making all parts of our theories of meaning and form and their relationships explicit.

In recent years a number of people have become interested in the possibility of combining a Montague approach to semantics and a transformational approach to syntax. Various tacks have been taken. T. Parsons was working for a number of years on providing a formal semantics for a transformational theory of English syntax. Partee (1976a) and others have taken the Montague framework for syntax as basic and worked out ways of grafting transformational operations onto it. Cooper and Parsons, in an important paper (1976), constructed fragments in two different versions of transformational grammar (roughly like 'generative semantic' and 'interpretive semantic' syntaxes) for the language of Montague's PTQ (1973), and proved the equivalence of the two with PTQ in their sense of strong equivalence (the fragments generate all the same strings and assign to them the same or logically equivalent translations in the intensional logic of PTQ.). Cooper (1975) considers much more generally the connections between the two theories and shows how to adopt many of the features (e.g. features) of transformational theory in a rigorous Montague framework. Hellan and Davis (in unpublished work) have been constructing a semantics for English comparatives based on the syntax worked out by Joan Bresnan in several important papers (Bresnan, 1973, 1975).

In recent work I have been following a somewhat different line. The attempts to weld a Montague semantics onto a transformational framework have so far all taken as given some version of the theory of transformational grammar that is derived from the so-called 'standard' theory of Chomsky's *Aspects* (1965). In several papers, I have suggested that the earlier theory represented by the earliest work of Chomsky—what we might call 'classical' transformational theory—had much to recommend it and that in fact it provides a way of doing syntax that can be quite easily adapted to a Montague way of doing semantics. (A number of writers had already pointed out parallels between the earlier theory and the work of Montague.) I make no claims about the superiority of this theory as against others on the market place, I claim only that it is an interesting alternative that deserves to be looked at again, with new aims in mind. It may turn out in the end that all our alternatives are provably equivalent, in which case we could stop arguing about which is better.

Before laying out the framework, I shall briefly review some of the differences between the standard theory of *Aspects,* later versions of the theory in both a 'generative' and 'interpretive' direction, including the most recent work on trace-theory, and the earlier classical theory. Then I will indicate briefly why I think the earlier model deserves another hearing. Finally, I will outline the way in which I think one can quite plausibly and naturally extend the theory in a way that makes it possible to build into it some of the attractive features of Montague grammar.

Classical transformational theory (as represented in Chomsky, 1957, and, more fully, in Chomsky, 1975 [1955]), was based on the idea that the best way to describe the syntax of a natural language was to give an explicit grammar for a certain set of maximally simple basic sentences (the *kernel*) and to describe more complex derived sentences by extending the basic set of kernel structures through certain structure-dependent rules called *transformations*. Discovering what the kernel structures of a language were was held to be an empirical problem, but Chomsky conjectured that continued research would show that evidence would converge on an answer to this question; in the early fragments that he and others presented the kernel structures were argued to be the simple active declarative affirmative sentences. This idea, which was followed out in a different way (i.e. not within a generative framework) by Zellig Harris, (1957, 1965) may be compared with the standard way in which a logician sets forth a recursive definition of the syntax of some artificial language. The recursive definition takes the form of first declaring a certain set of expressions to be (atomic) sentences or formulas, and then extending the set by *transformations* of the forms (i) If φ is a sentence, then $f(\varphi)$ is a sentence (or formula; or (ii) if φ and Ψ are sentences, then $g(\varphi, \Psi)$ is a sentence, where $\underline{f}$ and $\underline{g}$ are certain syntactic operations, for example prefixing a negative operator or forming the structure '$(\varphi \wedge \Psi)$'. Just as the logician describes certain operations as applying to single formulas (type i) and some as applying to pairs of formulas (type ii), Chomsky's early framework included *singulary* transformations like the negative and passive transformations, and *generalized* or binary transformations. Because of the vastly simpler structure of artificial languages, the transformations of the logician do not need the complex structure dependency of natural language transformations in most cases. But even here one can find closer analogues to the structure-dependent character of natural languages transformations, for example, in operations which substitute variables for variables or names, or in relational logics which include operations like forming the converse of a binary relation. The real difference is in the fact that the logician is stipulating the structure of his formulas as he constructs his language. The linguist is trying to discover the hidden structure of the *formulas* he is presented with, since they come at him simply as strings of elements with no overt structure (actually even this is an idealization). I say "analogues" to natural language transformations, since technically most of the logician's transformations are not grammatical transformations at all.

I find this an appealing and intuitively highly satisfying way of looking at the syntax of a language. This judgment is, of course, only a piece of autobiographical information, but in early work Chomsky argued for the general theory on grounds of native speaker's intuitions about whether one sentence was more 'basic' than another (e.g. passive is less basic than active, negative than affirmative) and about the 'transformational relations' between sentences (e.g. *Is John here?* is related by the question transformation to *John is here)*. In the language of Chomsky, the theory could claim 'explanatory adequacy' to the extent that the most simple and general account of the facts would lead to predictions about intuitions of that sort. The kernel sentences would be judged more basic, and transformationally related sentences were predicted to be judged as related in ways that nontransformationally related sentences weren't. I think there is little doubt that people have such intuitions, and they can be tested in various ways besides direct appeal to introspective judgments.

The first departure from this elegant scheme arose after it was observed that certain lexical elements never occur in simple kernel structures. One might make a case, for example, that *John wants to go* is just a more complex instantiation of the kernel structure underlying *John wants it,* but this approach seems pretty strained when we consider examples like *deem (John deems it necessary* but not **John deems that)*. It should be mentioned that it was a tacit assumption in early work that the set of kernel sentences would be finite, possibly with the exception of certain simple recursive structures like *very big, very very big, . . .* , hence that the major burden, if not the whole burden, of accounting for the unboundedness of natural languages would be carried by the transformations.

The way out of this difficulty was to posit the existence of certain 'dummy' elements in the kernel structures. One might assume, for example, that the kernel rules generated a structure underlying a string like this: *John deem DUMMY*. The dummy element was then simply a placeholder for a generalized embedding transformation. This approach was followed out in an important paper by Charles Fillmore (1963): Fillmore not only accepted this idea but proposed a certain organization of a grammar in terms of the ordering of rule components. Fillmore's paper was an attempt to solve the problem of providing some principled basis for the 'traffic rules' of a grammar (as they were then called). For example, Fillmore observed that in so far as anyone knew there was no evidence that any singulary transformation had to be applied to a 'matrix' sentence before an embedded structure was added to it, or that a certain singulary transformation had to be applied to an embedded structure after it had been embedded, except perhaps by virtue of the fact that it was now an embedded structure. Fillmore's proposal was this: Every embedding rule had to take as input one kernel structure (the *matrix*) and another derived structure (the *constituent)*. Only the latter might have undergone certain optional transformations (he made some other assumptions which I shall ignore here). He also noted that this assumption led to a cyclical application of transformational rules. Given a structure consisting of a sentence embedded inside another, the singulary rules must have applied to the constituent before it was embedded, and to the matrix after it has been embedded.

In the standard theory of *Aspects* and all post-*Aspects* transformational theories (and many nontransformational ones, such as the relational grammars of Postal and Perlmutter) a basic change was made. Rather than thinking of complex sentences as being built out of simple kernel structures by operations defined on pairs of structures (or, more generally, sets, as in conjunction transformations) it was assumed that the embedded sentences were already *there* at a certain descriptive level ("deep structure") and that a single set of transformations operated cyclically, bottom to top, on these structures to produce surface structures. This is a far-reaching change. I will single out two implications that are of importance for us here. First, the new theory no longer captured the notion of transformational relatedness in the direct way that the older model did (this point was made by Stanley Peters in a lecture several years ago at City University of New York). Second, the new theory opened the way to a much more abstract approach to the description of natural languages, in a way that I will explain presently. (The new theory was less restrictive than Fillmore's theory in a number of ways [Bach, forthcoming a] chiefly having to do with the possibilities of ordering and with the possibility of applying several deletion operations to a single embedded sentence.)

Note that in the older theory every embedded structure would have to be a viable candidate for a grammatical sentence of the language being described, otherwise the grammar would simply be empirically inadequate. In the new theory this was no longer the case. Since the transformations acted as a kind of filter, the base rules (the new counterpart to the kernel rules) generated an infinite set of structures, some of which might underlie no sentences of the language at all. From the point of view of 'sentence ecology' (*gratia* Avery Andrews) the older theory was much more conservationist. (Actually, in order to achieve empirical adequacy for particular choices of analyses the new theory had to include certain surface filters as well as using the filtering effect of the transformations.) For example, in the older theory one might derive a complex structure like *John wants to go to Carmel* by taking the structures underlying (say) *John Pres want Dummy* and *He Pres go to Carmel.* In this analysis the embedded structure underlies a perfectly good English sentence: *He goes to Carmel.* A popular analysis in the new theory (Bresnan, 1972) assumed that the underlying structure of the (already embedded) constituent sentence was something like this *For PRO to go to Carmel,* but of course, this underlies no simple English sentence. (The problem of empirical adequacy, which was never really faced, would lead to some such surface filter as this: "mark as ungrammatical any matrix without a tense, or with an initial complementizer.") Thus, the classical theory naturally incorporated a kind of property that I have called *local grammaticality*; we might call this more precisely *S-local grammaticality*: every embedded S-structure going into the make-up of a sentence must underlie a possible English sentence. The only kind of filtering allowed then could be based on a quite general principal: Sentences containing unreplaced dummy elements are ungrammatical. This might be thought to be letting abstractness in by the back door, but in fact the principle restricts the use of filtering to elements that can be the substituends of an embedding rule, and can even be thought of as a generalization of the idea that structures to which obligatory rules can still apply are ungrammatical (that's just what obligatory means). S-local grammaticality makes an essential difference in the mathematical properties of the model, as I have argued elsewhere (Bach, forthcoming a).

If, as I have argued, the new theory of *Aspects* was less restrictive than the classical theory, why was it abandoned? I believe that the real answer to this was the tremendous appeal of a hypothesis about the relation between syntax and semantics that was developed around the time of *Aspects*. Before looking at this hypothesis, let's consider a few questions about the role of semantics and syntax in transformational theory.

Most so-called semantic theories that have been proposed for transformational grammars by linguists are not semantic at all in the sense of the philosopher. They are instead translation schemes which map syntactic objects into other syntactic objects. These other syntactic objects must then be provided with a semantics in the sense of the philosopher or logician, that is, an interpretation, say in the model-theoretic framework or by the statement of rules for truth conditions. Most linguists stop before the interpretation. What the linguists' "rules of interpretation" really are are ways of associating a disambiguated language with the (in general) ambiguous language under consideration. (I will henceforth call the linguists' kind of rules *translation* rules, and reserve *semantic*, etc., for the rules concerned with interpreting some language, ambiguous or not. It is assumed generally that the interpretation is defined on some disambiguated language, although this is by no means a necessary or even empirically well-established assumption. See Cooper, 1975.)

The earliest proposals for a system of translation rules for transformational grammars were those of Katz and Fodor (1963). The scheme was set up for a classical syntax. Two types of "projection rules" were proposed. The first type (P I) applied to fully formed kernel structures: They were basically compositional and 'bottom-to-top,' making use of such notions as the grammatical relations of Subject and Predicate (configurationally defined), Modifier and Head and so on. The second type (P II) were associated with the transformations and provided a translation of the output as a function of the translation of the input(s). The result of this translation procedure was an object (a 'reading') which would presumably be the basis for a semantic interpretation. If a certain sentence was n-ways ambiguous, then the grammar and its associated translation rules would provide n different translations for the sentence. Katz (in this and later work) tried to provide an account of such notions as analyticity and consequence on the basis of the syntax of the "language of readings." The nature of the language of readings is of no consequence to us here (though of great importance in its own right). The P II rules fell into two types: Those associated with optional singulary transformations like the negative, or question transformations, and those which showed how to compose the translation of complex structures out of the translations of their parts.

Now, in a series of studies, various linguists had argued, within the framework of assumptions available at the time, that a number of transformations which clearly involved a change of meaning (negative, question) should be stated as obligatory transformations contingent on the presence of various 'real' or abstract elements in the underlying kernel structures. Katz and Postal (1964) took the step of arguing that *in general* this should be required by the theory, i.e. that no singulary transformations should be formulable which changed meaning. What this meant was that those P II rules which gave the meanings associated with optional rules could in every case be replaced by P I rules formulated for the underlying elements that "triggered" the transformation. Thus the only burden placed on the P II rules was to show how meanings of complex sentences were composed. In the standard theory, since the embedded structures were already *there* this meant that everything needed for the operation of the translation rules was *there* in the deep structure. Thus the stage was set for the so-called Katz-Postal hypothesis: Deep structure is the level at which the translation rules (projection rules) are defined. It followed from this hypothesis that no optional transformations could result in structures that carried different meanings from the untransformed structures. It also followed that if two sentences differed in meaning they must be derived from different deep structures.

The important point to note here is that the dropping of P II rules meant that a certain general claim was being made about the nature of the translation relation. Let us call this the *configurational hypothesis*:

I. Every translation rule is of the following form: Given a structure of such and such a sort, translate it into an expression of such and such a sort in the interpreted language.

I want to contrast this with a different view, what we may call the rule-by-rule hypothesis:

II. With every syntactic rule there is associated a unique translation rule, which gives the translation of the resultant expression as a function of the translation(s) of the input(s).

P II rules were of the latter sort. So also are the translation rules of Montague grammars like the fragment of PTQ.

It may not be self-evident that these two hypotheses are significantly different. But without further stipulations it is possible to formulate rules under one hypothesis that are impossible to formulate under the other and vice versa. For example, the configurational hypothesis has no restrictions on the complexity of the structures which may be the input to the translation rules or the 'direction' in which they operate. It is compatible not only with a strictly compositional 'bottom-to-top' procedure (as in Fodor and Katz' P I rules) but also with such theories as Hintikka's game-theoretical rules which unpack the meanings of sentences by means of a number of 'moves' which may go 'top-to-bottom' or even 'up and down' (Hintikka, 1973). The rule-by-rule hypothesis requires that the translation procedure mirror the syntax completely, but itself allows one to formulate rules which operate on the same syntactic structures, have the same syntactic output, and yield different translations. (This last possibility is disallowed in Montague's general theory, 1970.) So there really may be an empirical difference between the two and the linguist is faced with the familiar and difficult task of finding the right mix between freedom and restrictiveness to best match the facts of natural language.

The Katz-Postal hypothesis ran into severe difficulties almost immediately, chiefly with problems of scope and quantification. Two main directions were followed, called (not very felicitously) 'generative' and 'interpretive' semantics. The first group stuck with the Katz-Postal hypothesis and elaborated much more 'abstract' deep structures than had been countenanced before (e.g. G. Lakoff, 1971). If we restrict ourselves to scope problems, what the first group did was to assume different deep structures for the various readings of sentences like *Every man loves some woman*. The second group (e.g. Jackendoff, 1972) abandoned the hypothesis and allowed the translation relation to be defined on various levels: end of cycle, surface structure, deep structures.

In Chomsky's latest work (1976, forthcoming) there is again a single 'level' which determines Logical Form. It is intermediate between deep structure and surface structure, in the strict sense, but because of the presence of 'trace' elements which record the various locations of elements 'moved' in the course of a derivation, it includes information about the deep structure and (in general) information about every intermediate stage of a derivation. (This account is somewhat oversimplified.) Chomsky now postulates two levels relevant to semantic interpretation: Logical Form, roughly a representation of English sentences using labeled bracketings of elements which include English morphemes and various abstract elements like variables and trace elements. Logical Form is but one of the ingredients which go into a level of representation called Semantic Representation, presumably the latter is the language to be interpreted. In the case of the 'interpretive' rules that turn the 'enriched surface structure' into Logical Form, a structure goes through a number of intermediate stages.)

I don't intend to argue for or against the current approaches to the translation problem in the transformational tradition. What I am currently exploring is an alternative which follows a consequential choice of the rule-by-rule hypothesis, that is, I am taking exactly the opposite course from the one that has been followed by all transformational grammarians since P II rules were eliminated from the theory.

Classical transformational theory included among the structural descriptions assigned to sentences objects called transformation markers (T-markers). A T-marker is a record of the abstract transformational history of a sentence. Many writers have noted that T-markers are in some respects close analogues to the analysis-trees of Montague grammar. Both notions, viewed in general, may be thought of as incorporating an insight that goes back to Frege and has been emphasized by Geach, among others (Geach, 1962).[1]

The idea is that we can associate different *meanings* with different ways in which a sentence is built up out of the very same parts. Geach (1962) for example argues that *John loves Mary* can be analysed in two different ways: Under one interpretation we associate the 'predicable' _____ loves Mary with John; in the other we predicate John loves _____ of Mary. Both are valid ways of understanding the sentence and in some sentences involving quantifiers the two analyses satisfy different truth conditions. But there is no need to represent the difference by differences in syntactic structure, in the sense of labeled bracketings. One *can* do so, as in the standard use of quantifiers and parentheses in predicate logic, or in both the 'generative' semanticists' deep structures or the 'logical form' of current work by Chomsky and associates. But both Montague grammar and classical transformational theory provide a way of representing the differences in another dimension. In PTQ, *John loves Mary* has seven different possible derivations all leading to the same sentence (in this case, but not others, all logically equivalent). Classical transformational theory did not use T-markers for such purposes.

It is natural then to explore an extension of classical transformational theory which exploits this possibility for the sort of problem treated by Montague in PTQ. In the remainder of this paper I will outline a theory of this sort and then give an informal exposition of how one might treat a number of problems in such a theory (in Bach, forthcoming b, I have given a grammar of this sort for the fragment of PTQ).

Let's call the type of grammar to be considered here a KT-grammar (where "K" and "T" are memonic for Kernel and Transformation).[2] Such a grammar is a recursive definition of several sets of objects. Rather than thinking of the grammar as composed of a separate syntax and a rule-by-rule translation procedure, I will formulate the grammar by stating rules that define *structural descriptions*, each a pair, of which the first member is a syntactic structure—that is, a labeled bracketed string—and the second a translation of the structure into an interpreted intensional logic (I will have little to say about the latter here; I will take it to be of the same form as that of PTQ, but by no means do I agree with all the particulars of Montague's system). The general form of the rules is this:

If . . . is/are in the set of structural descriptions, then - - - is in the set of structural descriptions (where . . . is replaced by a specification of one or more pairs and - - - is a further pair)

(I assume but do not pursue here the idea that this scheme will be extended to incorporate representations of conventional implicatures in the manner proposed by L. Karttunen and Peters, 1975; in such an extension the structural descriptions would be not pairs but quadruples.) There is probably no theoretical significance in choosing to have rules simultaneously defining syntactic structures and their translations rather than taking some disambiguated representation such as analysis trees as the input to the translation rules. But there is a practical effect: I can't state rules that just give the syntax and put off doing something about the semantics until later. Thus I do not use either a notion of T-marker or analysis tree. If a structure is ambiguous then it will occur as the first member of a number of distinct structural discriptions.

The grammar is organized as follows:

(i)   The *lexicon* is the basis for generating the first set of structural descriptions called Kernel Structural Descriptions (KSD). Each entry in the lexicon is a triple; a representation of an element in the language described, a specification of its (lexical) syntactic category, and a translation of the item into the intensional logic. With every grammar we associate the general rule:

KR-0 If $\langle a, A, \alpha \rangle$ is a lexical entry, then $\langle [_A a], \alpha \rangle$ is in the set of kernel structural descriptions

(ii)   The *kernel rules* (KR-1, KR-2, ..., KR-n) then tell us how to build up the set by recursive rules such as this:

If $\langle [_A X_1], \alpha \rangle$ and $\langle [_B X_2], \beta \rangle \in$ KSD, then $\langle [_C [_A X_1] [_B X_2]], f(\alpha, \beta) \rangle \in$ KSD

The *then* parts of the kernel rules are confined to simple concatenations of the first members of the elements mentioned in the *if* part (possibly with additional elements, grammatical morphemes, etc.) inside of new pairs of labeled brackets. They are thus the analogues of the phrase structure rules of transformational grammars, and in fact we can represent them all in this more perspicuous form (cf. the example above:

$$C \rightarrow A\ B : f(\alpha, \beta)$$

Here and below, 'X_i' stands for an arbitrary string of labeled brackets and elements of the vocabulary.

I require that all rules be stated in such a way that the right members of the structures specified in the *if* part of the rule be variables over the whole translation of the structure and that these same variables appear in the specification of the resultant translation in the *then* part. What this means is that although we can look 'inside' the syntactic structures we are dealing with (this becomes essential in the transformations), we can't look inside the translation, nor can we delete elements from the translation or produce any internal modifications of the translation. This leads then to the next feature.

(iii)   The vocabulary of the kernel includes not just ordinary morphemes but several infinite sets of *indexed proforms*, which may be introduced either by lexical schemata or by rule schemata of the form "... proform$_i$ ...." Such schemata then stand for the infinite sets of entries or rules that we get by making some choice of an integer for i. The translations of such elements always involve variables in the intensional logic. The various sentential and desentential proforms play exactly the role in the syntax that the "dummy" elements played in classical transformational theory.

(iv) The transformations extend the set of structural descriptions as follows: From the set KSD we pick out all those structures that underlie sentences and noun phrases; these are the basis for a recursive definition of a further set, the set of SD's (in general). Each singulary transformation has the general form:

$$\text{If } \langle [_A \ldots], \varphi \rangle \in \text{SD, then } \langle t[_A \,\text{-}\,\text{-}\,\text{-}\,], g(\varphi) \rangle \in \text{SD}$$

where A is either S or NP (or either), '...' is a string of labeled brackets and variables (either X_i for any string including null, or W_i for any well formed labeled bracketing) and '$t[_A \,\text{-}\,\text{-}\,\text{-}\,]$' is the result of applying certain elementary operations on the particular string to which the transformation is applied, including a reduction in the sense of Peters and Ritchie (1973a). The general restriction on the translation part still applies, so the effect of a transformation must either be to leave the translation unchanged or to state some 'holistic' function on the entire translation of the input (e.g. we might have a negative transformation which, given a structure with the right member φ, yielded $\neg \varphi$ as its translation).

Embedding transformations look like this:

$$\text{If } \langle [_A \ldots \text{proform}_i \ldots], \varphi \rangle \text{ and } \langle [_B \,\text{-}\,\text{-}\,\text{-}\,], \Psi \rangle \in \text{SD}$$

$$\text{Then } \langle [_A \ldots t[_B \,\text{-}\,\text{-}\,\text{-}\,] \ldots], f\langle \varphi, \Psi \rangle \in \text{SD}$$

In all such rules the translation part of the rule makes use of lambda abstraction over the variable corresponding in the translation to the proform mentioned in the rule. The syntactic operation is always substitution of the second syntactic structure or some transform of it for the proform in the matrix.

Finally, conjunction transformations (which I won't talk about here) are defined for arbitrary sets of structures, all of the same syntactic category, and produce a new pair of brackets (with the same label) around a concatenation of the structures, possibly with intervening conjunctions.

(v) As in most versions of transformational grammar, I assume that there is a 'late' set of rules (call them M-rules) which carry out necessary operations like spelling out the effects of morphology, agreements, etc.

I assume that the terminal vocabulary of the transformational part of the grammar does not contain any indexed proforms. We then define the T-terminal SD's as those SD's whose left members are strings over the set of bracket labels and the terminal vocabulary, and the language of the grammar as the debracketization of the left members of the T-terminal structures.

I have constructed a KT grammar for the fragment of Montague's PTQ (Bach, forthcoming b). I don't want to burden you with a detailed set of rules in an unfamiliar notion, so I'll just talk informally about some examples.

Quantification of noun phrases is done in exactly the same way as in PTQ. An example of two analysis trees from PTQ for the sentence *Every woman seeks a unicorn* together with a sketch of the analogous derivations in the KT grammar (leaving out the translations) follows:

PTQ:

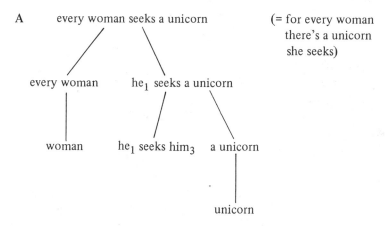

A   every woman seeks a unicorn   (= for every woman there's a unicorn she seeks)

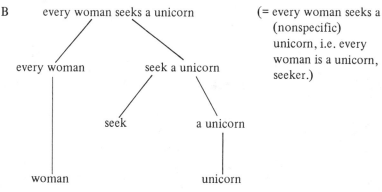

B   every woman seeks a unicorn   (= every woman seeks a (nonspecific) unicorn, i.e. every woman is a unicorn, seeker.)

KTG:

A′ Kernel structures:

NP: every woman
NP: a unicorn
S : she$_1$ Pres seek it$_2$

T-quantification: she$_1$ Pres seek a unicorn
T-quantification: every woman Pres seek a unicorn
M-rules every woman seeks a unicorn

B' Kernel structures: S: every woman   Pres   seek a unicorn
　　M-rules　　　　　　　　　every woman seeks a unicorn

The grammar assigns the same translation as PTQ does to the two analysis trees above.

Representations of the transformational histories of this sentence (T-marker) would be isomorphic to the analysis trees above:

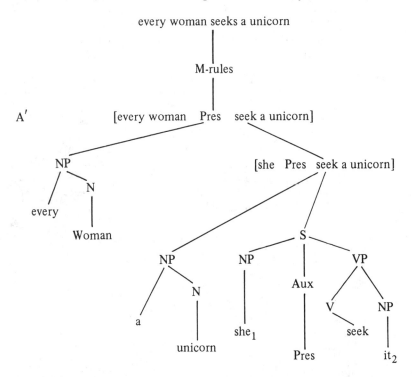

Here the leaves of the tree are the kernel structures, and the expressions at the nodes are shorthand for the structures that result from the application of the embedding rule (quantification). In the case of B', the T-marker would include only a record of the obligatory rules (in this case M-rules) and its single leaf would be the single kernel structure underlying the sentence.

We might compare these two treatments with the way transformational grammars following a configurational approach might represent the difference. Quasi 'generative semantic' underlying structures for the two readings might look like this:

DIAGRAM FOLLOWS ON NEXT PAGE

I say 'quasi' for two reasons. One, actual proposals were more complicated and assumed something more like a combination of relative clauses and 'predicates' like *every* (the above is a simpli-

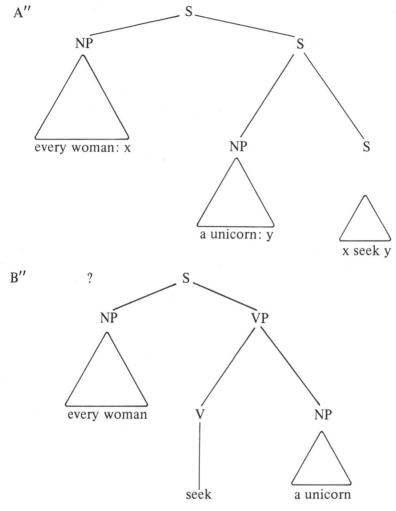

fied version of the structure given by the C-grammar of Cooper and Parsons, 1976). Second, (and this accounts also for the question mark) no specific proposals that I know of tried to account for the case in which the quantified noun-phrase was already there except (as in Bach, 1968) by positing a complex source for intensional verbs like *seek* (roughly, = *try to find*). If we ask how current theories like that of Chomsky, which follows out the interpretive approach, would handle the difference, we can give a very simple answer: The deep structure for all readings would be like B″, but optional rules of wide scope assignment would apply to get (among others) a structure exactly like A″.

There is an important difference between this treatment of quantification and that of Montague grammar (this difference holds also for other transformational frameworks in comparison to Montague grammar). Montague's general theory requires that his syntactic rules be total functions defined for every member of the syntactic categories mentioned in the *if* part of each rule. Transformational rules, since they can look at the internal composition of the structures to which they apply are defined only for those members of the general category (S or NP here) that meet the 'structural description' of the transformation (and meet certain general constraints on applicability which are stated once and for all by general linguistic theory). Thus, Montague's rules of quantification must be allowed to apply to every sentence, including outcomes which contain no pronouns at all. This means that every sentence such as *John loves Mary* has an infinite number of translations that arise by syntactically vacuous applications of quantification, that is, along with the nonquantified versions of the sentence and those in which various options are chosen for quantifying in *John* and *Mary*, the same English sentence will have associated with it translations that would correspond to sentences like those, under normal interpretations:

For every unicorn, John loves Mary

There is a fish such that for every unicorn John loves Mary and an infinite number of other equally absurd readings. Clearly, a descriptively adequate grammar must block this result. (Cf. Cooper and Parsons, 1976, for some discussion; similar remarks apply to vacuous applications of the relative clause rule to give noun phrases like *the man such that John loves Mary*).[3]

The *embedding rules* of classical transformational theory are handled by using instead of single dummy elements, indexed proforms which translate into expressions with variables in the intensional logic. For example, the derivation of a sentence with a *that*-clause goes like this:

Kernel structures: S_1:   John says that$_1$ (ignoring M-rules for now)

S_2:   Mary loves Bill

that-embedding: John says that Mary loves Bill.

If we translate that$_1$ as a propositional variable p_1 then the first structure can be translated as "John$'$ ($^\wedge$ say$'$ (p_1))" (where I use John$'$ etc., as shorthand for the translation of the item in the intensional logic, '$^\wedge\alpha$' means the sense or intension of α); the second structure is translated as "Mary$'$ ($^\wedge$love$'$ ($^\wedge$Bill$'$))." The translation rule associated with the embedding rule is this:

If S_1 translates as φ, and S_2 translates as Ψ, then the result of applying the *that*-embedding rule translates as $\lambda p_i \varphi(^\wedge\Psi)$, that is, 'the set of things that John says includes the proposition that Mary loves Bill'.

All other embedding rules operate on the same pattern. Thus to account for sentences like *John wants to catch a fish* we apply a rule that replaces a variable for properties of individuals (actually individual concepts) by the transform of a sentence with a pronominal subject:

Kernel structures: S_1:   John wants to to_2
                S_2: he_0 Pres catch a fish
<u>to</u> embedding: John wants to catch a fish

In this case the translation of <u>to_2</u> as a variable over properties forms the basis for lambda abstraction applied to the intension of the result of applying a second abstraction to the embedded sentence. Thus the translation is

$$\lambda q_2 \, [John' \, (^\wedge want' \, (q_2))] \, (\hat{x}_0 [\, x_0 \, (^\wedge catch' \, (a \, fish'))])$$

that is, the set of properties that John wants to have includes the property of catching a fish (the notation "$\hat{x}$" means the same as "$^\wedge \lambda x$").[4]

I don't want to try to motivate this treatment of complement verb phrases here, since that would get us into too many technical questions. But I would like at least to suggest that this way of handling embedding carries with it a possible alternative to an issue that has been hotly debated by linguists. The question is this: How are we to account for the way in which a sentence like (1) is understood:

1. Mary wants to catch a fish but Bill doesn't want to.

Clearly, at least one meaning of this sentence is that Bill doesn't want to catch a fish. One group of linguists has argued that the sentence arises by deletion; that is, that the underlying structure is something like (2):

2. Mary Pres want to catch a fish but Neg Bill Pres want to catch a fish.

And that the second occurrence of the phrase *catch a fish* is deleted under identity with the first. A difficulty with this analysis arises when we ask what 'identity' means. On the one hand, there are problems with sentences like this:

3. The chickens are ready to eat but the children aren't [ready to eat].

Clearly, the sentence with the bracketed material can be understood in a way that the sentence without it can't. Here it would seem that we need something more than pure formal identity. Another problem arises in cases like (4):

4. John wants to kiss his wife, but Bill doesn't want to.

Here, it seems as if the most normal interpretation is that it's Bill's wife rather than John's that Bill is reluctant to kiss. But clearly the *his* in the supposedly deleted second part does not have the same referent as the *his* of the first. An alternative then is to say that we generate structures with 'empty' elements in them and formulate interpretive rules that depend on other elements of the sentence (or even outside the sentence). A difficulty with this second approach is that on the one hand we need to allow ordinary transformations to apply to these 'empty' structures as well in order to account for cases where the antecedent expression has undergone a transformation, as in sentence (5):

  5. Bill was arrested by the police and but Mary wasn't.

We must assume that the 'empty structure' has also undergone Passive. But the application of Passive leaves morphological material in the otherwise empty structure, i.e. applying Passive to A (with "[ ]" standing for empty structures) gives us B:

  A: [   ] Past [   ] Mary
  B: Mary Past be [   ] ed by [   ]

and we have to do something about the bits and pieces left by the rule. The alternative I'm suggesting suffers from neither problem: It is to assume that just as pronouns that are like-indexed can 'pronominalize' so other indexed variables can be affected (i.e. in this case deleted). Thus we could derive the first sentence cited above like this:

Basis:	Mary Pres want to to$_3$ but Bill doesn't want to to$_3$
to deletion:	Mary Pres want to to$_3$ but Bill doesn't want to
to embedding:	Mary Pres want to catch a fish but Bill doesn't want to

Now although we have embedded just one occurrence of the phrase, the translation rules will form an abstract over the entire translation:

  [Mary' (^want (q$_3$)] but NOT [Bill (^want (q$_3$))]

Thus, the translation will carry with it the right meaning: What Mary desires but Bill does not is the property of being an x such that x catches a fish. This gives just the right results for the 'sloppy' reading of the sentence (4): Here the common property is the property of being an x such that x kisses x's wife. And we can account for the other reading (where Bill doesn't want to kiss John's wife by the proper ordering of to-embedding and quantification

Basis:	he$_1$ want to to$_3$ but Neg Bill want to to$_3$
to-deletion:	he$_1$ want to to$_3$ but Neg Bill want to
to-embedding:	he$_1$ want to kiss his$_1$ wife but Neg Bill

want to
Quantification: John want to kiss his wife but Bill doesn't want to.

Here the common property of being an x such that x kisses y's wife. What is of interest here is that the same rules that were formulated for the simple cases of embedding result in just the right answers for more complex cases. Moreover, the requirement that the translation of the inputs to a rule remain intact in the translation of the output ensures that the variables will remain in the right places.

The viability of this approach remains to be seen. I would like to close with some general remarks on the differences between the framework outlined here and more 'standard' transformational grammars on the one hand and Montague grammars on the other.

One major difference between this model and transformational grammars is the use of an infinite vocabulary of indexed proforms in the syntax. In this respect the model is more like those systems of 'generative semantics' which used variables in place of pronouns in the base (the models mimicked in the C-grammars of Cooper and Parson, 1976). It differs from them in dropping the insistence that all NP's get into sentences by replacement of variables. Transformational theories in the 'interpretive' tradition assume simple pronouns in the base (as well as various other proforms) and get an infinite set of variables only in the translation of structures into 'logical form'. Once we recognise that all of this is, strictly speaking, part of syntax there seems to be no a priori reason to choose one way rather than another. So the arguments must depend on empirical results of the usual sort. A clear answer can only come by first developing the various alternatives to the point where one can really see if they are different in any nonnotational way and if they are different looking for empirical consequences either of a straightforward factual sort or in terms of the degree to which the systems are able to capture 'linguistically significant generalizations'. I believe we are nowhere near being able to spell out the various proposals in sufficient detail to have any clear answers.

The model differs from the Montague theory in the way in which it singles out two syntactic categories, sentences and noun phrases, for special status. Montague grammars are definitions of all well-formed syntactic categories, and Partee (1976, forthcoming) has suggested a 'well-formedness constraint' which says something like this: A grammar must build up well-formed constituents from well-formed constituents (Montague did not follow this constraint in theory, but PTQ pretty much follows it).

This notion is different from the local-grammaticality idea mentioned earlier, even if we generalize 'S-local' and 'NP-local' to 'strictly local' (i.e. *every* constituent must underlie some well-formed output). What the KT grammar has in common with other transformational models and in contrast to Montague grammars is the idea that significant generalizations can be captured only if we allow the grammar to generate structures that differ from actual sequences found in the language and then map them by 'late' rules into actual sentences (or other structures). The strict well-formedness constraint requires that various basically morphological mappings be built into a variety of different rules.[5]

As far as the special status of NP's and S's is concerned, I think it can be argued that these categories should have special status. Every language has them, and they form the basis for the definition of a wide variety of further categories, whether in the fashion of categorial grammar or in some other scheme. Moreover, I believe that native speakers have much firmer intuition about the well-formedness and meaning of noun phrases and sentences than they do for other categories. Finally, the two categories are firmly anchored in two basic functions for all languages, the need to refer to things and to speak truly.

NOTES

*Preparation of this paper and part of the research reported on here was made possible by the Center for Advanced Study in the Behavioral Sciences and a grant from the National Endowment for the Humanities; I wish to thank Barbara H. Partee for helpful comments on an earlier draft of the paper, and Mary Tye for typing it.

1. I don't mean this as an historical remark. Chomsky (in 1975a, *Introduction*) writes that the more general notion of 'derivational history' was derived from his acquaintance with historical linguistics. Bloomfield's pioneering work on Menomini (Bloomfield, 1939) probably had the same source but was informed by the work of ancient Indian linguists like Panini. Discussions of models for the description of language, like that of Hockett, 1954, contain the idea of an 'abstract' order of operations.

2. The best way to become acquainted with Montague's work, which is written in a formidably concise way, is to read Thomason's introduction to Montague (1974) and Partee (1975).

3. In all fairness to Montague grammarians, I should point out that the above result can be avoided in various ways in a Montague grammar, and that a number of linguists working in this framework have dropped the 'total' function requirement, which has no linguistic motivation, whatever its technical appeal.

4. This idea incorporates Partee's derived verb-phrase rule but ties its use to particular embedding operations. It should be noted that this rule, generalized so as to apply to indexed *to*'s that can occur in other

187

places in sentences, allows us to get Montague's verb-phrase quantification without a separate rule.
5. Partee (forthcoming) allows for the possibility of certain very restricted
'morphological' mappings in her version of 'restricted' Montague
grammar.

REFERENCES

Bach, E. 1976. An extension of classical transformational grammar. In
Problems in linguistic metatheory. (Proceedings of the 1976 conference
at Michigan State University).
_____. Forthcoming a. "The position of embedding transformations
in a grammar" revisited. To appear in a volume of papers from the
International Summer School of Computational Linguistics (Pisa), ed.
Zampolli, A.
_____. Forthcoming b. Montague grammar and classical transfor-
mational grammar.
Bloomfield, L. 1939. Menomini morphophonemics. *Travaux du Cercle
Linguistique de Prague* 8, pp. 105-115.
Bresnan, J. 1972. Theory of complementation in English syntax. Unpub-
lished PhD. dissertation, M. I. T.
_____. 1973. Syntax of the comparative clause construction in
English. *Linguistic Inquiry* 4, pp. 275-343.
_____. 1975. Comparative deletion and constraints on transfor-
mations. *Linguistic Analysis* 1, pp. 25-74.
Chomsky, N. 1957. *Syntactic structures.* The Hague.
_____ 1965. *Aspects of the theory of syntax.* Cambridge: M.I.T.
Press.
_____ 1975 a. *The logical structure of linguistic theory.* New York.
_____ 1975 b. *Reflections on language.* New York.
_____ Forthcoming. On *wh*-movement. To appear in *Formal syntax*
(proceedings of the 1976 Irvine conference), eds. Culicover, P., Wasow,
T. and Akmajian, A.
Cooper, R. 1975. Montague's semantic theory and transformational syntax.
Unpublished PhD. dissertation, U. of Mass., Amherst.
Cooper, R. and Parsons, T. 1976. Montague grammar, generative semantics,
and interpretive semantics. In *Montague grammar* ed. Partee, B. New
York: Academic Press.
Fillmore, C. 1963. The position of embedding transformations in a grammar.
Word 19, pp. 208-231.
Geach, P. 1962. *Reference and generality.* Ithaca: Cornell Univ. Press.
Harria, Z. 1957. Co-occurence and transformation in linguistic structure.
Language 33, pp. 283-340.
Hintikka, J. 1973. *Logic, language-games, and information.* Oxford.
Hockett, C. 1954. Two models of grammatical description. *Word* 10,
pp. 210-233.
Jackendoff, R. 1972. *Semantic interpretation in generative grammar.*
Cambridge.
Karttunen, L. and Peters, S. 1975. Conventional implicature in Montague
grammar. Proceedings of the First Annual Meeting of the Berkeley
Linguistic Society, pp. 266-78.
Katz, J. and Fodor, J. 1963. The structure of a semantic theory. *Language*
39, pp. 170-210.

Katz, J. and Postal, P. 1964. *An integrated theory of linguistic descriptions.* Cambridge.

Kiparsky, R. and Kiparsky, C. 1971. Fact. In *Semantics,* eds. Steinberg, D., and Jakobovits, L. Cambridge.

Klima, E. 1964. Negation in English. In *The structure of language,* eds. Fodor, J. and Katz, J. Englewood Cliffs: Prentice-Hall.

Lakoff, G. 1971. On generative semantics. In *Semantics,* eds. Steinberg, D. and Jakobovits, L. Cambridge.

Montague, R. 1970. Universal grammar. In *Formal philosophy: selected papers of Richard Montague,* ed. Thomason, R. 1974. New Haven: Yale Univ. Press.

_____1973. The proper treatment of quantification in ordinary English. In *Formal philosophy: selected papers of Richard Montague,* ed. Thomason, R. 1974. New Haven: Yale.

Partee, B. 1976a. Some transformational extensions of Montague grammar. In *Montague grammar,* ed. Partee, B. New York: Academic Press.

_____ 1976b. Semantics and syntax: the search for constraints. In 1976 Georgetown Roundtable on Languages and Linguistics.

_____ Forthcoming. Montague grammar and the well-formedness constraint. To appear in the proceedings of the Third Groningen Round Table (1976) eds. Heny, F. and Schnelle, H.

Peters, S. and Ritchie, R. 1973a. On the generative power of transformational grammars. *Information Sciences* 6, pp. 49-83. _____

1973b. Nonfiltering and local-filtering transformational grammars. In *Approaches to natural languages,* eds. Hintikka, J., Moravcsik, J, and Suppes, P. Dordrecht: Reidel.

Thomason, R. and Stalnaker, R. 1973. A semantic theory of adverbs. *Linguistic Theory* 4, pp. 195-220.

ADDENDUM

Bach, E. 1968. Nouns and Noun phrases. In *Universal in linguistic theory,* eds. Bach, E. and Harms, R. New York.

Partee, B. 1975. Montague grammar and transformational grammar. *Linguistic Inquiry* 6, pp. 203-300.

Virginia Teller and Joan Bachenko

A COMPARISON OF THREE APPROACHES
TO THE INTERACTION OF SEMANTICS AND SYNTAX.[1]

(i) Problem Statement

Linguists have long been intrigued by the imperfect correspondences between semantic patterns and syntactic behavior
in natural language. Sapir (1921:38) found this lack of regularity
in such correspondences irksome but unsurprising:

> *The fact of grammar, a universal trait of language,
> is simply a generalized expression of the feeling that
> analogous concepts and relations are most conveniently
> symbolized in analogous forms. Were a language ever
> completely grammatical," it would be a perfect engine
> of conceptual expression. Unfortunately, or luckily, no
> language is tyrannically consistent. All grammars leak.*

Jespersen deemed this phenomenon a central linguistic concern.
"It will be the grammarian's task in each case," he stated, "to
investigate the relation between the notional and syntactic
categories" (Jespersen, 1924:55).

Jespersen's interest in the interconnections between
semantics and syntax has been carried over into modern theories
of language as one of the most important questions of grammar
construction. Is it the case that the semantic primitives are basic,
that semantic concepts determine syntactic behavior? Or is it
the case that the syntactic elements are primary, that syntactic
classifications predict semantic patterns? It could be that no
directionality exists in semantics-syntax interactions. In this
case a set of correlation functions might link the two aspects
of language.

There is no *a priori* solution to this problem. The question
of the precise interaction of semantics and syntax can only be
resolved through empirical investigation and the correct answer
found by testing formalized proposals against empirical data.

In this paper we will examine three different positions
on the relation between syntax and semantics along with evidence
for deciding which offers the best account of the syntactic and
semantic data of English. According to a *semantic hypothesis*
proposed by Kiparsky and Kiparsky (1970) and discussed by
Robin Lakoff (1973), semantic primitives determine syntactic
classes. Their central claim is that "the choice of complement
type is in large measure predictable from a number of basic

189

semantic factors" (Kiparsky and Kiparsky, 1970:143). The *lexicalist hypothesis* (Chomsky 1972, 1975, 1976), which represents the current position of transformational-generative grammar, does not specify the direction of semantics-syntax interactions. A set of semantic rules that apply at the level of surface structure correlates aspects of syntactic structure with aspects of semantic interpretation. In the model of *Montague grammar* developed by Partee (1973, 1975, this volume) there is a one-to-one correspondence between syntactic and semantic rules. For every syntactic rule there must be a unique semantic rule that assigns a semantic interpretation to the syntactic phrase.

In section (ii) we compare the lexicalist and semantic hypotheses on the issue of the semantic notion of factivity. In section (iii) we contrast the lexicalist hypothesis and Montague grammar using data from relative clauses and pseudo-cleft sentences.

(ii) Factivity and syntax: causation or interaction?

Kiparsky and Kiparsky (1970) proposed that a subset of English predicates can be divided into two classes, factive and non-factive, depending on whether the complement is presupposed to be true or not. The *factive* verb *amuse* in (1) presupposes that the complement *Joe is fat* expresses a true proposition, while in (2) the *non-factive* predicate *appear* merely asserts that this is the case:[2]

(1) It amuses us that Joe is fat.

(2) It appears to us that Joe is fat.

According to the Kiparskys, the semantic property of 'factivity' has syntactic consequences. Only factive predicates accept gerundive complements freely:

(3) a. factive: John ignored their smoking cigars.

*b. non-factive: *John alleged their smoking cigars.*

Extraposition is optional for factive verbs that take sentential subjects but obligatory for non-factives:

(4) factive:

a. That Clark won bothered Jane.

b. It bothered Jane that Clark won.

(5) non-factive:

*a. *That Clark won turned out.*

b. It turned out that Clark won.

Furthermore, only non-factives allow the complement subject to be raised to subject position in the main sentence:

(6) a. factive: *Sue is resented to need a new car soon.

b. non-factive: Sue is assumed to need a new car soon.

The factivity of verbs in the Kiparskys' grammar is reflected in their deep structures. Complements to factive verbs derive from structure (7a), while non-factive complements originate in structure (7b):

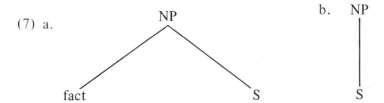

(7) a.   NP
       fact   S

b.   NP
      S

Factive predicates require a deep structure containing *fact*, and this extra constituent blocks extraction processes such as subject-raising.

Problems arise with this analysis when factive and non-factive verbs do not follow the expected syntactic paradigm[3]. For example, *discover* and *realize* align semantically with the factive group, but they align syntactically with the non-factives in rejecting gerundive objects:

(8) *John $\left\{ \begin{matrix} \text{discovered} \\ \text{realized} \end{matrix} \right\}$ their smoking cigars

Extraposition is optional, not obligatory, for such non-factives as *likely, certain, possible, true* and *false:*

(9) That Clark won is $\left\{ \begin{matrix} likely \\ certain \\ possible \\ true \\ false \end{matrix} \right\}$

Moreover, predicates such as *probable, charge* and *conclude,* all semantic non-factives, behave factively in that they do not undergo subject-raising:

*(10) *The congressman is* $\left\{ \begin{matrix} probable \\ charged \\ concluded \end{matrix} \right\}$ *to have broken the law.*

In her review of the Kiparskys' article, Lakoff (1973) cites similar counterexamples and maintains that the existence of exceptions renders the Kiparskys' hypothesis untenable. She suggests that if more than two categories of factivity are postulated (e.g. semi-factives), then semantic redundancy rules based on this finer breakdown of the factivity concept might account for the syntactic patterns:[4]

Then if we adopt the Kiparskys' theory we are necessarily forced to miss a generalization. But to discard their theory is to remain open to the possibility that a generalization can be found . . . based on the same redundancy rules. It is folly to formulate a theory that expressly denies us the chance for a generalization, when another theory might offer the (still unrealized, of course) possibility of one. (Lakoff, 1973:692)

We believe Lakoff's rejection of the Kiparskys' formulation is justified. Nevertheless, Lakoff shares with the Kiparskys the following assumptions about semantics-syntax interactions:

    (11) Semantic hypothesis
- a. Underlying representations are semantic in nature.
- b. Predicates are classified in terms of semantic properties.
- c. Certain semantic properties such as factivity determine the syntactic behavior of *verb + complement* constructions.

In contrast, the lexicalist hypothesis makes a very different set of assumptions about the grammar of complement constructions and the notion of factivity:

    (12) Lexicalist hypothesis
- a. Underlying representations are syntactic in nature. Deep structures determine the behavior of *verb + complement* constructions.
- b. Predicates are classified in terms of the syntactic environments in which they appear rather than any intrinsic semantic property.
- c. Certain semantic properties such as factivity correlate with aspects of surface structure strings.

It follows from the semantic hypothesis that, if factivity is indeed a semantic determinant of syntactic behavior, then factivity or non-factivity, once assigned to a predicate, should remain constant in any syntactic configuration in which that predicate occurs. This claim can be tested by examining the semantic interpretation of factives and non-factives in a variety of syntactic situations.

Consider first the situation shown in (13b), where the complement in a *verb + complement* construction is a noun phrase instead of a sentence:

    (13) a. Brando regretted [$_S$ that he refused the award]
        b. Brando regretted [$_{NP}$ his refusal of the award]

Since *regret* is on the Kiparskys' list of factive verbs, it is significant for our purposes that the property of factivity is preserved in the switch from a sentential complement to a noun phrase. Both (13a) and (13b) presuppose the truth of their complements.

Compare the analogous constructions with *believe,* a verb the Kiparskys list as non-factive:

> *(14) a. The guards believed [S the prisoner threatened to escape]*
> *b. The guards believed [NP the prisoner's threat to escape]*

In this case the non-factivity of *believe* is not retained in the change from a sentential to a noun phrase complement. When the complement following *believe* is a noun phrase, the *verb + complement* construction no longer receives a non-factive interpretation. There is no doubt that the prisoner has made a threat to escape, hence the noun phrase complement is understood as a factive. The truth of the complement is presupposed in the same sense as (13b).

Examples (14a) and (14b) show that non-factivity is not an invariant property of lexical items. In these sentences the interpretation of factivity or non-factivity relates directly to the syntactic structure of the complement. *Believe* receives a non-factive interpretation if the complement is a sentence; it receives a factive interpretation if the complement is a noun phrase.

These data are incompatible with the basic assumptions of the semantic hypothesis, but they are fully in accord with the lexicalist claim that semantic rules operating on surface structures correlate aspects of syntactic structure with semantic properties such as factivity. Since factivity or non-factivity in this case depends on whether the complement is a noun phrase or a sentence, rule (15) correctly specifies the interpretation of factivity:[5]

> (15)   *surface structure*   *reading*
>
> [S ...believe + S ...]   non-factive
> [S ...believe + NP ...]   factive

This initial observation concerning the relation between surface structure and factivity is corroborated by example (16). The source of ambiguity in this sentence lies in the two possibilities for complement structure (16a) and (16b):

(16) *We believe her promise to be good.*
    a. We believed [S *her promise to be good]*

    b. We believed [NP *her promise to be good*]

As a sentential complement *her promise to be good* may be understood in two ways. On one reading the sentence is para-phrasable as 'we believed that she made a promise that she will keep.' The second reading might be paraphrased as 'we believed that she showed good promise for the future.' In either case *believe* receives a non-factive interpretation. Sentence (16a) presupposes neither that she will keep her promise nor that she will be successful.

As a noun phrase complement *her promise to be good* refers to a specific action, namely, that she promised something, and what she promised was to be good. Sentence (16b) may be paraphrased 'we believed her promise that she would be good.' In this context, *believe* is understood as a factive, that is, it is presupposed that a promise was made.

The lexicalist grammar accounts for the ambiguity of (16) by assigning it two different complement structures, each of which correlates with a different factivity reading in accordance with rule (15). Such data, while compatible with the assumptions of the lexicalist hypothesis, cannot be accounted for under the assumption that factivity is a semantic constant.

There is additional evidence to support this conclusion. Consider examples like (17), noted by Kartunnen (1971):

(17) a. That his bride was not a virgin bothers Harry.

      b. His bride's not having been a virgin bothers Harry.

Bother is classified as a factive verb, and both of the examples in (17) presuppose that Harry's bride is not a virgin. There is no difference between *that* complements and gerundive comple-ments with the main verb *bother* in the present tense. A switch to the conditional tense, however, introduces a difference be-tween the complement types:

(18) a. *That his bride was not a virgin would bother Harry if he knew about it. (Luckily she was a virgin.)*

      b. *His bride's not having been a virgin would brother Harry if he knew about it. (Luckily she was a virgin.)*

Sentence (18a) presupposes that Harry's bride was in fact not a virgin, but (18b) does not contain this presupposition. It is non-committal as to whether the woman was a virgin. The statement *luckily she is a virgin* forms a contradiction when added to

(18a) because it denies the presupposition expressed in the complement, but no such contradiction arises in the case of (18b). The combination of conditional tense plus gerundive complement has converted a supposedly factive verb into a non-factive.

The Kiparskys themselves point out another syntactic factor that contributes to the interpretation of factivity. There is a general tendency for sentence-initial clauses to be understood factively. They use the example of *report*, a verb which occurs indifferently with factive and non-factive complements. In the Kiparskys' analysis the lexicon does not specify *report* as either factive or non-factive, and syntactically it participates in both complement paradigms. A speaker saying (19a) or (19b) takes no stand on the truth of the report:

(19) a. *The UPI reported that Smith had arrived.*

b. *It was reported by the UPI that Smith had arrived.*

But (20) normally conveys the meaning that the speaker assumes the report to be true:

(20) *That Smith had arrived was reported by the UPI.*

Although a non-factive interpretation of (20) can be teased out in various ways (for example, by laying contrastive stress on *by the UPI*), the unforced sense is still definitely factive.

The Kiparskys conclude:

> *These examples are interesting because they suggest that the factive vs. non-factive sense of the complement do not really correspond to the application of any particular transformation, but rather to the position of the complement in the surface structure . . . . It is much easier to say that the initial position itself of a clause is in such cases associated with a factive sense. (Kiparsky and Kiparsky, 1970:168)*

On this point the Kiparskys are in complete agreement with the lexicalist hypothesis. Moreover, the non-factivity or factivity of the complements in (19) and (20) appears to be a direct function of syntactic structure, not the other way around.[6]

We have now taken a first step toward answering the question of how semantics and syntax interact. We have shown that the semantic primitive 'factivity' is not an invariant property of lexical items. Instead the interpretation of factivity can be specified by semantic rules that correlate readings with aspects of the surface structure phrase marker. Among the syntactic factors that must be taken into account are the type of complement, the tense of the main verb and the surface structure position of the complement clause. It seems that the semantic patterns are more easily associated with the syntactic patterns if the semantic patterns are specified in terms of the syntactic patterns, just as in solving the equation $Y = 7X^3 + X^5$ it might be easier to start with values of X and solve for Y than to work from Y to X. Although the semantic attributes of certain classes of verbs undoubtedly play an important role in readings of factivity and non-factivity, it is a mistake to conclude from this fact that the syntax and semantics of constructions containing these verbs is solely determined by such properties.

Another issue which clearly separates the lexical and semantic hypotheses is the nature of underlying representations. According to premise (11a) of the semantic hypothesis, underlying representations are semantic in nature. If the meaning of a sentence is given by its underlying representation, then two sentences having the same reading must have the same underlying representation, and two sentences with different readings must necessarily have different underlying representations. This assumption forces proponents of the semantic hypothesis into the position that, given an underlying representation, no subsequent rule in the grammar can change the reading of a sentence.

For example, consider the operation of negative transportation, one of the rules that figures in the syntactic paradigm of factivity. Certain non-factive predicates, e.g. *likely* and *believe,* may undergo this rule, but it is applicable only if the input and output are synonymous, as in (21b) from (21a):

(21) a. *It is likely that Bill and Sue won't pass.*

b. *It is not likely that Bill and Sue will pass.*

In (21) it is understood that two people, Bill and Sue, will probably fail. This will be referred to as the *double-fail* reading. The double-fail reading is also present in (22) with the quantifier *both* added.

(22) *It is likely that both Bill and Sue won't pass.*

Note, however, the effect of applying negative transportation to (22) to produce (23):

(23) *It is not likely that both Bill and Sue will pass.*

Like (22), sentence (23) can be given the double-fail reading; it is possible that two people won't pass. But in (23) it is also possible that only one person is likely to fail. This *single-fail* reading was not present in the sentence before the operation of negative transportation.

The rule of negative transportation has added another reading to (22), counter to the assumptions of the semantic hypothesis. Numerous attempts in the literature to restrict the application of negative transportation to meaning-preserving

contexts have not succeeded. As Lakoff herself has noted:
*...The semantic evidence for negative transportation is
not as strong as it had seemed. ...Positing the existence
of a rule of negative transportation on the basis of
semantic evidence alone becomes even shakier and
more unsatisfactory than ever. (Lakoff 1969: 140, 141)*
The solution is straightforward in the lexicalist grammar.
There is no need for a rule of negative transportation. Surface
structure semantic rules interpret the scope of quantifiers and
negation. The surface order of constituents alone is relevant in
determining whether or not two sentences are assigned the same
range of readings. The relation between deep structure and surface structure readings may be one to one, or to many or many
to one. Dougherty (1975:163) formulated a quantifier interpretation rule which, when applied to the data we have been discussing, correctly correlates the surface order of quantifiers with
the appropriate interpretations:

(24)	surface structure	reading
	[$_S$... both NP and NP ... not ...]	double-fail
	[$_S$... not ... both NP and NP ...]	single-fail, double-fail

The data from negatives and quantifiers support the basic assumptions of the lexicalist hypothesis.

Lakoff claimed that counterexamples signaled "the
death knell for such a theory as the Kiparskys propose" (Lakoff,
1973:693). Based on the evidence we have presented, we suggest
that the bell tolls for Lakoff's theory as well. The counter-
examples to the syntactic paradigm indicate that factivity is an
unrealiable predictor of syntactic behavior. The discrepancies
between semantic prediction and syntactic reality are not
eliminated by the devices of the semantic hypothesis. Since
factivity is not a semantic concept that remains constant across
syntactic variation, it is not a viable criterion for the semantic
classification of verbs. Semantic primitives that are reliable
predictors of syntactic patterns may eventually be found, but
factivity is not one of them. The fact that syntactic rules can
alter the underlying semantic structure of a sentence undermines
the most fundamental premise of the semantic hypothesis.

In an attempt to salvage something from this state of
affairs, Lakoff asserted that "the facts are too complex for
beauty and elegance, at least in a theory such as the one espoused
by the Kiparskys" (Lakoff, 1973:693). She warned her readers
"to beware of the simple and the beautiful: given the state of
the field, you can bet it's wrong" (Lakoff, 1973:693). We disagree. Despite the intricate and subtle forms that semantics-

syntax interactions may take, it is a mistake to assume that complex data necessarily reflect a complex theory.

Certainly correspondences between the syntactic and semantic aspects of language do exist. Indeed it is highly desirable that the syntactic framework selected for a language should support a semantic theory. In Chomsky's words:

> . . . we should like the syntactic framework of the language that is isolated and exhibited by the grammar to be able to support semantic description, and we shall naturally rate more highly a theory of formal description that leads to grammars that meet this requirement more fully. (Chomsky, 1957:102)

We recognize the importance of the considerations Lakoff and the Kiparskys bring to bear in their proposals, but it is not the proper function of the syntactic component of a grammar to deal with these issues. They belong to a broader theory of language meaning and use.

The data of nominalization, tense, complement type and position, quantifiers and negatives support the conclusion that the lexicalist approach to linguistic theory is superior to the semantic hypothesis. The syntactic component of the lexicalist grammar operates without appeal to meaning. We therefore feel justified in concluding that an analysis of these data in terms of semantic primitives only leads away from explanation.

Montague Grammar and the principle of perfect correspondence.

The approach to semantics-syntax interactions that Partee takes in developing Montague grammar avoids the major pitfall of the semantic hypothesis. Instead of claiming that no syntactic rule can change the semantic representation of a sentence, Montague grammar claims that every syntactic rule affects semantic interpretation. Partee states the Montague position as follows:

> A central working premise of Montague's theory, carried over here, is that the syntactic rules that determine how a sentence is built up out of smaller syntactic parts should correspond one-to-one with the semantic rules that tell how the meaning of a sentence is a function of the meanings of its parts. (Partee, 1975:203)

The question of syntax-semantics/semantics-syntax directionality does not arise in Montague grammar. Montague grammar consists of a set of ordered pairs ⟨syntactic rule, semantic rule⟩ that assign syntactic and semantic descriptions simultaneously. The syntactic rules that combine phrase structure categories (e.g. Det, N) into larger constituent units (e.g. NP) are matched by semantic rules that assign meanings to each of the constituents and to the product of their combination. More complex syntactic rules such as movement, deletion and pronominalization transformations are likewise matched to more complex semantic rules that indicate what a given syntactic change adds to the meaning of a string.

The ⟨syntactic rule, semantic rule⟩ design of Montague grammar leads to an important methodological consequence:

If what looks like a single syntactic construction has diverse structural semantic properties, it must be split up into separate rules so that each rule has a unique corresponding semantic rule. (Partee, 1975:213)

The effects of this condition are severe. For any structure, the grammar permits only a single syntactic derivation which corresponds rule-by-rule with the semantic interpretation:

. . . the requirement that semantic interpretation rules correspond structurally to the syntactic rules can put very strong constraints on possible syntactic analyses . . . it is only in the connection between syntax and semantics that the grammar is constrained, but that constraint is strong enough that I think it is a serious, open question whether natural languages can be so described. (Partee, 1973:513)

(25)

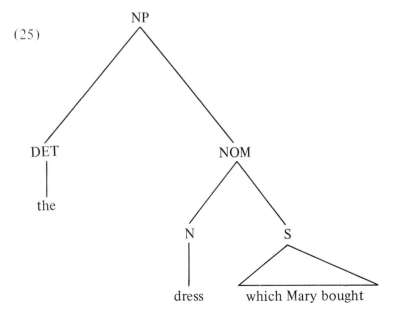

Data from relative clauses, pseudo-cleft sentences and reflexive pronouns provide a means for answering Partee's 'open question' and for evaluating Montague grammar as an alternative to the lexicalist hypothesis.

Let us begin with Partee's analysis of relativization. Partee contends that the structure in (25), where the major constituent break occurs between *the* and *dress which Mary bought,* is the only analysis consistent with the semantics of relative clauses.

Partee asserts that (25) means that there is one and only one thing which is both a dress and something Mary bought. To obtain this reading Partee proposes two syntactic formation rules. The first rule combines N and S into a NOM phrase while the corresponding semantic rule forms the union of 'dress' and 'something Mary bought.' The second rule adds the definite determiner to complete the relative NP and adds to the semantic analysis the notion that only a single object has the property designated by the NOM phrase.

An alternative structure often assumed in linguistic discussions has the major constituent break between *the dress* and *which Mary bought,* as in (26):

(26)

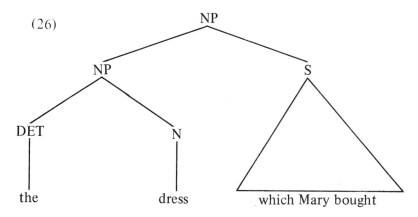

Partee argues, however, that this structure is wrong on semantic grounds. There can be no union of the properties described by N and S, and the interpretation of *the* includes the attached N but does not extend to S. If any reading is to be assigned to (26), it must be as an appositive relative clause (27), not a restrictive:

> (27) *The dress, which Mary bought, once belonged to Jane.*

Partee concludes that the Montague grammar approach, in which semantic facts can decide syntactic analyses, resolves a long-standing problem concerning the proper assignment of syntactic structure to relative clauses.

Partee's claim that semantic rules constrain the choice of syntactic analyses is challenged by Chomsky (1975). Based on data from plural NP's, Chomsky argued that the semantic evidence alone does not justify Partee's conclusions about the syntax of relative clauses. The bracketed phrase in (28), for example, is a relativized NP with a plural head:

(28) [NP *the dresses which Mary bought*] *are blue*

As it stands, Partee's analysis will not derive the relative NP in (28) because the semantic rule which accompanies *the*-adjunction incorrectly predicts that one and only one object has the property *dresses which Mary bought.* Chomsky (1975) suggests that this analysis can be made to accommodate plural relative clauses if it is assumed that *the* can refer to more than one object when the attached NOM indicates a cardinality greater than 1. This can be done, for example, by assigning NOM the feature [PL] for 'plural'.

With these amendments, the relative clause structure in (29a) aligns point by point with the interpretation in (29b):

(29) a.   b.

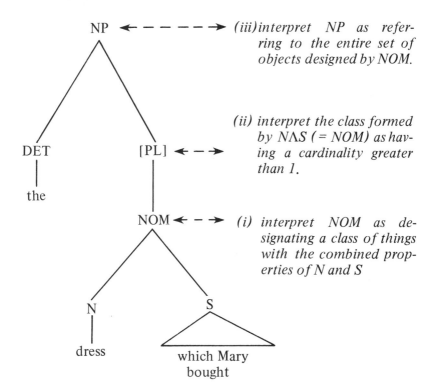

*(iii) interpret NP as refer-
ring to the entire set of
objects designed by NOM.*

*(ii) interpret the class formed
by N∧S (= NOM) as hav-
ing a cardinality greater
than 1.*

*(i) interpret NOM as de-
signating a class of things
with the combined prop-
erties of N and S*

The structure in (29a) satisfies the semantic requirements of Montague grammar. But (29a) is not a possible surface structure for the relative clause. [PL] must be associated with the noun, not NOM, since it is only the noun which occurs as a pluralized item in the surface. Hence, the surface structure of the relative clause in (28) must be essentially that in (30):

(30)

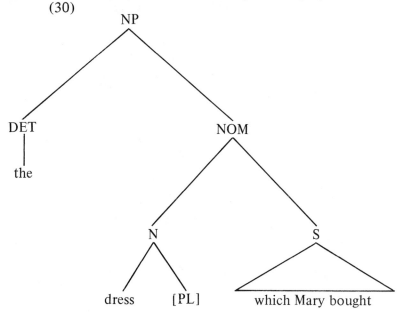

[PL] in (30) will not determine the cardinality of NOM since its scope is confined to N. The syntactic rule-semantic rule alignment is imperfect. While [PL] plays a crucial role in the semantics of NOM, syntactically it is a formal property of N. It follows that one-to-one correspondences do not exist for examples such as (28) because the correct grammatical analysis cannot be precisely matched with the semantic composition. Chomsky concluded: "There is no point-by-point relation between the surface syntax and the semantic structures, and no consequences of the suggested sort for syntactic analysis" (Chomsky, 1975:100).

Examples from plural NP's support the lexicalist position that syntactic and semantic rules are not mutually dependent. Syntactic structures generated by the lexicalist grammar are associated with semantic structures by rules that link aspects of the surface structure with aspects of semantic interpretation. Syntactic and semantic structures may coincide in composition or they may not, but syntactic analyses are not constrained either way. Chomsky reiterated this point:

> There is, in this case, a simple analysis of the semantics and also, I believe, of the syntax. The two are independent, though there is a natural, and no doubt quite general way to relate the two. But the syntax is not a reflection of the semantic structure. . .(Chomsky, 1975: 100)

Difficulties with the Montague model are not confined to relative clauses with plural heads. Pseudo-cleft sentences like those below add to the problems of the Montague approach (examples from Akmajiam, 1970);

> (31) What John threw away was a valuable piece of equipment.
> (32) What he wants his next wife to be is fascinating.

Each of these sentences appears to be 'a single syntactic construction'. Each, however, is ambiguous between what Bachenko (1976) termed a *focus* vs. *property* interpretation. For example, in (31) the predicate complement *a valuable piece of equipment* may simply refer to a specific thing that John threw away, and so fill in a semantic gap implied by the headless relative subject as in:

> (33) John threw away x; x = a valuable piece of equipment.

This focus reading may be paraphrased by the non-clefted sentence:

> (34) John threw away a valuable piece of equipment.

On the property reading *a valuable piece of equipment* does not refer to any particular object, but rather it stands for a property of some object whose identity is unknown. The relative clause *what John threw away* in this case is interpreted much like the relative NP's discussed earlier, that is, as a noun phrase that points to the class of things thrown away, with the predicate complement describing that class.

Similarly in (32), *fascinating* may be interpreted as an attribute of *wife* on the focus reading that again may be paraphrased by a non-clefted sentence, *He wants his next wife to be fascinating*. Or, with a property reading, he has fascinating ideas about what he wants his next wife to be.

These ambiguities in interpretation are not arbitrary. They are characteristic of the pseudo-cleft construction and systematically correspond with syntactic patterns such as the distribution of reflexive pronouns and tense and modal sequences.

A treatment within Montague grammar must therefore relate pseudo-cleft ambiguity to differences in the syntactic structure so that every ambiguous pseudo-cleft sentence will be derived by two different sets of syntactic rules, each with its own corresponding set of semantic rules.

A transformational analysis, similar to that of Akmajian (1970), offers Montague grammar an apparent solution to the formal description of pseudo-cleft sentences. Such an analysis accords with the principles of Montague grammar since it will correlate ambiguity with a transformational vs. non-transformational derivation. For example (31) as a focus sentence is derived by the pseudo-cleft extraction transformation, a rule that moves *a valuable piece of equipment* out of the relative clause and into the empty predicate complement position, as shown in (35)[7] . (36) shows the result of this movement.[8]

(35)

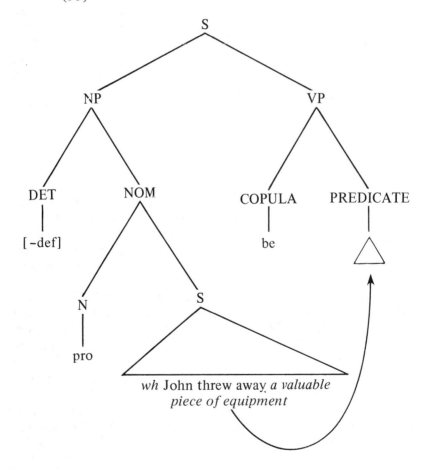

(36)

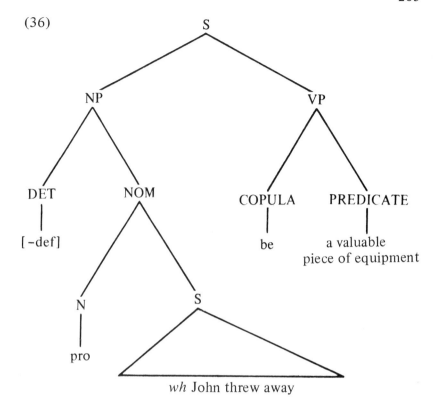

As a property sentence (31) is directly generated as the NP-be-NP copula structure in (36), with no movement of the predicate complement.

The semantics of pseudo-cleft sentences now fall neatly into place. The property reading in which a predicate complement functions descriptively can be uniquely associated with the (non-transformational) constituent structure rules that derive any copula sentence. The focus reading is uniquely associated with the pseudo-cleft extraction transformation, whose corresponding semantic rule will interpret the predicate complement as a focus phrase filling a semantic gap in the relative clause subject.

This analysis finds added support in the fact that it is the only one consistent with Partee's treatment of reflexivization. Reflexive formation in Montague grammar only occurs within simple sentences. The reflexive rule cannot apply across an S boundary in sentences like (37):

(37) [NP[S what John really likes to talk about]] is himself

To derive this focus pseudo-cleft sentence, Montague grammar must assume that the reflexive *himself* is first formed within the simple sentence *John really likes to talk about himself* and is then moved out by the pseudo-cleft extraction rule. Since only focus sentences permit reflexive pronouns in the predicate complement, this joint action of the reflexive rule and the extraction rule strengthens the Montague grammar position by correctly aligning reflexive complementation with the focus reading.

But, as we have alleged, this is only an apparent solution, because the assumptions of the transformational analysis lead to conflicting and irreconcilable claims about pseudo-cleft data. For example, a central assumption of the transformational analysis is that every focus pseudo-cleft has a non-clefted source which appears as a full sentence (e.g. *John threw away a valuable piece of equipment*) in the underlying subject relative clause. But many pseudo-cleft sentences have no non-clefted counterpart that could serve as a possible source. The examples in (a) of (38)-(40) are grammatical pseudo-cleft sentences, but their non-clefted (b) versions are ungrammatical:

(38) a. What I don't like about John is his grisly sense of humor.

b.*I don't like his grisly sense of humor about John.

(39) a. What I admire about him is his ability to cope with any situation.

b.*I admire his ability to cope with any situation about him.

(40) a. Who John wants Mary to describe is himself.

b.*John wants Mary to describe himself.

A transformational analysis cannot derive the (a) sentences without also deriving the (b) sentences. If the grammar blocks the non-clefted sentences in (b), then the focus pseudo-clefts in (a) cannot be derived since they will have no source. Either way, the transformational analysis fails to describe the facts of (38)-(40).

Similarly, focus sentences with existential *there* in the subject NP may have no non-clefted counterpart if the predicate complement is a definite noun phrase:

(41) a. What there was on the wall was John's picture.

b.*There was John's picture on the wall.

(42) a. What there was in the room was the clock that you gave me last Christmas.

b.*There was the clock that you gave me last Christmas in the room.

A transformational analysis cannot derive (41a) and (42a) since the rule for forming existential sentences requires that the NP replaced by *there* be indefinite. Along with (38)-(40), such sentences add to the evidence against the transformational analysis.

The distribution of data in (38)-(42) and the failure of a transformational analysis to account for them led Higgins (1973) to propose that the non-transformational derivation of property pseudo-clefts be extended to focus pseudo-clefts as well. With the pseudo-cleft extraction transformation eliminated, both types of pseudo-clefts will be assigned a syntactic structure roughly that of (36). It is left to other, non-transformational, rules to determine whether the structure is ambiguous.

Following the suggestions of Higgins (1973), Bachenko (1976) argued for a lexicalist-based analysis of pseudo-cleft sentences. In her analysis a single pseudo-cleft structure provides the input into two semantic rules, as shown in (43):

(43)

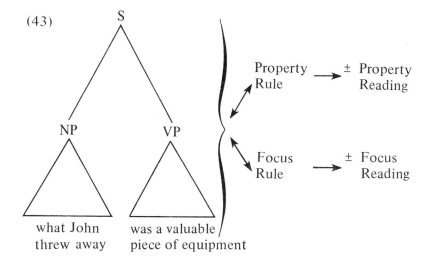

The output of the semantic rules specifies whether the structure receives a property reading, a focus reading, both or neither. A single pseudo-cleft construction may have one reading, more than one reading or no readings, depending on such factors as pronominal reference, both reflexive and non-reflexive, and the *verb + complement* structure within the headless relative clause. In any case, the ambiguity or non-ambiguity of a sentence is not a direct function of syntactic differences but rather of the particular rules that map elements of the syntax onto elements of a semantic representation.

Two assumptions central to the proposals of Higgins (1973) and Bachenko (1976) are first, that there need not exist a non-cleft version of any pseudo-cleft sentence and second, that one syntactic construction may receive more than one reading. While the proposals based on these assumptions constitute only a first step towards a complete theory, they nonetheless offer a productive direction for resolving problems about the formal description of pseudo-cleft sentences. The approach taken by Higgins and Bachenko is available within the lexicalist hypothesis because one-to-many relations are permitted between syntactic and semantic structures. But this analysis is not available within Montague grammar. The basic principle of Montague grammar requires that pseudo-cleft ambiguity be traceable to differences in syntactic derivation, an approach that we have shown leads to unacceptable consequences.

The data from relative clauses and pseudo-cleft sentences indicate that the requirement that a grammatical description provide for one-to-one semantics-syntax correspondences is too strong. In each case where Montague grammar has been tested it has failed precisely because of its insistence on rule-by-rule correlations. The lexicalist hypothesis, by contrast, does not impose such constraints on syntactic and semantic derivations. The syntactic and semantic components operate independently, although aspects of each are linked by rules that associate surface syntactic structure with a level of semantic representation. A lexicalist grammar, unlike a Montague grammar, does not preclude the possibility of finding answers to the questions we have posed. Again we conclude that the lexicalist framework is superior for developing theories of syntax, semantics and the connections between them.

(IV) Conclusion

Concerning the process of linguistic research, Chomsky wrote:

> *Precisely constructed models for linguistic structure can play an important role, both negative and positive, in the process of discovery itself. By pushing a precise but inadequate formulation to an unacceptable conclusion, we can often expose the exact source of this inadequacy and, consequently, gain a deeper understanding of the linguistic data. (Chomsky, 1957:5)*

From one point of view the results of this study may appear to be negative. No attempt has been made to refute the semantic hypothesis in its entirety or the Montague model of grammar, a task that would be impossible given the limited amount of evidence we have presented. Our goal instead has been to examine data from several areas of English which, while incompatible with the assumptions of the semantic hypothesis and Montague grammar, are consistent with the lexicalist hypothesis.

A central strength of these three alternative hypotheses is that from each it has been possible to derive testable claims about the relation between syntax and semantics and compare the results. We think these results demonstrate that the lexicalist hypothesis avoids the pitfalls of the semantic hypothesis and Montague grammar about semantics-syntax interactions. None of these alternatives yet offers a true account of these complex data. But we believe the lexicalist position, by making possible interactional rules such as (15) and (24), is superior and leaves open the door to eventual explanation.

NOTES

1. A shorter version of this paper, entitled "The interaction of semantics and syntax: an empirical question," was presented at the 1974 Summer Meeting of the Linguistic Society of America. We are grateful to Noam Chomsky, Ray C. Dougherty, Frederick Newmeyer and Hartvig Dahl for helpful comments.
2. Presuppositions are unlike assertions in that the presuppositions of a sentence remain constant under negation and questioning. Three different assertions are made in the examples below, but they all contain the presupposition that John has children:
    (i)   a. All of John's children are asleep.
           b. All of John's children are not asleep.
           c. Are all of John's children asleep?
   In order to be negated a presupposition must be denied explicitly:
    (ii)   a. All of John's children are not asleep because he doesn't have any children.
    The connections between presuppositions and factivity have been investigated in other sources, for example, Kartunnen (1971), Wilson (1972) and Reis (1973). We are focusing primarily on the discussions of Kiparsky & Kiparsky and Lakoff because in our opinion they offer the most concrete suggestions about the nature of semantics-syntax interactions.
3. The Kiparskys list the following examples of factive and non-factive predicates (pp. 143, 145):
    factive
    predicates taking sentences as subjects:
           significant, odd, tragic, exciting, relevant, matters, counts, makes sense, suffices, amuses, bothers
    predicates taking sentences as objects:
           regret, be aware (of), grasp, comprehend, take into con-

> sideration, take into account, bear in mind, ignore, make clear, mind, forget (about), deplore, resent, care (about)

non-factive

predicates taking sentences as subjects:

> likely, sure, possible, true, false, seems, appears, happens, chances, turns out

predicates taking sentences as objects:

> suppose, assert, allege, assume, claim, charge, maintain, believe, conclude, conjecture, deem, intimate, fancy, figure

4. A semantic redundancy rule states a semantic feature and lists the syntactic transformations that are optional, obligatory or ruled out in structures containing words marked for the semantic feature. For example, if the factivity paradigm were restated as semantic redundancy rules, the result might appear as follows:

[+factive] :   [±gerund formation], [±extraposition],
                 [−subject raising]

[+non-factive] : [−gerund formation], [+extraposition],
                 [+subject raising]

Verbs coded as [+factive] or [+non-factive] would be expected to exhibit the specified syntactic behavior.

Lakoff's solution to the Kiparskys' problem lies in establishing additional points on the scale of factivity. She finds that *discover* and *realize* should be classified as semi-factive rather than factive verbs. Given this additional distinction, a semi-factive redundancy rule might be devised to describe the syntactic behavior of these verbs, which differs from that of true factives. The problem is that *discover* and *realize* do not exhibit the same syntactic patterns. Subject raising may apply to *discover* but not to *realize:*

(i)   He was discovered to be unfaithful.

(ii)   *He was realized to be unfaithful.

So Lakoff's more refined semantic taxonomy still fails to bring semantic predictions in line with syntactic data. (See Teller, 1974, for a critique of Lakoff's theory of factivity and her framework for linguistic research.)

5. Some advocates of the semantic hypothesis have argued that there is a nominalization transformation that converts a complement with the structure of a sentence into a complement with the internal structure of a noun phrase. A rule of this sort is discussed in Kartunnen (1971), Lakoff & Ross (1970) and Ross (1969, 1970). A grammar that includes a nominalization transformation will assign identical underlying structures to the (a) and (b) strings in examples (13) and (14) and will derive the (b) strings from the (a) strings by the nominalization rule.

This analysis is consistent with the semantic hypothesis as long as the input and output of the nominalization transformation are identical in meaning. For a syntactic rule to effect a change in meaning would violate the premise that the underlying representation of a sentence completely specifies its semantic representation. But this is precisely what occurs in (14b). The nominalization transformation converts a sentence with a non-factive interpretation into a sentence that is understood as a factive. Example (14) calls into question both the nominalization transformation and the assumption of underlying semantic representation.

The lexicalist grammar does not contain a nominalization transformation. In accordance with Chomsky (1970), the complements in (14a) and (14b) will be assigned different deep structures by the rules of the base. The sentential complement will be generated as a base sentence, and the nominalization as a base noun phrase. In addition, the lexicalist hypothesis makes no claim that (14a) and (14b) must have the same meaning, since surface rules determine whether two sentences are assigned the same semantic interpretations.

Chomsky (personal communication) has noted that the factivity of NP-believe-NP structures is probably a special case of the referentiality of the object NP position after *believe*. If someone says, "I believe the news story," it is assumed that *the news story* is a referential expression, i.e. there is a news story. With a sentential complement *believe* may carry an intensional sense like *seek* or *hunt:*

> *I believe there is a unicorn in the garden (but maybe there aren't any).*
> *He's hunting a unicorn (but maybe there aren't any).*

Believe with a NP object does not have this intensional sense. All the more reason to treat the NP and S complements as entirely different base structures, eliminate the nominalization transformation and use surface rules to associate the intensional and non-intensional readings of *believe* with the appropriate complement structures.

6. The Kiparskys' observation about sentence-initial position holds for noun phrases as well. The factive sense is emphasized in (i), while (ii) elicits a non-factive reading. It is far more likely in the former than the latter that Bill has actually died:

> *(i) Bill's death was reported by the UPI.*
> *(ii) The UPI reported Bill's death.*

This circumstance may reflect a general tendency in English for surface structure subjects to be understood referentially, i.e. to be interpreted as referential expressions (see footnote 5). If so, then problems in determining the interpretation of factivity may be a subset of problems in determining conditions of truth and reference and may be related to broader questions concerning referring expressions in general.

7. For convenience, we assume that the pseudo-cleft transformation is an extraction rule like that proposed in Akmajian (1970), Grosu (1973) and Chomsky (1973), although it could as well be a deletion rule, following Peters and Bach (1968) and Ross (1972). The particular form is immaterial since our argument is aimed at transformational analyses in general. Detailed discussions of extraction vs. deletion can be found in Akmajian (1970) and Higgins (1973).

8. While Partee does not specifically discuss the structure of headless relative clauses, the structures in (35) and (36) are consistent with her analysis of full relative clauses and pronominal variables. The only innovation we have made is to substitute the abstract form *pro* and the element *wh* for two variables which in Montague grammar would be represented as subscripted variables he_i, with identical subscripts to indicate coreference.

REFERENCES

Akmajian, A. 1970. Aspects of the grammar of focus in English. Unpublished dissertation, MIT.

Anderson, S. and Kiparsky, P. 1973. eds. *A festschrift for Morris Halle.* New York: Holt.

Bachenko, J. 1976. Some semantic rules in the formal description of English pseudo-cleft sentences. Unpublished dissertation, NYU.

Bierwisch, M. and Heidolph, K. 1970. eds. *Progress in linguistics:* a collection of papers. The Hague: Mouton.

Chomsky, N. 1957. *Syntactic structures.* The Hague: Mouton.

_____1970. Remarks on nominalization. *Readings in English transformational grammar,* pp. 184-221.

_____1972. *Studies on semantics in generative grammar.* The Hague: Mouton.

_____1973. Conditions on transformations. In *A festschrift for Morris Halle,* eds. Anderson and Kiparsky. New York: Holt.

_____1975. Questions of form and interpretation. *Linguistic Analysis* 1: pp. 75-109.

_____1976. Conditions on rules. *Linguistic Analysis* 2: pp. 303-351.

Davidson, D. and Harman, G. 1972. eds. *Semantics of natural language.* Dordrecht: Reidel.

Dougherty, R. 1975. Harris and Chomsky at the syntax-semantics boundary. *Contemporary research in philosophical logic and linguistic semantics,* pp. 137-193.

Grosu, A. 1973. On the status of the so-called right roof constraint. *Language* 49: pp. 294-311.

Higgins, F. 1973. The pseudo-cleft construction in English. Unpublished dissertation, MIT.

Hockney, D. et al. eds. 1975. *Contemporary research in philosophical logic and linguistic semantics.* Dordrecht: Reidel.

Jacobs, R. and Rosenbaum, P. 1970. eds. *Readings in English transformational grammar.* Waltham: Ginn.

Jespersen, O. 1924. *The philosophy of grammar.* London: Allen & Unwin.

Kartunnen, L. 1971 Some observations on factivity. *Papers in linguistics* 4: pp. 55-69.

Kiparsky, P. and Kiparsky, C. 1970. Fact. *Progress in linguistics,* pp. 143-173.

Lakoff, G. and Ross, J. 1970. A derived nominal requiring a sentential source. *Linguistic Inquiry* 1: pp. 265-267.

Lakoff, R. 1969. A syntactic argument for negative transportation. *Papers from the 5th Regional Meeting,* Chicago Linguistic Society, ed. by R. Binnick *et al.,* pp. 140-147.

_____1973. Review of Bierwisch and Heidolph, 1970. *Language* 49: pp. 685-697.

Partee, B. 1973. Some transformational extensions of Montague Grammar. *Journal of Philosophical Logic* 2: pp. 509-534.

_____1975. Montague Grammar and transformational grammar. *Linguistic Inquiry* 6: pp. 203-300.

_____1980. Montague Grammar and issues of psychological reality. Developments in Semantics, ed. Stern and Orenstein. New York: Haven.

Peters, S. and Bach, E. 1968. Pseudo-cleft sentences. Unpublished MS, University of Texas.

Reis, M. 1973. Entanglement on factives. *Linguistic Inquiry* 4: pp. 261-271.

Ross, J. 1969. Guess who. *Papers from the 5th Regional Meeting,* Chicago Linguistic Society, ed. by R. Binnick *et al.,* pp. 252-286.

_____ 1970. On Declarative Sentences. *Readings in English transformational grammar,* pp. 222-277.

_____ 1972. Act. *Semantics of natural language,* pp. 70-126.

Sapir, E. 1921. *Language.* New York: Harcourt Brace.

Stern, R. 1980. *Developments in Semantics,* New York: Haven Publications.

Teller, V. 1974. A Methodological critique of recent work on factivity. Unpublished MS, New York University.

Wilson, D. 1972. Presuppositions on factives. *Linguistic Inquiry* 3: pp. 405-410.

PART III

CONCEPTUAL ROLE SEMANTICS

INTRODUCTION

When Frege introduced the problem of how the sentence "The morning star is identical with the evening star" can be informative even though the two terms involved have the same reference, he was anticipating a limitation in trying to explain an aspect of meaning—informative content—by using classical Tarskian referential truth conditions. The standard referential truth condition for the above sentence (i.e., "The morning star is identical with the evening star" is true if and only if "the morning star" refers to an object identical with the one to which "the evening star" refers), says nothing about the difference in meaning between the two terms. Something other than reference, either in the sense of *in addition to* or *instead of reference,* seems to be needed to solve this problem. Frege's own solution was to introduce senses over and above reference. Others, like Quine, Field, and Harman are skeptical about the existence of senses and have attempted solutions by appealing to the notion of *conceptual role.* Thus the difference in meaning between "the morning star" and "the evening star" is explained as being due to the different roles that the two expressions play in providing evidence, in making inferences, and in reasoning. However, conceptual role theorists are not of like mind on a number of issues. Of special importance is that they have different views of (1) conceptual role and (2) whether there is a need for classical truth conditions of a Tarskian kind in addition to role in a conceptual scheme and, if there is such a need, what is the relation between the Tarskian and the conceptual role components.

In addressing himself to these questions, Field distinguishes his view of conceptual role from those of Quine and Harman. In contrast to that of Harman who would dispense with giving truth conditions in favour of appealing to conceptual role, Field's proposal is more in keeping with a classical Tarskian semantics in that he would reinforce Tarski-like conditions with conceptual role considerations. In a word, the quarrel is whether or not conceptual role semantics should supplant or merely supplement referential semantics. A further difference between the views of Harman and Field is their account of conceptual role. Field, but not Harman, models his account of belief, the sensory impact on belief, and belief plus desires influencing action on the concept of subjective probability.

Field's treatment of conceptual role differs from Quine's as well. For Quine, the evidential considerations involved in conceptual role are narrowly construed in behavioristic terms, especially in terms of his notion of stimulus meaning. For Field the evidential considerations that contribute to the conceptual role account of meaning take in much more than the limited stimulus-response mechanisms to which Quine has recourse. Another difference between the two is that while Field shares Quine's qualms about intersubjective sameness of meaning, i.e., sameness of conceptual role, Field has none of the qualms Quine has about the possible inscrutability of reference.

Field's paper is a rich one containing many insights; there is one theme in it which is of value independently of the above considerations—his construction of a probabilistic semantics. In the first section and the appendix of his paper Field develops a referential probabilistic semantics with which he defines such concepts as validity for the sentences and reasoning of first-order logic by appealing to the epistemic concept of subjective probability. This venture at dispensing with truth is a decidely nonclassical i.e., non-Tarskian, approach to semantics. An attempt at such a semantics was made earlier in the century by Karl Popper in his *Logic of Scientific Discovery* (1959). However, Popper's results extended only as far as propositional logic. The significance of Field's paper is that he shows how to give a probabilistic interpretation to what many would say was all of logic, viz., first-order logic. The basic idea is that a valid sentence remains certain under every interpretation and a valid unit of reasoning is certainty-preserving under all interpretations. Though this probabilistic semantics is also the cornerstone of Field's approach to conceptual role, it is obviously of importance in its own right as an alternative to referential semantics of the more classical kind. Another volume in this series edited by Leblanc, Gumb and Stern consists of studies of Field's breakthrough (Essays in Epistemology and Semantics, 1983). The essays by Harman, Levin and Munz contain criticisms of Field's paper. Harman, in his comments on Field's paper, makes a number of points as to (1) whether subjective probability on its usual interpretation can account for the classical laws of logic and the logical constants, (2) the psychological reality of conceptual role semantics construed probabilistically, and (3) whether reference is a part of conceptual role.

Harman's first criticism is that Field begs the question of probabilistic semantics yielding the classical laws of logic (as opposed to nonclassical ones of an intuitionist variety). Harman claims that on the usual betting interpretation of subjective probability, Field unwittingly imports the notion of truth that his probabilistic semantics purports to dispense with. If Harman is right Field's claim to provide a semantics for the classical laws of logic while dispensing with truth has not been made. Harman's second criticism is that language users could not function with the notion of subjective probability as Field assumes they do. To establish that Field's probabilistic semantics has no psychological reality, Harman argues that the assignments of probability Field requires of native speakers would be astronomical. In his third criticism he gives an explanatory sketch of why theories of truth, as opposed to Field's probabilistic theory, account for the meaning of the logical constants. Last of all in his third footnote the issue of how to understand the relation of conceptual role to reference surfaces. Harman construes conceptual role so that it suffices without mentioning reference, but that is because he considers perceptual input physicalistically, in which case what are ordinarily taken as referents are part of his account of conceptual role.

An important theme in Munz's paper is that we do not have an adequate grasp of the concept of meaning. Munz brings this theme to bear on conceptual role accounts of meaning. He is critical of Harman's views and thinks that given the equally unclear character of conceptual role (even though it is open-ended enough to possibly fitu the concept of meaning) there is the difficulty of making a definitive judgment as to whether there is a good fit between the two. Munz regards Field's work as replacing Harman's, and goes on to note that Field's conceptual role plus Tarski-like truth conditions cannot, any more than Harman's conceptual role, be said to match, by itself, the unclear notion of meaning.

In his comments on Field's paper, Munz raises questions about Field's supplementation of conceptual role with referential semantics. Field's reason for introducing reference is to discuss certain questions of synonymy. Munz, in a Quine-like spirit, suggests that a healthy scepticism about synonymy would be a better way of dealing with these questions and would, in this case, allow us to dispense with the appeal to reference. More generally, Munz criticizes Field's attempted transition from subjective epistemic concepts to objective ones such as objective reference and objective (community wide) conceptual role.

In his comments on Field's paper Levin sketches some further sympathies and antipathies between the views of Field and Quine. Levin's main point, though, is that Field's account of meaning as conceptual role is in the positivist and pragmatist tradition and as such runs into similar difficulties concerning mathematical sentences. Roughly put, the point Levin makes is that the sentences of mathematics, such as the axiom of choice and the well-ordering principle can, in their remoteness from experience, be proven to be equivalent in a way that would indicate that they have the same meaning, i.e., the same conceptual role. But this similarity of conceptual role in this context does not and should not (trivially) yield sameness of meaning.

In another part of his essay Levin argues that it is a mistake to assume the concept of reference for mathematical sentences so that Platonic referents are counted as part of one's ontological commitment. Levin maintains that a semantics for mathematical sentences should be Tarskian without being referential in every case. His point is nominalistic in spirit, in order to avoid providing the classical referential account of sentences of mathematics which results in Platonism.

Alex Orenstein

Hartry Field

LOGIC, MEANING, AND CONCEPTUAL ROLE*

Michael Dummett has suggested (1973 in "The Justification of Induction") that, unless one believes that sense can be made of the notion of truth, one should not accept the laws of classical logic; for the only rationale there could be for accepting *those* laws (as opposed, say, to the laws of intuitionistic logic) is that they are precisely the laws that preserve truth. In this paper I will establish a result which, I think, disproves this suggestion. The result is that, in addition to truth-theoretic semantics of the sort made popular by Tarski, there is a way of doing semantics in terms of a purely epistemic notion, viz., subjective probability; and that, with respect to such a probabilistic semantics, classical logic is both sound and complete.

This result should be of interest to those who, like Harman (the 1975 "Meaning and Semantics"), are inclined to affirm (or to deny) the doctrine that

> . . . *meaning depends on role in conceptual scheme rather than on truth conditions. That is, meaning has to do with evidence, inference, and reasoning, including the impact sensory experience has on what one believes, the way in which inference and reasoning modify one's beliefs and plans, and the way beliefs and plans are reflected in action.*

For the most clearly understood models of

> *(i) belief,*
>
> *(ii) how the impact of sensory experience changes belief, and*
>
> *(iii) how beliefs together with desires influence actions*

now available are models in which the notion of subjective probability plays a central part. So if we can make sense of logic by using subjective probability rather than truth in our semantics, this would appear to support the view that semantics need not deal with truth conditions, that it need only deal with conceptual role.

This last view is not in fact one I want to defend. My view rather is that truth-theoretic semantics and conceptual-role semantics must supplement each other: Truth-theoretic semantics cannot account for certain differences in sense unaccompanied by differences in reference; and conceptual-role

*Thanks is due to the Journal of Philosophy for permission to reprint this article. This appeared in Volume LXXIV, No. 7 (July 1077).

semantics, though it deals nicely with questions of intra-speaker synonymy, cannot properly answer questions about inter-speaker synonymy or about relations between language and the world. But, taken together, I claim, truth-theoretic semantics and conceptual-role semantics provide an account of all the facts about meaning that there are. I will elaborate this view in the final section of the paper. (That section can be understood without too detailed a grasp of what comes before it.)

The general idea that a theory of meaning should have two distinct components, a truth-theoretic component and a conceptual-role component, is an idea that may be accepted even if the account of the conceptual-role component proposed in this paper (in terms of subjective probability) is rejected. Nevertheless, it is impossible to discuss the general idea in any but the most vague and impressionistic way without *some* fairly precise account of conceptual role, and the probabilistic account adopted in this paper has the virtue of simplicity. I suspect that my main conclusions about meaning would remain valid on other accounts of conceptual role as well.

I

The germ of the idea in this paper is to be found in Appendixes IV and V of *The Logic of Scientific Discovery* (Popper 1959). In these appendixes Popper gives what is *in effect* (though Popper does not think of it this way) a probabilistic semantics for the propositional calculus. But of course, the problem of providing a semantics for the predicate calculus is considerably more complicated.

Popper begins by considering a language L which has the formation rules of the propositional calculus, with $\neg$ and $\wedge$ as primitive. He then wants to consider a numerical function defined on the sentences of this language which obeys the laws of probability. Most axiomatizations of probability as applied to sentences start by assuming that logically equivalent sentences must have the same probability. Popper, however, does *not* make this a separate assumption—his idea is to adopt various other assumptions about probability, from which one can then *prove* that logically equivalent sentences must have the same probability. This point is extremely important, if we construe the assignment of probability values to sentences as part of a semantic interpretation of those sentences. For the whole point of giving a formal semantics for a language is to enable us to give sense to such notions as logical equivalence. We need to define logical equivalence in terms of the notions employed in the semantics, if the only way to explain the notions employed in the semantics (in particular, the notion of a semantic interpretation) was in terms of some independently understood notion of logical equivalence, then we would not have achieved our purpose.

The notion that Popper sets out to axiomatize, actually, is not probability but conditional probability. This makes a difference: For if one takes absolute probability as primitive and defines conditional probability from it in the usual way [viz., $P(A|B) = P(A \wedge B) / P(B)$], then one has to say that $P(A|B)$ is undefined when $P(B) = 0$; but if one takes conditional probability as basic, one need not do so. I think this makes Popper's approach attractive, for intuitively it seems that the conditional probability of A given B does sometimes exist even when the absolute probability of B does not. Suppose a point were picked at random from a cube. The probability of the point being on a particular vertical plane b through the cube would be zero (since the plane is "infinitesimally thin"); the probability of the point being in the top half of b (more accurately, the top half of the square common to b and the cube) is also zero. But the probability of the point being in the top half of b, given that it is on b, surely ought to be $\frac{1}{2}$. By taking conditional probability as basic, Popper can say this. Popper's notion of conditional probability is an extension of the usual notion, in the following sense: Popper's notion can be used to define a notion of absolute probability which obeys the classical laws; and if we take any two sentences A and B such that the absolute probability (in this derived sense) of B is nonzero, we can show that $P(A|B) = P(A \wedge B)/P(B)$. In other words, the conditional probability $P(A|B)$ has exactly the value it has classically when $P(B) \neq 0$; the *only* difference is that it is defined when $P(B) = 0$.

Popper's axiom system (actually a slightly more perspicuous variant of it, drawn from William Harper 1975) is

I. $P(A|B) \geqslant 0$

II. $P(A|A) = 1$

III. $\exists A \exists B (P(A|B) = 1)$

IV. If $P(A|B) = 1$ and $P(B|A) = 1$, then $\forall C(P(C|A) = P(C|B))$

V. $P(A \wedge B|C) = P(A|B \wedge C) \circ P(B|C)$

VI. $P(A \wedge B|C) \leqslant P(A|C)$

VII. $P(\neg B|A) = 1 - P(B|A)$, unless $\forall C(P(C|A) = 1)$

Let's define *A is certain* to mean $\forall C(P(A|C) = 1)$, *A legitimizes B* (symbolized $A \leqslant B$) to mean $\forall C(P(A|C) \leqslant P(B|C))$, and *A is equipollent to B* (symbolized $A \sim B$) to mean that A legitimizes

B and B legitimizes A. Popper then establishes the following theorem:

> (1) Equipollence is an equivalence relation, and $\neg$ and $\wedge$ are well-defined on the $\sim -$ equivalence classes.
>
> (2) These equivalence classes form a Boolean algebra in which $\neg$ and $\wedge$ play the role of complement and greatest lower bound, in which the class of certain propositions is the maximal element, and in which the ordering is given by $\leqslant$.

This is obviously an interesting result, but what precisely is its interest? Popper describes its interest as follows:

> . . .since a Boolean algebra may be interpreted as a logic of derivation, we may assert that *in its logical interpretation, the probability calculus is a genuine generalization of the logic of derivation* (356; italics his).

I think Popper's idea is this: There is *one correct* probability function P, and axioms I-VII partially characterize it; and the notions of certainty, legitimacy, etc., are to be defined as above *for this uniquely correct* P. On this construal, the notion of legitimacy is a strengthening of the notion of entailment formalized in the propositional calculus. If A deductively implies B, then A legitimizes B: That is part of the content of Popper's theorem. But the converse need not hold. For instance, on any plausible choice of "the uniquely correct P," "Jones is a bachelor" will legitimize "Jones isn't married," and "t is green" will legitimize "t is not red." These are not entailments (as that term is understood in the propositional calculus); but Popper seems to be suggesting that they are logical relations in some broader sense.

I don't much like this way of looking at the significance of Popper's theorem: I prefer to think of conditional probability functions as a means not of *generalizing* logic but rather of *providing a semantics* for it. Instead of regarding any one probability function as privileged (as "the correct" probability assignment), we quantify over *all* probability functions in deciding what inferences are good ones. To be more explicit, let us say that an *interpretation* of a propositional language is a conditional probability function, that is, a function satisfying axioms I-VII. And let us say that a sentence B is *certain under an interpretation* P (the probabilistic analogue of *true under an interpretation*) if $\forall C[P(B \mid C) = 1]$; equivalently, if $\forall C[P(C \mid \neg B) = 1]$. We can then say that a sentence is *probabilistically valid* if it comes out certain under *every* interpretation. With respect to this semantics, Popper's theorem shows that the propositional calculus is sound:

every theorem is probabilistically void. The semantics, and the soundness theorem, can be extended from statements to inferences, but first we have to define $P(\Gamma|C)$ where Γ is a *set* of sentences. It's clear enough how to do this: $P(\{A_1, \ldots, A_n\}|C)$ is just $P(A_1 \wedge \ldots \wedge A_n|C)$; and $P(\{A_1, A_2, \ldots\} |C)$ is just $\lim_{n \to \infty} P(A_1 \wedge \ldots \wedge A_n|C)$. We can now say that an inference from a set Γ of sentences to a sentence B is *legitimate under an interpretation* P if $\forall C[P(B|C) \geqslant P(\Gamma|C)]$, and that such an inference is *probabilistically valid* if it is legitimate under all interpretations. Again Popper's theorem establishes soundness: every inference derivable in the propositional calculus is probabilistically valid.

If we view conditional probability functions as providing the semantics of propositional logic, we want to ask about the completeness of the logic with respect to the semantics. But completeness is easy to establish, especially if we presuppose the fact that logic is complete with respect to *truth-theoretic* semantics. For given any truth-theoretic interpretation of a probabilistic language—that is, given an assignment α of truth-values to each propositional letter—we can construct a probabilistic interpretation P_α as follows: let

$$P_\alpha(A|B) \text{ be} \begin{cases} 1 \text{ if } B \supset A \text{ is true in } \alpha \\ 0 \text{ otherwise} \end{cases}$$

It is trivial to verify that P_α satisfies axioms I-VII, and that the sentences that come out true in α are precisely those which come out certain in P_α It follows that statements and inferences that are truth-theoretically invalid are probabilistically invalid as well.

II

How do we extend these results to the predicate calculus? The *general* idea is obvious. We first characterize a class of *reasonable* functions P mapping pairs of sentences of the predicate calculus into real numbers; by "reasonable" functions I mean functions which satisfy Axioms I-VII *and which have certain other properties, to be specified shortly*. We regard any such reasonable P as an *interpretation* of the language of the predicate calculus; and we define what it is for a sentence to be *certain under an interpretation,* and what it is for a sentential inference (inference from a set of sentences to a sentence) to be *legitimate under an interpretation,* precisely as we defined these things in section I. Similarly, *probabilistic validity* for sentences and for sentential inferences is defined, as in section I, as certainty or legitimacy under all interpretations.

Before we can raise the question of the soundness and completeness of classical logic with respect to probabilistic semantics, we must specify the class of reasonable P-functions.

An obvious partial characterization is

> (R)   For any language L that has the structure of the predicate calculus with $\neg$, $\wedge$, and $\exists$ as primitive, and any reasonable P defined on L,
> (r1) P satisfies Axioms I-VII
> (r2) For any variable x, any formula F of L containing only x free, any sentence C of L, and any singular terms $t_1, \ldots, t_n$ of L,
> $$P(\exists x F(x)|C) \geqslant P(F(t_1) \vee \ldots \vee F(t_n)|C)$$

But conditions (r1) and (r2), though clearly necessary for reasonability, are not sufficient. Consider, for instance, the sentence $\exists x(F(x) \wedge \neg F(x))$; since this sentence is a contradiction, it should have probability 0 conditional on any C (other than an absurd C, i.e. a C such that $\forall D(P(D|C) = 1)$). Yet there is obviously nothing in (r1) and (r2) that could force $P(\exists x(F(x) \wedge \neg F(x))|C)$ to be) 0; so we need to add some third condition to (r1) and (r2). What can this third condition be?

One possible third condition, of course, is that $P(A|C) = P(B|D)$ whenever A is logically equivalent to B and C is logically equivalent to D; but if our goal is to use the notion of reasonable P-functions in giving a *semantics* for the predicate calculus, any such appeal to the notion of logical equivalence (or logical truth, or any other such notion) is ruled out. But what other kind of condition *could* force $P(\exists x[F(x) \wedge \neg F(x)]|C)$ to be zero?

There is a substantial difficulty here that was not present in the truth-functional case. In the truth-functional case, Popper gave a bunch of laws (Axioms V through VII) that related the conditional probabilities of sentences to the conditional probabilities of their *subsentences.* This strategy is unavailable to explain why $\exists x[F(x) \wedge \neg F(x)]$ has to have probability zero (conditional on any C), because this sentence *has* no subsentences, it has only *subformulas,* and the notion of subjective probability cannot meaningfully be applied to unclosed formulas. An analogous problem arises in truth-theoretic semantics: truth makes no sense for unclosed formulas either. But there all we need to do is consider arbitrary functions f that assign objects to the free variables, and define truth-relative-to-f for each f. A natural suggestion for probabilistic semantics would be to pull the same trick, that is, to introduce a notion of the probability of an unclosed formula relative to an assignment f of objects to the free variables. But a moment's thought shows that this notion of probability relative to an assignment defies intelligible interpretation. For instance, let f be a function that assigns Hesperus (i.e., Phosphorus) to every variable. What is the probability, relative to f, of the formula "x = Phosphorus," for someone who doesn't know that Hesperus and Phosphorus are identical?

At this point, a Fregean might argue that the above difficulty would not arise if, instead of considering functions that assign arbitrary objects to variables, we considered functions that assigned *intensions* to variables: relative to a function that assigns the intension of "Phosphorus" to all variables, "x = Phosphorus" has probability 1; but relative to a function that assigns the intension of "Hesperus" to all variables, the formula has lower probability. (Carrying out this approach would require that we be able to talk of intensions that are not the intensions of any actual name: intensions would have to be construed as *possible* meanings for names.) Formally this approach might be made to work, but I do not consider it philosophically reputable to quantify over intensions in this way in developing probabilistic semantics. For part of the virtue of a probabilistic semantics is the light is sheds on the notion of meaning; if we had to appeal to meanings in the statement of the semantics, this virtue would be lost.

At this point, however, it will be helpful to bear in mind the idea that one important aspect of meaning is conceptual role. Of course, it is no good simply to mimic the formal approach found disreputable in the preceding paragraph, but using the term "possible conceptual role" instead of "intension"; that would be at least as disreputable. But a less *slavish* use of the conceptual-role idea suggests the right formal approach. Consider: the "conceptual role" of a name must be closely related to what counts as evidence for sentences containing that name, and to what sentences containing that name count as evidence for; and these things are determined by the conditional-probability relations between sentences containing the name and other sentences. If this is right, then a "possible conceptual role" ought to be closely related to a possible name together with a possible assignment of conditional probabilities to pairs of sentences for which at least one member of the pair involves the name. It would seem then that *by quantifying over conditional probability functions defined on expansions of the language we're interested in, we can get the effect of quantifying over possible conceptual roles*. The approach that follows is a development of this idea.

Let us say then that an *extension of a language L* is a language just like L except containing in addition an at most countable set of new names. (For convenience we allow the set to be empty, so that L is an extension of itself.) If L' is an extension of L and P is a conditional probability function defined on L, let an *extension of P to L'* be a function P' mapping pairs of sentences of L' into real numbers, such that $P'(A|B) = P(A|B)$ whenever A and B are sentences in L. With these notions we can now add a third clause to our earlier partial characterization (R) of reasonability:

> (r3) *For any variable x, any formula F of L containing only x free, any sentence C of L, and any number $q < P(\exists x F(x)\| C)$, there is an extension L' of L, and a reasonable extension P' of P to L' such that*
> $$P'(F(t_1)v \ldots vF(t_n)\| C) \geqslant q$$
> *for some terms $t_1, \ldots, t_n$ of L'.*

In thinking about (r3), it is important to realize that it does *not* say that an agent with a probability function P *must be in a position to introduce* the new names that (r3) requires: it says only that such names *could* be introduced without disturbing the original probability function or inducing violations of (r1) or (r2) in the expanded language. To see how (r3) works, return to our earlier example of the sentence $\exists x[F(x) \wedge \neg F(x)]$: we want to use (r3) to show that if, for some non-absurd C, $P(\exists x[F(x) \wedge \neg F(x)]|C)$ is some number p greater than zero, then P is unreasonable. Let q be a positive number less than p, and ask whether there is a reasonable extension P' of P such that

$$P'([F(t_1) \wedge \neg F(t_1)]v \ldots v[F(t_n) \wedge \neg F(t_n)]|C) \geqslant q$$

The answer is clearly 'no', for $[F(t_1) \wedge \neg F(t_1)]v \ldots v[F(t_n) \wedge \neg F(t_n)]$ is a *truth-functional* contradiction; so, by (r1) and Popper's theorem of section I, there can be no reasonable P' that gives it a nonzero probability conditional on any C. *Since the answer is 'no',* condition (r3) tells us that P itself is unreasonable, as desired.

It turns out that conditions (r1)–(r3) are the only reasonability conditions we need to impose on P-functions in order to yield a notion of probabilistic validity for which all the inferences licensed by classical logic come out valid. But we also want to be able to prove that *only* the inferences licensed by classical logic come out valid. We can't do this with (R) [which I now take to include clause (r3)] as it stands, since (R) says only that (r1)–(r3) are necessary conditions for reasonability; but we could do it if we added to (R) something that said that (r1)–(r3) were also jointly sufficient for reasonability. I will make this idea precise in the appendix, and then prove that the inferences licensed by classical logic are precisely those which are probabilistically valid.

III

The preceding sections, together with the appendix, show that one can develop a version of conceptual-role semantics in a precise enough form so that the soundness and completeness of classical logic with respect to this semantics can be proved:

We don't *need* to invoke truth to explain what's special about the laws of classical logic; we can invoke a purely epistemic notion instead. This fact may encourage skepticism about the utility of the notion of truth; or, if not that, it might encourage us at least to downgrade the role of truth in the theory of meaning and to try to get an account of meaning purely in terms of conceptual role. I will argue, however, for a somewhat different response.

One philosopher who does appear to believe in a purely conceptual-role account of meaning is Gilbert Harman. In a paper from which I quoted earlier, Harman argues that truth-theoretic semantics sheds much less light on meaning than is commonly supposed. More specifically, he argues that a theory of truth for a language L, in some metalanguage ML, tells us very little about meaning that is not revealed by a method for translating L into ML. In other words, all such a semantics does is to establish a few interlinguistic synonymies: It tells us (virtually) nothing about what meaning in L, or in ML, is.

The main support that Harman gives for this conclusion comes in his consideration of several popular attempts to show that truth-theoretic semantics does shed light on meaning—e.g., the line that understanding a sentence ("knowing the meaning of" the sentence) consists in knowing its truth conditions, and that therefore the meaning of the sentence must be its truth conditions. Harman demonstrates convincingly (see pp. 5-9 of his paper) that each of the attempts that he considers fails to show that a truth-theoretic semantics for L reveals any more about meaning than would be revealed by a translation manual into some antecedently understood language (e.g., English, or Mentalese). But all this shows is that need a better account of the relation between truth-theoretic semantics and meaning than is provided by the popular accounts.

Harman's position that truth-theoretic semantics sheds little light on meaning has a certain prima facie plausibility, if one assumes what I will call a *nonreferential version* of truth-theoretic semantics: a version whose paradigm is

(1) 'Beethoven wohnte in Deutschland' is true if and only if Beethoven lived in Germany.

If one thinks of truth-theoretic semantics in this way, then it is natural (though perhaps not correct) to think that truth-theoretic semantics can illuminate the meaning of "Beethoven wohnte in Deutschland" only insofar as it tells us that this sentence can be translated as "Beethoven lived in Germany." But there is another way of looking at truth-theoretic semantics which, apart from its other virtues, makes much clearer how truth theory and meaning theory are connected. This version of truth-theoretic semantics (I'll call it the *referential version*) takes as paradigm

> *(2)   'Beethoven lived in Germany' is true if and only*
> *if there are objects x and y and a relation R such*
> *that 'Beethoven' stands for x, 'Germany' stands*
> *for y, 'lived in' stands for R, and x bears R to y.*

(2) by itself does not of course tell us much about the meaning of "Beethoven lived in Germany:" It tells us nothing about this sentence which is not also true of "Caesar crossed the Rubicon." But it does hint at something that differentiates the meanings of "Beethoven lived in Germany" and "Caesar crossed the Rubicon:" viz., the fact that the words in those sentences stand for different objects and different relations. So we can say that the *referential meaning* of "Beethoven lived in Germany" is given by (2) together with a specification of the referents of the three components of this sentence. Similarly, of course, for a German sentence. To specify the referential meaning of a German sentence is *not* merely to specify what English sentences are synonymous with that German sentence: for it involves specifying a relation between the components of the German sentence and various extralinguistic things (e.g., Beethoven and Germany). That this is so becomes especially clear if we demand (as seems reasonable on independent grounds) that a *complete* theory of truth would have to include an account of the reference relation in nonsemantic terms. If we do demand this, then part of specifying the referential meaning of "Beethoven wohnte in Deutschland" is specifying that "Deutschland" bears this nonsemantically defined relation to Germany; and the question of whether "Deutschland" does bear this relation to Germany is surely a different question from the question of whether it bears a translation-relation to some English word.

   I take it as established, then, that to specify the referential meaning of a sentence of L is *not* merely to specify a translation of that sentence into some antecedently understood metalanguage. This leaves open the question of what, if anything, "referential meaning" has to do with *meaning*. Well, it is clear that to specify the referential meaning of a sentence is not *fully* to specify its meaning, for "Hesperus = Hesperus" and "Hesperus = Phosphorus" have the same referential meaning. Frege concluded from this that, in addition to postulating referents for words, we should postulate senses; but Frege's notion of the sense of a word is extremely obscure, so I prefer to explain the difference in meaning between "Hesperus = Hesperus" and "Hesperus = Phosphorus" by saying that these two sentences differ in conceptual role. Without some account of conceptual role, this is of course equally obscure; but the results of the preceding sections strongly suggest a certain account of conceptual role: Two sentences *have the same conceptual role* for a person if these sentences are equipollent with respect to that person's subjective probability function. That is, "Hesperus = Hesperus" and "Hesperus = Phosphorus" have different conceptual roles for me as long as my subjective conditional probability function has the property that there are sentences C for which the subjective probability of "Hesperus = Phosphorus" given C is lower than the subjective probability of "Hesperus = Hesperus" given C. Now what I want to say about meaning is that *the meaning of a sentence is given by its referential meaning together with its conceptual role.*

I said that, on my account, "Hesperus = Hesperus" and "Hesperus = Phosphorus" will differ in meaning (for a person with a subjective probability function P) if and only if there are sentences C for which $P(\text{Hesperus} = \text{Phosphorus}|C) \neq P(\text{Hesperus} = \text{Hesperus}|C)$: since the latter conditional probability is presumably 1 for each C, the two identities will differ in meaning on my account *if and only if there are sentences C for which* $P(\textit{Hesperus} = \textit{Phosphorus}|C) < 1$. Now, it seems pre-theoretically plausible that "Hesperus = Hesperus" and "Hesperus = Phosphorus" differ in meaning for everyone or virtually everyone. Let us see how well my account accords with this pretheoretic judgment.

Consider first those people who are not *sure* that Hesperus = Phosphorus, that is, those people who attach an absolute probability of less than 1 to "Hesperus = Phosphorus." It is clear that "Hesperus = Phosphorus" is not synonymous with "Hesperus = Hesperus" in *their* idiolects, on my account: for the absolute probability of A is just the conditional probability of A given any tautology, so any tautology is a sentence C for which $P(\text{Hesperus} = \text{Phosphorus}|C) < 1$. The interesting case, then, is the case of people who *are* sure that Hesperus = Phosphorus, that is, people for whom the probability of the sentence is 1. Now, I think we must grant that there *may* be people for whom "Hesperus = Phosphorus" really is synonymous with "Hesperus = Hesperus"–e.g., people who have simply resolved to use "Hesperus" and "Phosphorus" interchangeably come what may would be in this category. But let us consider someone who is not is this category, but is sure that Hesperus = Phosphorus. Such a person will certainly have some conception of what Hesperus (Phosphorus) is like–that is, there will be a number of descriptions that he thinks it satisfies. Now, I think it is pre-theoretically plausible that *if he really does use*

"Hesperus" and "Phosphorus" nonsynonymously, then he must associate (at least) one of these descriptions more closely with "Hesperus" than with "Phosphorus," and associate (at least) one other more closely with "Phosphorus" than with "Hesperus." This talk of "closeness of association" is vague, but I think that one plausible way to make it more precise (and at the same time make clear its semantic relevance) is to say that *if he were to discover that nothing satisfied both descriptions, he would no longer be sure that Hesperus = Phosphorus.* In other words: If we let C be the claim that nothing satisfies both descriptions, then *his conditional probability function has the property that* P(*Hesperus* = *Phosphorus*|*C*) *is less than* 1. This is enough to make "Hesperus = Phosphorus" differ in meaning from "Hesperus = Hesperus" on my account; so my account accords with pretheoretic conceptions.

The above arguments for the plausibility of my account of "Hesperus = Phosphorus" illustrates what I take to be the important grain of truth behind the description theory of names. By *the description theory of names* I mean the doctrine that, whenever anyone uses a name, the name as then used is synonymous with some description the speaker associates with the name. The description theory has recently come under heavy attack; so it is worth pointing out that nothing I have said commits me to anything nearly as strong as the description theory. Here are a few of the important differences between my view and the description theory:

(i) A speaker normally believes that a name he uses refers to a unique object; so if names are synonymous with descriptions that the speaker associates with the names, then these associated descriptions will have to be ones that the speaker believes uniquely refer. It may well be doubted that one can find such descriptions in all cases. On my account, however, there is no such requirement: the speaker might associate with 'Hesperus' and 'Phosphorus' only indefinite descriptions like 'a star sometimes seen in the west shortly after sunset' and 'a star sometimes seen in the north shortly before sunrise'; even if he believes both descriptions to be satisfied by many things, P(Hesperus = Phosphorus|there is no one star which is seen both in the west shortly after sunset and in the north shortly before sunrise) could easily be less than 1.

(ii) If names are synonymous with associated descriptions, then the referent of a name is the same as the referent of the associated description; that is, the associated description must be true of the object named. On my account there is no such requirement, and, in fact, in the example used in (i) the requirement is not met (since Phosphorus is a planet, not a star, and is seen in the morning in the east rather than the north). So my account does not suffer from the fact that we often have wildly erroneous conceptions of the objects we name.

(iii) If associated descriptions are conceived of as *synonyms* of names, we must be very careful to avoid circularity in choosing our associated descriptions: we must not associate 'denouncer of Catiline' with 'Cicero' and 'denouncee of Cicero' with 'Catiline'. But give up any pretense to synonymy and such "circularities" are perfectly acceptable.

(iv) In many cases there is a wide variety of descriptions that are closely associated with a name; for instance, with 'Shakespeare' we might associate 'the author of *Hamlet*', 'the author of *Macbeth*', 'the man who looked like such and such', etc. According to the description theory there is one such description that is synonymous with the name 'Shakespeare' on any given occasion of use; hence the description theorist has the thankless task of finding plausible principles for selecting "the one the speaker really had in mind." On my account, however, there is no such need; for in claiming that 'Shakespeare = Bacon' and 'Shakespeare = Shakespeare' are not synonymous (even for someone who firmly believes that Shakespeare = Bacon), I do not claim that there is only *one* sentence C such that the probability of 'Shakespeare = Bacon' given C is less than 1.

(v) The description theorist is forced to claim that on any occasion of use, 'Shakespeare = Bacon' is synonymous with some identify between descriptions, say 'the author of *Hamlet* = the author of *Novum Organum*'. It follows from this that the user of the sentence would have to hold that the conditional probability of 'Shakespeare = Bacon', given that the author of *Hamlet* $\neq$ the author of *Novum Organum,* was *zero*. My claim was much more cautious: I merely required that the conditional probability be less than 1. Roughly, I required only that either the discovery that the author of *Hamlet* $\neq$ the author of *Novum Organum* or some similar discovery weaken his confidence that Shakespeare = Bacon; the description theorist requires that some such discovery make him certain that Shakespeare $\neq$ Bacon. It seems to me that this stronger requirement is quite implausible.

In spite of its defects, the description theory of names has been held by a great many philosophers. I think that a main reason they have held it is that they have felt (correctly) that the explanation of the nonsynonymy of 'Hesperus' and 'Phosphorus' has to do with the fact that some descriptions are more closely associated with one of these names than with the other; and the only explanation they could think of for why this fact should be relevant to the difference in the cognitive meaning of the names (as opposed to the mere connotations of the names) was that the names were *synonymous* with the descriptions. An advantage of the idea that meaning involves conceptual role is that it provides us with another far less committal way to make the difference of "closeness of association" between names and descriptions relevant to issues about the cognitive meanings of names.

I have claimed that all differences in meaning between sentences with the same referential meaning are due to differences in conceptual role, and I have given a particular account of what a difference in conceptual role is: two sentences differ in conceptual role (for a person with subjective conditional probability function P) if they are not equipollent (under P). I have tried to illustrate the plausibility of this explication of sameness of conceptual role through the example of proper names, but there are also theoretical reasons to accept this as a reasonable explication. For if we do give this as our explication of sameness of conceptual role (and then identify sameness of meaning with sameness of referential meaning plus sameness of conceptual role), then sameness of meaning has a number of very nice properties, among them the following:

(a) *If A has the same meaning as B, then $\neg A$ has the same meaning as $\neg B$; and if in addition C has the same meaning as D, then $A \wedge C$ has the same meaning as $B \wedge D$. [Any violation of either of these principles would be a violation of the idea that the meaning of the whole is determined by the meanings of the parts.]*

(b) *If two sentences have the same meaning for a person at one time then, in the normal course of events, they will continue to have the same meaning for that person.*

(c) *If two sentences have the same meaning for a person, then no sensory stimulation could induce the person to believe one more strongly than the other (barring an "abnormal course of events" which we would intuitively regard as "changing the meaning of" one of the sentences).*

It is easy to see that if sameness of meaning were just equipollence, it would have all the three properties. That it would have property (a) is the content of part (1) of Popper's theorem. That it would have properties (b) and (c) depend on an assumption I will be making throughout the rest of this paper: that in the normal course of events people alter their probability functions in one of the standard ways—i.e., by conditionalization or by Richard Jeffrey's generalization of conditionalization. On this assumption, it is trivial to verify both (b) and (c). So (a)—(c) would hold if sameness of meaning were just equipollence; my proposal, however, has not quite been that we identify sameness of meaning with equipollence, for on my proposal sameness of meaning is equipollence *plus sameness of referential meaning*. Nevertheless, it is easy to see that the presence of this extra ingredient in meaning does not interfere with the validity of (a)—(c).

The general idea behind the account I have been advocating is that differences of meaning between referentially equivalent sentences are to be explained in terms of evidential considerations. This same general idea also underlies the account in §§9 and 11 of W.V. Quine's *Word and Object*. However, Quine uses a very simple behavioristic apparatus to implement the basic idea—the apparatus of stimulus-meanings—and this apparatus is not powerful enough to give very satisfactory results.

More specifically, Quine holds that we can give a fairly good account of intra-speaker synonymy for what he calls "occasion sentences" by saying that the sentences are synonymous if and only if they are "stimulus-synonymous"; i.e., if and only if any sensory stimulation that prompts assent to one will prompt assent to the other, and similarly for dissent. Quine notes, however, that stimulus synonymy is far too weak a requirement to yield a plausible synonymy relation for sentences *other* than occasion sentences. Now, equipollence is a much stronger requirement than stimulus synonymy: any two equipollent sentences are stimulus-synonymous [this follows from (c) above, together with the assumption that whether one assents to a sentence if queried depends solely on the probability that one attaches to that sentence]; but stimulus-synonymous sentences are certainly not equipollent in general. By replacing stimulus synonymy by the stronger requirement of equipollence, I have obviated the need of restricting the account of intra-speaker synonymy to occasion sentences. Moreover, even within the class of occasion sentences, my account of synonymy is sensitive to differences of meaning that Quine's account is insensitive to: compare his discussion of 'Buffalo nickel' and 'Indian nickel' in §11 with my discussion of 'Hesperus' and 'Phosphorus' above. For these and other reasons I think that my account is far superior in detail to Quine's, however similar it may be in spirit.

So far I have been extolling the virtues of including conceptual-role considerations in meaning. The next question I want to raise is whether I am right in thinking that referential meaning as well as conceptual role should be considered a component of meaning. There is an important prima facie objection to counting "referential meaning" as part of meaning. It is a bit complicated to state the objection properly to the doctrine in this form, however; so let me state it instead as an objection to a virtual corollary of my doctrine, namely the further doctrine that reference as well as conceptual role is a component of meaning for names and predicates. The prima facie objection to making reference an ingredient of meaning is that it seems to leave open the possibility that two names or two predicates with the same conceptual role for a speaker could differ in meaning for that speaker merely because they were casually connected to different objects (and hence referred to different objects); and this violates the plausible requirement that whether two names or two predicates are synonymous for a speaker ought not to depend on what goes on outside his head. All this objection really shows, however, is that we need a constraint on our theories of reference: it ought to follow from any adequate theory of reference that no two names or predicates that have the same conceptual role for a given speaker at a given time can refer (for that speaker at that time) to different things. I believe that this constraint is both plausible and easy to satisfy. For instance, consider Gareth Evan's version of the causal theory of reference: a name for a speaker refers to that object (if any) which is the dominant source of the set of all his beliefs that involve that name. This theory may already satisfy the proposed constraint; but, if not, a plausible modification of the theory which *does* meet the constraint is: a name for a speaker refers to that object (if any) which is the dominant source of the set of *all his beliefs that involve either that name or any other name that has the same conceptual role for him.* I think, then, that the proposed constraint is plausible; if so, then the inclusion of reference in addition to conceptual role as an ingredient in meaning in no way affects questions about the intra-speaker synonymy of names and predicates, and so the objection has no force.

So far I have given no reason *for* including referential meaning as part of meaning: why not hold, with Harman, that conceptual role is all there is to meaning? One answer is that if we do not include referential meaning in meaning we will get some unwanted synonymies. Suppose that for some reason some madman has developed a total certainty that everything is either red or green; if we let A be the sentence 'Everything is red or green', then his conditional probability function has $P(A|C) = 1$ for every C. It follows that, for every sentence B, $P(A \wedge B|C) = P(B|C)$ for all C; so if meaning were determined *wholly* by conceptual role, then every sentence B would be *synonymous* for the madman with that sentence conjoined with 'Everything is red or green'. This is very counterintuitive, and the most obvious way to avoid it is to include referential meaning within meaning: B and $B \wedge A$ clearly differ in referential meaning.

Unfortunately for my position, however, there is another way to avoid the consequence: modify the account of conceptual role by making it more fine-grained. One obvious way to do this is to say that two sentences have the same *fine-grained conceptual role* if (i) they have the same conceptual role (as defined previously), and (ii) they are built up in the same way from parts with the same conceptual roles. (The notion of conceptual role for the parts of a sentence was defined in fn 19.) It is hard to object to this proposal, and in fact something like it may be needed on independent grounds. (One might object to the details of the proposal, since, as David Lewis has remarked of an analogous proposal, it may yield a notion of synonymy that is *too* fine-grained to accord with our pre-theoretic judgments; but, as he also remarks, less fine-grained notions can easily be constructed by taking equivalence classes if we think this desirable.)

The upshot is that considerations of intra-speaker synonymy do not provide us with any very strong reason for including referential meaning within meaning. A better reason is this: a pure conceptual-role account of meaning does not accord with one of our most fundamental beliefs about meaning, namely, the belief that meaning determines truth conditions. To know whether the German sentence 'Beethoven wohnte in Deutschland' is true, it is natural to say that we need to know only two things: first, whether Beethoven lived in Germany; and second, what the German sentence means. This condition is met by an account of meaning that includes referential meaning as one component. But it does not appear to be met by any pure conceptual-role account of meaning: given only (i) the conceptual role that the string of symbols 'Beethoven wohnte in Deutschland' has for a given speaker and (ii) the fact that Beethoven lived in Germany, it is not at all clear how to determine whether or not the German sentence is true. In fact, it seems evident that such a determination is in principle impossible: for whether the sentence is true depends on what the terms in it refer to, and what the terms refer to depends on factors outside the speaker's head. (For example, if Evans is right, it depends on the casual role that external

objects and external properties have on the formation and retention of our beliefs involving these terms.) Meaning is a matter
not of conceptual role (i.e., role in individual psychology) but
of sociological role: one aspect of the sociological role of a term
is the role that term has in the psychologies of different members
of a linguistic community; another aspect, irreducible to the
first, is what physical object or physical property the term stands
for.

An important difference between the account of meaning
I've been advocating and a more traditional Fregean account is
that my account is compatible with a great deal of pessimism
about the clarity of the notion of inter-speaker synonymy.
Questions of inter-speaker synonymy are in part questions about
inter-speaker sameness of conceptual role—but that, I contend,
is an extremely unclear notion. The problem is that different
people have different subjective conditional probability functions: the machinery developed in this paper provides a natural
account of what it is for two sentences or two terms *within the
context of the same probability function* to have the same conceptual role; but I do not see any way to provide an account that
is both clear and useful of what it is for terms or sentences in
the contexts of *different* probability functions to have the same
role. My own inclination is not to try to provide such an account,
but to learn to live without the concept of inter-speaker
synonymy, and all other concepts in terms of which inter-
speaker synonymy could be defined. (The place that such concepts appear to be needed is in belief-desire psychology. I believe
that any such psychology formulated in terms of such concepts
can be reformulated so as not to employ them, and that there are
independent grounds for preferring the reformulated theory;
but I do not want to argue for this claim here.)

My pessimism about the prospects of giving a clear account of the notion of inter-speaker synonymy is very much in
the spirit of Quine's writings; but there is an important difference
between Quine's views and my own views on this score. On my
view, referential meaning is part of meaning, and provides a way
to make questions of intersubjective synonymy *in large part*
objective: terms in distinct idiolects are not to be regarded as
synonymous if they refer to different things. I'm sure that
Quine would object to this, since he finds the idea of intersubjective sameness of reference also suspect: cf. "the inscrutability of
reference." However, I have argued elsewhere that the phrase
"inscrutability of reference' covers two very different phenomena.
I argued that the first phenomenon (which I called "the conven-
tionality of claims about reference," but which is probably what

most people have primarily in mind when they speak of "in-scrutability") poses no problem for determining intersubjective sameness of reference, at least between languages of sufficiently similar structure. And I argued that the second phenomenon (which I called "genuine inscrutability") poses no problem either, if we replace the notion of reference with what I there called "partial reference." So neither phenomenon shows that there is any problem about intersubjective sameness of reference (except between languages of sufficiently different structure); but intersubjective sameness of meaning, insofar as it goes *beyond* sameness of reference or of referential meaning, is highly in-determinate, owing to the difficulty of clarifying the notion of intersubjective sameness of conceptual role.

I suspect that the extra determinacy that one gets by including referential considerations as well as conceptual-role considerations in one's account of meaning is extremely impor-tant to the theory of communication, in particular, to an account of how I can come to regard someone else's assertion of (say) "There are gravitational waves" (or some foreign equivalent) as evidence that there are gravitational waves. But I will not try to argue for this claim here.

I would like to close this paper with some brief remarks about (i) the relation between conceptual-role semantics and the verifiability theory of meaning, and (ii) the meanings of logical connectives. In *Experience and Prediction* Reichenbach elaborates two versions of the verifiability theory of meaning, both of which are based on the concept of probability. The official version is that two sentences A and B are synonymous if and only if, for every observation sentence C, $P(A|C) = P(B|C)$. The unofficial version—that is, the version that Reichenbach officially rejects but often lapses into—is that A and B are synony-mous if and only if, for every observation sentence C, $P(C|A) = P(C|B)$. This last criterion of synonymy (*positivistic synonymy*, I'll call it) says roughly that if two sentences have the same empirical consequences they are synonymous: this is the stand-ard positivist view of synonymy. The former criterion gives a much stronger relation of synonymy (*Reichenbachian synonymy*, I'll call it): it can be shown[26] that two sentences are Reichen-bachian-synonymous if and only if (a) they are positivistically synonymous, and (b) they have the same initial probability. This last requirement makes Reichenbachian synonymy rather useless as a weapon in the positivist's arsenal: you can't show that two theories which apparently differ in meaning but which have the same empirical consequences *really* are synonymous in Reichenbach's sense without first showing that the theories have the same initial probability; and any "metaphysician" who wants to deny that the theories are synonymous can do so by simply insisting on assigning them different initial probabilities. Reichenbach himself points out in one context how useless his concept of synonymy is as a critical tool (pp. 123/4, and esp. the footnote on 124); and whenever he himself tries to use his verificationism as a critical tool (as in §42), he does so by quietly slipping back into the positivistic notion of synonymy which he officially rejects.

But both the positivistic notion of synonymy and the Reichenbachian notion are formally quite bizarre: substitution of synonyms for synonyms in truth-functional contexts does not preserve synonymy. More specifically, if A is "synonymous" with B in either the positivistic or the Reichenbachian sense, and C is a nonobservational proposition, it need not be the case that $A \wedge C$ is "synonymous" with $B \wedge C$. It seems to me that this is sufficient reason to reject both "synonymy" notions as formally inadequate. In order to get a formally satisfactory probabilistic theory of meaning, one has to strengthen the synonymy relation even more than Reichenbach did: one has to require that $P(A|C) = P(B|C)$ not merely for all observation sentences C but for *all* sentences C. Roughly, then, we are saying that A is synonymous with B if, were we to assume any sentence no matter how nonobservational as "evidence," we would still regard A and B as equally likely. It is obvious that such a notion of synonymy has even less chance of being used as a critical tool than Reichenbach's had; consequently, even if I were to adopt a *purely* conceptual-role view of meaning (as I have not done), I would still not be resuscitating verificationism.

I now turn to the semantics of the logical connectives. On most versions of truth-theoretic semantics (whether nonreferential or referential) the recursion clauses are things like

(3) '⌐A' is true (relative to f) if and only if 'A' is
   not true (relative to f).

Harman's position is that (1) and the truth theory of which it is a part tell us nothing more about the meaning of "Beethoven wohnte in Deutschland' than that it has the same meaning as a certain English sentence; but that (3) gives a complete, nontranslational account of the meaning of '⌐'. This strikes me as a rather surprising combination of views: given Harman's views about the significance of (1), it would seem much more natural to say that (3) tells you nothing about the meaning of '⌐' that is not revealed by saying that '⌐' in the object language is to be translated into the metalanguage as 'not'. In any case, the idea that (3) does not really illuminate the meaning of ' ⌐' and 'not' but merely establishes a synonymy between them has considerable plausibility (whether or not it is correct). Is it possible to say something else about the meaning of '⌐' which is more obviously illuminating?

Recall that the way we established that truth-theoretic semantics really could say more about the meaning of 'Beethoven wohnte in Deutschland' than that this sentence could be translated in a certain way was to pass from a nonreferential version of truth-theoretic semantics [a version containing clauses like (1)] to a referential version [containing clauses like (2)]. The special problem with showing that truth-theoretic semantics illuminates the meanings of the logical connectives is that even most referential versions of truth-theoretic semantics treat the logical connectives by recursion clauses like (3); and these clauses are much more like (1) than like (2), in that the right-hand side of the biconditional contains a translation of the term whose meaning is to be illuminated. Can we come up with a more fully referential truth-theoretic semantics, a semantics that is referential even for logical connectives? Frege showed formally how to do this: truth-functional connectives refer to functions from truth values to truth values, and quantifiers refer to functions from "concepts" (i.e., functions from objects to truth values) to truth values. But this formal account really isn't of much help in illuminating the meanings of the connectives, for there seems to be no prospect of giving any interesting account of what it is for a word to "refer to" a function that maps T into ⊥ and ⊥ into T. Or, to put the point more accurately: it is hard to see how to give any account of "reference to" truth functions *unless we construe the claim that '⌐' refers to a certain truth function as really a claim about the role that '⌐' plays in our conceptual scheme.* And if we do so construe the claim, then we see that talk of "reference to truth functions" is an unnecessary diversion: what is really needed, if we are to give a more illuminating account of the meaning of '⌐' than is provided by (3), is to explain its meaning in terms of its conceptual role.

How then can we specify the conceptual roles of the connectives? One way to do this is to specify the probabilistic laws that the connectives obey; so we can look at rules (r1) to (r3) as specifying the meanings of the propositional connectives and of the quantifier. If we accept this as an account of the meanings of the connectives, then the soundness theorem shows that, in a nontrivial sense, the logical laws hold by virtue of meaning.

Gilbert Harman

PROBLEMS WITH PROBABILISTIC SEMANTICS

1. Subjective probabilistic semantics should yeild intuitionism.
Subjective probability is often explained in terms of betting: The
subjective probability of a proposition is supposed to represent
the odds one would require before betting for or against the
truth of a proposition. This suggests intuitionism, since what
settles a bet is not the mere truth or falsity of a proposition
but rather the *discovery* that the proposition is true or the
discovery that it is false. In this context, there is no point to a
distinction between truth and the discovery of truth. It is, of
course, the basic doctrine of intuitionism that there is no meaningful distinction of this sort. If subjective probability theory is
interpreted in terms of betting, then it ought to yield a form of
intuitionism. How surprising that Hartry Field (1977) should
claim that it yields classical nonintuitionistic logic instead!

Indeed Field claims even more implausibly that this
probabilistic semantics "disproves" a suggestion of Michael
Dummett's. Field states Dummett's suggestion as follows:
"Unless one believes that sense can be made of the notion of
truth, one should not accept the laws of classical logic; for
the only rationale there could be for accepting those laws (as
opposed, say, to the laws of intuitionistic logic) is that they are
precisely the laws that preserve truth." Field claims to disprove
this by presenting a subjective probabilistic semantics with respect
to which classical logic is sound and complete. But in his argument he makes a crucial assumption which not only begs the
question against the intuitionist but is false if one takes seriously
the interpretation of subjective probability in terms of betting.
Field assumes that any reasonable subjective conditional proba-
bility function P must satisfy the condition that $P(\neg B/A) = 1 - P(B/A)$ for nonabsurd A. Put in terms of betting, this says that
the subjective probability of discovering that B is false (given the
discovery that A is true) plus the subjective probability of
discovering that B is true (given the discovery that A is true)
should be 1. But this is not always so. These probabilities should
normally add up to something less than 1, since the subjective
probability of discovering whether or not B is true (given the
discovery that A is true) will normally be less than 1. So, the

crucial premise in Field's argument is false, if subjective probability is explained in terms of betting.

If Field is to make his argument go through, he will have to take his appeal to subjective probability more seriously. He will have to provide a different interpretation from the usual one in terms of betting. He will have to show that his crucial assumption is true, given that interpretation. Finally, if he is to show that Dummett is wrong, he will have to do all this without appealing to the sort of transcendent notion of truth to which the intuitionist objects. Surely that is impossible.

In my view, if a theory of meaning yields intuitionism, that shows that something has gone wrong. But there are further problems with subjective probabilistic semantics as a version of the theory that meaning is role in conceptual scheme.

2. *We do not and in principle could not operate in accordance with the principles of subjective probability.*

According to Field, "the most clearly understood models of

(i) belief

(ii) how the impact of sensory experience changes belief and

(iii) how beliefs together with desires influence actions now available are models in which the notion of subjective probability plays a central part." In connection with (ii) he refers to methods of changing probability assignments proposed by Richard Jeffrey and Paul Teller. The problem is that these methods involve an unwelcome combinatorial explosion. Given N unrelated atomic propositions, probabilities must be assigned to each of the various truth functional combinations of these propositions. This will require at least $2^N - 1$ explicit assignments, for example to all but one of the strongest conjunctions including each atomic proposition or its negation. If we were to operate in accordance with these methods, the number of explicit assignments needed would be an exponentially exploding function of the number of unrelated atomic propositions involved. Given a modest 300 unrelated atomic propositions about which we had some opinion we would need to make more explicit assignments of probability than there are atoms in the universe. Clearly we do not and in principle could not operate in this way. Instead we must resort to yes-no belief; we either believe something or we do not. That is how we are able to remember thousands of different things (Lewis 1975).[1]

The theory that meaning is role in conceptual scheme is the theory that the basic symbols with meaning are those mental representations used in thought and that other symbols have meaning because of some relation to such basic mental symbols, where mental representations have meaning because of their role in thought—how they are influenced by perception, how they lead to action, how reasoning involves them, and so on. An account of the content of particular mental representations is nothing other than an account of what makes a given mental state the particular state it is with that particular content. A theory of meaning as conceptual role is nothing other than a functional theory of the nature of our mental states (Harman 1973). [2] Since we do not function in accordance with the principles of subjective probability, an adequate theory of meaning as conceptual role will not be a probabilistic semantics.

3. Probabilistic semantics cannot explain why theories of truth shed light on the meaning of logical constants.

The truth functional analysis of logical connectives has rightly been thought to illuminate the meanings of these connectives. Tarski's account of truth in formalized languages has rightly been taken to make clear the meanings of the quantifiers. Kripke's truth conditional "semantics" for modal logic has rightly been thought to illuminate the meanings of modal operators of necessity and possibility. Davidson's account of the truth conditions of action sentences involving certain sorts of adverbial modification seems to shed light on the meaning of such sentences. Theories of truth conditions of the usual sort do tell us about the meanings of logical constants and the role logical form plays in determining the meaning of sentences. Such theories do not in the same way seem to tell us about the meanings of atomic predicates in the language.

The problem is why this should be so. A theory of truth of the relevant sort says such things as this:

> (1) "x is a horse" is satisfied by an assignment if and only if what that assignment assigns to "x" is a horse
>
> (2) "p and q" is satisfied by an assignment if and only if "p" and "q" are both satisfied by that assignment.

Why should it happen that such a theory tells us something significant about the meaning of a logical constant like "and" that it does not tell us about the meaning of an atomic predicate like "is a horse"?

A theory of meaning as conceptual role can offer the following sort of answer. One thing we do with mental representations is to reason with them. Reasoning can involve the construction of deductive arguments. The meaning of logical constants is determined by their role in the construction of such arguments. The validity of deductive arguments depends only on the meanings of the logical constants used and is independent of the meanings of nonlogical terms involved, such as atomic predicates. More precisely, the validity of these arguments depends on properties of logical constants like the property of "and" expressed in (2). The validity of arguments depends on the properties of logical constants that are stated in the usual accounts of truth conditions. That is why accounts of truth conditions shed light on the meanings of logical constants. They reveal the properties of logical constants that determine their functioning in the construction of valid deductive arguments.[3]

This, of course, is the barest sketch of an answer and much more needs to be said. But it should be clear that an answer of this sort requires taking seriously the idea that the meaning of an expression is the conceptual role of that expression, how it functions in thought. Field's probabilistic semantics cannot provide an answer of this sort since it does not concern itself with the way logical constants function in reasoning and that is because it is not really concerned with conceptual role at all.

NOTES

1. David and Stephanie Lewis understate the point when they observe, "Information-processing power is by no means a free good in unlimited supply, and we must resort to non-quantitative all-or-nothing belief as an economy measure."
2. Field argues that meaning must involve reference as well as conceptual role, but that is because he interprets conceptual role solipsistically, as a matter of "individual psychology." I prefer to treat conceptual role nonsolipsistically, counting as relevant to perceptual input, for example, not just nerve firings but the actual objects perceived and allowing also for other causal or genetic factors of the sort stressed by Kripke and others. See Harman, *Thought,* chapter four, especially pages 62-65.
3. Field clearly misrepresents this sort of account when he attributes to me the thesis that a clause like (2) by itself "gives a complete nontranslational account of the meaning" of a logical constant like "and".

REFERENCES

Field, H. 1977. Logic, meaning, and conceptual role. *Journal of Philosophy* 74, pp. 379-409.
Harman, G. 1973. *Thought.* Princeton: Princeton University Press. Lewis, D. Lewis and S. Lewis. 1975. Review of *Contemporary philosophy in Scandanavia. Theoria* 41, p. 57.

James Munz

HOW MEANINGFUL IS ENGLISH?

According to Carnap the study of natural languages is based on pragmatics. Constructing the (applied) syntax, semantics and grammar[1] of a natural language is a process of idealizing and abstracting from the pragmatic performance of speakers in the heat of their linguistic transactions. A grammar of a natural language is produced from a pragmatic onion by removing successive layers until the grammar is laid bare. As with removing layers from an onion, when to stop is not always evident. If we remove too much, nothing remains. If we remove too little, the grammar becomes excessively complex. Recently linguists have found it comforting to characterize the stopping point as that point at which the competence of the ideal speaker has just been exposed. I find this suggestion neither comforting nor illuminating, but be that as it may, linguists do stop and there is reasonable agreement in practice about where to stop.

My purpose here is to examine the relevance of conceptual role semantics—most particularly Field's version—to the study of natural languages. I propose to do this by considering the following questions. What is the relationship between semantics and the theory of meaning? What is the relationship between a comprehensive theory of meaning and a grammar? Can meaning be adequately explicated in terms of conceptual role? Can conceptual role be adequately explicated in terms of conditional probability functions as Field suggests? What is the relationship between descriptive semantics and grammar? What is the relationship between a natural language and logic?

By way of preface let me set down some fundamental beliefs about natural languages. A natural language is specified by giving its grammar. A grammar enumerates and describes the sentences of the language under study. Among the strings certified as sentences are many which will never be used by speakers. The grammar errs pragmatically in the other direction as well. If we call the pragmatic unit of language together with its context of production a discourse,[2] then there will be many linguistic fragments which appear in discourses set off by appropriate pauses or punctuation marks but which are not certified by the grammar as sentences. Some of these are fragments which work well enough when they can lean on neighboring passages which are certified as sentences or on extra-linguistic environments, but deprived of such support they are unacceptable. As defined by grammars, natural languages are relatively stable over time and change of speaker. The belief is widely held that a necessary condition for communication by speakers of a language is that they substantially share the grammar of the language and by virtue of this are said to speak the same language.

(i)

With respect to the first question—What is the relationship between semantics and a theory of meaning?—there is little to do but point out the divergence of opinions. Tarski lists meaning as a semantic property coordinate with truth, satisfaction, designation and consequence, and he claims, gratuitously, in a footnote, that meaning can be defined in terms of satisfaction (Tarski 1944). Quine (1953) suggests that semantics is composed of a theory of meaning and a theory of reference. Montague disagrees claiming that a theory of meaning "can most naturally be accommodated within pragmatics" (Montague 1974). According to Lewis semantics must treat truth conditions (Lewis 1970). The meaning of a sentence for Lewis determines its truth conditions. So a theory of meaning appears to be part of semantics for Lewis. Harman's position is not quite so clear. He identifies meaning with conceptual role and not with truth conditions, but he says "If by "semantics" we mean a formal theory of truth, we must not identify semantics with a theory of meaning" (Harman 1974). Field claims rather that a theory of meaning consists of conceptual role semantics together with truth-theoretic semantics (Field 1977). His position places meaning squarely within semantics.

The apparently equivocal position of meaning in relation to semantics is due, in part, to differing conceptions of the nature of semantics. A much greater share of the problem resides with the unclarity of the notion of meaning. Various technical and semi-technical senses of 'meaning' have been proposed; yet none has gained a position of dominance, and the various senses do not jointly constitute an inventory of what we presystematically call *meaning*. The term has not been adequately explicated. What is even more serious is that we even lack acceptable adequacy conditions for proposed definitions of meaning.[3]

(ii)

Even given the unexplicated notion of meaning, we can be more explicit about the relationship between a comprehensive theory of meaning and a grammar. At least a portion of what we call *meaning* in discourses—the pragmatic objects—will be lost in the removal of layers from the onion in the process of arriving at a grammar. To the extent that this is true English, as defined by its grammar, is less meaningful than the discourse of English.

That something is lost in the move to a grammar is clear from the following example. What does the following opening bid in a bridge game mean?

(I bid) two hearts.

As a performative it means precisely what it says. But there are other appropriate answers. It means that the bidder feels that he can take seven tricks with hearts as trump. It also means that the bidder has either a good, five-card heart suit with 25 points, or a good, six-card heart suit with 23 points, or a good, seven-card heart suit with 21 points. Clearly, at least the last two meanings will not survive the peeling away process. They will not be attributed to the sentence by the grammar of English. Yet the English speaking bridge player had better be aware of these meanings.

The particular example is not important, though I will return to it repeatedly. The reader can easily call to mind many examples of discourses whose meaning exceeds what we can reasonably expect a grammar to represent. The example is of interest in several respects. If the speaker lacks the required cards to support the bid, the bid is not false. Its truth conditions have nothing to do with the last two meanings we have given it—meaning need not determine truth conditions.

The important issue is how much of what we call *meaning* will be recorded in a grammar. I will argue that English has far less meaning than is commonly supposed. There is reason to suppose that among the kinds of meaning excluded from the language are logical form, consequence, validity and the like (see section vi). Precisely how much meaning is part of the English language is hard to say. It depends on a number of different factors: The technology of onion peeling, the trade off between scope, coherence, fit to the pragmatic objects, simplicity and how illuminating the resulting grammar is; what one intends to use a grammar for. When we take a language to be specified by its grammar or grammars, the question "How meaningful is the language?" has no helpful *a priori* answer. It also lacks a unique answer. Still we can say that a grammar will not exhaust meaning.

(iii)

Can meaning be explicated in terms of conceptual role as Harman contends? Conceptual role theory is attractive for a number of reasons. Yet one of the features which makes it a likely candidate for explicating meaning prevents us from giving a definitive answer to this question.

We noted that there are no clear adequacy conditions for definitions of meaning. This unclarity of the concept of meaning makes Harman's proposal appealing. "To specify a thought is to specify its role in . . . a conceptual scheme. To specify the meaning of a sentence of the relevant sort is to specify a thought, so to specify its meaning is to specify a role in a conceptual scheme" (Harman, *op. cit.,* p. 11). The speaker's conceptual scheme is "the system of concepts constituted by the speaker's beliefs, plans, hopes, fears, and so on, ways the speaker has of modifying his beliefs, plans, hopes, fears, and so on, and ways these modify what the speaker does" (Harman, *op. cit.,* p. 10).

If giving a comprehensive theory of meaning appears to be a monumental task, Harman's notion of conceptual role may have enough scope to be up to the task. There are reasons for thinking that the bridge bid and its kin are within its power. An opening bid of two hearts expresses the speaker's beliefs about tricks he can take, counts and distributions. It produces similar beliefs and hopes in his partner and contributes to his immediate plans. It is more likely to produce fears and associated plans for his opponents. It modifies what the speaker does for the rest of the hand, the meaning of following bids and the behavior of all the players.

The match between the unclarity of meaning and conceptual role as Harman formulates it gives rise to the hope that conceptual role will be strong enough. But the same unclarity blocks any definitive answer to our question.

Conceptual role theory has other appealing aspects. It is epistemically more realistic than traditional extensional theories. Speakers of natural languages do not know the extensions of many terms in their languages. They do not know the truth values of many of the sentences they use. Nor can speakers be viewed as having internalized Montague's intensions (Partee 1979). If it is unrealistic to assume that speakers have access to the extension of terms in natural languages, it is doubly so to assume that they have access to possible worlds.

There is another appeal of conceptual role theory which demands a measure of caution. Learning a language involves a coming to have beliefs and habits. But we must be careful here. Harman says,

> It would be a mistake to suppose that the relevant thoughts have an existence independent of the language in which one expresses them. Learning a language is not just learning a way to encode thoughts one already has. It is rather in part to acquire the possibility of new thoughts, thoughts that are *in* that language. That is why a language carries with it aspects of a world view. Learning a language is not to be distinguished from learning a theory (Harman 1974, p. 12).

No doubt no one, even Psammitichus's babies, have ever learned a language without simultaneously learning theories; yet not all one learns while one learns a language is part of the language as commonly conceived. There are facts (beliefs) about the language and facts (beliefs) about the world. Some of the conceptual relations within a conceptual scheme that determine conceptual role and meaning of sentences are not parts of the language. If we can represent the meaning of the bridge bid in a conceptual role theory, that does not make those meanings part of the language.

This point has a parallel in Tarski's semantics. For Tarski the specification of a formalized language may include axioms or primitive sentences and rules of inference. This view is harmless in connection with formalized languages for logicians are drawn to the study of a formalized language because of a prior interest in a theory formulated in the language. The transfer of this position to natural languages is not happy for it raises questions like "What are the axioms and rules of inference of English?" or for Harman, "What is the theory of English?" or perhaps for Field, "What is the logic of English?" We don't think of natural languages as having rules of inference or axioms. What Tarski calls a formalized language includes what we normally call a theory formulated in the language. Our normal approach to a natural language is not *via* a theory as is the case for formalized languages. We view natural languages as media which can be used to formulate theories.[4]

(iv)

Can conceptual role be explicated in terms of conditional probability functions as Field suggests? The great virtue of Field's paper is that he assigns precise content where Harman did not. For just that reason Field's proposal can not be an explication of Harman's conceptual role until Harman's position is elaborated in more detail. Field has provided a very plausible replacement for Harman's theory.

Can meaning be explicated in terms of conceptual role in Field's sense and truth-theoretic or referential semantics? Field contends rather forcefully that it can.

> But, taken together, I claim, truth-theoretic semantics and conceptual role semantics provide an account of all the facts about meaning that there are (Field 1977, p. 380) . . . *the meaning of a sentence is given by its referential meaning together with its conceptual role* (Field 1977, p. 391). I have claimed that all differences in meaning between sentences with the same referential meaning are due to differences in conceptual role, . . .
> (Field 1977, p. 394)

For just the reasons that the earlier form of the question was unanswerable, this form of the question is also unanswerable. The notion of meaning as well as the notion of "all the facts about meaning that there are" is too unclear to permit an answer. Field's claim is gratuitous.

What is the relationship of conceptual role semantics in Field's sense and a grammar? Consider again the bridge bid. It is apparent that the extra-grammatical meanings the bid has can be reflected in conditional probability functions; so conceptual role semantics will represent meaning which is not part of the language as we have defined it. There is one area in which conceptual role semantics may fall short of the account of meaning given by a grammar. The conditional probability function does not appear to be defined for non-trivial cases where the conditioning or conditioned sentences are non-declarative. On the face of it, Field's theory does not appear to provide an account of the meaning of non-declaratives. This problem may be surmountable if appropriate ways of associating non-declarative sentences with related declaratives (performatives, for instance), are found. In any case, this possible inadequacy is moot and I will ignore it subsequently.

We can take some important steps in clarifying the relationship between Field's theory and natural languages as defined by their grammars. Field establishes that a significant part of traditional semantics can be done without recourse to either reference or truth. In proving the soundness and completeness of first-order logic using only conditional probability, Field also conclusively refutes Dummett's suggestion that the laws of classical logic should only be accepted if one can make sense of truth (Dummett 1973) and at least one reading of Lewis' position that "Semantics without truth conditions is not semantics" (Lewis 1970). Still, Field feels that referential semantics is required as well. Field proposes two areas in which conceptual role semantics will prove inadequate. First, he says,

> . . .a pure conceptual role account of meaning does not accord with one of our most fundamental beliefs about meaning, namely, the belief that meaning determines truth conditions (Field 1977).

Truth conditions involve the objective reference of terms while conceptual role semantics deals with subjective beliefs. Field sees no way of reconstructing objective reference from subjective role. The need to augment conceptual role semantics with referential semantics is the wage of epistemic realism.

Second, while conceptual role semantics seems to provide an account of intra-speaker synonymy, it does not fare as well for inter-speaker synonymy. Speakers do not share conditional probability functions and, though each function may remain invariant under permissible transformations, it is hard to see how comparisons can be made between functions for different speakers (from different equivalence classes of functions). This problem is analogous to the problem of intersubjective comparisons of utility functions (Luce and Raiffa, 1964). Even the problem of determining empirically that two speakers shared the same class of conditional probability functions would be unmanageable. On Field's view including referential meaning is a partial solution to the problem. "On my view, . . . referential meaning provides a way to make questions of intersubjective synonymy *in large part* objective: Terms in distinct idiolects are not to be regarded as synonymous if they refer to different things" (Fielo 1977, p. 399). Sameness of referential meaning is a necessary condition for synonymy. Field is content to do without the notion of inter-speaker synonymy in so far as differences in inter-speaker meaning are not reflected in differences in reference.

Field's evidence for the necessity of including referential semantics is not convincing. Consider the problem of inter-speaker synonymy. Field is pessimistic both about the clarity of the notion and the clarity of the notion of sociological role (conceptual role for a community of speakers). Referential meaning is introduced as a practical way of refuting claims that two terms are synonymous. A more appropriate way of confronting such claims for those who, like Field, have a great deal of pessimism about inter-speaker synonymy and who have the courage of their conviction is to refuse to consider such claims until the notion is clarified and the pessimism dispelled. At present adding referential semantics is at best a move of convenience so far as inter-speaker synonymy is concerned.

The problem of stating truth conditions is more serious. Field argues convincingly that reference "depends on factors outside the speaker's head" and that objective reference cannot be reconstructed from subjective belief. When we change from an epistemological horse to an ontological one in mid-semantics we need the additional gear which referential semantics provides. Examining this point is important for a number of reasons.

Two of them are as much aesthetic as substantial. While Tarski usually doesn't talk about meaning, his attitude is that there is no absolute priority among the major semantic properties. They are interdefinable. His reason for beginning with satisfaction is convenience rather than priority. Field seems to be suggesting that when we come to meaning the situation changes fundamentally. There is, on his view, an independence of conceptual role and reference which appears to require a conceptual role-related property and a reference-related property for an adequate semantics. I find Tarski's attitude satisfying and am reluctant to give it up. Second, Field's insistence on the need for both conceptual role and reference is out of keeping with the spirit of the argument in the first part of his paper. He argues in a Tarskian spirit that important semantic properties, like soundness and completeness, can be defined using either truth or alternatively using conceptual role without recourse to a referential property. But his position changes in Section III. Some semantic properties can be defined using either only reference or only conceptual role; some require one (reference cannot be defined using conceptual role) and some require both (meaning).

There are two more substantial reasons to look at the problem of stating truth conditions. The problem touches on and illuminates central characteristics of Field's position. Where semantics for Quine consists of two subtheories, a theory of meaning and a theory of reference, Field sees a different division. Meaning pervades semantics which is divided into a theory of conceptual role and a theory of reference.

Meaning is a matter not of conceptual role (i.e., role
in individual psychology) but of sociological role:
one aspect of the sociological role of a term is the role
that term has in the psychologies of different members
of a linguistic community; another aspect, irreducible
to the first, is what psysical object or physical property
the term stands for. (Field, op. cit., p. 398)

But, as we will see shortly, the importance of individual conceptual role for Field is not that clear.

The final reason for looking at the problem of stating truth conditions is most important for my purposes. It clarifies the relationship between conceptual schemes and natural languages.

Consider first what an account of subjective *meaning—* meaning for an individual speaker—would be like. According to Field conceptual role theory, perhaps slightly modified, can give an account of intra-speaker synonymy. Conceptual role theory would also give us what the speaker believed to be true and his ontological commitments as well. But if we are to state objective truth conditions for the individual speaker's sentences we need some theory of reference. The theory of reference needed is not the theory of reference which is part of sociological role however. We have to know what objects the speaker applies his terms to, since he may not agree with society in the reference of his terms. But if speakers can differ over the reference of terms, then Field's pessimism about inter-speaker comparisons of conceptual role should extend to reconstructing sociological role reference from reference for a speaker. As I see it the heart of the problem is not that Field begins with a special kind of meaning but that he begins with a subjective, epistemic notion and then wants to address problems which are objective and public. So long as we address only problems of individual psychology it is likely that subjective conceptual role will be adequate. The change to an interest in objective, public ontological problems poses equal problems for subjective conditional probability and subjective reference. Field responds not by solving either problem but by leaping to sociological, objective reference.

Parallel to subjective conceptual role and subjective reference we can expect there to be sociological, objective conceptual role and sociological, objective reference. We can expect that, as intra-speaker synonymy is definable using only subjective conceptual role, inter-speaker synonymy is definable in terms of objective conceptual role.

Further, there are pressing reasons to try to define or partially define objective conceptual role. Field has made a step in that direction in his conditions rl-r3. These conditions specify when two speakers share the classical logic. Since, as I will argue in section 6, conditions rl-r3 are not language-specific, speakers of different languages share the same logic if their conditional probability functions satisfy rl-r3. Our belief that speakers of a language share a grammar—a belief that is more fundamental than the belief that meaning determines truth conditions—make the problem of specifying objective conceptual role more pressing.

The problem now is to see how grammar relates to conceptual role. A grammar can be viewed as stating language-specific conditions on conceptual schemes which must be satisfied if a speaker is to count as a speaker of the language in question. Some of these conditions are syntactic—having to do with the "shapes" of sentences in the domain of the speaker's conditional probability function. Some of these have to do with the meaning of terms and sentences. But the totality of grammatical conditions do not uniquely determine a conditional probability function any more than rl-r3 do. In section 6 I will argue that the grammatical conditions do not entail rl-r3. There is an alternative view for those who find talk of ideal speakers appealing. A grammar states conditions on the conditional probability function for a community of speakers. This function represents the ideal speaker. The conditions underdetermine the function. The function which represents the conceptual scheme for a community represents the belief structure of an ideal believer. While reference, either subject specific or objective, is not definable from subjective conditional probability until the nature of objective conditional probability functions is elucidated, the question of whether a theory of reference is needed for an adequate semantics cannot be answered.

(v)

What is the relationship between descriptive semantics and grammar? Assuming with Quine and Carnap that semantics contains a theory of meaning and assuming further that the theory of meaning in descriptive semantics includes "all the facts about meaning," it is obvious that on my view descriptive semantics is considerably more inclusive than what a linguist calls the semantics of a grammar. At this point the more interesting questions lie in connection with other boundaries. If in peeling the pragmatic onion to arrive at descriptive semantics some elements of meaning are lost, then my assumption is incorrect; though descriptive semantics is still likely to be more inclusive than the grammar. If in peeling no meaning is lost, then it isn't clear what remains uniquely in the domain of pragmatics. It may be for instance that any property in the domain of pragmatics may equally well be studied within semantics (though perhaps using different apparatus). This suggestion is not unreasonable when we remember that an axiomatization of first-order logic provides a syntactic account of the semantic property of being a logically true sentence.

Another issue is whether applied semantics deals with sentences of a language, theories in the language or discourses (pragmatic objects). A decision on this issue will effect the scope of semantics. If descriptive semantics deals with sentences then the gap between its contents and those of grammatical semantics will be smaller than if descriptive semantics deals with either theories or discourses. We noted earlier that Tarski includes theories. In the last section I will argue that a full concern with logic arises either with discourses or at least only with connected sequences of sentences.

The gap between descriptive semantics and grammar is important in another respect. If the gap is sufficiently great—for instance, if the grammar does not account for truth conditions, much of meaning, reference or the logician's classical semantic properties—or if the apparatus available in grammars is not at all like that used in clearly semantic studies, then the use of the term "semantics" by linguists in connection with grammars may be inappropriate. I am inclined to suspect that linguists ought to give up the term.

(vi)

What is the relationship between natural language and logic? This question will allow us to see how serious the shortfall of grammatical semantics is. In addition, it is often felt that the classical logic has some sort of special status with respect to natural languages. This view is pervasive enough that many linguists feel that assigning a logical form to sentences of a natural language is an important part of giving a semantic representation. The logical forms assigned to sentences by grammars which make such assignments are in the classical logic.

Implicit in this practice is the belief that the classical logic has such a privileged position with respect to natural languages that the classical logic is the logic of English and of natural languages generally. This view is indefensible for several reasons.

Let me begin with some obvious facts about Field's rl-r3. Field does not claim that any natural language has the structure rl-r3 require. He does not claim that $\neg$, $\wedge$, $\exists$ correspond to expressions of English or even to particular occurrences of expressions of English. Nor does he claim that English contains variables as required by r2 and r3.

Field's conditions are language-neutral. They apply to any language, natural or unnatural, whose sentences can appropriately be represented in the *system* Field is developing.[5] It is likely that in every natural language at least some occurrences of some of its sentences are appropriately represented in a direct way in first-order logic. Grice has taken a much stronger position. He claims that every occurrence of a declarative sentence of English can be assigned an appropriate logical representation in the standard logic. But different occurrences of the same sentence may receive different, possibly even contradictory, representations. The assignment of logical structure involves deductions from conversational maxims using extensive information about context of use. If Grice is right, the assignment of appropriate logical form is not made by the grammar. Even the fact that some sentence occurrences can be assigned correct logical forms directly is not strong evidence. Without prejudging the question of whether the classical logic is special as Field contends (*op. cit.*, p. 388) or has a special position with respect to natural languages, we note that one can do referential semantics for nonstandard logics as well. Modifying r1-r3 can provide the basis for conceptual role semantics for at least some nonclassical logics (see

Morgan's paper in Leblanc, Stern, Gumb, forthcoming). The extent to which this can be done for nonclassical logics using conceptual role is unclear at present.

One fairly common view of logic is that logic is a theory of reasoning. Corcoran has argued (Corcoran 1969) that we construct the theory on the basis of compelling passages of reasoning—sequences of sentences which are convincing proofs. On this view a logic is a theory about sequences of sentences. The logical representation given to a sentence in a natural language is appropriate or inappropriate only given the role the sentence has in passages of reasoning. When logic is viewed as dealing with the use of sentences in certain roles, we have reason to suspect that it is an extra-grammatical concern.

Further, it cannot be denied that there are passages framed in English which are proofs in nonclassical logics. When we begin with such proofs we construct other logics, and these logics are embodied in the pragmatic material from which grammars are constructed just as are proofs in the classical logic. Of course we cannot adopt arbitrary collections of rules as logics. There are conditions on admissible logics but these conditions are not linguistic. They are conditions on the psychology of conviction or on the notion of *following from* and the like.

Standard logic is an admissible logic with instances in the discourses of English, but there are other admissible logics which have instances in English discourses. Standard logic has no privileged position for English or any other natural language as specified by their grammars. Natural languages are, from the point of view of logic, like the perfect whore. A natural language has no logical personality of its own. Natural languages freely adopt any admissible logic their users wish.

If logic is not part of natural languages then there are significant consequences for the semantics of natural languages. Even should a grammar give truth conditions for its simple sentences (and standard grammars do not do even this at present), the normal recursive devices for giving truth conditions for complex sentences of formalized theories will not be available within grammars. Consequently it is unlikely that linguistic semantics will give truth conditions for sentences of natural languages.

NOTES

1. I have distinguished grammar from applied semantics and applied syntax because while a grammar may have a semantic and syntactic component, one of the questions I want to address is whether grammatical semantics is coextensive with applied semantics.

2. My use of "discourse" is nonstandard. It is normally used for a coherent sequence of sentences. I am aware of no established term for what I am talking about here, and I have impressed the term "discourse" into special service for the duration of this paper.

3. Tarski insists that definitions of semantic properties be materially adequate and formally correct. To guarantee material adequacy necessary and sufficient conditions must be given for the definition. No such conditions have been given for meaning.

4. We sometimes adopt the same view of formalized languages. This view is implicit when we say that two theories are formulated in the language of *Principia.*

5. What I call *representation* here is often called *translation.* The paradigm of translation is going from a sentence in one natural language to a sentence in another natural language. Because of the specialized function of the logical form assigned to a sentence, the term "representation" is more appropriate.

REFERENCES

Carnap, R. 1942. *Introduction to semantics.* Cambridge: Harvard University Press.

Corcoran, J. 1969. Three logical theories. *Philosophy of Science* 36, pp. 153-77.

Dummett, M. 1973. The justification of induction. *British Academy Lectures* LIX, pp. 201-232.

Field, Hartry. 1977. Logic, meaning and conceptual role. *The Journal of Philosophy* 74, 7, pp. 379-409.

Grice, H. P. Logic and conversation. Unpublished essay.

Harman, G. 1974. Meaning and semantics. In *Semantics and philosophy,* ed. Munitz, M. and Unger, P. New York: New York University Press.

Lewis, D. 1970. General semantics. *Synthese* 22, pp. 18-67.

Montague, R. 1974. *Formal philosophy.* New Haven: Yale University Press.

Partee, B. *Semantics*—mathematics or psychology? Forthcoming, Springer-Verlag.

Quine, W. V. 1953. *From a logical point of view.* Cambridge: Harvard University Press.

Raiffa, H. and Luce, R. 1964. *Games and decisions.* New York: Wiley.

Stern, R., Leblanc, H. and Gumb, R. Forthcoming. *Essays in epistemology and semantics.* New York: Haven Publications.

Tarski, A. 1944. The semantics conception of truth. *Philosophy and Phenomenological Research* 4, pp. 341-75, p. 354, fn. 20.

Michael Levin

A REMARK ON FIELD'S ACCOUNT OF MEANING

In "Logic, Meaning and Conceptual Role," Hartry Field suggests that a "probabilistic semantics" can provide an explication of "meaning" that is intrinsically natural and preserves our ordinary intuitions about meaning. Field also claims that his explication coheres with but improves upon Quine's "indeterminacy of translation," and shows that in a nontrivial sense logical laws hold in virtue of meaning. Systematic discussion of these last two matters is beyond the scope of the present paper. I do note in passing below some points of contact between Field's idea and Quine's; I also note in passing my qualm that the conditions on Popper functions have been so carefully contrived to yield (at least) the soundness theorem, and hence that Field has not shown that logical truths follow *nontrivially* from the meanings of the logical operators. This qualm is amplified by my intuition that, as a matter of usage, we would disqualify any translation which mapped an expression to one of our logical operators which did not satisfy the joint restrictions on probability functions and logical operators. But this is only a qualm, and I will not pursue it.

Beginning with the sentential case, Field requires that if sentences A and B have the same meaning, they must have the same referential meaning. To illustrate this requirement, suppose A is "$F(d)$" and B is "$G(e)$". Then A and B have the same referential meaning just in case the predicates "$F(x)$" and "$G(x)$" are coextensive, and "d" and "e" refer to the same object. Now, while sameness of referential meaning is clearly necessary for (intuitive) sameness of meaning, it is clearly not sufficient. But philosophers have long despaired of saying what more is required, or at least of so saying without appeal to such entities as senses and intensions, which are ontologically *de trop* and no clearer than intuitive sameness of meaning. Field suggests that the "what more" is this: A and B mean the same when they occupy the same conceptual role. More precisely, A and B occupy the same conceptual role when they confirm the same sentences to the same extent and are confirmed by the same sentences to the same extent: $(C)(P(A/C) = P(B/C))$ & $(C)(P(C/A) = P(C/B))$, where the quantified variable "C" is understood as ranging over some suitable language. This explication quickly extends to nonsentential items: Coreferential terms and coextensive predicates are synonymous if they preserve conceptual role under replacement. One could even construe "A's conceptual role" as denoting an object—perhaps $\langle \{P(A/C) : C \in L\}, \{P(C/A): C \in L\}\rangle$, for suitable language L—and then quantify over meanings in a language containing a modicum of set theory. But such reification is no part of Field's plan. Note, finally, that Field's apparatus yields no objectionable (to Quine) intersubjective synonymy notion, since $P(\_ \_ \_/---)$ is always a *personal* probability function. Moreover, as Field acknowledges in a footnote, even intrasubjective synonymy is far from firm, since a speaker's behavior may be compatible with more than one subjective probability function. Yet Field's account apparently permits more intrasubjective synonymy than Quine's reduction of synonymy to sameness of stimulus meaning. This is not altogether clear, however; it might always prove possible to trace a differential change in the conceptual roles of two erstwhile stimulus-syonymous expressions to some previous stimulation. Also, since Field is (rightly, in my view) sceptical of Quine's more specialized "inscrutability of reference" thesis, the inclusion of a reference component does not push his explication of meaning toward indeterminacy.

Field's account is intuitively attractive, falling in as it does with the pragmatist and positivist idea that the meaning or cash value of a statement is to be found by examining what would confirm or disconfirm it. As all philosophers know, the best way to find out what, if anything, an interlocutor means is to get him to commit himself on what, if anything, would be evidence for or against what he says. Similarly, we all take A = "All bachelors are neurotic" to differ in meaning from B = "All bachelors have brains in state b," and would continue to do so even if it is discovered that neurosis is uniquely correlated with b—so that "x is neurotic" and "x has a brain in state b" have the same referential meaning. This is so because we take certain kinds of social behavior as confirming A but not B. However, at least as weighty an intuition against the positivist account of meaning has been that it does insufficient justice to *mathematics*. Since, on the face of it, mathematical discourse is isolated from experience, or is at most an adjunct used in the articulation of properly empirical theories, positivists and pragmatists find themselves compelled to put very odd constructions on mathematics. And I think a version of this problem dogs Field's very sophisticated version of the pragmatist idea that the meaning of a sentence is its role in inquiry.

Consider any two provably equivalent mathematical sentences. A convenient enough pair, which I expect will be familiar to most readers, are the Axiom of Choice (AC) and the

Well-Ordering Principle (WOP). A conveniently strong form of AC says that there is a function which selects a member from every set in the universe; symbolically: $(\exists f)(x)(x \neq \phi \rightarrow f(x) \,\epsilon\, x)$ WOP says that for every set x there is a transitive, irreflexive, relation R such that every non-empty subset of x has an R-initial member. Intuitively, x is well-ordered if it is possible to arrange the members of x in such a way that every member of x is followed by a *next* member. The equivalence of AC to WOP is easy to see. First, assume AC, and pick a set x. Extract a member $f(x)$ and call this "the first member." From $x - \{f(x)\}$ extract a member $f(x - \{f(x)\})$ and call this "the second member." Proceed in this way until x is exhausted. You have well-ordered x. Now assume WOP. Define the set of ordered pairs $\{\, \langle x, \text{the first member of } x \rangle : x \text{ is a set}\,\}$. This set is the universal choice function promised by AC.

Since it is a theorem of Zermelo-Fraenkel set theory that AC $\equiv$ WOP it would seem that, for any sentence C of either ZF or one's overall background language, P(C/AC) = P(C/WOP). Moreover, since both AC and WOP are theorems of ZF we have at least that $(C)(\mathrm{P}_{ZF}(\mathrm{AC}/C) = \mathrm{P}_{ZF}(\mathrm{WOP}/C))$. Certainly, if we assume that the axioms of ZF are just about as certain as the laws of logic, we have $(C)(\mathrm{P}(\mathrm{AC}/C) = \mathrm{P}(\mathrm{WOP}/C))$. So the conceptual role played by AC is precisely that played by WOP; yet, intuitively, AC and WOP don't mean the same thing. Intuitively, they *say* quite different things. This is why the proof of their equivalence is nontrivial. In fact, there is a sense of "same conceptual role" even stronger than Field's in which AC and WOP have the same conceptual role. Consider any derivation in ZF of a theorem T in which AC is used. This derivation can be replaced by another derivation of T in which the occurrence of AC is replaced by the derivation of AC from WOP, and vice versa. In fact, all reasoning using AC can be dispensed with altogether, since anything derivable from AC can be derived *directly* from WOP, and *vice versa*.

In mathematics, where equivalences are provable, intuitively distinguishable sentences can occupy precisely the same conceptual role. So Field has not, after all, supplied a sufficient condition for "means the same," or "meaning." Much the same moral can be drawn for sameness of meaning for terms and predicates. If set S is provably identical to set S', any sentence using "S" will have the same conceptual role as the same sentence under replacement of "S" by "S'". Yet it can easily happen that "S" and "S'" are intuitively heteronymous. Thus, let "S" be "the cardinal number N" and "S'" be "the cardinality of the Nth level of the constructible hierarchy."

There are two reasons why it must not be thought that the neglected component of referential meaning can come to the rescue here. First, intuitively distinct but provably equivalent sentences can *also* have the same referential meaning. Thus, "ω is a member of some set" is equivalent in referential meaning to "ω is isomorphic to some ordinal," since it is a theorem of ZF that all and only those sets in the domain of the membership relation are isomorphic to some ordinal. This objection, however, is only a variation on the theme of provable equivalence already introduced. A deeper reason why Field would be ill-advised to fall back on referential meaning is that it is at least an open philosophical question whether the notion of "reference" has any application at all to the terms and predicates of mathematics. To put it as a dilemma: Either the notion of "reference" is vacuous, or an appeal to it in the present context involves mathematical Platonism. Just as Tarski's theory of truth is sometimes thought to express the correspondence theory of truth, so "'a' is an expression that refers" is sometimes thought to express realism about discourse in which the term "a" appears. It need not, however, just as Tarski's theory of truth need not be taken to express the correspondence theory. Just as any theory which assigns the same truth-value to "'p' is true" and "p" will satisfy Tarski's Convention T, so any theory whose language includes both "a" and a name for "a" can contain, as theorems, every instance of the Tarski reference schema:

"a" refers to a.

So if one *stipulates* that every instance of the Tarski reference schema must be true, one can (trivially) speak of the referential meaning of mathematical sentences, not in a way that involves Platonism, but also not in a way that carries one beyond the sentences themselves. If, however, reference is given more substance than is involved in merely satisfying the Tarski reference schema—and this is the line Field has taken elsewhere, as have Putnam and Boyd—then the claim that mathematical sentences have referential meaning has correspondingly more substance, so much so that commitment to Platonism is involved. (Benacerraf, for example, has argued that acceptance of a Tarskian account of truth for mathematical sentences involves Platonism.) And, despite the popularity that mathematical Platonism currently enjoys, it seems to me a very dubious doctrine. I myself would argue—although I cannot do so here—that the old Formalists were essentially right in holding that all there is to mathematics are the various formal systems, their internal deductive structures, and their interpretational relations to each other. But I don't need so strong a conclusion to make my main point:

Deployment of any strong notion of referential meaning to (say) distinguish WOP in meaning from AC would commit Field to Platonism, and no explication of meaning should be committed to one or another position on such a controversial philosophical problem.

The problem I've foisted on Field cropped up in the earliest work of proto-logical-empiricism. In the *Tractatus* Wittgenstein concluded that all tautologies mean the same thing because they all subtend the whole of logical space. In fact, two quite different tautologies could be used to make the same point I made with AC and WOP; I have concentrated on the more recondite examples because various normal form theorems can be used to maneuver (e.g.) all tautologies using the same number of distinct propositional letters into the same form. Someone could thus argue that there is no paradox in saying that all tautologies are synonymous, because at bottom all tautologies are one. But this last-ditch strategy is not evidently available for WOP and AC; the closest that one can come to transforming one into another is the mathematical derivation I outlined earlier.

A mathematician I put the problem to responded: "Why not allow WOP and AC to mean the same? Sameness of meaning is unclear anyway, and mathematicians, being extensionalists by inclination, care only that WOP and AC are provably equivalent." Tempting as such a response might be, it is not available to Field. To give such a response would be to give up the project of explicating "meaning" in a way which does justice to our ordinary intuitions about meaning. Certainly, no one can object to a *stipulated* notion of meaning—but Field promised us more, and in the preanalytic sense, AC and WOP differ in meaning. What is more, even if we decide that WOP *does* mean the same as AC, it is quite plain that *understanding* WOP is not the same as *understanding* AC. Since I take Field's project to be that of explicating "meaning" in a way that sheds light on the phenomenon of *understanding the meaning* of linguistic items, allowing AC and WOP to be synonymous because provably equivalent would leave incomplete the major part of Field's project. Finally, if one allows WOP and AC to mean the same, why not lapse completely and let *scientific,* empirically discovered identities determine synonymies? Why not say that "neurotic" and "having a brain in state b" mean the same, if it should turn out that the two are coextensive? But clearly we do draw the line here, letting our scientific discoveries determine *only* coextensiveness.

Field might try another tack: Denying that provably equivalent sentences do respond the same way to all possible evidence. There has recently appeared in the literature a reasonably well-articulated position called "mathematical empiricism," according to which empirical, even observational evidence can affect our credibility assessments of mathematical propositions. Mathematical empiricists–such as Putnam, Lakatos, Tymozcko and, implicitly perhaps, Quine–cite such phenomena as the trial-and-error methods of the great mathematicians, and the use of computers in solving the four-color problem, to show that observation, broadly but not vacuously conceived, can influence our mathematical beliefs. I do not know if Field wants any part of mathematical empiricism, but it might seem a way to rescue his analysis. But in fact it will not. Apart from the unusual cases that form the backbone of the mathematical empiricist's argument, the fact is that most mathematicians come to believe equivalences by proof, not experiment. Few mathematicians have ever altered their probability assessment of an equivalence or much else on the basis of observation. The only sort of case that springs readily to mind is a mathematician coming to doubt $A \equiv B$ because a distinguished colleague announces, without exhibiting, a counterexample. The most that can be said is this. Let O be the sentence "Machine m, which has proved itself infallible for five millenia, has announced that AC differs in truth-value from WOP." Then a reasonable probability function P will satisfy the condition $P(AC \equiv WOP/O) < P(AC \equiv AC/O) = 1$. This shows that AC and WOP differ in conceptual role for anyone whose belief structure is described by the one-place function $P(\_\ \_\ \_/O)$. But it is quite fantastic to suppose that more than a tiny minority of mathematicians have ever entertained the possibility O describes, or that their subjective probability functions admit of conditionalization with respect to O. Yet most mathematicians *already find* that AC differs in meaning from WOP. So the bare possibility of empirical mathematics, even if admitted, can offer no help to Field.

The proof-sketch I gave of the equivalence of WOP to AC tends to drive home the intuition that they differ in meaning: The proof of one involves a quite different *construction* from the proof of the other. Should we take this to suggest that Field's basic idea is right, and that what he has to do is offer a finer criterion for sameness of conceptual role than sameness of evidential function? Perhaps we should, but it is not clear in what direction Field should move. To refine sameness of conceptual role much further will lead Field to the conclusion that two sentences differ in meaning when they differ in *use*–and then he will have all the problems that attend the use of "use." It will do no good to say that AC differs in meaning from WOP because of how it is explained to the beginning mathematician, since the explanation of AC will presumably be equivalent to the explanation of WOP, and we will simply have pushed back by one step the question: Why don't two provably equivalent explanations mean the same? Similarly, it won't do (quite apart from questions of coherence with the rest of Field's program) to bring in the Gricean idea that WOP differs in meaning from AC because of what someone who utters "WOP" (as opposed to "AC") intends to get you to believe through infinitely nested recognitions of that intention. For suppose in uttering "WOP" I intend to get you to believe p (through recognition of my intention to get you to believe...), while in uttering "AC" I intend to get you to believe q. p and q here might either be something mathematical, or something to the effect that I *believe* something mathematical: both sorts of analyses have been advocated. Either way, this supposition will explain why WOP differs in meaning from AC only if we know why p differs from q: but this is our old problem come back again, since, presumably, p will be logically equivalent to q.

*I wish to thank James Bayley, Hugues Leblanc, Gilbert Harman, and my wife Margarita for their helpful comments and criticisms.

PART IV

COMPUTER MODELS
OF LANGUAGE USE

INTRODUCTION

The two essays in this section deal with computer models of "language use." The phrase "language use" is intended to demarcate quite different goals in the study of language from those ordinarily pursued by linguists, philosophers of language, and logicians. Thus Schank and Lehnert see their task as that of providing a model for how people understand actual texts and participate in actual conversations. In this vein Moyne states that the goal of computer models of language use is to provide an account of linguistic performance whereas most linguists and philosophers appear to be more interested in a theory of linguistic competence. Achieving these ends requires modelling such

Achieving these ends requires modelling such cognitive processes as parsing, inferring, memory, association, etc. To have a better idea of how this approach differs from that of the standard linguist or philosopher of language, consider as examples some of the strings and inferences for which this artificial intelligence model attempts to account. These are strings that are ruled out on transformational approaches, and inferences that would most likely be regarded as enthymematic (as incompletely stated), which are of little theoretical interest from the standpoint of theories of valid inference in logic or linguistics. Transformational accounts of linguistic competence are designed primarily to exclude ill-formed strings such as "was not" (which is not a well-formed sentence). But it is just such strings that a child uses in actual conversations in reply to a taunting "You were wrong!", and that computer models are designed to accommodate. This is accomplished by building into their models both contextual considerations and knowledge of the world. Yet another type of string that must be accounted for is an ambiguous one. Thus a computer model should disambiguate the sentence "Last night he broke the bank" which can in one context refer to breaking a piggy bank and in another to winning enough to close a gambling establishment.

As an example of the need for knowledge of the world Schank and Lehnert, and Moyne as well, want to provide a computer model of language processing which can account for inferring the sentence "John bought a sweater at a department store," from the sentence "John needs a sweater." To accomplish this they incorporate into their computer model information about the world, e.g. "He bought what he needed at a department store." (The example is a modification of one given by Schank and Lehnert.) In Schank and Lehnert's model this component is called "world knowledge," and in Moyne's description of his model it comprises the bulk of his "data base." The goal of these authors is to account for the inferences that people actually make and that computers can model by processing the relevant sentences.

In their essay Schank and Lehnert include critiques of standard transformational grammars and classical first-order logical languages as adequate models for achieving their own goals. Moyne, somewhat more circumspect, suggests that the difference of goals in providing a theory of performance rather than a theory of competence, makes the two approaches somewhat non-comparable.

A constraint on adequate computer models of language use is the need to develop computer programs that successfully realize the goals set. Thus Schank and Lehnert and Moyne include in their essays descriptions of functioning computer programs that process linguistic material such as the ambiguities and ill-formed strings people understand and use in conversations and inferences.

Alex Orenstein

Roger Schank and Wendy Lehnert

UNDERSTANDING AND
REPRESENTATION OF TEXT

When people read text or participate in conversation, a wide range of cognitive processes go into action. In order to study these processes, we are developing process models of natural language comprehension. These models have been implemented in various computer programs which read text and demonstrate their understanding by answering questions and producing summaries, translations into other languages, and paraphrases more detailed than the original text. This artificial intelligence approach to the study of language is producing theories of language and human memory organization which depart significantly from the theories of linguistics and cognitive psychology.

I. *Understanding in Context*

Our work is conducted under the assumption that all language, both written or spoken, is understood in context. Sentences within text are understood with reference to preceding sentences, and utterances are understood in terms of previous conversation, or what is known about the setting for that conversation. Contextual information is used in a number of ways. Context is needed to establish word senses, recognize causalities, generate inferences, and maintain conversational continuity.

More important, context is used to force an understander to miss ambiguities and use only the intended meaning of a sentence. This approach is counter to more formal models of language that seek to preserve and explain ambiguity. We seek, as do people, to avoid it and come up with the meaning intended by the speaker. As an example of this consider the following:

> *John hated to resort to his favorite piggy bank for the money he needed. But last night he broke the bank. John had never been very lucky at the casino. But last night he broke the bank.*

In building cognitive theories of language processing it is important to understand that sentences are not understood in isolation. When people read or hear sentences, they try to integrate the meaning of each new sentence into a unified structure. One way that sentences can be tied together is by establishing causal relationships.

John burned his hand because he forgot the stove was on.

John touched the stove inadvertently.

It is the causal relationships expressed in these sentences that make them virtual paraphrases of each other. We think of them as paraphrases because they refer to the same external events. Thus, our model of language is concerned with knowledge of the external world as much as it is with language.

John pulled into a gas station. The service attendant filled his tank and then he left.

In order to make sense of this we have to fill in a lot of information which is not explicitly stated. We must infer that John is driving a car. We must also infer that "his tank," refers to the gas tank of the car, and we assume that the gas tank was filled with gasoline. We also assume that it was John who left, not the service attendant. None of this information is explicit in the sentences; these are inferences which the reader makes in the process of understanding the sentences. If no such inferences were made, the sentences would not be understood. They would read something like this:

John slogged into a bath house. The manager filled his pockets and then he left.

The first story is understood without difficulty because the context of a gas station gives the information needed to make sense of what follows. In the second story, the context of a bath house does not facilitate making inferences about what the manager filled the pockets with, whose pockets were filled, or who left. The ability to make appropriate inferences is at the heart of language comprehension. We will return to the problem of inference-generation shortly.

A final use of context occurs in conversation, where rules of conversational continuity must be applied to previous dialogue in order to understand what is being said:

A: Did John get his PhD?
B: No.
A: Who did?
B: Nobody got John's PhD.

The last response is funny because it violates a rule of conversational continuity. This response answers the question "Who got John's Phd?" But an appropriate response would have addressed the question, "Who got their Phd?" Incomplete questions are common in actual dialogue and people rarely have difficulty interpreting them correctly. The processes which interpret incomplete questions depend upon previous dialogue and, therefore, rely on contextual information.

II. Using World Knowledge to Understand

In the last section we observed how understanding is sensitive to the context surrounding a sentence. In this section we will examine the actual processes of understanding more closely. Understanding a sentence requires conceptual knowledge of the entities and actions referenced. People have a great deal of mundane knowledge about the world which is used by the processes enabling us to understand language. Consider the following story:

> John needed a sweater. He went to a department store and asked a salesgirl for help. She showed him a number of sweaters. He found one which he liked and asked her how much it cost. It was $30. He asked her to gift wrap it.

After reading this story, it is easy to answer the following questions:

Q1: What did John want to buy at the department store?

A1: A sweater.

Q2: Who told him the price of the sweater?

A2: The salesgirl.

Q3: Did John buy the sweater?

A3: Yes.

Q4: How did he pay for it?

A4: I don't know—either by cash or check or credit care.

Q5: Was the sweater for John?

A5: Probably not.

Each of these questions asks for information which had to be inferred from the story. Inferences of this sort are made at the time of understanding (rather than at the time of question-answering). Furthermore, after hearing or reading a story, people have difficulty differentiating what was explicitly mentioned from what they inferred (Bransford & Franks, 1971).

Inferences are made on the basis of world knowledge. In this case knowledge was needed about shopping in department stores. We know that people who need certain items can go to a department store and buy what they need. Salesgirls are there to assist you and answer questions, and payment can be by check, credit card, or cash. If the item purchased is a gift for someone else, you can ask to have it gift-wrapped. The inferences needed to answer Q1-5 could not have been made without this very specific knowledge about department stores.

General world knowledge is used in natural language processing in order to make inferences and recognize causal connections. It is therefore crucial to develop theories describing how general knowledge about the world is stored in memory and accessed. In the next section we will briefly outline a theory of memory organization.

III. Knowledge Structures:
The Organization of Information in Memory

A theory of natural language processing which attempts to account for human inference processes must be concerned with the ways knowledge in permanent memory is applied during understanding. What kind of knowledge is used to understand natural language? How is this knowledge encoded and organized in memory? What are the processes which access permanent memory? Once knowledge is accessed, how is it used? These are critical questions which lead us to formulate theories of memory representation and memory organization.

The theory of memory organization which we are developing is a theory of knowledge structures. A knowledge structure is a representational device in memory which is used to encode a particular kind of knowledge. Two knowledge structures which we have developed in some detail are scripts and plans (Schank & Abelson, 1977).

Scripts and plans are theoretical structures which we are proposing as models of human memory organization. A vast amount of mundane world knowledge appears to be encoded in the form of scripts and plans. These constructs are being exploited as a means of organizing world knowledge in computers. Scripts are memory units which contain information about situations or activities frequently encountered. Scripts describe the expectations involved in situations such as going to a restaurant, shopping in a grocery store, or stopping at a gas station. People acquire most scripts through experience and use them both operationally in actually going to a restaurant) and cognitively (in understanding stories about restaurants). When we go to a restaurant, we have certain expectations about finding a table, ordering, being served, eating, getting a check, paying the check, etc. If we hear that John went to a restaurant and ordered a hamburger, we infer that he ate a hamburger unless we hear something to the contrary. While scriptal knowledge must vary from person to person according to variations in experience, there are quite a few standard scripts which are held in common as a cultural norm. Most people have the same restaurant script since restaurants are highly standardized.

The scripts which are important for natural language processing are those which a large population holds in common. Whenever a script is shared by people, it can be referenced very efficiently. "I went to a restaurant last night," conveys the events of the entire restaurant script to anyone who has that script.

Plans are used when scripts do not apply or fail to contain sufficient information. While scripts are tightly bound to well-specified situations, the same plan can be invoked in a variety of settings. For example, suppose you are trying to find a friend's house in San Francisco and you have the address but you've never been there before. There is clearly no script for this situation (since it is a novel situation) but you nevertheless know what sorts of things to do. You might invoke a plan which says to wander randomly until you hit the right street, but a better plan would entail knowledge acquisition. You need to find out where the street is. So you consult appropriate knowledge sources. If you have a map you look at it. If you don't have a map you might go about finding one, or you may opt for another knowledge source and try asking people if they can tell you. If you've asked ten people to no avail you might give up attempting to find it yourself and call your friend so he can tell you where he is or perhaps come and rescue you. The principles involved in this process are very general (by nature). The same planning structures could be used to find a particular office in the Pentagon, or to find a book in the library (without the possibility of being rescued by the book). Plans are extremely general procedures which are adaptable to a number of situations and are used when there is no standard routine to follow.

The processes which facilitate understanding a natural language use scripts and plans to generate expectations about what is likely to happen next. These knowledge structures are used as a foundation for predictive understanding. When we have a lot of relevant knowledge about a situation, we can make extensive predictions about what is liable to happen next. If we hear or read about such a situation, these predictions are used to generate inferences. Shared knowledge allows people to communicate information in natural language by implicit inference.

IV. Conceptual Representation of Information

We have outlined, roughly, the general memory structures in which mundane knowledge of the world can be stored. Now we will describe the representational system which is used to encode information within a knowledge structure. This system of conceptual representation is designed to capture the meaning of sentences. Conceptual meaning is independent of any particular natural language and does not rely on lexical entities.

Conceptual Dependency is a representational system that encodes the meaning of sentences by decomposition into eleven primitive actions (Schank, 1975). When two sentences are identical in meaning, the Conceptual Dependency representations for those sentences are identical. For example, "John kicked the ball," and "John hit the ball with his foot," will have identical Conceptual Dependency representations:

$$
\text{JOHN} <=> \text{PTRANS} <- \text{BALL} <- \begin{array}{l} -> \text{UNSPEC}_1 \\ \quad\quad\text{I} \\ \quad\quad\quad\quad\quad < \\ -< \text{UNSPEC}_2 \end{array}
$$

$$
\lceil\ -\ -\ -\ -\ -\ -\ \rceil
$$
$$
|\ \text{JOHN} <=> \text{MOVE} <- \text{FOOT}\ |
$$
$$
\lfloor\ -\ -\ -\ -\ -\ -\ \rfloor
$$

Cognitive memory processes operate on the meaning of sentences, not on the lexical expression of that meaning. It follows that simulations of human cognition must rely on conceptual representations of information. Conceptual Dependency facilitates necessary recognition processes on this level of conceptual representation. For example, if memory contains an encoding for "John bought a book from Mary," then the processes which access memory should be able to answer "Did Mary sell John a book?" on the basis of that encoding. This sort of recognition is trivial when "John bought a book from Mary," and "Mary sold John a book," have similar conceptual representations. In Conceptual Dependency these statements have nearly identical representations, as do other similar sentences:

John traded Mary a pen for a book.

JOHN < = > ATRANS ← PEN ← [→ MARY / → JOHN]

⇑ ⇓

MARY < = > ATRANS ← BOOK ← [→ JOHN / → MARY]

John gave Mary a pen in exchange for a book.

JOHN < = > ATRANS ← PEN ← [→ MARY / → JOHN]

⇑ ⇓

MARY < = > ATRANS ← BOOK ← [→ JOHN / → MARY]

Conceptual Dependency theory is not dependent on the particular set of primitives chosen, or the number of primitives used (although the strength of a given representational system is lost if the set of primitives used is too large). The primitive acts we use define one set of primitives which have proven to be effective in the knowledge domain of general mundane world knowledge. A set of seven object primitives have been proposed to augment the primitive acts of Conceptual Dependency (Lehnert, 1977). In the same way that primitive acts enable processes to recognize when two verbs describe conceptually identical events (such as kicking a ball and hitting a ball with your foot), object primitives make it easy to recognize conceptual similarities and differences between two objects. For example, a slot machine and a gum ball machine are similar insofar as they both take in coins, but they are dissimilar in terms of the objects they produce in return.

Decomposition allows us to recognize when events fulfill the expectations of predictive understanding processes. For example, in the restaurant script, we expect the waiter/waitress to bring the patron his meal. When this event is encoded in Conceptual Dependency, it is represented as a PTRANS. If we hear that a waitress carried the food to the table on roller skates, if she skipped to the table, shuffled to the table, or slinked to the table, we want to recognize all of these descriptions as events which match the scriptal expectation of the patron being served. Since all of these verbs are represented by a decomposition into PTRANS, this recognition task is easy.

Similarly, object primitives enable us to recognize when an object is appropriate for a conceptual prediction. For example, in the grocery store script, we expect the customer to take a shopping cart or basket when he enters the store. But if he uses a cardboard box, plastic bag or wicker basket instead, some recognition process must be able to understand that these are acceptable substitutions for a shopping cart or basket. This recognition is easy when objects are described by a decomposition into object primitives. Conceptually, we expect the customer to use any container that does not obscure its contents and which can be carried, pushed, or pulled. The grocery store script can describe such an object very easily in terms of object primitives. This object primitive description can be used to understand that a plastic bag is acceptable (it fulfills the conceptual requirements) but a pocket is not acceptable (it obscures its contents). If we hear that John went into a grocery store and put a candy bar in his pocket, we understand that John is not acting according to the grocery store script; higher memory processes then take over to understand that John is probably trying to steal the candy bar.

In prediction-based understanding systems, a representational scheme must encode information in a way which facilitates recognition processes. Recognition of conceptual information cannot be achieved by a system which is essentially lexical or one which does not reflect the language-independent meaning of verbs and nouns. Decomposition into primitives provides a way of encoding conceptual information crucial to the inference processes needed for language comprehension.

When text is processed, sentences are first parsed into Conceptual Dependency representations. These conceptualizations are then processed by script and plan appliers which generate a story representation on the level of knowledge structures. When a story can be understood in terms of scripts and plans, the Conceptual Dependency level of representation encodes a chronology of events while the knowledge structure level of representation encodes information about motives and intentionality. For example, consider the story:

John needed money. He got a gun and walked to the liquor store.

Full comprehension of this story will entail the following inferences:

    (1)   John wanted to get some money.

    (2)   John knew there was money in the liquor store.

    (3)   John intended to threaten the storekeeper with the gun in order to gain control of the store's money.

These inferences would be made on the basis of plans and incorporated in the story representation:

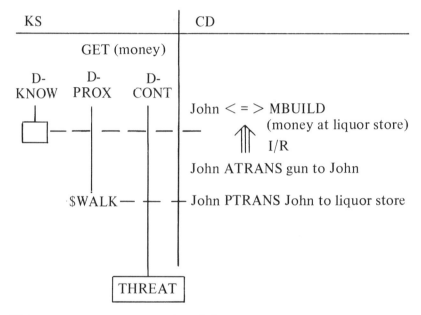

This representation says that John's goal was to acquire money by executing the GET plan box. This plan box decomposes into three delta-acts: delta-know, delta-proximity and delta-control (Schank & Abelson, 1975). That is in order to get something, you must know where it is, you must get to it, and you must take control of it. John knew there was money at the liquor store, he went to it by walking, and he intended to gain control of it by executing a THREATEN plan box. Plans exist as intentions on the part of the planner and as the guiding impetus for actions taken by the planner. Since the success or failure of plans influence subsequent plans and events in a story, it should be clear that there must be links between the events at the CD level and scripts and plans at the knowledge structure level.

V. Computer Programs That Understand Text

Our theories of knowledge structures and conceptual representation have been implemented in various computer programs which read English text and demonstrate their understanding by answering questions or providing summaries. Four of these programs will be described here: SAM, FRUMP, PAM, and POLITICS. Each of these programs generates a memory representation as it reads. After the processing of input text is completed, this memory representation is used by all subsequent processes (like question-answering or paraphrasing). No record of the lexical input text is retained by the system. In the following examples, the input stories given here are actual computer input. During Q/A sessions, English questions are input as they appear here, and all output summaries or answers are generated in English by the computer as shown.

SAM (Script Applier Mechanism) implements theories of script application to understand stories about stereotypic events (Schank et al. 1975, Lehnert 1975, Cullingford 1975, 1976, 1977). Once SAM has read a story, it can answer questions, summarize the story, produce a paraphrase of the story, or translate the story into Spanish, Dutch, Russian, or Chinese. The two stories given below are stories which have been input to SAM. The question answering sessions consist of questions input to SAM and answers that SAM returned:

STORY 1

John went to New York by bus. On the bus he talked to an old lady. When he left the bus, he thanked the driver. He took the subway to Leone's. On the subway his pocket was picked. He got off the train and entered Leone's. He had some lasagna. When the check came, he discovered he couldn't pay. The management told him he would have to wash dishes. When he left, he caught a bus to New Haven.

Q1: Why did John go to New York?
A1: BECAUSE JOHN WANTED TO GO TO LEONE'S.
Q2: How did John get to Leone's?
A2: JOHN TOOK A BUS TO NEW YORK AND THEN HE TOOK THE SUBWAY TO LEONE'S.
Q3: Did anything unusual happen on the bus?
A3: I DON'T REMEMBER ANYTHING.
Q4: Did anything unusual happen on the subway?
A4: A THIEF PICKED JOHN'S POCKET.
Q5: What did John order?
A5: JOHN ORDERED LASAGNA.

Q6: Did anything unusual happen at the restaurant?
A6: JOHN DISCOVERED THAT HE COULDN'T PAY THE CHECK AND SO HE HAD TO WASH DISHES.
Q7: Why couldn't John pay the check?
A7: BECAUSE JOHN DID NOT HAVE ANY MONEY.
Q8: Why didn't John have any money?
A8: BECAUSE A THIEF PICKED JOHN'S POCKET.
Q9: How did John get back to New Haven?
A9: JOHN WENT FROM LEONE'S BY SUBWAY AND THEN HE WENT TO NEW HAVEN BY BUS.
Q10: How was John able to take the bus to New Haven?
A10: PROBABLY JOHN HAD A TICKET.

STORY 2

A New Jersey man was killed Friday evening when the car he was riding swerved off Route 69 and struck a tree. David Hall, 27, was pronounced dead at the scene by Dr. Dana Blauchard, medical examiner. Frank Miller, 16, of 593 Foxon Road, operator of the vehicle, was taken by Flanagan Ambulance to Yale-New Haven Hospital. He was treated and released. The Branford Fire Department extricated the passenger from the vehicle. No charges were made. Patrolman Robert Onofrio is continuing the investigation.

Q1: Was anyone killed?
A1: YES, DAVID HALL DIED.
Q2: Was anyone hurt?
A2: YES, FRANK MILLER WAS SLIGHTLY INJURED.
Q3: Why was Frank Miller hurt?
A3: BECAUSE THE AUTOMOBILE HIT A TREE.
Q4: Did Frank Miller go to the hospital?
A4: YES, HE WAS IN YALE-NEW HAVEN.
Q5: How did Frank Miller get to the hospital?
A5: AN AMBULANCE TOOK HIM TO YALE-NEW HAVEN.

FRUMP (Fast Reading and Understanding Memory Program) is a program which skims newspaper stories (DeJong, 1977). FRUMP is a script-based system but it does not process every sentence as thoroughly as SAM does. FRUMP is interested in specific things, and it ignores information which is not relevant to its expectations. FRUMP summarizes articles in English, Russian, and Spanish.

STORY 3

1/12 Chihuahua, Mexico,—Officials here said today that the failure of an excursion train engineer to heed a stop signal was responsible for the collision with a freight train on Sunday that killed nearly a score of persons in Mexico, including two Americans.

The district attorney's office said two other Americans had been injured in the collision near the Barranca del Cobre in the Sierra Madre.

All the dead were Mexicans except the two Americans and two Britons. Most of those aboard were Mexican travel agents.

The Americans were identified as Mart Mortello of New York and Martin Ward whose hometown was still not available. The district attorney's office said the two injured Americans were Paul Joseph Callsen and Mary Callsen, both of New York.

FRUMP SUMMARY (English)
12 PEOPLE WERE KILLED AND 45 WERE INJURED WHEN A TRAIN CRASHED INTO A TRAIN IN MEXICO. THE ENGINEER WAS RESPONSIBLE FOR THE ACCIDENT.

FRUMP SUMMARY (Russian)
V ZHELEZNODOROZHNOI KATASTROFE V MEKSIKE 12 CHELOVEK BYLO UBITO I 45 RANENO. OTVETSTVENNOST ZA KATASTROFU VOZLOZHENA NA MASHINISTA.

FRUMP SUMMARY (Spanish)
HUBO 12 MUERTOS Y 45 HERIDOS CUANDO UN FERROCARRIL CHOCO CONTRA UN FERRO-CARRIL EN MEXICO. EL INGENEIRO FUE CULPABLE POR CAUSAR EL ACCIDENTE.

PAM (Plan Applier Mechanism) is a story understanding system which implements theories of plan application (Wilensky, 1976). PAM can paraphrase the stories it reads and answer questions.

STORY 4

John loved Mary but she didn't want to marry him. One day, a dragon stole Mary from the castle. John got on top of his horse and killed the dragon. Mary agreed to marry him. They lived happily ever after.

PARAPHRASE

JOHN WAS IN LOVE WITH MARY. SHE DID NOT WANT TO MARRY HIM. A DRAGON TOOK HER

FROM A CASTLE. HE LEARNED THAT THE DRAGON HAD TAKEN HER FROM THE CASTLE. HE MOUNTED A HORSE. IT TOOK HIM TO HER. HE KILLED THE DRAGON. SHE WAS INDEBTED TO HIM. SHE TOLD HIM SHE WAS GOING TO MARRY HIM. HE MARRIED HER. HE AND SHE WERE HAPPY THEREAFTER.

STORY 5

John disliked his job as a bank janitor. One day, a thief tried to rob the bank. John jumped on the thief and knocked him out. The bank president made John the bank guard. John enjoyed his new job.

Q1: Why did John knock the thief out?

A1: BECAUSE HE WANTED THE THIEF NOT TO HAVE THE BANK'S MONEY.

Q2: Why did the bank president make John the bank guard?

A2: BECAUSE THE BANK WAS INDEBTED TO JOHN.

POLITICS is a script-based system which accesses scripts about political situations in order to understand (Carbonell, 1977). This program can interpret situations according to a number of different political philosophies. When the same input text is interpreted by different ideologies, questions about the text will be answered differently according to the belief systems within those ideologies.

INPUT TEXT

The United States Congress voted to fund the Trident submarine project.

Q/A SESSION AFTER A RIGHT WING INTERPRETATION.

Q1: What did the U.S. Congress do this for?

A1: THE UNITED STATES CONGRESS WANTS THE UNITED STATES ARMED FORCES TO BE STRONGER.

Q2: Why should the U.S. be stronger?

A2: THE UNITED STATES ARMED FORCES SHOULD BE STRONG TO STOP COMMUNIST EXPANSION.

Q3: What should the U.S. do if Russia builds submarines?

A3: THE UNITED STATES SHOULD BUILD MORE SUBMARINES.

Q/A SESSION AFTER A LEFT WING INTER-
PRETATION:

Q1: What did the U.S. Congress do this for?

A1: THE UNITED STATES CONGRESS FEARED
FALLING BEHIND IN THE ARMS RACE.

Q2: What will Russia do next?

A2: RUSSIA WILL PROBABLY BUILD MORE
WEAPONS.

Q3: What should the U.S. do if Russia builds submarines?

A3: THE UNITED STATES SHOULD NEGOTIATE
WITH RUSSIA TO STOP THE ARMS RACE.

VI. Conclusions

The research presented here is concerned with the cognitive processes people use when understanding natural language. The approach taken here and the theoretical results we have obtained are very different from theories of linguistics. We will highlight some of these distinctions by contrasting our theories with the theory of transformational grammar as a process model of language, and the theory of first-order predicate calculus as a representational system.

Transformational Grammar

Transformational grammar (TG) claims to be a competence model of language. Although it is generally presented as a model of generation, its advocates often confuse generation with understanding as if these processes were inverse functions of each other. This confusion makes it very difficult to consider TG as a serious process model. But in spite of this fuzziness, it is clear that the task orientation behind TG is at the heart of its problems.

Chomsky states that the goal of TG is to distinguish the grammatical sentences of a language from the ungrammatical (Chomsky, 1965). The term "grammatical" is intended to refer to syntactic acceptability, not semantic acceptability. Some attempts were made to extend the TG model so that sensical sentences could be distinguished from the non-sensical (Katz & Fodor, 1964), but these extensions did not produce viable theories of semantic processing.

The task of distinguishing grammatical sentences from ungrammatical sentences is not a process central to human understanding and generation of language. People are perfectly capable of understanding and producing ungrammatical utterances. Since we are interested in modeling people, we would be very happy to create models which can be equally insensitive to rules of grammar.

Even if this task were important to a model of human language processing, it is clearly not sufficient. TG is not concerned with processes of inference, memory representation, or causal connectivity. In short, TG is not concerned with comprehension. While one might argue that the TG model could be extended to a more comprehensive model of human language processing, this is not a problem which linguists consider to be linguistics. TG was never intended to evolve into a model of human cognitive processes. Founded on the premises of the performance/competence distinction, TG attempts to isolate a formal description of language from the functional aspect of language as people use it. This separation has lead linguistics into the practice of pseudo-mathematics, and away from the study of language as a human communication device.

Predicate Calculus

While TG may be characterized as a theory that is wrongly motivated, the use of first-order predicate calculus as a representational system is an attempt to use mathematical logic for a problem which requires a process model approach. Predicate calculus is not suitable as a conceptual representation for a number of reasons. One major problem centers around the mathematical notion of truth and a resulting preoccupation with the use of propositions and truth values.

Predicate calculus forces us to think in terms of logical deduction where propositions are either true or false. This foundation is not very useful for theories of inference. An inference is an assumption which might be wrong. A deduction is an assumption which must be right. Trying to adopt the notion of a mathematical deduction to fit the requirements of inference generation is like forcing round pegs into square holes. Inference generation is not theorem proving.

Predicate calculus is also unsuitable because it results in representational systems which are essentially lexical. A lexical representation does not facilitate processes of recognition. For example, suppose a system is told that Shakespeare wrote Hamlet, and this is represented as [WROTE (SHAKESPEARE HAMLET)]. Now suppose we ask "Who was the author of Hamlet? If this question is represented as [AUTHOR-OF (*?* HAMLET)], the system will need some transformational rule to see that it has the information needed to answer the question. If a set of transformations were proposed which operated on lexical entities like WROTE and AUTHOR-OF, these transformations would have to effectively encode every conceivable relationship between all word pairs. If a new word were added to the vocabulary, transformations would have to be added relating the new word to every other word of the vocabulary. That is, the complexity of 'learning' a new word would grow linearly with the size of the vocabulary: the more the system knew, the harder it would be to learn more.

Even if a system of lexical transformations were found (no one has seriously tried to do this), the resulting system would become too cumbersome to function efficiently with any vocabulary of realistic size. Just as it would become harder to learn as vocabulary increased, it would also become harder to process simple sentences since more and more rules would have to be checked for possible application. This does not sound like a promising theory of language processing. The trouble with lexical meaning representations is that there is no understanding of the meaning behind a word. Processes of inference must operate on the level of conceptual content, not lexical manipulations.

A theory which claims to describe how people understand text or participate in conversation must describe cognitive processes. Theories of parsing, inference, remembering, forgetting, and association are all issues which must be studied in terms of process models. Artificial intelligence provides a paradigm in which theories of memory representation, causal connectivity, and memory structure can be tested and evaluated. From this perspective it has become apparent that language cannot be studied without regard for theories of human memory, knowledge, and cognition.

REFERENCES

Bransford, J. D. and Franks, J. J. 1971. The abstraction of linguistic ideas. *Cognitive psychology.* vol 2: pp. 331-350.

Carbonell, J. 1977. Ideological belief system simulation. Department of computer science: Yale University (Submitted to the Fifth International Joint Conference on Artificial Intelligence)

Chomsky, N. 1965. *Aspects of the theory of syntax.* Cambridge: MIT Press.

Cullingford, R. E. 1975. An approach to the representation of mundane world knowledge: the generation and management of situational scripts. *American Journal of Computational Linguistics.* Microfiche #44.

. . . . 1976. The uses of world knowledge in text understanding. *Proceedings of the Sixth International Conference on Computational Linguistics:* Ottawa.

. . . . 1977. Organizing world knowledge for story understanding by computer. Yale: Ph.D. thesis.

Dejong, G. 1977. Skimming newspaper stories by computer. New Haven: Yale Dept. of Computer Science.

Katz, J. and Fodor, J. 1964. The structure of a semantic theory. In *The Structure of Language,* eds. Fodor and Katz. Englewood Cliffs: Prentice Hall.

Lehnert, W. 1975. What makes SAM run? Script-based techniques for question answering. *Proceedings for Theoretical Issues in Natural Language Processing.* Cambridge.

.... 1977. The process of question answering. Yale: Ph.D. thesis.

Schank, R. C. 1975. *Conceptual information processing.* Amsterdam: North Holland.

Schank, R. C. and Abelson, R. P. 1975. Scripts, plans and knowledge. *Proceedings of the Fourth International Joint Conference on Artificial Intelligence:* Tbilisi.

Schank, R. C. and Abelson, R. P. 1977. *Scripts, plans, goals and understanding.* Lawrence Erlbaum Associates.

Schank, R. C. and Yale A. I. Project. 1975. SAM–A story understander. Research Report #43. Yale.

Wilensky, R. 1976. Using plans to understand natural language. *Proceedings of the Annual Conference of the ACM.* Texas.

J. A. Moyne

COMPREHENSION AND REPRESENTATION
OF KNOWLEDGE

An advantage of developing computer models for theories of natural language is that it compels the researcher to be precise and pay attention to many details which are often overlooked by theoretical linguists. This necessity for precision and completeness for computer implementation helps to focus on the outstanding problems in linguistic theory. The model builder, however, has to resort sometimes to ad hoc solutions in order to make the model work. Nevertheless, if the model helps to solve some problems, it would have served its purpose.

In this paper, we will discuss some aspects of a computational model for linguistic performance. The theory of performance or language use is contrasted with competence. Some of the models constructed by the author,[1] and others in the past, for communication with computers in natural languages have been based on the theory of competence and they have proved to be inadequate in some ways. Perhaps the most serious flaws in these models have resulted from posing them as models of man-machine communication with implicit or explicit claims for their generalization for immediate practical applications rather than tools of linguistic research. No such claims should be attributed to the proposal discussed in this paper. Furthermore, we will not even be concerned with the entire process of performance, but rather with some aspects of comprehension or language understanding, leaving out all considerations of production.

We have used the term *simple-English* in Moyne (1977) to refer to a special class of languages for man-machine communication. The notions about simple-English can be further formalized and worked into a model for performance. Let us assume a wellformedness relation R that binds a language L and a data base D. The data base can be regarded as a collection of information entities or the universe within which a language works or is perceptible. We can represent this relation as $R(L, D)$. The idea is that, given some system S and a data base D, there exists a language L such that the sentences (or utterances) of L are well-formed and can be interpreted only in the context of D. A corollary of this is that there are sentences of L which are not well-formed and not interpretable in the context of another data base D'. *Simple-English* is a generic name for the class of languages $= \{L_1, L_2, ..., L_n\}$ which has this relationship with a class of data bases $= \{D_1, D_2 ..., D_m\}$. Communication C for a system S could then be defined as $C = R (L_i, D_j)$.

We can now consider a performance model M as a virtual machine (e.g. a computer with its program or a simulated computer) with a virtual memory partitioned into n *pages*. We assume that computations can be carried simultaneously and independently in a number of pages. Other pages can be used as short-term and long-term memories for storage. Theoretically M is neutral with respect to a speaker or listener, but as a convenient computer model we will assume it to be a listener or acceptor model and its input to be written strings rather than utterances. What are the characteristics of M and how does it work? To start with, there must be some mechanism (grammar) for language analysis and understanding. It is well known that the grammar for performance is not identical with the grammar for competence. For performance we can impose the wellformedness condition stated above. Thus, there must be a language associated with each data base. That doesn't mean that if we have n data bases, we must necessarily have n distinct grammars describing n languages for communication with these data bases. The common features of all these languages can be factored into one component, but this component must then be augmented with specific rules and operations for each data base. For example, one problem for English that must be resolved in the context of each data base is the prevalence of ambiguities in many English sentences. [2]

It is assumed that in performance the analysis of utterances is not as uniform and complete as would be in a model of competence. In our model, input statements are received by M and are processed by methods to be described below. As soon as the input string is understood, which may be before the completion of the reading of the string and its analysis, the processing stops and the processing pages are cleared. Some results may, however, be stored in the background memory. This is, of course, in keeping with the psychological reality of perception. We often understand an utterance before we receive the whold signal. Furthermore, in performance a signal is not always a well-formed sentence in the sense of competence. Speakers make false starts, utter erroneous and incomplete sentences, make gestures, etc., the sum total of which is a continuous multi-level medium of communication. In our model, for practical reasons, we have to assume discrete and linear input strings which we will call *statements* to avoid confusion with the well-formed sentences of the competence model. Another general assumption is that complex statements are first reduced to kernel statements ("simple English") which are then processed for comprehension. However, the process of segmentation and kernel analysis is not so much based on syntactic (phrase structure) rules as is the case for competence models. Judging from what we know generally about comprehension, a performance model must depend on the characteristics and features of individual words and their association or co-occurrences, in the sense of Zellig Harris (1957).

Returning to our model, a statement received by M is first processed by a preprocessor which contains a lexicon including lexical rules and operations. The preprocessor partitions a statement S into a set of components $\{x_1, x_2, ..., x_n\}$ where each x_i may in turn be partitioned into subcomponents

$\{ x_{i_1}, x_{i_2}, ..., x_{i_m} \}$ such that at the level of x_i the processing is not completed until the processing of all its x_{i_j} subcomponents have been completed. Let us call this requirement the *completion condition* for reference purposes. This arrangement provides for the parallel processing of a number of components; yet it can preserve the hierarchical levels which are often needed in language analysis. Potentially all x_i can be processed simultaneously, but because of the completion condition and other delay factors, the processing of all x_i does not necessarily begin and end at the same time. The entire operation and the processing within each page is supervised and coordinated by a management procedure or operating system. So far, the model looks something like the sketch in Fig. 1. Obviously this figure is not the whole picture. What are the criteria for partitioning a statement into its components and subcomponents, and what is the nature of the processors that operate within each memory page of M? To answer these questions, we must add some details to our model M. We can presume the arrangement and working of the various components and subcomponents of the model in Fig. 1 to be analogous to a network of neurons where each node

INPUT

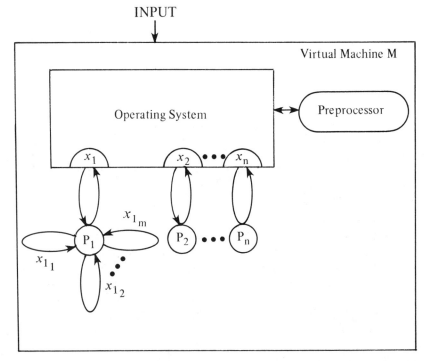

Fig. 1 A general sketch of the operations in M

n_i is provided with a threshold value θ_i, and each node will only fire a pulse or transmit data to the next node (level) when the value of the accumulation of the input pulses has reached the threshold value of that node. Fig. 2 can be regarded as a gross graphic representation of the grammatical apparatus for performance. An utterance is divided into a number of components and subcomponents for parallel processing. Notice that the processing of data in each processor (represented as x_i in Fig. 2) is dependent on three sources: The input data from the pre-processor/lexicon, the input data from the subcomponents x_{ij}, and the grammatical inferences, including predictions and probability factors. It is because of the last source that a processor may reach its threshold and transmit data to the next level prior to the completion of the data from the other two sources. In Fig. 2 the data from these multi-processors are transmitted along the g_i arcs to a processor node labeled *Perceptor*. This processor, in addition to its intrinsic grammatical apparatus, has devices for deriving grammatical inferences and predictions, applying probability factors, error correction, and input from external knowledge. The latter is the universe of human knowledge which plays a crucial role in language use and understanding. This also is an important source for understanding incomplete utterances and other signals which are not strictly "grammatical" by the standards of competence. The external knowledge for our model is comprised of the data bases that we have mentioned above. The output of this device is the semantic interpretation of the input statement.

This is not the place to go into more technical details of such devices.[3] In brief, we believe that the grammar for perception is a pattern grammar, and the model of understanding is a stochastic pattern recognition device augmented with the other components sketched in Fig. 2. On the basis of certain *keywords* and *keyphrases* such a recognizer for English, for example, can construct kernel sentences which are simple English sentences (now using the term *simple English* in its normal sense). Constructions such as noun phrases, prepositional phrases, and other syntactic units are recognized as a whole or as structured lexical units, rather than by the usual analytic/synthetic methods proposed for the competence model. This view simply carries the "lexicalist hypothesis" in linguistic theory one step further.[4] If idioms are lexical units and nominal constructions can be explained in terms of lexical operations (rather than transformations), so can these other constructions, at least in performance.

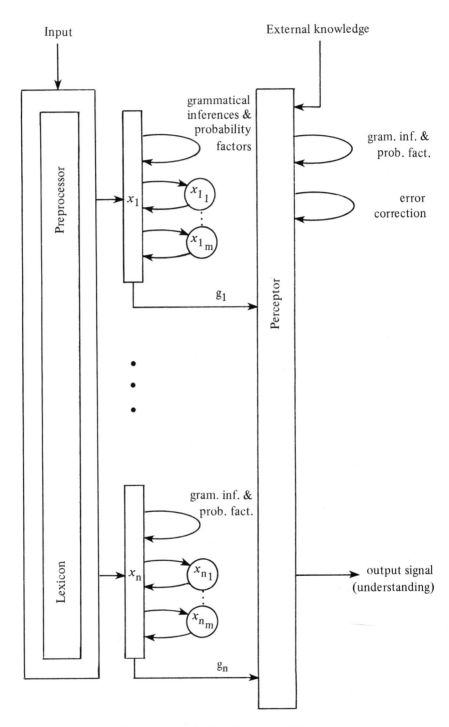

Fig. 2. Some additional details of M

It is interesting to note, in passing, that a number of early researchers who tried to provide for communication in English with computers used a keyword recognition approach. This approach was later abandoned in the face of criticisms that it was "unscientific" and was not based on proper linguistic analysis. It seems now that we can return to that approach with a proper formalization of the keyword analysis and with the addition of the necessary apparatus to take a realistic view of language use.

Notions about pattern recognition and kernel sentences are well known. The idea of pattern recognition in language perception was noted in a report by Chomsky and Miller (1957) and Harris postulated in 1957 that there were only seven kernel constructions for English with a few additional minor constructions and other elements. String transformations in Harris' theory can apply to any English sentence to produce the kernels. More recently, Chomsky states in *Aspects* that kernel structures play a distinctive and crucial role in language use.

For our model we can assume a limited number of "simple-English" structures constructed as receptor grids. A suitable pattern recognition device would select patterns from an input signal and fit them into appropriate grids; these are then passed on to the processor components in Fig. 2 for processing.

Finally, in Fig. 3 we give an example of an ambiguous sentence processed by a model currently under construction. The data base for this model is the telephone directory of Queens College with some additional data such as home addresses added to each entry. The following input sentence has the two readings (interpretations) listed below:

LIST THE NAMES OF ALL STAFF MEMBERS IN CHEMISTRY IN BAYSIDE.

(1) List the names of all staff members who live in Bayside and who are in the Chemistry Department.

(2) List the names of all staff members who are in the Chemistry Department which is in Bayside.

Compare the second reading with the sentence: *LIST THE NAMES OF ALL STAFF MEMBERS IN ROOM A20 IN THE COLLEGE.*

The input sentence is translated into the following two intermediate texts which represent the two readings respectively and which can be mapped into the structure of the data base.

(1) *V(NAME)   NAME,DEPT(CHEM)   NAME,CITY (BAYSIDE)*

(2) *V(NAME)   DEPT(CHEM), CITY(BAYSIDE)*

LIST NAMES OF ALL STAFF MEMBERS IN CHEMISTRY IN BAYSIDE

```
V(NAME)          NAME,CITY(BAYSIDE)          NAME,DEPT(CHEM)
   *** THE FOLLOWING RECORDS HAVE BEEN FOUND ***
      85.) SELMA A EICHHORN
     191.) DOROTHY S LASKIN
    ?
```

```
    V(NAME)     DEPT(CHEM),CITY(BAYSIDE)
                ***********************
     ERROR 7: ABOVE NODES ARE LOGICALLY UNRELATED
    ?
```

Fig. 3: Sample Sentence Processing

The data base is organized in a directed graph arrangement in which there is an arc connecting each name with various parts of the home address, but there are no arcs connecting departments with such addresses. The sentence is then disambiguated in the context of this data base. For the reading (1,1) names are printed; for the reading (2,2) there is a message saying that the Chemistry Department and Bayside are unrelated. This message and the printing of the second reading can be suppressed, if desired.

NOTES

This work was supported in part by a grant from the CUNY Faculty Research Fund under Grant No. 12306.
1. For a survey of some of the models previously constructed by the author see Moyne (1977); for a more general survey, see Minker (1977) and Moyne (1974).
2. For some details of ambiguities resolved in the context of discourse or data base see Moyne (1977). Other examples are provided in the article by Schank and Lehnert in this volume.
3. For further details see Moyne (1980).
4. Cf. Chomsky (1970).

REFERENCES

Chomsky, N. 1965. *Aspects of the theory of syntax.* Cambridge: MIT Press.

. . . . 1970. Remarks on nominalizations. In *Readings in english transformational grammar,* ed. Jacobs and Rosenbaum, pp. 184-221, Mass: Ginn and Co.

Chomsky, N. and Miller, G. A. 1957. Pattern conception. Report # AFCRC-TN-57-57. ASTIA Document # AD 110076.

Harris, Z. S. 1957. Co-occurrence and transformation in linguistic structure. *Language* 33:3, pp. 283-340.

Jacobs, R. and Rosenbaum, P. 1970. ed. *Readings in english transformational grammar.* Mass: Ginn and Co.

Minker, J. 1977. Information storage and retrieval: a survey and functional description. *SIGIR,* Association for Computing Machinery, Vol XII, #2, pp. 1-108.

Moyne, J. A. 1974. Some grammars and recognizers for formal and natural languages. In Tou, pp. 263-333.

. . . . 1977. Simple-English for data base communication. *International Journal of Computer and Information Science.* 6:4, pp. 327-343.

. . . . 1980. Language use: a performance model. *Int, J. of Comp. & Inf. Scis.* 9.6,483-505.

Tou, T. 1974. ed, *Advances in information systems science,* vol. 5. New York: Plenum.

PART V

NEW DIRECTIONS
IN TRANSFORMATIONAL
GRAMMAR

INTRODUCTION

Peters and Ritchie are two important figures in formal linguistics. Their work is difficult to appraise without some introduction to it. I will try to provide an informal account of their central ideas. We can then consider some of the implications of their work.

Linguists must tell us just what does and just what does not count as a sentence of some language or other under study, if they are to remain within the framework of assumptions demanding that they produce devices (grammars) which generate (or recognize) all and only sentences of a language. They cannot go "over" or "under the mark." It is not at all like going to your grocer and asking for a pound of tea and getting just a wee bit over (or under) and still feeling satisfied. Nothing could be more uncomfortable for the linguist. For with devices like grammars if you get "a bit over" then you are not describing (by generating, let us say) English, nor are you understanding what constitutes the set of English sentences.

What Peters and Ritchie prove, in very formal terms using applied automata theory, is that the grammars produced by Chomsky and his followers are inadequate. These grammars cannot "tell us," by generating all and *only* English sentences, precisely what English is like from a grammatical point of view. Instead, they seem to go on and generate virtually any sort of string, both English and non-English.

If this sort of thing goes on then it is no longer possible to locate English with any degree of precision (we do get English but we get it by default simply because we get so much more as well). However, a grammarian must tell us much more precisely than *this* just what constitutes English. It is not enough to say,

"Well, here is *English+* and somewhere in *English+* you will find English." Grammarians cannot proceed in this way for we assume all along that the way to find English, the only sensible way (and here we are beginning to empathize with the grammarian's intuitions) is to construct a grammar that generates the sentences of English. But this Peters and Ritchie tell us is precisely what Chomsky and his followers have failed to do.

Once grammarians learned of the Peters and Ritchie result they were at some pains to modify or "soften" the devices they constructed (so that they would no longer be quite so powerful). Suppose we provide the terminology needed to formulate the fundamental questions grammarians address and then suggest the sort of answer Peters and Ritchie gave. The fundamental question is—

Is a natural language recursive? (Is the set, S, of sentences recursive?)
One answer that linguists give is—
A natural language is recursive if there is an algorithm for generating sentences of the language.
But with this reply we must reformulate the question.
We can now begin to see just how to do this—
Is there an algorithm for generating the set, S, of sentences of a natural language such as English?

In order to understand Peters' and Ritchie's answer we must first make sense of terms like "language," "recursive," "algorithm," etc. This we attempt, quite informally, in what follows.

What is a language? It is a set of sentences formed over a well-defined alphabet. First we specify the vocabulary and then we admit that we can form strings or sentences over this vocabulary by joining or concatenating one item from the alphabet with another. We then select part of the set of all strings so formed. (Given a finite vocabulary V and the operation of concatenation over n-tuples of words out of V, one can form a denumerably infinite set of strings. A language is usually some proper subset of this set of strings.)

But how do we *present* a language to someone? If the set S of sentences is finite, we can simply *list* them (a list is a grammar). But what if it is infinite? We can't make an infinite list. But we need some device for generating the sentences from a finite vocabulary. And the device must itself be finitely representable or else we are simply faced with the same problem all over again. We tend to think of finitary representations of devices as either procedures or algorithms.

What then is a procedure? A procedure is a finite sequence of instructions that can be mechanically carried out. An example would be—

Suppose V = (a, b) and the instructions for constructing sentences from V are as follows: (i) you may take a and use it as a string, (ii) if you use a as a string you may then add a b to the right of it, (iii) after adding the first b you may either stop or continue adding a finite number of b's.

These instructions constitute a device and surely it is a finite device and it is a procedure—it is a finite representation. Notice that this finite representation terminates for any input. Not every procedure will terminate for just any input. But if a procedure does always terminate then we call it an algorithm.

One way to represent a language is to provide an algorithm that tells one whether a sentence x is in the language or not. If we do provide an algorithm which halts with the answer "yes" for sentences in the language and either does not terminate or else halts with "no" for sentences not in the language, then we have provided a way of recognizing the language.

A language is recursive *if there exists an algorithm for recognizing the language, and it is recursively enumerable if there exists a procedure for recognizing the language.*

Now we can put the question more precisely—

Assume S = the set of English sentences. Assume S is denumerable. Is S recursive? This translates to—is there an algorithm for recognizing S?

Now all along what Chomsky and his followers had assumed was that a natural language was recursive and that they were providing, in the transformational systems they developed, an algorithm for recognizing the language. What Peters and Ritchie have shown is that the natural language is not recursive but recursively enumerable relative to the existing grammars, which then provide only procedures and not algorithms.

The implications of this study for future work in linguistics has been profound. After the Peters/Ritchie result the search began for restrictions on the power of grammars. In some cases there was doubt about whether to apply the requirements of recursivity. In other cases questions arose about whether to characterize a language in terms of levels; in still other cases questions arose about how to write transformations.

There are, to say the least, a number of different approaches. One such approach involves reformulating the way one writes grammars so that there is less reliance on transformations and more on the lexicon. In his essay, Michael Brame (in this volume) takes a rather radical position in this respect. He explores the consequences for transformational theory of abandoning one particular transformation (called "Equui") for other, commonly accepted transformations. He shows by a reductio argument how if one abandoned Equui one would be forced as well to abandon a host of other transformations. This leads him to espouse a more lexically-oriented approach.

Other works exhibit *recursivity difficulties.* Hiż, in his latest essay (this volume), worries about translation. He feels the concept needs clarification, if it is to serve Richard Martin's program. (This would also be true of Donald Davidson's program.) In a recent work about Davidson (see *Truth and Meaning*, Clarendon Press, especially the essays by Davidson, Foster, and McDowell), both advocates and critics of Davidson's position talk, albeit vaguely, about translation. Translation into a suitable metalanguage would be a condition for Davidson's program. If the metalanguage were English (along with the object language) there would be no problem and the set of required translations would be recursive. On the other hand, the preferred metalanguage is not English and so, as suggested in essays in this volume (see Hiż, also Stern), there is some doubt that the translation functions would be even recursively enumerable. This could be very telling for attempts to interpret a theory of meaning as a theory of truth. R.M. Martin's position (first-order denumerabilism) also requires translations on this scale (if thought of as extended to cope with natural languages) and for the very same reasons might fail as well. (I don't think Martin would worry quite so much about whether his operators are recursively enumerable rather than recursive but I think it a matter for grave concern if they are not even recursively enumerable, and I hardly think they are that.)

Two other points about Martin: (i) The ability of some-one like Martin to create a set of metalanguages (assuming again the possibility of extending his system to English) and properly order them is a function of the possibility of determining just what would count as a name, a name of a name, a name of a sentence, a name of a name of a sentence, and so on. This presupposes that we can demarcate the class of names from, for example, the class of adjectives. But in other places in this volume (Stern) we show that the characteristic function on the class of names is neither recursive nor recursively enumerable.

(ii) Martin assumes that the whole tradition from Frege and Carnap on is a viable one, without attending to the properties (recursive vs. recursively enumerable vs. . . .) of the systems with which they are dealing. There can be little understanding of the feasibility of this tradition without some understanding of this sort. In "Meaning and Necessity," for example, Carnap describes the metalanguage M' in great detail; also in "The Logical Syntax of Language" a lot is made of translation and yet the entire program of this tradition in which Carnap is prime mover has very little to say about the formal properties (from the point of view of recursive function theory) of translations. Martin makes heavy weather of Hiż's lapses from this tradition calling them elsewhere "heresies." Hiż replies, fairly I think, that the whole notion of translation needs considerable work.

In many questions raised in this volume we are seeing constructivist complaints, both in syntactic and semantic matters. We already have a constructive tradition in syntax; we are beginning one in semantics. There are, of course, today a number of positions called "constructive," and a number of constructive gambits arising—in the logic of epistemic notions, in proof theory, in semantics, syntax, areas of science, mathematics of course, and in various reconstructions of psychological theories as well.

P. Stanley Peters and R. W. Ritchie

ON THE GENERATIVE POWER OF TRANS-
FORMATIONAL GRAMMARS

INTRODUCTION

In *Aspects of the Theory of Syntax*, Chomsky presents a theory of transformational grammar. The purpose of this paper is to formalize this notion of transformational grammar and to study the expressive power of these grammars.
In particular, we relate the languages generated by these grammars to classes of languages studied in recursive function theory.

The paper is arranged as follows:

Section 1 is an informal discussion of the nature of grammatical transformations and the manner in which they operate on phrase-markers. This material will be familiar to linguists.

Section 2 merely makes precise the concepts introduced in Sec. 1 with one difference. In informal discussion, phrase-markers are represented as trees to aid the reader's intuitions, but in Sec. 2 they are represented as labeled bracketings for technical convenience in later sections.

Section 3 merely recaps the definitions of phrase structure grammars, with emphasis on the manner in which they generate sets of phrase-markers.

Section 4 defines a transformational grammar to contain two components: a base component (consisting of a phrase structure grammar) and a transformational component (consisting of a finite ordered set of grammatical transformations). Furthermore, transformations are defined to apply cyclically in derivations converting step by step a phrase-marker generated by the base into a derived phrase-marker. If the latter contains no occurrences of a special sentence boundary symbol, it is a surface structure and the phrase-marker initiating the derivation is a deep structure

Reprinted by permission of the publisher, "On the Generative Power of Transformational Grammars", P. Stanley Peters, R. W. Ritchie, Information Sciences 6, 49-83, editor John Richardson, Copyright © Elsevier, North Holland, Inc.

underlying it. A transformational grammar then generates as its language the set of all strings which have a surface phrase-marker.

With these definitions as background, we prove in Sec. 5 that every recursively enumerable set of strings is the language generated by some transformational grammar. In Sec. 6 we examine the sets of languages generated by restricted types of transformational grammar and prove that the complexity of the language generated by a transformational grammar is no greater than the complexity of computation of the length of an underlying deep structure from a sentence. Section 7 is devoted to discussing some implications of these results for natural language in light of empirical studies linguists have made of a variety of languages. Empirical support is given for the hypothesis that natural languages are recursive.

The reader whose interest is primarily in the results of Secs. 5, 6, or 7 is encouraged to proceed directly to these sections after reading Sec. 1. Sections 5 and 6, which require properties of transformational grammars detailed in Secs. 2-4, begin with summaries of the relevant properties. The properties summarized at the beginning of Sec. 5 follow immediately from the definitions, while those of Sec. 6 are deduced at the end of that section.

1. TRANSFORMATIONS: INFORMAL DEVELOPMENT

As is usual in the formal study of grammars, we consider a language to be a set of finite strings over a vocabulary of *terminal symbols*, i.e. given a finite nonempty set V_T (the *terminal vocabulary*) we may form the set V_T^* of all finite sequences of members of V_T. Then a *language* is any subset of V_T^*. Phrase structure and transformational grammars also refer to another vocabulary of symbols, the *nonterminal vocabulary* V_N of phrase types or grammatical categories.

These grammatical categories appear in phrase-markers of strings in V_T^*, which represent their segmentation into phrases and the classification of these phrases into types. A phrase-marker may be represented as a tree in which the leaves are labeled with members of V_T and the other nodes with members of V_N. The sequence of leaves dominated by a node labeled with a nonterminal symbol A is a phrase of type A. Alternatively, the same information can be represented by a well-formed labeled bracketing (cf. Defs. 2.1 and 2.11). As an example of a phrase-marker, assume that we are given the nonterminal vocabulary V_N =

[S, NP, VP, N, A] and the terminal vocabulary V_T = [they, are, flying, planes] and consider the tree (1).

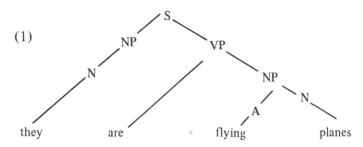

(1)

Phrase-marker (1) represents the information that, for example, *flying planes* is a member of the grammatical category NP, as is *they*. On the other hand *are flying* is not a phrase of any type according to (1).

Transformational rules are mappings of phrase-markers into phrase-markers (cf. Def. 2.14). Each such rule consists of two parts: a structural condition and a set of elementary transformations (cf. Defs. 2.8, 2.10, and 2.12). The structural condition of a transformation serves to determine whether or not the rule will apply to a given phrase-marker and, if so, how to factor the phrase-marker into sections to be rearranged, duplicated or deleted. These effects are achieved by application of elementary transformations to factors of the phrase-marker. In order to be a transformation, a paired structural condition and set of elementary transformations must meet conditions of compatibility, chief among them the condition of recoverability of deletions (cf. Def. 2.13). A factorization of a phrase-marker is induced by a factorization of its terminal string in the following way. Consider the factorization of the terminal string

(2) they are flying planes

into the four substrings X_1 = they, X_2 = are, X_3 = flying, and X_4 = planes. This induces the division of (1) into factors as indicated in (3) (cf. Def. 2.6). The factors are given in (4).

(3)

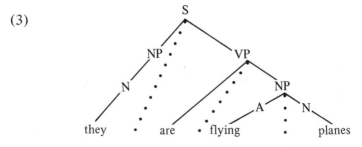

(4)

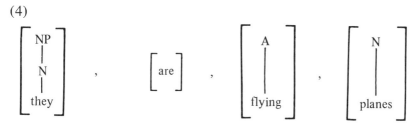

Notice that each tree factor is chosen so as to include the highest node dominating only terminal symbols in the corresponding string factor and that nodes which dominate two or more string factors do not appear in any tree factor. (cf. Def. 2.5 for corresponding concepts in terms of labeled bracketings.)

The factorization X_1, $X_2 X_3$, X_4 of (2) into three terms induces the factorization of (1) indicated in (5).

(5)

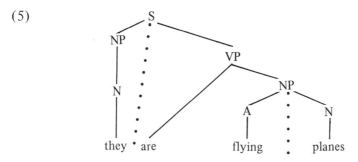

The first and last factors are the same as before but the second factor is (6) which is not a subtree of (1) but a forest of adjacent subtrees.

(6)

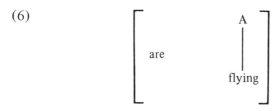

Such forests will arise not only as a single factor of a factorization but also as what we shall call a sequence of factors. The sequence of ith-jth factors of a tree factorization is defined to be the ith factor of the tree factorization induced by concatenating the ith through jth string factors (cf. Def. 2.7 of "contents," the corresponding notion on labeled bracketing). For example, (6) is the sequence of 2nd-3rd factors of (3) and (7) is the sequence of 2nd-4th factors of (3).

(7)

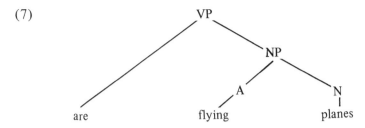

A structural condition will specify the properties a factorization of a tree must have if a transformation is to operate on it. These properties are expressed by employing three sorts of predicate: One sort specifies that a particular sequence of factors has a phrase of a certain type as its terminal string, another sort specifies that two sequences of factors are identical, and a third sort specifies that a sequence of factors possesses a certain terminal string. Each predicate is true only of factorizations with a specified number of terms and deals with particular sequences of these terms.

(a) For every nonterminal symbol A the predicate $A^n_{i \to j}$ is true of a factorization if and only if $1 \leqslant i \leqslant j \leqslant n$, the factorization has n terms, and a node labeled A dominates the terminal string of the sequence of ith-jth factors.

(b) The predicate $h \to i \equiv^n j \to k$ is true of a factorization if and only if $1 \leqslant h \leqslant i \leqslant n$, $i \leqslant j \leqslant k \leqslant n$, the factorization has n terms, and the sequence of hth-ith factors is identical to the sequence of jth-kth factors.

(c) For every string x of terminal symbols, the predicate $i \to j \equiv^n x$ is true of a factorization if and only if $1 \leqslant i \leqslant j \leqslant n$, the factorization has n terms, and the sequence of ith-jth factors has x as its terminal string.

Any Boolean combination of these predicates is a structural condition.

The action of a transformation on a tree to which it applies is determined by the elementary transformations it contains. Each elementary operates on factorizations of trees in one of three ways.

    (i) The deletion elementary $[T_d, (i,j)]$ deletes the sequence of ith-jth factors of a factorization.

    (ii) The substitution elementary $[T_s, (h, i), (j, k)]$ substitutes a copy of the sequence of jth-kth factors for the sequence of hth-ith factors if the latter is a subtree.

    (iii) The adjunction elementaries $[T_r, (h, i), (j, k)]$ and $[T_l, (h, i), (j, k)]$ attach a copy of the sequence of *j*th-*k*th factors to the right and left respectively of the sequence of *h*th-*i*th factors.

A set of elementary transformations may appear in a transformation if the sequences of factors on which they operate (indicated by the first pair of integers) do not overlap.

For a structural condition and a set of elementary transformations to form a transformation they must both deal with factorizations into the same number of terms and meet the condition of recoverability of deletions; namely, if the set of elementary transformations deletes or substitutes for a sequence of factors without leaving a replica of them in another position, then the structural condition implies that either an identical sequence of factors remains elsewhere in the tree or else the deleted sequence of factors had a member of a finite, preassigned subset of V_T^* as its terminal string.

[we omit Sections 2, 3, 4]

5. EVERY RECURSIVELY ENUMERABLE SET IS A TRANSFORMATIONAL LANGUAGE

Having defined transformational grammars we are now in a position to prove some theorems about their expressive power. We can distinguish two different aspects of expressive power: the first, called *weak generative capacity*, is the set of all languages which can be generated by transformational grammars: the second, called *strong generative capacity*, is the set of all sets of structural descriptions generated by transformational grammars.

The usual approach to the study of expressive power of a class of grammars is to investigate the weak generative capacity of the class. This is the approach we shall adopt. In particular we will compare the weak generative capacity of the class of transformational grammars with the set of recursively enumerable languages and with the set of elementary languages.

This section requires two facts about transformational grammars. First, that transformations are applied cyclically, each subsentence of a deep phrase-marker serving exactly once as the domain of application of each transformation. Second, that there is a transformation which alters a sentence if and only if it contains at least two terminal symbols the rightmost of which is a particular specified symbol and in this case deletes the symbol.

Our first theorem concerns the full class of context-sensitive based transformational grammars.

THEOREM 5.1. *Every recursively enumerable language is generated by some context-sensitive based transformational grammar, and conversely.*

Proof. The converse follows directly from our definitions by Church's Thesis. In somewhat more detail, one might carry out the enumeration as follows:

(1) effectively generate all pairs (n, x) where n is a positive integer and x is in V_T^*,

(2) as each pair appears, check effectively (say using the Turing machine constructed quite explicitly in Theorem 6.4) whether x has a deep phrase-marker in the desired grammar with no more than n subsentences,

(3) if x does have such a deep phrase-marker, output x, otherwise consider the next pair in the list being generated.

For the other direction, let L be any recursively enumerable language. We wish to construct a CS-based transformational grammar $\mathcal{G}$ such that $L = L(\mathcal{G})$. It is well-known (see, for example, [Ref. 7, p. 208, Theorem 0.3]) that there must be an unrestricted rewriting system G such that $L = L(G)$. In fact, G can even be chosen so that each rule is either of the form $\varphi X \psi \to \varphi Y \psi$ where X and Y are in V_N^* or of the form A $\to$ a where A is in V_N and a is in V_T. We will construct another URS G', such that $L(G')$ is closely related to $L(G)$. Let the terminal vocabulary of G' be $V_T \cup [b]$ where b is a new symbol, and the nonterminal vocabulary of G' be $V_N \cup [B]$ where B is also a new symbol. Let G' have the same initial symbol as G, and have the following rules:

I. if $\varphi \to \psi$ is a rule of G, then
   a) $\varphi \to \psi$ is a rule of G' if the length of ψ is not less than the length of φ
   b) $\varphi \to \psi B^n$ is a rule of G' if n = length of φ minus length of ψ is greater than zero
II. c) BA $\to$ AB is a rule of G' for all A $\in V_N$
   d) B $\to$ b is a rule of G'.

The following relation holds between $L(G')$ and $L(G)$ ($=L$): $L(G)$ is the set of all strings obtainable by deleting all occurrences of the symbol "b" from strings y in $L(G')$. To see that all members of $L(G)$ can be obtained in this way, note that given any $x \in L(G)$ there is an integer m such that $xb^m \in L(G')$; it is also easy to see that only members of $L(G)$ can be obtained in this way. Notice that every rule of G' has a right-hand side at least as long as its left-hand side. Therefore, by the proofs of Kuroda's Lemmas 2 and 3 (Ref. 7, p. 211) there is a CS grammar

$\mathcal{P}$ such that (i) $L(\mathcal{P}) = L(G')$, (ii) the only rules of $\mathcal{P}$ involving its initial symbol S are S → SA and S → S′ where A and S′ are nonterminals, and (iii) all other rules of $\mathcal{P}$ are of the form $CD → EF$, $C → E$, and $C → c$ where $C, D, E,$ and F are nonterminals and c is a terminal.

$\mathcal{P}$ will be the base component of $\mathcal{G}$. Let $\varphi \in \mathcal{L}(\mathcal{P})$ and let x be the terminal string of φ. Each initial substring of x is an S in φ (in the sense of "is a" defined after Def. 2.11) and thus each b in φ is the rightmost terminal symbol in some subsentence of φ. Now consider the transformation T which deletes b when it is the rightmost terminal symbol in a sentence (in the notation of Sec. 2, let T be $(2 → 2 \equiv^2 b, [[T_d, (2, 2)]])$. Although T does not necessarily preserve a copy of the symbol b, it satisfies the condition of recoverability of deletions by specifying that the deleted string must in every case be a single b. If we put $\mathcal{T} = (T)$ and $\mathcal{G} = (\mathcal{P}, \mathcal{T})$ then $L(\mathcal{G})$ is the set of all strings obtained by deleting each occurrence of the symbol "b" from each member of $L(\mathcal{P})$ $[= L(G')]$, since T applies cyclically to every phrasemarker φ in $\mathcal{L}(\mathcal{P})$ operating on every subsentence. Thus $L(\mathcal{G}) = L(G) = L$. This proves the theorem.

Theorem 5.1 was straightforward to prove since it did not involve any use of sophisticated properties of transformations. Its proof relied ultimately on an observation of Scheinberg's concerning the relation of recursively enumerable languages to context-sensitive languages. We can strengthen Theorem 5.1 considerably at the cost of a much more intricate argument. We state Theorem 5.2 here and prove it in Ref. 10.

THEOREM 5.2. *Every recursively enumerable language is generated by some context-free based transformational grammar, and conversely.*

The linguistic import of Theorems 5.1 and 5.2 is considerable. To get an idea of this import we must briefly look at the meaning of the notion "possible transformational grammar" for linguistics. In *Aspects* Chomsky states that the set of possible transformational grammars is the set of hypotheses which a child learning a language has available concerning the linguistic data he must explain. Learning a grammar consists of selecting one of these hypotheses on the basis of certain criteria. Theorems 5.1 and 5.2 show that the theory formulated in *Aspects* makes available to the child a hypothesis to explain any recursively enumerable set of data. It could be that the fact that the data will always be finite together with the criteria which are the basis of selection will prevent the child from ever learning a grammar which generates a nonrecursive language. But until the criteria of selection are more clearly stated we must consider the possibility that the child can actually learn any grammar made available given some set of data. In other words, until the criteria of selection are better defined, the theory of transformational grammar contained in *Aspects* should be taken as asserting that a child can learn a nonrecursive language. This is the linguistic import of the theorems in this section.

Such an assertion is quite strange, for it flies in the face of the intuitive meaning of recoverability of deletions. The intuitive meaning of this condition is that given a speaker who knows a grammar and given a string over the terminal vocabulary, the speaker can construct all structural descriptions for the string generated by the grammar and can furthermore determine that the grammar does not generate the string if this is the case. Chomsky states, somewhat tentatively, that there should be an algorithm to determine for an arbitrary possible grammar and an arbitrary string over the terminal vocabulary what structural descriptions the grammar assigns to the string, if any, as well as whether the grammar generates the string at all (Ref. 1, pp. 31-32 and footnote 18, p. 202). This is an even stronger condition than what we have called the intuitive meaning of the condition of recoverability of deletions. It follows from either of these conditions by Church's Thesis that each possible grammar generates a recursive language. Chomsky later says that conceivably the child has available a grammar for any recursively enumerable language (Ref. 1, p. 62). But even as he makes this statement, he adds that this "seems definitely not to be the case" (Ref. 1, footnote 37, p. 208) and he clearly expects the condition of recoverability of deletions as formulated in *Aspects* to require that every possible grammar generates a recursive language. Thus Theorem 5.1 can be taken as an indication of something amiss in the theory of transformational grammar as presented in *Aspects*. We have stated Theorem 5.2 here to show that these problems cannot be solved by restricting the base to be context-free.

For this reason, among others, it seems reasonable to us to search for conditions under which transformational grammars generate recursive languages. Another reason which supports this search is simply the desirability of restricting as much as possible the class of possible grammars without ruling out as impossible grammars which are required for any known natural language. Thus we should look not just for conditions under which transformational grammars generate recursive languages, but for such conditions as might conceivably be supported by empirical observations of linguists as to what types of transformational grammars are needed to describe known languages and what types are not. In the next section we investigate some such conditions.

6. THE DECIDABILITY OF TRANSFORMATIONAL LANGUAGES WITH BOUNDED CYCLING

It was shown in Sec. 5 that some nonrecursive languages are generated by transformational grammars. We now wish to study the nature of these grammars in order to determine which portions of the generative process are in fact effective, and isolate exactly those points at which the noneffectiveness enters.

Section 5 contradicts the following "plausible argument" that transformational languages are effectively decidable. To decide whether a given terminal string x is in the language generated by the transformational grammar $(\mathcal{P}, \mathcal{T})$ apply the following procedure:

(1) enumerate successively the well-formed terminal labeled bracketings over the vocabulary of $\mathcal{P}$;

(2) given such a well-formed labeled bracketing, decide whether it is strongly generated by $\mathcal{P}$, if not continue the enumeration in (1); if so, go to (3);

(3) apply the transformations of $\mathcal{T}$ to the given well-formed labeled bracketing and determine whether or not the last line of the transformational derivation obtained is a well-formed surface phrase-marker having x as its debracketization.

We now proceed to analyze this argument in order to determine why it does not in fact yield a decision procedure. In so doing, we shall isolate the one element missing from the argument, and then be able to formulate a necessary and sufficient condition for a transformational language to be recursively decidable.

This analysis uses a variety of properties of transformational grammars as defined in Sec. 4; however, we shall summarize in the following three lemmas all the results about grammars used in this section.

LEMMA 6.1. *If* $\mathcal{P}$ *is a context-sensitive grammar, then there is a constant* K_1 *and a Turing machine* Z_1 *on* $V_T \cup L \cup R \cup [\Delta]$ *which accepts* $\mathcal{L}(P)$, *rejects* $K_1 \mathcal{L}(P)$, *and uses at most* $K_1^{l(\varphi)}$ *tape squares on any input* φ *of length* $l(\varphi)$.

LEMMA 6.2. *If* $(\mathcal{P}, \mathcal{T})$ *is a transformational grammar, then there is a constant* K_2 *and a Turing machine* Z_2 *on* $V_T \cup L \cup R \cup [\Delta]$ *which accepts a tape of the form* $\Delta x \Delta \varphi \Delta \#^l \Delta$

where $x \in (V_T - [\#])^*$, $\varphi \in (V_T \cup L \cup R)^*$ and l is a positive integer if and only if φ is well-formed and there is a transformational derivation $(\psi_1, \ldots, \psi_t)$ with respect to $\mathfrak{I}$ such that $\varphi = \psi_1$, $x = d(\psi_t)$ and $l(\psi_i) < l$ for each $i = 1, \ldots, t$. Further the number of tape squares used is at most $K_2 l^2$.

LEMMA 6.3. *For every transformational grammar $\mathfrak{G} = (\mathfrak{P}, \mathfrak{I})$ there is a constant K_3 such that, if x is in $L(\mathfrak{G})$ and if s is an integer such that some deep phrase-marker underlying x contains at most s subsentences, then there is a transformational derivation $\varphi_1, \ldots, \varphi_t$ such that $\varphi_1 \in \mathcal{L}(\mathfrak{P})$, $d(\varphi_t) = x$, and further for each $i = 1, \ldots, t$, $l(\varphi_i) < K_3^s l(x)$.*

The reader who is interested in the results of this section and who is willing to accept these lemmas can read this section, with the exception of the proofs of these lemmas, without any knowledge of the definitions of Sec. 2, 3, and 4. No reference to those sections is made until the proofs of these lemmas, which are given at the conclusion of this section.

Consideration of the "plausibility" argument with which this section began (cf. Theorem 6.4 below) will show that the procedure does, in fact, yield a transformational derivation of each terminal string x which is in $L(\mathfrak{G})$, if the interpretation of clause (3) is that the procedure returns to (1) when the last line is not a surface phrase-marker of x. The flaw lies in the inability of this procedure to identify those strings not in $L(\mathfrak{G})$. When presented with any such string x the procedure will not terminate, but will instead continue enumerating and testing longer and longer candidates for the deep phrase-marker underlying x. If the process incorporated an effective method for determining from x when to stop enumerating in step (1) and conclude that x is not in $L(\mathfrak{G})$, it would constitute the desired decision procedure. The results of Sec. 5 thus make clear that there is no method for determining when to stop the enumeration. For example, there cannot be any effective method for computing from each x an upper bound on the length of the shortest deep phrase-marker underlying x, where this bound is taken to be zero when x is not a member of $L(\mathfrak{G})$.

Even though we know that it is not the case that *every* transformational grammar has associated with it an effective method for finding from an x an upper bound for the shortest underlying deep structure, some clearly do. In fact, this discussion indicates that the existence, for a particular grammar $\mathfrak{G}$, of such an effective method for obtaining these upper bounds is a sufficient condition for the language $L(\mathcal{G})$ to be decidable. The condition is also necessary, since if $L(\mathcal{G})$ is decidable one can, given x, apply the decision procedure and, if x is in $L(\mathcal{G})$, then continue by executing steps (1), (2), and (3) of the above procedure to obtain a deep phrase-marker underlying x, and hence an upper bound.

Thus, we will see that, although there is no decision procedure for arbitrary transformational languages, a modification of the fallacious "plausible argument" provides a necessary and sufficient condition that the language generated by a transformational grammar be decidable (cf. Corollary 6.6 below). We have phrased the condition in terms of length of deep phrase-markers, but in our rigorous treatment below we will use the linguistically more significant notion of number of subsentences of the deep phrase-marker—or, equivalently, number of cycles in the transformational derivation. We shall do this by showing that a bound on the number of subsentences, or of cycles, provides an upper bound on the length of an underlying deep phrase-marker.

We begin a more rigorous investigation of the argument given above by noting that Lemma 6.1 gives a Turing machine which performs step (2) of the procedure. At these and the remaining stages of this section, we will also explicitly note the amount of tape required by each Turing machine described in order to determine when the decision procedure for a particular transformational grammar will fall in a restricted class of procedures, such as the primitive recursive or elementary recursive ones. Lemma 6.2 shows that step (3) of the procedure can be carried out (within limited storage if there is an upper bound on the length of any line of a derivation). Lemma 6.3 gives an upper bound on the length of a deep phrase-marker (and on each line of a derivation from this phrase-marker to the terminal string) in terms of the number of sentences in the deep phrase-marker—equivalently, the number of cycles in the derivation. Theorem 6.4 produces a Turing machine which, given a string x and a number s, determines whether x has any deep phrase-marker containing s or fewer sentences. Corollary 6.6 justifies our remark that a necessary and sufficient condition is obtained for decidability of languages generated by transformational grammars in terms of computability of a bound on the number of sentences or cycles. Corollary 6.7 shows that if the bound is a very simply computable function of the input string, say elementary recursive, then the decision procedure is similarly easily executed, say is an elementary recursive one.

We begin with a proof of Theorem 6.4 from Lemmas 6.1, 6.2 and 6.3.

THEOREM 6.4. *For every transformational grammar there is a Turing machine Z, whose alphabet consists of the terminal symbols of the grammar together with a blank Δ, which accepts a tape $\Delta \, x \, \Delta \, \#^s \, \Delta$ if underlying x there is a deep phrase-marker containing at most s subsentences and which rejects $\Delta \, x \, \Delta \, \#^s \, \Delta$ otherwise. Further, there is a constant C such that Z uses at most $C^{C\,sl(x)}$ tape squares on this input.*

Proof. Let $\mathscr{G} = (\,\mathscr{P}, \mathscr{T}\,)$ be a transformational grammar. We shall construct a Turing machine Z' operating over the alphabet $V_T \cup L \cup R \cup [0, \Delta]$ which operates as desired, and appeal to the well-known result (stated and proved here for completeness as Lemma 6.8) that symbols may be removed from the alphabet of a Turing machine without affecting the function computed at the cost of a linear increase in length of tape. On input $\Delta \, x \, \Delta \, \#^s \, \Delta$, Z' arranges its tape as follows:

$$\Delta \, x \, \Delta \, \# \ldots \# \, \Delta \, 0 \ldots 0 \, \Delta \, 0 \ldots 0 \, \Delta \, 0 \ldots 0 \, \Delta$$

	s	$K_3^s l(x)$	$K_1^{K_3^s l(x)}$	$K_2 K_3^{2s} l^2(x)$
(1)	(2)	(3)	(4)	(5)

where K_1, K_2, and K_3 are the constants given in Lemmas 6.1, 6.2, and 6.3. The procedure is then to enumerate terminal labeled bracketings φ in increasing order in the position (3) and as each is produced, if it exceeds the space provided in position (3), reject the input, if not check in position (4) by Lemma 6.1 whether φ is in $\mathcal{L}(\,\mathscr{P}\,)$. If it is not, or if it contains more than s subsentences, continue the enumeration. If φ is in $\mathcal{L}(\,\mathscr{P}\,)$ and has at most s subsentences, then copy $\Delta \, x \, \Delta \, \varphi \, \Delta \, \#^{K_3^s l(x)} \, \Delta$ into position (5) and check by the procedure of Lemma 6.2 whether φ is a deep structure underlying x, and if not, continue enumerating. If x has a deep phrase-marker with no more than s subsentences, then Lemma 6.3 guarantees that there is one, φ, such that each line of a transformational derivation of x from φ is no longer than $K_3^s l(x)$, so that the procedures of Lemmas 6.1 and 6.2 can be carried out on the tape as set up by Z'. To obtain the constant C, we note that Z' uses $l(x) + s + K_3^s l(x) + K_1^{K_3^s l(x)} + K_2 K_3^{2s} l^2(x) +$

4 tape squares. Letting C be, for example, $K_1 + K_2 + K_3$, we have the theorem.

The Turing machine Z of Theorem 6.4 is almost the machine described by the fallacious "plausible argument" with which this section began—except that a number s is required as input in addition to the string x. We know that s cannot be eliminated for all transformational grammars, but we now proceed to eliminate s for certain grammars.

Definition 6.5. The *cycling function* $f_{\mathcal{G}}$ of a transformational grammar $\mathcal{G}$ is that function from V_T^* into the non-negative integers whose value on a string x is 0 if $x \notin L(\mathcal{G})$ and otherwise is the smallest number s such that some deep phrase-marker underlying x has s subsentences.

COROLLARY 6.6. *The following three conditions are equivalent for any transformational grammar*

    (i) *the language* $L(\mathcal{G})$ *is decidable,*
    (ii) *the cycling function* $f_{\mathcal{G}}$ *is recursive,*
    (iii) $f_{\mathcal{G}}$ *is bounded (pointwise) by a recursive function.*

Proof. Assume that $f_{\mathcal{G}}$ is bounded by a recursive function f. Given x, to decide membership in $L(\mathcal{G})$ compute $f(x)$ and apply the machine Z of Theorem 6.4 to $\Delta x \Delta \#^{f(x)} \Delta$, thus (iii) implies (i). To see that (i) implies (ii), assume that $L(\mathcal{G})$ is decidable. To compute $f_{\mathcal{G}}(x)$, output 0 if $x \notin L(\mathcal{G})$, otherwise set $f_{\mathcal{G}}(x)$ equal to the smallest integer s for which the machine Z of Theorem 6.4 accepts $\Delta x \Delta \#^s \Delta$. That (ii) implies (iii) is trivial since $f_{\mathcal{G}}$ bounds itself.

This corollary, which completes our discussion of decidability of transformational grammars, does not make use of the bound obtained on tape storage used in Theorem 6.4. This bound becomes $g(x) = C^{C^{f(x)}l(x)}$ when f bounds the cycling function, and g is not much more "difficult to compute" than is f. For example, if f is primitive recursive, or elementary recursive (in the sense of Csillag-Kalmar), so is g. Further, it was shown in Ref. 12 that functions computed by Turing machines for which the amount of tape used was elementary recursive are again elementary, and the extension to primitive recursive, though not drawn there is implicit, and was affirmed in Ref. 4. Hence we have the following corollary.

COROLLARY 6.7. *If $\mathcal{G}$ is a transformational grammar whose cycling function $f_\mathcal{G}$ is bounded by an elementary (primitive) recursive function, then $L(\mathcal{G})$ is an elementary (primitive) recursive language. (The same holds upon substituting $\mathcal{E}^n$ for any $n > 3$ for "elementary" or "primitive," where $\mathcal{E}^n$ is defined in Ref. 5.)*

7. SOME CONCLUDING REMARKS

We have seen that the ability of transformational grammars to generate nonrecursive languages, nonprimitive recursive languages, nonelementary languages, etc. resides in the fact that very short sentences may have very large numbers of cycles in their derivations, and thus a great amount of deletion may take place in the transformational derivation even though it is all "recoverable." Thus Corollaries 6.6 and 6.7 show that any restriction which limits the number of subsentences in the deep phrase-markers of strings generated by a transformational grammar can be interpreted as a stronger condition of recoverability of deletions. Available transformational grammars of natural languages do not make use of the power to take enormous numbers of cycles in the derivation of very short sentences. In fact, it appears that for every transformational grammar $\mathcal{G}$ written for a natural language there is a constant k such that the function $k^{l(x)}$ bounds $f_\mathcal{G}$. Since $k^{l(x)}$ is an elementary function the language $L(\mathcal{G})$ is elementary by Corollary 6.7; it is even in F_3, as can be seen from the proof of this corollary since $2^{l(x)}$ is in F_0.

These observations suggest that an appropriate line of research for the discovery of a more adequate condition of recoverability of deletions would be to search for empirically supportable restrictions on transformational grammars which would guarantee that the cycling function of such grammars be bounded by an exponential or polynomial function. This would become especially interesting if the length of the deep phrase-marker were linear in the terminal string x. Then we would know that the languages generated by these grammars were context-sensitive since this restriction would permit checking of base and transformational components to be done nondeterministically in linearly bounded storage.

We relate our results to some remarks and proposals of Putnam [Ref. 11]. There he noted that every recursively enumerable language is generated by a transformational grammar and made several suggestions for conditions which would restrict the transformational languages to being recursive. We will return to his reasons for desiring such restrictions. He suggested two conditions (Ref. 11, p. 42) (i) that the transformational rules be made "cut-free" in the sense that the output of a transformation never be shorter than its input and (ii) that there be constants n_1 and n_2 for each transformational grammar such that at most n_1 terminals can be deleted by any transformation and at most n_2 deletion transformations can be applied in any derivation.

Empirical considerations clearly rule out both of these as restrictions on the definition of a transformational grammar. Noting this, Putnam proposed that the class of transformational grammars be defined so that they satisfy a "cut-elimination" theorem. We can interpret this rather broadly to mean that for every grammar $\mathcal{G}_1$ in the class there is another grammar $\mathcal{G}_2$ such that (i) $L(\mathcal{G}_1) = L(\mathcal{G}_2)$ and (ii) there is a constant k with the property that for every $x \in L(\mathcal{G}_2)$ there is a deep phrase-marker φ underlying x with respect to $\mathcal{G}_2$ such that $l[d(\varphi)] < kl(x)$. We now see that any grammar satisfying such a cut-elimination theorem generates a language which more than being recursive is context sensitive. This is so because a non-deterministic linear bounded automaton can determine both that a labeled bracketing φ is strongly generated by a context sensitive grammar and that it underlies a given string x if the automaton has enough tape to write φ (since the $C^{Csl(x)}$ sections of the tape in the proof of Theorem 6.4 are used only to check deterministically all possibilities, and hence are dispensable in nondeterministic operation.) However, we have no way of settling the question whether grammars of natural languages satisfy a cut-elimination theorem.

Thus, let us return to the point discussed at the end of Sec. 5, where we concerned ourselves with the question whether all natural languages are recursive. Putnam offers an argument (Ref. 11, pp. 39-41) that natural languages are recursive. His argument involves several highly debatable assumptions and in addition is in reality an argument that the set of sentences of a natural language acceptable to a speaker under performance conditions is recursive rather than an argument about the set of sentences specified as grammatical by the speaker's competence (Ref. 1, pp. 3-4, 10-15). We are able to circumvent these difficulties and offer a new argument based on empirical research in linguistics.

There has been a great deal of work describing the competence of native speakers of a variety of natural languages by transformational grammars. As we have noted, all these grammars seem to have exponentially bounded cycling functions. Thus, if one makes the empirically falsifiable assumptions (a) that every natural language has a descriptively adequate transformational grammar, and (b) that the languages investigated so far are typical as regards the computational complexity of their cycling functions, then it follows that the set of grammatical sentences of every natural language is recursive, in fact predictably computable and in F_3 at worst. There is a great deal of empirical evidence to support assumption (a) and we see no reason to doubt (b); thus we feel that this argument is empirically well supported. It provides strong justification for our feelings expressed at the end of Sec. 5 that recoverability of deletions should restrict natural languages to being recursive. It is worthy of note that the assumptions of this argument are not philosophical but empirical in nature.

Thus we can justify the intuition of virtually all linguists that natural languages are recursive. This provides motivation for the desire, as seen for example in (Ref. 1, footnote 37, p. 208), of transformational linguists to restrict deletions so that transformational languages are recursive. Although we have shown that the restrictions currently imposed on deletions do not accomplish this, our results provide guidance for research into this problem.

REFERENCES

Noam Chomsky, *Aspects of the Theory of Syntax,* M.I.T. Press, Cambridge (1965).

Noam Chomsky, *Current Issues in Linguistic Theory,* Mouton, The Hague (1964).

Noam Chomsky, On certain formal properties of grammar, *Information and Control* 2, 137-167 (1959).

Alan Cobham, The intrinsic computational difficulty of functions, *Logic, Methodology and Philosophy of Science* (Proc. 1964 Internat. Congr.), North-Holland, Amsterdam (1965) pp. 24-30.

Andrej Grzegorczyk, Some classes of recursive functions, *Rozprwy Matematyczne,* Warsaw (1953).

S. C. Kleene, *Introduction to Metamathematics.* Van Nostrand, Princeton, N.J. (1952).

S. Y. Kuroda, Classes of languages and linear-bounded automata, *Information and Control* 7, 207-223 (1964).

Rozsa Peter, *Rekursive Funktionen,* Akademia Kiado, Budapest (1951).

Stanley Peters, A note on the equivalence of ordered and unordered grammars, *Harvard Computation Laboratory Report to NSF, No. 17* (1966).

Stanley Peters, and R. W. Ritchie, On restricting the base component of transformational grammars, *Information and Control* 18, 483-501 (1971).

Hilary Putnam, Some issues in the theory of grammar, *The Structure of Language and Its Mathematical Aspect* (Roman Jakobson, Ed.), American Mathematical Society, Providence, R.I. (1961).

R. W. Ritchie, Classes of predictably computable functions, *Trans. Amer. Math. Soc.* 106, 139-173 (1963).

John R. Ross, A proposed rule of tree pruning, *Harvard Computation Laboratory Report to NSF, No. 17* (1966).

Michael K. Brame

THE BASE HYPOTHESIS
AND THE SPELLING PROHIBITION:
Sentential Subjects, Extraposition, Expletives, and Auxiliaries

Introduction

Recent research in syntax suggests that much of the work of a large number of previously postulated transformations should be taken over by the lexicon. The thrust of my comments today are in harmony with this work and, in fact, my own work suggests an extreme position in respect to how much of the transformational component must be relinquished in favor of a more lexically oriented approach.

In broaching this topic, I would like first to recapitulate several arguments which I advanced during the course of my Fulbright-Hays lectures several years ago. These arguments turn on the nonexistence of Equi, a rule posited by transformationalists working within the framework of the standard theory of transformational grammar. Of considerable interest are the consequences of abandoning Equi, which I intend to review. They culminate in a more radical conception of grammar and ultimately in a constraint on the functioning of transformations which results in enjoining a healthful respect for the integrity of lexical items.

I want to go on to provide new arguments for my contention that many structures which are transformationally derived in the standard theory should in fact be base generated. In particular, I want to argue that a basic generalization goes unexpressed if we assume the existence of rules such as Affix-Hopping and there-Insertion and that therefore the relevant structures must be base generated if the generalization is to be expressed. I also wish to argue that VP gaps are base generated. From this result it will again be shown that the earlier conclusions follow.

If time permits, I would like to go on to propose a new analysis of sentential subjects and related phenomena. I wish to show that a wide range of data previously described by constraints such as Ross's Sentential Subject Constraint and Island Internal S Constraint, Emonds's prohibition against multiple application of root transformations, Horn's NP Constraint and global Pruning, etc., can in fact be eliminated by a straightforward elaboration of the base. These results, if they can be sustained, have consequences for the classical conception of Extraposition. It will no longer be possible to assume that extraposed clauses are transformationally derived. Rather, in consonance with my initial development, Extraposition must be abandoned in favor of a lexical treatment.

1. The Base Hypothesis

Within the standard theory of transformational grammar, a problem of overgeneration emerges. This problem has not really been faced up to. It concerns the following examples.

(1) a.   John tried to avoid the issue.
    b. *John tried for Mary to avoid the issue.
(2) a.   I will persuade you to recognize the superiority of an Elna.
    b. *I will persuade you for John to recognize the superiority of an Elna.
(3) a.   Mary wants us to provide genever for everyone.
    b. *Mary wants us for Harry to provide genever for everyone.

The problem is to avoid generating examples such as (1b), (2b), and (3b), while allowing for (1a), (2a), and (3a). Various constraints have been proposed to accomplish this, but none of these constraints touches the heart of the problem. They simply amount to redescriptions of the basic problem.[1] Rather than proposing new constraints which serve no independent purpose, we might alternatively question some of the basic assumptions which contribute to the generation of the ill-formed examples. Thus, taking (1a) as a representative example, we might ask why (1b) should even arise as a problem for the standard theory? The answer in this case is quite obvious. Example (1b) arises because (1a) is derived from an underlying structure incorporating a sentential complement, as illustrated in (4).

(4) a. John tried [$_S$ for John [$_{VP}$ to avoid the issue]$_{VP}$]$_S$

    b. John tried [$_S$ for PRO [$_{VP}$ to avoid the issue]$_{VP}$]$_S$

Whether one adopts (4a), as in the standard theory, or (4b), as in the extended standard theory, the very fact that *try* can be lexically subcategorized so as to select an S-complement gives rise to new problems connected with ill-formed sentences such as (1b), and likewise for (2) and (3). However, if one rejects this basic assumption and adopts instead what is recognized to exist on the surface, i.e. a VP-complement as the underlying subcategorization associated with *try*, then the question of the ungrammaticality of (1b) does not even arise. Likewise, if *persuade, want*, etc., are subcategorized so as to select NP VP-complements in the case of (2a) and (3a), then the question of the ungrammaticality of (2b) and (3b) does not even arise. Rather, (2b) and (3b) are out for precisely the same reason as the following examples are out.

    (5) a. *I saw Mary for John to leave.

       b. *Mary pinched me for Harry to speak up.

       c. *They all recognized Bill for us to forget our grudge.

Thus, *persuade* and *want*, like *see, pinch,* and *recognize,* do not select NP S-complements, although the former do select NP VP-complements.

We see, then, that not only must the standard and extended standard theories contend with examples such as (1b), (2b), and (3b), but that the means that these theories employ to avoid such examples amounts to a loss of generalization inasmuch as the constraints proposed to rule out such examples do not generalize with mechanisms proposed to rule out examples such as (5a-c). By contrast, the approach that I have advocated (Brame 1976) avoids the ill-formed examples in a general straightforward way. Predicates such as *try* select VP-complements and predicates such as *want* and *persuade* select NP VP-complements.

Such an approach has further consequences. Consider the well-known problem with the following examples.

    (6) a. Who do you want ___ to see John?

       b. *Who do you wanna see John?

As has been pointed out often, reduction and contraction is prohibited in the presence of a removal site as in (6b). Now, if there is indeed a rule of Equi, we would expect (7b) to be ill-formed just as is (6b).

    (7) a. Do you want ___ to sleep?

       b. Do you wanna sleep?

But (7b) is fully grammatical, suggesting that no equi-NP was in fact present in the structure underlying (7b). Consequently, we are led to conclude that there is no rule of Equi. It then follows without theoretical elaboration that (7b) is possible, whereas (6b) is not since there is no removal site in the case of (7b), as opposed to (6b), which does exhibit a removal site. This explanation strikes me as natural and straightforward. It requires no theoretical subtlety. It demands no theoretical elaboration to write off (7b) as counterevidence. Things follow without employment of theoretical prophylactic. It is the difference between an explanation and a description.

There are some important consequences of our conclusion that Equi does not exist. Consider, for example, the following examples.

(8) a. Mary was examined by the doctor.

    b. Mary tried to be examined by the doctor.

(9) a. They expected Jimmy to rip us off.

    b. Jimmy was expected by them to rip us off.

It is generally assumed that (8a) derives from its active counterpart via a transformation called Passive. But consider the derivation of (8b).

(10) a. Mary tried [$_S$ the doctor to examine Mary]$_S$ ⇒ Passive

    b. Mary tried [$_S$ Mary to be examined by the doctor]$_S$ ⇒ Equi

    c. Mary tried ___ to be examined by the doctor

To derive (8b), utilizing the Passive transformation, we arrive at stage (b) of (10), which requires Equi to derive the desired results. Thus, if Passive exists, then Equi exists. But we have concluded that Equi does not exist. Therefore, we must conclude that Passive does not exist. It follows, then, that passive structures, like VP structures, should be generated directly. This is not at all an undesirable consequence. In fact, if passives are generated directly, there is no need for an agent deletion transformation since agents need not be generated at all by base structures (Brame 1976, 133).

Let us now turn to (9a) and (9b). Examples such as (9a) are generally derived by a transformation which raises the NP subject of the complement into the object position of the matrix S. Let us call this putative rule, *Raising to Object Position*, or ROP for short. Notice that ROP is also utilized in deriving (9b). The requisite derivation is given in (11).

(11) They expected [$_S$ Jimmy to rip us off]$_S$ ⇒ ROP

    They expected Jimmy [$_S$ to rip us off]$_S$ ⇒ Passive

    Jimmy was expected by them to rip us off

Thus, if we assume that there is a rule of ROP, then we need Passive to yield the desired results in (11). But there is no rule of Passive because there is no Equi. Consequently, there is no ROP.

Similar conclusions obtain for other transformations that do not make essential use of variables—what I will call *local transformations.* Thus, consider the following examples.

(12) a. Mary tried to appear to be calm.

    b. Every child was given a dime.

    c. He tried to be easy to please.

    d. There was believed to be jelly between his toes.

By reasoning completely analogous to the foregoing, it is possible to conclude on the basis of such examples that there are no rules such as Raising to Subject Position (hereafter RSP), Dative, and *there*-Insertion. Thus, consider (12a), on the assumption that RSP applies in the course of its derivation.

(13) a. Mary tried [$_S$ it to appear [$_S$ Mary to be calm]] $\Rightarrow$ RSP

    b. Mary tried [$_S$ Mary to appear [$_S$ to be calm]] $\Rightarrow$ Equi

    c. Mary tried ___ to appear to be calm

Again, we see, quite clearly, that Equi is a consequence of RSP in such cases. Thus, if we are to maintain our assumption that there is no rule of Equi, then we must also give up RSP and search for an alternative account of the range of data that it explains. Or, turning to (12b), under the assumption that Dative moves an NP leftward, we obtain the following derivation.

(14) a. Δ gave a dime to every child $\Rightarrow$ Dative

    b. Δ gave every child a dime $\Rightarrow$ Passive (and Δ-deletion)

    c. every child was given a dime

Here we see that if Dative applies to (14a) to yield (14b), then Passive must subsequently apply so as to derive (14c). But above we concluded that Passive does not exist since Equi does not exist. Hence if Dative is contingent on Passive, there can be no Dative in the form assumed for this derivation. And likewise for Object Shift. Thus, consider the derivation associated with (12c).

(15) a. He$_i$ tried [$_S$ it to be easy [$_S$ Δ to please he$_i$] $\Rightarrow$ Object Shift

    b. He$_i$ tried [$_S$ he$_i$ to be easy [$_S$ Δ to please] $\Rightarrow$ Equi

    c. He tried ___ to be easy to please

After Object Shift has applied to yield (15b), Equi is needed to provide for the desired surface structure. Thus, Object Shift must be eliminated also if Equi is given up. And, finally, it is possible to arrive at a similar conclusion with respect to there-Insertion, as indicated in the derivation of (12d).

(16) a. Δ believed [$_S$ jelly to be between his toes] $\Rightarrow$ there-Insertion

    b. Δ believed [$_S$ there to be jelly between his toes] $\Rightarrow$ ROP

    c. Δ believed there [$_S$ to be jelly between his toes] $\Rightarrow$ Passive

    d. there was believed to be jelly between his toes

Derivation (16) illustrates a contingency of there-Insertion on ROP and Passive which, recall, do not exist if Equi does not exist. Proceeding on the assumption that Equi does not exist, we conclude that there-Insertion does not either.

Thus, we see that the consequences of giving up Equi are somewhat drastic. One could perhaps take these conclusions as a reductio ad absurdum argument against abandoning Equi, but I will accept the correct alternative hypothesis and assume that all structures previously derived by local transformations must in fact be generated as base structures. Let us call this approach the base hypothesis.

Base Hypothesis: All structures previously derived by local transformations are in fact generated by phrase structure rules.

The base hypothesis was first advanced in the course of my Fulbright-Hays lectures in the fall of 1973 and later published as (Brame 1976). If one accepts the base hypothesis, a question arises as to just what replaces the traditional local transformations. I will have more to say about this in the sequel. Here, however, I wish to provide several additional arguments to support the base hypothesis.

2. Affix-Hopping and there-Insertion

In this section new evidence will be adduced to support the base hypothesis. First, let us consider the putative rule known as Affix-Hopping, which was initially proposed and formulated in Chomsky (1975, 1957). The key is that Affix-Hopping is a local transformation in our sense. That is, it does not make essential use of variables and therefore, according to the base hypothesis, is not a transformation. There is, in fact, some evidence indicating that auxiliaries can be generated in English directly by base rules and that direct generation is desirable. This approach makes use of a more sophisticated theory of the lexicon, one approach being that developed in (Hust 1976, 1977).

By way of presenting the evidence, let us note first that the standard theory misses a significant generalization. Consider, for example, the following ungrammatical cases.

(17) a. *John is being drinking beer.
   b. *John's being drinking beer all day surprises me.
   c. *Being drinking beer all day, John is slowly going under.

Consider first (17a). How is this example prohibited within the framework of the standard theory? It is blocked by virtue of the phrase structure rules expanding Aux, as in (18).

(18) Aux → tense (M) (have en) (be ing)

Since two instances of be ing cannot be generated by rule (18), example (17a) will never arise subsequent to Affix-Hopping. Thus, one mechanism, namely, phrase structure, is utilized to block (17a). However, a totally different mechanism must be utilized to block (17b) and (17c), since (presumably) the gerund-ive and participial phrases in such examples are derived via transformation from sentential sources in the standard theory. In fact, Chomsky (1970, 16, fn. 6) quite explicitly remarks that examples such as (17b) are blocked by a special constraint:

(19) Forms such as *John's being reading the book* (but not *John's having been reading the book*) are blocked by a restriction against certain -ing -ing sequences (compare *John's stopping reading, John's having stopped reading,* etc.)

Thus, examples (17b) and (17c) are ruled out by a special restriction on -ing -ing sequences, constituting one mechanism, whereas example (17a) is ruled out by a totally different mechanism, phrase structure. This amounts to a loss of generalization. The significant generalization for all the examples appears to be that being does not select ing-complements. This generalization could be expressed if being were a lexical item, but it goes unexpressed under the traditional approach utilizing Affix-Hopping.

I will briefly sketch one possible lexical approach below. But first let us turn to a second set of examples which bear on the base hypothesis.

(20) a. There was a boy being arrested.
b. *There was being a boy arrested.
c. There were to be three boys arrested.

Examples such as these pose critical problems for the standard theory of transformational grammar, where expletive there is inserted via transformation. Within such an approach adopting there-Insertion, special conditions (and complications) must be associated with this rule in order to keep it from applying and producing (20b). One might ask how such restrictions could prohibit (20b) and yet allow (20c). If we assume that such restrictions are in fact formulable so as to account for the data in (20), we must still conclude that such an account leads to a loss of significant generalization inasmuch as it fails to provide a general account of the examples in (20) and those in (21).

(21) a. It was a boy being arrested.
b. *It was being a boy arrested.
c. It was to be a boy arrested.

Apparently (21b) must be ruled out by a mechanism completely independent of there-Insertion, if there is inserted transformationally in (20). However, the correct approach would utilize the same mechanism to rule out (21b) and (20b). This mechanism entails generating existential sentences directly. It thereby supports the base hypothesis which provides for direct generation of existentials.

A tentative account of the data can be sketched by making

use of Hust's theory of the lexicon along with a version of Emonds' approach to auxiliaries in English. Tentative phrase structure rules are provided in (22).

(22) a. S̄ → Comp S
    b. S → NP Aux VP
    c. VP → V VP . . .
    d. Aux → tense (M)

Lexical entries are represented as trees and lexical items are taken to be individual leaves of lexical trees. By Hust's precipitation convention, "all features of a node A in a lexical entry are assigned to all nodes dominated by A" (Hust 1976, 51). Thus, a simplified representation for refuse ~ refusal is, according to Hust, the following.

(23)

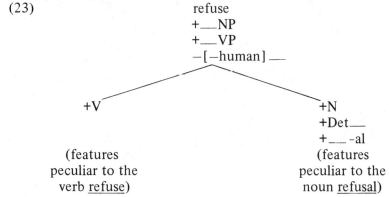

Hust supplements his lexicon with a set of redundancy rules (suggested by Chomsky in earlier work). Thus, for example, +N in (23) can be filled in by redundancy rules on the basis of the presence of the feature +Det__. It is to be emphasized that individual lexical items are leaves of trees such as (23). Together with the precipitation convention, then, a lexical entry will be a constellation of syntactic and phonological (and perhaps semantic) features. It is to be noted that morphological features such as +__-al in (23) are considered to be part of the lexical entry itself after feature precipitation (as opposed to a context for lexical insertion). Thus, the lexical entry for *refusal*, after precipitation, is [+__NP, +__VP, −[−human]__, +N, +Det__] together with the phonological sequence *refusal.*

A similar approach can now be taken in the case of auxiliary elements in English. It will be assumed that active participles such as *eating, having, being,* etc., are dominated by the category V, that past participles such as *eaten, had, been,* etc., are dominated by the category V, and that nonderived verbs such as *eat, have, be,* etc., are dominated by V. This elaboration entails a slight modification of rule (22c).

(24)

$$VP \rightarrow \begin{Bmatrix} V \\ \bar{V} \\ \bar{\bar{V}} \end{Bmatrix} VP \ldots$$

The lexical entry for *eat* and its related participles can now be tentatively given as follows:

(25)

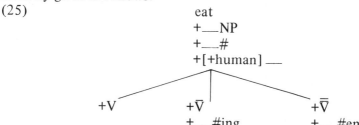

```
                              eat
                           +__NP
                           +__#
                           +[+human] __

        +V               +V̄                    +V̄̄
                      +__#ing              +__#en
```

Actually, (25) is redundant in various ways. For example, the participial endings can be omitted provided we supplement the lexicon with the following redundancy rules.[2]

(26) $[+\bar{V} \rightarrow [+\_\_\#ing]$
     $[+\bar{\bar{V}} \rightarrow [+\_\_\#en]$

Thus, *eat, eating,* and *eaten* are all considered to be individual *lexical items,* although the fact that all three select identical complements is expressed in terms of a single *lexical entry.* That is, the precipitation convention will associate the relevant contextual features of the root node of (25) with its leaves.

Now let us consider how the correct order of auxiliaries is predicted within the approach sketched here. In this case, be can be given the tentative representation in (27).

(27)

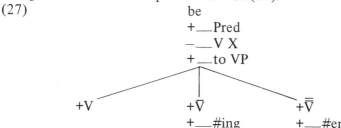

```
                               be
                           +__Pred
                           -__V X
                           +__to VP

        +V               +V̄                    +V̄̄
                      +__#ing              +__#en
```

Of interest here is the feature $[-\_\_V\ X]$. This feature will prohibit sequences such as *John was eat the beans* but will allow *John was eating the beans* and *John was seen.* Thus, *be* can be followed by active and passive participles. This is also true of *been*, as predicted by feature precipitation.

(28) a. *John has *been eat* the beans.
     b. John has *been eating* the beans.
     c. John has *been seen.*

Likewise, by feature precipitation we expect a similar state of affairs to hold for being.

(29) a. *John is *being eat* the beans.

b. *John is *being eating* the beans.

c. John is *being taken.*

Of course, the fact that (29b) is ungrammatical is just the problem described earlier in terms of (17a). But, now we may account for (29b)-(17a), as well as (17b) and (17c) with one general redundancy rule.

(30) $[+\bar{V}] \rightarrow [-\_\_\bar{V}\ X]$

This rule may be taken as a formalization of Chomsky's restriction noted in (19); however, by giving up Affix-Hopping and by treating the distribution of auxiliaries lexically, we succeed in expressing all of the facts in (17) by the same means, namely, by (31), whereas the standard theory requires two separate mechanisms.[3]

Let us now also return to (20b) and (21b). Recall, the standard theory must rule out (20b) by constraining there-Insertion without, however, blocking (20c), and it must rule out (20b) by a different mechanism since there-Insertion is irrelevant in this case. Both of these examples, (20b) and (21b), can be ruled out by a natural extension of the redundancy rule (30) and, consequently, there is indeed a deeper generalization missed by the standard theory.

Let us assume that Pred is expanded according to the following rule (31).[4]

$$(31)\ \text{Pred} \rightarrow (\text{NP}) \begin{Bmatrix} \text{VP} \\ \text{PP} \\ \text{AP} \\ \text{A}_{\text{SD}} \end{Bmatrix}$$

Let us assume further that expletive *there* is generated directly in subject position by base rules and that there is no rule of there-Insertion. Then (20a) and (21a) are allowed by virtue of the lexical entry for *be* in (27). The same distribution should hold for *being* and *been*. However, in the case of *being*, as in (20b) and (21b), the presence of Pred leads to ungrammaticality. But now we may simply extend the redundancy rule (30) in the following way.

(32) $[+\bar{V}] \rightarrow [-\_\_\bar{V}\ X, -\_\_\text{Pred}]$

Thus, by (32), active participles, in particular *being*, will select neither active participles nor predicate phrases as their complements. This analysis thus succeeds in ruling out (20b) in precisely the same way that it rules out (21b), a generalization missed in the standard theory. This mechanism also accounts for the examples in (17).

Additional examples, brought to my attention by Robin Cooper, make it necessary to further revise (32). These examples include the following.

(33) a. I do not approve of there being two knives on the table.

b. There being nobody at home, we left.

Such examples show that the prohibition against predicate complements is not absolute in the case of active participles, but rather contingent on the presence of an overt auxiliary element such as *tense* or *modal.* Therefore, it is necessary to alter (32) so as to express this fact.

(34) $[+\bar{V}] \rightarrow [-\_\bar{V} X, -NP \text{ Aux}\_\text{Pred}]$

It appears that a number of facts can be handled adequately within the framework advanced here. The generalizations that emerge, however, depend crucially on base generated existential sentences. This is a conclusion reached on independent grounds in section 1, a conclusion which is consistent with the base hypothesis and argued independently in (Jenkins 1972) and (Brame 1976).[5] The data adduced in this section therefore support this hypothesis.

Before turning to additional evidence for base generated structures previously derived by transformation, let us consider the following examples mentioned in Akmajian and Wasow (1975) and elaborated in Iwakura (1977a).

(35) a. Sam was being examined by a psychiatrist and Bill was __ too.

b. *Sam was being examined by a psychiatrist and Bill was being __ too.

Akmajian and Wasow fail to express a basic generalization concerning the full range of relevant examples involving VP phenomena, as Iwakura (1977a) shows. However, Iwakura also fails to express the generalization since he requires at least two mechanisms to rule out the structures which would otherwise be generated. Thus, for Iwakura (35b) is out because *examined by a psychiatrist* is not a single VP constituent within his framework, an assumption which can be questioned, and (36) is out because of a special condition which he associates with VP-Deletion.

(36) *Which bothers you more: John's having taken a drug, or Bill's having __?

If we consider VP gaps to be base generated, say, in terms of Δ, both (35b) and (36) can be ruled out by the same means. We need only revise the redundancy rule (34) so that *being* will not select Δ.

(37) $[+\bar{V}] \rightarrow [-\_\bar{V} X, -NP \text{ Aux}\_\text{Pred}, -\_\Delta X]$

If this approach is correct, it shows that VP's should not be deleted, as assumed earlier. Rather, VP phenomena must be treated interpretively as argued in recent work. Moreover, this conclusion has consequences which bear on the base hypothesis, for consider the examples listed in (38).

(38) a. They said that Mary appears to be sick and she does
       __.

    b. Joe was examined by a quack and Bill was __ too.

    c. They said there was an elephant in the yard and there
       was __.

    d. Mary was given a message and Sue was __ too.

According to the approach advocated here, the gaps in (38a-d) are generated as Δ. But if this is indeed the case, then Raising to Subject Position, Passive, there-Insertion, and Dative cannot account for the data exhibited in the right conjunct of each of these examples. Thus, the relevant structures must be base generated, a conclusion arrived at on independent grounds in section 1.

3. Extraposition and Sentential Subjects

    In the foregoing it has been suggested that structures previously derived by local transformations are in fact base generated. (Local transformation means a transformation which does not make essential use of variables.) Now what about the putative rule of Extraposition? This transformation has been stated with variables in the literature of transformational grammar. However, there is an important difference between Extraposition and other rules stated with variables, such as Question Formation, Relative Clause Formation, Topicalization, etc. The variable in Extraposition could in principle be replaced by a disjunction of constant terms, although this is not the case for Question Formation, Relative Clause Formation, etc. To put it differently, in Ross's terms Extraposition is bounded, whereas the other rules are not.

    Now, if we take essential variable to mean unbounded essential variable of the type found in Question Formation, Relative Clause Formation, etc., then Extraposition is a local transformation in the relevant sense and therefore, accepting the base hypothesis, should not be considered a transformation. Rather, extraposed S's should be base generated and sentential subject S's should also be base generated. This position is taken in Brame (1976, 142).

    Let us now turn to some evidence which supports the base generation hypothesis in this case. First, it is important to observe that S's and VP's are not NP's, a position defended in Emonds (1970, 1972) on the basis of examples such as the following.[6]

(39) a. *They told *that everything would turn out for the best* to the children.

    b. They told the children *that everything would turn out for the best.*

    c. They told *a story* to the children.

    d.   They told the children *a story*.

(40) a. *He blamed it on *that Bill was too strict*.

      b. He blamed it on *Bill's strictness*.

(41) a. *It was *that John refused to see the light* that bothered us.

      b. It was *John's refusal* that bothered us.

(42) a. *You promised *to be quiet* to Mary.

      b. You promised Mary *to be quiet*.

      c. You promised *a new hat* to Mary.

      d. You promised Mary *a new hat*.

These data indicate that S's and VP's are not NP's since they would be expected to exhibit the identical distribution of NP's if they were. Thus, in (39c), the true NP *a story* can occupy the immediate post verbal slot in the sentence, but this is not so in the case of (39a), indicating that the italicized phrase is not an NP, etc.

    Let us accept Emonds' straightforward explanation for this range of data and proceed to the crucial examples.

(43) a. That John was sick bothered Mary.

      b. *Did that John was sick bother Mary?

(44) a. That John dislikes artichokes surprised you.

      b. *Which artichokes did that John dislikes surprise you?

(45) a. That it bothers the teacher for John to smoke is quite possible.

      b. *That for John to smoke bothers the teacher is quite possible.

(46) a. That he forgot his lesson proves that John was not serious.

      b. *It proves that John was not serious that he forgot his lesson.

Some of these examples, and in some cases all of them, have been discussed and treated by grammarians working within the transformational framework. These grammarians include Ross (1967), Emonds (1970, 1976), Higgins (1973), Kuno (1973), Horn (1975), and Iwakura (1977b). It seems to me that all of the analyses advanced have failed in one way or another to express the basic generalization underlying the full range of data.[7] Accepting the base hypothesis, we can attempt to express the generalization in terms of phrase structure.

    Let us recall that in Emonds' earlier work (1970, 69), it was argued that sentential subjects are not dominated by NP in surface structure. Thus, Emonds argued that an example such as *For the house to be painted would irritate him* should be represented in surface structure as (47).

DIAGRAM (47) FOLLOWS ON NEXT PAGE

(47)

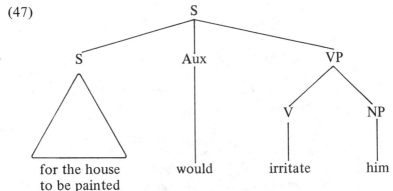

for the house
to be painted   would   irritate   him

According to Emonds (47) is derived by a rule which is essentially the inverse of Extraposition, where S is substituted for the NP
subject. However, adopting the base hypothesis, let us now
assume that Emonds' surface structure is in fact the base generated structure.[8] That is, let us assume that S's and VP's can be
generated directly as subjects where the relevant categories are
not dominated by NP. To resolve the difficulties that arise in
connection with (43)-(46), however, let us introduce the category $\bar{\bar{S}}$, which will play a crucial role in explaining the relevant
data.

(48) a. $\bar{\bar{S}} \rightarrow \begin{Bmatrix} \bar{S} \\ VP \end{Bmatrix}$ Aux VP

    b. $\bar{S} \rightarrow$ Comp S

    c. S $\rightarrow$ NP Aux VP

    d. VP $\rightarrow$ V $\begin{Bmatrix} \bar{\bar{S}} \\ \bar{S} \\ VP \\ . \\ . \\ . \end{Bmatrix}$ ...

Now let us see how this reanalysis explains all of the data tabu-
lated in (43)-(46) without recourse to special constraints such as
Ross's Sentential Subject Constraint and Island Internal S Constraint, Emonds's constraint on root transformations, Horn's
NP Constraint and global Pruning, etc.

    Consider first (43b). Since *that John was sick* is a sentential
subject, Comp is unavailable for the root $\bar{S}$ which dominates it,
and consequently a question cannot be formed. For exactly the
same reason, a <u>wh</u>-question cannot be formed and thus (44b)
cannot be derived. Example (45b) also cannot be generated
since the sentential subject $\bar{S}$ cannot be expanded to yield a
second sentential subject by rule (48b). Finally, (46b) is avoided
by virtue of the fact that VP cannot be expanded by rule (48d)

to provide two sentential complements. In sum, we see that all of the relevant examples are explained quite naturally by phrase structure. This analysis should be compared with the proposals found in the literature mentioned above.

Additional support for the position outlined here is gleaned from the following examples.

(49) a. I imagine for one to work that hard would require a lot of effort.

b. I suppose to do that would require a good deal of manual dexterity.

c. I guess that the night is black demonstrates that the universe is expanding.

d. I imagine that Bill works hard shows that he is German.

Many speakers apparently accept some sentences such as these with embedded sentential and VP subjects, although there is variation from speaker to speaker. Other examples are clearly ungrammatical for all speakers.

(50) a. *I resent for you to leave would bother her.

b. *It is surprising for you to say that would annoy him.

c. *It bothers me that John left proves that he was not serious.

The fact that we do obtain different results for different predicates, say *imagine* vs. *resent*, indicates that we are dealing with a lexical phenomenon (i.e., with subcategorization). But the reanalysis sketched out in the foregoing makes just such an approach_possible since rule (48d) has been introduced to provide for $\bar{S}$. Thus, *imagine, guess,* etc., but not *resent,* etc., can be subcategorized to select $\bar{S}$, providing for (49a-d), but not for (50a-c).

The new analysis admits a further prediction which is borne out. It predicts a contrast between the examples in (51) and those listed in (49).

(51) a. *I imagine that for one to work that hard would require a lot of effort.

b. *I suppose that to do that would require a good deal of manual dexterity.

c. *I guess that the night is black demonstrates that the universe is expanding.

d. *I imagine that that Bill works hard shows that he is German.

These data follow from the fact that $\bar{\bar{S}}$ does not directly dominate a Comp node as does $\bar{S}$. Hence, the complementizers such as *that* and *for* in (49) are all associated with the sentential $\bar{S}$ which is dominated by $\bar{\bar{S}}$. This explanation appears to me to be quite natural and straightforward. If correct, it should lend credence to the analysis advanced in this section.

4. The Spelling Prohibition

In sections 3 and 4, new evidence has been provided to support base generated structures which were previously derived via transformation. In this section a general constraint will be suggested which has the effect of favoring the analyses outlined above. The Spelling Prohibition will, in fact, have the effect of prohibiting the previous transformational analyses which have been impugned by the evidence adduced in the previous discussion. This constraint can be initially formulated as follows.

Spelling Prohibition (weak form): Transformations cannot spell out morphological material (or effect the spelling out).

The effect of the Spelling Prohibition is to ensure that all morphological material is present after lexical insertion. Thus, the presence of morphological material such as the expletive *there* and the passive *be en* is contingent on phrase structure and the lexicon, a result which is consistent with the arguments of previous sections. Consequently, the Spelling Prohibition makes classical transformations such as <u>there</u>-Insertion and Passive unavailable to the theory, a desirable result.

The Spelling Prohibition has consequences for many other transformations proposed in the literature. For one, it disallows a rule switching *some* to *any* as suggested in earlier work such as Klima (1964). Rather, *any* must be introduced directly into phrase structure. That there is no rule turning *some* to *any* has been argued in Lakoff (1969).[9] Another proposed transformation which is prohibited by the Spelling Prohibition is Comp-Placement, which was originally proposed in Rosenbaum (1967). The fact that Bresnan (1970, 1972) has shown that complementizers such as *that, for,* and *wh* must be present in phrase structure shows that the Spelling Prohibition (hereafter SP) makes a correct prediction in this case. SP also rules out the possibility of deriving NP's such as *John's picture* from relative clause constructions such as *the picture that John has* as proposed in early work and accepted in Chomsky (1970, 40) and suggests base generation as per the base generated possessives involving intrinsic connection discussed by Chomsky. This follows from the fact that the morphological material *'s* would otherwise have to be inserted by the transformation. Other elements are also prohibited as transformationally inserted elements, such as the *of* in *several of John's proofs of the theorem* (Chomsky 1970). Bresnan has in fact suggested that *of* should not be inserted by transformation (1973). Again we see that SP makes the correct prediction. SP likewise prohibits deriving *who, what,* etc., from *wh-someone, wh-something,* etc., as argued in Chomsky (1964). Chomsky has shown that *who* and *someone, what* and *something,* etc., bear a close relationship in that they exhibit many distributional similarities, one illustration of which is given in (52).

(52) a. Harry will meet with *someone else.*

    b. *Who else* will Harry meet with?

    c. *Harry will meet with *a girl else.*

    d. *Harry will meet with *the adviser else.*

In (52) we see that *else* can cooccur with *wh*-words and with *some*-words. This fact could be explained if *who, what,* etc., derived from *wh-someone, wh-something,* etc. However SP disallows such a derivation, and therefore we might expect to find a difference in distributional properties. We do, indeed, find a distinguishing environment.

(53) a. *Who the hell* broke my typewriter?

    b. **Someone the hell* broke my typewriter.*

(54) a. *What in tarnation* are you talking about?

    b. *You are talking about *something in tarnation.*

(55) a. *Where in the name of God* did Sam buy that Okito box?

    b. *Sam bought that Okito box *somewhere in the name of God.*

Such examples again show that SP makes correct predictions. Proceeding, we see that SP also disallows *do*-Support as a transformation in any of the variant formulations in which *do* is inserted by transformation. Rather, according to SP, *do* must be introduced in base structures. Rules such as Case-Marking, Subject-Verb Agreement, and other agreement rules are also prohibited by SP. Rather, case violations, agreement violations, and the like should apparently be treated by a checking or filtering mechanism, as suggested in Bresnan (1971) and Brame (1977). The classical approach to pronominalization and reflexivization is also disallowed by SP. This accords with much recent research which shows that pronouns, reflexives, and reciprocals should be base generated. Base generation of such pronouns and anaphoric pronouns, including *so,* is a direct consequence of SP, thus lending further credence to its correctness. Finally, SP has the virtue of prohibiting lexical decomposition, which plays a prominent role in generative semantics. Thus, for example, Seuren writes that generative semanticists "posit a great deal of transformational syntax inside, or behind, lexical items, especially verbs (1974);" advocates of this lexical decomposition approach derive the (b) examples of (56)-(59) from structures akin to the corresponding (a) examples.

(56) a. John struck Bill as being similar to a gorilla.

    b. Bill reminded John of a gorilla.

(57) a. The sauce came to be thick.

    b. The sauce thickened.

(58) a. John caused Harry to die.

b. John killed Harry.

(59) a. Mary persuaded Bill not to go.

b. Mary dissuaded Bill from going.

Considerable internal evidence has been adduced in Brame (1976, ch. 1) to demonstrate that lexical decomposition cannot be maintained without loss of significant generalization. The fact that SP is consistent with these language specific independent arguments further supports it as a basic constraint on the functioning of grammars.

It is possible, and conceivably correct, to strengthen SP in the following way.

Spelling Prohibition (strong form): Transformations cannot spell out or alter morphological material.

The strong form of SP has the added effect of prohibiting deletion of morphological material as well as substitution for morphological material. Thus, substitution of a sentential complement for *it*, according to one version of Raising to Subject Position and Raising to Object Position is prohibited, a result consistent with the conclusions of section 1. Similarly, Object Shift, which substitutes an object NP for *it* so as to derive sentences such as *John is easy to please* from *it is easy to please John* is disallowed, a result which again coincides with the conclusions of section 1. Of course, the deletion approach to Object Shift phenomena, as proposed in (Lasnick 1974), is also prohibited by the strong form of SP (cf. Brame 1976 for discussion). The strong form of SP also disallows Extraposition, albeit somewhat indirectly, since it-Deletion is prohibited. Alternative approaches involving spelling out of *it*, as in (Chomsky 1965), are ruled out by the weak form of SP. Dative is also disallowed since deletion of *to* or *for* is ruled out, as are alternative approaches which spell out *to* and *for*. Finally, the deletion approach to VP gaps is also ruled out by the strong form of SP.

We see, then, that SP has consequences consistent with the (language) internal arguments advanced in (Brame 1976) and in the preceding sections. This convergence provides considerable motivation for SP and, therefore, it is advanced as a universal constraint on the functioning of transformations.

5. Lexicalism vs. the Inverse Cycle

In view of the fact that a large number of transformations must be abandoned in favor of base generated structures, we might ask just how the explanations provided by the classical transformations are to be expressed. Before attempting an answer to this question, it is important to recognize just what it is that the classical transformations account for, in view of the fact that there is a good deal of misunderstanding on this point.

Let us take Passive as the basis of discussion in this section.

It is often asserted that transformational rules account for paraphrase relations or synonymy relations which hold between the sentences related by transformation. The truth of the matter is that paraphrase and synonymy remain as vague today as they were before the advent of transformational grammar. Transformations provide no insight into putative relations such as paraphrase and synonymy. Others have argued that grammatical relations are preserved under transformation, yet such advocates fail to indicate to what extent such relations yield insight into any interesting questions or how they resolve outstanding issues. It seems, therefore, that we must recognize that classical transformations have served one and only one basic function and that is the syntactic function of accounting for distributional generalizations by avoiding repetitive statements involving co-occurrence phenomena.[10] For example, in the case of Passive, it has been assumed that if an active verb selects an NP as direct object, its passive counterpart will select that NP as subject. And if an active verb does not select an NP as object or fails to select a specific kind of NP as object, then the same facts will hold for the subject of the passive counterpart. Thus, because (60a) allows *the beans* as object of *eat*, (60b) allows *the beans* as subject of *be eaten*. And, equally important, because (61a) does not allow *sincerity* as object of *eat, sincerity* is not allowed as subject of *be eaten*.

(60) a. John ate the beans.

    b. The beans were eaten by John.

(61) a. John ate sincerity.

    b. Sincerity was eaten by John.

Since the foregoing is a distributional argument, it is quite obviously a syntactic argument. Now, if passives are derived from actives, then the convergence of distributional facts follows as a consequence and need be stated only once in the grammar, namely, before the Passive rule applies. However, if Passive is abandoned in its classical formulation, then how can the syntactic generalizations be expressed? One answer to this question was provided in Brame (1976), where both actives and passives are base generated in conformity with the base hypothesis of section 1. In lieu of the classical rule of Passive, its inverse was proposed which had the effect of converting base generated passives into structures identical to actives. It was at this deep level of derived actives that the co-occurrence restrictions were checked, thus expressing the basis generalization inherent in (60)-(61).

Another possibility was suggested in Brame (1976, 132): "Granted that passives are generated directly, it remains to relate them to corresponding actives. One approach would be to formulate a lexical redundancy rule taking a form quite similar to the

Passive transformation itself." Recently Bresnan (1973) has provided an explicit statement of such a redundancy rule and has suggested that all local transformations be supplanted by lexical redundancy rules, thus accepting the base hypothesis. Let us identify the redundancy rule approach with the lexicalist hypothesis which was initiated in Chomsky (1970). This position can be informally stated as follows.

Lexicalist Hypothesis: All co-occurrence generalizations previously expressed by local transformations are expressed by lexical redundancy rules.

The inverse cycle and the lexicalist hypothesis are contrasted schematically in (62).

(62)

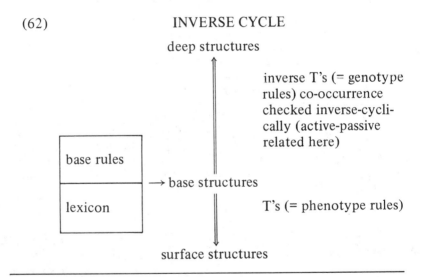

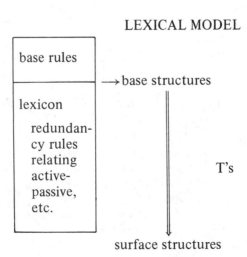

There is a certain naturalness to the lexicalist model depicted in (62). Local transformations are typically local by virtue of the fact that a particular lexical item, usually a predicate, serves as the locus of the transformation. It is quite natural to express the locality of such phenomena in that area of the grammar where lexical items are represented and where unboundedness cannot be expressed, namely, in the lexicon. Then, it is no longer a mystery why certain lexical items typically serve as the locus of local transformations.

Now, however, we must ask if there are any empirical arguments favoring one approach over the other. In the case of Passive, there appears to be some evidence favoring the lexical model. To see this, let us return to the lexical entry for *eat* as (25) in section 2. By feature precipitation, the past participle *eaten* will be positively specified for +__NP, whereas in fact the NP object must assume the subject position in this case. Otherwise, a grammar incorporating (25), along with base generated past participles, will give rise to ungrammatical strings such as *NP was eaten the bananas*. To overcome this difficulty, just as we posited lexical redundancy rule (34) to account for additional distributional characteristics of $\bar{V}$, we may now do likewise for $\bar{\bar{V}}$.[12]

$$(63) \quad [+\bar{\bar{V}}] \rightarrow [\alpha [f] \, \_\_] \, / \, \left\{ \begin{array}{c} \underline{} \\ +\_\_NP \\ \alpha \_\_ [\underline{f}] \end{array} \right\}$$

This redundancy rule is of course the lexical analogue of the transformational rule known as NP-Preposing or the inverse rule known as NP-Postposing. By accepting the lexical approach to participles outlined in section 2, we are thereby forced to choose the lexicalist model depicted in (62).

There is further evidence that this conclusion is not only desirable, but that it allows us to express a much deeper generalization. Note first that adjectives in *-able* which are derived from verbs exhibit one characteristic feature of passives. When the V of the adjective sequence selects NP as object, the related adjective itself selects this NP as subject. Chomsky (1970) noted this redundancy and proposed a lexical approach.

> . . . insofar as a subregularity exists regarding selectional rules in the case of -able, it can be formulated as a lexical rule that assigns the feature [X__] to a lexical item [V-able] where V has the intrinsic selectional feature [__X].
>
> Chomsky (1970, 56)

Chomsky's rule has been formulated by Hust (1976, 67) as approximately the following.

(64)
$$[+\underline{\quad}\#\underline{able}] \rightarrow [\alpha\,[\underline{f}]\underline{\quad}] \; / \; \begin{Bmatrix} \underline{\quad\quad} \\ +\underline{\quad}NP \\ \alpha\underline{\quad}[\underline{f}] \end{Bmatrix}$$

Hust has gone on to show that unpassive adjectives exhibit identical selectional properties. Thus, he was able to express the two sets of co-occurrence restriction by one general rule, repeated here as (65).

(65)
$$\begin{Bmatrix} [+\underline{\quad}\#\underline{able}] \\ [+un\#\underline{\quad}\#\underline{ed}] \end{Bmatrix} \rightarrow [\alpha[\underline{f}]\underline{\quad}] \; / \; \begin{Bmatrix} \underline{\quad\quad} \\ +\underline{\quad}NP \\ \alpha\underline{\quad}[\underline{f}] \end{Bmatrix}$$

Of relevance for the present discussion is the fact that rule (63) can now be collapsed with Hust's rule (65), thus expressing a deeper generalization.

(66)
$$\begin{Bmatrix} [+\overline{\overline{V}}] \\ [+\underline{\quad}\#\underline{able}] \\ [+\underline{un}\#\underline{\quad}\#\underline{ed}] \end{Bmatrix} \rightarrow [\alpha[\underline{f}]\underline{\quad}] \; / \; \begin{Bmatrix} \underline{\quad\quad} \\ +\underline{\quad}NP \\ \alpha\underline{\quad}[\underline{f}] \end{Bmatrix}$$

The fact that a deeper generalization is naturally expressed within the lexical framework provides some justification for favoring it, at least in the case of passives.

6. The Transformational Component

If local transformations are to be replaced with lexical redundancy rules, one might ask what transformations remain. A rather natural answer to this question is embodied in the following constraint on the form of transformations.

Variable Constraint: All transformations make essential use of unbounded variables.

Thus, rules such as Question Formation, Relative Clause Formation, Topicalization, and the like, all of which make essential use of variables which are unbounded, are the remaining candidates for the transformational component. This result is natural when contrasted with the observations of the preceding sections. Thus, unlike local transformations, no single lexical item serves as the locus of the long-distance rules. Hence, long-distance rules could not, in principle, be expressed as lexical redundancy rules. By contrast, given the Variable Constraint as a constraint on the form of transformations, local transformations no longer qualify as transformational rules.

These conclusions may prove too strong and additional analyses with precise formulations of the rules in question are needed before a final determination can be made. For example, there are some root transformations such as Subject-Aux Inversion which do not qualify as transformations by the Variable

Constraint. Perhaps it would not be pointless to consider the feasibility of base generating all relevant structures of a local character by elaborating the base, as was done in section 3 with respect to sentential subjects and extraposed S's.

There is furthermore a model of grammar which is also worthy of serious consideration. This model can be thought of as a hybrid of the two models depicted in (62) and is laid out in picture form in (67).

(67)   INVERSE LEXICAL MODEL

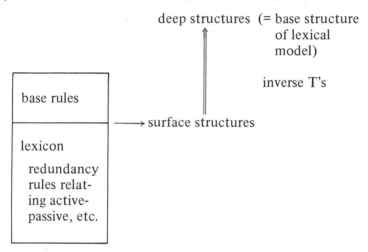

If the Variable Constraint can be maintained, then the inverse lexical model is appealing for the following reason. By treating long-distance rules in an inverse fashion, we succeed in expressing a generalization which cannot be expressed in the standard theory, as argued in (Brame 1976). To see this, consider the following ungrammatical strings.

(68) a. *John saw the boy (who) Mary likes the girl.
      b. *What did they see the parade?
      c. *It was the car that I parked the truck in the garage.
      d. *Harry I saw Sue yesterday.
      e. *That she would do such a thing I believe Harry to be impossible.
      f. *They said she was examined by Dr. Qu, and examined by Dr. Qu she was arrested by the police.

Against the examples in (68), the following grammatical sentences should be contrasted.

(69) a. John saw the boy (who) Mary likes.
      b. What did they see?
      c. It was the car that I parked in the garage.
      d. Harry I saw yesterday.

e. That she would do such a thing I believe to be impossible.

f. They said she was examined by Dr. Qu, and examined by Dr. Qu she was.

Now how does the standard theory rule out the examples in (68)? According to (Chomsky 1965), (68a) is ruled out by the filtering function of transformations. Thus, special boundary symbols suffice to ensure identity in relative clauses and if the boundary symbol is not erased by application of Relative Clause Formation, which itself requires identity, then the internal occurrence of the boundary symbols will be sensitive to a filtering device, thus blocking the example. However, other examples in (68) will be ruled out by different mechanisms. Thus, (68b) will be blocked by virtue of the fact that *what* originates as the object of the verb *see*, which does not allow two objects. Hence by purely lexical considerations, (68b) is ruled out, as are some of the other examples in (68). But this surely constitutes a loss of generalization. An adequate theory would rule out all of (68) by the same basic mechanism. If we generate the examples in (69) directly, that is, if the *who* in (69a) is generated in Comp position, *what* in Composition in (69b), *the car* in focus position in (69c), *Harry* in the topicalization position in (69d), etc., then it is possible to rule out all of (68) by purely lexical considerations, as advocated in Brame (1976).

NOTES

1. To take just one example, consider Lakoff's absolute exception mechanism advocated in Lakoff (1970). Lakoff marks predicates such as *try* with ad hoc absolute exception features so that they will obligatorily meet the structural description of Equi. In other words, *try* is syntactically irregular within Lakoff's framework for appearing in the structures in which it appears. For summary and criticism of proposals for dealing with examples such as (1b), (2b), and (3b), see Brame (1976, 94-97, 103-107).

2. Many details and redundant properties of lexical items are being glossed over here in order to avoid unduly burdening the exposition. For example, irregular past participles are listed ad hoc and cannot be predicted, whereas the feature $+\bar{V}$ for present participles is itself redundant. A detailed discussion of these and other properties of the auxiliary system in English is provided in Brame (in preparation).

3. The so-called doubl-ing facts have been discussed by Ross

(1967), who proposes a global rule to account for the relevant data. Both Emonds (1973) and Milsark (1972) have demonstrated that a nonglobal account is superior. Pullum (1974) has adduced new evidence. In Brame (in preparation) the controversy is reviewed and it is shown that the doubl-ing facts all follow naturally from an approach similar to that advanced here, i.e. from a more sophisticated theory of the lexicon together with redundancy rules and constraints on what can constitute a subcategorizational feature.

4. Rule (31) is tentative and by no means exhausts the predicate phrase, which has been neglected in transformational studies. The inclusion of (NP) within the Pred phrase may be incorrect, as assumed in (Milsark 1972).

5. It was Emonds (1970) who first noted and attempted to come to grips with examples such as the following:
   (i) a. Some boys were doctors.
       b. *There were some boys doctors.
   (ii) a. An elephant was small.
       b. *There was an elephant small.

Emond's explanation was based on structural considerations and the structure-preserving hypothesis. To create the ungrammatical (b) examples required a violation of the structure-preserving hypothesis, which is possible only in the case of root transformations (and minor movement rules) within Emonds's framework. Jenkins (1972) attempted to account for the same phenomena utilizing Emonds's basic observation concerning phrase structure. However, for Jenkins, expletive *there* is base generated with no rule of *there*-Insertion. Thus, the (b) examples could not arise because the phrase structure rules could not give rise to the relevant structures. Recently, Milsark (1972) has perceptively noted that some analogous sentences are well-formed.

   (iii) a. (All over the world) there are people hungry.
         b. (After the banquet) there were several people sick.

Milsark indicates that such examples tend to argue against base generated existentials; however, such a conclusion does not appear to me to follow. Milsark divides the adjectives into two classes: those that permit *there* as in (iii), which he calls *state-descriptive* (SD), and those that do not as in (ii), which he calls *property* (P) predicates. This distribution is reflected in rule (31) of the text by the inclusion of A_{SD}, signifying the class of state-descriptive adjectives. However, Milsark considers the distinction to be semantic in nature. If so, there is no reason why the semantic explanation cannot be expressed in terms of the base generated structures in the absence of a rule of *there*-Insertion. Thus, I can see no way in which such examples argue against base generated existentials.

6. Emonds's correct assumptions concerning the nonNP nature of sentential complements is questioned in Higgins (1973) and Horn (1975). The relevant arguments are refuted in Brame (in preparation). Emonds himself abandoned his analysis of the relevant examples in (1976) for an inferior analysis. See (Brame, in prep.) for discussion and arguments against Emonds's more recent analysis.

7. It should be noted that although I disagree with Iwakura's ingenious analysis in (1977b), he was the first to recognize that there is indeed a deeper generalization to be expressed. Iwakura also provides much penetrating criticism of Horn (1975).

8. Alfredo Hurtado has informed me that he also has made this assumption for the grammar of Spanish.

9. This point holds for the general process of Negative Incorporation proposed by Klima, Ross, and others. For a discussion of how examples such as *John has any money* are to be blocked, see (Brame 1977).

10. Excellent discussion of this point can be found in Hust 1976).

11. Several classical transformations were formulated as redundancy rules during the course of my Fulbright-Hays lectures at the Rijksuniversiteit te Utrecht in 1973; however, the project was terminated by my failure to work out the relevant facts concerning Equi.

12. Details concerning Aux and other material are omitted here. See (Brame, in prep.).

REFERENCES

Akmajian, A. and T. Wasow 1975. The constituent structure of VP and Aux and the position of the verb *be*. *Linguistic Analysis* 1:205-245.

Brame, M. K. 1976. *Conjectures and Refutations in Syntax and Semantics.* Elsevier-North Holland, New York.

Brame, M. K. 1977. Alternatives to the Tensed-S and Specified Subject Conditions. *Linguistics and Philosophy* 1:3.

Brame, M. K. (in preparation). *Base Generated Syntax.*

Bresnan, J. W. 1970. On complementizers: Toward a syntactic theory of complement types. *Foundations of Language* 6:297-321.

Bresnan, J. W. 1971. Sentence stress and syntactic transformations. *Language* 47:257-81.

Bresnan, J. W. 1972. Theory of complementation in English syntax. Doctoral dissertation, MIT.

Bresnan, J. W. 1973. Syntax of the Comparative clause construction in English. *Linguistic Inquiry* 4:275-343.

Bresnan, J. W. 1977. Toward a realistic model of transformational grammar. Paper presented at the Bell Telephone Convocation at MIT.

Chomsky, N. 1975. *The Logical Structure of Linguistic Theory.* Plenum Press, New York. (Condensation of 1955 manuscript.)

Chomsky, N. 1957. *Syntactic Structures.* The Hague: Mouton.

Chomsky, N. 1964. *Current Issues in Linguistic Theory.* The Hague: Mouton.

Chomsky, N. 1965. *Aspects of the Theory of Syntax.* Cambridge, Mass.: MIT Press.

Chomsky, N. 1970. Remarks on nominalization. In *Readings in English Transformational Grammar,* R.A. Jacobs and P.S. Rosenbaum, eds., Waltham, Mass.: Ginn. Page references to reprinted version in *Studies on Semantics in Generative Grammar,* N. Chomsky, The Hague: Mouton.

Emonds, J.E. 1970. Root and Structure-Preserving Transformations. Doctoral dissertation, MIT.

Emonds, J.E. 1972. A reformulation of certain syntactic transformations. In *Goals of Linguistic Theory,* S. Peters, ed., 1972. Englewood Cliffs, N.J.: Prentice-Hall.

Emonds, J.E. 1973. Alternatives to global constraints. *Glossa* 7:39-62.

Emonds, J.E. 1976. *A Transformational Approach to English Syntax.* New York: Academic Press.

Higgins, F.R. 1973. On J. Emonds's analysis of extraposition. In *Syntax and Semantics* 2, J.P. Kimball, ed. New York: Seminar Press.

Horn, G.M. 1975. On the nonsentential nature of the POSS-ING construction in English. *Linguistic Analysis* 1:333-387.

Hust, J.R. 1976. A lexical approach to the unpassive construction in English. Doctoral dissertation, U. of Wa., Seattle.

Hust, J.R. 1977. Lexical redundancy rules and the unpassive construction. *Linguistic Analysis* 3:000-000.

Iwakura, K. 1977. The auxiliary system in English. *Linguistic Analysis* 3:000-000.

Iwakura, K. 1977. The syntax of complement sentences in English. *Linguistic Analysis* 3:000-000.

Jenkins, L. 1972. Modality in English syntax. Doctoral dissertation, MIT.

Klima, E.S. 1964. Negation in English. In *The Structure of Language: Readings in the Philosophy of Language,* J.A. Fodor and J.J. Katz, eds., Englewood Cliffs, N.J.: Prentice-Hall.

Kuno, S. 1973. Constraints on internal clauses and sentential subjects. *Linguistic Inquiry* 4:363-385.

Lakoff, G. 1970. *Irregularity in Syntax.* New York: Holt, Rinehart, and Winston.

Lakoff, R.T. 1969. Some reasons why there can't be any *some-any* rule. *Language* 45:608-15.

Lasnik, H. and Fiengo, R. 1974. Complement object deletion. *Linguistic*

Inquiry 5:535-71.

Milsark, G. 1972. Re: Doubl-ing. *Linguistic Inquiry* 3:542-49.

Milsark, G. 1977. Toward an explanation of certain peculiarities of the existential construction in English. *Linguistic Analysis 3:*

Pullum, G.K. 1974. Restating Doubl-ing. *Glossa* 8:109-120.

Rosenbaum, P.S. 1967. *The Grammar of English Predicate Complement Constructions.* Cambridge, Mass.: MIT Press.

Ross, J.R. 1967. Constraints on variables in syntax. Doctoral dissertation, MIT.

Ross, J.R. 1972. Doubl-ing. *Linguistic Inquiry* 3:61-86.

Seuren, P.A.M., ed., 1974. *Semantic Syntax.* London: Oxford University Press.

PART VI

ANIMAL COMMUNICATION AND LANGUAGE

Animal Communication and Language

INTRODUCTION

There are a number of ways to study language. It is important to be aware of their similarities, differences and shortcomings. There are three major areas to consider: Experimental, semiotic and linguistic. Under experimental approaches I wish to consider two difficulties, one with the experiments directly, and the other with the philosophical and terminological grounding for the experiments (this is something that has been worrying experimenters recently).

EXPERIMENT

(a) Terminology

One difficulty experimenters have sensed with efforts to provide evidence for animal languages is that no one seems to be clear about just what is a 'language'. There are a number of problems. One is that although this is a technical term of philosophers it is also a technical term of linguists. This has introduced untoward confusion since everyone seems to use it differently. Another problem is that there is some not inconsiderable confusion about how to identify a language. A third involves difficulties with just what properties to attribute to a language.

Experimenters have become quite sensitive to these difficulties and some have asked for clarification. Let me suggest some of the difficulties with proposals about 'language' by providing three examples.

(1) From the point of view of the mathematical linguist a language is simply a *set* of strings. However, this is a very "thin" view of language.

Whether from habit or reflection language users tend to think of a language, not as an unordered heap of strings, but as having structure. This appears a rather simple requirement but to this day the full implications (and difficulties) of this view have not been fully appreciated. And once we do begin to study language from this perspective (we do so here in this example) we find a number of problems, in particular relative to current methodological assumptions about language (we continue studying difficulties, particularly of this sort, in the second example). One fundamental question that arises more and more often, and that to date has received no clear answer, is just how much structure to impose. After all, we are talking about languages as if they were structured entities. Fair enough. But which structures shall we impose? What is it that is structurally required if we are to admit that some set of strings, S, is a language? (Notice that elsewhere in this volume and, I suspect, for very similar reasons, Munz has comparable worries about just how much structure to invoke for a theory of meaning.) Let me give an example. Suppose X is a domain of strings and F a relation we would like to impose on X. What properties shall we assign F? The statement below, not without problems, assigns F some properties and rather reasonable ones, too, before other worries ensue.

(I) $(x)(y)(w)(-Fxx$ & $(Fxy$ & $Fyw \to Fxw)$ & $(x)(\exists y)(Fxy$ & $-(Fxy \to Fyx)))$

At first glance this seems to be a rather reasonable set of demands for F. Our third condition, for example, asks only that every sentence be related to at least one other sentence. Well, why not? After all, we did ask for structure and how better to insure structure than by requiring that each sentence be "tied" to some other sentence? Yet (I) demands that anything that is a language have an infinite set of strings? Do we want to be held to this condition? Suppose we waive it below

(II) Fxx & $(Fxy$ & $Fyz \to Fxz)$ & $Fxy \to Fyx$ & $(x)(\exists y)(Fxy)$

But now that we modify the condition in this way we have still another worry, we admit finite languages and a question arises about whether we want this, given the rather special sense that we sometimes attach to "language." Some of the difficulties with construing languages as finite will be considered in the second example.

(2) One difficulty with the above view on finite languages is that is we are also allowed to operationalize "mean" and "say," and if we are allowed to think of a language as a communication system embedded in (other) systems of behavior (the favorite model for this sort of thing is Wittgenstein's notion of a language as something embedded in the life of a culture), then there would be no problem whatever in assigning virtually any species right down to bees, ants, protozoan, etc., languages, if we also admit that we are not restricting the methods of encoding to the written and verbal, and *this* sort of restriction would be an excessive anthropomorphizing of our methodology. Notice that we have a few very reasonable methodological assumptions—about admitting finite languages, about methods of encoding, etc.—coupled with the Wittgensteinian approach.

Experimenters and others have quite legitimately worried about whether we want to broaden the extension of "language" in this way. Is this at all enlightening? It certainly seems to be just the sort of thing that is confusing many experimenters. Does not *language* lose something of its intended exclusiveness if we extend its use in this way? There are other, related difficulties. This extension is based on what seem rather sound, nearly indispensable (to those theorists sanctioning the ideas) principles (that we admit finite languages, etc.) plus one other assumption—that Wittgenstein's idea of a language is a useful model. Many people who hold these principles do also hold Wittgenstein's view, and this gives us precisely the problems Wittgenstein's view would engender if coupled with these other principles. The dilemma is that on the one hand we feel we ought to abandon or modify some of the principles, on the other we are loathe to do so, so reasonable-seeming do they appear. But it is hardly reasonable, some say, to think of humans and protozoans as both having languages. What also exercises philosophers and an increasing number of experimenters who do occasionally worry about the same sorts of problems that captivate the philosopher, is that if they propose a hypothesis or classification, there ought to be something that does not fit—they hardly expect that a vastly large number of items counting as species behavior, for almost any species, could count as language. Notice that if we don't restrict method of encoding, if the behavior is systematic, is a subsystem of other systems, can be thought of in terms of 'messages', has structure, then with a few, easily met other conditions whatever meets these criteria is a language, and an unfortunately large number of things do meet these criteria. When the experimenter then turns to the philosopher and asks for a definition of some sort that he can live with, he is reflecting these worries. But it is difficult to see just what to do with these principles. Which one(s) should we abandon, if any? I suppose I am prepared to abandon some, in extremis, but they are all so reasonable-seeming. It is particularly difficult to see what to do about the Wittgensteinian assumption. (Notice what hangs on these principles. We finally have a broad mathematical notion of information. We can now collect a variety of systems together as languages, and do so formally. Psychologists and others pursue this and a good deal that was not information-theoretically based is now so based.) The information theoretical approaches do have several implicit methodological principles—they look at language very broadly, and they think of language *and* thought as isomorphic and as subsystems of larger environments. But then we are on the road to calling just about everything a language. And note, it seems perfectly reasonable to think of a language as having an environment, as a subsystem, then, of a larger system. But this, coupled with other equally reasonable ideas, generates the difficulties discussed above.

(3) As our last example we consider problems with identifying languages. Philosophers have tried to account for meaning by, for example, providing models and mappings to elements of the models. In this they already *assume* that what they are dealing with is both a language *and* a meaning-bearing system. And this is all right as far as it goes and for the purposes for which it is devised. But our problem here is a bit different in that we are trying to decide how one would locate a language. That is, suppose we are given a set X and we hold there are relations over X, hence a two-tuple (X, R). We don't know whether (X, R) is meaning-bearing and even if we did, we don't know that it is a language. Our task then seems clear enough. We then locate other meaning-bearing systems (those we assume have this property) and then provide a mapping onto (X, R). Suppose, for example, we looked to a set of systems, Z, Z', etc. Suppose Z were a Boolean algebra. We are inclined to think *these* are meaning-bearing, whether rightly or wrongly I don't dispute now. (We are inclined, for example, to talk of Boolean logics, L, when we mean a Boolean algebra of propositions where the Boolean lattice operations of meet, join and ortho-complementation correspond to logical operations.) In virtue of a mapping of Z onto (X, R) we might begin to think that (X, R) could very well have the properties we attribute to meaning-bearing systems. And why not? After all it has properties like those of Z which, presumably, we do think is meaning-bearing. Now, assuming this worked, we might feel

sufficiently confident about this sort of approach and devise still other systems, Z', Z'', etc., with still other operations and properties of interest (they too seem meaning-bearing in virtue of their properties) and define homomorphisms γ, γ', γ'', etc., between these systems and (X, R). We would, assuming we continue along this line, then feel even more reassured, for now we have a number of systems, all ostensibly meaning-bearing, and all seem to provide "insight" into (X, R) under these mappings. (And how else do we locate meaning-bearing systems that are also languages?)

However, there is a difficulty with this. We assume we can start with some standard (meaning-bearing?) system and then by exhaustively tacking on other properties found under mappings to still other putative meaning-bearing systems, find ourselves with a language (or rather certify that we had one all along). But Z, Z', Z'', etc., also map to the real numbers. The fact that we have created a mapping of some system or other $(Z, Z'$, etc.) to another system (X, R), or the reals, or whatever, does nothing to distinguish the reals or subsystems of the reals from (X, R). The mappings themselves enable us to tie Z, Z', etc., to a number of systems including the reals and do not isolate a distinguished system that is both meaning-bearing and a language. Indeed, the reals are not a language and there is some doubt as to whether they are meaning-bearing in the required sense.

Thus, the gambit of mapping a set of entities with some set of distinguished or interesting properties onto an ostensible language system, won't enable us to identify the system as a language because then we would be obliged to do so for some subset of the reals as well. On the one hand, the principle of "exhaustion" does seem a reasonable one (if we can't begin with a rather familiar system, explore its properties under homomorphisms to other familiar systems, and tack on properties to the first system as we acknowledge that some homomorphism exists until we "realize a language," then how are we to proceed?) for we contend only that we identify (X, R) as a language by mapping it onto a sufficient number of other systems of interest that are meaning-bearing and have "relevant" properties (language-like properties, presumably). The assumptions seem reasonable enough but they don't enable us to locate a language with any degree of precision. They enable us to locate so much more that we get out languages by default and not because we have isolated language-related properties.

b. Some Recent Experimental Work

If this begins to give the reader some sense of the problems encountered by experimenters (and others) from one direction, suppose we take a look at some experimental work performed with animals. First consider recent work done with rhesus monkeys. This consists of efforts to study homologous areas of the brain to see whether human speech arose from vocal centers controlling vocalization in other animals. The results are somewhat unilluminating for this research seems to assume that speech is the primary discourse mode of the other animals. The researchers then go on to isolate speech centers and observe the vocal behavior of monkeys with very discouraging results for the relations between different species seems rather thin. And surely this *is* a bit odd for speech might not be the primary discourse mode of monkeys so that attempt to find homologies can fall apart entirely (as it seems to have done). The results of such failures are curious—failing to find the connections they seek and surprised (indicating that they are still convinced that the connections *ought* to have been there) the theorists begin to posit "evolutionary jumps," "gaps," and so on. It would be more interesting, however, to explore many discourse modalities and find the brain areas controlling these. It is a rather unhappy methodology that insists on analogies given dubious assumptions and then, analogies failing, introduces inviting, though dubious, new theoretical gambits.

A more cautious and certainly more welcome note comes from Marler who claims that, after all, we know so little about the semantics of animal communication that perhaps we ought to concentrate on other discourse modalities, besides speech, and other means of encoding. Comparisons deriving from this sort of study might prove more fruitful, he thinks.

Assumptions about uniformity of discourse modalities and methods of encoding, and the appropriate channels of communication to study carry over in much of the literature. But these very same assumptions, minimizing the number and the kind of discourse modalities, introduce some rather trying difficulties for experimenters. To see this suppose we turn to the Gardners, et al., and the study of chimps. There have been some very considerable claims made here: That chimps have language, for one, claims about intelligence, for another. A number of workers have remarked about the untidiness of these experiments. Several, including the linguist Thomas Sebeok, have focused attention on one particular theme: Sebeok and others point out that the experimenters seem to have ignored other encoding systems and channels of communication that were, in fact, operative at the time of the experiment, and that what has excited the experimenters, all of whom have made rather elaborate claims about animal communication has been nothing more than a rather sophisticated version of the Clever Hans phenomenon. In cases of this sort the animal—ostensibly communicating—is merely picking up (*unfairly*) cues from the trainer that have been over-looked. This suggests that experimenters (and theorists) may need semiotic techniques in formulating criteria for how to determine whether animals use language. We shall pursue this in section 2 below.

SEMIOTICS: CLEVER HANS

Clever Hans figures centrally in Sebeok's account so we ought to be clear just what it means. Let me construct a fictitious account of a talking chimp and then generalize what is happening in order to get at the Hans phenomenon. Suppose we have a chimp, Alexander. We want to see whether Alexander counts. Imagine a room in which Alexander and I (his trainer) are working. We admit at least one observer. I face Alexander and say "Count to three, Alexander," and Alexander proceeds to raise and lower his arm three times. We all conclude that Alexander counts; a slew of journal articles follow. What might be objectionable about all this? What is Clever Hans? Suppose I have been assuming all along that there is only one operative channel of communication and just one significant modality of communication. When deciding what Alexander is doing I look only for signs emanating along this channel (and so do you the observer) and we ignore the trainer (me). In the usual Hans phenomenon the trainer is signalling in rather complex ways and doing so along a number of different channels, and at least one of these channels is entirely unexpected (from both the observer's and trainer's points of view). But the chimp is watching all of this very closely. He notices, for example, that the trainer has altered his breathing and noticing this and using it as a cue then raises and lowers his arm until the trainer's breathing has returned to normal. Of course the trainer's breathing gets faster as soon as he asks the chimp to count (the trainer is a bit nervous) and then returns to normal just as the chimp counts to three. Further breathing cues are no longer in evidence (why should they be, the trainer is now satisfied and no longer nervously responding to the situation by altering his breathing patterns) and the chimp then stops "counting." But surely he is not counting, he is merely moving his arm along with his trainer's breath stops.

Now this is Hans and this, they say, is what has been going on in a good deal of the animal experimentation we have been hearing so much about (I suspect it goes on as well in psychotherapy where, as Laing and others acknowledge, we know very little about the interview process; translated to semiotic terms this might read—when we make various posits, the unconscious being one, based on the ostensibly closed set of data "uncovered" in the interview, our data base is too narrow for we are gathering data by attending to too few of the actually operative channels of communication.) The whole Hans phenomenon turns out to be semiotic exotica and an excellent analytic tool, applicable both to studies of language and communication.

DISTRIBUTIONAL ANALYSIS

There are a number of approaches to the problem of whether animals other than man communicate. The Hans phenomenon and the semiotic tools described constitute but one. Another, more formal, and in a way more general method, can be found in Fiengo's paper. We might, as he suggests, attempt a distributional analysis of the calls of different species, isolate languages for each species and grammars for these languages. We might then distinguish various properties different grammars and languages have in common and correlate with these findings distinct senses of "having language." We could begin to look for significant analogues, in other species, with human language ability (they might not, of course, exist but the procedure might enable us to see whether or not they do). Sebeok's method would enable us to isolate the relevant channels along which the calls operate. Once we do this we could then begin to employ Fiengo's suggestions.

Raphael Stern

Robert Fiengo

ON "HAVING LANGUAGE"

That other animals can communicate with our species and that
we can communicate with them are not matters of controversy.
We might doubt whether a dog intends us to understand the state
it is in when it whines during our dinner, but surely a definition
of the term "communication" need not be so restrictive as to allow only what is intended. And we might doubt that a dog is as
quick to perceive the intent of our messages as we are to perceive
the intent of his, or wonder what he is trying to tell us, or marvel
at his reaction to messages we were not consciously aware of
sending. Such circumstances, if empirically confirmed, suggest
that the "communication spaces," the sets of messages which can
be sent or received, overlap in the two species, not that they are
identical.[1]

It is probable that the reason that our normally argumen-
tative species has fought so little over the question whether we
and other animals communicate is due largely to the vacuity of
the claim that we do. We might question whether a starving cockroach would beg, or could even conceive that there are other living organisms which could provide food. But the term "communication" is a plastic one, and that a cockroach can, at least, respond to our actions is not in doubt. If we allow our perception
of goal-directed response to a stimulus as evidence for communication, our species and the cockroach have an active, if narrow,
channel of communication.

While granting communicative abilities to other organisms
without a second thought, the question whether other species
have Language has been hotly contested. Scientists agonize over
such questions as "to be sure, that chimpanzee can order its behavior in a certain way, but does it have Language", but never
over such questions as "to be sure, that chimpanzee can order its
behavior in a certain way, but does it have Communication". We
infer that participants in such debates must attach some quite
special significance to the predicate "have Language" and that
the predicate does not, in their opinion, have the width of application which "have Communication" enjoys.

Is there a sense of the term "have Language" in which we
can say that humans and other species "have Language"? This
question is quite different from the much more commonly asked

question: "Are humans the only species which has Language". The first question, in particular, does not assume that the term "have Language" is well defined as a property of more than one species but rather calls the very notion into question. The first question would seem also to be the prior one; if we cannot make sense of the central notion, raising the second question is without point.

We know, of course, that there are languages which humans speak naturally and we, in general, use geopolitical terms such as French, Spanish, etc., to distinguish them. But no one who argues that non-humans have Language means by this that they *naturally* acquire languages such as these. Two alternative conceptions dominate the literature. On the one hand, there are those who hold that there is a notion of Language which can be defined in inter-specific parameters and a set of species whose behavior might meet these criteria. On the other side are those who would use the term "have Language" as an essentially human attribute, the question then being the extent to which other species can acquire it.

While the second research program derives much of its interest from the demands it places on "learning theory" to explain the acquisition of complex abilities, the first is probably best viewed as being within the domain of comparative biology. Taking this viewpoint, we may ask whether (say) the language abilities of species X and species Y are analogous or homologous, whether species X is genetically prepared for its language ability, etc., just as we might ask similar questions concerning the ability to fly. Answers to these questions would correctly be taken as pertinent to such general concerns as the nature of the interaction between biological preparedness and the environment as well as to the reconstruction of the history of speciation itself.

To ask such questions as those raised in the previous paragraph correctly is as important to our understanding of these matters as is the collection of the data relevant to deciding them. The former task will be attempted in this paper; I will attempt to sketch a cross-specific explication of the notion "have Language" and then pose the relevant questions accordingly. As will be seen, while it is a fairly simple matter to arrive at an account of this notion from a theoretical perspective, in practice there would be many difficulties in carrying out a research program constructed along the lines suggested. I have no desire to minimize these difficulties, some of which will be described below. In fact, I do not rule out the practical possibility that the program of research advocated simply cannot be pursued. There are grounds for optimism untainted by velleity, however, and I believe an optimistic stand to be appropriate here. Lastly, I should say that, while I find the alternative program of research, in which other species are trained variants of human language, to be relatively devoid of interest, it is clearly not one which is in principle opposed to the one which will be sketched here. Its interest appears to lie in the successes or failures of various training programs, not in what it tells us about other species. We will return to this question below; now we should get on with our task.

Let us begin by considering the distributional analysis of the calls of a non-human species.[2]

Suppose that we ascertain that a certain set of calls $c_1, ...,$ c_n has the effect of guarding territory from other members of a species. Suppose further that we identify a set of properties $p_i, ..., p_k$ which $c_1, ..., c_n$ share and that we notice that there are other logically possible but unobserved calls $c_{n+1}, ..., c_x$, distinct from $c_1, ..., c_n$, which also share $p_i, ..., p_k$. We may now test the properties proposed. Suppose that we construct synthetically members of $c_{n+1}, ..., c_x$ and find that the species behaves identically with respect to these as it does to members of $c_1, ..., c_n$. This would appear to constitute confirmation of our proposal; if the species behaves differently with respect to the previously unobserved calls, we might question whether the properties proposed were the correct ones. But, assuming confirmation, we could now say that we had initiated a research program in which $c_1, ..., c_x$ is the proposed language of the species, and $p_i, ..., p_k$ the proposed grammar of that language.

By asserting that some language L has a grammar, I mean only to assert that there is some finite specification of the sentences (calls) of L. I do not assume that it is a necessary property of grammars, therefore, that they generate an infinite number of sentences. If L is a finite language, then L itself can be considered a grammar of L, or, in the usual parlance, the "list grammar of L". This does not rule out, obviously, the possibility that a finite language might allow a more revealing specification than a list. Furthermore, in this traditional mathematical sense of the term, it is not necessary that a grammar "relate sound and meaning". Lastly, although the examples to be discussed involve the communicative use of Language, I do not consider it to be analytic to Language that it have communication as a use.

Now note that we have allowed ourselves the ability to identify territorial calls by referring to the behavior of organisms. Would behavioral criteria suffice in general to identify what are and are not the calls of a species? As we have no science in which the term "behavior" is defined within an explanatory theory, we can hardly hope to ask this question precisely. Consider the narrower question whether behavioral criteria suffice to identify all and only the sentences of English. If by "behavior" one includes the reported intuitions of native speakers of English concerning the properties of their language, the answer is that statements of such behavior are data with which one can construct a theory which provides such an identification. Such data appear to be necessary but not sufficient to such a construction. The existence of behavioral limitations of memory, attention, etc., complicate this task but do not render it impossible. If, on the other hand, we define reported intuitions as not being behavior, it would appear that behavioral criteria would not even be necessary to the construction of a grammar.

Since we lack, in general, reported intuitions of members of other species concerning the properties of their calls, we are, in effect, in the same position with them as we would be if the intuitions of native speakers of human languages were eliminated as possible data for the construction of grammars. Although various postures have been struck concerning the possibility of achieving formulations of grammars without appeal to the intuitions of native speakers, there are no substantive proposals of this sort. We conclude that the problem of determining which parts of the behavior of another species constitute its calls is a serious one.

There is a related difficulty. We wish to say that a particular sentence of English is the same sentence whether it is shouted or whispered, spoken by a female or male, even though acoustically these calls would differ. In order to express the type of which various performances of a sentence are tokens, we have phonetic transcription, an alphabet of symbols which are independent of these parameters as a score is independent of the various performances of a piece of music. A spectrographic display does not make this idealization; it does not characterize the experience of a member of a species in the domain of its own language. The problem is this: How are we to characterize the calls of a non-human species in such a way that we can identify tokens of the same type?

It is clear that appeal to the meanings of the calls will not help. Since for our own species the same phonetic string can carry more than one meaning and the same meaning can be carried by distinct phonetic strings, it is surely clear that the type-token distinction will not be effected by meaning alone if our own species is to be included in our study. More important, however, is the difficulty, if not impossibility, of imputing meaning to the calls of other species. Consider the case of the territorial call. Suppose we have a member of a species which respects the territorial call of another member. Can we infer from this alone that the first knows the meaning of the call of the second? Indeed, can we infer that the call has meaning at all? Surely not. Imagine the species were somewhat different and, instead of emitting calls, constructed brick walls around its territory. We would not be entitled to infer that other members knew the meaning of the wall if they respected the territory. In general, from the fact that an object has a certain use, we cannot infer that the user knows the meaning of the object. We will say more of this in a later section.

Can acoustic similarity be of aid in the case of those languages where sound is the medium? Consider as an example the catalogue of chimpanzee and gorilla vocalizations presented in Marler (1976)[3].

Marler in several instances conflates distinctions made by Lawick-Goodall "either because they seem acoustically indistinguishable, because they intergrade without clear separation, or because they are different renditions of the same basic call by male or female, or by particular age-classes." One can easily imagine grounds for disagreement between Lawick-Goodall and Marler (or with both these views) and these grounds might be of a fundamental nature. It might be pointed out that two calls which seem indistinguishable to humans may indeed be perceived as quite distinct by chimpanzees or gorillas. Indeed the possibility cannot be ruled out that these species perceive categorical distinctions in sets of calls which to the human ear seem to "intergrade without clear separation."[4] There are, then, reasonable grounds for skepticism, as I imagine Lawick-Goodall and Marler would agree.

Of what potential help would the social organization of a species be in determining its calls? In the case of the gorilla, there are, it appears, striking differences between sexes and age groups in the use of calls. Older male gorillas, the so-called silverbacks, contrast with the younger blackbacked males and the females with respect to vocal behavior. The silverbacks also appear to dominate a quite rigid social hierarchy. In the case of chimpanzees, however, where social structure is relatively loose, the full range of vocal behavior is apparently distributed through all age classes and both sexes. But the fact that certain behaviors are characteristic of certain social groups but not others could serve as evidence only that the groups emit (perhaps only partially) different languages, the problem now being to identify the calls in each of these.

The problem may be appreciated if we imagine a Martian who, studying English speakers, notes that males tend to belch while drinking beer in front of televisions, and that females do so much less frequently. The Martian might now ask the question whether the belch is a call of the English-speaking male. If the

Martian had made much progress on the analysis of the English language, it would know on phonological grounds that the belch could only very unnaturally be included as a part of English. But the Martian might wonder whether English-speaking males might not have *another* language, of which the belches observed would be a part. It is, however, precisely this sort of motivation that we lack in the case of non-human species.

It is probably in the studies of the perceptual abilities of other species that the best evidence can be found to identify their languages. In a recent study, Zoloth, et al. (1979) contrast the perceptual ability of Japanese macaques (Macaca fuscata) with that of other species of monkey. Two variants of the macaque coo call, one called smooth early (SE) and the other smooth late (SL) were identified. While the two calls are "similar in most acoustic dimensions", they differ in relative position of the peak frequency inflection—in SE's the peak is in the first two-thirds of the call while in SL's this occurs in the final third. Another difference between the calls selected was identified: the starting frequency. One group had a low starting pitch (<600 Hz), the other a high starting pitch (>600 Hz). The general finding was that "if the discrimination task was based on the position of the peak in the call, Japanese macaques learned the task readily. However, if starting pitch was the relevant dimension, the Japanese macaques experienced much more difficulty. Mirror image results were obtained for the comparison species."[5]

It seems clear that studies of this sort could lead to a general theory of perceptual constancy in the Japanese macaque. Although correctly pointing to the possibility that these differences are culturally transmitted rather than the result of innate predisposition, they hypothesize that, as in the case of humans, the Japanese macaque manifests an "interplay of innate and learned perceptual predispositions."[6]

It furthermore seems clear that a description of the perceptions of this species in its own language, a sort of phonetic transcription, could in principle be inferred. By identifying the acoustic ranges within which a species enjoys categorical perception, a discrimination between those behaviors which are not within the genetic preparedness of the species and those which are could be hypothesized. Whether it would be possible in practice to identify tokens of the same type within the latter class I will not speculate, and there is the further difficulty that a species might not exploit for its language the *entire* acoustic space for which it is genetically prepared. Nevertheless, it seems clear to me that investigations of the type Zoloth et al. undertook are at present the most secure forms of evidence for the identification of the language of a species. It would be bizarre indeed to hypothesize a species which is genetically prepared in perceived acoustic dimensions X but whose language is drawn from perceived acoustic dimensions Y, where X and Y are distinct. The coincidence of these two in the species observed in this manner underlines this bizarreness. If we consider a species whose grammar is *learned*, the "inferred phonetic description" of the calls of the species is itself a (partial) characterization of the *experience* of (members of) the species—precisely the data upon which (members of) the species base their knowledge of the grammar. Thus, in this case, we have the cognitively appropriate characterization of the language.

I am sensible of the fact that the theory of categorical perception in humans has come under some attack. Carney, Widin, and Viemeister (1977) have argued, for example, that listeners can be trained to perceive a supposedly categorical continuum noncategorically or to shift categorical boundaries. Strange and Jenkins (1977) review cross-language studies which suggest that speakers of different languages place categorical boundaries at different locations along the same acoustic continuum. These studies, if accepted at face value, refute the hypothesis that the categories of language perception are both innate and immutable. But *this* theory of categorical perception, while perhaps the strongest, is also quite implausible. A more defensible conception would be one in which the theory posits a set of categories which determine the properties of the *initial* perceptions of the language learner in its domain, and which allows refinement of these categories, either through experience or genetically determined maturation. The categories for which humans are genetically prepared would, on this view, constitute the initial hypothesis concerning the categories of the language to be learned, the unmarked system with respect to which the adult categorical system would be a marked variant. Taste discrimination, which is in part delimited by genetic preparedness, can be refined through courses in wine tasting, to give a partially analogous case. In any event, the results of the studies cited are not inconsistent with this more plastic conception of categorical perception, which I continue to consider the explanation for the phenomena which originally suggested it.[7]

Suppose then that our optimism is not misplaced and that it is possible to perform distributional analyses of the calls of other species. Associated with each species we would have a set of languages and a set of their corresponding grammars, as illustrated in the figure below:

$$\text{Species}_1 \quad [\ 1_1^1, 1_1^2, ..., 1_1^n\ ]\ [\ g_1^1, g_1^2, ..., g_1^n\ ]$$
$$\text{Species}_2 \quad [\ 1_2^1, 1_2^2, ..., 1_2^m\ ]\ [\ g_2^1, g_2^2, ..., g_2^m\ ]$$

$$\vdots$$

$$\text{Species}_x \quad [\ 1_x^1, 1_x^2, ..., 1_x^y\ ]\ [\ g_x^1, g_x^2, ..., g_x^y\ ]$$

We have allowed for the possibility that some species will manifest several distinct languages, each of which would have a grammar provided for it. This possibility is no doubt realized, not only in the human species, but in others as well. There are species of bird, for example, within which "dialectal" variation has been observed;[8] in our terminology, there are birds which exhibit distinct languages (sets of calls), depending, in some cases, on the bird language heard during their critical periods.

The grammars isolated will be various. Some will be the result of interaction of the biological preparedness of a species with its environment, that is to say, it will be learned. Other grammars will seem totally innate, without the requirement that there be exposure to instances of the language. Still others will appear to be totally learned, without any biological preparedness. Again, some languages will be stimulus-bound, while others will be controlled only by the will of the organism, if we wish to acknowledge the existence of such.

We are now enabled to ask certain questions of comparative biology. The following are of particular interest to us:

1. *Is it in general true that, if several languages are manifest in a particular species, that there are formal analogies between the grammars of these?*

2. *Is it in general true that, if distinct species possess languages which serve a particular function, there are formal analogies between the grammars of these?*

3. *Is it in general true that languages which are stimulus-bound have grammars which are formally analogous across the various species? Do these grammars tend to be list grammars?*

4. *Is it in general true that languages which are learned have grammars which are analogous across the various species?[9] Are the grammars of languages which appear innate formally analogous?*

Many questions such as these could be asked, and, with sufficient knowledge of the abilities of species, given coherent, empirically based answers, but it would be presumptuous to attempt to answer them before the relevant distributional analyses are performed. We may, however, now give sense to the notion "having Language" which was the original task which we set for ourselves.

Assume that, among the grammars of all the species, we find certain subsets of formally analogous grammars. We may let G_i stand for a set of analogous properties shared by various g's (grammars). We may say that various grammars belong to G_i, while others belong to G_j, etc. To belong to G_i will be to "have Language$_i$"; to belong to G_j will be to "have Language$_j$". Notice that we do not *require* that there will be, in any significant sense, such sets of analogous properties between grammars. Rather, we state that *if* there are such formal analogies, and we are able to set up G's to express these, we may use the term "have Language" with precision. Notice also that we have not assumed that the term "have Language" is absolute. Rather we have acknowledged the empirical possibility that there are several such realizations, several such clusterings of species' abilities. And notice that it might turn out that of three grammars g_m, g_n, g_o, there is a G_i to which g_m and g_n belong and a G_j to which g_n and g_o belong. We allow, then, for the possibility that G_i and G_j might overlap.

A further point must be made. We have said that two species "have Language$_i$" if the grammars of their languages belong to G_i. But, it might be asked, what is the relevance of grammar to the notion "having Language"? Why not refer to the properties of the language itself, e.g., what concepts it can express, whether it is finite or infinite, etc.

One such proposal will be considered below. Here I wish to give some positive reasons for the terminological choice I have made.

I assume that those who approach without prejudice the question whether various species "have Language" want to know whether, or to what extent, the properties of those species are biologically analogous or homologous. They wish to compare species with respect to this property just as they wish to compare the various species with respect to such properties as "having Flight." These questions are posed within the general context of the goals of determining the possible variations which life forms can manifest and the history of speciation which has led to the variations we observe. In particular, they wish to know the possible structures and the probable evolutionary histories of the brains of these species. They understand that the behaviors which certain brain structures enable a species to manifest will constitute either selective advantages or detriments. But while the utility of these behaviors may help explain why certain evolutionary changes occur, it is with the nature of the biological structures themselves that the program is concerned. On one interpretation of the term, grammars are theories of the abilities of biological structures. Their languages are not (at least in the interesting case where these are infinite). Consequently we analogize at the level of grammar, not language, given our orientation.

A certain analogy with historical linguistics is appropriate here. Imagine that the world were altered in such a way that we lacked any evidence (ancient documents, etc.) concerning the human languages of the past but retained the ability to observe present variation. By determining the nature of present variation, we could plausibly draw inferences concerning the history of the interactions of the human language communities. Upon analysis, it might be found that certain grammars differed only in superficial respects while certain classes of grammars revealed more fundamental variation. Using such comparisons, an historical account of present variation could be inferred. It is true that such an account would not make use of the *best* evidence, which would be a direct observation of the history of the human species.[10] But it would allow a type of argument which could be productively counterposed to hypotheses concerning the development of other species attributes, where information is similarly vague. The comparisons would, of course, be between the *knowledges* of the various languages, not between the languages themselves. It would, in other words, be between *grammars*, as it has become common in the field of historical linguistics to insist. To come to the point, similar forms of inference are in principle possible if applied to inter-specific variation. It would certainly seem plausible to advance an account of the speciation of the nonhuman primates, if the grammars of their natural languages are as simple as they appear.[11]

Let us return, finally, to our original question, which may now be stated as follows: is there some G_i such that the grammar of the natural language of humans and the grammar of the natural language of some other species belong to it? Unless the analogous properties specified by G_i are of the most trivial sort, such that any two grammars might belong to it, I believe that the answer to this question will be an unqualified no. Let me hasten to inform those well-meaning, liberal-minded souls who would assign the honor of "having Language" to other species with the same spirit they would show in giving money to the poor (and with the same amount of fanfare) that I believe that bees will also be shown to be unique. And let me hasten to inform those chauvinists who believe that through our linguistic uniqueness we have further evidence that the human species is the crown of creation, that from a biological point of view such evaluations are totally inappropriate. I believe neither that all species are "the same under the skin" with respect to language, nor that, having made the empirically necessary distinctions, we have any objective way of evaluating some species as "better" than another. We will return to this last point later, but let me now point out that if by the "goodness" of a biological trait we mean the extent to which it provides a selective advantage, then "goodness" will vary with environment and be relative to species. Bee language appears to be "good" for bees, at the moment, but if the environment were altered in such a way that bee language provided incorrect instructions for the location of honey, it would be "bad", if that is its function. The notion "good for organism X in environment Y" seems useful, but not "good no matter what the species or environment".

My belief that the human language ability will find no significant analogue in other species is based partly on an appraisal of what has been discovered concerning the grammars of human languages rather than on a comparison of this with the grammars of languages of other species. The required sort of distributional analyses have not in general been done on other species, and future research could prove me wrong. Work on the theory of human language has, however, shown that there is a rich and highly articulated set of formal parameters which human grammars uniformly manifest, and none of these parameters seems even to intersect in an interesting way with any property observed or even alleged to exist in any other species. It seems unlikely, given this, that we have linguistic relatives very close to us.

The distinction between the position advocated here and that advocated by the liberal on the one hand and the chauvinist on the other can be put, perhaps overly dramatically, as follows. The liberal would wish to claim, particularly if Language were given a functionalist definition in terms of communication, that many, if not all, species have Language. The chauvinist, on the other hand, would wish, having identified some property thought to be essential to human language, to view it as defining Language and expect to find Language only in the "higher species". I maintain, contrary to both of these views, that it is an empirical possibility that the only other species whose grammar belongs to the G_i to which we belong is (say) the locust. Just as Flight is scattered among the mammals, birds, and insects, a scattering of Language among the various species is not ruled out in principle.

The chauvinist point of view is of more immediate interest to the issue at hand, since it has representatives, in particular Premack, who have brought forth fairly detailed definitions of "having Language". But before considering Premack's position, an example of the liberal viewpoint is in order.

A better example of the "looks like therefore is" fallacy can hardly be found than the position taken by Gardner and Gardner (1977):

Thus, we do not assert that our chimpanzee subjects use the signs of Ameslan, we do not argue from analogy, we do not base our conclusions on the assumptions of any linguistic theory. Instead, we can marshal a very large body of empirical evidence and independent linguistic analysis, all agreeing with the conclusion that the communicative gestures of our chimpanzees would be called signs if they were used by human children and that the chimpanzees use signs in a rudimentary, childish form of Ameslan. [12]

This criterion, of course, as it is divorced from "the assumptions of any linguistic theory", in other words, as it is divorced from any scientific understanding of the domain which it claims to pronounce on, is far too loose. What prevents us from concluding that parrots speak English, since what they do "would be called" English if humans did it? Why not conclude that humans can fly, since, if a bird "jumps" ten feet we call it flight? If the criterion the Gardners propose is simply to ask people to vote on whether they think certain chimpanzees have Ameslan, then their conclusion depends on the electorate they choose.

The position of David Premack is more interesting, and it deserves attention.

Premack's position, as put forth most completely in his book *Intelligence in Man and Ape* (1976), is in essence as follows. "The two most basic language exemplars," he tells us, "are reference relations and a sentence generating capacity. . . . the first basic evidence for language, reference relations, can be expressed by two factors:

1. Arbitrary items (words) can serve as information retrieval devices, in the limiting case, providing as much information about their associated referent as is contained in the referent itself.
2. The kind of items for which words can serve as information retrieval devices in the human case are agents, objects, actions, and properties." [13]

In elaboration of Factor 1, it is apparently the ability of subjects to "match attributes of objects to names of objects as well as to the intact objects themselves" in match-to-sample tests that Premack considers criterial.

Concerning sentence-generating capacity, Premack states: "if the species could do no more than commit to memory some fixed inventory of admissable strings of words this would be of little interest and would not be evidence for language. The achievement is interesting only if, in order to explain it, we are forced to infer that the species has induced a theory which enables it to produce in principle indeterminately many sentences."[14]

As the reader will probably have inferred by now, it is Premack's belief that "man is the only creature with a known natural language."[15] He explicitly rejects an approach similar to the one sketched in this essay: "An appealing possibility is to define language as a general system and then distinguish the human variant of the general system from other possible ones."[16] He continues, however, by pointing out that the "exolinguist", whose task it would be to characterize languages that might suit other species, would be limited, in that the exolinguist speaks only one of the possible forms. In Premack's words: "In attempting to describe languages different from the human one, he has the problem of using language X to formulate Y, Z, ..., etc. How different from X (the formulating language) can Y (the language to be formulated) be? All the concepts of Y must be formulated in terms of concepts from X. Every lexical item in Y, every grammatical class, and every rule concerning grammatical operations must be stated in terms of lexical items, grammatical classes and rules from X. This, so far as I can see, sets a disappointing limit on how far Y can depart from X. It appears to say that the only departures from human language of which we can conceive are reductions on human language, in terms of either lexicon, or syntax, or both."[17]

Since no history is given as to how one would come to adopt this, to be sure, clear-cut position, we had best consider closely its implications.

Let us use the following diagram to mean that language$_j$ is a reduction of language$_i$.

According to Premack, the species languages will form a hierarchy, with humans (H) at the pinnacle, as in the following diagram:[18]

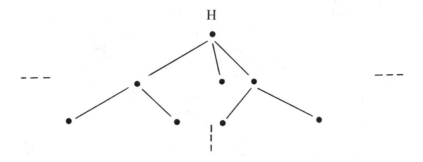

We might even have a "great chain of linguistic being," if reduction is along only one dimension, as follows:

Recall that Premack assumes that human language is the only natural language. Thus any account of the natural language abilities of the species would take the human ability as quintessential.

Premack has, then, an anthropocentric conception of species differences, which itself is the result of the assumption that the exolinguist is limited by the language he speaks. The reductions which Premack has in mind are conceptual reductions, in general. He gives one example involving the transaction of giving, where his claim is that various different "partitionings" of the human conception of this are not significantly different and another involving an hypothesized language in which modifiers are made primary and the objects of modification secondary.[19, 20]

Must we accept Premack's assumption and the anthropocentrism which it leads to?

Consider a partially analogous case. Due to the descriptive power of mathematical formalism, we are enabled to discuss the properties of (say) eight-dimensional solids. We cannot, so far as

I am aware, picture these to ourselves. Yet we can posit and discuss the properties of such alternatives to the natural human conception of space. The analogy of topology to the theory of the concepts of natural language breaks down, of course, due to the non-existence of the latter. But suppose there were such a theory (a possibility with which Premack surely must agree). Then we would expect that various parameters of it could be altered in perhaps bizarre ways to yield conceptual structures which were neither human conceptual structures nor reductions of these. We see then that when Premack says we *must* be confined in our ability to imagine alternatives to human language, he cannot mean that this is a logical necessity; at most, this would seem to be a practical limitation. Now if, in describing the semantic properties of an object language, we wish to set up a metalanguage with which to "talk about" the object language, we will apparently need a metalanguage containing semantic terms which *refer to* the object language. But the object language need not, in principle, contain these terms, and metalanguages can be constructed (or hierarchies of these) which are arbitrarily "far away" from the original object language.[21]

But why accept even a practical limitation? Why not focus on possible alternatives to the syntactic conditions which define human language, a domain which is relatively well understood within cognitive psychology. We can imagine a language so constructed that questions are formed by a rule which moves any constituent to the front of the sentence just in case the constituent is a prime number of constituents from the beginning, a device outside of the range of human variation. Again, we have good reason to believe that there is a general constraint on human language which accounts, in the case of English, for the contrast between *he believes himself left* and *he believes himself to have left*. It is simple to imagine the constraint being reversed, with the result that a non-human class of languages would be described. Finally, we are able, if we wish, to imagine languages of which the human language would be a reduction by adding a condition to those motivated for the human case.

Notice that when we consider alternatives to the human ability in the domain of syntax, we are in no way forced to anthropocentrism; we do not have to accept this arbitrary analytic limitation. If our goal is to characterize the distinctions between the natural abilities of the species, which are the results of their distinct evolutionary histories, we surely do not wish to *assume* that their distinct evolutionary histories have, by some miracle, converged in a hierarchical pattern. If it were true, it would be a startling fact, which would raise many more questions than it would answer.

374

Since Premack's program appears to have no relevance to any attempt to account for the differences and similarities of the natural abilities of the species, we must wonder what his program is about. I believe the answer to this question lies in the success or failure of the operational methodology used to train his subjects, but an evaluation of these matters is not our present concern, which is to distinguish Premack's conception from the one sketched here.

I will conclude by stating again that we are a long way from giving the term "having Language" an empirical foundation in comparative biology. Much popular debate on the question of whether a particular species "has Language" therefore seems quite premature. It does, however, seem fairly clear what kind of definition is appropriate, just as it is clear what kind of definition is not.

NOTES

*I wish to thank Charles Cairns, James Higginbotham, Jerrold Katz, Robert May, David Premack, and Michael Studdert-Kennedy for helpful discussions of the topics contained in this essay.

1. Note that by establishing that there is such overlap, we can conclude very little concerning the general communicative ability of either species. To use a simple analogy, a pie-slice shape may be thought of as the overlap of a circle and a diamond, but countless other shapes might overlap with the same result.
2. I will use the term "call" in a very general sense to include the sentences of human language, bee dance, the sentences of Ameslan, etc. The problem of identifying the calls of other species is partially treated below.
3. Cf. Marler (1976), p. 241.
4. In fact, just such a proposal has been made recently by Zoloth, *et al.*, (1979). Cf. p. 871, below.
5. Zoloth, *et al.*, p. 871.
6. *Ibid.*, p. 872.
7. Cf. Liberman, *et al.*, (1967), and Studdert-Kennedy, *et al.*, (1970).
8. Cf. Marler (1970). As Studdert-Kennedy notes, "For insight into the origins of language, the frank analogues of birdsong may have more to offer than the possible homologues of ape signs," and, as Leiber (1979) has provocatively pointed out, "Maybe we share more with chordates in general then with mammals in particular."
9. A positive answer to this question would suggest the existence of a species-general "learning theory". The manifest differences between the grammars of humans and birds make it unlikely that such a positive answer will be found, however.
10. Note that we respect the method of historical linguistics even though it must often cope with precisely the limitations of data posited here.
11. If the accounts of the languages of chimpanzees and gorillas which Marler presents is even close to correct, we note that they seem to share much; there is probably a fairly richly structured G_i to which the grammars of these species, and presumably others, belong. As neither

species seems to share any interesting grammatical attribute with humans, a comparison of their relative abilities with respect to humans would seem able to reveal very little. This point will become relevant when Premack's research is discussed below.

12. Gardner and Gardner (1977), p. 7.
13. Premack (1976), p. 14. I am somewhat unclear what Premack means to exclude here.
14. *Ibid.*, p. 14. Apparently Premack is using the term "sentence generating capacity" in such a way that only a grammar with an infinite language has this property.
15. *Ibid.*, p. 37.
16. *Ibid.*, p. 19. Gardner and Gardner asked signers fluent in Ameslan for their opinions concerning the competence of their subjects.
17. *Ibid.*, p. 20.
18. We might imagine two reductions of human language, neither of which is a reduction of the other.
19. Premack (1976), p. 333-335.
20. Those who find the great chain of being a convenient metaphor in general for the variation they observe will be happy to learn that Koko the gorilla has received scores of 95 and 85 (five months apart) on the Stanford-Binet Intelligence Scale. Possible cultural bias has been blamed (cf. Patterson and Cohn (1978)). Nevertheless, I consider this the *reductio ad absurdum* of the claim that this test measures human cognitive ability. If all we can say of variation between the cognitive abilities of humans and gorillas is that it is along one linear dimension, we have a quite unrevealing cognitive theory indeed.
21. Cf. Tarski (1944).

REFERENCES

Carney, A. E. Widin, G. P., and Viemeister, N. F. 1977. Noncategorical perception of stop consonants differing in VOT. *Psychological Review.* 62: pp. 961-970.

Chomsky, N. 1977. *Reflections on language.* Pantheon Press.

Gardner and Gardner. 1977. Comparative psychology and language acquisition. In *Annals of the New York Academy of Sciences*, ed. Salzinger and Denmark.

Green, S. 1975. Variation of vocal pattern with social situation in the Japanese monkey (Macaca fuscata): a field study. *Primate behavior* Vol 4, Academic Press.

..... 1975. Dialects in Japanese monkeys: vocal learning and cultural transmission or locale-specific vocal behavior. Z. *Tierpsychol.* 38, pp. 304-314.

Lenneberg, E. 1972. On explaining language. In *Biological boundaries of learning*, eds. Seligman and Hager. Appleton Century Crofts.

Liberman, Cooper, Shankweiler, and Studdert-Kennedy. 1967. Perception of the speech code. *Psychological Review* 74, pp. 431-461.

Leiber, J. Language and models of the mind. Unpublished ditto.

Limber, J. 1977. Language in child and chimp. *American Psychologist.*

Marler, P. 1972. A comparative approach to vocal learning: song development in white-crowned sparrows. In *Biological boundaries of learning*, eds. Seligman and Hager. Appleton Century Crofts.

..... 1973. A comparison of vocalizations of red-tailed monkeys and blue monkeys, *Cercopithecus ascanius* and *C. mitis*, in Uganda. Z. *Tierpsychol.* 33, pp. 223-247.

..... 1976. Social organization, communication, and graded signals: the chimpanzee and the gorilla. In *Growing points in ethology*, eds. Bateson and Hinde. Cambridge Univ. Press.

. . . . .1977. The evolution of communication. In *How animals communicate*, ed. Sebeok, T. Indiana Univ. Press.

May, R. 1978. Invited comments on "Does the chimpanzee have a theory of mind" by David Premack. Conference on Methods in Philosophy and the Sciences, The New School for Social Research, New York.

Patterson and Cohn. 1978. Conversations with a gorilla. *National Geographic* (Oct.).

Premack, D. 1976. *Intelligence in ape and man*. Lawrence Erlbaum Assoc.

Strange, W. and Jenkins, J. 1978. The role of linguistic experience in the perception of speech. In *Perception and experience*, eds. Pick, H. and Walk, R. New York: Plenum.

Studdert-Kennedy, M. The beginnings of speech. In *Behavioral development*, eds. Barlow, G., Immelmann, K., Main, M., and Petrinovich, L. New York: Cambridge Univ. Press.

Tarski, A. 1944. The semantic conception of truth. *Philosophy and Phenomenological Research* 4.

Zoloth, Petersen, Beecher, Green, Marler, Moody, and Stebbins. 1979. Species-specific perceptual processing of vocal sounds by monkeys. *Science* (May).

Thomas A. Sebeok

LOOKING FOR IN THE DESTINATION WHAT SHOULD HAVE BEEN SOUGHT IN THE SOURCE

Gibt es nicht gelehrte Hunde?
Und auch Pferde, welche rechnen
Wie Commerzienräthe? Trommeln
Nicht die Hasen ganz vorzüglich?
Heinrich Heine
Atta Troll (Cap. V,
Quatr. 15)

The notorious but unimpeachably corroborated case of Pavlov's mice raises, in capsule form, a variety of fascinating issues with far-reaching ramifications in several directions, but with particularly serious implications, several of which are well worth restating and pondering further (cf. Sebeok 1977b:192-201), both for the foundations and research methodology of contemporary semiotics.

The facts, as reconstructed by Gruenberg (1929:326-327), Zirkle (1958), and Razran (1959) are straightforward enough. Pavlov, convinced that acquired characters could be inherited, thought at one time that this process might be demonstrated by inducing conditioned reflexes in mice and then counting the conditioning trials required through successive generations. His expectation, in conformity with the Lamarckian model of information transmission then, as later, favored in the USSR (Razran 1958), was that the numbers would significantly decrease. Accordingly, he caused an assistant of his, one Studentsov (who appears in the history of science solely as an obscure although, for present purposes, emblematic figure confined to this single episode), to conduct a series of experiments over five generations of mice, the astounding results of which the collaborator then reported to the 1923 Soviet Physiological Conference, as expressed by the following dramatically cascading figures (rounded out later by Pavlov himself): 300, 100, 30, 10, and 5.

The intellectual milieu in which Pavlov worked and, of course, the very assumptions he brought to the investigation of the problem, accounts for his remissness in not instantly questioning the results, let alone repudiating the conclusions, obtained and announced by his "over-zealous assistant" (Razran 1959:916). "It seems reasonable to assume," Razran continues (*ibid.*), "that Pavlov would not have been so gullible if he had not shared the Lamarckian predisposition, common to Russian bioscientists—and to the intelligentsia in general—even before the Revolution, and if he had reviewed critically the general evidence on the topic. . . ." Only in 1929 did this uncompromisingly empirical scientist, whose honesty was never in doubt, indeed who, in a famous lecture, as far back as April 23, 1921, on the basic qualities of mind deemed indispensable to a scientist, put in a leading place exceptional facility in constructing scientific hypotheses—the capacity, that is, "to get behind the facts," as he used to say (Frolov 1938:256)—set forth publicly an alternative hypothesis to explain the astonishing data emanating from his laboratory. As related in Gruenberg's *The Story of Evolution* (1929:327, fn. 1), "[i]n an informal statement made at the time of the Thirteenth International Physiological Congress, Boston, August 1929, Pavlov explained that in checking up these experiments it was found that the apparent improvement in the ability to learn, on the part of successive generations of mice, was really due to an improvement in the ability to teach, on the part of the experimenter! And so this 'proof' of the transmission of modifications drops out of the picture, at least for the present."

This little tale of self-deception—a variant of what Merton (1948) has dubbed the self-fulfilling prophecy, a phenomenon which was later most creatively and ingeniously explored by Rosenthal (e.g., 1976:136-137) and Rosenthal and Jacobson (e.g., 1968:36), but which is perhaps best known by the tag, Clever Hans Fallacy—evokes certain urgent lines of inquiry which continue to be neglected by semioticians, as well as most other students of human and animal behavior, at their peril. The issue is such an important one because the Clever Hans effect informs, in fact insidiously infects, all dyadic interactions whatsoever, whether interpersonal, or between man and animal,[1] and by no means excepting the interactions of any living organism with a computer.[2]

In what follows, I will confine my observations to the three salient features suggested by the Pavlov episode which seem to me to be especially instructive for a general theory of signs. The first of these has to do with the notion of deception, especially within or at the perimeter of the academy, and the importance of being able to recognize different kinds and degrees thereof, ranging from out-and-out fraud for financial gain (say, royalties) and preferment (in the form, for example, of a doctorate), as in a scintillating instance of fictional ethnography, cleverly unwrapped by de Mille (1976; cf. Truzzi 1977). Imposture is sometimes alleged where facts remain forever bafflingly insubstantial while nonetheless mortally damaging, as in the melodramatic Paul Kammerer scandal made famous anew by Koestler (1971): Was the principal in the case deliberately trying to perpetrate a swindle, or was he an ingenuous yet suicidal victim of his own Lamarckian tendencies, or did he have a Studentsov in his lab, and, if so, was this putative staff member doctoring critical specimens of *Alytes obstetricans* either to please or to discredit (*ibid.* 124) his master? No possibility can be entirely excluded, just as we shall never know whether Claudius Ptolemy is the most successful fraud in the history of science, as Robert R. Newton recently argued, or the greatest astronomer of antiquity, as Owen Gingerich reaffirms. The question hinges on whether Ptolemy systematically invented or doctored earlier astronomers' data in order to support his own theories, whether he was unknowingly deceived by a dishonest assistant, or selected, for pedagogical purposes, just the data which happened to agree best with his theory (Wade 1977).

From a semiotic point of view, the deliberate exercise of fraud and deceit—the traditional confidence game or, as this is known to its practitioners, the con—is less interesting than self-deception and its far-flung consequences. For centuries, of course, one very special and continuing form of the con has been perpetuated upon marks by an operator using a tame, trained, domesticated animal, such as a horse, as his or her pivotal prop. A celebrated equine in point, popularized in a ballad published on November 14, 1595, was Morocco, "Maroccus Extaticus, or Bankes [John Banks', the operator's] Bay Horse in Trance," whose astonishing feats, suspected of verging on magic, were graphically portrayed in 1602, by Jean de Montlyard, Sieur de Melleray, in a long note (transcribed in Halliwell-Phillipps 1879: 31-36) to a French translation of the Golden Ass of Apuleius. If contemporary accounts are to be believed, both Banks and Morocco were burned upon orders of the Pope, as alluded to by Ben Jonson in one of his *Epigrams*: "Old Bankes the juggler, our Pythagoras,/Grave tutor to the learned horse, Both which,/Being, beyond sea, burned for one witch . . ." (1616). Pepys witnessed just such a horse, operated for profit nearly a century later, as noted in his *Diary* for September 1, 1668: "So to the Fair, and there saw several sights; among others, the mare that tells money, and many things to admiration; and, among others, come to me, when she was bid to go to him of the company that most loved a pretty wench in a corner. And this did cost me 12 *d.* to the horse, which I had flung him before, and did give me the occasion to baiser a might belle fille that was in the house that was exceeding plain, but forte belle." And Christopher (1970, Ch. 3) entertainingly relates the adventures of "the most discussed animal marvel of recent times," a mare named Lady, and her operator, Mrs. Claudia Fonda.[3] Although Dr. Joseph Banks Rhine declared Lady "the greatest thing since radio,"[4] and that she possessed ESP, the skillful conjuror and historian of magical entertainment exposed the technique used by Mrs. Fonda, an obvious trick—obvious, that is, to mentalists—sometimes employed by mediums and known as pencil reading.

Christopher's key sentence reads (*ibid*. 45): "If Dr. Rhine was interested in testing for ESP, he should have ignored the horse and studied Mrs. Fonda." He is restating here a basic principle, explicitly recognized already in 1612 by a certain Samuel Rid, the author of a wondrously sophisticated instructional manual, or how-to-do-it book, of whom, alas, nothing further is known. This book, *The Art of Juggling*, ought to be made required reading for all would-be semioticians; here I will reproduce only a brief passage of commentary on the exploits of a performing horse, presumably Morocco:

> *"As, for ensample, His master will ask him how many people there are in the room? The horse will paw with his foot so many times as there are people. And mark the eye of the horse is always upon his master, and as his master moves, so goes he or stands still, as he is brought to it at the first. As, for ensample, his master will throw three dice, and will bid his horse tell you how many you or he have thrown. Then the horse paws with his foot whiles the master stands stone still. Then when his master sees he hath pawed so many as the first dice shews itself, then he lifts up his shoulders and stirs a little. Then he bids him tell what is on the second die, and then of the third die, which the horse will do accordingly, still pawing with his foot until his master sees he hath pawed enough, and then stirs. Which, the horse marking, will stay and leave pawing. And note, that the horse will paw an hundred times together, until he sees his master stir. And note also that nothing can be done but his master must first know, and then his master knowing, the horse is ruled by him by signs. This if you mark at any time you shall plainly perceive."*

Let me underscore Rid's last sentence: "This if you mark at any time you shall plainly perceive." The point is that, until the advent of Oskar Pfungst (1965 [1907]), no scientist that we know of had the insight to ask an animal—in this instance, Clever Hans, the horse of Herr von Osten—a question to which the inquirer himself did not know the answer. It turned out that, no matter how severely skeptical the audience, whether unschooled or expert, was, it was the observer who had involuntarily and unknowingly signed to the observed to stop tapping at the precise instant where the message destination—alive to the correct answer—expected the message source to cease emitting. "This," Polanyi (1958:169-170) says, "is how they made the answers invariably come out right" (continuing: "this is exactly also how philosophers make their descriptions of science, or their formalized procedures of scientific inference, come out right").

Actually, Lord Avebury, in the 1880s, came very close to rediscovering the correct solution in his experiments with Van, his black poodle, supplemented by his casual inspection of other dogs, some score of years before Pfungst, who himself regarded Van "as a predecessor of our Hans" (1965:178). Avebury had the right attitude to begin with, "that hitherto we have tried to teach animals, rather than to learn from them: To convey our ideas to them, rather than to devise any language or code or signals by means of which they might communicate theirs to us" (Lubbock 1886:1089). He sensitively discerned that when a dog—or a chimpanzee (see Thomson 1924:132) for that matter—is taught how to "count," the operator need not, in fact, ordinarily does not, "*consciously* give the dog any sign, yet so quick [is] the dog in seizing the slightest indication that he [is] able to give the correct answer. . . . Evidently, the dog seize[s] upon the slight indications unintentionally given" (*ibid.* 1091).

Avebury, furthermore, shrewdly connected these observations "with the so-called 'thought-reading' " (*ibid.*), one variant of which, commonly known as "muscle reading," came eventually to be investigated in painstaking detail by three prominent Berkeley psychologists, Edward C. Tolman among them. "Muscle reading" was shown to crucially hinge on the performer's perception of motor signs of an exceedingly delicate character, signs, moreover, "unintentionally" communicated to him "by each of the persons who acted as his guide" (Stratton 1921; discussed further in Sebeok 1977b:200-201).[5] It is established by now beyond serious doubt that the working ingredient of many other mind reading acts—much in the manner of the children's game of Hot and Cold—consists of unwitting and inadvertent nonverbal signs transmitted from audience to "psychic"; nor is this surprising, "since people constantly pass nonverbal signals to each other through such things as changes in their tones of voice and body movements. In fact, this nonverbal communication forms the basis of a well-known magic act. One performer, for example, asks to have his check in payment for a show hidden in the auditorium in full view of his audience. He then comes on stage and finds the check by reading the nonverbal cues of the audience as he wanders closer to or farther from the check" (Kolata 1977: 283, interviewing Persi Diaconis, who is both a prominent mathematician and magician; the identical illusion is discussed, in his somewhat hokey style, by Kreskin [1973:80-84], describing how "I concentrate on reading every direction, every clue, and sensitize myself to hear or see any supportive factors beyond the perceived thought. . . . It can be likened to a highly stimulating game of charades . . ."). This example is far from insignificant, since, as Diaconis emphasizes (*ibid.*), it suggests an enormous problem area of "how much usable information is being transmitted in this way and what the best guessing strategy is," and which arises in many contexts other than parapsychology—in fact, whenever and wherever organisms interact.

As to the mental operation of guessing, it was none other than Peirce (1929:269-270) who had emphasized that "[i]ts full powers are only brought out under critical circumstances," a claim he went on to substantiate in a colorful extended narrative of a true personal incident in which the great philosopher was metamorphosed into a master sleuth (for the full story, see *loc. cit.* 267-282).[6] As one of his editors summarizes the anecdote, it concerned "the theft of [Peirce's] coat and a valuable watch from his stateroom on a Boston to New York boat. He says that he made all the waiters stand in a row and after briefly talking with each, but without consciously getting any clue, he made a guess as to which one was guilty. The upshot of the story is that after many difficulties, and by making more successful guesses, he proved that his original guess had been correct" (Peirce 7.40n15; cf. 7.45). What Peirce attempted to do by talking briefly with each man in turn was, as he put it, "to detect in my consciousness some symptoms of the thief" (*loc. cit.* 281). His expectation was that the crook would emit some unwitting index, but Peirce also stressed that his own perception of telltale signs, while he held himself "in as passive and receptive a state" (*ibid.*) as he could, had to be unconscious, or, to use a preferred term he suggested, unself-conscious, "a discrimination below the surface of consciousness, and not recognized as a real judgment, yet in very truth a genuine discrimination . . ." (*loc. cit.* 280). He mentions two conjectural principles that may furnish at least a partial explanation for his successful application of "this singular guessing instinct. I infer in the first place," he concluded, "that man divines something of the secret principles of the universe because his mind has developed as a part of the universe and under the influence of these same secret principles; and secondly, that we often derive from observation strong intimations of truth, without being able to specify what were the circumstances we had observed which conveyed those intimations" (*loc. cit.* 281-282). In Peirce's incomparably insightful fashion, the first principle adduced provides the ultimate evolutionary rationale for the workings of the Clever Hans effect, while the other addresses its specifically semiotic roots.

The work on deception by illicit communication in the laboratory recently adumbrated by Pilisuk and his collaborators (1976) surely is on the right track, but merely scratches the surface of deception being a pervasive fact of life characteristic of experimental studies of human and animal behavior; Rosenthal (1976:156), for instance, admits that "[d]eception is a necessary commonplace in psychological research," although I believe that he tends to substantially underestimate (*ibid.* 388) potentially harmful consequences, particularly in the context of placebos, which may have decided toxic effects and even the power to produce gross physical change (cf., e.g., Beecher 1955:1606), as well as of the dubious role of double-blind "controls."[7]

The first general lesson of the Pavlov episode thus boils down to this: Be ever on the lookout against deception, but beware, above all, of self-deception. The second moral is expressly methodological, and may be best understood in a semiotic frame. It has been formulated, as we saw, in more or less the same way by Rid, Avebury, Pfungst, Christopher, and stated perhaps most comprehensively in the title of this article. Pfungst (1965:xxx) and his chief, the eminent psychologist Carl Stumpf, distilled the essence of their investigation by recognizing and admitting that the Hans Commission made the initial mistake of "looking for, in the horse, what should have been sought in the man." In physics, one speaks of couplings between the observer and the observed, and keeps asking how the former affects the latter. In psychological jargon, the experimenter becomes a proxy for "man," while "horse" can stand for any subject, whether human or animal (Rosenthal 1976). In anthropological, folkloristic (Fine and Crane 1977), and even linguistic (Sebeok 1977b:196), fieldwork, we are concerned with the distorting influence of elicitor upon native informant. In a clinical setting, we are interested in what the agentive physician's (or quack's or shaman's) personality and paraphernalia contribute towards the healing of the patient/client (Sebeok 1977b:196-197; *id.* 1978). In the argot of the con, the police wants to know how does the operator "take" the mark? All of these dynamic/dyadic relationships between living systems have specific commonalities ultimately modeled on, or, more exactly, programmed after, the one universal dependence relationship which must be both basic and paradigmatic: The cybernetic cycle that prevails between mother (or other caretaker) and child. The nature of this system, "in which one partner assumes the functions of sensor and regulator for the other one and vice versa," was first outlined by Th. von Uexküll (1978), in an attempt to account for the efficaciousness of placebos. All of us are assumed to be reliving and reiterating the early months of our extrauterine existence, when gesturing, posturing, vocalizing, and eventually articulating wicca words like "mama," produced something from nothing—milk and toys, for instance—"out of the blurry, remote world of the adult gods," in Wagoner's (1976: 1598) apt and evocative conceit.

Although von Uexküll states his hypotheses in exceedingly fruitful semiotic terms, it is likewise in obvious conformity with psychoanalytic theory, which suggests consideration of this primal program as a reactivation of a pivotal early experience and one which "may be a permanent available pattern of social interchange in human life, which is not confined only to child-mother or patient-doctor relationship." Plausible as this formula appears, it nevertheless leaves the question most often asked about the seemingly miraculous placebo effect and comparable forms of therapy open—say, the "laying on of hands" (currently taught at the graduate level at the New York University School of Education, Health, Nursing and Arts Professions) or "mother's kiss or voodoo drums, leeches, purgatives, poultices, or snake oil" (Moertel et al. 1976:96)—or, indeed, the workings of one's belief in Christian Science (Sebeok 1978): namely, how are the semiotic agencies and habiliments transmuted into physiologically operational mechanisms? The answer was foreshadowed in Janet's (1925:1:43-53) discussion of the value of miraculous methods of treatment, from the shrine of Aesculapius to Lourdes. Cannon's classic article (1942) on the cause of "voodoo" death notwithstanding,[8] much fascinating research remains to be done at the borders of the sign science with the life science before this problem can be wholly resolved.

Another area of role-demand where the von Uexküll paradigm is palpably manifested is in hypnotic and posthypnotic responsiveness. As in the placebo effect—for, as Paul Sacerdote emphasizes, "hypnosis may be in many ways the most powerful of placebos" (Holden 1977:808)—the audience, or, using a semiotic term with a broader charge, context (cf. Fisher 1965:85), serves at least four functions that combine to reinforce the realization and maintenance of so-called hypnotic behavior; these were conveniently summarized by Sarbin and Coe (1972:96-97), but may be assigned to a wider category of effects sometimes called *artifacts*, such as increased motivation and role-playing, in contrast to *essence*, which, if it really exists, refers to what is more or less vaguely known as "an altered state of consciousness," or sometimes "cortical inhibition" or "dissociation" (Orne 1959). Artifacts are systematic errors stemming from specifiable uncontrolled conditions—a bouquet of subtle cues emanating from both the experimental procedure and the experimenter. Thus investigation has revealed that the paraphonetic features selected by the source—viz., forceful or lethargic tone of voice—constitutes a ruling variable which must, if feasible, be carefully controlled (Barber and Calverley 1964). The hypnotized subject exhibits the behavior which he thinks the hypnotist expects of him, or, more accurately, what he thinks hypnosis is. The phrase "demand characteristics" is applied to this invigorating idea in the history of hypnosis research (Sheehan and Perry 1976), to which Jaynes' (1977:385) notion of the "collective cognitive imperative" corresponds exactly.

The intimate mutual gaze of lovers furnishes one example among many of how his fundamental paradigm is played out in young adulthood: The reason why both a boy and a girl spend so much time peering closely into each other's eyes is that "[t]hey are unconsciously checking each other's pupil dilations. The more her pupils expand with emotional excitement, the more it makes his expand, and vice versa" (Morris 1977:172). The pupil response is, as a rule, unknowingly emitted as well as, even more often, unknowingly perceived (Janisse 1977; Sebeok 1977a:1067-1068). Hip dudes, metaphoric "cats," wear dark glasses, or "shades," like the Chinese jade dealers of yore, to conceal their excited pupil dilation and thus to project a cool look—one that demands heightened participation of their "transparent" interlocutors.[9]

Semiotics, which is commonly defined as the study of any messages whatsoever, whether verbal or not, must be equally concerned with the successive processes of generation and encoding on the part of the most various sources, whether human or not; with the transmission of any string of signs through all possible channels; and with the successive processes of decoding and interpretation on the part of the most various destinations, whether human or not. What the Pavlov tale reminds us of is the peculiar force of the linkage joining any source with any destination. In marveling at the accomplishments of animals—especially hand-reared dolphins in the 1960s and great apes in the 1970s—

trained to engage in two-way communication with man, attention to the behavior of the human has all too often been either shunted aside by deliberate misdirection (imposture) or ignored in innocence (self-deception). Thus many people cherish the belief that police dogs are infallible as trackers, enabling them to recognize the trail of a stranger after getting the scent. However, in one historic experiment (Katz 1937:8-10), it turned out that the man in charge of the police dogs had provided unwitting cues: In other words, "it was not the dog guiding the man, but the man guiding the dog owing to his preconceived opinion about the result to be expected."[10]

Those who stage-manage the circus antics of apes have known for centuries what scientists who aim to instill manually encoded and visually decoded verbal communicative skills in such animals have still scarcely grasped. It is widely imagined, for example, that imitation of the human model in learning situations of this sort is critical. On this issue, Hachet-Souplet (1897:83-84, 91), author of the standard textbook on dressage, quotes Buffon: " 'Le singe, ayant des bras et des mains, s'en sert comme nous, mais sans songer à nous; la similitude des membres et des organes produit nécessairement des mouvement qui ressemblent aux nôtres; étant conformé comme l'homme, le singe ne peut se mouvoir que comme lui; mais se mouvoir de même n'est pas agir pour imiter'. . . . Du reste," the canny author concludes, "le public se laissait prendre à cette ruse innocente." When the subject patently fails to imitate the trainer, this imperfection, too, is reinterpreted to fit with the anticipated design. Patterson (1977), for instance, instructed Koko to smile for a photograph. Her gorilla signed "frown" or "sad." The psychologist's explanation of this contrary behavior was not at all that Koko responded erroneously; Patterson's preconception of her design constrained her to assert that negative occurrences of this sort "demonstrate [the ape's] grasp of opposites." With dialectic unfolded in this vein how can you lose?[11]

What actually happens, as Hediger (1974:40) keeps patiently repeating, is that whoever poses the question about the linguistic accomplishment of apes "often already has preconceived ideas about the outcome of the experiments, indeed, he must frequently have possessed such ideas before being able to set up the experiment in the first place. Another factor is the choice of suitable experimental animals. It is up to him to choose a suitable species and individuals, treat and prepare them in a definite way. In this, the 'context' . . ., are already included many possibilities of influence by channels still largely unknown to us." The modish mirage of the Pathetic Fallacy, or the attribution of human characteristics to objects in the natural world, especially to the speechless creatures populating it, reinforced in ways that are more or less well understood (cf. Sebeok 1977b:197-199, 201-202n3), is so powerful that observers are not uncommonly prone to report a Barmecidal feast of signs where the more candid among them admit to having perceived none. Thus Stokoe (1977:1)–a leading expert on Ameslan–remarks about some infant chimpanzees: "These baby chimps sign as they move–very rapidly; and we often found that we had seen a sign or a sequence of two or three signs without consciously realizing that we had in fact seen it." Stokoe's encounter with baby Dar and bantling Tatu is disturbingly reminiscent of my own experience in the early 1960s with dolphins in Miami's long defunct Communication Research Institute. In that laboratory, *Tursiops* was being trained to mimic the speech of a human investigator by standard operant conditioning technique. Numerous rumors and some reports were put in circulation to the effect that the animals, especially Elvar and Chee-Chee, were indeed capable of reproducing words "appropriately." Of Elvar, it was avouched, for instance (Lilly 1963:114): "He does not reproduce a word in 'tape-recorder' fashion or in the fashion of a talking bird. In one's presence he literally [*sic*] analyzed acoustic components of our words and reproduced various aspects in sequence and separately." Perhaps mistaken for a mark, I was permitted to observe one training session, and later to listen to recordings of several previous sessions. I heard only random dolphin noises, no dialogue. My puzzled demurral was countered by the assertion that these coastal porpoises articulated much too fast for their emissions to be interpreted by the human ear unaided: understanding presupposed analysis by means of the sound spectrograph and oscillographic methods. It was shown a decade or so afterwards that the papers published in scientific journals by this Florida research group "provided no solid evidence in support of [such] speculations" (Wood 1973:91). The project was, accordingly, scratched, in 1968, altogether. The long shadow of Clever Hans darkened that undertaking from the start, as is perfectly patent from a sentence the principal had printed in italic type: "*And he* [i.e., Elvar] *first did it* [i.e., spoke] *when and only when we believed he could do it and somehow demonstrated our belief to him*" (Lilly 1963, *ibid.*).

Stokoe (1977, *ibid.*) drew another methodological conclusion from his observation in Nevada, or, more accurately, the lack of it: videotape or film "can never be an adequate substitute for trained live observation. ..." This, however, holds only if the inevitability of voluntary and involuntary influence upon the animals being experimented upon is objectively and critically recognized and assessed at every turn, and if all conceivable media of communication between men and animals are kept in constant view. Concerning the work Stokoe describes, and the like, it is not enough to exclaim in awe on what the chimps do; the real challenge is to uncover—the relationship being reciprocal—what the University of Nevada team, for one, is up to.

The use of recording devices is no panacea, of course. As F.J.J. Buytendijk's scrutiny of a film of a fight between a mongoose and cobra established, the reaction time of their coordinate exchange of some messages is so short that it can neither be viewed by human observers nor re-viewed even in slow motion. This is explicable in terms of the concept of zero signifier (Sebeok 1976:118): "these dissimilar combatants behaved part of the time like a pair of dancers, in which each anticipated the other's next movement" (Hediger 1974:38), that is, their reaction time was reduced to naught. Hediger believes that something similar takes place in the circus, for example, between a skilled trainer causing a panther sitting on a pedestal to strike out with a forepaw and withdrawing in exquisite accord with that movement, or a springboard acrobat adjusting his leap to the blow of the elephant's foot at the other end of the plank. In his keen observations on movement coordination, or microsynchrony, in human social interaction, Kendon (1977:75) has noted the same kind of foreknowledge: "The precision with which the listener's movements are synchronized with the speaker's speech means that the listener is in some way able to anticipate what the speaker is going to say. . . ."

Hediger's mention of channels focuses attention on yet a third dimension of the Pavlov yarn. It is insufficient to shift one's attention back from the destination to the source. It is essential to consider, as well, the means whereby the two are conjoined. Although the visual, auditory, tactile, and chemical mechanisms of rodent communication, for instance, are understood to a degree (Eisenberg and Kleiman 1977:637-649), no one, least of all the principals, had the slightest idea how, precisely, Studentsov unwittingly disciplined Pavlov's mice; neither was Rosenthal (1976:178) able to determine to his satisfaction how his "bright" and "dull" rat subjects were differentially educated by his naive students: "We cannot be certain of the role of handling patterns as the mediators of the experimenters' expectancies, nor of whether such other channels as the visual, olfactory, and auditory were involved." As to this, we can but reiterate Hediger's query and observation (1974:39): "How many channels exist between man and animal? We know little more today than we did half a century ago, i.e., that many other channels exist besides those of optic and acoustic question. On account of the inadequacy of our sense organs and the apparatus at our disposal, such channels remain for the moment unknown. It is known, however, that many apparently quite objective laboratory experiments have given, and continue to give, false results for the very reason that many experimenters believe themselves aware of and able to control all the channels of communication existing between those conducting the experiment and the animal involved."

The following principles deserve, in consequence, attentive consideration:

1) Any form of physical energy propagation can be exploited for communication purposes (Sebeok 1972:40, 67, 124).

2) Channel selection is governed and constrained by the source encoder's sensorium. The source decoder will generate an acceptable reproduction of the source output if endowed (at least in part) with a correspondingly functioning sensorium.

3) It is reasonable to assume that messages are routinely transmitted between organisms through hitherto undiscovered or as yet scarcely discerned channels. One arresting case in point is the electrical channel, "a new modality" (Hopkins 1977:286), the multifaceted communicative functions of which are in the process of being actively disclosed.

4) The range of each of man's sense organs is significantly exceeded by those of a host of other animals. Hediger (1974:32) cites Pfungst as having demonstrated that the horse is capable of perceiving movements in the human face of "less than one fifth of a millimetre." Pierce and David (1958:102-103) relate amusingly how a trio of electronics experts learned about the ultrasonic stridulation of crickets, drawing from this story the moral "that we hear only what we can hear, and that there may be a great many obvious differences among sounds which must forever escape our ears," wisely adding: "[t]o some degree we hear what we expect to hear." Parallel comparisons can be adduced, *mutatis mutandis*, about the human eye, to say nothing of the olfactory field.

5) Man has invented a variety of technical aids to enhance the ineffectualness of his channel capacity. However, such intensifying equipment "has frequently been shown to have been a [further] source of error . . ." (Hediger 1974:30).

6) Before resorting to cheap *ad hoc* paranormal rationalizations, a sophisticated, if time consuming, research program must be conducted to pin down the mechanism actually at work in each instance. Elegant and exhaustive investigations of this character are illuminatingly inventoried in Vogt's and Hyman's

(1959, Ch. 6) psychophysical exegesis of the movement of the dowsing rod in water witching (cf. Gardner 1957:101-113). The contrary is illustrated by the widely publicized case of Rosa Kouleshova (Pratt 1973:63), who was reputed to be capable of "seeing," particularly reading, through her fingertips. Astute press-agentry led to a global rash of other reported "dermooptical" manifestations (Sebeok 1977b:201), in the early 1960s, all of which turned out to be phony. "X-Ray Eye Act" is the professional designation of hoaxes of this nature,[12] where the performer can easily open his or her eyes and is able to look down both sides of the nose; blindfold magic can be achieved with seemingly impenetrable coverings like bread dough, silver dollars, wads of cotton, powder puffs, folded paper, sheets of metal, adhesive tape, and, of course, a variety of cloth shields.

The small but influential segment of mankind that can afford leisure for the contemplation of such matters longs to establish communication links in two opposite directions: With the rest of animate existence (plant forms, involving phytosemiosis, as well as animal forms, involving zoosemiosis), in the matrix of which our lives lie inalienably embedded; and with supposititious extraterrestrial civilizations. Leaving unearthly aspirations and efforts aside (cf., e.g., Ponnamperuma and Cameron 1974; see pp. 213-215 for selected references to "interstellar communication languages"), one can confidently assert that the fundamentals of code-switching between our species and not a few others are adequately understood, not just intuitively—that kind of comprehension was the imperative semiotic prerequisite for domestication—but also scientifically, thanks, in the main, to Hediger's brilliantly creative lifelong spadework (cf., *inter alia*, Hediger 1974, and the references given in Sebeok 1976:219-220). Two-way zoosemiotic communication is thus not at issue, but such communication between man and animalkind by *verbal* means is quite another matter. The fascinating paradox of language-endowed speechless creatures has been iteratively resolved in myth and fiction, but not in reality. That search, for a resolution of the authentic kind, has lately taken a disturbingly pseudoscientific turn. An account of the socioeconomic reasons for this craze, interesting though it may be, of "humanizing" pets, quasi-feral terrestrial and marine mammals, and an occasional tame bird,[13] falls outside of the scope of this article.

Leo Szilard's satirical story about "The Voice of the Dolphins" (1961) and Robert Merle's thriller about *The Day of the Dolphin* (1967) are chimerical treatments of the same theme in what may well be called the Decade of the Dolphin. In the 1970s, writers have, fittingly, emerged from the brine. Peter Dickinson's "chimpocentric" tale of detection, *The Poison Oracle* (1974), where the action hinges on the linguistic capacity of an ape, and John Goulet's affecting book, *Oh's Profit* (1975), the hero of which, a gifted young signing gorilla, is pitted against the merciless forces of a singularly sinister coalition of linguists, are modern transfigurements of Jules Verne's diverting (if today seldom read) parodic SF pastiche, *The Great Forest* (originally published with his *Le Village aérien*, in 1901). This work was inspired by the genuine, if eccentric, exploits of Richard L. Garner, who, in 1892, left America on a field trip for Gabon, where he lived in Libreville for two years. He then proceeded upcountry, where he was sheltered at a mission of the Fathers of the Holy Ghost, located on the banks of the Ogowe. In due course, he published (Garner 1892) a book on the "speech" of monkeys. His studies were themselves an odd mishmash of valuable observations, pure inventions and colorful humbug: "Peut-être a-t-on souvenir de l'expérience à laquelle voulut se livrer l'Américain Garner dans le but d'étudier le langage des singes et de donner à ses théories une démonstration expérimental," Verne questions tongue-in-cheek, and then goes on to invent a lunatic proto-ethologist, one Dr. Johausen (obviously Garner, but in Teutonic guise), who journeys to Central Africa to seek out "le pretendu langage des singes." Predictably, he finds just what he was expecting to find—speaking monkeys—but with a difference: "Ce qui les distingue essentiellement des hommes [est qu'ils] ne parlaient jamais sans nécessité." In passing, Verne makes some exceedingly prescient observations about language and cognition, intelligence and verbal propensity, and animal communication in general. The story ends with an ironic twist: Johausen's expectations are indeed fulfilled and he even rises to become the ruler of the beasts, Sa Majesté Msélo-Tala-Tala, but the cost he has to pay for his achievement is enormous. The price is the loss of his most precious possession, his own language, which is to say, his humanity: "Il est devenu singe . . . ." Thus, in an unending cycle, does Pop Art burlesque scientific lore while Big Science apes (*le mot juste*) the presentiments of Pop Culture—no less in today's ecologically remorseful USA than in yesteryear's Lysenko-ridden USSR.

The road from Russian rodents to American apes is paved with good intentions, but for an innocent onlooker, trained in the sign science, at least three signposts pointing to a need for ventilation loom behind and ahead, each beckoning to as yet insufficiently explored byways at the dangerous intersection of two synergetic causes of error: The Clever Hans Fallacy and the Pathetic Fallacy. The trio of problems that seem, from a semiotic point of view, to cry out for immediate, impartial, intensive in-

vestigation are: the destructive pitfall of self-deception, the pre-
dominance, in dyadic encounters, of the source over the destination, and the paucity of accurate knowledge about the multiplicity
and range of natural channels connecting both extremities of the
communication chain.[14]

NOTES

1. In view of the now hardly controvertible fact, underlined once again by
   Hediger (1974:27-28), that the Clever Hans effect in "animals is only
   explainable by the continually repressed fact that the animal—be it
   horse, monkey or planarian—is generally more capable of interpreting
   the signals emanating from humans than is conversely the case," it is
   irksome to repeatedly come across reports fatuously stating that "[i]n
   order to avoid the results of suggestion [certain] investigators decided
   to use animals rather than humans as their experimental organisms"
   (this in reference to mice, in a test of "laying-on-of-hands" healing, as
   reported by Rhine [1970:316-317]).
2. Cf. Weizenbaum's (1977) telling remark about the "power of . . . [his]
   computer program [being] no more and no less than the power to de-
   ceive," and the constant, inevitable, yet apparently discounted intrusion
   of Clever Hans cues into the Lana experiment intended to be conducted
   by means of an "impersonal" computerized system—see, e.g., Rumbaugh
   (1977:159, 161), and the acerbic comment on this project by Gardner
   and Gardner (1977:44), alleging that his "results . . . presented thus far
   are more parsimoniously interpreted in terms of such classic factors as
   Clever Hans cues. . . ." The Gardners claim that, to the contrary, testing
   procedures they themselves developed rule out this and kindred alternative interpretations. The procedures they refer to presumably involve
   the "double-blind" design, adapted from psychopharmacological re-
   searches. The objectivity of this method, however, though comforting,
   is altogether illusory; see, e.g., Tuteur 1957-1958. So what we have here
   is a blatant case of, paraphrasing Cervantes, the pot calling the kettle
   black.
3. As recently as 1975, one still finds books on communication between
   man and horse imbued with the Clever Hans Fallacy. Thus Blake (1975,
   Ch. 10) devotes an entire chaotic chapter to "telepathy in horse language." He describes, no doubt accurately, his experiences with a horse,
   Weeping Roger (*ibid.*, Ch. 7), but goes on to imply an absurd explanation: "I discovered that I could direct [this stallion] where I wanted to
   go just by thinking it. I would steer him to the left or right or straight
   ahead simply by visualizing the road. This was the first time I had consciously experienced telepathy with a horse" (*ibid.* 126). Elsewhere
   (*ibid.* 94), he remarks, "I was always at one with him." Plainly, all the
   constituents for a Clever Hans setup are present, but Blake still finds it
   necessary to resort to ESP instead of the correct semiotic explanation,
   which he apparently knows nothing of.
4. Perhaps echoing Upton Sinclair's (1930:4) technologically puerile yet
   by virtue of that very fact endearing simile, comparing ESP to "some
   kind of vibration, going out from the brain, like radio broadcasting."
   This imagery has its ultimate source in Democritus.
5. On "muscle reading" as explanation for other pseudo-occult phenomena,

such as the movement of a Ouija board, table tipping, and automatic writing, see Gardner (1957:109), who speaks of the "unwitting translation of thoughts into muscular action. . . ." See also Vogt and Hyman (1959, Ch. 5). Regarding the most flashy of contemporary "psychics," the Israeli stage-performer Uri Geller, see Marks and Kammann (1977: 17), who similarly conclude that "[p]arsimony dictates the choice of normal explanations for the phenomena described. . . . Geller's procedures allow him to use ordinary sensory channels and ordinary motor functions." Incidentally, James ("The Amazing") Randi, a top flight Canadian conjurer, has publicly duplicated all of Geller's feats. Concerning Peirce's disapprobation of telepathy, "with its infrequency and usual deceptiveness" (Peirce 7.686), and of kindred psychic doctrines and claims, see his extended if apparently incomplete essay on "Telepathy and perception" (*ibid.* 597-686).

6. Peirce's detectival procedure is compared in detail, in a forthcoming paper by Sebeok and Umiker-Sebeok (1978), with the famous "method" of Sherlock Holmes, wherein the similarity is accounted for by virtue of their common roots in Natural Semiotics (including medical). Kreskin (1973:27-28) incidentally sketches a stage illusion, *Guilty*, which unfolds precisely according to the strategy devised by Peirce, in applying which, Kreskin claims, it is "impossible for the 'guilty' person not to give himself away. . . ." For a flagrant case of real life abuse of "telepathy" in law enforcement, seemingly motivated by social prejudice, see Posinsky (1961).

7. Cf. fn. 2, above; I intend to return in much more depth elsewhere to these complex semiotic topics, which I had occasion to discuss but briefly before (Sebeok 1977b:196-197, and 1978).

8. Huxley, who professes to believe in the existence of ESP (1967:282), and appears perversely unaware of Cannon's highly significant study of a quarter of a century earlier than his, nevertheless gropes toward an analysis of voodoo in semiotic terms: "Is it . . . possible that symbols," he asks, meaning icons, "by containing the field of relationships and providing the ground of consciousness, are responsible for what we call ESP?" (*ibid.* 302). Discussion of the etiology of voodoo death continues in anthropological and other circles; for a summary of the recent literature and latest interpretations, see Lex 1974.

9. See Umiker-Sebeok (1978) for a detailed treatment of the elaborate semiotic code for partial or total eye concealment by means of eyeglasses and other devices in American culture.

10. One side effect of this 1913 experiment was a decisive improvement in the training of police dogs and in their consequent accuracy in tracking. Katz's conclusion is, of course, equally applicable to any "muscle reading" act. The performer may have a spectator take hold of his hand believing that "he is being led by the magician, but actually the performer permits the *spectator to lead him* by unconscious muscular tensions" (Gardner 1957:109). The best muscle readers, like the famous Eugen de Rubini (whose case I discussed in Sebeok 1977b:200-201), may dispense with physical contact altogether, relying on far more illusive guiding cues, such as tremors of the floor, faint sounds of feet, movements of arms and clothing, and/or those made by changes in breathing (Rinn 1950:531). The workings of several variants of the Clever Hans theme were known to scientists of the stature of Michael Faraday (table turning) and Michel Eugene Chevreul (the magic pendulum) by at least the early 1850s (Hansel 1966:33-34).

11. Parents who act on the assumption that their child is bright appear to

proceed in just this way. I recently observed an infant of 17 months being fed beef. Her mother interrogated her, "What's this?" The daughter replied, "Chicken." The mother observed, "She loves to tease me!" She then followed this remark up with a further unsubstantiated general comment: "She enjoys making a game out of oppositions." Bingham (1971) has shown that preverbal children are addressed in a carefully accommodated register by mothers who judge that *their* infants have the capacity to understand quite a bit, but not by mothers who set a lower estimate on *their* infants' capacity.

12. In part no doubt inspired by Jules Romains, the French writer, who was obsessed with "paroptic" vision, or "eyeless sight." His book on this subject (Romains 1920; American version, 1924) was widely read in the postwar years here and throughout Europe.

13. Chauvin-Muckensturm 1974:207 explicitly compares the drumming code she imparted to her Greated Spotted Woodpecker to the man-monkey performances variously shaped by the Gardners and Premack, stressing that *"le bec est au moins l'égal de la main du chimpanzé."* This woodpecker is French. It will not have escaped notice, however, that the happily defunct myth of dolphin discourse, as well as the currently continuing promotion of primates to the status of a putatively (Limber 1977) productive *animal loquens*, have been confined, so far without a single exception, to the United States.

14. Several leading themes developed in this paper were touched upon in different lectures and seminars given, during the Fall of 1977, at the University of Kansas (week of October 10), Texas Tech University (October 17), and the University of Texas-Dallas (October 18). Some were also presented, in synoptic form, under the title "Natural Semi-otics," at the 76th Annual Meeting of the American Anthropological Association, suited to the context of an all-day Symposium on the "Semiotics of Culture: Toward a New Synthesis in World Anthropology" (co-organized by Drs. D. Jean Umiker-Sebeok and Irene Portis Winner, and held in Houston, December 1). A substantially revised and expanded version of that talk will be published in a special 1979 issue of *Semiotica*, featuring the array of papers, linking sign theory with culture theory, delivered at this Symposium.

REFERENCES

Barber, T. and Calverley, D. 1964. Effect of *E*'s tone of voice on "hypnotic-like" suggestibility. *Psychological Reports* 15, pp. 139-144.

Beecher, H. 1955. The powerful placebo. *Journal of the American Medical Association* 159, pp. 1602-1606.

Bingham, N. 1971. Maternal speech to pre-linguistic infants: differences re-lated to maternal judgments of infant language competence. Unpublished paper. Cornell University: Ithaca.

Blake, H. N. 1975. *Talking with horses: a study of communication between man and horse*. London: Souvenir Press.

Cannon, W. 1942. "Voodoo" death. *American Anthropologist* 44, pp. 169-181.

Chauvin-Muckensturm, B. 1974. Y a-t-il utilisation de signaux appris comme moyen de communication chez le pic epeiche? *Revue du Comportement Animal* 9, pp. 185-207.

Christopher, M. 1970. *ESP, seers & psychics*. New York: Thomas Y. Crowell.

de Mille, R. 1976. *Castaneda's journey: the power and the allegory*. Santa Barbara: Capra Press.

Eisenberg, J. and Kleinman, D. 1977. Communication in lagamorphs and rodents. In *How animals communicate*, ed. T. A. Sebeok. Bloomington: Indiana University Press.

Fine, G. and Crane, B. 1977. The expectancy effect in anthropological research: an experimental study of riddle collection. *American Ethnologist* 4, pp. 517-524.

Fisher, S. 1965. The role of expectancy in the performance of posthypnotic behavior. In *The nature of hypnosis*, ed. Shor, R. and Orne, M. New York: Holt, Rinehart and Winston.

Frolov, I. 1938. *Pavlov and his school*. London: Paul, Trench, Trubner.

Gardner, M. 1957. *Fads and fallacies in the name of science*. New York: Dover.

Gardner, R. and Gardner, B. 1977. Comparative psychology and language acquisition. In *Psychology: the state of the art*, eds. Kurt Salzinger and F. Denmark. New York: Annals of the New York Academy of Sciences.

Garner, R. 1892. *The speech of monkeys*. New York: Charles L. Webster.

Gruenberg, B. 1929. *The story of evolution: facts and theories on the development of life*. Garden City: Garden City Publishing Co.

Hachet-Souplet, P. 1897. *Le dressage des animaux et les combats de bêtes, révélation des procédés employés par les professionals pour dresser le chien, le singe, le cheval, l'éléphant, les bêtes féroces, etc.* Paris: Firmin Didot.

Halliwell-Phillipps, J. 1879. *Memoranda on Love's Labour's Lost, King John, Othello, and on Romeo and Juliet*. London: James Evan Adlard.

Hansel, C. 1966. *ESP: a scientific evaluation*. New York: Charles Scribner's Sons.

Hediger, H. 1974. Communication between man and animal. *Image* 62, pp. 27-40.

Holden, C. 1977. Pain control with hypnosis. *Science* 198, p. 808.

Hopkins, C. 1977. Electric communication. In *How animals communicate* ed. Sebeok, T. Bloomington: Indiana Univ. Press.

Huxley, F. 1967. Anthropology and ESP. In *Science and ESP*, ed. Smythies, R. New York: Humanities Press.

Janet, P. 1925. *Psychological healing: a historical & clinical study*. New York: Macmillan.

Janisse, M. 1977. *Pupillometry: the psychology of the pupillary response*. New York: Halsted Press.

Jaynes, J. 1977. *The origin of consciousness in the breakdown of the bicameral mind*. Boston: Houghton Mifflin.

Katz, D. 1937. *Animals and men: studies in comparative psychology*. London: Longmans, Green.

Kendon, A. 1977. *Studies in the behavior of social interaction*. Lisse: Peter de Ridder Press.

Kinney, A. ed. 1973. *Rogues, vagabonds, & sturdy beggars*. Baree, Mass: Imprint Society.

Koestler, A. 1971. *The case of the midwife toad*. London: Hutchinson.

Kolata, G. 1977. Mathematics and magic: illumination and illusion. *Science* 198. pp. 282-283.

Kreskin. 1973. *The amazing world of Kreskin*. New York: Random House.

Lex, B. 1974. Voodoo death: new thoughts on an old explanation. *American Anthropologist* 76, pp. 818-823.

Lilly, J. 1963. Productive and creative research with man and dolphin. *Archives of General Psychiatry* 8, pp. 111-116.

396

Limber, J. 1977. Language in child and chimp? *American Psychologist* 32, pp. 280-295.
Lubbock, John [Lord Avebury]. 1886. Note on the intelligence of the dog. *Report of the Fifty-fith Meeting of the British Association for the Advancement of Science*. London: John Murray.
Marks, D. and Kammann, R. 1977. The nonpsychic powers of Uri Geller. *The Zetetic* 1/2.9-17.
Pratt, J. 1973. *ESP research today: a study of developments in parapsychology since 1960*. Metuchen: The Scarecrow Press.
Razran, G. 1958. Pavlov and Lamarck. *Science* 128, pp. 758-760.
.....1959. Pavlov the empiricist. *Science* 130, pp. 916-917.
Rhine, L. 1970. *Mind over matter: psychokinesis*. New York: Macmillan.
Rinn, J. 1950. *Sixty years of psychical research*. New York: Truth Seeker.
Romains, J. 1920. *La visions: extra-rétinienne et le sens paroptique; recherches de psychophysiologie expérimentale et de physiologie histologique*. Paris: Nouvelle Revue Frangaise.
Rosenthal, R. 1976. *Experimenter effects in behavioral research*. New York: Appleton-Century-Croft.
....., and Jacobson, Lenore. 1968. *Pygmalion in the classroom: teacher expectation and pupils' intellectual development*. New York: Holt, Rinehart and Winston.
Rumbaugh, D. ed. 1977. *Language learning by a chimpanzee: the Lana project*. New York: Academic Press.
Sarbin, T. and Coe, W. 1972. *Hypnosis: a social psychological analysis of influence communication*. New York: Holt, Rinehart and Winston.
Sebeok, T. 1972. *Perspectives in zoosemiotics*. The Hague: Mouton.
.....1976. *Contributions to the doctrine of signs*. Lisse: Peter de Ridder Press.
.....1977a. Zoosemiotic components of human communication. In *How animals communicate*, ed. T. A. Sebeok. Bloomington: Indiana University Press.
.....1977b. Ecumenicalism in semiotics. In *A perfusion of signs*, ed. Sebeok. Bloomington: Indiana University Press.
.....1977c. Displaying the symptoms. *Times Literary Supplement*, No. 3, 939, September 9.
.....1978. Jakob von Uexküll: neglected figures in the history of semiotic inquiry I. In *Semiotk III. zeichentypologie*, ed. Tasso Borbé, Munich: Wilhelm Fink.
....., and Umiker-Sebeok, D. Jean. 1978. "You know my method": C. S. Peirce and Sherlock Holmes: consulting semioticians. *Semiotica* (forthcoming).
Sheehan, P. and Perry, C. 1976. *Methodologies of hypnosis: a critical appraisal of contemporary paradigms of hypnosis*. Hillsdale, N.J.: Erlbaum.
Sinclair, U. 1930. *Mental radio*. Pasadena: Upton Sinclair.
Stokoe, W. 1977. First hand reporting from the field . . . *Signs for Our Times* 46, p. 1.
Stratton, G. 1921. The control of another person by obscure signs. *Psychological Review* 28, pp. 301-314.
Thomson, J. 1924. Zoology (animal behaviour). In *The life-work of Lord Avebury (Sir John Lubbock)*. London: Watt.
Truzzi, M. 1977. Review of de Mille 1976. *The Zetetic* 1/2, 86-87.
Tuteur, W. 1957-1958. The "double-blind" method: its pitfalls and fallacies. *The American Journal of Psychiatry* 114, pp. 921-922.

Uexküll, T. 1978. Terminological problems of medical semiotics: In: *Semiotik III. zeichentypologie*, ed. Tasso Borbé. Munich: Wilhelm Fink.

Umiker-Sebeok, D. 1978 [March]. You're only as old as you look: age displays in American culture. Paper presented to the Annual Meeting of the Central States Anthropological Society, Bloomington, Indiana.

Vogt, E. and Hyman, R. 1959. *Water witching U.S.A.* Chicago: University of Chicago Press.

Wade, N. 1977. Scandal in the heavens: renowned astronomer accused of fraud. *Science* 198, pp. 707-709.

Wagoner, D. 1976. The literature of legerdemain. *Times Literary Supplement*, No. 3, 902, December 24.

Weizenbaum, J. 1977. Computers as "therapists." *Science* 198, p. 354.

Wood, P. 1973. *Marine mammals and men: the navy's porpoises and sea lions*. Washington: Robert D. Luce.

Zirkle, C. 1958. Pavlov's beliefs. *Science* 128, p. 1476.

DUE DATE

OCT 2 0 1990			
OCT 1 8 1990			

COLLECTIVE BARGAINING
IN THE
BASIC STEEL INDUSTRY

**A Study of the Public Interest and
the Role of Government**

GREENWOOD PRESS, PUBLISHERS
WESTPORT, CONNECTICUT

Library of Congress Cataloging in Publication Data

Livernash, Edward Robert.
    Collective bargaining in the basic steel industry.

    Commonly known as the Livernash report.
    Reprint of the 1961 ed. published by the U. S. Dept.
of Labor, Washington.
    1. Collective bargaining--Steel industry--United
States. 2. Strikes and lockouts--Steel industry--
United States. I. Title. II. Title: Livernash
report on collective bargaining in the basic steel in-
dustry.
[HD6976.I52U54 1976]   331.89'046'91420973   76-9742
ISBN 0-8371-8913-6

Originally published in 1961 by United States Department
of Labor, Washington, D.C.

Reprinted in 1976 by Greenwood Press,
a division of Williamhouse-Regency Inc.

Library of Congress Catalog Card Number 76-9742

ISBN 0-8371-8913-6

Printed in the United States of America

TABLE OF CONTENTS

FOREWORD

Public apprehension over the frequency, length, and effects of strikes in the basic steel industry prompted me, shortly after the onset of the 1959 strike, to set in motion the study upon which this report is based. I asked Professor E. R. Livernash, of Harvard University, one of the Nation's experts on labor-management relations, to direct a comprehensive study of the way in which the collective bargaining process, and Government intervention, had worked in the basic steel industry.

During the past year, Professor Livernash and his group developed the study and the report with no restrictions from the Department of Labor other than a very general injunction at the outset: to produce a careful and objective work which would serve the broadest interests of the public with respect to the character of steel collective bargaining and the public policy problems which it raised.

The study and the report exemplify the right of a free people to make searching and critical public inquiry through a public agency into matters of public concern. That such a study can involve one of America's major industries, one of its largest labor unions, and the operations of its Government is testimony to the vitality of our free institutions.

The basic conclusions of the report are indeed noteworthy. One is that the long-range economic effects of past steel strikes have left no permanent scars on our economy. Another is that the negotiated settlements in steel, when properly understood, have had minimal effects on wages and prices in the economy. These two conclusions lead inevitably to a third: that the consequences of the steel bargain have their effects primarily on the parties, and the strikes which from time to time may accompany the negotiations do not warrant the public consternation and outcry that have occurred in the past.

Of course, Professor Livernash and his study group quite properly point to the possible danger to defense activity which a prolonged steel strike might inflict. But they recommend further serious exploration of partial operation of the steel industry during a strike as a possible solution to the problem of meeting defense needs.

The fundamental recommendation of the report is to urge continued free play of collective bargaining, with no untimely public intervention. Apart from the defense problem, the report finds no overriding public interest in such negotiations, or in strikes which may result, until they reach a truly critical stage (depleted inventories and widespread unemployment). But it is at this time that private pressures on the parties to settle are substantially irresistible. The private pressures have been found to rise coordinately with the public interest and thus provide an appropriate climate for mediation— the only form of Government intervention that in the past, when timely, has proved to be effective.

If the report can help to acquaint the public and Government officials with the circumstances and the practical economic realities which attend a steel strike, the parties to steel bargaining will have in the future to reckon with a much more sophisticated public, and with Government policies which sternly place upon the parties their full responsibilities for mature bargaining and peaceful settlement of their differences.

JAMES P. MITCHELL
Secretary of Labor

PREFACE

In 1953, at a dinner held in Pittsburgh on the occasion of the 51st birthday of David J. McDonald, president of the United Steelworkers of America, Benjamin Fairless, then chairman of the board of U.S. Steel, suggested that "* * * unless we can improve our collective bargaining methods and wipe out this endless and senseless succession of strikes, the righteous wrath of public opinion will someday descend, with crushing force, upon both our houses * * *"

During the 7 years prior to this comment and the 6 subsequent years, there were several industrywide strikes in the steel industry. The most recent one, which lasted for 116 days in 1959, prompted the Secretary of Labor, in the summer of that year, to inaugurate within the Department of Labor, but under outside direction, the study upon which this report is based. As publicly expressed at the time, the Secretary's objective was clear: "The American people need to know why the steel industry is continually plagued by strikes and what actions, if any, management and labor in the industry, or Government, can or should take to correct the situation."

The organization of the report reflects the purpose of the study. Following a brief profile of the parties, there is an examination of the frequency and intensity of postwar steel strikes compared with those in other industries and a limited analysis of the effect of steel strikes on the economy. A second phase of the study explores various facets of collective bargaining in the industry, including such matters as the development of the industry's labor policy, the organization and structure of the Steelworkers, strike techniques, bargaining structures, contract administration, and the areas of conflict and accommodation revealed by a close scrutiny of the history of negotiations since 1937. In the third part of the report the economic results of collective bargaining are reviewed: the level of settlements, the comparative status of earnings, the impact of employment and other costs upon prices, and the inflationary dimensions of wage-price policies. The fourth section contains a review of the role of Government in steel labor disputes. A summary, which also expresses some judgments and opinions as to the functioning of bargaining and the appropriate role of Government, has for convenience been made in chapter 1.

A few words explaining the methods pursued in making the study and writing the report are in order. In the fall of 1959, after the Secretary had expressed his feelings concerning the need for the study, he assembled a group of Government officials, academicians, and others (excluding representatives of the parties), all of whom had an interest in collective bargaining and the role of Government in labor disputes. The group spent 2 days in conference, discussing various aspects of the steel situation and the value of making the type of study the Secretary had proposed. It reached the conclusion that the study should be made and that the Department of Labor should make it. Thereupon a director for the project was appointed from outside the Government and a small staff was set up within the Bureau of Labor Statistics to supervise the work and prepare the report. Secretary Mitchell, it should be emphasized, accorded the group complete freedom to develop the character of the study and its content. The locus of the study in the BLS was consistent with the traditions of that agency which, almost from its establishment in 1884, engaged in studies of labor relations problems in specific industries, including steel. A steering committee of nongovernmental persons was established to meet regularly with the project director and to advise him. Twelve background papers were prepared. Those relating to economic subjects were written by special consultants engaged specially for the study; papers relating to collective bargaining were staff-written. In connection with the latter, numerous interviews were conducted with representatives of the parties and other individuals who have been close to steel collective bargaining. The final report was drafted from these papers and from the interviews.

Thus the report as finally published represents the contributions of many individuals. The steering committee members, whose helpful advice was available during the entire course of the project, included Harold L. Enarson, administrative vice president, University of New Mexico; George H. Hildebrand, professor of economics, Cornell University; Charles L. Schultze, associate professor of economics, University of Indiana; and George P. Shultz, professor of industrial relations, University of Chicago.

The staff loaned for the study consisted of John C. Davis, manpower adviser in the Office of the Secretary of Labor; Lawrence R. Klein, editor-in-chief of the Monthly Labor Review, Bureau of Labor Statistics; and Charles M. Rehmus, a commissioner in the Federal Mediation and Conciliation Service. In general, those portions of the report related to collective bargaining and to the role of Government were written by Messrs. Klein and Rehmus, with Mr. Davis handling those concerned with economic analysis. King Carr was on loan from the Bureau of the Budget for the planning stages of the study.

Background papers on the indicated subjects were prepared by the following persons:

W. Halder Fisher and Associates, economic impact of steel strikes; Morris A. Horowitz, Northeastern University, steelworker earnings; Harold M. Levinson, University of Michigan, pattern influence of steel collective bargaining; Louis Lister, Columbia University, production costs and productivity in steel; Garth L. Mangum, Brigham Young

University, contract administration in steel; Frank E. Norton, University of California at Los Angeles, steel prices and inflation; Loyle A. Morrison, former chief of investigations, U.S. Tariff Commission, foreign competition in steel; George Seltzer, University of Minnesota, influence of basic steel settlements on other Steelworker contracts; Abraham Siegel, Massachusetts Institute of Technology, steel collective bargaining in foreign countries; Robert M. Weidenhammer, University of Pittsburgh, steel technology, markets, and financing. In addition, the Department of Commerce prepared a study on problems of partial operation of the steel industry.

In addition to all of the above individuals who were attached to the study in a formal capacity, grateful acknowledgment should be accorded scores of other busy persons, too numerous to mention separately, who devoted time and talent by granting interviews and critically reading manuscript: representatives of the United Steelworkers and the steel companies, Government officials, arbitrators, and others closely connected with the subject matter. Special recognition should be made, however, of the continuous assistance provided by Philip Arnow, assistant commissioner, and staff members of the Bureau of Labor Statistics, and by the Library staff of the Department of Labor.

Responsibility for the content of the report is basically my own. It was a foregone conclusion that neither the approach to the report nor its findings and implications would be universally approved. No study of a subject matter so sensitive and so charged with conflicting views could anticipate a better fate. For myself and those associated with the project, I can only offer the assurance that our approach was open-minded and that our conclusions represent sincere beliefs. Those connected with the work would be the first to concede that their efforts are subject to the imperfections of all human effort.

It is hoped that what has eventuated from this task of some 14 months will serve a public good. At the very least it should reveal to the thousands of citizens who are periodically perturbed over steel strikes the essence of the controversy and its essential complexity. Perhaps the more fundamental conclusions will be of assistance to the parties. Finally, the report should make clear the limitations on the role which Government can play in the resolution of the problems of the parties.

E. Robert Livernash,
Professor of Business Administration
Graduate School of Business Adminis-
tration
Harvard University
Project Director

Part I

INTRODUCTION

CHAPTER 1

SUMMARY AND CONCLUSIONS

This report is written with continued confidence in the process and progress of free collective bargaining. It is reasonable to expect that the substantial mutuality of the long-term interests of the parties to collective bargaining in steel will bring a reduction of conflict. Also, the problem of national emergency strikes appears to have been declining in importance in this country and should continue to decline.

Collective bargaining for most major industries in the United States is only about 25 years old. The record of experience over this period is not one to cause alarm. It is one which, on balance, has shown a steady growth of accommodation. This is reflected predominantly in the development of much more orderly day-to-day relations within a framework of increasingly stabilized contract language and contract interpretation. Conflict continues, however, over the economic terms of settlement. In recent years there has been increasing firmness in management positions. This change coincides with an intensification of competition in the economy and with the growth of excess manufacturing capacity. It corresponds also with more intense concern over the problem of inflation. The 1959 steel strike took place against the background of these factors.

The broad possibilities and alternatives with respect to future collective bargaining relationships in steel are: (1) Drastic legislation which would variously preclude industrywide bargaining, limit the right to strike or the scope of strikes, apply antitrust legislation to unions, compel arbitration, allow seizure, or establish governmental determination of wages and prices—all of these embody far-reaching limitations of free collective bargaining; (2) less fundamental changes in existing legislation aimed at improving mechanisms to facilitate settlements and avoid strikes in important disputes; (3) improved understanding between the parties, with a consequent reduction in conflict; (4) continued conflict comparable in frequency with the past.

This study does not lend support to the future success of limited legislative changes. Formal and early Government intervention, discussed subsequently, has not prevented strikes. Continued frequent conflict, with its attendant crisis atmosphere and with probable disillusion as to the accomplishments of limited Government intervention, could make some type of drastic legislation a more likely eventuality. This may well be true regardless of whether the public interest would best be served by such legislation. By far the most constructive alternative is the achievement by the parties of a reduction in conflict.

3

A minimum of Government intervention will assist the parties in achieving this goal. Even if conflict is not substantially reduced, its consequences are of primary concern only to the parties. The public interest, as will be developed, can easily be exaggerated.

The Content of the Report

Part I of the report describes briefly the basic steel industry and the union. It poses in capsule form two major problems with which collective bargaining must deal. These problems are: (1) To adjust future settlement terms to the changed competitive conditions in the economy and in the industry; and (2) to mitigate problems of employee insecurity, particularly those resulting from the accelerating pace of technological change. These problems pose somewhat contradictory objectives and involve controversial issues.

Part II analyzes the impact of steel strikes and concludes that they have not been of serious magnitude so far as the economy as a whole is concerned. Although national defense projects pose something of a special problem which requires a thorough consideration of the feasibility of partial operation during strikes, the consumer of products made from steel has in fact been protected by a considerable inventory cushion.

Part III discusses the development of the industry's labor policy, the history of the United Steelworkers of America, the mode of bargaining, substantive areas of accommodation and conflict, and some limited aspects of contract administration. With so much public concern over conflict, a balanced review requires special emphasis upon the progress which the parties have made—progress toward resolution of issues through negotiation and progress in establishing orderly day-to-day contract administration. The degree of progress has certainly matched that recorded in other leading industries. The explanation for strikes must be sought in the negotiating environment and the contract goals of the parties rather than in the day-to-day relationship between them.

The relatively centralized bargaining structure in basic steel has been influenced by the particular history, policies, and objectives of the Steelworkers union, and by the economic environment of the steel industry. The union from its inception has been quite centralized with respect to its internal administration, its negotiation objectives within basic steel, and its attitude toward strikes. With respect to contract administration, however, it has been quite decentralized. United States Steel's position in the industry, including its substantial price leadership, coupled with an industry tradition of uniform wage adjustments among companies, constituted an economic environment which no doubt influenced the union in its development of an industrywide orientation toward bargaining. Government regulation during World War II, and in later instances of intervention, appears to have reinforced and contributed to the tendency toward centralization of major settlements. In whatever manner these influences are evaluated, a form of industrywide bargaining has been the result.[1]

The substantive issues which have led to breakdowns in negotiation, as analyzed in chapter 7, have not been notably different from those arising in other industries. The importance of steel in the economy, the importance of steel negotiations within the framework of collective bargaining, and the importance of steel prices within the price structure have intensified issues and complicated their resolution. These circumstances, in association with industrywide strikes, have brought to steel the most unique problem which the parties have had to face; namely, the unusual degree of involvement of collective bargaining with Government influence and intervention. There can be no question, after a review of the experience of the parties, that intervention of Government into price determination and into collective bargaining has greatly complicated the resolving of issues through collective bargaining and has been a source of conflict in and of itself.

Part IV examines: (1) Hourly earnings and wage and benefit settlements in steel and other industries; (2) employment costs, steel prices, and competition; and (3) the influence of steel prices on inflation. These subjects are discussed subsequently in this chapter. The conclusion with respect to the economic analysis of settlements is that the independent influence of steel upon wages and prices in the economy has not been of major proportions. The public interest in wage and price decisions in steel is considerably protected by competitive forces.

Part V explores the effects of Government intervention in steel disputes. Most of the commonly suggested forms of intervention have been tried at one time or another in steel disputes. During World War II, the National War Labor Board employed, in effect, a form of compulsory arbitration, though clearly under special circumstances. Factfinding with recommendations was used in the 1946 and 1949 disputes and by the Wage Stabilization Board in 1952. Factfinding without recommendations and injunction under Taft-Hartley were used in the 1959 dispute. Seizure was attempted in 1952. Mediation has been used in various of the disputes. The record in

---

[1] Bargaining structures in the United States are exceedingly diverse and complex. While these structures have been influenced by union and management policies, they reflect in large measure differences in the character of product competition among and within industries. It is these wide differences which make the effects of any legislative modification of bargaining structures so difficult to determine and appraise.

steel provides very little support for early intervention to facilitate settlements and avoid strikes.

The conclusion of this study indicates the desirability of a minimum of intervention. The reasons for this conclusion will be developed in this chapter and, in more detail, elsewhere in the report. Nevertheless, it should be stated at the outset that it is not possible to take a position against all or any Government intervention. With the potential effects of industrywide strikes, it is not realistic, even in time of peace, to state that the Government should not intervene in some manner at some point of time in some future steel dispute. The issues involve the frequency of intervention, its timing, and its form.

The following four sections highlight the major subjects investigated during the course of the study. Included in these discussions are most of the major conclusions flowing from the report. The final section of this chapter briefly itemizes these conclusions.

The Impact of Steel Strikes

There have been five major strikes in the postwar years: 1946 (26 days), 1949 (45 days), 1952 (59 days), 1956 (36 days), and 1959 (116 days). A meaningful comparison of the frequency and duration of strikes in steel with other industries cannot be made because of differences in bargaining structure and contract duration. However, the record in steel is not one to inspire a high degree of public confidence in and support for collective bargaining.

An important public question is whether Government intervention is required purely and simply to prevent or end a strike. The answer to this question depends upon the effects of steel strikes. The impact of any particular steel strike will vary with its duration and will depend upon the relation of production to capacity and upon inventory levels in steel and related user industries. The following dimensions of the problem will be examined briefly: (1) The direct effect upon steel production over a period of about 1 year centered at the time of the strike; (2) the effects upon final product sales of durable goods; (3) the longer-run effects upon steel demand; (4) the costs to the parties; (5) the secondary unemployment effects; and (6) the effects upon national defense.

A steel strike shuts down almost the entire industry. However, it is clearly not correct to measure the loss of steel production by examining only the strike period itself. There may be anticipatory production prior to the strike and will be catch-up production after the strike. It is not possible statistically to separate with any precision strike-related variations in production from cyclical and other variations. Possible long-term market losses, noted subsequently, cannot be measured. Nevertheless, experimentation with estimates of what steel production might have been had there been no strike leads to the judgment that the probability of net loss over a period of about 1 year is small.

The probability of little or no net final-product loss for the economy from steel strikes is indicated by a study of quarterly data on production, final sales, and inventory change for the durable goods component of the gross national product and of other data. While the postwar steel strikes show up quite clearly in production, it is difficult to discern any clear-cut effects upon final sales, even for the 1959 strike, though this strike did result in some delays. Steel inventory has unquestionably provided a significant cushion in past steel strikes. Since this inventory is in turn supplemented by the finished goods inventories in user industries, it is clear that final purchasers of such goods have been amply protected.

Aggregate data do not prove that there were no shortages of particular products during the longer steel strikes. The 1952 and 1959 strikes unquestionably caused some construction delays and product shortages. For this and other reasons, national defense is discussed subsequently. But economic data do not indicate any serious general effects stemming from the strikes.

Whether or not there were some longrun and permanent effects upon the steel industry from strikes or anticipation of strikes is impossible to determine. Substitute materials may have gained some permanent advantage from steel shortages. Imported steel may have strengthened its position in domestic markets. Some durable goods purchases may have been given up. These types of possible effects, though not believed to be marked, are hidden in longer-term trends.

The fact that strikes appear to have had no serious permanent effects upon the economy does not imply that the strikes have not resulted in costs to the parties. The companies have special shutdown and start-up costs. There are various service, material, and overhead costs which continue during the strike. Production at a fairly constant level over a period of time is more efficient and less costly than the fluctuating production related to the strike. Interruption in the flow of materials and special inventory costs should also be mentioned. For the employees, there is no necessary balancing of income even if total production requirements over a period of time were identical with or without a strike. Some particular employees might gain in income because of the strike and some might lose. Layoff also can involve unemployment and SUB compensation. In addition, employees can to some extent offset strike loss of pay with vacation pay.

One of the more serious effects of steel strikes is secondary unemployment in closely related industries, such as transportation and mining. As the strikes are prolonged and steel inventories depleted, producton can also be curtailed in steel-using industries. Again there is no way by which the net amount of secondary unemployment can be measured because there usually are offsetting gains in secondary employment prior to and after steel strikes. In general, the extent of secondary unemployment due to steel strikes is believed to have been exaggerated.

One of the most difficult aspects of steel strikes to analyze is their impact on national defense. For example, in the 1959 strike there were Government affidavits to the effect that the strike caused postponements in the delivery dates of critical defense items. The Steelworkers union protested vigorously as to the generality of the allegations in the affidavits. Also what may or may not have been true with respect to past strikes is not necessarily pertinent to future strikes.

Obviously a steel strike can adversely affect national defense, although the general public is in no position to assess such consequences. The most crucial question to be answered is the feasibility of partial operation to meet defense needs during a strike.

A special report made by the U.S. Department of Commerce for this study points out that there are three types of problems posed by partial operation—technical, economic, and administrative. Technical and economic problems clearly require consideration of the possibility of partial operation only on the assumption that entire plants be allowed or required to operate. If entire plants are opened, the technical and economic problems largely disappear. If entire plants operate, considerable nondefense steel will be produced. The determination of what plants would operate, what employees would work, and what customers would get the nondefense steel poses administrative and equity problems, but these problems, while difficult, do not seem insuperable.

In other words, it does not seem beyond the range of possibility to guard against the danger of delay in critical defense projects by partial operation. If defense officials felt that a steel strike involved a threat to national security, it might be practical to keep open or reopen plants producing critical items. Under most circumstances it is doubtful if this would require operation of more than a small fraction of the industry's capacity. If partial operation could not be achieved by voluntary agreement, it might well be possible under present injunction procedures.

The feasibility of partial operation should be given serious study by the parties and by the Government. The contention is not that it can be done easily but that its problems should be judged against the alternatives of total intervention and the risk of delay in important defense projects.

In summary, it appears that: (1) The actual adverse economic effects of steel strikes have usually been overestimated; (2) partial operation in the interest of national defense should be given far more serious attention than has been the case to date; and (3) a major reason why steel strikes have had so little measurable impact is that when a strike approaches a critical stage, pressures upon the parties to settle become substantially irresistible.

Experience With Government Intervention

The Government may intervene with one or more of the following objectives: (1) To avert or stop a strike if it threatens a national emergency; (2) to aid in the process of bargaining and facilitate a settlement; and (3) to encourage terms of settlement believed to be more in accord with the public interest than a privately negotiated settlement. In response to some combination of these objectives the Government has intervened, or exerted influence, in all of the major steel strikes.

The national emergency problem in steel has two primary dimensions—one of national defense and another of widespread curtailment of production in user industries upon exhaustion of steel inventories. Partial or complete operation may be regarded as essential in the interest of national defense. Widespread curtailment of production in user industries has not been a serious problem since pressures at this critical stage result in settlement. The record of intervention to avoid strikes or to attain settlements before this critical stage is reached is not an encouraging one.

Early intervention to avoid strikes typically has taken the form of mediation or factfinding with recommendations. Neither has been effective. Recommendations, contrary to the usual argument, have not been tantamount to compulsory arbitration. They have not served to crystallize public opinion in such fashion as to compel the parties to accept. The issue of accepting or not accepting a particular recommendation has become a new source of conflict. While it can be argued that recommendations have served to narrow the issues in dispute, clearly they have been unsuccessful in achieving steel settlements without strikes.

The anticipation of intervention modifies each party's approach to negotiation. Neither party wishes to weaken its position if intervention is regarded as probable. The parties behave quite differently in negotiations when they anticipate formal intervention than when they do not.

With this history and these attitudes toward intervention, it is very difficult to be optimistic with respect to the fruitfulness of any form of early intervention to facilitate the settlement of disputes. The imposition of neutrals, as distinct from a situation in which parties voluntarily seek the assistance of neutrals, would appear more likely to intensify conflict than to aid in the resolution of issues.

It is most difficult to define terms of settlement believed to be "in the public interest." Several disputes in steel, however, have been complicated by this issue. Shortly after World War II, wage control was abandoned but price control retained. Bargaining under these circumstances contributed to strikes in various industries and made their resolution difficult. The conflict was sharp in steel and the President's suggested wage settlement in 1946 was made effective only with the virtual abandonment of price regulation. A similar difficulty was encountered during the 1952 negotiations. In various negotiations the influence of Government officials and their pronouncements with respect to steel prices have appeared to complicate the resolution of disputes.

The economic implication of settlements will be discussed subsequently, but the possible conflict in intervention objectives between securing a settlement and encouraging terms of settlement believed to be in the public interest must be recognized. During periods of peace, and in the absence of thoroughgoing wage and price control, no form of noncompulsory intervention can be effective unless it largely accepts the equities of the issues as argued by the parties. Attempts to achieve settlement on terms deviating considerably from the views of the parties are not likely to be effective.

In collective bargaining in steel, intervention has itself been a source of conflict. It seldom appears even-handed to the parties. Over the years, it appears to have been more resented by the industry than the union. The industry has objected to the wage and price implications of intervention and has felt that on issues of principle neutrals have more often compromised the industry position. The union in 1959 felt that the injunction considerably favored the companies.

The only form of intervention which has produced settlements in steel has been high-level mediation, perhaps aptly described as mediation "with a club". This form of mediation is similar in many respects to mediation in general. It involves no public statement of proposed terms of settlement. Its fundamental purpose is to move each party from fixed positions. It differs from many instances of traditional mediation in that it is not highly dependent upon presenting novel alternatives to the parties.

The significance of "high-level pressure" may nevertheless have been exaggerated in respect to steel strike settlements. It would appear to be far less the pressure of high office than the pressure of circumstances upon the parties which creates the settlement. The advantage of high-level mediation is that the parties have seemed to feel their prestige enhanced by working out a settlement under these auspices rather than through traditional mediation. But a consequence is that the high-level intervenor then is charged with some public responsibility for the settlement reached.

Is the experience of the past likely to be much modified in the future by modest changes in the mechanism for handling national emergency disputes? It is argued that if the President had various alternative choices as to the mechanism to be used to resolve such disputes, the probability of resolution would be improved. The major arguments advanced in favor of this proposal are the advantages of uncertainty and flexibility. However, the realistic list of such alternatives would add little to the existing procedure other than "legalizing" factfinding with recommendations. Most of the difficulties experienced with intervention apply equally to a package approach as to an individual approach. The probabilities of keeping the parties guessing also seems somewhat unrealistic. Suggesting the use of an extreme form of intervention as a threat to induce a negotiated settlement may not be received with an equal or compelling repugnance by each party. Introducing a variety of alternatives may also encourage intervention and hinder the process of accommodation between the parties. So far as steel is concerned, there is little ground for optimism with respect to any mechanistic type of solution.

In summary: (1) Early noncompulsory intervention tends to frustrate and hinder the process of negotiation and it has neither secured settlements nor avoided strikes; (2) Minor modifications in the mechanism for handling national emergency disputes hold little promise for altering this conclusion; (3) Late, informal, and mediatory intervention has produced settlements and appears to be least harmful to achieving a pattern of private agreement.

The Economics of Settlements

The economic terms of steel settlements are of interest for this study: (1) to assess their impact upon wages and prices in the economy, and (2) to indicate their significance in the relationship between the parties.

The effect of collective bargaining in general upon the increase of wages and prices in the postwar economy has been much debated. Since all periods of inflation are characterized by both wage and price increaes, and since statistical leads and lags shed relatively little light on the problem of causation, much is left to judgment.

The immediate post-World War II and Korean periods of wage-price increases appear, in the opinion of most economists, to be attributable primarily, but not exclusively, to monetary influences and excess aggregate demand. The period of inflation following the 1954 recession was associated with the investment expansion of those years, and does not appear to have involved excess aggregate demand. During this period the influence of cost upon prices is more significant than in the earlier period, but there were still important demand influences in certain sectors of the economy. To the extent that collective bargaining in general has contributed to inflationary wage and price increases in the economy, collective bargaining in steel must share in this responsibility. While this general problem is recognized, this study is concerned with steel's independent influence within this framework.

There are decided difficulties in an examination of this narrower problem. These difficulties involve judgment in assessing pattern influences. The clearest instances of pattern setting and following are to be found within narrowly defined industries and segments of industries. For example, settlements with U.S. Steel have set the pattern for the basic steel industry. There are also varying degrees of pattern influence throughout the jurisdiction of given unions. With respect to the Steelworkers union, the basic steel pattern has been followed quite generally in aluminum and metal containers, but there has been much pattern deviation within steel fabrication. Complex combinations of bargaining and competitive product and labor market influences have produced varying degrees of pattern following and pattern deviation within the jurisdiction of the larger industrial unions.

Most difficult to analyze is the pattern influence among various unions in different industries. There is again a combination of bargaining and economic influences which defy completely satisfactory separation. The relative importance of the steel and automobile industries has given rise to the view that the settlements negotiated in these two industries exert widespread influence beyond their industry and union contexts. The relative ease with which a few important bargains can be followed in the press and by the public, as compared with the time and technical persistence required to follow a more complete picture, contributes to this point of view.

To appraise steel's influence, trends in hourly earnings in various industries were first analyzed. The increase in earnings in steel was similar to that in other durable and highly organized industries prior to 1955. There was, however, a marked relative increase for steel in the period from 1954 to 1959. This relative increase was attributable in large part not to basic wage rate increases, but to revision and extension of incentive plans, the introduction of Sunday and holiday premium pay with continuous operations, and to other similar variables. The increase in earnings, as distinct from wage rates, had no discernible repercussions beyond the basic steel industry. It contributed significantly, however, to employment cost increases in steel.

The timing and amounts of wage and fringe settlements over the postwar years were next studied. Steel did not lead in the timing or the amount of settlement to any marked degree prior to 1955. It was not possible to ascribe to any particular union or industry leadership in the first postwar "round" with its various factfinding boards and ultimate selection by the President of the crucial settlement figure. In 1947 and 1948, the automobile industry provided the focal point for the convergence of major settlements. In 1949, the steel factfinding board established an influential pension and insurance figure, but this became a basis for settlements in other industries prior to the negotiated settlement in steel. Since 1950, major wage settlements have closely approximated the amount yielded by the automobile wage formula which has persisted over these years.

The pattern influence, the economic appropriateness, and the equity of the automobile wage formula can be debated. It can be argued that it contributed to inflation by accentuating the wage-price spiral, that it moderated inflation by restraining collective bargaining settlements, or that it closely approximated and predominately reflected underlying economic conditions. It may or may not have been appropriate as a wage guide for other industries. It was, however, an important independent influence. Major settlements in durable and other highly organized manufacturing industries did not in fact deviate substantially from it.

In the years 1955–58, wage rate increases in steel did exceed the automobile formula by some 9 to 13 cents. This increase had repercussions predominately within the jurisdiction of the Steelworkers union. Most clearly it did not pull the remainder of the economy with it. The fact that, as it turned out, the 1959 settlement in steel involved no wage rate increase for that year, and considerably moderated the annual employment cost increases previously prevailing, moved steel in the direction of closer conformity with the automobile formula. For the years 1955–59, total effective wage rate increases in steel were below coal, aluminum, shipbuilding, can, meatpacking, and agricultural implements, but were above other important industries.

Though statistics cannot reflect all of the dynamic influences of one union or industry upon another, the results of this study indicate that if it were possible to abstract steel from the collective bargaining environment of the postwar years, it is very doubtful whether wage and other settlement terms in the economy would have been much modified. While judgments with respect to broad pattern influences cannot be dogmatic, steel appears much more to have been conforming to, rather than establishing, major wage trends in the economy.

By the same token, with the context of collective bargaining as it existed, the impact of increases in employment costs upon steel prices could hardly have differed substantially from that which in fact took place. Employment costs in steel constitute some one-third of average realized price. It would require, therefore, quite unrealistic assumptions as to what employment cost increases "might have been" to derive a 10 percent plus or minus assumed change in steel prices over this span of years.

As noted in chapter 10, steel prices have increased markedly in the postwar period. These increases in large measure reflect increases in employment, material, and capital costs, and have been largely unavoidable. Regardless of the reasons for price increases, however, even large price increases in steel, as analyzed in chapter 11, have only small effects upon the general price level in the economy. Within a range of realistic discretion open to the parties in collective bargaining, and to the companies in the determination of prices, their decisions have hardly had a measurable effect upon the general price level.

In making the foregoing statements, it is recognized that various settlements in collective bargaining, and various decisions with respect to price policy, can be debated. For example: Were the 1955 and 1956 contract settlements too high? Should the union in 1959 have given priority to noncontributory insurance relative to greater protection for employees? Did the companies increase cash flow and profits too much during the years 1955–57? Has the industry expanded too rapidly? Should the industry have increased cash flow to a greater extent in the earlier postwar years? Should the industry have spent more on research and development? Answers to questions of this type must be placed in perspective. In the first place, there are no simple answers that do not contain controversial public policy implications. Second, answers within a range of realistic discretion have minimal effects upon the general price level. Third, answers are of predominant importance only to the steel companies, steel employees, the steel union, and steel users.

Decisions in collective bargaining, and as to prices, are highly important to the parties. Adjusting the terms of settlement to the increasingly competitive conditions in the industry and the economy has already been singled out as a major problem for the parties, as has employee insecurity. The increase in the intensity of competition with respect to steel is discussed in chapter 10. Steel users, however, viewed over any reasonable period of years, are significantly protected by the compulsions of competition.

In summary: (1) Collective bargaining settlements in steel have not been a predominant independent influence in establishing or modifying wage trends in the economy; (2) the wage and price effects of steel settlements, and industry decisions with respect to price policy, when realistically interpreted, have had a minimal independent effect upon the price level in the economy; (3) the increasingly stringent compulsions of competition provide important protection for steel users; and (4) a major problem confronting the parties in collective bargaining is to adjust to the increasingly competitive environment in a manner best suited to protect their mutual longer-term interests.

The Negotiating Relationship

During 1957, an industry leader in steel negotiations stated, somewhat facetiously but with an element of bitterness, that the difficulty in steel was that the union would not allow the industry to win a short strike and that the Government and the industry's customers would not allow it to win a long strike. He might have added that from the industry's point of view the price which had to be paid to avoid a strike or to settle a short strike had, upon occasion, been higher than the industry's long-term interests warranted. From the union's point of view it has sometimes felt that the industry had not bargained with a genuine intent to settle prior to a strike. Neutrals have at times concurred in both of these opinions.

Neither the companies nor the union desire a strike. No one feels the pressures and criticisms to the degree of those responsible for calling or taking a strike. Also, neither party as a general rule wants Government intervention in a dispute.

If neither party wants a strike, and neither wants Government intervention, why have both taken place so frequently in the past? Each party would answer the question by pointing to the unreasonable position taken by the other party prior to a strike. This is not, however, a complete explanation. To the extent that a single generalization appears valid, it is that pressures upon the parties to avoid a strike have frequently been less compelling than those which develop in connection with the strike's resolution. The following paragraphs develop this point.

The negotiating relationship which exists in steel is different from the much more common situation prevailing in most other industries.

If, for example, a major industrial union is negotiating with a single large company, that company is faced with the decision of whether to take a strike while its competitors continue to operate. The union is faced with the realization that a long strike will be required to obtain even a small liberalization of the company offer. Increasingly, as experience with collective bargaining has developed, both parties in a major single-company negotiation recognize that they must either reach a settlement or undertake a long and costly strike for what will likely be a very small change in the previous offer. Normally, the pressures to avoid a strike are compelling enough to bring about a settlement.

There is less pressure to avoid a strike in steel, however, because steel strikes are industrywide and virtually all companies are shut down. In addition, the parties have not usually anticipated a long strike because of the national emergency characterization of such strikes with consequent Government intervention. Of the five major postwar strikes, three have lasted roughly 1 month, one lasted approximately 2 months, and the 1959 strike lasted more than 3 months. In this last instance a long strike was widely anticipated and steel-using industries had deliberately built up large inventories, making a strike of such duration possible.

Consider somewhat more specifically the broad outlines of the last several negotiations. After the 2-month strike in 1952 and the change in union leadership, there was no serious anticipation of a strike in 1953, and negotiation functioned effectively. A strike was likewise not anticipated in 1954, a recession year, and none resulted. In 1955, a strike was not anticipated. The union became unexpectedly militant, however, and to avoid a major strike in a year of peak demand for steel the companies went above, it is believed, what they considered to be a reasonable wage offer relative to settlements in other industries. In 1956, the companies presented a large package in a 5-year contract proposal. The belief again is that they strongly hoped to achieve a settlement largely within the framework of the original proposal. This proved not to be possible, and a strike resulted. At the end of a month, and at least partially influenced by the desire to avoid Government intervention, they gave, in a 3-year contract, substantially all that had been included in the original 5-year package. In 1959, they anticipated a strike, took a very firm position in prestrike negotiation, and the longest strike in steel history resulted.

It would seem that there is only one way out of the dilemma of avoiding frequent strikes which is consistent with the preservation of the present system of bargaining. In essence, the parties must recognize the longrun futility and danger of frequent strikes. In this process they can be assisted greatly by a public policy which avoids early and formal Government intervertion. Under such circumstances it should not be too difficult to avoid short strikes. The parties should be sufficiently flexible in their positions to anticipate any concessions they would be willing to make as a consequence of a 1-month strike.

Avoiding medium-to-long strikes is an entirely different matter. In this process the parties would be greatly assisted by a public policy which limited intervention, if a strike reached a truly critical stage, to an informal mediatory procedure. But avoiding medium-to-long strikes probably implies that the union, from the point of view of a single dispute, would accept something less than it could get by such a strike. No matter how hard the companies might strive to make pre-negotiation offers on which they would stand, regardless of the length of the strike, growing secondary unemployment might force concessions from the companies as well as from the union. However, a Government policy allowing medium-to-long strikes, and limiting intervention to a mediatory form, considerably increases the pressures to avoid strikes.

While the conclusions of this study indicate that the consequences of steel strikes to the public need not cause alarm and are typically exaggerated, the crisis atmosphere which is created can outweigh a logical appraisal. A succession of long steel strikes can easily lead to a political situation which demands drastic legislation. The consequences of such legislation are very difficult to appraise, but they are not appealing because they substitute the uncertain consequences of public power for private responsibility.

It is difficult to appraise the present state of the negotiating relationship. In some respects attitudes have hardened. On the other hand, explorations of issues under the two committees set up under the 1959 contract are continuing. Although most observers are not overly optimistic as to the results, neither party will desire to take the responsibility for breaking off the work of these committees. It is to be hoped that the committees will make a meaningful contribution to mutual understanding.

In summary: (1) The exaggerated national emergency interpretation of steel strikes, with consequent Government intervention, has tended to reduce the compulsions for avoiding strikes; (2) a public policy which avoids early intervention and limits its form to mediatory procedures at truly critical stages of strikes encourages the parties to avoid strikes; and (3) if the parties do not improve their negotiating relationships, the political consequences of continued frequent strikes may lead to some form of drastic legislation regardless of the wisdom and necessity for such legislation.

Conclusion

The conclusions of this chapter can best be emphasized by an unqualified statement of the major points from the section summaries:

1. The actual adverse effects of steel strikes on the economy have not been of serious magnitude. A major reason why steel strikes have had so little measurable impact is that when a strike approaches a critical stage, pressures upon the parties to settle become substantially irresistible.

2. Partial operation in the interest of national defense should be given far more serious attention than it has in the past.

3. Early intervention tends to frustrate and hinder the process of negotiation and has neither secured settlements nor avoided strikes. Late, informal, and mediatory intervention has produced settlements and appears to be least harmful in achieving a pattern of private agreement.

4. Minor modifications in the mechanism for handling national emergency disputes hold little promise for altering the above conclusion.

5. Collective bargaining settlements in steel have not been a predominant independent influence in establishing or modifying wage trends in the economy.

6. The wage and price effects of steel settlements, and industry decisions with respect to price policy, when realistically interpreted, have had a minimal effect upon the price level in the economy.

7. The increasingly stringent compulsions of competition provide important protection for steel users.

8. A major problem confronting the parties in collective bargaining is to adjust to the increasingly competitive environment in a manner best suited to protect their mutual longer-term interests.

9. The exaggerated interpretation of the national emergency dimension of steel strikes and resulting Government intervention have tended to reduce the compulsions for avoiding strikes relative to the pressures for ending them.

It is significant that the public interest has not been seriously harmed by strikes in steel, or by steel collective bargaining agreements, despite common public opinion to the contrary. Minor changes in existing legislation will not provide demonstrably superior results in the avoidance of future steel strikes. Moreover, the problems involved do not seem to indicate the necessity for the more drastic forms of governmental intervention that are sometimes proposed. In the light of these conclusions it is hoped that the public and its representatives will be very cautious in approving legislative changes affecting the existing collective bargaining system.

CHAPTER 2

THE PARTIES

As an aid to understanding the issues which confront the industry and the union in steel collective bargaining, the following few pages are devoted to brief sketches of the parties concerned and even briefer statements of certain pressing and long-term problems which beset them.

The Industry

Steel provides the skeletal frame and sinews of American industry, and steelmaking itself is a main bulwark of the economy. The industry assumes this importance because its product, in some form, has generally been more suitable for more purposes at a cost more favorable than its substitutes. Even with inroads made upon its markets by aluminum, plastics, glass, wood, and paper, steel is paramount among metals and basic to the fabrication of most consumer and industrial products as well as numerous construction materials. Because it supplies this basic wherewithal, the actions of the steel industry in the fields of prices, wages, production, and labor relations can be of significant importance to other industries. In turn, the steel industry itself is sensitively responsive to changes in the business cycle.

Net fixed assets of the industry in 1959 were valued at close to $8 billion. Estimates of the present cost to replace plant and equipment run as high as $45 billion. Sales for 1959 were more than $14 billion, of which about $8 billion constitute value added above cost of raw materials. Annual expenditures for new equipment and construction were more than $1 billion in 6 of the preceding 10 years. Steel has been required to meet heavy capital requirements to cover expansion and replacement and to develop iron ore reserves. Capital investment per production worker, in part because of higher costs, has more than doubled in recent years.

Steelmaking capacity in the United States is prodigious. Expressed in ingots, it is about 150 million tons annually, equal to about a third of the world's potential. But capacity usually exceeds demand by a considerable margin.

Since 1901, utilization has ranged from 19 percent (1932) to 100 percent (1951). During about a third of this century the rate was 65 percent or less. Yet steel capacity in absolute terms has been growing—nearly 90 percent in the past quarter-century. The increase in capacity in tons per capita of population over the same span of years has been about one-third.

Manufacture of steel ingots takes place in more than half the States, but Pennsylvania and Ohio are still the major centers, with 45 percent of the Nation's capacity. Other important States include Indiana, Illinois, Maryland, Michigan, New York, Alabama, California, and West Virginia.

Most plants in the steel industry are large. More than two-thirds of all steelworkers are in plants employing 2,500 or more workers. Plants of the four largest companies (U.S. Steel, Bethlehem, Republic, and Jones and Laughlin) account for nearly 60 percent of the industry's ingot capacity; the 10 largest companies account for 80 percent. There are, however, more than 250 firms which make or finish steel.

Large plants and multiplant operations are generally desired by the industry for economic reasons. Steel can ordinarily be produced with greater efficiency if all of the operations, from the coking of coal and the smelting of iron ore in the blast furnace to the final processing into any of the innumerable steel-mill products, are performed in one location. In addition to the technical advantages of size, there are also managerial and sales advantages to be achieved through multiplant operations of a given company. It is costly to ship steel, and a firm desirous of nationwide sales can distribute its product with least expense from several production units located in various regions. This requirement of size largely accounts for the concentration of production in a relatively few plants. The cost of new, fully integrated steel facilities is inordinately high and provides a formidable financial barrier to new entries to the industry. Moreover, there is scant opportunity for significant product differentiation among companies. These factors combine to create the particular economic environment within which collective bargaining and competition must function.

An almost endless variety of shapes, sizes, and qualities emanates from steel plants, in many stages of finishing. They range from massive steel plates for warships and large pipe for oil transmission to woven wire fencing and finishing nails. This very diversity of product and processes complicates steel mill operation. Capacity must be adequate to handle orders to completion and to meet peak demand for any given item. The threat of unused capacity presents a constant challenge to the industry to improve quality, reduce costs, and expand sales, while competition in technology continuously creates added capacity.

Shifts in the consumption of steel products have followed changes in the industrial development of the country. Construction of railroads and industrial plants placed emphasis on rails and structural steels. As late as the midtwenties, railroads used more than 20 percent of all finished steel; by the latter half of the fifties the percentage had dropped to about 4. Automobiles, meanwhile, increased in relation to the total—from approximately 14 to close to 20 percent. Technological developments like the continuous hot strip mill and the electrolytic tin plating line have enabled sheets and tin plate to compete with other materials and permitted the widespread use of tin cans and home electrical appliances: the percentage of the total finished-steel production used by the container industry, for example, almost tripled between 1923 and 1959.

Such change in product utilization has been reflected in the composition of the steel industry work force, which traditionally consisted of large masses of unskilled labor and a smaller contingent of skilled workers. There appears to have been a considerable reduction over the last quarter-century in the proportion of unskilled labor required. More recently there has been a stabilization of the number employed in labor grades 5 to 10 at about 49 percent of the total, a slow increase in employment above grade 10, owing to the more complex maintenance requirements of more mechanized processes, and a slight diminution below labor grade 5, to approximately 21 percent. Salaried employees in the past 2 decades have grown from 10 percent to 20 percent of the total.

Total employment in the industry during the past decade has averaged over 600,000, but has not increased significantly as a trend since World War II, except in white collar occupations. Overall, the steel labor force is losing ground in relation to output because of increased efficiency owing to technological change. Employees in steel are also subject to severe cyclical unemployment.

The steel industry does enjoy, however, a stability among its employees. Nearly 5 out of 8 production workers with continuous service at the beginning and end of 1959 had been with the same employer for more than 10 years. But it is an aging work force; 43 percent were at least 45 years old; close to 18 percent were 55 or over.

At the turn of the current century, with the formation of the United States Steel Corp., the basis for the modern industry was laid. Many of the smaller, less efficient firms were absorbed; others were competition casualties. In 1901, U.S. Steel dominated the industry's capacity, with two-thirds of the total. Today the ratio is less than three-tenths, although the corporation itself is much larger. It has in some periods been outpaced in developing new products and has been apprehensive of antitrust action by the Federal Government, causing it to pursue a cautious policy toward mergers. On the other hand, competitors such as Bethlehem, Republic, National, and Jones and Laughlin grew larger through mergers. Armco and Youngstown were enlarged to meet specialty needs: sheet and pipe and tubing.

Inland, Colorado Fuel and Iron, and the newly organized Kaiser Steel expanded to meet fast-growing, steel-hungry regions. Nevertheless, U.S. Steel still plays a dominant price leadership role in the industry. For decades it has led in labor policy and, since the recognition of the United Steelworkers of America, in contract negotiations.

The steel industry, vast and complex, faces serious problems in terms of its own industrial and economic situation, and many of these problems are part and parcel of its policies in negotiating with the union. Industry negotiators must bargain with a profound sense of responsibility for the effect of their decisions on the industry and upon the national economy, in addition to their sense of social responsibility for their employees and fiduciary responsibility for vast capital investments.

The Union

Compared with the industry, the United Steelworkers of America is a very young arrival on the industrial scene—less than a third the age of United States Steel. Like most unions, however, it owes its existence to the insecurities of the industrial system. There have been many attempts to meet the need for organization in steel, but unions had died aborning or had been incapable of coping with either the industry's opposition or its changing character.

The Steelworkers was formed in 1936 as an organizing committee of the old CIO—a part of the surging drive of workers in the mass production industries of that era to join industrial unions. It was formally established as an international union in May 1942. In the 25 years since its genesis, the union, with more than a million members, has become one of the three largest in the United States. Two factors were influential in achieving this stature. During its formative years a large part of its financing came from the United Mine Workers of America and the new union was subject to the firm but experienced guardianship of that organization. One circumstance resulting from this relationship was the presence of Philip Murray, a vice president of the Mine Workers, who led the Steelworkers until his death in 1952. Murray enjoyed the complete support of the membership, a fact which gave the union stability, a reputation for responsibility, and freedom from the factional rows which sapped the energies and injured the reputations of some of the other newly organized CIO affiliates. This early influence can still be detected in the Steelworkers. Some of the current top leadership have UMW backgrounds and the organizational structure and bargaining technique were derived from the mine union. It appears that the Steelworkers has successfully amalgamated the diverse ethnic groups which make up the basic steel labor force and which were such a deterrent to unionism during organizational efforts of the past.

Members of the Steelworkers are organized into about 3,000 locals. Administration of international policy is carried on through 29 district offices. There are three international officers who, with the district directors, and the national director for Canada, comprise the international executive board, the supreme authority of the union between biennial conventions. A Wage Policy Committee of 163 serves to funnel rank-and-file sentiment concerning contract demands to the union officers. Local unions are administered by a uniform complement of officers. In addition to elected officials, the union avails itself of the services of a large organizing, professional, and clerical staff—about 1,200 divided between international and district offices.

Membership eligibility comprises all the nonsupervisory occupations, including white collar workers, in the industries in which it claims jurisdiction. These industries extend far beyond basic steel into steel processing and fabricating, aluminum, copper, iron mining and ore shipping, containers, certain other transportation, and miscellaneous manufacturing enterprises. But the hard core of membership (about 50 percent) is in basic steel where the union has organized plants accounting for 92 percent of total national ingot capacity.[1]

Detailed constitutional procedures govern the Steelworkers. Conventions are held every 2 years to establish basic policy. Delegates are elected by the local unions in proportion to their eligible membership, by referendum vote or local union meeting. Local union officers are elected for 2-year terms by the same methods. International officers are elected for 4 years by referendum vote of good-standing members; any such member may run for office provided he is nominated by the membership of at least 40 local unions. District directors serve 4-year terms and are chosen by referendum vote within the district after nomination by at least five locals. The Wage Policy Committee (a nonconstitutional group), except for the ex officio members, is selected by district conferences immediately after the international convention and serves until the signing of the next wage agreement, which must meet WPC approval.

Union dues and initiation fees are in line with those of other industrial unions. They are set by the constitution at $5 a month, with a $5 fee to join. Dues have not been increased since 1956. By constitutional stipulation, all funds collected are sent to the international union office, from which a remission is made: 40 percent on initiation fees and half on dues. About 30 percent of the share which the inter-

---

[1] Armco Steel and Weirton Steel have the bulk of the capacity not organized by the Steelworkers.

national retains is used for operating expenses; the districts are given about 40 percent, and the remainder is placed in a reserve, mainly in Government bonds. Net worth at the beginning of 1960 was in excess of $26 million, exclusive of the cash and properties owned by the locals. Even prior to any legal requirements along these lines, the Steelworkers' constitution required reporting and accounting to the membership of union funds, at both local and national levels, as well as independent auditing.

The Steelworkers is a vigorous, progressive union, conscious of the fact that it has won its position in relation to the industry as a result of many struggles which have tested the loyalty of its members. It pays no strike benefits in the manner of the Typographical Union or the Machinists, for example, but major portions of the membership have remained on strike for long periods of time without any outward sign of wavering.

A union summary of some of the benefits that have been achieved for its members in basic steel collective bargaining agreements was published in its newspaper, Steel Labor, for August 1960. In 1936, common labor rates were 47 cents an hour and overall average earnings 66 cents. There were no paid vacations, holiday, Sunday or overtime premium pay, insurance, severance pay, shift differentials, jury pay, reporting pay, supplemental unemployment benefits, seniority rights, or organized grievance procedure. The provisions for such items in the current contract (described in detail in appendix A) provide a startling contrast. The union might have added that it had jointly worked out with steel management a job classification system providing equal pay for equal work in practically all basic steel plants.

Far from being merely a "bread-and-butter" union, the Steelworkers offers its members a wide variety of services, some personal, some beneficial to the local unions as such. It provides research materials for collective bargaining, contract administration, legislation, and other purposes. An extensive educational program offers, among other opportunities, labor institutes on the campuses of 48 universities for the training of local-level leadership. A 24-page monthly newspaper is circulated to members. There are special staffs providing legal counsel, assistance to retired members, guidance on arbitration, job evaluation and incentives, direct help on workmen's compensation and technical aid on safety and health hazards on the job. On one occasion the international union arranged for the Pittsburgh Symphony to tour several steel communities for the benefit of members. The union maintains an active interest in foreign affairs and international labor relations; for example, it has participated in the training of 200 Indian engineers who will be employed in the steel industry of that country. A helpful role in community life has been achieved by local units of the union through identifiable participation in the leadership of community funds, Red Cross Chapters, hospitals, school boards, economic development committees, and various other organizations dedicated to civic betterment. Perhaps one of the most foresighted and altruistic of the union's programs is the series of annual college scholarships its locals and districts offer to children of members—125 totaling $126,000. There are also numerous examples of special donations for works unrelated to union activity, such as the purchase of equipment for a physician who desired to test school children for heart murmur, and the half-million-dollar contribution to a hospital drive.

In basic steel, much of the work is arduous and performed under extremes of temperature and other industrial hazards, though it should be noted that the safety record is extremely good. Employment is subject to considerable fluctuation, and although hourly earnings are high in comparison with other manufacturing industries, annual earnings can be adversely affected.

About a fifth of all workers in basic steel are unskilled and about 3 out of 10 are skilled. Nearly 2 out of 3 are on incentive pay, and earnings for these workers average about 22 percent over base rates. Wage earners with seniority in the basic steel industry averaged a bit more than $5,300 in 1957 and about $500 less in 1958. The effect of cyclical unemployment on annual earnings is indicated by the fact that in 1957 only about 9 percent of wage earners received less than $3,600; in 1958 the percentage was 22.

The union has apparently solved many of the problems all unions face, such as industry acceptance, union security, and membership solidarity, but other important issues bearing on collective bargaining and related to both the economic problems of the industry and the social and economic fortunes of its members remain for it to solve. Solution of these problems requires, as with the industry negotiators, exceptional leadership courage and foresight.

Mutual Problems

Reference has been made in the foregoing brief profiles to serious and unsolved problems which have an important if not decisive bearing on the attitudes and policies of the parties in negotiating a labor contract. Generally speaking, they can be viewed as problems of mutual concern. The broad basis for these problems is discussed in several of the ensuing chapters.

One such problem is the market situation in which the industry must seek to operate profitably. Although the demand for steel has been growing, the rate of growth has been declining in relation to gross national product. This decline can be attributed partly to the general shift in demand from goods to services, partly to the competition which steel meets from other materials, and partly to the change in character of steel-using products.

The adversity of its market position has been a factor in prompting the steel industry to curtail or abandon less efficient production units, to make others more efficient, and to invent new product uses. This course has entailed large expenditures for new equipment and processes and for market and product research. Such capital requirements have been influenced by substantial increases in the costs of materials, services, and labor. As a consequence, and in part to achieve and maintain what the industry regards as a reasonable return on capital, steel prices have risen markedly, even though gains have been achieved through technological advances.

All of these factors—growing capacity relative to demand, increased product competition, continued competitive necessity for technological advance, and rising costs—have continued to be matters of grave concern to the industry in recent years and have heightened the bargaining conflict over the costs of the economic package emanating from negotiations. They have also prompted the industry's reassessment of its work rules and crew-size practices, matters which remain unresolved from the 1959 negotiations and strike.

It is both natural and understandable that these industry problems, and the moves to meet them, should create problems of grave concern for the employees and their union, since they accentuate both the reality and the fear of job insecurity.

The core of the industrial relations problems in the steel industry is the shrinking work force required to produce enough steel to fill the industry's orders. The stresses such a situation places on union-management relations are clear. There is pressure on management by the union to maintain job security. Regardless of other matters which concern the union in pursuit of service to its members, job security or the cushioning of job insecurity is normally the heart of its efforts. This can take the form of such demands as shorter working hours; longer vacations; continuation of past crew sizes; and improvement of pension, severance pay, and unemployment benefits. To the extent that these objectives are achieved in a planned, orderly, bargained manner, they help serve the purpose of the union in regard to employment security. But each of them, once achieved, intensifies management's efforts to reduce costs in order to remain competitive in the face of its present and future market position. The problem has been complicated by management prerogative issues which arise. Significantly, technological unemployment was not specifically listed as an item to be explored by the joint Human Relations Research Committee established by the 1960 contract.

Industrial peace in the steel industry, as indicated in chapter 1, may well depend in large part on a mutually satisfactory progress with respect to these conflicting goals. Certainly a workable understanding, however devised, to alleviate basic strike-producing issues such as this one, could prove more beneficial to all concerned than periodic strikes which in the past have resulted in Government intervention to work out settlements which on occasion were stop-gap compromises with economic imperatives.

The monumental challenge to the parties in the solving of this overriding problem and many subsidiary problems is abandonment of certain positions which over the years have become stereotyped to the point where they are regarded as inviolable principles. Efforts toward resolution of these issues may result in intensified conflict or the development of mutually acceptable long-range objectives and understanding.

Part II

THE IMPACT OF STEEL STRIKES

CHAPTER 3

STEEL STRIKES AND THE ECONOMY

The very initiation of this study clearly reflected public concern with the number and economic effects of strikes in basic steel. Since the end of World War II there have been 10 negotiations in which the Steelworkers had the right to strike. There have been five major strikes:[1] 1946 (26 days), 1949 (45 days), 1952 (59 days), 1956 (36 days), and 1959 (116 days). Any collective bargaining relationship which results in such a ratio of strikes to negotiations raises questions with respect to the underlying causes and effects of such a record.

The number of strikes, however, did not provide in itself the motivation for this study. Although the frequency rate in steel appears high, a review of Bureau of Labor Statistics data in important negotiating situations in the country reveals a few companies in other industries with a comparable frequency rate. To frequency must be added the industrywide character of the strikes. In basic steel alone about a half-million workers have been direct participants. In recent years, the Steelworkers has also included in its stoppages iron mines, ore carriers, and certain fabricating subsidiaries of basic steel companies. Almost immediately affected in an indirect way are employees of certain coal mines and railroads. Thus, the strikes are in some degree multiindustry in effect and nationwide in extent.

The frequency and scope of the strikes must, of course, be coupled with the strategic importance of steel in the economy—its importance in national defense, in the gross national product, and in the country's price structure—to indicate the range of legitimate concern with respect to the possible effects of strikes. These effects, in turn, are highly important in considering the appropriate role of Government in collective bargaining.

An attempted statistical study of the frequency, duration, and intensity of strikes in steel and in other industries does not add substantially to the commonsense judgment of the record noted above. A major question is the method of comparison and its meaning, since negotiation in most major industries is on a single-company basis and strikes are not industrywide. Comparable negotiations do take place in railroads and coal, but railroad negotiations and strikes are

---

[1] This count, based on BLS data, excludes the 1955 stoppage which, although involving about 400,000 employees, lasted only 1 day. In subsequent discussions of industrywide strikes, the work interruption of 1955 is also excluded. The reasons for this distinction are that it was exceptionally brief, was not sanctioned by the international union, and part of the cessation of work was due to layoffs in anticipation of a strike.

procedurally controlled by the Railway Labor Act, and the relation of railroad service to the economy virtually precludes an industry-wide strike. Coal is reasonably comparable with steel, except that the coal contracts do not carry specific and automatic termination dates.

Bituminous coal and steel each had the same number of negotiations and about the same number of industrywide strikes during the 14 years between 1946 and 1959. Reducing the time lost because of work stoppages to a percentage of available worktime (a rough measure of strike intensity) for the entire period reveals that steel had the better record: 4.4 to 5.9, although it should be noted that the last industrywide strike in coal took place in 1952 and that the record in coal was heavily influenced by the 1946 and 1949 strikes when 20.5 and 16.7 percent of the available work time was lost.[2] Omitting the 1-day stoppage in 1955, steel strike time-losses as a percent of available worktime have run between 7 and 8 percent in strike years, except in 1952 (14 percent) and 1959 (27 percent).

Using the "time-lost" measure to compare steel with several other important industries indicates, for the postwar years, a far better overall record for motor vehicles (1.3 percent), agricultural machinery (2.5 percent), electrical machinery (0.8 percent), tires and tubes (1.8 percent), meat products (0.7 percent), and oil refining (0.6 percent). A crucial difference in this comparison is in the scope of the strikes. It is perhaps significant in this connection that steel strikes have not been of inordinate duration in comparison with those taking place against certain individual companies in the industries just listed. For example, there were strikes lasting for 113 days at General Motors in 1945–46, 102 days at Chrysler in 1950, 60 days at General Electric in 1945–46, 85 days and 156 days at Westinghouse in 1945–46 and 1955, 67 days at Armour and Swift in 1948, 60 days at Goodrich in 1959, and from 16 to 330 days at International Harvester and Allis Chalmers in 6 different years.

So far as the vital statistics of steel industry strikes are concerned—frequency, duration, and intensity—the parties to steel bargaining suffer by comparison with many other economically important industries because of their collective bargaining habits—simultaneous bargaining and industrywide strikes. If U.S. Steel is considered sepa-

---

[2] Strike statistics are based on BLS published reports for appropriate years. Work time "lost", of course, is a designation of convenience. No one can accurately measure in an industry where a product is involved how much "time lost" during a strike is made up in advance in anticipation of the strike (see below), or how much is made up subsequent to a settlement to build up depleted stocks.

BLS defines estimated working time as the average number of days typically worked by most employees times the average number of workers employed during the year. Saturdays, when not customarily worked, Sundays, and established holidays as provided in most union contracts are excluded.

rately, its 5 major strikes in 11 negotiations in 14 years represents about the same frequency as such companies as Swift, International Harvester, Firestone, and Goodrich. But if, for example, the Big Four rubber companies, which bargain individually, are considered together, there were 12 strikes against various major companies in the rubber industry during the negotiation years between 1949 and 1959.

Each industrial relationship develops its own unique habits and traditions resulting from the uneven historical contribution of many streams of influence—social, psychological, economic. Thus, frequency, duration, and intensity of strikes may be dependent on any combination of many factors—bargaining structure, size of bargaining unit, length of contract, the past experience of the parties, the issues at hand, and the attitudes and skills of the parties in administering the expiring contract and negotiating the new one. Criticism based on steel strike statistics—or any strike statistics—must take these factors into account and give them their proper weight, especially in making comparisons with other industries.

The physical features of steel strikes present a large and, in some respects, awesome contour. It is not a record which has inspired public confidence in and wholehearted support for collective bargaining, but it remains for the following examination and analysis to determine whether the economic impact of strikes warrants the grave national apprehension with which they are often viewed.

Impact of Steel Strikes on the GNP

The reminder of this chapter examines the impact of steel strikes on the physical output of the economy.

The opinion is widely held that the Nation cannot afford the production that is lost because of strikes, particularly in industries which supply essential products or services. There are others who believe that these alleged losses have been greatly exaggerated. This part of the study attempts to test the often made generalization that steel strike causes serious, unrecoverable losses. (Chart 1)

Obviously the impact of strikes varies. It is different for different industries. It is affected by the business cycle. It is affected by the state of the labor market, the product market, and the capacity situation. Consequently, this effort to appraise the impact of past steel strikes does not necessarily provide conclusions that can be applied to all strike situations.

It also must be made clear that this chapter deals only with the economic impact of strikes. In the first place, the analysis does not extend to the economic effects of settlements, both strike and nonstrike. The wage, price, and cost implications of settlements are considered subsequently in the report. In the second place, the question of

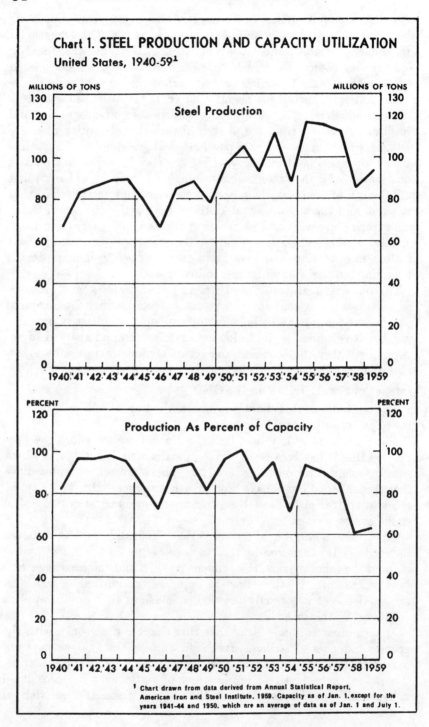

Chart 1. STEEL PRODUCTION AND CAPACITY UTILIZATION
United States, 1940-59[1]

Steel Production

Production As Percent of Capacity

[1] Chart drawn from data derived from Annual Statistical Report,
American Iron and Steel Institute, 1959. Capacity as of Jan. 1, except for the
years 1941-44 and 1950, which are an average of data as of Jan. 1 and July 1.

whether there have been net losses from steel strikes in aggregate national production and income is not identical with the question of whether or not the parties have incurred serious losses. Some of the considerations which bear upon this latter question are noted in the following paragraphs.

That these strikes have not been as serious as generally believed arises from the available inventory cushion which has also in some instances been built up in anticipation of the strike. Also following the strike, production is made up by operating at higher levels than would otherwise have prevailed.

A major difficulty in analyzing the impact of steel strikes is one of balancing excess anticipatory and catch-up production against the curtailed production during the strike. Assume, with respect to a particular strike, that the deficiency of production during the strike is exactly matched by excess production before and after the strike. Under this assumption, there would be no output loss on balance over the time period involved. But so far as the parties are concerned it does not follow that the strike would not have had its costs. To the companies there are various special "shutdown" and "start-up" costs. Certain out-of-pocket costs are incurred during the strike, such as, payments to employees whose activities continue, cost of utility services, and certain fixed costs, as interest and insurance. There may well be special inventory costs. There may be excess costs associated with the dislocation in the flow of raw materials and special overtime and other costs. The costs of operating at a "normal" rate before, during, and after the strike would almost certainly be less than the costs associated with widely fluctuating rates of operation. Often marginal facilities must be used during production peaks immediately before and after strikes. There can be better production planning when overall production is maintained at a relatively even keel and the work force can be better utilized.

For the employees there is likewise no clear balancing of income and employment. Some steel industry employees may suffer an employment and income loss closely proportional to the duration of the strike. For some employees, added hours of employment and enlarged income may balance lost hours and income. Some employees may gain in employment and income because of the strike. The use of vacation pay to offset loss of income during a strike and unemployment compensation for possible alternative layoff further complicates the comparison. It is clear that costs and losses to the parties pose questions over and beyond those involved in assessing the impact on the economy.

In addition, with respect to any specific steel strike, the fact that there may have been no serious, overall losses to the economy as indicated by aggregate measurements does not mean that particular construction projects, particular companies making specialized products, the merchants in particular communities, employees in specific industries, and other types of specialized and localized situations may not have been damaged in greater or lesser degree by a strike. A very important question of this type relates to the impact of steel strikes on national defense. This particular question is discussed later in this section. Beyond examination of national impact, no effort is made to evaluate the effects on particular localities.

In the next place, the secondary effects of steel strikes are exceedingly complex to trace. The problem of the degree of substitution of other products for steel is in this category. Temporary shortage of steel may have encouraged the permanent use of substitutes for steel. In the 1959 steel strike we know that some employees in industries using steel were temporarily laid off. It is not possible to know how much of this unemployment was caused by the stoppage in the steel industry and how much was due to seasonal, or other, factors. Neither do we know to what extent employees in industries competing with steel had more time at work in 1959 and 1960 than would have been the case had there been no steel strike.

For these reasons it is not possible to quantify with any confidence the employment or income that was lost because of the strike; particularly since the world "lost" to have significance must be interpreted to mean losses that were permanent and not offset or recovered during the time period before or following the strike period.

Likewise there may be permanent production losses which cannot be qualified. Particular types of steel imports could become established in the domestic market during strike shortages. Substitute materials might gain permanent advantages. Some durable purchases might be foregone. The evidence does not establish, however, that the long run trend of steel output was modified by these strikes.

Finally, even though steel production may balance out over a period of time, some temporal dislocations in production may have adverse effects. A long strike most certainly would produce some such dislocations. This point is discussed to some extent subsequently, but primary attention is given to the major question of the balanced effect on national product.

The Direct Measurement of Strike Losses

The ideal way to measure the magnitude of the losses caused by steel strikes is to make a reconstruction of what the situation would have been had there been no strike and compare this with what actually happened. Strikes in steel are characterized by a very low level of activity.[3] But anticipation of a strike may lead to an inventory build-up by customers and by the industry. After a strike, production activity is higher than would otherwise have been the case until inventories have been restored.

Thus, to measure the effect of the strike on production it is necessary to consider (a) the period of prestrike anticipation, (b) the period of strike stoppage, and (c) the period of post-strike make-up, none of which is characterized by normal (i.e., not strike related) activity. Thus a crucial part of any reconstruction is the determination of the time period over which the reconstruction must extend. This strike period must be long enough to embrace the three indicated stages and short enough to exclude any significant part of the period of interstrike normalcy.

To select the right time period is exceedingly difficult. Yet, failure to make a proper selection seriously affects the results. A meaningful projection of "what production would have been" had there been no strike, across the strike and the post-strike period, must eliminate seasonal and cyclical influences.

This point is illustrated by the recent situation in the industry. The years 1957-58 were unaffected by strikes. Under recession influences in 1958, the year prior to the strike year, production declined and the industry operated at about 61 percent of capacity, as the average for the year. But, during the first 6 months of 1959, the period just prior to the strike, production as a percent of capacity, averaged 87.8. Following the settlement, production jumped within 2 months to about 96 percent of capacity, and continued at high levels until the inventory situation was balanced. But it is significant that within 4 months after the strike, production began to decline. By July 1960, production as a percent of capacity was much lower than the 1958 average. (Chart 1, p. 34.)

Steel production was reconstructed for various postwar steel strikes. The method used was to base the reconstruction on production indexes for various industries. The difficulties encountered were (1) a production index whose cyclical movements were closely related to steel was also affected by the strike, (2) a production index for an industry not closely related to steel did not show cyclical movements closely related to steel, and (3) the results of the reconstruction varied with the time span of the reconstruction. Any particular reconstruction is subject to debate, but the judgment was reached that the likelihood of any serious loss in steel production, for the strike periods considered, when measured over the prestrike, strike, and post-strike

---

[3] During the 1959 steel strike the plants that continued in operation had an ingot capacity of about 15 percent of the total.

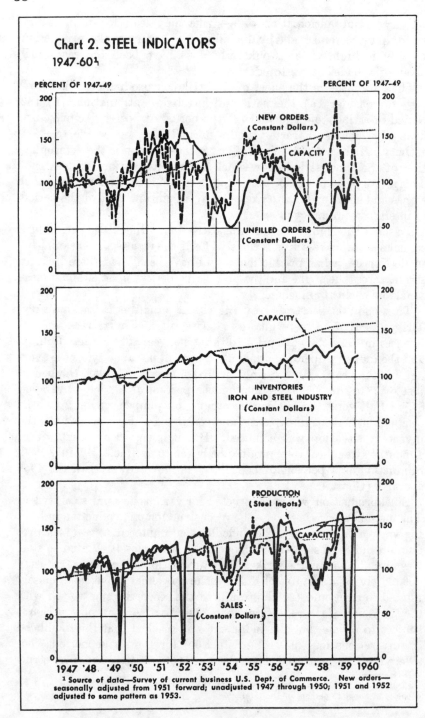

Chart 2. STEEL INDICATORS
1947-60[1]

PERCENT OF 1947-49   PERCENT OF 1947-49

NEW ORDERS
(Constant Dollars)

CAPACITY

UNFILLED ORDERS
(Constant Dollars)

CAPACITY

INVENTORIES
IRON AND STEEL INDUSTRY
(Constant Dollars)

PRODUCTION
(Steel Ingots)

CAPACITY

SALES
(Constant Dollars)

1947 '48   '49   '50   '51   '52   '53   '54   '55   '56   '57   '58   '59 1960

[1] Source of data—Survey of current business U.S. Dept. of Commerce. New orders—
seasonally adjusted from 1951 forward; unadjusted 1947 through 1950; 1951 and 1952
adjusted to same pattern as 1953.

period, is quite remote. Chart 2 showing, among other variables, production, sales, and capacity monthly on a 1947-49 base from 1947 to 1960, allows the reader to exercise his judgment by a rough comparison of these variables. It should be noted that this chart does not show the actual relationship between production and capacity at any given time, but only the relative growth in the two components when 1947-49 is used as the base.

Effect on Steel Using Industries

A significant test of the economic impact of steel strikes can be made by an analysis of the effect of such strikes on industries dependent upon steel for their raw materials. If such industries continue to operate normally, both during and after the strike period, the evidence would suggest strongly that there had been little or no impact on them except that they may have paid premium prices for steel or maintained excess inventory at added cost. To make this test three sets of statistics were considered:

(a) Quarterly constant dollar expenditures on the total durable goods component of the gross national product.

(b) Quarterly constant dollar sales of consumers' durables and producers' equipment.

(c) Changes in durable goods inventory.

Expenditures for Total GNP Durable Goods

Chart 3 shows the quarterly totals of final expenditures on all durable goods industries, expressed in constant dollars of 1954 purchasing power, for the 1947–59 period. Four major steel strikes (1949, 1952, 1956, and 1959) occurred during this interval. The 1949 strike did not reduce that year's sales of durables below the 1947–48 level, although it may have delayed the start of the ensuing upswing. The 1952 strike did not prevent a continuance of the post-1949 up-movement. It is impossible to say with any assurance whether the strike of 1956 softened the 1954–57 cycle upswing. In any case there was only a slight reduction of durable goods sales during the strike period. The most severe strike to date, that of 1959, may have contributed partially to the cyclical upswing in final sales indirectly through inventory accumulation and may have been partially responsible for the dip in final sales subsequent to the strike. However, if we begin with 1950, and leave out of consideration the cyclical troughs of 1954 and 1958, final durable goods sales have tended to increase at a smoothly decreasing rate. This behavior would be expected in view of the durable goods deficits which resulted from World War II and which were gradually made up in subsequent years, allowing also for the Korean enlargement of the level of defense spending.

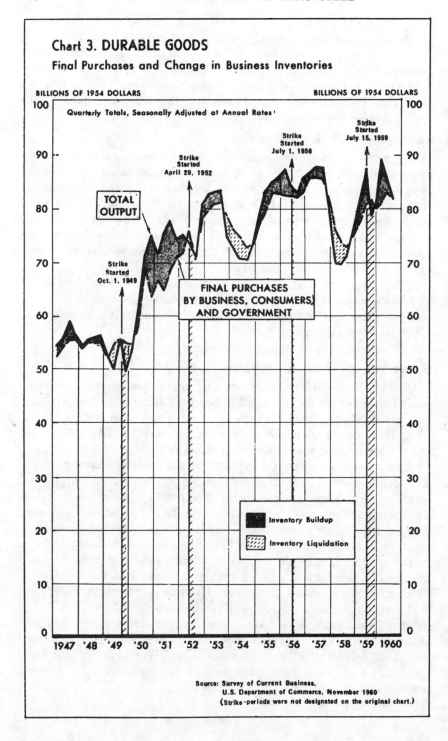

Chart 3. DURABLE GOODS
Final Purchases and Change in Business Inventories

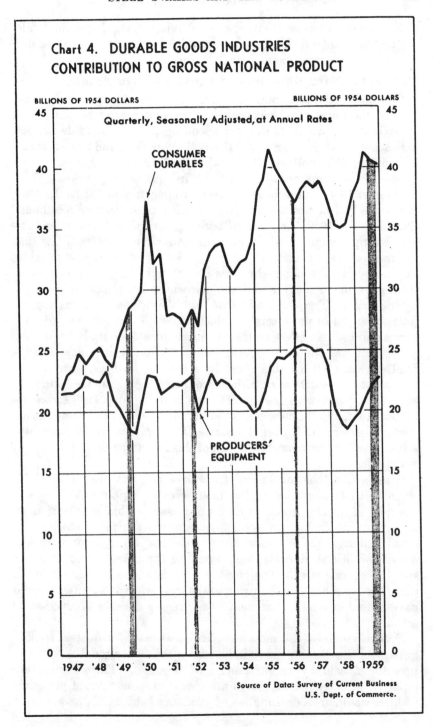

Chart 4. DURABLE GOODS INDUSTRIES
CONTRIBUTION TO GROSS NATIONAL PRODUCT

BILLIONS OF 1954 DOLLARS   BILLIONS OF 1954 DOLLARS

Quarterly, Seasonally Adjusted, at Annual Rates

CONSUMER
DURABLES

PRODUCERS'
EQUIPMENT

1947 '48 '49 '50 '51 '52 '53 '54 '55 '56 '57 '58 1959

Source of Data: Survey of Current Business
U.S. Dept. of Commerce.

No precise interpretation of the behavior of the large final sales aggregate is intended. The important point is the obvious protection for final purchasers through inventory.

Expenditures for Durables and Producers' Equipment

Consumers' durables and producers' equipment production in constant dollars may also be examined. These data are more influenced by strikes than would be the corresponding data on final sales. These series are shown in chart 4 for the 1947–59 period, and are expressed in constant 1954 dollars. The major steel strikes of this period affected the last quarter of 1949, the third quarter of 1952, the third quarter of 1956, and at least the last two quarters of 1959. In 1949, the strike had no noticeable effect on either producers' or consumers' durables. In 1952, the flows of both producers' and consumers' durables dipped slightly below the rates in previous quarters. The 1956 strike gives no indication of affecting the flow of producers' durables in that year. Consumer durables had already begun a down-movement prior to the strike, and that movement was not noticeably altered by the strike. The severe strike of 1959 likewise had no apparent impact on output of producers' durables, although it may have had some direct and indirect effect on the consumer durables output fluctuation which followed the 1958 cyclical trough. We may conclude, as with final sales for all durables, that it is difficult to discern any major impacts on production of either producers' or consumers' durables over these years with the qualification that the long 1959 strike, its anticipation, and the subsequent readjustment, no doubt affected somewhat the entire GNP over the course of several quarters by accentuating inventory movements. Much of this inventory change, however, was cyclical.

Summarizing the conclusions from these two analyses: There is no evidence that the strikes of the 1950's created serious restrictions in the flow of durable goods to final purchasers. This is an extremely significant conclusion, since one obvious way in which the steel strikes could influence the ultimate desires of producers or consumers to acquire additional durable assets would be through their effect on the supplies of raw steel. The obvious implication as to past strikes is that they have been settled prior to the time when their effects would have caused critical curtailment of aggregate durable production or sales.

Probably one of the most sensitive measures of any steel strike's impact on the durable goods industries is the monthly dollar value of inventories held by manufacturers of durables. These figures are reported in current dollars and are classified as purchased materials (which would include supplies of customer-held steel), as goods in

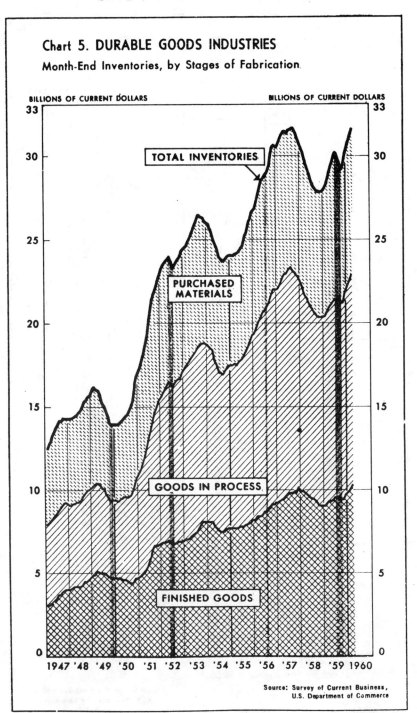

Chart 5. DURABLE GOODS INDUSTRIES

Month-End Inventories, by Stages of Fabrication.

BILLIONS OF CURRENT DOLLARS

BILLIONS OF CURRENT DOLLARS

TOTAL INVENTORIES

PURCHASED MATERIALS

GOODS IN PROCESS

FINISHED GOODS

1947 '48 '49 '50 '51 '52 '53 '54 '55 '56 '57 '58 '59 1960

Source: Survey of Current Business,
U.S. Department of Commerce

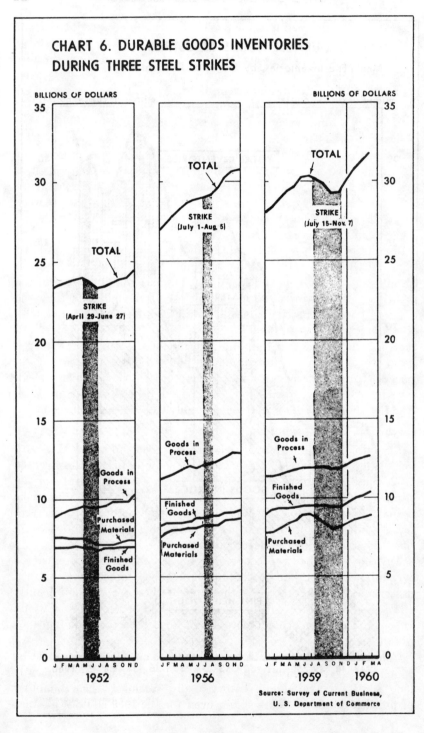

CHART 6. DURABLE GOODS INVENTORIES
DURING THREE STEEL STRIKES

Source: Survey of Current Business,
U. S. Department of Commerce

process, and as finished durable goods. Durables are produced from a wide range of raw materials, of which steel, although important, is only one. Therefore, when shortages of raw steel force durable goods producers to draw down their inventories, this should become apparent. The ultimate impact on flow of production can be traced from raw materials through semifinshed goods to final output by means of these inventory statistics (see charts 5 and 6). These statistics have been presented on a cumulative basis in chart 5 and by series in chart 6. It will be noted in the first chart that goods in process and raw materials contribute most of the cyclical movement to the inventory level, while finished goods inventories follow much more closely a trend of gradual expansion. Only in 1952 and 1959 were there distinct downmovements in inventory levels which were associated with those years' strikes.

In chart 6, the three classes of durable producers' inventories have been plotted separately, without accumulation. This chart makes it easier—both because the series are noncumulative and because of the greatly enlarged vertical scale—to trace the strike effects. Near the middle of the 1952 strike period, inventories of purchased materials (including steel) ceased to follow their prestrike trend upward; and they did not resume that trend until the strike was settled. The 1956 strike did not have as clear an effect; but the 1959 strike clearly reversed the prestrike increase in materials inventories. Thus, we can say that these inventories were unaffected by the strikes in 1956, slightly affected in 1952, and considerably affected in 1959.

Impact on Inventories

In terms of semimanufactured goods (goods in process) inventories, the 1956 strike likewise failed to show impact. However, in 1952, these inventories were already falling—and their rate of decline appears to have been accelerated. Near the end of the 1959 strike period, some reduction took place in semimanufactured goods inventories which probably was strike-related; but it was much less severe than the decline which affected materials.

Turning to finished goods inventories, each of these strikes registered even milder impact than on the previous stage of fabrication. In fact, it becomes difficult to say whether any of these strikes significantly affected the availability of finished goods. Any such influence would appear to have been evident more as a failure to rise than as a tendency to fall.

Comparing the evidence in chart 6, there is one clear generalization which emerges: The duration of none of these strikes was sufficiently long relative to available inventory to affect seriously the availability of finished durables. This is true even for the 1959 shutdown which was the longest one in history. It is obvious, of course, that prolongation (especially of the 1952 and 1959 strikes) would have had more serious consequences. It is also clear that anticipation of the 1959 strike accentuated total inventory accumulation but not significantly with respect to finished goods.

Other Relevant Data

Additional reasons for believing that these steel strikes did not result in serious hardship to the economy are shown by several other statistical indicators: (a) steelmaking capacity, (b) steel production, (c) sales of steel manufacturers, (d) new orders placed, and (e) unfilled orders. Although these indicators are not all available in comparable units, most of them can be reduced to a useful degree of general comparability.

In chart 2, these series have been plotted on a monthly basis for the period 1947 through the first quarter of 1960. This chart is made up of three panels with capacity appearing in each. Steel productive capacity increased steadily from 1947–49 by slightly more than 50 percent of that average before the end of 1959. Although not absolutely steady, this rate of increase has been more nearly stable than that of any of the other series studied. In contrast, the industry's output and sales have fluctuated sharply around a level or slowly rising trend. From time to time, peaks in the rate of steel production have utilized the industry's full capacity,[4] but the average levels of steel output and sales have fallen further and further below it. It is also noteworthy that the level of inventories held by the iron and steel industry itself has gradually moved upward,[5] and significant steel inventories are held by consuming industries. The upper panel of the chart relates new orders and unfilled orders for steel to steelmaking capacity. There have been a few exceptional peaks in new orders, which otherwise have tended to fluctuate violently around a level trend; unfilled orders tend to follow a downward trend. As can be seen from the top panel of chart 2, after the severe strike of 1952, buyers of steel placed unseasonably high demands (seasonally adjusted new orders deflated) on the industry in June of 1953 and 1954. The most likely explanation is that these purchases, timed for delivery just before current labor contracts expired, were placed to anticipate a strike-induced interrup-

---

[4] The steel industry in the base period 1947–49 operated at about 89 percent of capacity and the chart must be read with this in mind.

[5] It is to be expected that, as steel production rises, and even if no planned increase in inventory holdings had been undertaken by steel producers, inventories also would rise. Inventories held by steel producers include raw materials (ore, fuel, etc.), goods in process (i.e., the flow of raw and semifinished materials through the plant), and finished goods (primarily those awaiting shipments, plus small "cushion" inventories). Each of these quantities inevitably would tend to increase or to decrease with the level of activity. Inventory data does not show the large stock of steel held by steel-using industries.

tion of steel supplies. These purchases entered customer-held inventories which already were tending to expand because of generally favorable business expectations.

Effect of Foreign Imports

Imports of steel alleviate to only a slight extent the effect of curtailment production during a strike period. Historically, the United States has been a net exporter of steel mill products, although this situation was temporarily reversed in December 1958 until the spring of 1960,

The steel strike of 1959 did induce an increase in imports. We imported almost 4.4 million tons, or over twice that of the previous record year of 1951. The 1959 imports were about 2½ times their 1958 volume. Probably most of this increase of 2¾ million tons was induced by the strike.

During the first 8 months of 1959, total imports of 2.7 million net tons represent only 4.9 percent of the net new supply of steel products (i.e., industry shipment of steel products, plus imports minus exports), as compared with 2.9 percent in 1958 and 1.5 percent in 1957. Thus, supplies from foreign sources, in total, provide only slight relief during a steel strike period. In addition, foreign imports are concentrated in a relatively few shapes and forms. Specialized items, particularly, those needed for defense, can seldom be furnished at all. In many instances, even if steel products can be supplied from abroad, there is too great a time lag between the time that orders are placed and deliveries are made for foreign supplies to be of much help, even though some American consumers of steel have set up contingent contracts with foreign producers in light of the recurring emergencies here.

Effect on National Security Programs

Steel is indispensable in the manufacture of many defense items, such as missiles, ships, tanks, launching sites, aircraft, and atomic reactors. Obviously, a curtailment in the flow of steel, if it came at a time close to the outbreak of war, could have very serious effects on our defense efforts. A strike during a cold war period, such as the one in 1959, may or may not have serious consequences. That the 1959 strike involved costly delays that resulted in postponements in the delivery dates of critical defense items was attested to by the Secretaries of several Government Departments and Agencies. Among these were the Secretaries of Commerce and Defense in affidavits filed in the District Court of the United States when testimony was being taken relative to invoking the injunction provisions of the Taft-Hartley Act. The union objected strenuously to the generality of these affidavits.

The question is not whether a strike in an industry such as steel could affect negatively our national security programs. Obviously this is possible if they lasted long enough and if no steps were taken to mitigate their effects. Judgments as to the seriousness of interruptions in past situations are not of particular value as to the future. The true focal question posed is whether the entire strike must be ended in the interest of national defense, or whether partial operation to meet defense needs is feasible. If feasible, it could be agreed to or compelled, for example, in the absence of agreement, by special use of injunctive procedure.

Partial operation poses (1) technical problems, (2) economic problems, and (3) labor-relations and administrative problems for the companies and the union. It is generally agreed that these problems are insurmountable if only defense items as such are produced. On the other hand, if some civilian production is restored the technical and economic problems could probably be met. In an analysis of this subject undertaken for us by the Department of Commerce, the conclusion was reached that it is technically and economically feasible to meet defense needs through partial operation provided the plants which are kept open are permitted to produce their normal output and are not confined in their operations to producing defense items only. Some special problems might remain, such as maintaining an appropriate supply of steelmaking coals. The question becomes, however, primarily one of whether opening up a sufficient number of plants to meet critical defense needs leaves extremely serious problems of a labor-relations and administrative character. It is difficult to accept the conclusion that these equity and administrative problems are insurmountable. The potential for meeting defense needs by this method warrants careful exploration of the problem by the parties and by the Government. Such exploration should be undertaken now. It should not wait until there is a shutdown of operations.

Conclusion

Although there have been rather frequent strikes in basic steel which pose problems with regard to labor relations and Government intervention, a very important related consideration is whether the economy can stand strikes in steel. It is our opinion that the economic impact of strikes on the economy are usually seriously exaggerated. Too often the losses of production, employment, and wages are evaluated in a context which assumes that there would have been continuous high-level operation had there been no strike. Such losses, as noted previously, if they are to be placed in a realistic focus, must be weighed over a time span that encompasses a period prior to the strike, the period of the strike, and a period long enough following the strike to permit restoration of inventory. The secondary effects of strikes must be evaluated in a context which recognizes the extent to which industry is subject to seasonal and cyclical forces, the fact that American industry generally operates well below capacity and the fact of inventory accumulation at several stages beyond basic steel itself. Viewed in this perspective most strikes can last much longer (even in an industry as basic as steel) than is generally believed before the economy will be seriously hurt. History in steel indicates that once strikes really begin to be seriously felt over wide segments of the economy, pressure from those affected will in most instances bring about a settlement.

Free collective bargaining necessitates the right to strike. The cost of strikes must be kept in perspective. The freedom to strike is in our society the major deterrent to strikes. Any effective alternative involves drastic legislative modification of free bargaining and is far from having no economic costs. National defense, as previously stated, presents a special problem for which partial operation should be most seriously considered. Fundamentally, it should be recognized that the pressures upon the parties to settle are substantially irresistible when a strike reaches the critical stage.

Part III

COLLECTIVE BARGAINING IN STEEL

CHAPTER 4

DEVELOPMENT OF THE INDUSTRY'S LABOR POLICY

Introduction

In 1937, the annual report to stockholders of the United States Steel Corp. contained an innovation—a section entitled "Employee Relations." Half laconic, half apologetic in tone, its seven paragraphs announced that the corporation had signed an agreement with the Steel Workers Organizing Committee (SWOC) of the Committee for Industrial Organization. Significant portions of the announcement follow:

> For several years it has been the policy to negotiate with the representatives of *any* group of employees and with *any* organization as the representative of its members. [Emphasis supplied.] Prior to 1937, written contracts had been entered into with the * * * representatives of the so-called "captive" mines. Contracts in writing were entered into [with the Employee Representation Plans] in November 1936. * * *
>
> In accordance with this policy, contracts were entered into in March of 1937, expiring February 28, 1938, between the steel manufacturing subsidiaries and the [SWOC] as the collective bargaining agent for those employees who are members of the Amalgamated Association of Iron, Steel, and Tin Workers of North America.

Thus the new "employee relationship" was rationalized. But it proved not to be quite that simple.

A decade later, in 1947, the contracts between the corporation (along with most of the basic steel and steel fabricating companies) and the union—now known as the United Steelworkers of America—indicated a relationship both complex and, despite a month-long strike in 1946, reasonably cooperative. The parties had collaborated for about 3 years in producing a monumental job classification manual and job evaluation system as part of an intricate program to correct wage rate inequities. They had also agreed contractually to joint plant safety committees, joint studies of seniority, social insurance, and job administration, and quarterly joint meetings of top officials to assay the administration of the agreement. They pledged to "encourage the highest possible degree of friendly, cooperative relationships * * *" Their statement of aims ended with a pronouncement that "as men of good will with sound purposes" they would work to "protect private enterprise and its efficiency in the interests of all, as well as the legitimate interest of their respective organizations within the framework of a democratic society in which regard for fact and fairness is essential." [1]

It should be noted that the above sentiments represented the high point of a relationship covering a quarter-century, with antecedents reaching back into the 19th century and with much of its history written in black or crimson.

The Industry's Pre-SWOC Labor Policy [2]

"* * * Before 1901 there was a national union which dealt with individual employers. Now there is one great corporation whose negative action, at least practically fixes standards for the whole industry." [3]

This capsule characterization by Fitch, with its reference to the U.S. Steel, not only establishes a line of demarcation in the progress of the industry's labor relations policy, but in a general way describes a situation which has persisted through the years. Two other commentators, carrying forward a discussion of the consequences of this turn of events, pointed out that "bargaining between big unions and big corporations often leads to internal centralization of decision-making and policy determination." [4]

United States Steel subsidiaries, at the time of the formation of the corporation in 1901, employed more than half the steelworkers in the country. Their experience in union and labor relations, even though affecting exceptionally large numbers of workers, should not be presumed to be a prototype for the entire industry; there was not even consistency in practices among U.S. Steel plants. Nevertheless, there are common threads of labor policies and situations which can be considered typical for the bulk of the industry at about that period.

The corporation's initial labor policy was conditioned by three factors: the Amalgamated was threatening a strike; the corporation was hypersensitive to public opinion because the public and the Government were critically evaluating the new colossus; within the corporation the directors were split between the banking interests and the operating officials. The latter held an antagonistic and intransigent

[1] Agreement between United States Steel Corp. and the United Steelworkers of America, 1947.

[2] The ensuing paragraphs are based chiefly on the following sources: J. H. Fitch, *The Steel Workers*, Vol. 3 of *the Pittsburgh Study*, Russell Sage Foundation, New York, 1910; Carroll R. Daugherty, Melvin G. de Chazeau, and Samuel S. Stratton, *the Economics of the Iron and Steel Industry*, McGraw-Hill Book Co., 1937; Robert R. R. Brooks, *As Steel Goes*, Yale University Press, 1940; and John A. Garraty, "U.S. Steel Versus Labor: The Early Years," in *Labor History*, Vol. 1, No. 1, Winter, 1960.

[3] Fitch, op. cit., p. 192.

[4] Frederick H. Harbison and Robert Dubin, *Patterns of Union-Management Relations*, Science Research Associates, Chicago, 1947, p. 184.

attitude toward the work force. The bankers, although opposed to unionism, were in favor of winning the loyalty of workers through blandishments, and with the support of J. P. Morgan, whose authority was supreme, this group's approach ultimately won out. Corporation policy, while amenable to continuation of existing union relations, was opposed to extension of unionization. Morgan himself, in a conciliatory mood, met with T. J. Shaffer, president of the Amalgamated, when the union struck all plate, sheet, and hoop companies. In the face of management agreement to wage demands, the union refused to compromise on other issues and extended the strike to the entire corporation (an action which the AFL, through Samuel Gompers, criticized). The union, ill-organized and ineptly led, lost— ignominiously.

After the defeat of the union, the corporation in 1902 promulgated an intensified program of welfare benefits under the leadership of George W. Perkins, its chairman.

The Perkins program included an installment-buying stock ownership plan which provided bonuses and dividend credits prior to full ownership. Later there were also pension and accident benefits, a safety program, reduction of Sunday work, a move toward an 8-hour shift, home financing, and cash savings plans, to exemplify a policy embodying what the corporation termed "the most enlightened view of an employer's responsibility."

During the depression of 1908 the corporation resisted pressure from its own operating heads and from the industry as a whole to cut wages. But at the same time it fought another Amalgamated strike in a bold and successful effort to force the union out of the last 14 mills in which it had recognition. For the next 35 years it was to pursue an adamant open shop policy. It did, however, continue its policy of "enlightened responsibility," even to the extent, in 1911, of permitting a dissident stockholder to make a resolution (which was approved) to investigate charges of "inhuman" working conditions. The corporation in fact did appoint an investigating committee which in 1912 praised the corporation's welfare work while condemning the 7-day week and 12-hour shift.

The ouster of the union from all corporation subsidiaries, according to Fitch, "had no direct bearing on the policies." [5]   He contends that the motive was the "desire for administrative control." The Amalgamated, he insists, was trying to interfere in a manner "inconsistent with necessary business methods." [6]   One can place some credence on this contention, given Fitch's warm approbation of unionism

---

[5] Fitch, op. cit., p. 200.
[6] Ibid., p. 205.

and the predilection of the Amalgamated for doing the improper thing at the most inappropriate time.

The employees were enthused by neither the corporation's labor practices nor its welfare policies, according to Garraty. In 1919, when U.S. Steel employees were part of more than 360,000 out on strike, there was evidence that paternalism had not bred loyalty. Its failure he ascribes in part to the caste and economic differences between men and managers, onerous hours and working conditions, changing technology, and speeded production.

In the face of all this, why did not unionism secure a solid base in the industry? So far as the U.S. Steel experience is concerned, there were a number of factors, most of which also obtained in the remainder of the industry.

Unionism could not take root because the company was opposed to it and took positive measures to prevent its establishment. There were also reasons implicit in the union's history and policies. Among these were fear of reprisals through discharge and blacklisting; espionage; and a studied policy on the part of management for an efficacious "mix" of ethnic groups. There was also the barrier raised by the Amalgamated itself through membership restrictions and stubborn refusal to expand beyond the ironworkers' skills in the face of changing technology.

In summary, the labor policy from 1901 through 1930 was (1) an attempt to prevent the spread of unionism and to destroy it; and (2) to win the loyalty of the employees through welfare, fringe benefits, and paternalism. The policy on the first point was almost completely successful; it failed on the second. Paternalism could not fill the void left by the retreating and evaporating Amalgamated. What it could not do was exorcise the spectre of unemployment. Security from job loss was the objective of the workers and was to provide the motivation for most union actions to this day, and probably for so long as unemployment plagues the work life of the employee.

Failure of the welfare-paternalism gambit became more acutely noticeable as the economic depression worsened in the early thirties. With the passage of the National Industrial Recovery Act in 1933, with its Section 7(a) guaranteeing workers the right to organize and bargain through representatives of their own choosing without interference or coercion by employers, unionism again became a possibility.

Reaction of the steel industry to the new Act's labor section found expression in a veritable boom in employee representation plans. By the end of 1934, according to Brooks [7] there were 93 such plans cover-

---

[7] Brooks, op. cit., p. 79.

ing 90 percent of all steelworkers. In 1932, Daugherty reports, there had been only seven plans.[8] He is careful, and probably correctly so, to dissociate them from the usual opprobrium attached to company unionism. The steel companies' policy in espousing the ERP's was, in the main, to thwart or divert any propensity on the part of their workers for "outside" unionism, and still remain within the letter of the new law. Indeed, even before the depression, Brooks notes, some officers of U.S. Steel were beginning to look with favor on establishment of such plans.[9] The NRA, giving at least strong moral support to trade unionism as official Government policy, accelerated this exploratory thinking into pragmatic action.[10] The problem faced by most companies was to provide for representation and at the same time influence the organization without overtly exercising control. The fact that most plans were organized by the companies to meet the threat of the NRA is attested by the termination clauses in most of the plans. These specified that the plans would "remain in full force and effect during the term of the National Industrial Recovery Act * * *" [11]

The employee representatives did not engage in collective bargaining as such, although the general 10 percent wage rate increase in the industry in 1934 originated as an ERP demand. Contracts were not negotiated or written.

In 1934 and 1935, there was a significant series of interplant, inter-company, and interarea meetings of ERP's, usually held with the frowning and apprehensive disapproval of the companies concerned; for these conventions reflected an aggressiveness and community of interest amongst the workers which trod perilously close to the very attributes of independent unionism which the companies had tried to fend off by establishing the plans.

ERP's operated under the handicap of administrative and inherent organizational weaknesses which dissipated their potential influence just short of affecting short-term industry labor policy. As one plan's

---

[8] Daugherty, op. cit., p. 1005.

[9] Brooks, op. cit., pp. 78–82.

[10] Bethlehem was the only sizable company with a plan dating back to 1919. Frederick H. Harbison, who has done much research in this period, says in *Collective Bargaining in the Steel Industry*, Princeton University Press, 1937, pp. 1–2, that most companies "found difficulties in developing . . . a complex management technique of group relations which [Bethlehem] had taken nearly 15 years to evolve." Harbison also credits the ERP's with some accomplishments in behalf of the employees. Certainly they became more assertive and demanding than management envisioned as a role for them. In his doctoral thesis (*Labor Relations in the Iron and Steel Industry, 1936–39*, Princeton, 1940, p. 18.) he relates the gleeful (and probably facetious) observations of one steelworker that the fore-man of his department had not knocked down a single worker since the plans were introduced!

[11] Daugherty, op. cit., p. 1019.

leader put it, the ERP's were able to get new soap containers in the shower rooms—but no soap.[12] But the ERP's definitely did enter into and influence, indirectly, long-term labor policy.

Steel industry management had banked heavily on the ERP's: they filled the vacuum left by the exit of the Amalgamated; they could provide a cooperative vehicle for company policy; and they served the requirements of Section 7(a) without the more odious possibilities. But management fully anticipated that the ERP's would remain within tractable limits. Thus Daugherty quotes Charles M. Schwab of U.S. Steel:

* * * We make our own labor unions. * * * We discuss matters, but we never vote. I will not permit myself of being in the position of having the labor dictate to the management. But the remarkable thing is that in all the sifting of complaints through such an organization * * * we find in 70 percent of the cases the workmen are right.[13]

Brooks notes that Arthur H. Young, vice president of United States Steel for labor relations, likened the employee representation plans to the "sound and harmonious relationship between a man and his wife," [14] an unhappy analogy which doubtless left critics of the plans ample latitude for quips.

Some steel executives discovered unsuspected virtues in the ERP's. One suggested that "just because [they] were put in to protect us against outside unions, don't make the mistake of thinking that's their only value to us now. We've gotten a real education out of our experience. We hadn't realized, as we grew bigger, how far away we had drifted from personal contact with the men in the plant." [15]

The ERP's were a mixed blessing as an industry policy, because, as Daugherty points out it is a mistake to presume that company unions will remain docile, stereotyped, and company-oriented.[16] In the end, they wore thin as a barrier to "outside" unionism, abraded on the one side by the NRA Code-inspired restlessness of the men and the competition of those same "outside" organizers, and bruised on the other by a rather desperate industry practice of meeting demands—if they were not too many or too onerous.

Steel companies also were in an uncomfortable predicament during NRA days. They first of all disliked and distrusted Government intervention in their labor affairs. Yet they wished even more to avoid the public criticism which would result from a defiance of the Codes

---

[12] Brooks, op. cit., p. 87.
[13] Daugherty, op. cit., p. 989.
[14] Brooks, op. cit., p. 78.
[15] Daugherty, op. cit., p. 989.
[16] Ibid., p. 971.

or the exposure of their policies before a public tribunal. A company officer put the whole problem thus:

* * * Ten years ago we would have fired every union member and sympathizer * * * and we'd have had the organizers run out of town on a rail * * * Now we have to have some other damned good excuse before we fire a union man. We hate like hell to get all that publicity that comes when you're hauled up before a labor board. Another thing, there's a spirit of freedom among our employees we didn't suspect existed * * * So we're learning subtlety * * * A big problem is to convince foremen and people who are for us out in the community that the old days are pretty well over. * * * There's a good chance that these employee representation plans, if they continue to work out so well, will do away with most of or all the necessity for [espionage], at least inside the plants. * * * We'll continue to learn from [the men themselves] the really important things that are on the workers' minds * * * as long as they are convinced we are on the level with them.[17]

The steel Code, formulated in the summer of 1933, brought unionism its first real opportunity in the industry since 1919, even though employee representatives, through union officials or otherwise, were not part of the private meetings at which the labor sections were negotiated by industry and Government officials. Despite the weakness of unionism (chiefly the remnants of the Amalgamated), the industry was skittish over joint union participation in discussion of Code matters. On one occasion the chief executives of several steel companies, to avoid a situation which might be construed as "recognition," walked out of a meeting called by the Secretary of Labor, because AFL President William Green entered the room in his capacity as a representative on the Labor Advisory Board.[18]

There was, however, a reaction (albeit feeble) in the Amalgamated to the restlessness of the men in the plants.[19] By July 1934, militants in its ranks had pushed it to a strike threat, and the Government established a special Steel Labor Board in an effort (successful) to forestall a walkout which might impede the recovery progress. The board failed in other respects, but its failure resulted from union leaders'

---

[17] Daugherty, op. cit., pp. 995–96.
[18] Ibid., p. 260.
[19] Daugherty, p. 969, called the Amalgamated "outmoded, inconsistent, patched up * * * in general unsuited to meet the needs of industrial unionism in the iron and steel industry. * * *" It is of passing interest to note that the U.S. Bureau of Labor, in its *Report on Conditions of Employment in the Iron and Steel Industry in the United States, Vol. III: Working Conditions and the Relations of Employers and Employees*, p. 15, had this to say as of 1910: "* * * [T]hey are almost entirely without organization. * * * The Amalgamated Association of Iron, Steel, and Tin Workers, it is true, still exists, but * * * it possesses little strength, except in a very narrow field.

purblind stubbornness rather than the steel industry's unwillingness to compromise.

Daugherty relates an amazing story of successive offers by Carnegie Steel Co. (later Carnegie-Illinois) to the Amalgamated through the Steel Labor Board.[20]

The board with variable success had arranged for a half dozen tenuous agreements with the Amalgamated to deal for its members in certain plants of six companies. The agreements were secured only by letters to the respective locals, acknowledging that hours, wages, and working conditions would remain in effect, or by memorandums kept by the parties. In October 1934, faced by representation election petitions from the Amalgamated in several large plants, the board attempted to work out an industrywide open shop recognition agreement.

On October 26, the Carnegie Co. agreed on behalf of itself and the industry (except Weirton Steel), to "negotiate with members of any organization, as such." It made it clear that the organization could bargain only in behalf of its own members and that "the company does not engage to make any term contracts; it will, however, hold an open mind upon this subject provided no demands are made for a closed shop agreement." It also agreed that signing such a contract would not prejudice the Amalgamated's majority representation principle, and recognized the board's jurisdiction to the extent of its powers under congressional and Presidential authority.

This wording was a long step from the companies' two previous offers made in August and mid-October. The first had not contained the vital promise to bargain with the union as an organization. The second offer had, but the union rejected the offer because there was no commitment to hold a representation election. Thereupon, the company on November 3 removed the equivocal language concerning the Steel Labor Board and recognized it "as the tribunal in the first instance to hear and adjust complaints * * * which cannot otherwise be adjusted." In return it asked for "a truce in the general labor situation during the life of the NIRA."

A week later, a fifth company offer was submitted which omitted the previous refusal to sign a term contract. The union, on November 14, then submitted a counterproposal calling for a board-conducted representation election, with sole bargaining rights to the winner, and board decisions on unsettled noneconomic grievances to be final and binding.

The sixth company proposal, on December 4, recognized the board's binding arbitral rights (but reserved "legal rights" of both parties)

[20] Ibid., pp. 1040–46.

and included a firm contract to June 16, 1935, or during "the present life of NIRA." It also agreed to bargain on wages. In return, it asked the Amalgamated to forego election petitions, without prejudice to its majority rule principle. Although the union again turned the offer down, the board thought the parties were close enough to meet face-to-face at the White House, and such a conference was arranged for December 18. A final company draft was submitted. It dropped the "legal rights" reservation in regard to board decisions while asking the union to hold election requests in abeyance. Despite the repeated company concessions, the union stood stubbornly firm on the winner-take-all election, and on this issue the negotiations were broken off.

The foregoing bit of history is important for several reasons.

1. The companies' desire for labor peace was intense enough to be paid for with union recognition, a term contract, and government intervention.

2. The companies indicated willingness for an industrywide agreement.

3. The companies, although they foreclosed an election to widen the bargaining unit, offered the Amalgamated almost everything United States Steel gave John L. Lewis in its contract with SWOC 18 months later, plus industrywide bargaining.

4. The Amalgamated (and the AFL) by its tenacity over the majority rule vote waived an opportunity not only to rehabilitate the badly eroded foundations of its existence but to change the entire development of unionism in the industry.

Enter SWOC

As it was, its fateful decision created a situation in which steel labor was ripe for the confidence which the resonant oratory and almost mythological personality of John L. Lewis inspired. It was a labor force ripe but wary. One worker had expressed these sentiments, considered by Daugherty as typical of the "northern native white workers above 40 years of age":

Most of the men would join an outside union right now if the right one came along * * * a union with low dues and with real leaders who would give us a lot of say about local affairs and who would be at least as interested in us as in holding office. Till such a union turns up, a lot of the men are going to hold back and a lot are going to wait and see what they can get out of these company unions.[21]

As noted in the next section, the SWOC campaign, although well-financed and well-run, was not overly successful. All the more sur-

---
[21] Daugherty, p. 937.

prising, then, was the announcement that, as a result of private conversations between John L. Lewis and Myron Taylor, chairman of the board of U. S. Steel, an agreement had been signed on March 2, 1937.[22]

In retrospect, it is relatively easy to enumerate many of the reasons why the citadel of the open shop surrendered to "outside" unionism:

1. Production and profits, after years of depression, were favorable and there was an excellent chance for the corporation to improve its competitive position. This opportunity was enhanced by the prospect of substantial British orders anticipatory of war production.

2. The political climate favored the union. The Wagner Act had been passed and was operative. The La Follette committee hearings had created a public opinion condemnatory of steel company personnel practices. The New Deal program had been enthusiastically reaffirmed by the presidential electon of 1936. In many State administrations—notably Pennsylvania—there were governors friendly to the CIO. (In Pennsylvania, Thomas Kennedy, Lieutenant Governor, was also vice president of the United Mine Workers; Governor Earle had proclaimed the right of the SWOC to hold meetings with the protection of the police power of the State.) Charges of illegal support of the ERP had been made to the National Labor Relations Board against Carnegie-Illinois by the SWOC.

3. Within the industry, the SWOC had manipulated the ERP's to the point of unreliability or collapse—in some instances to a state where management preferred the stability of established unionism and responsible leadership. (U.S. Steel had already experienced John L. Lewis' union leadership in the captive coal mines.) Success on the part of the United Automobile Workers Union, another CIO organization, in its strike against the General Motors Corp., was doubtless an example which gave the industry considerable food for thought.

4. There is credibility to the speculation that Myron Taylor, board chairman of U.S. Steel, with a business background outside the steel industry, was less imbued with antagonisms toward union recognition than some of his colleagues and predecessors.

By virtue of NLRB elections the union won exclusive bargaining rights in a few companies (e.g., Jones and Laughlin, Sharon, and Pittsburgh Steel), but the sequel to the Carnegie-Illinois contract was

---

[22] Details of the contract and further rationalization of the corporation's action are to be found in appendix A.

on balance not a happy experience for SWOC. The "Little Steel" companies (Republic, Youngstown Sheet and Tube, Inland, Bethlehem, and National) resisted a signed agreement, and ensuing strikes beginning in May 1937 failed.[23] But for the renewal of the U.S. Steel contracts in 1938, the successful resistance of the Little Steel companies could have proved disastrous for the union. The strikes were ill-timed: public support of the CIO had weakened; an economic recession was in the making; and Little Steel, on principle, was determined to refuse SWOC signed agreements until legally required to do so. Indeed, it was not until 1942, and then with Government help (through the War Labor Board) and the added stimulus of wartime exigencies, that signed agreements were achieved.

Creating New Attitudes

It is emphasized by Brooks that 36 years of antiunionism by a corporation cannot be wiped out overnight.[24] Steel companies are vast and sprawling enterprises, and translation of top corporate policy through the various layers of the corporate hierarchy to ultimate supervision resulted in the loss of much of what was intended at the top to be the companies' attitude in direct dealing with the union at the lower levels. He contends that there was no uniform labor policy, a shortcoming which "is not the consequence of bad faith on the part of the large corporations * * *. It is the result of the absence of a uniform policy, thoroughly understood, thoroughly accepted, and thoroughly enforced from top to bottom."[25] Such failure of communication could only result in chaotic and irresponsible contract administration.

Another contemporary observer, who at that time was the union's research director, speculates on the role of the foreman: "For years the absolute ruler in his department, [he] is now subject to the scrutiny of the workers [who have been] denied * * * the right to question an act of their foreman." The workers now "confer with him on an equal footing and appeal to his superiors if he does not give them satisfaction."[26] Thus the foreman too must adjust himself to the new ways of collective bargaining. Managerial status was suddenly placed in jeopardy. It has been succinctly stated that "the sharing of authority with the union becomes * * * to a degree, a de-

---

[23] Details of these strikes are to be found in appendix A. National Steel was never struck and only one plant of Bethlehem was closed. The Inland case was resolved by a company letter to the Governor of Indiana in which Inland agreed to compulsory arbitration of unsettled grievances and unilaterally accepted what was tantamount to the contract terms of SWOC in agreements signed with other companies.

[24] Brooks, op. cit., p. 194.

[25] Ibid., p. 195.

[26] Harold J. Ruttenberg, "The Strategy of Industrial Peace," *Harvard Business Review*, Winter, 1939, p. 164.

fense of personal prestige and status. It is this which explains in good part the emotional tirades, the small quarrels, the points of pride on which settlement efforts collapse and long strikes are precipitated." [27]

Changing Attitudes

The edgy wariness and suspicion which characterized the relationship of the parties between 1937 and 1940 was at least partially dispelled by the control over industrial relations exercised by the War Labor Board. But this was an enforced change and by itself probably not sufficient to effect a genuine shift in attitude on the part of either the union or the major companies. They were by force of circumstance brought together as litigants under the discipline of a quasi-judicial body. Mutual recognition and imposed orders were not substitutes for mutual acceptance and negotiated settlements freely arrived at through bargaining and accommodation.

There were other forceful factors, however, which tended to melt any frozen attitudes between company and union. Force of circumstance also threw them together for joint war work on production and manpower problems in an atmosphere more conducive to respect, trust, and appreciation of each other's institutional roles. And, of course, there was the rapid growth of union power itself.

To the extent that the public utterances of John A. Stephens, former vice president for industrial relations at U.S. Steel, bespeak company policy on labor matters over the years, they can be considered indicative of the development of that policy.[28] It is of at least passing interest that not until 1942 did his public addresses on industrial relations subjects allude to unions; there was no specific mention of the United Steelworkers of America until 1943.

In that year Stephens told the Conference on Manpower Stabilization, in New York, that management had an obligation to accept the realities of the day and make the best of the situation, because "when employees as in U.S. Steel have indicated by substantial majorities a union preference, there is incumbent on management the responsibility of making the union relationship as responsible, agreeable, and constructive as is possible, without deviation from sound principles or compromise with what is right. It is, of course, essential that principles not be confused with prejudices." [29]

A year and a half later, before the Bishops' Conference on Capital and Labor, in Washington, with acceptance of unionism taken for

---

[27] Harold L. Enarson, *Fact-finding as a Technique for Settlement of National Emergency Disputes*, 1951, unpublished doctoral dissertation, p. 21.

[28] John A. Stephens, *Speeches Before Groups Outside the United States Steel Corp.*, Vol. I, January 1938–August 1949. U.S. Steel Corp.

[29] Stephens, p. 84.

granted, he began surveying the boundaries of responsibilities and prerogatives. Having attained stature, he said, labor should develop responsible leadership and "adult judgment,"[30] He decried labor's bargaining encroachment on what should be legislative action in broad social fields. Labor might harken well to the retribution meted out to management for "overbearing" attitudes. Self-restraint would be the wiser course.[31]

After the 1946 strike, in a talk to the Industrial Training Directors Association, in Cleveland, Stephens spoke almost musingly of the need in his own company for a mutuality of interest. This was anticipatory of the 1947 "era of good feeling contract." He admonished, however, against union demands generated by interunion rivalries. "Many leaders of labor may today run well ahead of rank and file members in formulating demands."[32]

There was a strong suggestion, in a speech to the American Management Association, in New York, that the 1947 agreement reflected the willingness of U.S. Steel to pay a substantial price for good will and the mutuality of interests referred to during the previous year. "United States Steel approached the recent negotiations hoping to find a way to peaceful conclusions. We were convinced that after years of war and Government control, there was need to demonstrate that the interests of Management and Labor could be reconciled with regard for their respective rights and privileges."[33] He contended that the company considered alternate courses of action in terms of what would best serve the broader interests of the economy—extension of the contract without change, or a wage increase. The corporation evaluated the possibilities, and weighing the union's probable reaction to no change in the light of "improved profits and higher living costs," concluded that a strike should be avoided. "Reasoned judgment permitted no other conclusion. * * *

"Prior to and during the negotiations we realized, whether rightly or wrongly, that we were burdened with a responsibility broader than to United States Steel alone. We considered that * * * our negotiations might to some degree influence the framework within which private enterprise and unionism might operate in the future * * * that our results might influence the economy for some unpredictable period. * * *"[34]

Stephens in this talk gave ungrudging praise to the union, which, in terms of the times, "has been one of the better labor unions * * *

---

[30] Stephens, p. 112.
[31] Ibid., p. 113.
[32] Ibid., p. 125.
[33] Ibid., p. 134.
[34] Ibid., p. 135.

[whose] officers believe that agreements made are agreements to be observed. * * * We think we see a union increasingly concerned with removal of basic causes of difficulties in the administration of labor agreements. And * * * we have progressively seen in reasonably clear perspective, some of those things which we must do to aid in building responsible unionism and better labor-management relations. We have seen also some things we should do cooperatively with the union." [35] He tempered this encomium by a general recommendation for legislative "regulation of union power and competitive tactics." He thought that unions had grown "under political and competitive influences not conducive to temperate progress * * * [and that] it is not too surprising that opportunism has too often dictated action * * * [and] discipline sometimes begets opposition. Disgruntled members are fair and easy prey for raiding competitors." [36]

Significantly, he conceded that union survival is dependent on union security, but he regarded maintenance of membership (which the union had achieved via War Labor Board order in 1942) as an improper device for union security. The Corporation continued the security clause in the 1947 agreement to prevent the union from interpreting denial of it as "a desire to destroy it [the union]." The issue of individual freedom was basically involved in compulsory membership, and thus became a matter which should be solved by legislation. [37]

In summary, the position of U.S. Steel at the end of 1947, taking Stephen's public speeches as reasonably representative of management attitude, was as follows: determination to get along with the union, to cooperate with it, to go to considerable lengths to avoid strikes. At the same time it expressed apprehension over the competitive features of unionism which tended to beget demand born of political necessity. It also was fearful of its responsibility to the country at large because of the pervasive effect of its wage settlements on other steel companies and other industries.

Speaking to the Philadelphia Chamber of Commerce in 1948, Stephens concluded that labor itself "quite realistically, will admit that a politically governed movement cannot conduct its affairs as if it were a commercial venture." This fact makes negotiations difficult because the desirable end-point "should be a labor agreement which will stabilize the relations of the parties thereto for a period of time." He wished that the union would "abandon * * * the studied whipping up of attitudes among its membership. But I don't expect that they

---

[35] Stephens, p. 136.
[36] Ibid., p. 136.
[37] Ibid., p. 140.

can, or will, in periods of high, profitable business activity or competitive unionism." [38]

He hammered repeatedly on the theme of the political nature of unionism. In the fall of 1948, before the Boston Chamber of Commerce, he decried the shirking of leadership responsibility in the disciplinary and grievance-processing fields, calling this nonfeasance "a major obstacle to wholehearted employer-employee acceptance and cooperation." [39] He limited his concept of union responsibility, in a talk at Williamsburg, Va., to "union responsibility in making, administering, and observing * * * agreements; responsibility toward the fullest development of the country's production enterprises, and responsibility for constructive, cooperative effort toward solution of our problems in a way calculated to preserve private enterprise, a prosperous economy, and democratic freedoms." [40] All this, he thought, was embodied in Section I of the contract, and what it meant was that the company accepted the union, the union needn't feel obliged to beat the company image to "keep safe from attack by management * * *." [41]

Perhaps his thoughts on this score were adumbrations of the collapse of the vaunted "statement of attitudes" section of the 1947 contract. His fond hopes for mutuality of interests foundered in the bitterness of the 1948 wage settlement and the 1949 strike.

Certainly disillusionment had set in before the 1949 strike, which took place in the fall of that year. In an address to the Advanced Management and Trade Union Groups at Harvard, in April 1949, he suggested that the public attacks by the union against the industry led to a reappraisal of U.S. Steel's position on cooperative relationships. Perhaps the position and hope for its workability had been "naive." [42] He pointed to polemics by union spokesmen against the industry on the very issues which had been the basis for cooperation and joint action. "All in all [the attack] leads me to the conclusion at this time that if there is to be success in the cooperative route * * * there must, as a condition precedent, occur a resolution within the union circles of the question whether the trade union is to be just that or * * * emerge * * * purely as a political force. * * *" [43]

The Current Position

There is little doubt that the hard feelings engendered by the 1948 refusal of the industry to grant a wage increase (the contract prohibited a strike over wages) and the strike over pensions in 1949 (the

---

[38] Stephens, p. 152.
[39] Ibid., p. 164.
[40] Ibid., p. 168.
[41] Ibid., p. 183.
[42] Ibid., p. 182.
[43] Ibid., p. 183.

industry claimed pensions could not be an issue under terms of the contract) had a marked influence on the attitudes of the parties. The situation lent support to the observation made at the first of the quarterly meetings that men were sentient human beings, "delicately adjusted," and that mutual objectives could not thrive in an atmosphere "of bullying and brow-beating." Hardened positions on the union shop became crucial in the 1952 strike. The industry resisted on principle. As explained in 1955, by Stephens, U.S. Steel was "pleased to have employees join the Steelworkers' Union," but the corporation wanted to protect the individual employee's "right to decide. * * *" [44] However, the industry did grant a modified union shop in 1956, as part of the strike settlement. The gradual development of union security is discussed in detail in chapter 7.

It was during the early fifties that U.S. Steel became restive over the constraints of the 2B clause in the contract. Stephens, in an appearance before the Senate Banking and Currency Committee in April 1952, complained that "certain provisions called 'local working conditions' were being abused by the union in the grievance and arbitration procedures." [45] The company's attempt to make changes in the local work practice provisions of the agreement was hampered, he testified, because the union made discussion of changes conditional on its wage demands.

The local work practice issue was a serious one with U.S. Steel, and the corporation had gone so far as to offer the following in payment for relief from the local work practices clauses: "* * * [to make] every effort to see to it that [men displaced by crew size reductions] are given other work of their choosing; [to preserve] their wage rate through a training period if no opportunity is open to them * * * so they may pick up again and have equally as good an opportunity for the future. We want the right to be competitive * * * to progress through change. * * * We are perfectly willing * * * to let the arbitrator determine whether anybody has been wronged, whether [the change instituted] has been reasonably exercised as a reasonable responsibility of management. * * *" [46] The union, of course, wanted such opportunities extended to employees technologically displaced as well as to those released through a relaxation of 2B.

Despite the 1949 and 1952 strikes and some cooling of the relationship between the parties, the labor policy of U.S. Steel (as of the industry as a whole) was still one of accommodation. There was an unprecedented visit by Stephens and officials of Bethlehem and Jones

---

[44] Stephens, Vol. II, p. 445.
[45] Ibid., p. 379.
[46] Ibid., pp. 395-6.

and Laughlin to the union's Wage Policy Committee, near the end of the 1952 strike, to explain the industry's last offer in negotiations; there was agreement between Murray and Fairless to renew the quarterly meetings; and there was a projected arrangement for a joint tour of plants by the two leaders. All of these manifestations of good will were more than surface gestures. Unfortunately, the death of Murray in late 1952 precluded immediate fulfillment of the joint tour plans, and the quarterly meetings foundered. But the plant visits, ultimately made by McDonald and Fairless, were designed, in Stephens' words, spoken in 1955, "to put to rest one basic influence against better relations—a belief among union officials, employees, and, to a degree, supervision, that U.S. Steel had never fully accepted the union and should a propitious time arrive, would seek its destruction." [47]

By 1958 a change had taken place in the entire mood of the parties' relationship, which by the terminal date of the 1959 strike had developed into one of hostility. Interestingly, the basic industry policy determinants appeared to be the same in 1959 as in 1952. Then, the industry had pressed for regaining lost management prerogatives, revision of Section 2B, an overhauling of incentive rates and crew sizes. Stephens had even enunciated in 1953 the belief that so incensed the union when reiterated in 1960: that the industry had a responsibility to communicate with its employees, apart from the industry's relationship to the union—that labor-management relations operated in two dimensions:

> We do not "believe that the fact of the union lessens the need for management leadership. * * * To the contrary, we believe that * * * a union relationship enhances the need to work patiently and in all proper ways with individuals. * * * Such a course, we believe, does not involve a contest for loyalties with the union as an institution. * * * We believe that the motivations and policies of the union aggregate should spring from an informed membership which places a high degree of trust in management. * * * Whether or not we succeed, logic * * * requires that we continue to try. * * *" [48]

Comparison of this statement, made shortly after the 1952 strike, with those of Conrad Cooper and William G. Caples, vice presidents of U.S. Steel and Inland Steel, respectively, reveals little significant difference in content. Yet the earlier talk did not evoke the disturbed union reaction that followed the speeches given a half dozen years later.

[47] Stephens, p. 449.
[48] Ibid., pp. 435–6.

By 1958, both conditions and individuals had changed. The guidelines for determination of industry policy had in considerable measure passed to other hands. The strength of the forces underlying postwar expansion could no longer be taken for granted. Investment programs in steel, previously undertaken with confidence, had produced an increasing gap between production and capacity. Steel had been unable to match in 1956 and 1957 its production record of 1955, and the 1958 recession decline was serious. Management attitudes became more determined as a result of these changes.

The industry is worried about its right to manage and the abridgment of that right as a deterrent to cost cutting. It feels, as Thomas F. Patton, president of Republic Steel, put it, that this right will "come under even heavier attack." [49] Moreover, it feels that it failed to make any progress in communicating its fears and needs to its employees through the union leadership. Now it wants to try a direct approach. This is not ipso facto an antiunion move. The companies are concerned about the gulf between management and workers in relation to industry problems. And they are concerned about the worries of their employees, according to Patton:

> The unseen rabble rouser in the 1959 crisis was fear: fear of layoffs, the speedup, the loss of seniority, the loss of dignity and personal freedom * * *
>
> We found that we were dealing with the fear of the company itself—that same company that provided their jobs in the first place * * *
>
> * * * Only when men understand the reason behind the company policies are they likely to support those policies, instead of blindly following the union line. [50]

The key word, of course, is "blindly."

Cooper's enunciation of policy on management rights and management's relation to the work force in regard to industry problems and employee personal work problems is likewise not subversive of union rights or unmindful of the union's function:

> It is a matter of people and their attitudes—the degree of respect they hold for one another * * * their willingness to recognize that one man's * * * aspirations cannot be isolated from * * * the industry of which he is a part.
>
> And believing this, I am equally certain that the entire problem of wasteful practices is a job that must be tackled both by the

---

[49] *Communication Countdown*, Proceeding of the Joint Session of the Industrial Relations Committee and Public Relations Committee of the American Iron and Steel Institute, New York, May 1960, p. 47.

[50] Ibid., p. 50.

companies *and the union.* * * * It is a job that must be [correctly] done * * * lest the wheels of competitive misfortune spin us beyond the point of no return [emphasis supplied]. It is a question which must be answered to provide real job security for the steel workers.

Clearly this is not a job that can be done amidst conflict and strife and sterile argument about management's rights. The need is for recognition and discharge of obligations.

Being obligated to employees and the stockholders, management cannot pass that obligation on to the union leaders or anyone else. Faulty contract language which stands in the way of management's ability to discharge its obligation is not in the interest of the employees or anyone else. We live in the hope that our union friends will come to recognize this basic truth.[51]

The union too faces serious problems in relation to membership and the disemployment of members, and each side complains that the other does not even care to understand either the seriousness or the nature of the problems. Each has reached a point close to frustration and despair. Hence, from the viewpoint of change over the short run, industry labor policy appears to the union to have become antiunion. An evaluation of the industry's labor policy indicates, however, that even those points which the union considers abhorrent are pursued by the industry on the assumption that the union will remain the strong and the chosen agent of its employees.

As noted in chapter 1, progress in collective bargaining in the United States over the last 25 years has been considerable. Particularly clear has been the growth of orderly day-to-day relations under increasingly constant contract language and interpretation. In recent years collective bargaining has been in a process of readjustment to a more competitive environment with elements of increased employee insecurity. It is too soon to attempt any appraisal of results. Temporarily, conflict has been intensified. Steel is participating in this change. But viewed over a span of 60 years, the change in the industry's labor policy has been revolutionary indeed, and the pessimism over the future which is currently prevalent can appropriately be tempered by the viewpoint of that perspective.

[51] *Management's Obligation to Manage,* an address by Conrad Cooper before the Canadian Manufacturers Association, Toronto, June 6, 1960.

CHAPTER 5

DEVELOPMENT OF THE UNITED STEEL-WORKERS OF AMERICA

Antecedents

Unionism of a sort in steel is more than a century old. The oldest steel union on record, with the classical name of Sons of Vulcan, was secretly formed of puddlers in 1858. In 1876, it formed the most powerful unit in the merger of the United Nailers, the National Union, Iron and Steel Roll Hands of the United States, and the Association Brotherhood, Iron and Steel Heaters, Rollers, and Roughers of the United States. The new organization was ultimately called the Amalgamated Association of Iron, Steel, and Tin Workers of North America. Peak membership was 24,000 in 1891. Three factors inhibited its growth. Membership was restricted to specific skills, and the constituent organizations never fully appreciated the occupational shifts which were taking place with the advent of steel manufacture. Disastrous strikes in 1892 (Homestead) and 1901 (U.S. Steel) left a permanent weakness. Irresponsible contract administration and bad judgment in gauging the significance of employers' offers and resistance power led to poor relationships and lost opportunities at critical stages of the union's history. The union became so ineffectual that during the AFL's general organizing drive and strike of 1919–20 it somewhat petulantly played a minor and largely ignored role.

The genesis of the United Steelworkers of America took place amidst the despair and turbulence and mass unemployment of the 1930's, and was nurtured by the New Deal counterdepression measures. It was not a product of Government action, however, but rather a powerful effort within the American labor movement to organize mass production workers into industrial unions. The impulse for this effort reflected the mood of the workers themselves. Government policy, through Section 7a of the National Industrial Recovery Act (NIRA), had encouraged this mood, but the real impetus came from the dynamic and imaginative drive of the Committee for Industrial Organization, led by John L. Lewis. The CIO was also active and successful in automobiles, oil, rubber, flat glass, electrical equipment, shipbuilding, and nonferrous metals.

The present Steelworkers Union, although it in 1942 formally absorbed the old Amalgamated (along with its debts), bears no resemblance in form, attitudes, or influence to its predecessors of the 19th century. It was formed in 1936 as an integral part of a nationwide

73

multi-industry drive for industrial unionism, which meant that for the first time unskilled labor was admitted to affiliation on an equal basis. It resulted from a more militant, astute, and carefully planned campaign than had been attempted previously. And it proved to be enduringly successful. These characteristics can be traced to seasoned leadership. Behind the efforts of the CIO were the brains, experience, and material resources of some of the most successful and established trade union leaders in America.

The 1935–37 Campaign

John L. Lewis and his associates in the United Mine Workers of America (notable among whom were Philip Murray, vice president of the union; Thomas J. Kennedy, secretary-treasurer; Van A. Bittner, John Brophy; P. T. Fagan, Ora Gassaway, David J. McDonald, and William Mitch) dominated the organizational drive in steel. Lewis' motives were frankly expressed on more than one occasion. The fate of unionism in the captive coal mines of U. S. Steel depended in large part on a supporting organization in basic steel.

The AFL's will to organize steel in this period was weakened, as it had been in earlier periods, by craft jealousies and a general fear that potentially powerful international unions or even a group of independently charted Federal locals within mass production industries could end craft dominance of the AFL. There was much discussion in the AFL throughout 1935 and the first half of 1936 anent organizing steel, but each proposal foundered on self-serving objections.

Lewis knew full well that the exigencies of the situation as well as the temper of the men required on all-inclusive organizational structure. Early in 1936, he offered to contribute, on behalf of the Mine Workers, one-third of an AFL organizing fund of $1.5 million, if the drive were headed by vigorous and sophisticated leadership and if the resulting union were industrial in character. The offer was not accepted. Lewis thereupon began to deal directly with the Amalgamated in the name of the CIO. The upshot was that the Steel Workers' Organizing Committee (SWOC), which included Amalgamated representatives, was formed by the CIO.[1] The date was June 4, 1936. The first meeting was held 13 days later.

---

[1] Until the United Steelworkers was formed in 1942, the SWOC maintained the fiction of recognizing the "jurisdiction" of the AAISTW, by issuing charters in its name. The agreement with the Amalgamated called for such an arrangement. At the time of signing the agreement, all parties were still bona fide AFL constituents, and the Amalgamated held the AFL charter for steel. There was, in fact, a dual set-up. The Amalgamated retained its identity, and technically all new members became its members. But SWOC had exclusive right to direct the drive and to control revenues. The first contract between U.S. Steel and SWOC refers to the latter as agent for the Amalgamated. Mention of the relationship continued in subsequent contracts until 1941. Final dissolution of the

Lewis saw to it that the SWOC, whose success was crucial to the accomplishment of CIO objectives, received the best he could offer in talent and financing. From his own Mine Workers he appointed Philip Murray and David J. McDonald as the two officers (president and secretary-treasurer) along with Van A. Bittner, John Brophy, and Patrick T. Fagan; the Amalgamated Clothing Workers gave Leo Krzycki; the International Ladies' Garment Workers, Julius Hochman; and, pro forma, Michael F. Tighe and Joseph K. Gaither of the Amalgamated Association were also included. A "line of credit" of a half million dollars was established for the committee by the UMW.

It was fortunate for the new group's future that it was thus endowed because, while the opportunity was propitious, the situation it faced was complicated and the opposition formidable. The events which transpired were indeed, as one student of the period put it, "the stuff of America's labor history."[2]

Steel labor and steel labor relations, as SWOC found them, were in ferment. The labor and Code provisions of the NIRA, the existence of Employee Representation Plans, factional fights within the Amalgamated, genuine grievances over working conditions, the contagious countrywide push of labor for unionization, and overall the spectre of the CIO—all contributed to this.

Several deterents to organization faced the SWOC at the outset of its maiden venture in 1936:

(1) The history of unsuccessful prior efforts to organize and the determination of the industry to fight off the new effort.

(2) The conscious practice of the industry in or near large cities of ethnic "mixing" of the labor force as a basis for hiring, with the practical effect of keeping the workers divided.

(3) The "cordon sanitaire" thrown up by the companies through the use of labor espionage and exchange of employment information.

(4) The welfare plans.

(5) The lack of experienced local union leadership.

Among the advantages favoring the SWOC in overcoming these handicaps were:

(1) The working conditions prevailing in much of the industry—accident-producing hazards, extremes of temperature, and tiring working hours.

Amalgamated was voted by that organization as of June 30, 1942, and formal absorption by the Steelworkers of Amalgamated locals were ordered consummated by July 15 of that year.

[2] Robert Spencer, *Bargaining with the Government; A Case Study in the Politics of Collective Bargaining in the Basic Steel Industry, Unpublished doctoral dissertation*, University of Chicago ,June 1955, p. 8.

(2) The personnel practices which aroused resentment—petty graft and favoritism in hiring and layoffs; lack of training opportunity and seniority consideration for promotion and transfer; low take-home pay occasioned by deductions for such items as sick benefits, housing, and fuel, work clothing and other company-store purchases; frustrated efforts to check tonnage and piece rate computations.

(3) The ferment in the ERP's, reflecting the general movement of workers throughout the country to organize and to press for wage increases and a redressing of grievances.

(4) The presence of a friendly National Government and an especially friendly State Government in Pennsylvania.

(5) The willingness of the United Mine Workers to supply funds and leadership.

(6) The nonrestrictive basis for membership and the waiving of initiation fees.

The SWOC campaign has been characterized as "one of the best managed organization drives in American trade union history."[3] It was aggressive, imaginative, and fast-moving.

The strategy of the union was to utilize the ERP's as a bridge to the men and to win over its leadership. Tactically, through sympathizers in the ERP's, it harassed management at every opportunity by exploiting the grievance procedure, insisting on verbatim reports of ERP meetings for later propaganda campaigns, enlarging and controlling key committees; and forcing through wage and hour demands. In short, the plan was to cajole, needle, shame, and, if necessary, buy action from the ERP's, taking credit for successes and pointing to the need for the SWOC when efforts failed. Generally, management was kept on the defensive.

When enough control of plant ERP's had been obtained, the SWOC moved to coordinate them through companywide and areawide committees. When, for example, the company refused travel funds for the Carnegie-Illinois ERP executive committee's trip to attend a meeting of a central committee (whose existence did not have the company's blessing), the SWOC offered to furnish the funds. Finally forced into accepting the idea of central committees, management supported a plan for them, but in the Pittsburgh-Youngstown area promptly lost control of it to SWOC-oriented forces in one skirmish of what was almost an internecine struggle between SWOC and anti-SWOC factions in the ERP's.

---

[3] Harbison, *Collective Bargaining in the Steel Industry*, op. cit., p. 3.

Exit ERP

By October 1936, both the SWOC-controlled and company-inclined ERP's of Carnegie-Illinois in the Pittsburgh and Great Lakes regions had submitted formal demands for a 62½ cents-an-hour rate for common labor and an $1.12 a day increase for all other classes. Management was on the defensive, attempting to quiet the ferment in the ERP's, forestall and minimize a wage increase, and overcome the basic handicap (of which SWOC was fully cognizant) created by the task of conveying a new policy to lower levels of management, especially foremen, in matters of workaday plant problems and grievances.

Following the election of that year, U. S. Steel, upon action of its board of directors, offered an average 10 percent increase, to be written into 1-year agreements with the ERP's of all subsidiaries, with wage rates tied to an escalator formula. Many company unions, including the just-organized Pittsburgh Council, rejected the proposal.

The SWOC had seized upon the wage offer and ridiculed it as a gesture designed to take the edge off the union drive. It also assailed the escalator clause as a device to freeze inadequate living standards. In the face of such opposition and despite pressure to obtain ERP signatures on an agreement, the corporation in many cases was forced to establish the new rates unilaterally.

Keeping on the offensive, the SWOC then decided it had squeezed the maximum advantage from the ERP infiltration. Its control of representatives had reached a claimed 1,534 out of 2,500 and its own membership was a modest 82,000. The new strategy was to go after the ERP's and destroy them. In pursuance of this aim, the SWOC, late in 1936, instituted charges against Carnegie-Illinois with the National Labor Relations Board on the ground that its ERP was illegally dominated by the company.

The Hardship of Success

Yet success was not completely self-generating and automatic for SWOC, despite obvious ancillary effects of the contract with U.S. Steel and despite the U.S. Supreme Court decision upholding the constitutionality of the Wagner Act, both of which events combined to administer the coup de grace to ERP's. Reliance upon direct membership solicitation, even with no initiation fees and a lax attitude toward the $1 a month dues, brought considerable less than sensational results.

The failure in connection with Little Steel, noted in chapter 4, put the union on the defensive for the first time, and the rather loose organizational structure within which it had operated revealed some gaping fissures. Although by mid-1937 SWOC had contracts with companies employing about half the production workers in the industry and real earnings were at an alltime high, these achievements were somewhat in advance of actual organizational accomplishments. There probably were by no means dues-paying members commensurate with contract coverage. Galenson points out that as late as November 1940 the SWOC, although covering 600,000 workers by agreements, had only 250,000 dues-paying members.[4]

Early Influences

Because of the loose organizational structure and the inexperience of the local lodge officials, the early bargaining relationship was frequently a tenuous affair—somewhat in the nature of a holding action by the calmer, more experienced higher officials against the more precipitous local leadership made eager by a newly won freedom and a newly discovered status.

To understand the early structure of the SWOC, the dichotomy between the top leadership and the membership should be explained. The SWOC was not an autonomous, member-controlled union. Its affairs were shepherded by the United Mine Workers of America who furnished the greater part of its finances and staff, and the imprint of the miners was discernible in its early leadership, attitudes, and tactics. There was a tight control from the top which took the form of a benevolent autocracy. Dues were collected locally and sent in to the national headquarters, with 25 percent then remitted to local lodges. No formal, representative convention was held during the first 18 months the SWOC operated. When, in December 1937, a convention was held, it was a "wage and policy" convention at which discussion of plans for a permanent organization was not on the agenda. The constitutional convention was not held until 1942. (As a matter of fact it was in 1946—11 years after SWOC was first established and 10 years after its first contract with U.S. Steel—that a steelworker was first elected as an international officer.)

Tight control by Murray and the Mine Workers at that time was a manifestation of more than the desire to keep a controlling hand on the "property" to protect the "investment." There was a deep concern over the inexperience at the local level and the ability of the new local leadership to handle its authority and its obligations in contract administration. Murray realized full well that the road to contract renewal was paved with a solid reputation for responsibility—and the precarious situation in which SWOC found itself after its early success demanded contract renewal. It was natural then, given the

---

[4] Walter Galenson, The CIO Challenge to the AFL, Harvard University Press, 1960, p. 113. Brooks in As Steel Goes, op. cit., p. 162, contends that between 1937 and 1939, the largest dues collection in any month showed paid-up membership equal to only half of those who had signed membership cards.

almost exclusive UMW leadership above the local level,[5] and the UMW reputation for disciplined adherence to contract terms, for Murray to create a new union in the mine workers' image. Moreover, he had before him the unfolding drama of near destruction visited upon the United Automobile Workers by factional fighting for control of leadership and by irresponsibility in contractual relationships.

During the 1950 convention of the union, Murray, in meeting the complaint of some delegates over local autonomy in contract approval, made this revealing statement: "We don't do as a lot of organizations do * * * with respect to the collective bargaining processes. The policy of the Steelworker's Union * * * is the policy of the United Mine Workers * * * I happen to be one of those who assisted in that organization's policy for * * * 28 or 30 years and the mine workers never raised objections to the policy because they found out in the end that they were able to get more out of it." [6]

Was the tight control exercised by Murray and his United Mine Workers associates warranted by the situation in SWOC? A realistic appraisal would conclude that it was. The finances of the organization, from the point of view of self-support, were shaky and mainly reliant on the largesse of the UMW.[7] Membership in a disciplined dues-paying sense was very weak and the power situation often varied from plant to plant within a given company (union security in any form was not to come until 1942, when the War Labor Board ordered maintenance of membership, and a modified union shop not until 1956). By late 1937, the CIO as a whole had lost much of the early magic spell its initials had conjured up. SWOC was at that time anything but all-powerful and invincible. Most of the rank and file lacked experience and faced the double jeopardy of an unskilled plant bargaining posture with management and a new-found political opportunity in its own internal relationships. Management attitudes did not help in this situation.

The union at the top made an honest and zealous effort to obey the contract and handle grievances intelligently. In furtherance of the latter effort, the union issued a handbook for shop stewards which Brooks terms "a model of union statesmanship." [8] Brooks also cites examples of union efforts in the early days to educate grievance com-

---

[5] Proceedings, Second Wage and Policy Convention, 1940, p. 28, revealed that two-thirds of the district directors were still being paid by the UMW as of May 1940.

[6] Proceedings of the Fifth Constitutional Convention of the United Steelworkers of America, 1950, p. 275.

[7] Murray at one point informed the organization: "Your union * * * is living to a very substantial degree on borrowed money." Later, on the same occasion, he said "The miners of this country have given that money, my friends * * *" (Proceedings, First Wage and Policy Convention, 1937, pp. 131–32.)

[8] Brooks, op. cit., p. 210.

mitteemen of local lodges to help management in improving efficiency.[9]
But the union leaders encountered some hostility from a rank and file
still smarting under its recollection of the old management image.
Workers' suspicions of management lingered for a long time after
formal union recognition and retarded real understanding between
the parties.   The barrier between them resulted from unfamiliarity.

A perceptive student of this period in the bargaining relationships
in steel makes this observation:

> In summary, the union considered its prewar gains in the steel industry as
> hardly more than letters of introduction to management, since the fact of
> recognition and negotiation in certain areas was scarcely acceptance of the
> principle of collective bargaining by the companies.   Actually, more progress
> * * * was reached with some smaller companies which were less able to resist
> the demands of the union and whose executives discovered that positive
> cooperation with the union was insurance against disunity within the plants,
> and for stable production in the future.   Management representatives of the
> large firms, schooled by generations of hostility toward unions, found them-
> selves faced with building new industrial relations departments and policies
> squaring with the facts of the SWOC's existence.   Likewise, inexperienced
> and over-militant local union officers were called upon to develop constructive
> patterns of dealing with the companies.
>
> Collective bargaining in America's steel industry was in its infancy on the
> eve of World War II.   Incompletely accepted or misunderstood by manage-
> ment, the union felt itself under assault and insecure, without means to
> stabilize its membership and assure itself of a regular financial status.[10]

Reasons enough, one must conclude, for Murray to be wary of full
autonomy and democracy.   "Our union is young," he said, "it is growing, and we must exercise care in the development of this child until it
reaches its maturity." [11]

A question for consideration, of course, is whether there were too
rigorous controls, too much suppression of rank and file sentiment, too
centralized authority for even the tenuous hold the union had on institutional security.   In short, was the "maturing" of Murray's "child"
retarded by parental apprehension and restraint?

Growing Pains

Steelworkers conventions were and are very large and somewhat
unwieldy delegate affairs with as many as 3,500 officially in attend-
ance.   Organization and chairmanship of such a constituent body is
extremely difficult.

Review of the eight conventions chaired by Philip Murray between
1937 and 1952 reveal a struggle between the national officers—who

---

[9] Ibid., pp. 213–15.
[10] Robert C. Spencer, *Bargaining with the Government: A Case Study in the Politics of
Collective Bargaining in the Basic Steel Industry,* 1955, unpublished doctoral dissertation,
University of Chicago, pp. 16–17.
[11] Proceedings, First Wage and Policy Convention, op. cit., p. 10.

keenly recognized the inner weaknesses of the union and its formidable external opposition—and the delegates from the locals. The latter were striving for local autonomy and a more democratic source of power. In all of this political counterpoint, there was never an intent to challenge Murray's position or authority in the union. He was venerated and his wishes respected. It is apparent from his approach to problems coming before conventions of the Steelworkers that he was aware of this special regard which he commanded, and he was not loathe to exploit it. Yet it is equally clear that many delegates were restive and disturbed over the tight reins by which they were led and that their adversative posture was responsive to rank and file pressure. The reiterated complaints voiced in the conventions were concerned with dues distribution, local approval of contracts, procedural limitations on resolutions, and national office control over local administration.

When the long-sought constitutional convention did come in 1942, Murray, in the face of strong sentiment for local election of organizers, threatened to resign, as he had over the issue of immediate independence at the Wage and Policy convention of 1940, if such a procedure were adopted. He stated unequivocally that the organization was not mature enough to carry the heady wine of democratic decisionmaking. It would be a mistake, he said, for the delegates to assume "that the functions of your organization have been so stabilized that we can run the gamut of every known kind of democratic procedure, even to the point of license in the operation of our affairs.

"I don't mind telling you * * * that your interest still needs some safeguarding in this man's country. My personal judgment is that your situations are not sufficiently well-stabilized [to elect] all your representatives. * * *

"I would not want to assume the hazards incident to directing * * * this mighty organization with a provision incorporated in the constitution requiring the election of all my field representatives * * * I am not kidding * * * I am not talking to you as a politician looking for a job. * * *" [12]

Murray, of course, was largely correct. But he did not, in rejecting the plea for elected organizers, face up to the considerable resentment which resided in the locals against international organizers and representatives in the field.[13] Nor did he meet the fears of delegates in regard to the perpetuation of a bureaucracy which potentially existed in the powers of the president authorized by Article IV of the constitution. In part Murray was attempting to keep the Communists

---

[12] 1942 Convention, pp. 219–33.
[13] The first constitution changed the designation of local units from lodges to locals.

out of places of influence in the districts. But the whole weight of his fellow officers' arguments—and they were numerous—against the election proposal was "Trust Murray." "Murray knows best." "Pass it because Phil wants it." These fears were not transitory. Four years later the convention received 55 separate resolutions which in some manner would restrict the power of the president.

Early convention debate brings to light more than a hint of dissatisfaction over real or assumed bypassing of local unions and faulty communication with the national office. Some of the instances, of course, resulted from inevitable foot-faults in big-organization operations. Others may have been more deliberate. There were frequent complaints of local agreements being negotiated or modified without knowledge of the local concerned.

One rule of convention procedure, in effect from the outset, had the clear intent of keeping delegates from amending reports and resolutions as reported out by administration-appointed committees: amendments or substitute resolutions from the floor were not permitted.

The constitution and the desire for changes in it was apparently an early source of agitation among members. At the 1946 convention there were 1,014 resolutions submitted for constitutional changes.[14] At the next convention there were more than 1,600.[15] The significant point was that in neither year was it deemed necessary to distribute in advance the recommendations of the Constitution Committee so that the delegates could study the changes the administration was willing to make. The purpose, apparently, was to prevent "unwise" amendments from sliding through the convention.

One aspect of central control which was especially galling to the membership and which was a source of controversy between the locals and the international officers from the beginning was the practice of having all dues money sent to the international office and a percentage (at first 25 percent) remitted to the locals. The convention delegates complained about the method and the size of the remission percentage.

In 1944 Murray after debate on the per capita remissions, which covered 11 pages in the proceedings, enjoined the delegates to "get this bellyache out of your system * * * quit this biennial 'beef' * * * let's stop this biennial practice of coming back into national conventions trying to tap the International till." [16]

As late as 1952 he castigated the delegates who were resisting his plea for a dues increase: "It may be that there are some people here who hesitate to vote for a dues increase * * * Well, those characters are just about as dangerous to this organization * * * as John

---

14 1946 Convention, p. 211.
15 1948 Convention, p. 231.
16 1944 Convention, pp. 250-60.

Stephens [chief U.S. Steel negotiator] is.   You can't play that sort of double game in this Union." [17]

The frequent Murray admonitions against the dangers of inexperienced leadership taking over became embodied in official policy at the first Wage and Policy Convention.   "We feel," the Scale Committee (which was also the Policy Committee) commented, "that we have been fortunate thus far in having been provided with the services of experienced and capable leaders by the Committee for Industrial Organization.   We are mindful of the fact that our organization has been built so rapidly in the past 18 months that there has not been sufficient opportunity for the development of leadership from within our own ranks * * *." [18]   The hostility of the industry was cited as a reason.

Yet the new auto union faced at least equally hostile management with green leadership from within its own ranks.   The two unions—steel and auto—present interestingly divergent institutional practices and policies, although both had their genesis in the same ebullient period.   Despite these historical divergencies, both unions have come out at about the same place in terms of achieving inter-union democracy, discipline, and influence in their respective industries.   But the UAW during its first decade was riven with the factional feuds of contending leadership blocs.   At times it was perilously close to a break-up.   Hence it might be fairly concluded that the Murray leadership welded the Steelworkers into stability and probably guided it to earlier and more complete acceptance by the industry than might have been the case had it followed the UAW path.

It is not to be implied that the early Murray policies solved the union's internal problems for all time or that they had no negative aspects.   The union sought and utilized an organizational form and method of operation which it believed best suited to the industrial situation in which it found itself at the time.   The union now has had 25 years in which to develop local and international leaders of experience in negotiation, contract administration, and union operation.   As noted in chapter 2, it has attained financial and membership security and has developed an able and diversified central-organization service staff.   Rank-and-file vitality remains strong enough to insure democratic procedures.   There is reason to believe that the coordinated talents of its elected officers and staff specialists are equal to the task of formulating the long-range plans necessary to accommodate the best interests of the membership to the multifold problems which will attend future collective bargaining.

[17] 1952 Convention, p. 305.
[18] 1937 Convention, p. 151.

CHAPTER 6

THE MODE OF BARGAINING

The Approach to Bargaining

Union demands, in theory, are formulated by an elected International Wage Policy Committee, a descendant of the old Scale Committee which itself was heritage from the Mine Workers. [1] In practice, according to union officers who currently or in the past have served on the committee, the WPC is a sounding board through which the union rank and file can voice their dislikes and desires in regard to contract demands. The real policymaking and negotiating power in the union resides in the international officers and in the International Executive Board. Most persons interviewed regarding the WPC, however, were certain that the committee has more authority currently than during the earlier years of the union and that its debates are more meaningful.

The actual bargaining sessions at which the terms of the basic contract are negotiated begin with an almost ritualistic formality. Scores of people from both sides participate. The union presents its demands—some specific, some in very general terms, with numerous officials and staff experts speaking. The meeting then adjourns while the companies study the proposals. On a stipulated date the parties reassemble to hear the companies' response to the demands. Ordinarily negotiations open formally 60 days prior to contract expiration, and the ceremonial aspects of the sessions consume a considerable amount of time. Gradually the size of the negotiating groups diminish to a few on each side—in the most recent negotiations the international officers and general counsel of the union and the industry committee of four.

In the past, during the Murray-Stephens era, there was a great deal of private and personal negotiating prior to and during the period of regular bargaining sessions, especially as negotiations were heated up under the pressure of approaching strike deadlines. Deals proposed and agreed to under such circumstances, of course, must be sold to the respective principals. With Murray it was seldom a problem. He might receive argument, but never defiance. He held the power in the union and enjoyed the full backing of the membership. Even

[1] Despite the historical importance and the physical size of the Wage Policy Committee, there is no specific constitutional provision for its existence. Its continuation is dependent on convention resolution alone. Union representatives have told of resentment by basic steel members of the WPC against the influence members from fabricating plants have in formulating demands affecting basic steel. Fabricating plants were struck in conjunction with basic steel plants only once—in 1946.

in the 1949 strike, when the pension issue did not fire the rank and file with enthusiasm, the members struck solidly. Stephens could count on a more difficult selling job. His commitment rested not only on the sanction of his own company, but on that of many companies—in practical effect, on that of an industry. To the extent that U.S. Steel exerted leadership, the center of authority rested in corporate officers. According to many observers interviewed, the finance committee of U.S. Steel made the decisive policy decisions on the industry side.

There is the weight of opinion of many observers that a shifting both of bargaining technique and of authority has taken place in steel relationships, beginning about 1956. On the union side, the voices of the Wage Policy Committee and of the Executive Board—especially the latter—have become more forceful. It is more difficult for the union president to commit his organization to a settlement in advance of consultation with his Executive Board. On the industry side, there is an expressed feeling that a greater sharing of decisionmaking occurs under the group bargaining arrangement.

Structure of Bargaining

Bargaining structure in basic steel is undergoing a metamorphosis. As noted earlier, the Steelworkers union from its genesis had set industrywide bargaining as a desirable goal, but it could not overcome industry opposition. The almost unvarying practice in the past had been for U.S. Steel to take the leadership in negotiations and settlements. Bargaining committees of other companies ordinarily marked time with their union counterparts until the settlement on a basic contract with U.S. Steel had been achieved. Having assumed the role of industry leadership, U.S. Steel carried the burden of conflict with the union over issues of principle to a greater extent than did the other companies.

It should be emphasized, however, that the situation has not been quite as stereotyped as the foregoing generalization might suggest. There have been frequent variations from the U.S. Steel settlement on both wage and nonwage items to meet special situations, and there were occasions when a company other than U.S. Steel led in the settlement.

There are, in fact, many differences between companies which necessitate or make desirable individual bargaining. For example, a few generalizations are written into the basic contract on seniority, but for the most part the particular type of seniority is left for local plant agreement. Different approaches in incentive negotiation have been taken by different companies. But, in the opinion of the officers of one large firm, individual company negotiations on most issues would put the companies at a great disadvantage.

During World War II and the Korean War, Government boards confronted with steel-industry labor relations presentations made an effort as a sheer matter of efficiency to get the industry to act as a unit. They met with partial success. U.S. Steel continued to lead, but an industry coordinating committee was established. There was an indication as early as 1947 that U.S. Steel considered itself a reluctant dragon so far as its leadership role was concerned. John Stephens noted the corporation's "bellwether characteristics" and what he termed attendant "hazards." [2]

A source close to steel negotiations claims that Stephens and Fairless for many years had favored industrywide bargaining, but could not win over the rest of the industry. Apparently U.S. Steel didn't relish either the responsibility for setting the pattern for each settlement or the tedious procedure of extra meetings and consultations which the initial bargain imposed on the corporation. Consultation was cumbersome and artificial, and may well have worked to the disadvantage of some of the companies, since there was a tendency toward upward trading to the best provisions operative within the industry.

Stieber holds that the industry's reasons for avoiding genuine industrywide bargaining varied with the changing status of the union during three distinct periods.[3] Between 1937 and 1941, the union was too weak to enforce industrywide bargaining. Its organization of the entire basic steel industry was not accomplished until 1941 and the union as such was still an organizing committee with no permanent structure and little real influence. This might be termed the toehold period.

From 1942 to 1946, the toehold became a handhold, with the union pushing for the industrywide goal as an aid to securing its equal pay for equal work objective. Industrywide bargaining received some further impetus between 1947 and 1954 because of the considerable degree of wage standardization achieved through the job evaluation program, but industrywide bargaining faced the barrier of some remaining area wage differentials and other elements of resistance.

In 1955 the first open and substantial move toward industrywide bargaining was achieved when the union, after prior consultation with U.S. Steel, announced that David J. McDonald would serve as chairman of each negotiating committee and that all negotiations would be held in Pittsburgh. Stieber, who is a former steel union staff member, conjectures that McDonald, having inherited the mantle of Philip

---

[2] John A. Stephens, op. cit., pp. 133–4.
[3] Jack Stieber, *Company Cooperation in Collective Bargaining in the Basic Steel Industry,* in Labor Law Journal, July 1960, pp. 614–21.

Murray when the latter died in 1952, was consolidating his political position in the union in relation to district directors, who normally would handle negotiations with individual companies. Concentration of bargaining sessions in one locality also gave the union's top officers tighter control over the uniformity of contract terms.

Twelve major companies in 1956 arranged to have a committee of four represent them in bargaining on major issues. Although Stephens, chairman of the industry committee, contended without real force of fact or conviction that each company was bargaining for itself in the same room, the ultimate memorandum of agreement was with all 12 companies. U.S. Steel still led the industry team with 2 members to 1 each from Bethlehem and Republic.

In 1959, a four-man industry committee was drawn in the same proportions from the same three companies and again represented a dozen major concerns—this time on all contract terms. But the union demurred, wishing to hold to only major items, leaving lesser issues to individual company bargaining. Some individual company bargaining took place, but progress was impossible in these meetings.

Stieber's paper suggests that the companies' 1959 recognition of the advantages of concerted action must be based on more than the union's solid and central control over the work force, a *fait accompli* of nearly two decades' duration. He suggests as plausible explanation (1) diminution of intercompany contract differentials; (2) fear of a union strike policy of one-at-a-time; and (3) a challenge to U.S. Steel's domination of bargaining sessions and to its policy of accommodation under Fairless and Stephens.

A strong likelihood exists that industrywide bargaining will continue as an industry policy and perhaps become even more formalized than was the case in the 1959 negotiations. For one thing, the joint committees set up under the 1959 contract are continuing bodies, and on the industry side are representative of 11 companies (a separate arrangement was established for Kaiser Steel), a factor conducive to both extension and permanency. For another thing, the advantages of joint bargaining are incomplete without strong and positive mutual aid, including the policy of "a strike against one is a strike against all." Finally, the development of long-range policies may be facilitated by a group approach.

It should be emphasized that bargaining as discussed above applies mainly to the basic steel companies. Captive iron mines, ore carriers, and certain other non-steel-producing subsidiaries are not included in the bargaining units of basic steel companies. In many instances, contracts for the steel fabricating plants are negotiated separately on a local basis, usually under the supervision of the district director.

The policy in respect to subsidiary fabricating companies is mixed.[4] Basic steel contract terms are followed in varying degrees of conformity by other firms which negotiate with the steel union, whose jurisdiction goes beyond the steel fabricating plants to the container, aluminum, and copper industries. Containers and aluminum have generally followed the pattern established in basic steel (1959 was a notable exception).

In the main, union officials concede that there is wide variation from the basic steel contract in the case of the fabricating plants. "There is an effort to use the substance of the basic contract so far as possible in the case of subsidiaries of basic steel, *and to make whatever other local deals possible*, so long as they don't conflict with the provisions of the basic, however. *In some cases a fresh start is made on a contract*, but these are influenced by the basic." [Emphasis supplied.]

According to a staff representative, "there are extensive contract variations—on wages, fringes (especially SUB), and pensions, which lag behind the basic settlement pattern. Use of clause 2B varies among fabricators, but the arbitrators for these firms tend to follow the 2B decisions of basic steel, even in the absence of such a clause * * *."[5]

Strikes and Industrywide Bargaining

Most union officials consulted on the matter of single-company versus industrywide strikes feel that the former are not feasible. Basic steel is not a consumer commodity and the source or brand-name of the product is of little concern to the purchaser. One industry executive expressed the opinion that his company would lose a large percentage of its customers if it were struck separately. A real fear of permanent loss of markets and jobs overhangs the union's policy in this regard. Despite certain tactical advantages it might enjoy from "whip-saw" strikes, the union is deterred by the success of past practice in industrywide strikes, the political consideration of placing the strike burdens overwhelmingly on the same locals, and the strong possibility of some sort of industry mutual-aid plan reducing the pressure on the struck concern. There is also the frequently heard theory, difficult to appraise because the union has expressed a desire to avoid such action, that an important strategic objective of the union is Government intervention.

---

[4] For example, in recent years the subsidiary fabricating units of U.S. Steel, Bethlehem, and Republic have negotiated settlements concurrently with those of the basic parent companies.

[5] It is very difficult to generalize on the pattern influence of basic steel contracts on steel fabricating company settlements because of the variegated product and local labor market influences. An article on this subject by George Seltzer, based on his paper prepared for this study, is to be found in the February 1961 *Monthly Labor Review*.

Thus, bargaining in steel takes place with the possibility of a more-than-industrywide strike or the threat of one. The scope of a steel strike includes most of the basic steel industry, certain other manufacturing plants of these companies, ore boats, and iron mines. In other chapters, the direct and indirect economic effects of steel strikes are discussed. The actual and potential consequences of a strike of such magnitude also have a telling effect upon the national state of mind. It is this widening fear of the effects of strikes which creates the political pressures helping to force Government intervention to settle the strike. Most industry officials interviewed for this study have suggested that Government intervention has been a union strike-goal. Some union officials, although not expressing official union policy, have expressed the belief that "without Government intervention the union cannot win." All agree, as one district director put it, that "one of the prime weapons is shutting off the supply of steel completely."

The gradual development of a form of industrywide bargaining in steel conceivably can be interpreted essentially as an industry response to industrywide strikes and the growing power of the union. This interpretation raises the question as to whether the union's power is thus made greater than it would be if the union were to bargain separately with leading companies and to strike companies singly. Any judgment on this question is speculative. Unions in most manufacturing industries practice a policy of separate bargaining and separate strikes. Most unions hold the view that industry bargaining strengthens the companies more than the union. Coordinated bargaining among companies in some manufacturing industries other than steel is developing not because the union strikes all companies simultaneously but because it does not.

It is not clear that the character and form of strikes in steel is an adequate explanation of the development of industrywide bargaining. The question is a particularly difficult one, however, because the potential national crisis character of strikes in steel may well increase the effectiveness of industrywide strikes in steel compared with other industries. There are, however, compulsions toward centralization on both the industry and the union side. Price leadership on the part of U.S. Steel, a logical consequence of its position in the industry, created strong compulsions toward an initial form of bargaining which concentrated upon U.S. Steel. The union's strike policy may have developed with the conscious or unconscious belief that the economic environment of the basic steel industry precluded effective action except on an industrywide basis. Companies other than U.S. Steel would have been in a difficult position to bargain without concurrence in their position by U.S. Steel.

With these various forces favorable to centralization, formal group bargaining offers advantages to both sides. It allows greater opportunity to develop long-range objectives. It perpetuates, however, the national emergency problem. As discussed in chapter 1, drastic legislation modifying the bargaining structure in steel is one possible future alternative. These few words on the compulsions toward centralization indicate that it is by no means clear that the bargaining power of either of the parties would be modified decisively by drastic legislative proposals. It is impossible to say just what the major longrun effects would be. But it is felt that such action would not present an obvious or easy solution to bargaining problems in steel.

The Battle for the Public Mind

In every steel strike or even in negotiations in which a settlement is achieved without a strike, there is a contest for moral support from the public. This struggle begins even before negotiations commence. In fact, in one way or another, it is constantly in progress. Public support is an extremely useful weapon for either party, whether the battle cry be cutting of crew sizes, halting of inflation, winning of a pension, or granting of a union shop. The extent of public support secured in a steel strike is roughly proportional to the measure of blame ascribed to one party for the inconvenience suffered by the public as a result of the strike.

It may well be that the union has an initial advantage in the publicity war, assuming competence and astuteness in its campaign, than does the industry. Under normal circumstances the union already has the staunch support of its members. This gives momentum to its drive for public support. The industry must not only win the public at large but its employees as well. William G. Caples pointed this out clearly: "We believe that if we are to reach understanding with our employees, we will not do it through the union. We shall do so only by directly communicating with employees. * * * A right largely defaulted since 1935. * * * We encourage our employees to raise their voice in national, state and local politics—why not in union politics? * * *" [6] Conrad Cooper agreed: "We cannot hope to reach understanding with our employees through the union leaders. We must reach understanding with the union leaders through the development of understanding with the employees they represent." [7] There are keen observers who believe that during the 1959 negotiations the industry argument first convinced and then lost the credulity of both the employees and the public.

---

[6] *Communication Countdown,* op. cit., p. 2.
[7] Ibid., p. 17.

Both parties to the 1959 negotiations began their publicity buildups early with nationwide newspaper ads. Many people—including some union leaders—believe the union approach, stressing industry profits and the need for a wage increase, misjudged the public temper. The language at times bordered on the vituperative: "We accuse the Steel industry of deliberate and wilful abuses of honorable collective bargaining [June 15] * * * The steel companies have an organized plan to take away individual rights of every steelworker * * * They [the companies] vaguely hinted at a 'modest' wage bribe if the Steelworkers would take a disastrous backward step which would wreck every gain the Union has made in its long history * * * the infamous 8-point 'Break the Union' proposal * * * designed to reduce workers to industrial slaves [July 22] * * * Their arrogance, greed, and desire for personal gain would make old-time 'steel barons' blush with envy * * * purposely deceitful * * * irresponsibility to its workers, its stockholders, and to the Nation." [August 7]

Cooper made the comment that "there seems to be less room for emotional, glamorizing appeal of headline-catching nature in the presentation of management's case than in the union's * * * There is popularity in seeming to fight for the worker, even though the item sought, if won, may ultimately injure the worker. And there is always news value in conflict." [8]

The union addressed rhetorical questions to various entrepreneurs, asking what an extra billion dollars would do for their sales. To the dairy industry, for example, it pictured ice cream and milk shakes as part of the American "way of life," and noted that all people required "generous supplies of milk, eggs and butter." The ad then expressed the "hope to buy more of your health-giving products" if only wages of steelworkers were increased. "Remember," it concluded, "the more you earn, the more you buy." [9]

This line was grist for the industry's publicity mill. The early theme was the relation of wages to inflation and the industry's obligation and desire to halt the decline in purchasing power thus generated. A series of advertisements accused the union of striking for more inflation ("That is the issue * * * the real issue * * * at stake in the steel strike."), claimed widespread approbation of its point of view on the inflation flight ("By a 20 to 1 margin you supported [via "thousands" of letters] our stand against inflation."), and pointed to the pattern-setting and cumulative effect of a wage increase in steel ("An inflation-

8 *Communications Countdown*, op. cit., p. 15.
9 Advertisement in *New York Times* for Mar. 23, 1959, p. 25.

ary wage increase in steel today would mean higher living costs for everyone.")[10]

A number of union officials concede that the companies' anti-inflation line had a convincing effect on a substantial segment of the union membership and the general public. The spectre of inflation was sufficiently frightening to some employees to weaken the desire for a wage increase. There had never been a widespread sympathetic understanding by the general public of the need for a wage increase for workers whose $3 an hour average earnings (irrespective of annual earnings) had been so thoroughly publicized.

But having clearly scored in the early propaganda battle, the industry promptly threw its advantage away by allowing the emphasis of the argument to be shifted from inflation to work rules.[11] This issue, constituting a threat to crew sizes and employment security, created apprehension among employees, which the union was quick and vigorous to exploit. It was also a complicated issue which could not generate popular support or interest. One corporation officer, commenting on the serious introduction of the work rules demand into the negotiations, said that work rules were injected without appreciation of their crucial bargaining significance. McDonald instantly realized that he had a ready-made issue handed to him and "could hardly wait to get out of the room to exploit it."

The purpose of this discussion is to point to the overweening importance attached to the slogans and contentions uttered in extremely expensive and widespread propaganda battles.[12] In point of fact, steel negotiations, wholly apart from their effect on the industry or the national economy, have become contentious public issues, with the

---

[10] Advertisements appearing in 400 papers on July 20, Aug. 7, and Aug. 12, as reproduced in a brochure entitled *Where the Steel Companies Stand* [undated], published by the Steel Companies Coordinating Committee, pp. 5–7.

[11] In an exceptionally candid talk, Phelps Adams, vice president, public relations, U.S. Steel, had this to say:

"By early June it was evident that the public was with us to a very large extent; but it was also evident that the negotiations were hopelessly deadlocked. So came the letter of June tenth setting forth the companies' eight-point proposal. Despite all that has been said about the strategic wisdom or unwisdom of that proposal, no one who knows the facts can doubt, I believe, that it was a sincere and worthwhile effort * * * to meet the demand of the union leadership.

"McDonald, however, seized upon it as a heaven-sent black snake whip [a play on McDonald's charge at the Taylor board hearings that the demand to eliminate section 2B from the contract was management's effort to use a black snake whip on the backs of the workers] with which to lash his men into anger against the companies, and thus to win the rank-and-file support he had so far lacked.

"And we in public relations were caught with our * * * well, let's say with our defenses down. For this we had made no advance preparation. * * *" (*Communications Countdown*, op. cit., p. 29.)

[12] The controversies in steel collective bargaining are so complicated that the attempts of the parties to reduce the issues to slogans which have popular appeal really result in a beclouding or a distortion of the essential problems. Sloganeering is designed for the emotional reactions and does not stimulate reflective thought or serve as a guide to understanding.

parties conducting campaigns, such as those described, which are ends in themselves and are won or lost or abandoned in a sphere remote from the bargaining table. Yet they are not unconnected to the bargaining process. They have become a sort of bargaining superstructure which, depending on circumstances, can be an encumbrance or an aid. Negotiations, in short, are two-plane affairs. On one plane the traditional bargaining takes place, responsive to the vis-à-vis of daily encounter and to the application of policy. On the other plane is the public relations campaign which tests the acceptability of policy and then sells it. In this process the parties retain public relations firms who supervise the preparation of advertising copy, press releases, brochures, public opinion polls—all the logistical planning and accoutrements which are attached to a major advertising and merchandising campaign.

The public posture the parties strive for, casting each other constantly in the role of devil, makes it increasingly difficult for them to be conciliatory in public or to communicate effectively in private. Thus an entire complex of pressures, built up in ever-increasing constraint, is generated by the public encounter of the parties. There probably is a fertile field for study by social scientists to determine the degree to which the difficulties of industrywide bargaining in steel are also intensified by a national crisis psychology inculcated by the propaganda vendettas of the parties.

It may be that the need for the importuning of public support by the parties is self-generating and can take the form of a public defense of a position or a justification for an advance to higher ground. For example, the Steelworkers over the years has enjoyed exceptional success in the outcome of negotiations. Its achievement record is high. But it may be true that success begets demand and that there is a point where membership demand can rise beyond the potential of the union to achieve or the industry to grant more. Such a situation could lead to an attempt to create public pressure to support the position taken. In such a situation, can the union itself call a halt without risking internal political difficulty, or conversely, daring to proceed, can it afford to fail?

Similarly, if the industry elevates ordinary bargaining positions to the status of principles from which there can be no retreat, the frozen situation results in a serious bargaining impasse. Here too there is an attempt to marshall public support for the "positions of principle." The result is a further solidification which makes the ultimate necessity for maneuver as difficult to acknowledge as it is to achieve.

A good case could be made for the contention that the battle for public support, though it may redound to the benefit of either party, is destructive of the beneficial functions of collective bargaining. To the extent that the result of the contest is to create a crisis atmosphere, irrespective of an intent merely to win public support, the intervention of Government to force a settlement on the parties is hastened by dint of political pressure. This could vitiate a free play of bargaining power.

CHAPTER 7

AREAS OF ACCOMMODATION AND CONFLICT

The three preceding chapters have covered the background of collective bargaining in basic steel, and the way in which it has developed. This chapter moves to the area of what bargaining has produced. It is a general summary and analysis of what appear to be the major successes and limitations in the relationship between the United Steelworkers of America and the steel industry. It is based upon the history of their negotiations between 1937 and 1959, contained in appendix A.

Areas of Accommodation

In some areas the parties seem to have made a real accommodation by finding means fundamentally to resolve longstanding basic issues. Among these areas are basic wage structures, safety, insurance, pensions, supplemental unemployment benefits, and to a considerable degree, seniority. Although important disagreements remain and occur between the parties on each of these subjects, methods of resolution of differences have been created such as to make it unlikely that major strikes will occur over any of them in the future. In several of these areas this accommodation has been assisted by a special joint committee set up by the parties to study the problem and report prior to a given year's negotiation.

Wage Structure

The first and most important of these committees operated over a period of years to work toward the equalization of basic wage rates within individual companies and, eventually, within the industry. This history has been recounted in appendix A and will not be repeated here. In summary, it is sufficient to say that in 1947, after almost 2 years of constant negotiations, the steel producing subsidiaries of U.S. Steel and the United Steelworkers concluded an agreement on the classification of jobs for the purpose of eliminating wage rate inequities both within and between plants. The same system of job description, evaluation, and classification was later applied to almost all of the Nation's basic steel plants and has produced substantially identical classification results for 90 percent of all hourly paid steel employees. This agreement has survived modification by later committees and in collective bargaining, the pressures of the outside labor market, and technological change. Although recent unsuccessful efforts to negotiate changes have produced some conflict, it remains perhaps the outstanding achievement of these parties, and represents a combined application of industrial engineering and collective bargaining without parallel in American industry.

Safety and Seniority

The 1947 basic agreement between U.S. Steel and the steelworkers also provided for permanent continuing plant-level joint committees on the subjects of safety and seniority. Both of these appear to have had some success. The area of seniority has never been a subject of serious controversy in national negotiations and the basic agreement relating to seniority has been modified only slightly in the last decade. Problems in regard to seniority are often a subject of controversy in some local negotiations. In an industry such as steel in which cyclical fluctuations in employment are characteristic, it is noteworthy that neither layoffs nor recalls are outstanding sources of grievances. It is nevertheless likely that the decreasing employment requirements of the industry will cause seniority to become a far more significant problem in the future than past agreement in this area would indicate. The chances are strong, however, that the parties will maintain a high degree of accommodation in this area.

The plant-level joint committees on safety appear to have succeeded to the satisfaction of the parties. The industry accident record is approximately one-half that of the United States all-manufacturing average, in large part owing to the continuing safety engineering and training programs established by the companies, which are fully supported by the union. When the joint safety committees were originally set up the union seized upon them as an opportunity to make anticompany propaganda, but this has not been characteristic of its approach to safety problems in the later years of the relationship. The basic clause in the U.S. Steel agreement relating to safety has not been significantly modified for many years. A corporate level joint committee on health and safety was created in 1956, but has been largely inactive.

Pensions, Insurance, and SUB

The basic agreements on insurance and pensions were negotiated in 1949, following the strike of that year involving the issue of employee contribution to these programs. In 1953, the parties agreed to establish a special joint committee to study the operation and shortcomings of the two programs. This committee was to report prior to the 1954 negotiations. As a result of the findings of this committee, the parties were able peacefully to negotiate substantial modifications in the insurance and pension plans in 1954. Although there was some disagreement during the negotiation, fundamentally they were not greatly apart on the changes that had to be made, the ways in which changes should be accomplished, and the cost involved. Benefits under both programs were improved in 1956 and 1959. Additionally, the long controversy over joint contribution was ended in 1959 when the insurance program was made noncontributory. The joint committees on pensions and insurance continue in operation to the present time, although discussions on these subjects have to a considerable extent in recent years been carried on outside the committee framework. During recent years neither the insurance nor the pension program appears to have been subject to the kind of controversy that leads to strikes. The cost of both, of course, becomes part of the total package involved in negotiation. The existing programs provide benefits that are substantially equal to or better than those provided by other major American industries. Moreover, joint discussions relating to medical care have been taking place.

In 1956, an unusual 52-week supplemental unemployment benefit plan was negotiated following the initiation of a comparable plan in the can industry. When disagreements concerning the operation of the SUB plan arise, they are commonly the subject of hard-fought arbitrations, the results of which are then generally applied throughout the industry.

Judgments with respect to what constitutes areas of conflict or accommodation are subject to differences of opinion. Conscious as they are of their disagreements in this area, the parties do not completely agree with our treatment of this subject. Nevertheless, in our judgment, there has been sufficient agreement with respect to basic objectives in regard to such programs to warrant emphasis in the report on the degree of accommodation achieved.

Long-Range Committees

The parties' experience with joint study committees oriented to solve a specific problem has been good. The only exception was the incentive inequity negotiation in U.S. Steel. This is not equally true of general joint committees set up at the highest level to consider the long range relationship of the parties, but, nevertheless, the provision for the committees, and in modest degree their accomplishments, should be noted as an effort toward accommodation.

Several times over the years the parties have agreed to undertake continuing discussion of areas of mutual concern. As a part of the 1947 settlement U.S. Steel and the union agreed to meet quarterly, to discuss long-range problems of the steel industry. No more than two inconclusive meetings had been held when the frustrations attendant upon the 1948 wage reopening soured the relationship. A resumption of these meetings had been planned for the fall of 1952 when the death of Philip Murray intervened. Subsequently Fairless and McDonald made a good-will tour of U.S. Steel plants. Once again in 1953, and at several other times in years following, regular informal meetings were planned, but they always were discontinued because of animosities arising in contract negotiations or because of disinterest.

The settlement of the long 1959 strike included agreement on two committees that are to study basic problems of joint concern to the parties. The controversial local working conditions issue was referred to a joint study committee to be headed by a neutral chairman. By the end of 1960, one year later, the parties had agreed thus far to do without a neutral chairman, but had reported no other agreement. A joint Human Relations Research Committee was also established to study and recommend solutions for problems such as medical care, equitable wage and benefit adjustments, job classification, seniority, incentives, and other problems. It is too early to determine what will be the result of the studies of these committees. It is difficult to be too optimistic. On the other hand, some important explorations of problem areas are being undertaken by the Human Relations Committee. At the very least there will be an improved understanding of each party's point of view in the areas they study.

Potentially this committee could work out a basis for a cooperative approach to some important problems. The committee is a novel one in that it is an outgrowth of the newly developed industry bargaining group. It involves a cooperative approach among the companies as well as jointly with the union. Some problems of individual companies are no longer theirs alone, but are of joint concern to all. This factor should encourage a joint approach to the union to solve mutual problems. It is to be hoped that the advantages of working outside the tension of negotiating atmosphere will be fruitful.

Other Areas of Accommodation

As discussed subsequently in chapter 8, most areas of day-to-day union management relations are reasonably resolved within the steel industry. Incentives, crew size, and production standards are related areas of low accommodation, but the day-to-day problems should not be exaggerated. With continuous operations and enlarged vacation benefits, work scheduling presents problems which make a satisfactory level of adjustment most difficult. The issue of subcontracting is intensified by unemployment. But in the overwhelming number of situations, orderly day-to-day industrial relations prevail. Discipline, transfer, work assignment, layoff, promotion, and most aspects of the problem areas noted above do not create other than a normal number of routine grievances. Although some wildcat strikes continue to

occur, the problem appears to be of decreasing importance. The grievance procedure functions quite satisfactorily in most plants and the
arbitration system is highly developed. The years have seen the development of orderly relations which in most plants continue quite
independently of the record of industrywide strikes. There is thus
considerable general accommodation in contract administration based
upon growing stability of contract language and its interpretation and
application.

Areas of Conflict

The sources of conflict between the basic steel industry and the Steelworkers in the years of their relationship have been varied. Among
them have been wages, prices, and profits; responsibility for inflation;
union security; the timing and method of Government intervention;
and in some cases and to some degree the bargaining attitudes of the
industry and union leaders and their respective negotiators. Finally,
and probably most important, are the fundamentally differing economic attitudes that each party brings to and represents at the bargaining table.

The first of the following sections summarizes these economic differences, which are the heart of collective bargaining difficulties.
These, of course, have their impact on the parties' approach to all
other issues. The remaining sections then treat various of the other
issues which seem to have been recurring sources of conflict over the
years.

Economic Attitudes

The following brief paragraphs contrast basic differences in approach and viewpoint on fundamental economic issues between industry and union leaders. Some of these points may overstate or
understate the strength of belief of the parties generally on an issue.
Others may not be characteristic of the beliefs of some or many individuals on each side. In general, however, they represent valid generalizations about the basic beliefs that each side brings to the
collective bargaining table.

The size of the economic package has been the predominant recurring source of conflict in steel. Involvement of wages and prices
with Government control or influence is discussed in the next section.
Clearly it has intensified the wage conflict.

Union leaders, sincerely viewing the union preeminently as an institutional device for the improvement of the standard of living of
the employees, bring to the bargaining table a strong purchasing-
power view of wages. In this view, most wage increases are good for
the country.

Management, on the other hand, sees in investment the predominant key to growth. It tends to support the view that wage increases should not force price increases. These views carry over to profits. Union leaders tend generally to regard profits as "too high." Management tends to resent the continuous wage squeeze on profits and looks upon wage increases of all kinds, including escalator clauses, as being the primary cause of postwar inflation. Union leaders see management as grossly distorting the impact of wages as a cause of inflation. They see management as using wage increases as an excuse for price increases large enough to add to profits. They see any lack of purchasing power as a source of imbalance in the economy, threatening depression and deterioration of existing living standards and a halting of progress.

The above paragraphs are, of course, oversimplified. Differences in attitude and various forms of economic conflict are inherent in a free society. On the other hand, it is to be hoped that the range of difference in opinions can be narrowed to diminish conflict. Somewhat closer agreement on the means to reach balanced growth for the economy—fundamentally a mutual problem—should be possible.

Wages, Prices, and Collective Bargaining

Because of its preeminent place in the economy, there is more general interest in the economic decisions of the basic steel industry than in those of any other American industry. This has forced the dominant industry leaders, particularly U.S. Steel, to be concerned with the opinions of other businesses, the general public, and Government whenever it makes a decision in the wage or price field. This aspect of steel economic decisionmaking has always had an extremely significant impact on its success or failure in collective bargaining with the Steelworkers.

Governmental pressures, from both executive and legislative branches, have been brought to bear on aspects of the wage and price relationship almost continuously over the years of the collective bargaining relationship. In 1937, at least in part because of Government pressure, the industry abandoned plans to reduce wages. In 1938 and 1939 the "monopoly power" and price policies of the industry were seriously questioned as a part of the Temporary National Economic Committee investigations. In 1941 the industry felt the Government was urging it to increase wages while holding prices steady. When a wage increase was finally agreed upon, the Government suddently froze steel prices, the first major industry to be so treated.

During World War II steel prices were held almost constant: price stability was more pronounced in steel than in any other major industry. Yet twice the industry was ordered by the War Labor

Board to increase wage and fringe costs. At the end of the war, the Government decontrolled wages and held prices frozen. The 1946 negotiation resulted in a strike when the Government recommended wage increases without a change in price policy, and the strike was settled only after the Government retreated to virtual price decontrol.

During 1947 and 1948 the industry bore the brunt of the Administration's attack on inflation. Both President and the Congress investigated the industry's price policies and charged it with lack of public responsibility. Under this pressure in 1948 U. S. Steel made a slight reduction in prices and refused to grant a wage increase. It succeeded only in incurring the rancor of the union by so doing and later in the year reversed both decisions. In 1949 a Government fact-finding board recommended substantial increases in fringe costs, although no wage increase, at a time when the industry was experiencing a minor recession. In late 1950, the industry negotiated with the union on wages and the Government on prices: when a price increase was informally approved the industry had no difficulty in quickly completing wage negotiations. In 1952 the Government once again recommended a wage increase while limiting the amount of price increase, and once again the industry forced Government to recede from its position by withholding a wage offer. Had this position been maintained it alone would undoubtedly have caused a strike. The strike which actually followed was primarily over other issues.

During 1953, 1954, and 1955, governmental price pressure was largely absent. In the first 2 of these years a peaceful settlement was reached: in 1955 a work-stoppage lasted only 1 day. In 1956, however, governmental concern over inflation was again brought to bear on the collective bargaining relationship. Once again the industry took a strike that was settled after the Government, concerned with the outcome of the election and the impact of the strike on the economy and on defense production, in effect accepted the fact that settlement would result in a susbtantial wage and price increase. In 1959, the administration strongly encouraged a noninflationary settlement. Partially in response to this, and partly in view of its own economic situation, the industry proposed a 1-year wage and benefit freeze, and again took a strike. As in 1956, the administration decided that the paramount issue was settlement of the dispute, and recommended that the industry consider increasing its offer.

Because of the pressures from Government of the sort noted in the preceding paragraphs, for the period from 1940 to 1948, steel prices for many types of products were probably below what the market would have borne. This was particularly true in the years immediately following World War II, when a thriving "gray market" for many types of steels existed. In general, of course, the steady overall trend of steel prices has been upward for 25 years, based both upon increasing costs and the industry's need to finance replacement, modernization, and expansion of facilities. However, and again in response to outside pressure, U. S. Steel, the industry leader, has never sought to maximize profits in the short run. Instead, the industry has chosen to defer its price increases until a time of apparent major cost increase, when increases were politically most justifiable. With but one exception since 1937, the industry has always announced general price increases immediately following its labor contract settlements. This decision has tended to shift the public opprobrium for increased prices to the union.

This policy was not followed in the spring of 1948. A congressional investigation led by Senator Taft condemned the increases. Industry leaders maintained throughout the hearings that the increases were necessary, and apologized only for their "political visibility." Later in the same year prices were once again raised following the wage increase granted to employees: no substantial criticism was raised. After every subsequent negotiation prices were immediately raised except after the strike settlement in January 1960. The "mistake" of making a general price increase at a time other than when it could be rationalized by labor cost increases has not been repeated. But, by the same token, conflict with the union has been intensified.

The Steelworkers, of course, has repeatedly denounced the industry for its policy on timing of increases, insisting that most of the total increases were based on anticipated cost increases which were in many cases never realized, and the industry's desire to accumulate capital and to increase profits.

Thus, charges and countercharges as to which of them is responsible for inflation has become one of the major sources of conflict between these parties. This is particularly the case at the level of the public relations campaign in which each engages to enlist the support of the public and thereby the Government on its side. This conflict has been intensified over the years (a more detailed analysis of this subject is in chapter 6) and has had the effect of crystalizing each party's position to the extent that it is increasingly difficult for them to compromise in face-to-face bargaining.

The history of wage-price relationships and their impact upon negotiations in the basic steel industry permits the following observations:

1. If Government has not attempted to bring pressure to bear upon steel prices, there has been considerable likelihood that the parties would reach a settlement through collective bargaining,

though this must be qualified to take account of the business climate.

2. If Government controlled steel prices and yet encouraged or permitted wage increases creating labor cost increases, a strike has been virtually inevitable as has been modification of the Government's price position to settle the strike.

3. If Government has brought pressure to bear on steel prices, the industry has tried to hold cost increases to a minimum, thereby increasing the possibility of a strike.

4 Conflict over the responsibility for inflation has created intensive public relations campaigns. The parties appear to have become prisoners of their own strategy upon occasion, making a settlement through collective bargaining without Government intervention more difficult.

5. When the Government has been forced to intervene to prevent or halt a strike, it ordinarily has been forced to approve or take the responsibility for a wage-price increase as the price of settlement.

The history of bargaining relationships in the steel industry is such that, absent a system of compulsory arbitration or wage and price controls, the Government must be aware that it faces a dilemma when it intervenes. If the Government's concern is to avoid steel strikes or to end them as soon as possible after they occur, then the Government must be prepared to accept the cost and price consequences. If, on the other hand, the Government's concern is to avoid mounting inflation and it takes steps to see that any wage increases negotiated are "noninflationary," then it must be aware that when a strong industry faces a strong union a strike may frequently result. Additionally, different agencies and individuals within the Government have frequently taken inconsistent positions, creating an element of uncertainty which has greatly complicated the bargaining process. Clearly the Government and the public cannot have it both ways.

The Government's past efforts to achieve simultaneously price stability and industrial peace have not been conspicuously successful. It is possible, of course, the changed political or competitive conditions might reduce the seriousness of the dilemma. Additionally, various individuals endorse different ways out of the dilemma ranging from the prohibition of industrywide bargaining and strikes, through enlarged powers of the Government to control or influence wages and prices, to allowing the parties greater freedom under peacetime conditions. The summary chapter of the report deals further with this problem.

Union Security

Union security, as a source of conflict in the steel industrial relationship, is of more historical than current importance. Nevertheless, the history of conflict over this issue is of some significance in evaluating the role of Government and of Government-sponsored recommendations in this as well as in other collective bargaining relationships.

The agreement negotiated in 1937 between the SWOC and U.S. Steel was for "members only." With the exception of a few plants where the union had won NLRB-held elections and represented all the bargaining unit, for the next 5 years "members only" was the rule in all steel plants where the SWOC had representation. In fact, throughout most of these years the union's prime goal was to maintain its security by getting its contracts renewed. No real contractual improvements were negotiated in the industry until 1940 and after.

Not until the early part of World War II was the union security clause in the basic steel agreements improved, and then not through collective bargaining. In accordance with policies established in some other disputes the National War Labor Board established maintenance of membership as the standard union security clause, first in the "Little Steel" case, and later for U.S. Steel and others in the industry. This award became a source of conflict between the industry and the union for a number of years. The industry never really acquiesced in the decision and insisted that the union had obtained from Government what it never could have obtained in collective bargaining. In 1944, some companies proposed that the maintenance-of-membership clause be deleted from the agreement, although this was not a unanimous industry request. The WLB rejected the requests and ordered no change in the maintenance-of-membership clause throughout the rest of the war period.

Interestingly enough, union security did not become a serious issue when the whole basic steel contract was open for renegotiation in 1947. The union did request the union shop, but apparently was not insistent upon it. The industry, in the interest of harmony, decided to forego a request for deletion of maintenance of membership. The result was that in the major contract renegotiation that occurred in that year union security changes were shunted aside in the final settlement.

The major dispute over union security in the steel industry occurred in 1952. The whole contract was open for the first time since 1947, and the union's request for the union shop was one of many issues over which the parties deadlocked. When the issue went before the Wage Stabilization Board, the Board originally hoped to return it to the parties for further negotiation. If the parties failed to agree, they were to return to the WSB for a further recommendation. When this compromise proved unacceptable to either party, the Board found that a recommendation favoring the union shop was the price of getting the union's agreement to the other parts of its award. When the Board's award recommending that the parties negotiate a union shop clause was made public, the industry seized upon this part of the award as one of the major criticisms in its public attack upon the WSB recommendations. During a great part of the period which followed the WSB recommendation the industry was attempting to force the Government to modify its wage-price policy, and its attack on "compulsory unionism" was only part of its total opposition to the Government. However, it would be a mistake to assume, as some have, that union security was only a smoke screen and not a real issue with the industry. Considerable agreement between the parties as to the size of the economic package, and tentative approval by the Government of a $5.20 price increase was reached approximately when the strike began, and in essence the industry took the first 4 of a 6 weeks' strike on the issue of union security. Despite the fact that, as the union continually reminded them, they had long had union shop agreements in the captive mines and with other unions, the steel industry was not going to give the union shop to the Steelworkers. At least not by Government suggestion and pressure.

Finally, after the strike had gone on for a month, Bethlehem Steel took the initiative in trying to settle with the union for a modified union shop. Their tentative agreement ultimately became the basis for agreements throughout the industry. The last 2 weeks of the 1952 strike were concerned with problems relating to incentives and the fair-day's work negotiation, and only incidentally with completing the details of the new union security clause.

The result of the union security settlement of 1952 was that over the next several years the union succeeded in obtaining what was, for all practical purposes, a full union shop. Well over 90 percent of all production workers in the industry joined the union, compared with approximately 80 percent in the previous 5 years. Almost none took advantage of the periodic opportunities to withdraw. In 1954, the contract was again completely open for renegotiation. Once again the union asked for a full union shop but it was a recession year and the union had to place primary emphasis upon obtaining some sort of economic gains. Union security, therefore, did not become a serious issue in the negotiations. It was not granted, and the realities of the situation were such that the union did not press for it.

In 1956 the long controverted issue of union security in basic steel was finally settled, "not with a bang but a whimper." The steel industry strongly desired a long-term contract. One of the union's objections to the industry's proposal for a 5-year agreement was that it did not contain a full union shop. When the month-long strike over the size of the economic package and length of the contract was finally settled, the industry had capitulated and given the union virtually a full union shop. By this time the industry apparently realized that the principle it had defended so long no longer had much reality. To all intents and purposes all employees were already in the union. Continued maintenance of the principle of individual choice protected few individuals and only served to maintain the animosity of the union. After many years, the steel industry finally was able to eliminate union security as a continuing source of conflict in its collective bargaining relationship. In 1959, after some negotiation, the parties agreed upon the agency shop in "right-to-work" States.

There seems no prospect that the issue of union security will again become a serious area of conflict between these parties. So far as continued existence is concerned, the union is now secure. This does not mean, however, that the industry accepts the union as positively desirable, or as a necessary partner in certain phases of managing the enterprise. Realistically, most major industries such as steel recognize the fact that unions will continue to exist. The problem facing sensible management, as they see it, is to find some method of living peacefully and constructively with the union. Under fairly typical conditions of belief such as those just described the union is not insecure, but neither is it welcome.

The long history of controversy over union security in basic steel contains several instructive points. First, it illustrates that basic steel, like many other industries, is capable of taking an extended strike over an issue of principle unrelated to immediate dollars and cents. Although it is common among industrial relations specialists to deprecate conflicts over "principles," some of the disputes and strikes that are most difficult to settle occur over them. The principle of voluntary union membership was stoutly defended for nearly 20 years. The retreats were gradual and were often forced upon it. Capitulation, when it finally came, was the result of an accumulation of minor retreats rather than one large lost battle.

Second, with reference to the role of Government, the union security controversy illustrates the difficulty that arises when outsiders try to establish a new basic element in a collective bargaining relationship. Outsiders—whether Government fact-finders, mediators, or private arbitrators—can make suggestions to the parties as to entirely new contractual provisions. Labor and management, however, properly regard it as their own prerogative to set the basic framework of the agreement and almost never welcome the setting of this framework by an outsider. One of the major reasons why union security became such a major source of conflict was that industry felt that the Government continually favored the union in forcing ever-stronger union security clauses into the contract. To the extent that this was true, the Government helped create the very disputes it was trying to avoid.

Leadership and Bargaining Attitudes

Assessment of the impact of individual leadership upon the success or failure of a given collective bargaining negotiation is at best a matter of speculation. Judgments of necessity are matters of opinion and inference rather than demonstrable fact. Nonetheless, the backgrounds, beliefs, and intentions of leaders and negotiators are generally conceded to be important. It must not be forgotten, however, that leaders will be subject to the economic and institutional pressures existing at the time. The individual negotiator is somewhat flexible, but the framework within which he moves is largely fixed. With these caveats and reservations, the following section is a summary attempt to indicate a few major points at which individuals and their approach to issues may have had some impact upon the success or failure of basic steel negotiations.

The nature of leadership affected the earliest industry-union relationship. Most observers have concluded that one of the significant factors in the decision of U.S. Steel to recognize the SWOC was that Myron Taylor, then Chairman of the Board of U.S. Steel, came from a different background from that of the leaders of the Little Steel companies. Taylor was a finance specialist rather than a lifelong steel man, and was not imbued with the antiunionism characteristic of most industry leaders. His purpose was to stabilize U.S. Steel and to make it profitable and he was more concerned with industrial peace than in the "principle" of keeping outside unionism out of the mills. Additionally, at least to a degree, he was able to understand and get along with John L. Lewis. A sufficient degree of trust resulted so that the two were able to make an agreement. This relationship can be contrasted with the Little Steel leaders, most of whom refused even to meet with Lewis. One cannot conclude, however, that differences of leadership background and attitude were the sole reason behind the U.S. Steel-SWOC agreement and the Little Steel strike. It can be argued equally well that U.S. Steel made a rational economic choice among several not-too-agreeable alternatives, and that the economic forces had changed by the time the union tried to organize the rest of the industry.

In subsequent years, particularly during most of the 1940's, Philip Murray was a significant figure in the steel collective bargaining relationship. During the war years, Murray had cooperated with the Government and, to a degree, with the industry. By so doing he gained a reputation as a leader of "responsible unionism." This reputation strengthened his already existing political relationship with the Government, and made it more difficult for the industry to attack him personally. There is little question that Murray's reputation for honesty and responsibility stood his union in good stead both in its collective bargaining relationship with the industry and its ability to maintain a sympathetic relationship with the Democratic administration. Yet the fact that the industry recognized and decried this relationship with the Roosevelt and Truman administrations became an important source of industry-union conflict in and of itself.

During the same period of years a new director of industrial relations became the negotiator for U.S. Steel and, in effect, a leading spokesman for the industry. By 1947, John A. Stephens was apparently able to convince the corporation that it was good business to negotiate an agreement which represented a genuine attempt to establish a permanent peaceful relationship with the union. As a result of this effort Murray and Stephens came to understand one another. Although it suffered several hard bumps, the relationship between Stephens and Murray continued to grow over the next 5 years. In 1948, the union felt the industry had broken an implied promise when it refused to grant a wage increase. In 1949, the industry felt the union had broken an explicit promise when it brought pensions into the negotiations as an issue. Nevertheless, during most of these years Murray and Stephens were able to settle many problems through private meetings and good faith efforts to convince their respective constituents of the merits of many of the other's positions. Murray's death in November 1952 broke an established relationship pattern that might well have continued to improve substantially over the coming years.

In the period between 1953 and 1955 there appears little doubt that the leadership of U.S. Steel was one factor that helped to create a peaceful collective bargaining relationship. Benjamin Fairless had become the chief executive officer of the corporation. He and John Stephens agreed on the need to attempt to reach a rapprochement with Murray's successor, David McDonald. The new president of the Steelworker's union was of different temperament, abilities, and background than Murray, and lacked Murray's strong foundation of personal loyalty among the workers. He too found a lessening of tension desirable in the first years that he dealt with the industry. Both industry and union found it to their joint advantage to get along fairly peacefully in the next few years of negotiation. These factors, partly personal and partly institutional, along with changing economic and political factors, resulted in two consecutive peaceful negotiations followed by a third in which a stoppage lasted for only 1 day. But which of the many factors bearing on success were paramount would be impossible to demonstrate.

By 1956, Fairless had retired and had been replaced by Roger Blough. Similar changes had taken place, or were about to take place, in the leadership of many of the major steel producing companies. Between 1955 and 1959 the chief executives or chief negotiators of half of the major companies changed. In addition to this factor, which made for an unsettled relationship, the industry's general economic position changed.

The year 1955 has turned out to be steel's peak production year up to the present time. It was a prosperous year. It was a year in which the economic compulsion upon the industry to avoid a strike was extremely great. Negotiation was confined to wages. The hope was for a peaceful settlement and a wage offer above the automobile industry wage settlement was made. But the union, sensing its advantage, suddenly turned militant and drastically changed the posture it had assumed in 1953 and 1954. The industry yielded in the face of this militancy and gave about double the automobile settlement, considered on a wages-only basis. The total cost was less than for autos, but the automobile settlement was predominately in the fringe area.

In 1956, with the entire contract open for negotiation, and lagging behind autos in fringes, the industry knew that the price of peace would be high. The industry also wished a long term contract both from a labor relations point of view and also to provide an opportunity peacefully to carry out an extensive capital investment program. Under these circumstances they sought a peaceful settlement. They put together a large total package stretched out over a 5 year term to allow for reasonable absorption. At the time it was proposed there was some reason to believe that it would be acceptable to the union, although no certain commitments had been made on either side. However, the union reacted in a militant manner, dubbing the offer "too little, too long, and too late." In retrospect it is possible that a somewhat more flexible industry approach might have produced a satisfactory settlement, but the new bargaining mechanism which was evolving on the industry side appeared to be too cumbersome and time-consuming for the ready formation and easy modification of the industry position. In any event, a strike resulted, and the settlement, under some influence of the informal governmental pressures noted in the previous section, telescoped the package into 3 years and added what was for all practical purposes a full union shop.

The events of 1959 cannot be understood except in the light of the 1955 and 1956 settlements which, in combination with wage escalation, were extremely expensive, and the change in economic conditions. Investment programs undertaken with optimism began to raise questions as the gap between production and capacity grew.

It no doubt appeared to the industry, particularly to the new industry leadership, that their efforts over the years since 1952 to develop constructive relations with the union had been singularly unsuccessful. What they seemed to have achieved was a decidedly high level of costs in a far more competitive environment. It is in the light of this background that 1959 should be viewed.

In 1959, the 12 largest steel companies bargained for the first time on a publicly unified basis. The committee which coordinated bargaining was composed of one representative from each of the 12 largest producers. The actual negotiating team had four members, two from U.S. Steel, one from Republic, and one from Bethlehem. The necessity for advice and consultation between the negotiating team, the coordinating committee, and the chief executive officers of the companies in and of itself made for some difficulties in communication within the industry. The most experienced negotiator is apt to have trouble if it takes him days to change his position or make an agreement. Industrywide bargaining is a difficult technique at best, and usually improves through experience over a period of years. The industry's administrative arrangement complicated its approach and confronted the union with an arrangement foreign to its accustomed method of reaching settlements.

The situation may have been further influenced by the fact that John Stephens, the longtime industry spokesman, had been replaced by R. Conrad Cooper of U.S. Steel. Yet the industry negotiating arrangement appeared to give to Cooper little opportunity to act as a free agent. One must be very cautious about placing undue importance upon individual leadership as a source of conflict. Attitudes hardened in 1959 essentially because of costs and competition. As in any negotiation, the particular strategies proposed by individual leaders may have increased or reduced the possibility of a peaceful settlement. Whatever the causes, the result in 1959 was futility protracted over a period of many months.

The problems inherent in industrywide bargaining may continue as a source of difficulty, although these should be eased in the years to come. Perhaps the most difficult problem in multiemployer bargaining is to discover a feasible method of determining group policy and exercising group authority. In 1959 the steel industry used a process of joint decisionmaking strongly led by U.S. Steel and one or two others of the Big Four. Satisfactory group decisions in industrywide bargaining require flexibility within a well-developed long-range program. This can only be accomplished by careful prior consideration of the authority to be given to negotiators and of procedures for assuring fair considerations of the interest and problems of all members. A further essential is that negotiators be given sufficient authority and leeway in their instructions to enable them to bind the industry on points which are not of fundamental importance to the interests of all. Whether or not the basic steel industry can accomplish this kind of equitable, yet flexible, technique remains to be seen. The present approach has great potential for the development of a long-range program; it has the danger that industry agreement on future contract proposals may be reached only on an unimaginative basis.

Incentives and Work Rules

The introduction of job evaluation into the steel industry created a systematic and orderly basic wage rate structure. If work in the industry had consisted predominately of nonincentive jobs, the rationalization of wages would have been accomplished. However, about 65 percent of all steel production and maintenance employees are paid under some type of incentive arrangement which yields earnings over and above the base rates. This fact created problems that had to be dealt with immediately after the standard hourly wage rates were established in 1947. Much time and effort in subsequent years was occupied in the attempt to reach agreement on principles as a necessary prelude to the ultimate elimination of inequities on incentive jobs. The effort to negotiate basic incentive principles was largely unsuccessful, and aspects of the failure still create conflict between the union and some companies in the industry.

From mid-1947 through 1950 the Joint Wage Rate Negotiating Committee of U.S. Steel and the Steelworkers union worked to complete the task of "developing the principles for determining a fairday's work" as required in the 1947 agreement. For various reasons this effort was almost totally unsuccessful:

(1) The incentive negotiations were started too soon after the completion of the inequities agreements. The parties had not had the opportunity to assimilate the basic and far-reaching changes installed by the earlier agreements, and thus the incentive negotiations took place in a time of too great upheaval.

(2) There was not the same compulsion on both parties to press for an early settlement of the incentive issue as there had been in the case of inequities in base rates. In the first case the union could foresee greater earnings; in the latter the industry hoped to make

some cost reductions while maintaining or improving average incentive yield.

(3) The steelworker leadership was apparently not prepared to assume the responsibility with management for the installation of new incentives, particularly in the case of plans which were not acceptable to the local grievance committees.

(4) The union's negative attitude toward the renegotiation of incentives resulted partially from the fact that incentive workers already felt some resentment since they had not shared in the monetary gains of the wage classification program.

(5) The steel industry as a whole was divided on the treatment of incentives. U.S. Steel could not speak for the whole industry to the same degree that it had on base rates.

(6) The parties did not have available to them in the incentive negotiation a Government directive order and a Government supervising commission as it had had in the case of the inequities negotiation. Some major issues between the parties with respect to job classification had been resolved by the WLB order.

(7) The era of good feeling and mutual respect which had prevailed during the inequities negotiations did not carry over into the incentives negotiations. The bad feelings engendered by the 1948 wage reopening and the 1949 strike over pensions probably carried over to the incentive negotiations.

The failure of union and management to agree either upon general principles or in specific cases that earnings on given jobs were inequitable led to a stalemate in negotiation. While U.S. Steel went ahead with the introduction of new and revised incentive plans, the union as a matter of policy brought a grievance over all such cases. This still left the parties with the day-to-day problem of the replacement of existing incentive plans and the installation of new incentive plans. Disagreement in carrying forward incentive revision led to the submission and resubmission of the problem to several different arbitrators. Their awards did lead to a case-by-case solution of the problem, although providing no industrial engineering principles for resolution of the overall controversy.

The next round in the incentive controversy was fought before the Wage Stabilization Board in the early months of 1952. The WSB accepted neither the union nor the company position and referred the incentive issues back to the parties without majority recommendation. To assist the parties in their negotiations the public members of the panel gave them an opinion to serve as a guide for resolution of the issue. The public members suggested that the parties should abandon the effort to agree on a set of guides to the setting of performance standards, and that U.S. Steel should proceed on the basis of principles of its own choosing, subject to challenge through the grievance procedure. Subsequent agreement to give up the effort to define, except on a case-by-case approach, the term "equitable incentive compensation," broke the log jam of grievances within U.S. Steel.

It should not be assumed that no progress was made in the rationalization of the incentive structure because of the failure to agree upon an industrial engineering definition of equitable incentive compensation and the inability to carry out a program to identify and remove inequities in incentive earnings. This entire disagreement went on within a framework in which it had been agreed to substitute "new" incentives for "old" incentives. In some situations the right to install new incentives was optional with the company, in some situations obligatory, and in some cases it required mutual agreement. Agreement was also achieved with respect to the 1947 increase not to give to workers on "old" incentives that portion of the increase resulting from increasing the labor grade increment. As a result of this wage agreement, the yield on old incentives declined relative to that on new incentives, facilitating the introduction of new incentives. Also the rates under the job classification plan had "submerged" some incentive plans and had reduced the yield as calculated on the new hourly rate structure. In the years between 1947 and 1956, incremental increases were added to the minimum guarantee and to hourly earnings but were not added to the base rate, and therefore not compounded in incentive earnings. In 1956 all incentive workers received a compounded increase.

To a considerable extent new incentives have now been substituted for old incentives. The new incentives are all based upon or related to a standard hour measurement, displacing a variety of older forms, and are generally judged to be technically superior to the incentives which they replaced.

Disagreement as to principle was also decidedly more acute within U.S. Steel than in other companies. Some companies, such as Bethlehem, postponed the entire issue of incentive revision. Jones and Laughlin and the union agreed upon an equipment utilization approach, as, very recently, has Bethlehem. Following U.S. Steel's lead, most companies went ahead replacing old with new incentives but not becoming involved in the negotiation of principle or being subjected to the degree of grievance challenge which took place in U.S. Steel.

Wage incentives, production standards, and manning are related areas of low adjustment between management and unions in many collective bargaining relationships in American industry. No other incentive industry is known which has tackled the job of revision on the scale attempted in steel. The fact that increasing progress has been made in incentive revisions may well be regarded as more noteworthy than the disagreements which have been involved. It can hardly be doubted, however, that the negotiation failures in this area put considerable strain on the improved relationship which U.S. Steel and the Steelworkers had achieved in working out the job evaluation program.

In interviews with company and union officials various partial "explanations" have been given as to why the local working conditions issue was introduced into the 1959 negotiations. One such explanation relates the crew-size issue directly to incentive administration and to the failure of the earlier incentive negotiations to give to management a relatively free hand to carry through an industrial engineering program. Another regards the issue as a part of give-and-take bargaining strategy that misfired. A third states that the primary motivation came from companies not restricted by 2B and not wanting to be restricted. Still another relates it to a 1959 arbitration decision ruling that new local working conditions were created even after the original 1947 cutoff date. A general explanation places the entire matter on the plane of an argument over a basic principle of management rights.

It is impossible to write a chapter on accommodation and conflict in steel negotiations and ignore the now-famous 2B issue. It is equally impossible to "explain" the issue when people very close to the negotiation advance, with unquestioned sincerity, conflicting and divergent views. The 2B clause is by no means a common type of contract provision in labor agreements in this country. While "past practice" is used by arbitrators in interpreting and applying the substantive provisions of contracts, it is unusual to find such practices expressly protected by a contract provision. This alone could have led the companies to desire strongly to eliminate the clause. The union, by earlier success in achieving extension of the clause to the contracts of steel companies which had not had it, increased the number and solidarity of companies opposing it. The lack of a test of reasonableness where there had not been a change of conditions clearly was regarded by management as improper. Furthermore, management felt it undesirable that the clause resulted in a large number of arbitrations even where there had been a change in condition. On the other hand, arbitrators have not applied the test loosely and companies win many of the cases which are brought. One company which had had the clause for some years, but had been unusually careful in its administrative practices, reported that as of 1959 it "couldn't have cared less." Another company, literally buried in hundreds of oral and written practices and agreements, saw no way out of its difficulties except by modification of 2B. One company with a good many thousands of employees reported that with a free hand as to the contract it might potentially reduce its labor force by as much as a few hundred employees. The union saw in the clause protection of many reasonable conditions of work. Clearly, it found widespread employee support for its position.

In a limited sense, the 1959 dispute over the 2B clause can also be viewed as a symbolic issue. Even if it cannot be evaluated in specific dollars and cents terms, it may have reflected a general desire on the part of management to regain a greater degree of power vis-a-vis the union in managing the plants. For example, there are numerous areas of minor technological change which, even though permitted by the labor agreement, cannot be made without encountering counterpressure from employees and, in some fashion, from the union. If the industry had won its demand on the changes in the 2B clause, the relative balance of power would have shifted in some degree to the industry. The making of the endless variety of minor changes which management views as its prerogative would thereby have been greatly facilitated.

The 2B dispute remained unresolved when the 1959 strike was settled, and was referred to a joint committee for study and such recommendations as the parties can mutually agree upon. From an outsider's point of view only a few generalizations about the dispute over the clause appear possible. It is a reasonable concluson that the clause does not protect widespread inefficiency because such inefficiency does not exist. In the few instances where it is demonstrable that high labor costs make a plant or company noncompetitive, much more than a revision of 2B is required to solve the problem. On the other hand, although it is doubtful that changes in 2B would have the sweeping potential for harm to existing conditions which the union attached to it, it is true that some cost savings would undoubtedly result from an improved basis for adjusting to technological change. If the parties cannot agree upon this phase of a joint approach to the problem of adjusting to change, it remains as a potentially serious issue in future negotiations.

CHAPTER 8

CONTRACT ADMINISTRATION

No detailed study of contract administration was made in connection with this project. Such a study would have been a major task in and of itself. However, there were certain questions relating to contract administration which require some judgments. These were: (1) Have the relatively frequent breakdowns in negotiation and consequent strikes in steel carried conflict into the plants, resulting in relatively poor day-to-day labor relations? (2) Has the centralized form of negotiation in the steel industry made it difficult to resolve contract administration issues through negotiation? and (3) Are there at present contract administration issues which can be expected to create important negotiating issues?

These questions were discussed with labor relations officials in five of the large steel companies and with some national officers and staff representatives of the Steelworkers. The discussions were judged in the light of several years of study in connection with a Brookings Institution project on the impact of collective bargaining on management. In the course of that study interviews were held with several hundred labor relations and union officials in about 150 different companies and 40 unions in various industries.

The Development of Orderly Plant Labor Relations

In regard to general public understanding, the most important point to emphasize is the quite widespread establishment of orderly day-to-day labor relations throughout American industry which have been developed through a very substantial body of rights and obligations under labor contracts. The modern labor movement in the United States burst upon the country during the 1935–45 decade, during which labor union membership grew from some 3 million to 15 million. In retrospect, over the past 25 years there have been overlapping stages such as (1) organizing, (2) contract-development, and (3) adjustment. Conflict has diminished and orderly day-to-day relations largely established.

Labor agreements, initially little more than recognition documents, have expanded into substantial bodies of rules. The contracts are, however, in many respects skeletal in character. They are supplemented by managerial policies, local supplementary agreements, precedents established in grievance settlements, local practices and arbitration decisions. The practice of final and binding arbitration of grievances arising under the contract has, over the years, grown

119

from a novel experiment to almost universal practice. Contract language has become more detailed and interpretations have become more stable. To get a broad view of the "web of rules" collective bargaining has created in steel, one should peruse the *Steelworkers Handbook on Arbitration Decisions*, recently published by the union, a 517 page digest and analysis of selected decisions.

There is a tendency to think of collective bargaining too exclusively in its negotiation context, and, particularly in terms of strikes over economic issues, forgetting or grossly underestimating the significant evolution in contract administration which has taken place. To be sure, there remain elements of conflict in contract administration. Managements feel that in important respects their discretion has been too limited. Unions push for new and broader limitations. But the extremely hectic day-to-day relations of the organizing stage and, to a degree, of the contract-development stage, are generally a thing of the past.

In broad outline, contract administration in basic steel does not differ from that prevailing in other major industries. Contract negotiation has produced frequent strikes but has not retarded the growth of orderly and for the most part friendly and constructive day-to-day relationships. No small part of the explanation of this fact is that steel management has never attempted to break the union in any of the postwar strikes. The recognition struggle in "Little Steel" was the last of the no-holds-barred strikes. Although strikes in steel may be described as industrial warfare, they have followed a civilized form of warfare. They typically involve an orderly shutdown of facilities, certain maintenance work during the strike, no attempt by the companies to operate during the strike, token picketing with amenities such as coffee and radio facilities occasionally furnished by the company, a strike settlement, and an orderly resumption of work. By and large the employees, while they support the union, appear to be glad to resume work and in no mood to carry resentment back to the job. Of course, most postwar steel strikes have been relatively short. The approximate 2-month strike in 1952 was something of an exception and the almost 4-month 1959 strike was decidedly an exception. Most strikes have not involved a severe financial drain upon the employees, particularly in view of high prestrike and poststrike earnings.

There are, of course, the usual company and plant variations in the quality of contract administration within basic steel as in other industries. There are some plants and companies in basic steel in which the cumulative effects of concessions given under the threat of wildcat strikes and other pressure tactics have produced a noncompetitive level of costs. Wildcat strikes in steel in some degree present a special problem. The threat in a grievance discussion to walk out of an open hearth or blast furnace, with its attendant costs and dangers, may have made the control of such strikes particularly difficult. On the other hand, those managements which have faced this problem squarely report their ability to close down safely any facility in the mill and to successfully control wildcats by consistent disciplinary action. All managements are able to control wildcats much more effectively today than some years ago, and commonly with union agreement as to policy.

Some plants in steel have very high grievance rates. A plant management confronted with a factional fight in its local union is likely to have high grievance activity. For example, some managements have developed and applied more effective labor relations policies than others. Some local unions are much more militant than others. Thus, plant-to-plant variation in the quality of labor relations makes generalization very speculative. Possibly steel, because of its wage incentive system and continuing revision of incentives, has had a somewhat more difficult contract administration problem than have some other industries, but orderly relations have nevertheless been established. This substantial improvement has been remarkably uninfluenced by the frequent strikes.

The Relation of Negotiation to Administration

The larger the negotiation framework, the more difficult becomes the resolution, through negotiation, of special problems facing the various smaller units within the scope of the bargain. It is for this reason that supplementary local agreements on such problems as seniority systems are commonly associated with multiplant agreements in large companies. The matter is one of degree, since all contracts establish general rules or principles only with respect to many important phases of labor relations—a simple "just cause" disciplinary clause is as appropriate in a multiplant as in a single plant contract. When several companies join in a single contract, differences in what is regarded by both company and union as appropriate policy, as well as differences in problems, further complicate the satisfactory resolution of issues.

For most of the postwar years, the steel industry followed a bargaining practice of pattern-setting by U.S. Steel and pattern following by the rest of the industry. This type of bargaining limits the opportunity for negotiation once the pattern is set. U.S. Steel could balance economic offers against desired contract language. Among the other companies, no economic bargaining leverage remained to deal separately with the problems of particular companies and those of individual local unions. Also the form of pattern bargaining in basic steel has been much more inclusive than in most industries. In steel the pattern mechanism tended over the years to carry the entire contract, not just the economic settlement, to all major companies. This point should not be overemphasized because there are, and always have been, some significant contract differences among major companies. However, though neither the other companies nor the union may have thought the U.S. Steel language the best possible from their respective points of view, it was frequently the only basis for agreement. An additional consideration is the industrywide orientation which exists within the union and, to a lesser degree, among the companies. By way of contrast, the automobile industry follows a set pattern, but negotiation is much more company-centered than in steel.

The companies and the union react quite differently to the compulsion of pattern following in those contract areas where there is no compatible mutual interest in special negotiation. The companies are conscious of their inability to negotiate on particular issues of concern to them. They are conscious of the union's power to insist upon favored language and to demand just "one more thing" before signing. The union is conscious of its inability to improve upon the U.S. Steel contract, and its inability to meet special local demands.

There have been a number of instances in which the union has secured concessions in particular companies by its willingness to strike. There have been a few instances where companies have been willing to take a strike to improve contract language. For example, in 1947, Inland Steel obtained stronger sanction for discipline in the event of wildcat strikes. Most recently, Pittsburgh Steel, by persuasion and willingness to take a special strike, obtained economic concessions with respect to incentive compensation. But, once a pattern has been set, there is little opportunity for further negotiation.

The trend, in this type of situation, is toward a uniform master contract with perhaps some expansion of the coverage of supplementary agreements. The situation at present is that both companies and union continue to accept clauses they would like to change rather than risk a work stoppage over the issue. For clauses of this type the new industry-group form of negotiation, possibly resting upon a substantially uniform contract, is probably superior to the pattern mechanism. In substantive areas where both parties desire to diverge, and there is scope to negotiate, supplementary agreements are appropriate. An interesting trend in this direction is the growth of company agreements on wage incentive principles and administration. Although it is fair to conclude that there is some frustration over the centralized negotiating framework for resolution of particular issues, the parties appear to be moving toward an improved basis for the negotiation of common problems and toward separate negotiation, where feasible.

It would be easy to exaggerate the problems the companies and the union have encountered through highly centralized and pattern-dominated negotiation in resolving "noneconomic" issues. For the most part, contract terms are satisfactory. There are several reasons for this. First, U.S. Steel and the Steelworkers have negotiated contract terms which, on the whole, have been reasonably balanced. Second, as analyzed in chapter 7, conflict has chiefly centered in economic issues and issues of principle. The parties have achieved a high level of accommodation with respect to most aspects of contract administration. Finally, the contract (in those important areas in which the contract language is general or limited) has left considerable latitude for variation through administration, which has been decidedly decentralized.

One of the most interesting aspects of the Steelworker's organization is the contrast between its approach to negotiation and to administration. Over the years it has become highly centralized in its approach to negotiation, but it is still highly decentralized in its approach to administration. Contract administration for all plants of all companies in a district operates through the district director's office. An international representative from this office will typically handle the contract administration problems for a given plant. This leads to a high degree of local autonomy with no strong unification on the union side with respect to the various plants of a given company. On the union side, there is a considerable gap between leadership in negotiation and leadership in contract administration. Although this is filled to some extent by staff guidance, as illustrated by the new arbitration handbook, locals most certainly are masters of their own destiny in living under the contract.

Perhaps local autonomy in contract administration is in some sense a counterbalance to centralized negotiation. Problems of most immediate concern to employees, such as handling work assignments, production standards, incentive earnings, manning, work schedules, the administration of plant rules, discipline, etc., are resolved through company policy, grievance settlements, local agreements, and arbitration. While the basic contract establishes some ground rules, much of the substance is left for local determination.

There is one additional influence in this situation. Once the arbitration level is reached, similarity in contract language and permanent umpire systems of long standing seem to create much more industry-wide precedent influence for decisions than is true in most industries.

An element of centralization reappears at this level in contract administration.

An interesting comparison can be made with the Automobile Workers, in which there has been somewhat more decentralization by company in negotiation and more centralized control in administration. Each bargaining system has grown within its own environment, but what the Steelworker locals may lack in autonomy in negotiation they sometimes more than make up in autonomy in administration. No completely opposite contrast is intended, but there does appear to be a difference in degree.

Bargaining systems evolve in response to many influences. The steel system has its own elements of uniqueness. It has its own problems. A local union has little influence or control over basic contract terms and neither does local plant management. But local autonomy through local adaptation of policy and through the grievance procedure creates about the same plant-by-plant variations as are to be found in comparable industries.

Important Contract Administration Issues

Discussion with a limited number of union and industry officials tends to support the view that the relatively high degree of adjustment in negotiation of most contract administration issues pointed out in chapter 7 is paralleled by adjustment in day-to-day relations with respect to these same issues. Grievances with respect to wage rates for new and changed jobs, and those relating to employee classification and assignment, while important in number, are resolved within the principles established by the cooperative wage study. Pension, insurance, and other benefit plans, although they have their administrative problems, are low grievance areas (though grievances involving important principles are serious in nature) and reflect the adjustment developed. The union's specialized staff plays an important role in administration. Layoff and promotion systems are difficult to administer, particularly with fluctuations in employment, but both parties are flexible in their approach through local negotiation. Subcontracting problems increase with employees on layoff. Work and vacation schedules are difficult to administer in a continuous process industry. Any agreed-upon rules will leave elements of unrest because not every employee can have a preferred schedule. The plant-committee approach to safety has been decidedly successful. Disciplinary grievances create no more problems than in other industries. Arbitration is well established and the same arbitrators have served in most companies for some years.

Unquestionably the wage incentives area is, and has been for some time, the most difficult contract administration issue. Wage incentives at times impinge upon the local working practice clause, and also become the indirect cause of grievances arising under other contract sections. It is difficult, however, to give a brief and balanced account of wage incentive problems.

One reason that wage incentive grievances stand out is that issues in other areas have been reasonably well resolved. Perhaps more important, the companies have been in the process of revising and improving their incentive structure. A third reason is that changing technology, methods, and products require continuous adjustment in production standards. Technology has also been changing the character of work, creating jobs which are difficult to compensate under an effort philosophy.

The steel industry is not alone in its problems with the incentive system. The combination of union challenge through the grievance procedure with the economic and production conditions prevailing during and since World War II has led to the development of many demoralized wage incentive plans in which the average incentive yield has grown, the average effort level has declined, inequities in earnings and effort have developed, and "off-standard" time has increased. Some incentive plans have lost all vestige of their original purpose. Judged by the operation of incentives in some companies in other industries, incentives in steel are not generally demoralized and they are being improved.

Special problems have developed in the revision of the incentive plans, such as (1) the upward revision of incentive yield; (2) the establishment of new and the replacement of old incentives and the removal of inequities; (3) the extension of incentive coverage; and (4) the effort philosophy and the type of incentive payment. Relating to the first problem, steel has been in the process of revising upward the average incentive yield as new incentive plans replace old incentive plans. At the end of World War II, incentive earnings had increased relative to the earnings of nonincentive workers. The standard hourly rates established under the job classification program raised the guaranteed rate for incentive jobs and the relative level of earnings of nonincentive workers. The earnings on some low-yield old incentives were "submerged"; that is, they fell below the newly guaranteed rates. The average yield of old incentives calculated on the new wage scale fell, and substantially corrected the incentive vs. nonincentive inequity so far as an average relationship was concerned. The manner of handling the wage-increment wage increases for incentive workers who were under old incentive plans further reduced the average yield of the old incentives and facilitated the introduction of new incentive plans. The average yield on old incentive plans in several companies seems to be approximately 17 percent.   The average yield on new incentives appears to be close to 22 percent.

The change from old to new incentives is a constructive revision of the incentive structure, but it is expensive and adds to the cost of wage increases.   It also created disagreement over what constituted equitable incentive compensation.   Most companies also believe that not all incentive plans should be designed to produce the same percentage yield and they generally do not wish to bind themselves to some fixed percentage figure.   The union, particularly at the local level, wishes to get as much as possible out of the incentive revision program, and wishes to protect vested interests.   Without attempting to develop the complexities of this problem, it should be emphasized that the parties are moving toward an improved incentive structure, and they do not face the problem existing in many incentive plants of reducing the entire level of incentive earnings.   For the industry as a whole, the incentive yield is not abnormally high.   A few companies (e.g., Pittsburgh Steel) and a few plants, however, do have a severe problem of reducing a noncompetitive level of incentive earnings.

The revision program had to face the issue of removing inequities among jobs.   Since the yield on many old incentives was on the low side, it was possible to remove "low-side" inequities and this reduced the relative significance of inequities on the "high-side."   But naturally the companies wanted to isolate and remove gradually the "high-side" inequities in the old incentive structure.   In this effort they were largely unsuccessful.   Where "high-side" old incentives have been revised, the companies have had to build into their new incentives an out-of-line job differential to preserve the old level of earnings for the old level of effort.   Although the number of such differentials is not so large as to create an impossible problem, the companies obviously will make continued efforts to remove these guarantees.   In principle, the companies, spending considerable money to remove "low-side" inequities, resented the union's unwillingness to yield on this issue.

The third and fourth problems grow out of the considerable change technology is making in the character of work.   More and more the effort burden is being taken over by the employee-operated machine.   The worker frequently does not have to pace the machine to turn out more work.   This is not true of all work, nor all technological change, but it has had meaningful effect within steel.   Assume, for example, an employee controls a rheostat to operate a slitting machine.   To turn out more products, he turns up the rheostat, but he can hardly be regarded as working at an "incentive level of effort."   If work is broken down into "work time," "attention time," and "standby time," a larger part of the daily hours seems to be falling in the last two categories, and "work" in itself is becoming less arduous.

To continue the slitting-machine example, it may be desirable for the company to pay an incentive premium to encourage minimum downtime and maximum production to get minimum capital cost per unit of product, but it becomes difficult to defend this payment as being one for added or incentive effort. This kind of payment leads all employees to desire incentive payment and to feel they are entitled to it. One local union paper demanded, for example, that all dayworkers be included in the "profit-sharing incentive plan."

Managements, in response to this employee attitude, have differed in their desire to extend incentive plans. Some managements have felt that they could gain from such extensions and have developed plans to include a high proportion of the work force. On the other hand, some managements have been reluctant to expand coverage. However, if one company introduces incentive plans in coke ovens and blast furnaces, the pattern influence is strong. The result has been a growth in incentive coverage, with variations among companies and plants.

Where incentive has been introduced into areas and jobs with controlled processes and production, the only way management could gain was through doing the required work with fewer man-hours. But this road may be blocked by the crew-size restriction in the local working practices clause. Frequently, management can negotiate a crew reduction in return for incentive coverage. If it cannot, it is not obliged to put in the incentive. But if it puts in the incentive on a low-yield basis, it may be held not to be paying equitable incentive compensation.

Some companies have also, with union encouragement, moved to an equipment utilization basis for much of their incentive compensation. On this basis, the only payment consideration is the rate of production from the machine or equipment. If the equipment is operated at practical capacity (with some variation in definition), all employees are paid maximum incentive pay for all hours worked. If an effort basis is used for incentive compensation, attention time but not standby time is compensated at an incentive rate.

It is evident from the above paragraphs that it is not easy to determine the basis for incentive payment, nor is it easy to distinguish incentive work from nonincentive work. In such a setting, management frequently wishes to establish some incentive plans with lower level normal yields and other plans with higher level normal yields. The union wishes high yield plans for all employees for all hours worked.

Cearly, both managements and the union are struggling with difficult problems in the incentive area and there are no perfect answers. There is no difficulty in understanding why the revision of incentive plans and their administration should produce a relatively high fraction of all grievances. It is not a question of poor union-management relations [1] but rather of a difficult administrative problem. But revision of plans is being completed, thus diminishing the scope of the problems. Also, there have been some successful negotiations with particular companies on principles and policies. There will be continued negotiation on incentive issues, largely on a company-by-company basis, and there will be continued difficulty in administration. However, progress is being made in the incentive area. Nor is it the type of issue which is likely to produce an industrywide strike. Also, in repetition, incentives in steel are not grossly distorted or demoralized—they are better than those in a number of other industries—but the path toward improvement has been expensive, has encountered some thorny problems, and creates a major difficulty in contract administration.

This chapter concludes with a brief discussion of the administrative significance of the local working practices issue. The crew-size issue has already been mentioned, but it should be qualified. In the event of technological change (a change in underlying conditions), the companies are not held to a fixed crew. Incentive revision based upon technological change is thus not bound. It is only in the extension of incentive (and proposed revision not based on technological change) that the fixed-crew ruling can halt or make difficult the establishment of plans.

It is difficult to judge the administrative seriousness of the local practices issue. Of the few companies with which we have talked, all are concerned on the basis of principle, but several say that it is not very serious with them in terms of efficiency. One company (not U.S. Steel) was most decidedly concerned. But in this company the problems would not be eliminated by removal or modification of the contract clause. For example, this company is burdened by a plant-wide type seniority system and many costly seniority practices. It is also troubled by many types of oral and written agreements and practices. While the management might make some progress, absent a local practices clause, it most certainly would face a challenge from the union concerning many issues under various parts of the contract. The very militant local obtained concession after concession from management, typically through pressure and wildcat strikes. Man-

---

[1] In plants where union-management relations are poor, conflict is likely to focus strongly on incentive administration.

agement faces a difficult task in this plant, but its problems go far beyond the scope of the local work practice clause.

In addition, various examples of costly local practices cited by industry representatives turn out in fact to be cases in which management did not exercise its right under the contract. Again, as an example, in one plant of one company firemen are employed on diesel locomotives. The company purchased mirrors to mount on the cabs and proposed taking the firemen off the locomotives. They undoubtedly had the right to remove the firemen under the contract but backed down in the face of a threatened strike. Other practices cited, such as coffee breaks, turn out to be management initiated in the interest of efficiency.

It is true that the local practice clause provides a vehicle for harassment. Many grievances can be brought under this article if the local so desires. Its alleged violation is often attached to grievances brought primarily under other articles. But, again, if a local union is of a mind to harass management through the grievance procedure, it has many avenues of approach open to it.

Our belief is that the administrative handicap of the clause, for the industry as a whole, is not widespread. This does not make the clause "right" or "wrong," but appears to be a reasonable assessment of the most typical situation.

In those few plants with widespread elements of inefficiency, and there are such plants in every industry in the country, the union is faced with the necessity of allowing management to lower its costs and improve efficiency or suffer more severe consequences through competitive loss of business.

The hope remains that the industry and the union will be able to evolve a balanced approach in adjustment to technological change. Monetary concessions are one avenue of approach, though the companies with their 52-week supplementary unemployment benefits and with severance pay have gone far in this direction. The more difficult tasks are working out ways and means for senior employees to retain useful and efficient employment in the face of advancing technology and, simultaneously, of allowing the companies to achieve full benefit from new technology.

Part IV

ECONOMIC IMPLICATIONS OF STEEL BARGAINING

CHAPTER 9

HOURLY EARNINGS AND WAGE ADJUSTMENTS

This chapter first discusses hourly earnings in basic steel. The focus is upon the trend of steelworkers' earnings in the postwar period as compared with the trend of earnings in other industries. One purpose is descriptive: How have steelworkers fared in comparison with workers in other industries? Another purpose is analytical: Can comparisons of various time periods and various groupings of industries provide clues as to wage forces operating in the economy?

Although the study of relative earnings gives perspective, hourly earnings fluctuate for many reasons and this analysis needed to be supplemented by a study of wage adjustments. If, as was the case, steel earnings ran about parallel with all durable goods during the years 1945–55, could a study of the timing and amounts of wage adjustments (and major fringe benefit changes) establish whether steel was leading or following in this succession of events? In the 1955–59 period, when steel earnings advanced sharply in relation to other industries, what wage forces were in operation and what were the effects? In addition, a special study was made of the pattern influence of basic steel upon steel fabrication. In other words, after a review of trends in earnings, the chapter turns more directly to an analysis of the wage influence of steel in the economy.

Hourly Earnings of Steel Workers [1]

The Period 1922–35.—To place the interindustry wage structure of the American economy in modest historical perspective, brief consideration is given to the relationship between steel earnings and those of other selected industries in the period 1922–35. Comparisons are given only between the terminal years, but annual data show similar trends. (Data are from the National Industrial Conference Board and are not precisely comparable with those for the 1934–59 period. The later data are from the Bureau of Labor Statistics whose industry series generally began in 1929.)

With one exception, there were relatively similar increases among selected durable goods industries in earnings in both cents per hour

---

[1] This section is based upon a study paper by Morris A. Horowitz, Northeastern University, entitled, *The Earnings of Steel Workers in the Postwar Period.* Much of the following is excerpted directly from the study paper with compression and with a few changes and additions.

and percentage terms. Excluding foundries, the increases ranged from 15 cents for chemicals to 22 cents for rubber, with iron and steel at 16 cents. The relative increases ranged from 29 percent for automobiles to 38 percent for rubber, with iron and steel at 32 percent. For this period there was no significant widening of differentials among these various durable goods industries. (See table I.)

Comparisons were also made between iron and steel earnings and earnings in selected nondurable goods industries. Unlike the situation among the durable goods industries, there were sizable changes in differentials among the nondurable goods industries and between iron and steel and the other industries. Except for hosiery and knit goods, all other of the selected nondurable goods industries showed significantly lower increases than iron and steel. (See table 2.)

TABLE 1.—*Average gross hourly earnings in the iron and steel industry compared with selected durable goods industries, 1922 and 1935*

Industry	Average hourly earnings		Hourly increase, 1922–35	
	1922	1935	Amount	Percent
Iron and steel	$0.50	$0.66	$0.16	32
Agricultural implements	.49	.67	.18	37
Automobile manufacturing	.59	.76	.17	29
Chemical manufacturing	.46	.61	.15	33
Electrical manufacturing	.50	.67	.17	34
Foundries and machine shops heavy equipment	.60	.63	.03	5
Rubber manufacturing	.58	.80	.22	38

SOURCE: National Industrial Conference Board, *Wages, Hours and Employment in the United States, 1914–1936*, 1936.

TABLE 2.—*Average gross hourly earnings in the iron and steel industry compared with selected nondurable goods industries, 1922 and 1935*

Industry	Average hourly earnings		Hourly increase, 1922–35	
	1922	1935	Amount	Percent
Iron and steel	$0.50	$0.66	$0.16	32
Boot and shoe manufacturing	.48	.57	.09	19
Cotton manufacturing, North	.40	.45	.05	12
Hosiery and knit goods manufacturing	.35	.52	.17	49
Paper products manufacturing	.43	.52	.09	21
Silk manufacturing	.45	.53	.08	18
Wool manufacturing	.46	.52	.06	13

SOURCE: National Industrial Conference Board, *Wages, Hours and Employment in the United States, 1914–1936*, 1936.

For the same period, 1922–35, a third comparison was made. Table 3 shows average hourly earnings in iron and steel and in selected miscellaneous industries. As with nondurable goods, these industries showed varied increases but, with one exception, did not reach the level of increase in iron and steel. Printing, newspaper and magazines, did exceed the increase in iron and steel in absolute figures (17 cents as against 16 cents), but had a lower relative increase (25 percent compared with 32 percent).

It is evident from these data that for this period, earnings in iron and steel moved relatively uniformly with virtually all other durable goods industries, but moved up faster than most industries in the nondurable and in the miscellaneous groups. Thus, within the selected group of durable goods industries there was little distortion of the wage structure. Even in the absence of union organization in most of the industries compared for this period, durable goods industries showed a relative advance.

TABLE 3.—*Average gross hourly earnings in the iron and steel industry compared with selected miscellaneous industries, 1922 and 1935*

Industry	Average hourly earnings		Hourly increase, 1922-35	
	1922	1935	Amount	Percent
Iron and steel	$0.50	$0.66	$0.16	32
Furniture manufacturing	.48	.54	.06	12
Leather tanning and finishirg	.45	.56	.11	24
Lumber and millwork	.45	.50	.05	11
Meatpacking	.44	.57	.13	30
Paint and varnish manufacturing	.51	.58	.07	14
Paper and pulp manufacturing	.46	.53	.07	15
Printing, book and job	.63	.74	.11	18
Printing, newspaper and magazines	.69	.86	.17	25

SOURCE: National Industrial Conference Board, *Wages, Hours and Employment in the United States, 1914-1936,* 1936.

The Period 1934–59.—Examining the broad sweep of the 1934–59 period, a changing picture of the interindustry wage structure of the economy emerges. In view of the long period involved, this is not unexpected, since some industries may be expanding much more rapidly than others whereas some industries may actually be declining. Average hourly earnings in basic steel and in selected industries for 1934 and 1959 are shown in table 4, along with increases by industry for specified periods within the 25-year period.

In 1934, hourly earnings in basic steel were higher than those in all-manufacturing and in durable goods industries, but were lower than those in four of the six selected industries for which data are available. Automobiles, tires and inner tubes, petroleum refining, and shipbuilding exceeded basic steel by amounts ranging from 6 to 13 cents. By 1959 basic steel's hourly earnings at $3.08 were the highest of the group, with petroleum refining second at $2.98. Automobiles was fourth highest, with earnings at $2.70—38 cents below basic steel. The last two columns of table 4 show the actual and percentage increases over the 25-year period, by industry. Average hourly earnings in basic steel rose by $2.45, or 389 percent, 22 cents more than petroleum refining, the second highest industry. In relative terms, tin cans with a rise of 430 percent exceeded basic steel, but this rise was only $2.15, starting from a low wage of 50 cents an hour in 1934. Meatpacking, also starting from a low wage (55 cents), rose by 376 percent, the relative increase closest to that of basic steel. Although it is clear that the 1959 earnings in basic steel was highest, as was its monetary increase over the 25 years, the question is when did this significant increase take place. Was it a gradual rise over the whole period, or was it a sudden jump in a relatively short period of time?

Columns 3 and 4 show cents per hour and percent increases for the prewar period, 1934–40. Both shipbuilding and automobiles, greatly affected by the defense buildup, showed increases higher than basic steel, whereas tin cans and meatpacking were lower. This prewar pattern was rather mixed, with steel falling between the high and the low.

The war years, 1940–45, showed a different pattern, undoubtedly as a result of the Government's wage stabilization program. There was a rather uniform movement of wages during the period, with variations in a relatively narrow range. Of interest during this period is that the increases in earnings in all-manufacturing and in durable goods industries exceeded those in all the selected industries, including basic steel. The shift of employees to defense industries undoubtedly increased the average for all-manufacturing and possibly durable goods.

In the postwar period, 1945–49, basic steel still showed no extraordinary increase, compared with other industries. While steel earnings increased by 47 cents, or 40 percent, petroleum rose by 58 cents, or 45 percent, and tin cans, by 48 cents, or 52 percent. Except for shipbuilding, which was in a postwar slump, increases in the other industries were within 3 cents of those in basic steel.

Compared with the 1945–49 period, the next 5 years (1949–54), showed larger cents-per-hour increases for all industries except petroleum refining, which had an unusually large rise in the preceding period. The increase in basic steel earnings was on the high side, with a rise of 55 cents, or 33 percent, but tin cans exceeded steel with an increase of 57 cents, or 41 percent. In cents per hour, increases in tires and inner tubes and in meatpacking were within 2 cents of steel, and on a percentage basis meatpacking exceeded steel, 38 percent compared with 33 percent. Shipbuilding had the lowest increase with a rise of 46 cents, or 28 percent.

TABLE 4.—*Average gross hourly earnings in basic steel and in selected industries, 1934 and 1959, and increases by selected periods, 1934–59*

Industry	Average hourly earnings		Increase in hourly earnings											
			1934-40		1940-45		1945-49		1949-54		1954-59		1934-59	
	1934	1959	Amount	Percent	Amount	Percent	Amount	Percent	Amount	Percent	Amount	Percent	Amount	Percent
Basic steel	$0.63	$3.08	$0.21	33	$0.34	40	$0.47	40	$0.55	33	$0.88	40	$2.45	389
Automobiles	.69	2.70	.25	36	.32	34	.44	35	.49	29	.51	23	2.01	291
Tires and inner tubes	.76	2.95	.20	26	.31	32	.47	37	.53	30	.65	26	2.19	298
Petroleum refining	.75	2.98	.22	29	.32	33	.58	45	.50	27	.61	26	2.23	297
Chemicals and allied products	(1)	2.41	---	---	---	---	---	---	.48	34	.50	26	---	---
Tin cans	.50	2.65	.12	24	.29	47	.48	52	.57	41	.69	35	2.15	430
Meatpacking	.55	2.62	.14	25	.26	38	.45	47	.53	38	.69	36	2.07	376
Shipbuilding	.72	2.60	.28	39	.36	36	.26	19	.46	28	.52	25	1.88	261
All manufacturing	.53	2.22	.13	24	.36	54	.38	37	.41	29	.41	23	1.69	318
Durable goods	.56	2.38	.16	29	.39	54	.35	31	.46	31	.46	24	1.82	325

1 Earliest data are for 1947 when earnings averaged $1.23.

SOURCE: U.S. Department of Labor, Bureau of Labor Statistics.

Up to that point (1954), the increases in steel earnings were not far out of line with those of other industries. The increases over this 20-year period were as follows:

| | Hourly increases, 1934–54 | | Average hourly |
	Amount	Percent	earnings, 1954
Basic steel	$1. 57	243	$2. 20
Automobiles	1. 50	217	2. 19
Tires and inner tubes	1. 51	199	2. 27
Petroleum refining	1. 62	216	2. 37
Tin cans	1. 46	292	1. 96
Meatpacking	1. 39	251	1. 94
Shipbuilding	1. 36	189	2. 08
All manufacturing	1. 28	242	1. 81
Durable goods	1. 36	243	1. 92

Again referring to table 4, the statistics on increases for the 1954–59 period show a completely different picture of basic steel than existed in any of the previous periods. Here, for the first time, the increase was greater in steel than in the other selected industries, and higher by a significant amount, in both cents per hour and percentage terms. Steel earnings rose by 88 cents, or 40 percent, with meatpacking the closest follow-up showing an increase of 69 cents, or 36 percent. The rise in steel earnings was thus 19 cents higher than in meatpacking, and 37 cents higher than in automobiles, the traditional rival of basic steel. The 88-cent increase in steel averaged better than 17 cents a year for this 5-year period. Since no other industry consistently showed larger increases than steel in the previous periods studied, the unusually large rise of 88 cents brought the 1959 average hourly earnings in basic steel significantly above any of the other industry.

A similar comparison of steel earnings and earnings in miscellaneous industries and industry groups is shown in table 5. Just as basic steel showed a particularly large increase in 1954–59, so did bituminous coal mining in 1945–49, when earnings rose by 70 cents compared with only 47 cents in steel. And even in the most recent period, 1954–59, earnings in bituminous coal mining rose by 77 cents, only 11 cents less than the increase in steel. Over the 25 years, earnings increased by $2.58 in this industry 13 cents in excess of the increase in basic steel. Although overshadowed by the steel increase in 1954–59, the increases in building and construction earnings had been consistently higher than those in steel in the three previous periods, resulting in combined increases for the 25-year period only 3 cents below steel. The 1959 average hourly earnings in building and construction, $3.22, was still higher than in basic steel. The increases in steel during 1954–59, however, far exceeded those in the other miscellaneous industries.

TABLE 5.—*Average gross hourly earnings in basic steel and in selected miscellaneous industries, 1934 and 1959, and increases by selected periods, 1934–59*

Industry	Average hourly earnings		Increase in hourly earnings											
	Base period[1]	1959	1934–40		1940–45		1945–49		1949–54		1954–59		1934–59	
			Amount	Percent	Amount	Percent	Amount	Percent	Amount	Percent	Amount	Percent	Amount	Percent
Basic steel	$0.63	$3.08	$0.21	33	$0.34	40	$0.47	40	$0.55	33	$0.88	40	$2.45	389
Bituminous coal mining	.67	3.25	.21	31	.36	41	.70	56	.54	28	.77	31	2.58	385
Nonmetallic mining	.47	2.18	.10	21	.32	56	.41	46	.46	35	.42	24	1.71	363
Building and construction	.80	3.22	.16	20	.42	44	.56	41	.66	34	.62	24	2.42	308
Electrical work	1.20	3.70			.36	30	.65	42	.71	32	.78	27		
Textile mill products	1.19	1.57							.17	14	.21	15		
Lumber and wood products	1.27	1.97							.36	28	.34	21		
Furniture and fixtures	1.23	1.82							.34	28	.25	16		
Paper and allied products	1.34	2.20							.41	31	.45	26		
Printing and publishing, etc.	1.84	2.70							.43	23	.43	19		
Leather and leather products	1.14	1.61							.24	21	.23	17		
Apparel and other finished products	.54	1.52			.32	59	.32	36	.18	15	.17	13		

[1] Base periods for the industries were as follows: 1934—*Basic steel, bituminous coal mining, nonmetallic mining, and building and construction;* 1940—*Electrical work, and apparel and other finished products;* 1949—*Textile mill products, lumber and wood products, furniture and fixtures, paper and allied products, printing and publishing, etc., and leather and leather products.*

SOURCE: U.S. Department of Labor, Bureau of Labor Statistics.

Comparison by Industry Groups

In the previous discussion some note has been taken of the relative increase of earnings in the durable goods industries. In addition to a comparison of industries in the durable and nondurable categories, comparison was made between high- and low-concentration industries and between industries with a high and low degree of union organization. As expected, industries producing durable goods, industries with high concentration, and industries with a high degree of union organization (involving much overlapping as to industries) showed larger increases than their opposites. While there are many detailed differences among all these industries, the increase in steel earnings for the 1954–59 period stands out in all the comparisons.

Steel Earnings 1954–59

As is well known, changes in gross hourly earnings are no simple reflection of changes in basic wage rates. During the years 1955–59 inclusive, negotiated increases in basic steel amounted to 61 cents.[2] However, gross earnings in steel, it will be recalled, increased 88 cents from the base year 1954 to 1959, 27 cents in excess of negotiated increases. It has been estimated that premium pay (overtime, holidays, and the Sunday premium) accounted for about 14 of the 27 cent increase.[3] The Sunday premium, an expensive item in a continuous-process industry, is estimated at about 6 cents. The increase in shift differentials added about 1 cent. The increase in employment in the higher job classes also increased earnings by 2.5 cents. Over this 5-year period, the composition of the work force changed as follows:

	1954 percent	1959 percent
Job classes 1–4	23. 4	20. 9
Job classes 5–10	48. 8	48. 9
Job classes 10–32	27. 8	30. 2

The incentive yield in 1954 amounted to 16 percent. Revision of incentive plans, discussed in connection with contract administration, increased incentive yield to 21 percent in 1959. Incentive coverage was 49 percent in 1954 and 63 percent in 1959. The combined effect of extending incentive coverage and increasing the yield was equivalent to about a 10 cent increase in average earnings for all production employees. Although these are rough estimates, it is believed that they portray reasonably well the various influences which have produced the gain in earnings over negotiated increases.

---

[2] Includes the increase in incentive earnings resulting directly from the increase in base rates.

[3] This estimate and other estimates in the calculation are based on American Iron and Steel Industry data.

In summary, the comparison of increases in earnings in steel with those in other industries revealed no marked deviation up to 1954. Steel maintained a favorable position among durable goods and all-manufacturing industries, but up to that year the percentage gains in steel, in durable goods, and in all-manufacturing were essentially identical. However, beginning in 1954 steel earnings gained markedly. Among the manufacturing industries, flat glass with an increase of 70 cents and meatpacking and cans at 69 cents appear to come closest to steel's 88 cents. Negotiated wage increases account for approximately 61 of the 88 cent increase in steel. Revision and extension of incentive plans account for about 10 cents, the Sunday premium with continuous operations, about 6 cents, and other smaller items, the remainder.

A major focus of interest in this chapter is the importance of the relation of wage and fringe adjustments in steel to other industries. It should be pointed out, however, that steel's relative gain in 1955–58, and particularly in 1955–59, is far more marked with respect to hourly earnings than with respect to negotiated wage increases.

The relative gain in earnings had serious employment cost consequences within basic steel including its effects upon wage-related fringe benefits. But, so far as can be determined, the increase in earnings as such had no influences beyond the steel industry itself.

During the years 1955–58 negotiated wage increases in steel exceeded those in the automobile industry and in other leading industries not closely associated with the Steelworkers union. The settlement of the 1959 negotiations considerably reduced steel's superior wage position. The significance of the negotiations of these years is discussed subsequently. Table 6 is included at this point to indicate roughly the difference between an earnings and a negotiated wage increase comparison.

Steel's Pattern Position

The fact that steel earnings have, for much of the postwar period, moved approximately in line with earnings in other durable goods industries is interesting, but does not answer the question of whether steel has been leading or following in the establishment of the trend.[4] If steel was primarily "locked into" a position by settlements already made and was thus confirming and continuing trends already developing or developed, there is no strong reason to believe that steel had substantial independent wage influence upon the economy. If, on the other hand, steel continued to establish new and higher levels of settlements, pulling the economy with it, much more serious questions are posed.

---

[4] This section is based upon the study paper by Harold M. Levinson, University of Michigan, entitled, *The Role of Collective Bargaining in the Steel Industry: Pattern Setter or Pattern Follower?*

TABLE 6.—*Total negotiated wage increases effective in 1955–58 and 1955–59, selected companies and industries*

1955–58		1955–59	
Company or industry	Cents per hour	Company or industry	Cents per hour
Aluminum Co. of America	67	Bituminous Coal	75–83
Bethlehem Shipbuilding	64	Aluminum Co. of America	73
U.S. Steel	60	American Can	67
American Can	58	Bethlehem Shipbuilding	65
Swift and Co	55	Swift and Co	65
Bituminous Coal	50–55	Pacific Shipbuilding	61
Pacific Shipbuilding	51	U.S. Steel	61
International Harvester	51	International Harvester	60
General Motors	48	General Motors	57
Rubber (4 companies)	43	Sinclair Oil	56
General Electric	43	Rubber (4 companies)	53
Sinclair Oil	42	Pacific Longshore	53
Pacific Longshore	42	General Electric	52
Lockheed Aircraft	38	Lockheed Aircraft	49
Anaconda Copper	37	Anaconda Copper	44
Libbey-Owens-Ford	29	Libbey-Owens-Ford	37
Anthracite	21–29	Anthracite	36–43

SOURCE: Bureau of Labor Statistics data.   Incentive earnings effect of wage increases of approximately 3 cents included for U.S. Steel.

The Levinson study was based upon some 30 companies, or groups of companies, representing important industries. Data were primarily from the BLS *Wage Chronology* Series. Manufacturing predominates, though some nonmanufacturing is included. Although not representative of the entire economy, the sample is a significant one for an investigation of steel's influence with respect to important manufacturing industries.

The magnitude and timing of negotiated wage and major fringe changes were analyzed in detail for the postwar years. While fringe items presented problems and prevented precise comparison, their omission would have introduced greater error. This report does not include the detailed documentation of the findings of the study, but gives summary statements for various periods.

Pattern Setter or Follower [5]

Summary, 1945–September 1949.—Four major points stand out with respect to this period:

1. In each year a substantial number of contracts were negotiated over a 5- or 6-month period prior to the agreements in the steel industry. These earlier contracts usually covered clothing, textiles, shoes, petroleum, and longshoring, though other sectors were also sometimes included. On the other hand, final agreements in most of the large mass production, durable goods sectors were usually postponed until after a "key" bargain was signed with a leading firm in the steel or automobile industry.

---

[5] Taken directly, but with substantial omissions and minor modifications, from the Levinson study.

2. Despite some variations in the magnitude of the wage-fringe improvements negotiated during the first several months of each "round," the majority usually fell within a range of from 3 to 5 cents, within which the key bargain in steel or automobiles later fell. In this sense, the agreements in steel in 1946 and 1947 and in autos in 1948 tended to reflect and codify already existing trends rather than to create or contribute to a new and different level of wage-fringe adjustments. Even in 1946 and 1947, when the steel agreements were usually considered to be key bargains, their exact terms had been reached earlier in some sector of the automobile industry.

3. Once the key bargain was negotiated, it became the basis for the same, or very similar settlements in a large number of other industries; what previously had been a range of settlements became a more exact standard, with relatively small deviations.

The strong tendency for the several mass production industries to cluster very closely is evident in summary data for automobiles, steel, aluminum, meatpacking, electrical equipment, rubber, copper, and farm equipment. In addition, the three branches of the textile industry, men's and women's clothing, and the rail unions also fell within or very close to this total pattern.

4. Some companies and industry sectors showed a consistent tendency to move independently of these general trends. Dominant among these were anthracite and bituminous coal and petroleum refining, each of which consistently exceeded the pattern. In addition, Atlantic and Pacific longshoring and the railroad nonoperating unions pulled far ahead of the mass production industries as a result of the wage increases introduced in late 1948–early 1949 which were not matched elsewhere.

At the other extreme, the aircraft and shipbuilding industries, both hard hit by the cessation of war production, consistently fell below the pattern level, although the 1949 Lockheed "makeup" contract improved its relative position considerably. The shoe manufacturing and hosiery firms also negotiated relatively low wage-fringe improvements during most of the early postwar period.

The Late 1949–50 Insurance Round.—The analysis of the role of the steel contract in the 1949–50 insurance round can best be developed along two lines. First, to what extent did the 10-cent package of fringe benefits represent any new or different level of benefits than had already been developing elsewhere in the economy? And second, what was the role of the steel agreement itself as an initiator or as a follower in the establishment of the specific pattern involved?

On the first question, the weight of evidence strongly suggests that the isurance pattern did establish a generally higher level of wage-fringe adjustments. In fact, it has been noted that until the late 1949 pension-welfare agreements, several negotiations had resulted in no changes whatever. This trend was also supported by the relatively high rate of unemployment and the mildly declining Consumer Price Index (CPI), which brought no net wage increase under the General Motors contract. In this respect, the widespread insurance programs initiated in late 1949 did represent more of a "breakthrough" than the previous rounds.

Even this conclusion must be qualified to some degree by the fact that pension and welfare plans of various types had been established by several firms long before 1949. Most of these plans, however, had been introduced unilaterally by management, and many provided relatively low benefits, limited coverage, and involved only small employer contributions. Collectively bargained noncontributory pension plans were rare—concentrated particularly in clothing and coal mining; certainly no trend had yet developed in the great bulk of unionized industries. Considering in addition the nature of the underlying economic conditions in 1949, it seems most doubtful that a 10-cent wage or fringe "package" would have been negotiated at that time, in the absence of strong union pressures.

Assuming this to be the case, what was the role of the steel industry in this development? Clearly, both the importance of the steel industry in the economy and the threat of the union to press its demands by a strike, focussed the issues on steel despite the fact that similar demands were being pressed in many other industries at the time. Also, once a steel factfinding board was appointed, all other major industries "marked time," pending its report. In this sense, the steel industry did bear considerable responsibility for the 1949 pattern.

When the Board's findings were finally made, however, it was in the Ford Motor Co. that the first agreement was signed embodying its recommendations, closely followed by a Goodrich settlement increasing the company's total welfare contribution to 10 cents an hour.[6] It was not until a month later that the first break came in the original resistance offered by the steel industry to the noncontributory principle. In this context, therefore, the role of steel was that of a follower. Considering these general circumstances and the sequence of events involved, therefore, the major responsibility for the 1949 break through is perhaps best viewed as the joint result of pressures in

---

[6] Actually, Ford had indicated its interest and willingness to accept a noncontributory pension plan as early as 1947, when it agreed to set aside 8 cents an hour for this purpose. At that time, however, the plan was rejected by the UAW membership, which preferred a straight wage increase.

several sectors, but with the major responsibility resting on the steel and automobile sectors.

The Korean Period and 1953.—Superimposed upon the "working through" of the pension-welfare round during the latter half of 1950 was a new series of wage increases arising partly out of the gradual recovery from the 1949 recession, but more particularly as a result of the entry of the United States into the Korean War in June 1950. From January to June, the rate of unemployment fell sharply from 6.7 to 5.3 percent; by October 1950, it had fallen to 4.1 percent and to 3.1 percent by April 1951. In addition, the CPI resumed its strong upward movement, rising from 100.7 in March 1950, to 106.9 in December, and to 110.8 by June 1951.

These economic developments found their most immediate reflection in collective bargaining under terms of the General Motors contract, which was signed on May 23, 1950.

It was against this background that negotiations were begun in the steel industry in October 1950. Within a few weeks (by November 30) a wage increase averaging 16 cents plus reduction of the North-South differential was agreed upon, to be effective for the period to December 31, 1951. Shortly thereafter, somewhat more liberal 1 year settlements were made in aluminum [7] (15 cents plus 6 holidays), coal mining (bituminous 20 cents, anthracite 23 cents), and Bethlehem Shipbuilding (22½ cents).[8]

The 16-cent adjustment in steel represented a greater increase than had prevailed up to that point; in general, increases in other industries were in the 9- to 13-cent range (plus pensions and welfare). Nevertheless, the steel settlement must again be viewed much more as a reflection of basic trends than as a major factor affecting them. At the time of the steel contract, there was every reason to expect continuing pressure on the price level, and hence a continuing upward movement of wages in the automobile and other industries having automatic cost-of-living adjustments and wage reopeners. Further, even in the unlikely event of a stable price level, an additional improvement factor of 4 cents was to be instituted in the automobile industry in May, bringing the total automobile increase to at least 15 cents over its 1948 level.

That the steel agreement reflected rather than originated the wage movements of the period is given ample support by the developments of the subsequent 6 months. In the automobile, farm equipment, and electrical equipment industries, added wage increases of 8 to 12 cents

---

[7] The offer in aluminum appears to have been prior to steel as was a nonferrous adjustment.

[8] The settlement in Bethlehem Shipbuilding, however, was largely justified as a "makeup" for the below-pattern agreements of 1946–48.

were introduced under contract provisions predating the steel agreement and hence unrelated to it. In these industries, the final total of wage increases by June 1951, substantially exceeded the steel level. Further, under the wage regulations instituted by the Wage Stabilization Board, which had been established by Executive order in September 1950, wage increases in several other sectors were permitted to compensate for the rising cost of living and to permit improvement factors negotiated prior to the wage stabilization program. Many of these sectors also negotiated wage adjustments in excess of the steel standard. The conclusion is inescapable that wages moved strongly upward under pressures quite independent of steel and that the late 1950 steel agreement did not significantly affect these trends. The same pressures on the labor supply and on the cost of living continued through the remainder of 1951 and into late 1952.

Viewed in the light of the wage trends which had developed since the prior steel settlement in late 1950, and considering the nature of underlying economic trends as they existed at the time, there appears to be little grounds for the view that the 1952 steel contract was out of line, or that it contributed to a new and higher pattern of wage-fringe benefits.

During the latter half of 1952, the cost of living, improvement factor, and related increases which might reasonably have been anticipated at the time of the steel contract did in fact materialize, although the rate of increase slowed somewhat. In General Electric, General Motors, International Harvester, and Glenn L. Martin, increases of from 2 to 8 cents were given on these grounds, resulting in final levels at the end of 1952 of from 30 to 35 cents, plus fringes. While a small steel advantage averaging perhaps 2 or 3 cents remained, a continuation of these trends into 1953 would have eliminated it.

As matters developed, however, the Consumer Price Index took an unexpected turn downward during the first quarter of 1953, with the result that those firms in which wages were tied to the CPI introduced wage reductions or, if an improvement factor was also involved, the net wage increase was reduced. The result, of course, was to increase slightly the wage advantage of the steel industry and of others having fixed rate contracts. The differences involved, however, were quite small and in large part, the result of the unexpected decline in the CPI.

In general, this relationship continued through the remainder of 1953. The dominant bargain of the year occurred in the automobile industry in May, when the 5-year contracts negotiated in 1950 were voluntarily reopened and more liberal wage and fringe benefits introduced. The effect of these changes yielded a net package increase of approximately 6 cents as of May 29 (after taking into account a 1-cent cost-of-living wage reduction and skill differentials) plus more liberal cost-of-living-improvement factor provisions. During the latter half of 1953, further cost-of-living increases brought the total for the year up to 9 cents.

Shortly after the General Motors' voluntary reopening, a wage increase of 8½ cents was negotiated in steel. At this point, the steel agreement seems clearly to have been in excess of the automobile package, and there were no strong grounds for believing that future cost-of-living increases would make up the difference, since the price level had remained virtually stable over several months. Potentially, therefore, the 1953 steel settlement did provide the basis for a higher level than previously prevailed. As before, the same or similar adjustments quickly followed in Bethlehem Shipbuilding (7 cents), Aluminum (8½ cents), Sinclair (9 cents), Anaconda (7½ cents), and others. The automobile formula, on the other hand, was more closely followed by General Electric (6 cents), rubber (5 cents plus fringes), and Armour (5 cents plus fringes).

The rise in the CPI during the latter half of 1953, however, again brought the automobile pattern to within only a few cents of the steel level, and again based upon criteria generally unrelated to steel. Thus, despite the small wage advantage of the steel industry at the end of 1953, and of the few industries closely related to it in bargaining, it is doubtful that it had contributed in any important degree to a higher wage-fringe level than would have prevailed otherwise. Nevertheless, some tendency in this direction did become evident during the year.[9]

The 1954 Recession.—The second postwar recession in the United States occurred in 1954, although it had begun to develop with the cessation of hostilities in Korea in mid-1953. The rate of unemployment, which had been below 3 percent during the first 6 months of 1953, rose to 4.5 percent by December of that year and to about 6 percent in mid-1954. In addition, the CPI again reflected a very mild downward movement.

With the exception of the automatic wage adjustments in the automobile and International Harvester contracts, no major agreements were signed in the firms under analysis prior to the steel settlement on June 29. Up to that time, and after taking account of the annual improvement factors, net wage increases of only 3 cents had been, or were due to be introduced in automobiles and Harvester; furthermore,

---

[9] A few important deviations from the 1953 pattern may be worth brief note. The International Harvester Co. refused to go along with the automobile policy of voluntary renegotiation, so that its net wage gain during 1953 was only 3 cents. In both branches of coal mining, severely depressed conditions resulted in the continuation of the prior contracts without change; in these industries, however, previous terms had been so substantial that they were still left with negotiated benefits far in excess of the steel pattern.

even more than in 1953, nothing in the conditions of the labor market or in price trends gave indication of upward pressures to come. The steel contract, however, provided for a wage increase of 5 cents, plus elimination of the North-South differential, an increase in minimum pensions from $100 to $140 a month (including a maximum deduction of $85 for Federal benefits) and an increase of 2 cents an hour in the company's contribution to the health and welfare program. Both the wage increase and the liberalization of various types of fringes were adopted by several other firms during the following 6 months; whereas in a few others, only a wage increase was introduced.[10]

Did the steel contract of 1954, then, provide the impetus for another small upward shift in the wage-fringe pattern? At least with respect to wages, the answer would appear to be "yes," although the General Electric offer of May 24 of 2.68 percent should also be recognized. However, by the end of 1954, the steel margin had increased to 5 or 6 cents over the GM automatic approach—a small margin, but a definite one. The matter of fringes is much more difficult to evaluate, because of the considerable variations among the benefit provisions of different firms, and because of differences in the proportion of costs provided by the companies. Using the General Motors program as perhaps the best basis of comparison, both the pension and welfare standards set up in steel in 1954 appear to be slightly better than those in the automotive firm. As against this, however, is the fact that the improved pensions set up in automobiles in 1953 applies to workers already retired; those established in steel in 1954 did not. In any case, the differences in fringe benefits were quite small. The year 1954, nevertheless, appears to have established wage standards in steel generally in excess of those prevailing, or expected shortly to prevail, elsewhere in the mass production industries.

Summary.—Taken as a whole, collective bargaining in the steel industry during 1949–54 was not a major factor in new and higher patterns of wage-fringe benefits. This was particularly true during the Korean War period, which was characterized by rapidly rising prices and low unemployment, and during which time the greatest increases in wages and fringes occurred. The role of the steel industry was much greater, however, in the insurance round of 1949–50, and its influence became more evident, though it was still relatively small, in late 1953 and 1954.

While it is not possible to measure accurately the total value of the increases in wage and fringe benefits in the several concerns involved, the bulk of firms fell within a fairly narrow range, although

---

[10] As in 1953, a few sectors—coal mining, Sinclair, and the railroads—had no changes.

the dispersion was greater than in the immediate postwar years. At the upper limit once again were both branches of coal mining and of longshoring, the former despite the fact that no increases had been negotiated in 1953 and 1954. At the lower end, on the other hand, were the railroad nonoperating unions, which had enjoyed one of the highest wage increases in the earlier period, and the roadmen among the operating unions, whose workweek had not been reduced and who consequently had not received any compensating increase in hourly wages. Also in a relatively poor position were two aircraft firms—Lockheed and North American—where no broad pension plans had as yet been negotiated.

Between these extremes were the major large mass production industries in which the role of "patterns" was strongest. Highest among these were three closely tied to the steel bargain—U.S. Steel itself, Aluminum, and Bethlehem Shipbuilding. In addition, Glenn L. Martin and North American Aviation had above average benefits, probably in part as a makeup for the poor experience of this industry during 1945–48. At the middle and lower end of this large central group were General Motors, International Harvester, General Electric, Armour, and others which had fallen somewhat behind in the 1953 and 1954 negotiations.

The years 1955 to 1959.[11]—Settlements in 1955 prior to the automobile and steel negotiations had been running at about a 10-cent level. Automobiles and steel raised the level of settlements with automobiles leading but with steel going ahead of automobiles on a wages-only basis. The 1955 automobile package of approximately 20 cents about doubled the previously existing level of settlements. The 15-cent wage increase in steel allowed some automobile "catch up" for 1953–54 gains in steel, but, considered as a wage adjustment under a reopening clause, provided a special wage gain for steel.

The 3-year 1956 contract in steel was noteworthy in its fringe concessions, particularly the pension improvement, the Sunday premium in a continuous-operations industry, and the 52-week supplementary unemployment benefit plan, but it also provided the basis for further wage gains in steel relative to the automobile formula. Annual wage gains in steel were 2 to 3 cents a year above automobiles. As noted in table 6 steel gained some 12 cents an hour over the automobile industry in the 1955–58 period.

The point of fundamental interest with respect to steel's wage gains in the 1955–58 period is that the impact was limited essentially to those industries in which the Steelworkers union exerted a major influence. This is indicated by an examination of table 6. The

---

[11] Based upon but not taken from the Levinson study.

wage gains under the 1955 and 1956 settlements, while creating the most significant dual wage influences during the postwar years within this sector of the economy, most certainly did not pull all durable goods, much less the entire economy, to higher levels of wage settlements.

During the 1959 steel negotiations and strike, developments in collective bargaining continued elsewhere. Several long-term contracts signed in 1958 resulted in wage increases clustering around the 10 cent level. This same level was also closely approximated in a large proportion to newly negotiated contracts.

The provisions of the 1959 contract settlement, reached in January 1960, represented a considerable downward modification of wage standards which had prevailed under the 1956 contract and in relation to the timing of wage adjustments in other industries. Wage rates, but not employment costs, were held nearly stable over a 2½-year period from July 1958 to December 1960. For the years 1955–59 steel, on a wages-only basis, was not greatly ahead of automobiles. Also a novel limitation of cost-of-living adjustments was instituted. The December 1960 and October 1961 cost-of-living adjustments were limited to 3 plus 3 cents minus certain potential insurance cost increases. Although from a realistic point of view, employees in steel in 1959 received the equivalent of about an 8.5 cent wage increase because of company payment of employee insurance contributions, the total package was smaller than under the 1956 contract as noted below.

On the basis of estimates of the value of 1959 fringes, a maximum total package of approximately 39 cents including the estimated insurance escalation/cost-of-living allowance is indicated for the 3-year period from June 30, 1959, to June 30, 1962, or an increase of slightly more than 12 cents a year. This may be compared with a total wage increase of about 45 cents during the prior 3-year contract, and to a total wage-fringe-employment cost increase of between 80 to 85 cents during this same period. Even if cost-of-living allowances were omitted from each period, the 1959–62 package would be about 29 cents compared with approximately 65 cents for 1956–59. While a comparison with other industries involving future years cannot be made, clearly the most recent steel contract involves a considerable reduction in employment-cost increases as compared with the 1956 contract.

Some Concluding Observations

The analysis of hourly earnings and wage and fringe adjustments in this chapter has had the limited objective of attempting to appraise Steel's independent influence upon wage and fringe levels in the econ-

omy during the postwar years.   It can be argued that this approach
begs the more fundamental question of the general and total effect
of collective bargaining upon wage and price trends in the economy.
In a sense this is true, but, as noted below, any judgment as to this
more fundamental question is highly speculative and controversial.

Unions did not create the so-called wage-price spiral.   Increases
in the general price level have always been associated with increases
in wages.   The wage-price spiral is much closer to a definition than to
an analysis of inflation.   Leads and lags in the relative movements
of wages and prices throw very little light on the question of causation.   In relation to these general observations, it is interesting that
the statistical application of the automobile wage formula to manufacturing from a 1910 base produces an extremely close fit to the
actual trends and movements of money wages which have taken place
over the years.

Arguments over the causes of wage-price increases in the economy
have frequently been phrased in terms of the relative importance of
"demand pull" and "cost push" in the operation of the wage-price
mechanism under collective bargaining.   An important phase of this
argument is an analysis of the movements of the major components in
the Consumer Price Index.   The considerable importance of food and
service prices in the movements of this Index (areas less closely associated with collective bargaining) lend support to a demand pull
emphasis for much of the postwar period as does analysis of excess
aggregate demand and monetary influences in the immediate postwar
and Korean increase in prices.   On the other hand, the continuous
pressure of unions on employment costs, and wage increases in excess
of increases in output per man-hour for the economy, lend support
to a cost-push emphasis, particularly in the price increase following
the 1954 recession.   It is thus impossible to separate demand, cost,
and collective bargaining influences in a convincing manner though it
is believed that most economists place major emphasis upon demand
factors for much of the postwar period.

Although this larger question clearly needs to be recognized the
more limited question is more significant for this study.   It also must
be recognized as a complex one.   Steel's independent influence on wage
and price trends and levels is not subject to precise appraisal.   Even if
steel's influence has been predominantly one of reinforcing existing
trends or levels, rather than modifying or creating them, it nevertheless can be judged quite important in the dynamic interplay of wages
and prices.   On the other hand, it is believed that the review of developments contained in the chapter lends considerable weight to the

view that steel's independent influence on wage trends in the economy has not been a crucial one.

In the first place, steel's influence can be exaggerated by looking only at trends in hourly earnings over recent years. The sharp relative advance of hourly earnings in steel in 1954–59 was clearly of decided consequence with respect to the increase in wage and fringe employment costs within steel, but there is no evidence that this trend in hourly earnings exerted influence beyond basic steel.

In the second place, steel does not appear to have initiated increases in wage levels which had significant consequences beyond the jurisdiction of the Steelworkers union. Even within the union jurisdiction pattern influences did not operate in any simple fashion, particularly with respect to steel fabrication.[12] Wage increases in major manufacturing industries were much more closely associated with the operation of the automobile wage formula than with negotiations in steel. It can be argued that the automobile formula restrained collective bargaining influences that would otherwise have prevailed or that it accentuated the rise in wages and prices. But it was a formula approach to wage determination embodied in long-term contracts and operating quite independently of steel. Wage settlements in major industries other than automobiles would not be expected, either for collective bargaining or for economic reasons, to have matched in exact fashion adjustments in automobiles. Wage forces do not operate in this simple fashion. In fact, even the similarity of settlements may be attributed to similar underlying economic conditions or to pattern influences. Whatever the causal relationships, if it were possible to abstract steel from the economy it is difficult to support the view that wage trends in the economy would have been meaningfully modified. Much the same can be said with respect to fringe benefits, although the leads and lags in the liberalization of benefits have no benchmark comparison such as the automobile wage formula.

In the third place, granted the economic and collective bargaining influences existing during the postwar years, it is difficult to defend the position that steel wages and benefits "might have been" much different from what they were. Steel might not have advanced beyond

---

[12] This statement is based on a study paper by George Seltzer, University of Minnesota, entitled *The United Steelworkers and Union-Wide Bargaining.* He demonstrates that pattern following has varied with geographic location, size of firm, union leadership, union policy, general business conditions, ability-to-pay of particular companies, product competition, and labor market conditions. Pattern following also has varied in content. It was strongest in wage elements, weaker on fringes, and weaker yet on contract terms. Ten years after basic steel introduced pensions many fabricators had no pension plans. Relatively few fabricators had a local-practices clause. Many fabricators introduced paid holidays prior to basic steel, showing influences other than steel. It is far from accurate to think of pattern following in steel fabrication as a carbon copy of what happens in basic steel. See footnote 5, chapter 6.

automobiles in the 1955–58 period. The increase in employment costs might have been somewhat less for the 1955–59 period. Any such assumption is highly controversial. But, recognizing the arbitrary and controversial basis for judgment, it is difficult to postulate employment cost increases that would have been more than 10 percent lower than those prevailing. As will be noted in the next two chapters, a difference of this amount, though decidedly important to the parties, is not of sufficient magnitude to warrant interference on public policy grounds with the operation of free collective bargaining.

CHAPTER 10

EMPLOYMENT COSTS, PRICES, AND
COMPETITION

This chapter has two major purposes. One purpose is to examine the impact of increases in employment costs upon steel prices. To give perspective to the effect of employment cost increases on prices, the influence of material and service costs, capital costs, taxes, and profits upon prices is examined. This examination will be related to the previous discussion of wage changes and increases in average earnings. A second purpose, to which the latter part of the chapter is devoted, is to examine the changing competitive position of the steel industry in domestic and foreign markets.

A massive amount of statistical information is available bearing upon costs and prices in steel. For purposes of this report a reasonably simple statistical framework showing the relationship among cost components in these operations concerned solely with steelmaking is needed. Unfortunately, the data necessary for a complete analysis of this character are not available.

The decision was made therefore to approach the problem in two stages. First, changes in steel employment costs will be related to average realized price per ton of steel produced. Data for doing this are available but, unfortunately, data are not available to extend this approach to cover material costs and return to property.[1]

After analyzing employment costs related to all steelmaking activities, it is necessary to broaden the approach using data covering the consolidated activities of the steelmaking industry. Relevant data for this approach are provided in the Annual Statistical Report of the Iron and Steel Institute wherein they publish consolidated statistics on revenue, employment costs, material costs, return to property, and so on. The AISI statements cover all the affiliated interests of the parent companies with approximately 95 percent of the total industry capacity.

This second-stage analysis will use revenue per ton shipped which in turn will be broken down into employment costs per ton shipped, material and service costs per ton shipped, and so forth. An internally consistent analysis is possible by this approach, although the figures do include activities not directly related to steelmaking. This

---

[1] Data used are taken from *Background Statistics Bearing on the Steel Dispute*—Bulletin No. S–1. U.S. Dept. of Labor. The estimates used cover all steelmaking activities.

approach does, however, indicate how much revenue the industry received and how it distributed this revenue.

It must be pointed out, however, that changes in average revenue per ton shipped, average material and service costs per ton shipped, employment costs, and other costs are not measures of price and cost changes per se. For example, the BLS index of basic steel prices shows an increase of 178 percent from 1940 to 1959. Average revenue per ton shipped increased 190 percent during the same period. Over this same period the product mix shifted somewhat from lower value to higher value products.

The qualification with respect to costs is even greater. For example, average material and service cost per ton shipped will reflect not only the difference between an average price and a price index, as with average revenue, but also changes in utilization of various materials and services. The cost of coal per ton shipped will rise with increases in the price of coal, but will fall with improved technology which utilizes less coal per ton of steel. Cost of transportation will rise with increases in such service charges, but it will also rise if, on the average, raw materials and products are transported over greater distances. In other words, an average cost concept reflects, in addition to price changes, the advantages which the industry has achieved through improved technology in the utilization of materials, labor, and capital and other influences on utilization.

Since the cost concept used in the chapter discounts for "productivity" improvements, and since "productivity" has been much discussed in connection with "noninflationary" steel settlements, a brief discussion of that subject is introduced prior to the analysis of revenue and costs.

The Productivity Concept

Concern in recent years with the question of economic growth and price stability has led to a continuing interest in productivity as related to wages. Many feel that productivity, as measured in terms of output per worker, should be given substantial weight in negotiating wage agreements. Available information tends to show that for the Nation over the longrun, real wages do increase at about the same rate as worker productivity. Since this is the case, the question arises as to the role of this concept in helping determine wages in the steel industry. This section examines the problems related to the use of the productivity concept in the steel industry and its feasibility in wage settlements.

The concept of productivity for the entire economy which is most commonly used is a measure of change in output per man-hour. There are a host of statistical problems involved in measuring output per man-hour for the economy. Let us assume that an output measure for the private economy has been achieved which holds constant the composition of that output. Let us also assume that a measure of man-hours worked has been achieved which is consistent with the measure of output. If the change in output per man-hour for the economy is then calculated for a span of years, what has been measured? It would appear that what has been measured is the average decrease in man-hours required to produce a composite unit of product. Very little is implied as to the reasons for this change. All of the forces which could contribute to an increase in total output, except a change in man-hours, are reflected in the change in the measure.

It would be expected that changes in output per man-hour for the economy over, say, 1, 2, or 3 years would be heavily influenced by the ratio of actual production to capacity to produce, that is, by cyclical forces. Over a long period of years changes measured at points of approximate full capacity for the economy would presumably reflect primarily labor-saving technological change and increases in physical capital per man-hour.

What assumptions are necessary if this measure is used to evaluate noninflationary wage settlements? Employment costs per hour worked, including the costs of all fringe benefits, could rise on the average for the economy by the trend increase (to exclude cyclical influences) without increasing the trend of labor cost per unit of output for the economy. But is this adequate to allow stable prices? Not unless material and capital costs, including profits, have remained constant.

For the economy as a whole, material and indirect service costs become labor and capital costs. Clearly this is a most important distinction in terms of the economy as a whole in contrast with any single industry. Steel in particular has had very large material cost increases. But what about capital costs? Output per man-hour for the economy as a whole can be used as a guide to employment cost increases which are consistent with stable prices, only if the physical capital used and its cost per unit of output remain constant over time and only if constant return on capital is regarded as appropriate in relation to increasing real wages. To measure the capital-output ratio is difficult but this ratio in physical terms appears to have been reasonably constant in the postwar years. Increases in the cost of capital, however, have been caused by and have contributed to the upward movement of prices. Most economists would accept as appropriate a constant return on capital in relation to increasing real wages.

Although the output per man-hour concept in its use as a guide for national wage policy is blurred by capital cost considerations, it has analytical usefulness in this connection. Nevertheless, there is in reality no single guide to national wage policy which can be supported. An inclusive national wage policy would need to consider the stage of the business cycle, whether there is a need to expand investment or consumption, what is happening to our balance of payments, past and present inflationary pressures, and so on. The search for a comprehensive formula approach to national wage policy is not likely to be fruitful.

While output per man-hour for the economy has a limited application to steel bargaining as a general test of inflationary significance, output per man-hour in the steel industry does not have this economy-wide significance. Output per man-hour in steel can only be conceived as one of many variables indicating the economic condition of the industry. No productivity measure, for the economy or for the industry, can be endorsed as an adequate guide to wage policy. However, the use of the steel figure in bargaining, warrants its discussion.

It so happens that output per wage employee man-hour changes in steel, variously measured, have moved approximately within the same range of change as output per man-hour in the economy, also variously measured. For all employees, the increase has been somewhat less than for the economy as a whole. See chart 7.

If employment cost increases in steel were held to the trend increase in output per man-hour changes in steel, other costs might still advance, necessitating price increases. Material and service cost increases, either indirectly caused by wage increases in steel or independent of such increases, could necessitate a price increase unless they were offset by material-saving technological changes within the industry. Capital costs to achieve all types of technological and other improvements in both methods and products might cause capital costs to rise per unit of output and necessitate an increase in prices. It should be emphasized that although productivity gains in a specific industry do provide elbow room for negotiation, output per man-hour changes in a given industry cannot, alone, determine its wage policy.

A measure of "productivity" in steel, as it is factually reflected in steel prices, could not appropriately be restricted to a partial productivity measure relating only to the utilization of labor. It is for this reason, among others, that all costs and revenue have been portrayed on a per-ton shipped basis. This does not measure productivity in steel in its multitudinous dimensions, but it does allow for such changes. It shows cost increases over and beyond the savings achieved in the utilization of the input factors.

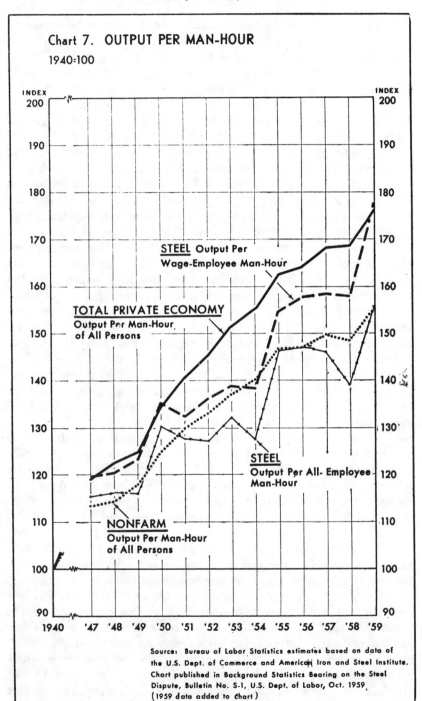

Chart 7. OUTPUT PER MAN-HOUR
1940=100

STEEL Output Per
Wage-Employee Man-Hour

TOTAL PRIVATE ECONOMY
Output Per Man-Hour
of All Persons

STEEL
Output Per All- Employee
Man-Hour

NONFARM
Output Per Man-Hour
of All Persons

1940 '47 '48 '49 '50 '51 '52 '53 '54 '55 '56 '57 '58 '59

Source: Bureau of Labor Statistics estimates based on data of
the U.S. Dept. of Commerce and American Iron and Steel Institute.
Chart published in Background Statistics Bearing on the Steel
Dispute, Bulletin No. S-1, U.S. Dept. of Labor, Oct. 1959.
(1959 data added to chart)

While productivity changes in relation to price must be viewed in terms of the cost of all factors of production, it is nevertheless true that particular interest attaches to output per man-hour. This is because changes in this measure of productivity have become so closely associated with steel bargaining and because of general interest in the character and timing of changes in the utilization of man-hours. It was hoped initially to study intensively these changes, but this has not been possible. Some points, however, can be noted.

Investment per employee in steel has increased markedly during the postwar years. Such investment, both on a physical and on a value basis, appears to have increased considerably more than for the economy as a whole, but output per man-hour in steel has not increased in any spectacular manner. It has increased, as noted, somewhat less than for the whole economy. This suggests that investment is undertaken for a variety of reasons. Much investment in steel has been undertaken to obtain new sources of ore and to use lower-grade ores. Much investment has gone into improvements in the quality and into diversification and multiplication of steel products. Some improvements in process, however, which have produced substantial increases in output per man-hour, and promise even greater improvements, have not involved particularly heavy capital outlays.

Yet, broadly speaking, over time there appears to be a close association between capital expenditures and production worker costs. From 1947 to 1957, for example, all-manufacturing spent an average of 7 percent of its annual value added by manufacture on capital expenditures. Production worker costs in this period fell from 41 percent to 36 percent of its value added. This was a reduction of about 12 percent. Steel in the same period expended about 13.5 percent of its value added on capital. Its production worker costs fell from 55 percent to 41 percent, a decline of about 25 percent. In contrast, the apparel industry with 2 percent a year capital expenditure had no reduction in production worker costs. In fact, such costs rose by 2 percent for the period.

Output per man-hour in steel, as measured by any of the indexes used (see chart 7) clearly changes with the level of capacity. But the major advances in output per man-hour come, as in other industries, with recovery from recession. Conceptually, with technology constant, output per man-hour may be thought of as a curve relating output per man-hour to capacity of operation with less efficient utilization of labor at lower capacity points. Laborsaving technological changes shift this curve so that less labor is required at all levels of capacity. (It might also change its shape.) But changes over time in output per man-hour do not appear to reflect a gradual and steady shift of this curve. It seems to move in jumps in cyclical recovery periods. The payoff in laborsaving improvements seems to come in not rehiring in accordance with the former relationship after a recession. This is not said critically, but only to raise the speculative point that if in fact technological changes come regularly, rather than intermittently, gradual change in utilization of labor would in fact yield considerable cost savings in its time dimension, and would create less cyclical unemployment. Steady adjustment to technological change would in fact reduce both employee hardship and costs.

In brief summary, the only output per man-hour relationship which provides even a broad, qualified guide to wage policy is output per man-hour for the economy. Productivity change in steel, as related to steel prices, must encompass all factors of production. Change in output per man-hour in steel is a very complex concept, not easily related to any single variable. It is not a concept that by itself provides a definitive guide to wage policy in steel.

Basic Steel Prices and Employment Costs

Basic steel prices rose by 178 percent from 1940 to 1959. Average realized price per ton increased about 207 percent during the same period. Employment cost per unit of output (wage payments and fringe benefits, offset by increases in output per man-hour) for wage employees rose about 145 percent from 1940 to 1959 (first half). For all employees, the increase in employment cost per unit of output to June 1959 was about 170 percent.[2] Employment costs for all employees have increased more than for wage employees alone because of the increase in the relative importance of administrative, professional, and clerical personnel. (See table 1.)

In evaluating the relationship of employment costs to steel prices (and to average realized price), it should be noted that total employment costs of steel companies as a percentage of average realized price have averaged something like 35 percent during the period under consideration. Before World War II, they represented about 37 percent of total revenues; during most of the postwar years they ranged from 32 to 37 percent. Only in the recession year of 1958, with the sharp drop in utilization of capacity, did the ratio increase substantially—to 37.5. With recovery and greater capacity utilization, the percentage declined in early 1959 to a level somewhat below the postwar average.

---

[2] Calculations supplied by Louis Lister, Columbia University, using a slightly different methodology, show employment costs for all employees rising 188 percent for the entire period 1940 through calendar year 1959.

TABLE 1.—*Employment costs, basic steel prices, average realized price per ton and percent of capacity utilized (steel operations only) 1940 and 1947–59*

Year	BLS index of basic steel prices	Average realized price per ton [1]		Employment cost [2]				Operating rate (percent)
				All employees [3]		Wage employees		
		(Dollars)	(Index)	(Dollars)	(Index)	(Dollars)	(Index)	
1940	100.0	$58	100.0	$21.81	100.0	$17.78	100.0	82.1
1947	131.4	88	151.7	32.05	146.9	25.69	144 4	93 0
1948	150.0	101	174.1	34.57	158.5	27.56	155.0	94.1
1949	162.6	107	184.4	36.69	168.2	28.09	157.9	81.1
1950	171.2	114	196.5	35.98	164.9	28.44	159.9	96.9
1951	184.6	125	215.5	40.21	184.3	31.93	179.5	100.9
1952	188.6	129	222.4	45.48	208.5	34.78	195.6	85.8
1953	203.6	135	232.7	46.14	211.5	35.87	201.7	94.9
1954	212.7	139	239.6	51.06	234.1	37.71	212.0	71.0
1955	222.9	142	244.8	47.13	216.0	35.93	202.0	93.0
1956	241.4	155	267.2	50.92	233.4	38.36	215.7	89.9
1957	264.6	165	284.4	56.17	257.5	41.80	235.0	84.5
1958	273.8	173	298.2	64.92	297.6	46.68	262.5	60.6
1959	[4] 278.4	178	306.8	[4] 58.93	[4] 270.1	[4] 43.64	[4] 245.4	63.0

[1] The average realized prices per ton for the years 1947 and 1949 through 1959 were derived from census data with adjustments for the years 1947, 1949, 1950, and 1954 to reflect the estimated amount of wire products made in the steel industry during these years so that the data would be comparable with other years. Prices for the years 1940 and 1948 were estimated with the estimates based on movements of the BLS wholesale price indexes for steel mill products.
[2] From *Background Statistics Bearing on Steel Dispute*—Bulletin No. S-1 U.S. Department of Labor—Source of data: Bureau of Labor Statistics estimates based on Iron and Steel Institute data.
[3] Assumes supplementary contributions per man-hour for all employees in steel operations same as for all employees covering all operations of steel companies.
[4] First half 1959.

Since the ratio of employment costs to average realized price has been roughly 35 percent, the increase in employment costs from 1940 through 1959 would explain something like one-third of the 178 percent rise in steel prices over this period.

Costs Related to Revenues: Consolidated Activities

An analysis of employment cost not confined solely to steelmaking operations shows a fairly close relationship to the trends observed when considering steelmaking activities only. Employment cost (all employees) per ton shipped when considered in this context rose 184 percent from 1940 to 1959. (See table 2.)

Since it is evident from this that only a small part of the steel price increases since 1940 can be attributed to increases in employment costs, consideration is now given to the part that increases in costs of materials and services may have played in such increases. The relation between increases in employment costs and material and service costs will also be considered briefly.

Purchased materials and services, including transportation, accounted for between 43 and 47 percent of total revenues during the 1940–59 period. Although varying from year to year, this category as a whole represented the largest single element of cost.

As shown by table 2, material and service costs per ton of steel shipped increased 205 percent from 1940 through 1959. Material costs accounted for 44 percent of total revenues in 1940, but the percentage has been higher in most postwar years with a range of about 44 to 47 percent. The lowest percentages were attained in the recession years 1954 (43 percent) and 1958 (42 percent): the percentage that material costs are of total revenues usually declines during recessions whereas that for employment costs increases.

If we accept 45 percent as roughly the approximate proportion that material costs are of total revenues, it follows that material cost increases accounted for roughly one-half of the rise in steel prices from 1940 through 1959.

Combining the effects of the increased costs of employment and materials it appears that they absorb something like 80 to 85 percent of the steel price increase that has taken place from 1940 through 1959.

Material Costs Related to Steel Employment Costs

In view of the fact that as a trend over the years, material costs appear to rise slightly more than employment costs, consideration was given to the question of whether there is any causal relationship between the two. We were unable to prove or disprove any such relationship.

In most of the postwar years material costs per unit of steel shipped increased more than steel employment costs on the 1940 base. However, there were substantial differences in timing and in amount from one year to the next. Material costs went up more than steel employment costs in some years and less in others; in still other years the two moved in opposite directions. A study of the behavior of the two indicates:

1. In contracting years, when steel employment costs rise sharply, and with some exceptions, material costs tend to rise weakly, or less than their percentage increase during years of peak or plateau.

2. Material costs have dropped in 3 of the 4 years of expansion following a decline. Hardly a typical year, 1959 was the exception.

3. Material costs have shown a pronounced tendency to rise during peak or plateau years, except for 1957. But although they rise most in such years, steel employment costs rise most in contracting years. But both classes of cost show a tendency, different in degree, to rise when business conditions approach the end of a boom.

4. Although steel employment and material cost are both influenced by the business cycle, each variable appears to react to its own particular pattern rather than to a common pattern. The relationships between them appear to be erratic and variable, floating rather than fixed. No determinate connection between them is apparent.

Not enough detailed price data related to various types of materials are available to permit the drawing of firm conclusions respecting

TABLE 2.—*Steel revenue and production costs, 1940 and 1947–59*

Year	Revenue [1] (in millions)	Revenue per ton [3]	Cost per ton shipped		
			Total	Employment (all employees)	Materials and services
1940	$3,235	$73	$58.92	$27.19	$31.73
1947	6,674	113	95.75	42.02	53.73
1948	8,080	130	108.41	45.69	62.72
1949	7,391	135	111.87	47.93	63.94
1950	9,485	139	110.10	46.46	63.64
1951	11,782	154	121.84	50.32	71.52
1952	10,803	164	139.46	57.67	81.79
1953	13,091	166	134.29	57.26	77.03
1954	10,532	170	136.82	63.15	73.67
1955	13,960	170	132.07	57.66	74.41
1956	15,160	189	150.62	63.56	87.06
1957	15,468	199	158.22	71.39	86.83
1958	12,442	210	170.12	81.67	88.45
1959	14,088	212	174.15	77.28	96.87

Indexes (1940=100)

Year					
1940	100	100	100	100	100
1947	206	155	163	155	169
1948	250	178	184	168	198
1949	228	185	190	176	202
1950	293	190	187	171	201
1951	364	211	207	185	225
1952	334	225	237	212	258
1953	405	227	228	211	243
1954	325	233	232	232	232
1955	431	233	224	212	235
1956	469	259	256	234	274
1957	478	273	269	263	274
1958	385	288	289	300	279
1959	435	290	296	284	305

Year	Return to property				
	Net income per ton	Cost per ton			
		Depreciation	Interest on long term debt	Nonfederal taxes	Federal taxes
1940	$5.88	$3.93	$0.89	$1.69	$2.04
1947	6.97	4.04	.30	1.54	4.76
1948	8.68	4.84	.32	1.67	6.25
1949	9.73	5.07	.39	2.05	6.88
1950	11.38	4.78	.36	1.93	11.37
1951	8.90	4.88	.36	2.10	16.69
1952	8.20	6.82	.65	2.27	7.33
1953	9.31	7.76	.68	2.42	12.63
1954	10.28	10.81	.85	2.78	9.57
1955	13.36	8.95	.64	2.60	13.44
1956	13.87	9.31	.64	2.81	13.01
1957	14.54	9.07	.83	3.52	12.89
1958	13.29	11.50	1.34	2.99	12.39
1959	12.46	9.98	1.42	3.87	12.10

Indexes (1940=100)

Year					
1940	100	100	100	100	100
1947	119	103	34	91	233
1948	148	123	36	99	306
1949	165	129	44	121	337
1950	194	121	40	114	557
1951	151	124	40	124	818
1952	139	173	73	134	359
1953	158	197	76	144	619
1954	275	275	96	164	469
1955	227	228	72	154	659
1956	236	237	72	166	637
1957	247	231	93	208	632
1958	226	293	150	177	607
1959	212	254	160	229	593

[1] Net billing value of products shipped and services.   [3] Rounded.

Source: 1959 AISI Statistical Report.

price movements of materials manufactured internally in contrast with those purchased externally. On the basis of the data available we could not establish any clear-cut correlation between employment and material costs.

Return to Property

As previously noted, employment and material costs together account for something like 80 percent of total revenue. Depreciation, depletion and amortization account on the average for about 4 to 5 percent. Interest and charges on long term debts accounted for approximately 2 to 4 percent until 1958 and 1959, when it became considerably higher. The remainder, roughly 12 to 15 percent, represents the gross profits, before taxes, share of total revenue.

State, local, and miscellaneous taxes account for something less than 2 percent of total revenues. Federal income tax, as a percent of total revenue, has varied widely but in recent years has accounted for roughly 6 percent.[3] Thus, the remainder (net profits) amount to something like 5 to 7 percent of total revenues. We now turn to an analysis of this residual share.

Steel Industry Profits

Two ratios are commonly used in comparing profits from industry to industry—profits in relation to sales, and profits as a return on net worth or stockholders' equity.[4] The difference between net worth (frequently used by private business) and stockholders' equity (as used in Federal Trade Commission and Securities and Exchange Commission reports) is relatively small, involving the treatment of certain types of special reserve funds.

During the postwar period, steel industry profits (after taxes) per dollar of sales have been higher than the comparable ratio for all-manufacturing (chart 8). The difference has widened during recent years, starting in 1955. The ratio for all-manufacturing and for the steel industry declined from the peak level of 1950.

In comparing steel industry profits as a percent of sales with the same ratio for all-manufacturing, account should be taken of the relatively high capital requirements in steel production. Profits in relation to sales must be higher in industries with high capital requirements in order to yield a given return on investment. Available published data indicate that capital investment per dollar of revenue is about one-quarter higher in steel than in manufacturing as a whole.

---

[3] As can be seen from table 2, Federal taxes as a percentage of total cost per ton of steel have risen almost 500 percent since 1940.

[4] In order that the profits data be on a comparable basis, this analysis will be based on Federal Trade Commission and Securities and Exchange Commission reports.

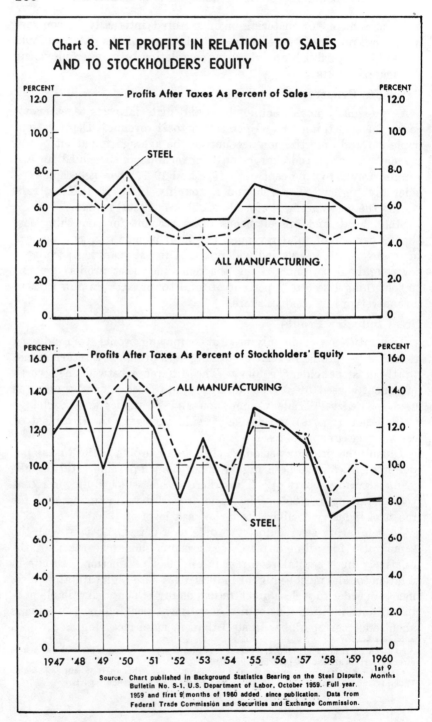

Chart 8. NET PROFITS IN RELATION TO SALES
AND TO STOCKHOLDERS' EQUITY

Source. Chart published in Background Statistics Bearing on the Steel Dispute,
Bulletin No. S-1, U.S. Department of Labor, October 1959. Full year.
1959 and first 9 months of 1960 added since publication. Data from
Federal Trade Commission and Securities and Exchange Commission.

Net profits as a rate of return on stockholders' equity in the steel industry have been lower than those in all-manufacturing during most of the postwar years (chart 8). Supplementary data, not shown in the chart, suggest that the steel profit ratio was also lower than that for all-manufacturing in 1940. The steel profits ratio slightly exceeded the ratio for all-manufacturing in 1955, 1956, and 1957, then fell to a low point in 1958.

The profit comparisons made above have been influenced somewhat by changing methods of depreciation allowances, such as accelerated amortization, which have resulted in increased deductions for depreciation. They also have been influenced obviously by changing prices and changing production levels.

Competitive Problems Facing the Steel Industry

Foreign Competition.—The steel industry in the United States has for many years supplied the great bulk of this country's requirements of steel mill products. It is estimated that in the thirties, imports on the average supplied only about 1 percent of the domestic consumption of steel mill products; the percentage, however, varied considerably from year to year. In 1932, at the bottom of the Depression, imports had declined less from previous years than domestic production. In that year imports are estimated to have accounted for slightly more than 2 percent of the domestic consumption, the highest ratio imports to the country's consumption in any year of the interwar period. In all years of the later thirties, imports supplied less than 1 percent of the country's consumption of steel mill products. Although foreign markets have never been of major importance to this country's steel industry, exports of steel mill products have usually been much greater in tonnage, and greater still in terms of value, than the imports. It is estimated that in prewar years from about 3.5 to 6.5 percent of the domestic production of steel mill products was exported. In the years 1935–37 this country's annual exports of steel mill products averaged about 1.6 million net tons, valued at about $110 million, while our annual imports of steel mill products averaged about a quarter-million tons valued at approximately $15 million.[5]

During World War II, our annual exports of steel mill products ranged from 7 million tons (1942) to 4.8 million tons (1945). Imports during the war dropped to a small fraction of their former levels, with most of the small amount coming from Canada.

After 1945, our exports of steel mill products remained substantially above their prewar level until 1949. Since then they have fluctuated irregularly from year to year, but in all years until 1959 they

---

[5] United States Tariff Commission, *Iron and Steel*, Report No. 128, Second Series, pp. 133–142.

approximated or substantially exceeded the volume of the peak years (1929 and 1937) of the prewar decade.

Imports recovered in the years after 1945, and in 1949 were of approximately average tonnage for immediate prewar years. In 1950 under the stimulus of the high United States demand that accompanied Korean hostilities and increased rearmament expenditures, imports attained a volume of over 1 million tons—over double that of 1929, and about four times that of the average of the thirties. In 1951, with the continuing high demand in this country and with the domestic steel industry operating at practically full capacity, more than 2 million tons of steel mill products were imported. The 1951 imports represented a record level up to that time, and thereafter imports, like exports, have varied irregularly from year to year.

Table 3 shows the shipments of steel mill products by domestic steel mills and United States exports and imports in the years 1950–59 and in the first 7 months of 1960.

TABLE 3.—*Steel mill products—United States production, imports, exports, and apparent consumption, 1950–59 and January–July 1690*

[In thousands of net tons of 2,000 pounds]

Year	Production [1]	Imports	Exports	Apparent consumption	Ratio of—	
					Imports to apparent consumption	Exports to production (percent)
1950	72,232	1,014	2,639	70,607	1.4	3.7
1951	78,929	2,174	3,051	78,052	2.8	3.9
1952	68,004	1,182	3,918	65,268	1.8	5.8
1953	80,152	1,670	2,907	78,915	2.1	3.6
1954	63,153	784	2,659	61,278	1.1	4.2
1955	84,717	970	3,871	81,817	1.2	4.6
1956	83,251	1,334	4,156	80,429	1.7	5.0
1957	79,895	1,153	5,175	75,872	1.5	6.5
1958	59,914	1,705	2,687	58,932	2.9	4.5
1959	69,377	4,392	1,508	72,261	6.1	2.2
1960: January–March	23,967	1,400	528	24,839	5.6	2.2
April	6,742	331	235	6,838	4.8	3.5
May	6,272	272	320	6,224	4.4	5.1
June	5,921	213	282	5,752	3.7	6.5
July	4,710	177	331	4,556	3.9	7.0

[1] Shipments of steel-mill products by U.S. producers as reported by American Iron & Steel Institute.
Source: Annual and monthly statistical reports of the American Iron & Steel Institute.

Recent Variations in Imports.—Attention is called particularly to the data in table 3 relating to the period since 1957. In 1958, despite the sharp decline in United States production and consumption, this country's imports of steel mill products increased by almost 50 percent from its 1957 volume. This increase was partly due to the fact that, during the recession, the export prices of most steel mill products in the major foreign steel-producing countries were sharply reduced; the prices of most domestic steel mill products in this country were maintained early in the year and in August were increased.[6] A major factor in the increase in imports was the improved availability of foreign steel resulting from a concurrent decline in demand in many countries and continued increase in productive capacity.

In 1959, our imports of steel mill products again increased—to more than 2½ times the 1958 volume. Anticipation of the 1959 steel strike probably began somewhat to stimulate imports before the actual shutdown in July. In any case, the large increase in imports in the second half of the year was probably attributable to the stoppage of operations in the bulk of the domestic mills during the strike. Orders placed abroad in anticipation of a longer strike or of its resumption in 1960, were also factors responsible for sustaining imports at swollen volume well into the first half of 1960. The monthly volume of the imports declined sharply after March, and in July they were below the average monthly volume of 1958. The export prices of foreign steel producers seem generally to have hardened somewhat early in 1959 and showed a more definite rise later in the year, but they remain substantially below the 1957 levels and below the levels of United States domestic prices. (An exception to this statement appears in the case of cold reduced sheets which have been important in United States exports but not in imports.)

The following tabulation reproduced from a bulletin issued by the Business and Defense Services Administration of the Department of Commerce shows imports of steel mill products by month in 1959 and the first 7 months of 1960. (See table 4.)

TABLE 4.—*Monthly trend of United States foreign trade in steel mill products, 1959–60*

[In thousands of net tons]

Year	Exports		Imports	
	1959	1960	1959	1960
January	177	158	229	465
February	185	168	241	471
March	193	203	287	464
April	196	235	359	331
May	183	320	385	272
June	212	382	410	213
July	176	331	430	177
August	64		424	
September	60		366	
October	48		362	
November	70		460	
December	130		539	
Total for first 7 months	1,322	1,797	2,341	2,393
Total for year	1,694		4,392	

[6] Economic Commission for Europe, Steel Committee, *The European Steel Market in 1959*, Table 3.

Recent Variations in Exports.—In 1957, with high levels of business activity in most foreign countries and a moderately high level in this country, 5 million tons of steel mill products were exported from the United States. This was the highest level of exports since 1947. In 1958, with the business recession in most of the Free World, this country's steel exports fell to little more than half the volume of 1957. In 1958 exports of steel mill products from some of the other major steel-producing countries of the Free World also fell somewhat from their 1957 volumes, but those of others (Belgium-Luxembourg, France/Saar and Japan) increased. Although the data for some countries are not yet available, it appears that the total volume of exports of steel mill products from countries of the Free World in 1958 decline 10 percent or more from 1957.

Probably a major factor in the fall in the share of Free World exports accounted for by the United States in 1958 was attributable to the reduction of prices on export sales by foreign producers while the prices on export sales by this country's steel producers were somewhat increased. In the first half of 1959, this country's exports of steel remained at about the average level of 1958. In the second half of that year, exports were of course curtailed to very low levels as a result of the strike in the domestic industry. The dearth of orders from abroad during the strike because of uncertainty as to delivery dates was also probably responsible for the continued low level of exports into the early months of 1960 despite the recovery of business activity in most foreign countries which began in the second half of 1959. The trend of monthly exports was upward during the first half of 1960, and the average for May, June, and July was well above 1958. In light of the continued generally higher level of United States export prices compared with foreign export prices, this would appear to be a rather unexpected recovery. A large part of this country's exports, however, have consisted of tin plate and cold rolled sheets, on which in general the United States export prices have been lower than the foreign export prices.

The Balance of Trade in Steel Mill Products.—Other statistical information relating to United States imports and exports of steel mill products is shown in table 5. This table gives the quantity, value, and average value per short ton of United States imports and exports of steel mill products in 1958 and 1959, and the first 6 months of 1960. For the first time in many decades, this country's imports of steel mill products in 1959 exceeded the exports of such products not only in tonnage but also in value. This situation continued into the early months of 1960, but with the monthly imports decreasing and the exports increasing, the balance of trade, in terms of value, returned to the pre-1959 status in April 1960. In May and later months exports exceeded imports in both quantity and value. As is pointed out later, the different grades and higher quality of products imported accounts in large part for the substantially higher average unit values of exports.

TABLE 5.—*Steel mill products—United States exports and imports, quantity, value, and average unit value, 1958, 1959, and January–June 1960*

	Imports			Exports		
	Quantity (thousands of net tons)	Value (thousands)	Average unit value	Quantity (thousands of net tons)	Value (thousands)	Average unit value
1958	1,705	$192,494	$113	2,687	$547,741	$204
1959	4,391	515,440	117	1,508	342,777	227
1960:						
January	465	63,327	136	158	34,099	216
February	471	63,455	135	167	35,807	214
March	464	62,726	135	203	45,207	224
April	331	44,608	135	235	50,636	225
May	272	36,675		320	62,677	196
June	213	29,443		382	73,134	191

SOURCE: Monthly releases of the American Iron and Steel Institute. Data compiled from statistics collected by the Department of Commerce.

Attention is also called to the much higher average unit values of the exports than of the imports. The values of imports from which the average unit values are derived are foreign values, i.e. values of the goods at the foreign ports of exportation. (In order to arrive at the values at which the imports are delivered to consuming interests in the United States, one would usually have to add ocean freight, import duties, importers' commission, and local delivery charges.) The lower average unit values of the imports are probably in part attributable to the fact already mentioned, that in recent years the foreign export prices on most steel mill products have been lower than United States export prices. Undoubtedly, however, a more important factor has been that the exports consist in greater part than the imports of relatively high priced products, such as tin plate, cold rolled sheets, seamless pipe and tubing, and electrical sheets. Our imports also include some high priced steel mill products such as bars of high speed tool steel, seamless tubes for the manufacture of roller bearings, and flat wire or strip for the manufacture of safety razor blades. Although the imports of some of these items may be important to the domestic trade in such products, they constitute a relatively small part of the total imports. They do, however, account for a much larger part of the value than of the quantity of the imports.

Nonprice Factors in International Competition

One difficulty in analyzing the competition between the steel industries of different countries is the fact that a number of factors in addition to price must be taken into account. In the United States, the steel industry has been developed in coordination with the expansion of the large domestic market for steel mill products. The domestic steel-producing plants have therefore, been adapted and located appropriately to supply the large and diverse requirements of most domestic markets. In addition, the domestic producers have been to some extent protected from foreign competition by the tariff and transportation advantages. As a result of these considerations, neither foreign steel producers nor domestic importers have developed the marketing facilities that enable them to respond quickly to the large domestic demands for different steel products. Many of these products must conform to precise specifications in order to meet specific needs of the consuming industries.

Related to the consideration above referred to is the fact that it is not economical or feasible for consumers, producers, or middlemen to maintain inventories of many steel products commensurate with requirements for more than limited periods. The result is that most steel mill products are usually produced to scheduled orders for delivery. The steel mill products used in heavy construction orders are usually placed only after the construction contracts are closed. Again, in the case of steel mill products used in the production of highly fabricated products, such as machinery and vehicles, orders for steel tend to be placed only after estimates of the demands for the fabricated products are made and production schedules formulated. Under these circumstances, the usual ability of the domestic mills to respond to domestic orders on shorter notice than foreign mills is a substantial advantage. Because of this and the familiarity of the domestic steel producers with the requirements of domestic consuming enterprises and the familiarity of the latter with the services and products of the former, many of the large domestic consuming enterprises would frequently not be prepared to shift to foreign sources of supply even if there were considerable price advantages. Foreign steel mill products of some types therefore can penetrate some United States markets only with difficulty and only then when offered at substantially lower delivered prices.

Of course, factors of the sort referred to in the preceding paragraph are more important in the case of some products than others. For example, products such as barbed wire and nails which are delivered to many small consumers and where conformity to precise and diverse specifications is not a factor, foreign products compete on more nearly equal terms with domestic products. Somewhat similar situations prevail with respect to steel pipe used in house construction and small structural shapes and bars of common grades of steel, that is to say with regard to some of the products which are handled largely through the so-called warehouse trade, and which are of generally low value.

Somewhat similar situations as those described above have prevailed in all the major steel-producing countries though most probably in somewhat lesser degree because of their smaller geographical area and because of the smaller size and, in some cases, less diversified character of their steel industries.

The structure of domestic prices of steel mill products is such as to encourage imports to serve demands at seaboard points and particularly on the West Coast and other areas such as Florida and other South Atlantic points which are distant from domestic mills. The West Coast mills with their higher mill base prices would seem to be particularly vulnerable to import competition, and a substantial part (about a third) of the imports from Japan were entered in that area in the past couple of years. It is somewhat surprising that imports have not been concentrated to a greater extent in those areas. Of course, in 1959 when the increased imports were largely attributable to the shutdown of the domestic industry, the conditions were conductive to indiscriminate imports into all sections of the country.

A feature of the structure of prices maintained by the domestic mills which differs from the practice in prewar years is that the same or somewhat higher prices have in recent years been maintained on export as in domestic sales. This has probably been a major consideration affecting the sharp decline in United States exports of steel mill products in 1958 when as previously indicated the export prices of continental European and Japanese steel mill products were sharply reduced.

The Immediate Outlook for Import Competition.—Since the hardening of foreign export prices that began in late 1959, the influence of the 1958 recession abroad in tending to stimulate United States imports of steel mill products has been reduced. The available information, however, indicates that the general export prices in the principal steel exporting countries on bars, shapes, and plates, but not on cold rolled sheets and some other products, remain below domestic prices contrary to the situation before the 1958 recession. Moreover, the prices of the principal foreign steel producing countries on sales in their domestic markets for the heavier types of hot rolled products are also apparently somewhat lower than domestic prices. The current prices here and abroad, however, appear to be such as to discourage large imports of such products as reinforcing bars and structural shapes. To be sure, as in previous nonrecession years, it is probable that limited amounts of such products may be available for export to the United States at below the quoted prices. When account is taken of ocean freight charges, import duties, dealers' commissions, and the discounts at which foreign products usually have to be sold to overcome buyers' resistance, it does not seem likely that imports will be a much greater factor in United States markets than they were before 1958. That is to say it is reasonable to suppose that most such imports will supply limited demand near ports of entry, especially those at which the delivered prices of domestic products are highest relative to delivered prices at points closer to producing mills.

Domestic Competition.—If competing products are increasingly purchased as substitutes, steel consumption will become more elastic relative to price. Available evidence suggests that steel products are facing increasing competition in our domestic markets.

Steel ingot production has not grown as rapidly as constant dollar Gross National Product in the years 1919–59—145 percent for steel compared with 221 percent for the GNP. However, if the increase to 1957 (a more normal year) is considered, the increase for steel is 197 percent compared with the 221 percent for the GNP. From 1940 through 1957, the production of steel ingots increased 67 percent whereas the GNP increase was about 107 percent. However, if the increase to 1955 (the year of highest ingot production) is considered, the increase for steel is 207 percent compared with 196 percent for GNP.

Total industrial production rose approximately 300 percent from 1919 to 1957. This compares with the 197 percent increase in the production of steel ingots. For the period 1940 through 1957, the increase of 67 percent for steel compares with an increase of 130 percent for total industrial production.

Thus, steel production has not kept pace with the growth of the economy as measured by GNP, nor with industrial production as measured by the Federal Reserve Board Index. On the other hand, neither phenomen is surprising in view of the rapid expansion of the services component of GNP, and the growing complexity of industrial production relative to quantitative material usage.

The above comparisons are not entirely satisfactory because of technical limitations. It may be more meaningful to compare pounds of ingots produced per capita. The level reached in 1929 of 1,014 pounds is only slightly lower than the 1,056 pounds of ingot production per capita in 1959. However, the period 1947–59 showed an average annual per capita production of 1,221 pounds compared with 804 pounds for the 1919–29 period, an increase of 52 percent.

Although steel output, in tonnage, has lagged the increase in GNP, a comparison of dollar sales of steel products with GNP for the years 1940–57 shows a different picture. For this period the GNP in current dollars rose 340 percent whereas total steel revenue increased 378 percent. Whether steel demand and hence output would have advanced more favorably if steel prices had risen less can only be conjectural even though the evidence shows that a number of important competitive products that have been growing much more rapidly than steel have advanced less in prices.[7]

A comparison of steel shipments from 1947 to 1959 clearly points up the fact that steel is lagging behind its competitors. Using 1947 as a base, steel shipments in 1959 were up only about 12 percent; plywood increased 220 percent; plastics (vinyl) 525 percent; plastics (polystrene) 796 percent and portland cement 80 percent. (See table 6.) In part, the larger percentage gains for some of these items result from the very low bases established for them in 1947. Also, much of their growth has not been at the expense of steel.

TABLE 6.—*Shipments of steel and competing minerals*

[Quantities shipped 1947=100]

Year	Plywood	Vinyl	Urea	Poly-strene	Phonelics	Portland cement	Aluminum plate and sheet	Total steel
1947	100.0	100.0	100.0	100.0	100.0	100.0	100.0	100.0
1948	113.1	121.8	110.1	153.0	92.9	109.9	114.1	105.5
1949	118.1	162.3	163.6	221.6	75.6	110.0	71.0	92.4
1950	158.9	229.3	240.9	327.3	122.2	121.5	111.1	115.3
1951	175.0	252.8	275.4	346.4	135.6	130.1	96.6	129.3
1952	186.5	213.1	261.6	362.6	109.6	134.0	97.7	111.4
1953	229.8	278.1	284.7	424.4	144.5	139.2	123.1	133.0
1954	233.1	281.0	303.2	436.8	117.0	146.3	102.4	104.6
1955	290.4	376.7	368.3	532.1	149.9	158.1	138.8	138.8
1956	331.2	406.6	377.1	567.8	150.7	166.3	141.1	135.7
1957	320.1	452.6	375.7	590.5	141.9	155.7	125.4	131.1
1958		446.3	395.2	631.6	139.3	165.3	122.2	99.5
1959		625.6	482.8	896.4	174.1	180.4	159.0	112.4

SOURCE: Data on *plywood* are from the National Lumber Manufacturer's Association; *vinyl, urea, polystrene, and phonelics,* from the U.S. Tariff Commission beginning July 1948—prior thereto U.S. Department of Commerce, "Survey of Current Business," *Portland cement,* from the U.S. Department of Interior, Bureau of Mines; *aluminum plate and sheet,* from the U.S. Department of Commerce, Bureau of Census, and Business and Defense Services Administration; and *steel,* from the American Iron and Steel Institute.

[7] Using an electronic computer we made an effort to determine the relationship between demand for steel and the price trends of competing materials. The results failed to show any clear-cut relationship. The reason was that the competitive materials are used more often as components of manufactured goods which are made largely, or at least in part, from steel. For example, aluminum and plastics are increasingly replacing iron and steel in automobiles but for 52 pounds of aluminum in a car, there are still some 3,400 pounds of iron and steel in today's standard sized car. If, because of a recession or a steel strike, the output of cars is relatively low, aluminum consumption does not increase at the expense of steel, but rather declines in proportion.

Some reasons for the lower demands for steel compared with various competing products are found in the trend toward smaller size as exemplified by compact cars and the use of thinner wall pipe by the oil and gas industry. To meet the competition of concrete and prestressed concrete the steel industry developed a lighter and stronger carbon-grade structural steel. Such developments call for less steel tonnage to meet the demands even though the price per ton may be higher because of the increased costs.

Conclusions

The purpose of this chapter is not to make a detailed analysis of costs and prices in the steel industry. Its purpose is to provide background for an analysis of the results of collective bargaining and to briefly review competitive economic developments that might affect it in the future.

The previous chapter analyzed hourly earnings and steel's wage position. On the basis of the findings of that chapter, which found that general wage movements in the economy have not been affected substantially by steel's independent influence, it is difficult to postulate, as a rough guide, that steel employment costs "might have been" more than 10 percent lower than actual. A 10 percent reduction in such costs would not reduce total costs more than 5 percent even allowing for some induced reduction in material costs. It is not argued that these figures are exact. The contention is, however, that any reasonable assumptions as to the special gains the steelworkers have achieved through collective bargaining have not had a major effect upon the level of steel prices. This, of course, does not imply any answer as to the total effect of collective bargaining in all industries upon prices in the economy. Nor does it imply that employment cost increases have not caused serious concern to steel managements in their increasingly competitive situation.

The same type of conclusion holds with respect to profits. Any "excess" profit which might be attributed to the steel industry has not had a significant impact on steel prices. It is recognized that depreciation policy and internal financing can be debated. Most obviously, steel had had a difficult task in meeting the problem of impact of inflation upon replacement costs. Their response has been well within what might be termed reasonable business discretion.

There is also little ground for criticism of the industry with respect to internal financing. Not only is internal financing the common practice of much of manufacturing industry (table 7), but for most of the postwar years it appears that steel did not have a profit rate sufficiently attractive to have raised equity capital externally without damaging the interests of existing stockholders. The industry, with its cyclical fluctuations, can hardly be criticized for not desiring the burden of fixed charges on large bonded debt. Finally, steel has had a difficult task in anticipating appropriate future capacity requirements. It may be that optimism, public criticism, and competition have established a capacity level that is temporarily high in the light of developing competitive conditions and trends. Nevertheless, while lower capital investment would have allowed some limited price reductions, these would have been small. Because of the important position the steel industry occupies in meeting the defense requirements of the Nation it is much to be preferred for them to err on the high rather than the low side in making decisions relating to expansion.

Increases in steel prices have been caused primarily by cost increases. The size of steel price increases differs from those of many other industries because of the fact that steel has had substantial increases in material costs. In a period of rising prices or in a period of price regulation, Government attitude toward price increases has been strict. The typical regulatory approach has been to hold price increases to a direct or limited pass-through of cost increases already incurred. This has produced conflict between the industry and the Government, particularly since price-increase policy and collective bargaining have been so closely associated.

Obviously, while price policy can be debated in the short run, in the long run all cost increases must be met. Steel has done no more than this. But to cover its cost increases in the postwar years it was necessary for steel to increase its profit margins if its rate of return

TABLE 7.—*Sources and uses of funds by 18 large steel companies compared with all-manufacturing, 1946-58*

[Percent distribution]

Uses of funds	18 large steel companies	All manu- facturing
Plant and equipment expenditures	75.2	68.0
Inventories	12.0	15.9
Receivables	4.2	12.2
Cash	1.5	2.2
Government securities	3.3	—.3
Other assets and uses	3.8	2.0
SOURCES OF FUNDS		
Retained earnings	35.2	39.6
Depreciation	37.7	33.1
Capital stock	4.5	2.5
Bonds and mortgage loans	8.8	11.3
Bank loans:		
short-term	.4	2.5
long-term	.4	1.0
Trade payables	3.6	5.3
Federal income tax liabilities	4.7	.4
Other liabilities and sources	4.7	4.3

SOURCE: Data for 18 large steel companies from Federal Reserve Board Data for all-manufacturing from Department of Commerce.

on capital were to be comparable with the return on American capital generally.

The most serious problem facing the parties is that of adjusting to the developing competitive forces acting upon the steel industry. Extensive technological change is in progress; more change is on the horizon. Changes in the size and nature of many consumer products appear to be lessening the demand for steel. Substitute materials are further reducing demand. The problem of foreign competition has various dimensions. Perhaps the most serious may prove to be the loss of important export markets.

Whether the steel industry can maintain itself against the growing competition of these various products and against foreign competition depends to some extent on its own research and development successes. Technological advances in steel might have dramatic effects in lowering costs, improving quality, and stimulating new uses. Ability to maintain and expand the market for steel would also seem dependent upon the ability of the steel industry to lower its costs and to pass lower costs on to buyers in the form of lower prices. The outcome of the struggle that lies ahead cannot be foreseen. But it seems clear that steel demand will not be as inelastic relative to price as it has been in the past.

CHAPTER 11

STEEL PRICES AND INFLATION

Collective bargaining in steel could have inflationary impacts by (1) establishing wage-fringe levels in steel which pull up the wage-fringe level in the economy through steel's pattern-setting influence, or (2) by the effect of employment and other cost increases upon steel prices which in turn result in indirect price increases throughout the economy. The first influence has already been discussed. The second is the subject of this chapter.

The relationship of steel prices to postwar inflation has been the subject of considerable controversy in recent years. A number of studies have been made assessing the impact of the increase in steel prices on various price indexes. These studies have become controversial.

The study made for this project cannot be summarized in adequate fashion, but in our judgment it was so well reasoned that it is included in its entirety in the following section. The conclusion drawn from the attached study is that any independent wage-price influence on the economy which might be attributed to steel has had extremely small effects upon the price structure of the economy.

Impact of Steel Prices on Inflation

The view has been expressed frequently that the rise in steel prices since World War II has been an important contributor to inflationary tendencies in the United States. It is recognized that steel is a key material input into many industrial processes in the production of the Nation's output, particularly in the case of durable goods purchased by households, business firms, and governments. This widespread prevalence of steel in our economy plus the fact that finished steel product prices have risen 109 percent from 1947 to 1959 while consumer prices have risen only 30 percent leads to the inference that steel prices have had an important influence on the overall price performance of the Nation.

Our purpose here is to trace the impact of a change in steel prices on overall prices both over a short time and over more extended periods.[1] An attempt is made to specify some of the more important conditions that determine the quantitative influence on inflation of a rise in steel prices. Some estimates are made of the effect of an

---

[1] Text of a study paper by Frank E. Norton, University of California, Los Angeles. Graphic material is omitted. The technical appendix accompanying the study is available upon request to the Department of Labor.

increase in steel prices on various price indexes. These are supplemented by an empirical study of the behavior of a selected list of steel-using product prices during the postwar period with especial attention to the recessions of 1953–54 and 1957–58 and the subsequent recoveries therefrom. Before undertaking this analysis, some pertinent aspects of the concept and measurement of inflation are considered.

The Concept and Measurement of Inflation.—Inflation is usually defined as a persistent overall upward movement of prices. The concept most often refers to a wide universe of prices where the average movement is upward although some prices may be falling. Concern with economic welfare and the normative performance of the economy, however, leads to other notions of inflation that are less comprehensive.

Alternative Notions of Inflation

Many would maintain that the most relevant concept of inflation is that which refers to changes in the prices of all the Nation's final products. In this instance, the prices refer to the newly produced goods and services included in the gross national product. Only final product prices are included because intermediate products are considered to be used up in the production of final products. If this notion of inflation is accepted, the appropriate price index for the measurement of inflation is the gross national product implicit price deflator. This, conceptually, is the most comprehensive measure of inflation.

Particular significance is usually attached to consumer prices because everyone is a consumer despite other roles he may play in the economy. Given consumer income, the welfare of the consumer is influenced by the prices of products and services he purchases. A rise in the prices of items consumers typically purchase will reduce his real income which in turn has an adverse welfare effect and may also affect unfavorably the aggregate demand for the Nation's output. If one focuses attention on these considerations, the relevant price index is the Consumer Price Index or perhaps the personal consumption expenditures implicit price deflator. The CPI is the price index with which the layman is most familiar and is widely used in escalator clauses of labor contracts and income negotiations generally.

Finally, one might take the position that inflation should be defined as a rise in the average level of prices at the primary market level. In order to avoid duplication, however, it would be advisable to consider only finished products, thereby excluding intermediate materials, supplies, and components as well as crude materials for further processing. Consequently, movements of the Wholesale Price Index of finished goods would serve best as a measure of inflation at this market level. This price index is of limited coverage because it does not measure the price movements of retail transactions, transactions for services, construction, real estate, and transportation.

Some Properties of Price Indexes To Measure Inflation

The Consumer Price Index and the Wholesale Price Index are generally well known and the details of their essential properties are available elsewhere.[2] They are both variants of a Laspeyres price index.

The implicit price deflators call for some comment. These deflators have variable weights because of the indirect way they are derived. The implicit deflators are obtained by deflation of the expenditure components of national product in as much detail as possible by appropriate price indexes frequently drawn from the component price series of the CPI and the WPI. Since the expenditure components in many instances are available in less detail than the prices, it is necessary to combine various price series into composites. The weights assigned to the various indexes are proportional to their relative importance in terms of expenditures in the base year. Consequently, the weights of the implicit deflators vary in proportion to the expenditures each year on goods and services. For this reason, the implicit deflators give a pure measure of price change only when comparisons are made with the base year. Other comparisons are affected by some change in expenditure patterns as well. Thus, because of this weight system, the implicit deflators take on some of the characteristics of a Paasche price index.

An important offset to its implicit weight system deficiency is the comprehensiveness of the GNP deflator. Among other items, it includes the prices of construction, exports and imports, and the remuneration of Government employees which are usually omitted from other indexes or covered only in part.

The subsequent quantitative estimates of the effect of steel price increases on inflation make use of all four of these price indexes mentioned here, namely, the gross national product implicit price deflator, the personal consumption expenditures implicit price deflator, the Consumer Price Index, and the wholesale price index of finished goods.

Propagation of Steel Price Increases in the Economy.—A rise in steel prices may contribute to inflationary tendencies in the economy via several principal routes. In addition to the impact of the steel

---

[2] See for example, H. E. Riley, "The Price Indexes of the Bureau of Labor Statistics," U.S. Congress, Joint Economic Committee, *The Relationship of Prices to Economic Stability and Growth* (Washington : Government Printing Office, 1958), 107–116.

price rise on the prices of steel-using products and ultimately final product prices, it may induce changes in the prices of substitute and complementary products which on balance may thus lead to magnified changes in final product prices. Moreover, once the final product price level or important sectoral components thereof has moved up significantly, additional mechanisms begin to operate to further the inflationary movement. These matters will be discussed in the next section as a prerequisite to the empirical analysis of a rise in steel prices on various price indexes and on the prices of steel-using products.

Final Product Prices and Price Structure

A notion of the interrelationship between steel prices and final product prices can best be developed initially by relating the problem to national income accounting concepts.

An increase in the final product price level, given the level of output in the Nation, means by definitions based upon the national income accounting framework, that the sum of gross values added in the economy has increased. We may think of the gross value added in the Nation as divided into three separate parts: That originating at production stages below the steel industry; that originating in the steel industry proper, and that originating at production stages above the steel industry. Thus inflation, at any stage of production or in any industry, means a rise in the price of value added in the particular segment of the economy.

An increase in steel prices may reflect an increase in value added in the steel industry itself or a rise in value added at production stages below the steel industry. This is true because all value added below the steel industry is an intermediate product to the industry and involves payments for products and services purchased from other firms at lower stages of production. These intermediate products to the steel industry represent, of course, an important part of its costs. Consequently, inflation may be said to originate in the steel industry only if its value added rises, given its rate of output. Those increases in steel prices which merely reflect a rise in the price of value added at lower production stages are associated with inflationary conditions in other industries.

For our present purposes, we may consider the gross value added in any industry to consist simply of wages, profits, depreciation charges, and indirect business taxes. The concept of "wages" is taken to include all employee compensation; that of "profits" to include corporate profits, income of unincorporated businesses, and interest; that of "depreciation charges" to include depreciation allowances proper and other minor items usually included in capital consumption allowances. Still other relatively small items may be considered to be truncated into one of these larger variables. Gross profits may conveniently be defined as the sum of profits plus depreciation charges.

From the above concepts it follows that a rise in the value added in any industry may be due to either a rise in wages or a rise in gross profits apart from changes in indirect business taxes. Since we are assuming output to be given, this is equivalent to a rise in unit labor costs or gross profit margins per unit of output. Therefore, a rise in the price of value added may be broken down into a rise in wages (short for unit labor cost) or a rise in gross profit margins; and the rise in wages or profit margin may be either autonomous or induced in nature.

The magnitude of the impact of an increase in steel prices on final product prices depends in large part upon whether the value added at production stages above the steel industry is interrelated with changes in steel prices. In short, is a rise in steel prices, reflecting increased value added in the steel industry and below the steel industry, simply passed forward or is the value added above the steel industry also increased? Is there a simple pass-through of steel price increases in the price structure or is there a pyramiding? Furthermore, are the prices of substitute and complementary products at the intermediate product price levels changed as a result of steel price changes? To determine the influence of a change in steel prices on the final product price level, we need to know its probable repercussions on both the vertical and horizontal aspects of the price structure.

Price Policies and Price Flexibility

When steel prices rise, the extent to which final product prices rise is significantly dependent upon the price policies of business firms at production stages above the steel industry. It may be useful to consider how cost, on the one hand, and demand, on the other, may influence price formation in markets deviating to some degree from the concept of pure competition.

Typically, prices are determined in such circumstances, by adding a "markup" to "cost." Whether the concept of cost, upon which the markup is taken is only unit variable cost or unit fixed cost, as well, it is clear that in the long run unit fixed costs must be taken into account. No firm, over an extended period, will consider writing off at intervals the value of investments responsible for the unit fixed costs. They must have sufficient inducement to make investments which will lead to further unit fixed costs in the future otherwise they will operate for only a limited period. Consequently, cost in terms of the concepts specified above will include explicitly unit labor costs and the unit intermediate product costs; it may also include unit fixed costs. In any event, the sum of the profit margin plus unit costs (however defined) must take into consideration all unit costs and provide a sufficient rate of return over longer periods of time.

It is likely that the size of the markup over cost will depend to some extent upon the various conditions of demand facing individual firms. These relate primarily to the nature of the market structure for the particular product, the state of demand for the specific industry, and the characteristics of aggregate demand for the Nation's output at the time.

In those stages of production above the steel industry, such market structure properties as the direct-price elasticity of demand for the particular industry, and the potential price reactions of rival sellers to the price changes of one another determine in part the extent of the markup. A seller encountering a significant cost increase is more likely to raise his price by more than the rise in cost when the industry demand is fairly price-inelastic and when rival sellers will also readily raise their prices.

The state of demand for the particular industry will likewise have an important bearing on the extent of the price rise following a cost increase. Where demand is growing rapidly over time so that little or no excess plant capacity exists, price increases tend to be greater than would otherwise be the case.

Likewise, the movement of aggregate demand for the Nation's output will influence the markup taken. A strong overall demand will make possible larger price increases and vice versa. Persistent excess plant capacity usually tends to inhibit price increases.

Assuming profit margins in production stages above the steel industry are not excessive to begin with, one might expect a simple pass-through of a steel price increase as the minimum impact. This is another way of saying that profits per unit of output would remain constant at all stages of production above the steel industry. However, if the demand for products in all these stages rose because of the growth of industry and aggregate demand so as to maintain output at the initial level, we might expect a pyramiding of the steel price increase as a result of percentage markups. Thus, profits per dollar of sales would remain constant at all production stages above the steel industry. Such a markup would be in keeping with profit maximization by individual firms.[3] The longer the period of time allowed for

---

[3] Let $p(x)$ =product price, $c(x)$ =total variable cost, and $r(x)$ =$p(x)$. x =total revenue.

Then $\mu = \dfrac{p(x) - \dfrac{c(x)}{x}}{p(x)}$ and $\eta = \dfrac{p(x)}{x \cdot p'(x)}$

Where μ =markup as a percentage of price and η =direct price-elasticity of demand. If $c'(x) = \dfrac{c(x)}{x}$, in the relevant range and the firm maximizes profits, $\mu = -\dfrac{1}{\eta}$. The statement above is strictly valid only if we specify isoelastic changes in demand.

adjustment of prices to the steel price increase, the more likely they are to move up by this amount.

Apart from the effects of an increase in steel prices on final product prices, discussed above, such a change would have some influence on substitute and complementary products for steel. A rise in steel prices tends to raise the prices of substitute products and to lower the prices of complementary products relatively to those of their products. One would expect still further indirect repercussions of a change in steel prices when the price system as a whole is considered, but these effects probably would tend to be small in comparison with those already cited.[4] Again, however, we would have to translate such changes into changes in final product prices by taking account of the markups taken over cost from the production stage at which these induced price changes occurred.

What then are the conditions for a stable final product price level when steel prices increase? It is clear that if steel prices rise, some other prices must fall if the overall level of prices is to remain unchanged. To have a stable price index, such converse movements must also be compatible with its weight system. The set of prices moving upward must be compensated by a set of prices moving downward in terms of their weight in the price index. This involves implications with regard to price flexibility.

If aggregate demand for the Nation's output is given, and the same level of employment and output are to be maintained, there must be sufficient downward price and wage flexibility in some sectors to compensate for the rise in prices in other sectors resulting from the rise in steel prices, to maintain a stable price index. If prices and wages are not sufficiently flexible downward, the price level will remain higher and some reduction in employment and output will take place. To achieve both goals simultaneously, namely, the same level of employment (and output) and the same price level, requires an absolute fall in some other prices.[5] The prospects of achieving the required drop in prices and wages thus depends on price and wage policies. The more sectors of the economy possessing a substantial downward rigidity of prices, the greater the price adjustment required of the remaining flexible price sectors. It is probably true that the number of sectors manifesting relatively rigid prices downward will

---

[4] See John R. Hicks, Value and Capital (Oxford: The Clarendon Press, 1950), especially Chapters IV, V, and VIII.

[5] Oscar Lange, Price Flexibility and Full Employment (Bloomington: Principea Press, 1944), gives the most precise statement of the theoretical relationships involved. A. C. Pigow, "The Classical Stationary State," Economic Journal, LIII (1943), 343–51 introduced the real balance effect for the first time in an aggregative model which is easily translated into more strictly Keynesian model terms.

decline as aggregate employment and output decline to increasingly lower levels and as such a situation endures. The markups taken over cost in product markets are probably responsive to excess plant capacity; and the bargaining power of unions in labor markets is likewise no doubt responsive to some extent to unemployment. Unfortunately, the amounts of excess plant capacity and unemployment required to achieve price stability may not be socially acceptable. In such instances, the monetary and fiscal authorities find it necessary to validate some rise in the price level.

Further Repercussions of an Increase in Steel Prices

Once a rise in final product prices has taken place, certain additional mechanisms will be set in motion which will contribute to further inflationary tendencies in the economy. Perhaps the most obvious are certain feedback effects of an institutional character on factor costs. A rise in the CPI will lead to an increase in money wages rates at all stages of production where escalator clauses exist. Other types of escalation clauses in contracts pertaining to construction will have a similar effect on construction costs.

Money wage rates not "geared" to price indexes will tend to rise also through the adjustment of the wage structure to the escalated money wage rate increases. The extent to which this will be offset depends upon the degree of downward flexibility of money wage rates to unemployment in other sectors of the economy.

Feedbacks of a less "built-in" character are particularly important with regard to gross profit margins. As the prices of capital facilities rise and new plant and equipment is put in place, depreciation charges at all production stages will rise because of the gradual rise in the book values of the business capital stock. This rise in depreciation charges will show a distributed lag behind that of the increase in plant and equipment prices. It is also true that over more extended periods of time, net profit margins plus interest charges per unit of output would be expected to rise in proportion to the value of the capital stock so that the same rate of return is maintained. These effects taken together will have a further influence on the overall level of final product prices providing aggregate demand for the Nation's output does not become substantially deficient for extended periods of time.

The preoccupation of business firms with internal financing of capital facilities may exert a separate influence on prices from that mentioned above. Price policies may involve a markup aimed at providing retained earnings plus depreciation allowances sufficient to finance the largest part of current capital expenditures. This, of course, will take account of the payout ratio and the debt-equity ratio necessary to furnish a yield on new equity funds sufficient to obtain external equity funds as well. Thus, although the price policy must run in terms of net profit margin plus depreciation allowances, only retained earnings plus depreciation allowances are available for the financing of capital assets in the business sector.

To the extent that the above net profit margins plus depreciation allowances tend to be excessive because of the attempt to finance capital expenditures from internal funds, two further developments may be induced. First, wage rates may tend to rise more rapidly. The significance of this for secondary price increases is obvious. Second, over a more extended period, overinvestment via internal funds may result in excess plant capacity. This means that the business capital stock will be larger in those areas where this circumstance prevails and that therefore depreciation charges may be larger, thus raising prices further in the long run.

Finally, to the extent wage agreements in the steel industry tend to be pattern setting, the rate of increase in wage rates in other parts of the economy may be enhanced via this route with subsequent increases in prices.

Quantitative Estimate of Influence of Steel Prices on Overall Prices.—This section presents certain empirical materials which may prove helpful in evaluating the influence of a rise in steel prices on inflation. First, an attempt is made to estimate the quantitative effect of an increase in steel prices on various price indexes. Second, an analysis is made of the response of the prices of various steel-using products to increases in steel prices under varying conditions of demand. The purpose of the latter analysis is to assess the validity of certain assumptions underlying the methodology employed in the former analysis. It should be clear in any case that it is impossible at present to evaluate quantitatively the incidence of all the theoretical considerations previously discussed.

Effect of Steel Prices on Price Indexes

In terms of our discussion concerning the concept and measurement of inflation, it was decided to estimate the influence of steel price changes on three price indexes: the gross national product implicit deflator, the personal consumption expenditures implicit price deflator, and the Consumer Price Index. Some estimates pertaining to the wholesale price index of finished goods recently published by Otto Eckstein and Gary Fromm are also included.[6]

---

[6] Otto Eckstein and Gary Fromm, *Steel and the Post War Inflation*, U. S. Congress, Joint Economic Committee, Study Paper No. 2 (Washington: Government Printing Office, 1959).

The methodology used is similar to that employed by Eckstein and Fromm at one point in their study.[7] The procedure relates to the analysis of the relationship between steel prices and final product prices presented previously. It considers the price change in an aggregate to be a weighted average of the changes in value added per unit of its components. Thus the price change of an aggregate may be broken down into two parts: the price change attributable to steel, which is the product of the price change in steel value added per unit and its weight in the aggregate; and the price change due to all other products, which in turn is the product of the price change in value added per unit of these other products and their weight in the aggregate. The weights used are value added weights.

The weight of steel was taken to be 2 percent of the GNP although the exact ratio of steel value added to GNP was 1.7 percent as of 1954. The weight of steel taken for personal consumption expenditures and for the CPI was based fundamentally upon the input-output analysis of the Bureau of Labor Statistics. It was determined by multiplying the total value added in steel in 1954 by the percentage of gross iron and steel output to final demand absorbed by households in 1947 and dividing the resultant product by personal consumption expenditures for 1954.[8] Because the weight of steel in household expenditures as determined on the basis of the input-output categories does not allow for steel used in new residential construction and because there appears to have been an upward trend in the use of steel in many consumer durable goods since 1947, alternative weights were also used. While the basic weight of steel in household expenditures as determined by the input-output study was one third, the analysis was also undertaken using the alternative weights of two-fifths and one-half.

Table 1 presents selected findings from the analysis of the effect of steel price changes on various price indexes. The question was posed: How much would each of the price indexes have changed if steel prices had changed no more than all other prices exclusive of steel for the periods, 1947–58 and 1953–58? For each price index and for each period, the table shows the actual and hypothetical price changes. The hypothetical price changes are derived in substance by replacing the actual contribution of steel in terms of its actual price change during the period in question by a hypothetical contribution of steel in terms of the price change of all other items. In this table, the results for the personal consumption expenditures implicit price

---

[7] Eckstein and Fromm, op. cit., p. 14, fn. 9.

[8] See W. Duane Evans and Marvin Hoffenbrg, "The Interindustry Relations Study for 1947," *Review of Economics and Statistics*, XXXIV (1952), Table 3, p. 124.

deflator and the CPI are based upon a weight of steel in household expenditures of two-fifths. A table in the technical appendix gives the results for alternative weights of one-third and one-half. Also value added per ton of steel is used here as a measure of steel price change, while other results based upon a special BLS index for steel mill products is presented in the appendix table.

Table 1 suggests that the quantitative influence of steel price increases on final product prices in both periods under review was modest. If steel prices had moved in accordance with all other prices, the general price rise would have been from 2.4 to 4.8 percent lower for the 1947–58 period and 2.4 to 5.0 percent lower for the 1953–58 period depending upon the measure of overall price change used. All alternative weights and steel price change definitions used give results falling within these ranges.

The estimate drawn from Eckstein and Fromm pertaining to the wholesale price index for finished goods gives an exaggerated notion of the contribution of steel price increases to overall price movements.[9] Apart from the limited coverage of the price index in which all of retail trade and all or part of services, communications, wholesale trade, transportation, finance, and construction are excluded, the method actually used takes changes in the sum of steel value added plus intermediate product costs as a measure of the relevant steel price change. Consequently, changes in steel prices attributable to changes in the prices of materials, supplies, freight—all purchases from other industries—are included as well as those which are due

TABLE 1.—*The effect of increases in steel prices on price indexes, 1947–58*

Price index	Percent change in index, 1947–58		Percent change in index, 1953–58		Percent decreases in index if steel prices had changed like all other prices	
	Actual	Hypothet-ical [1]	Actual	Hypothet-ical [1]	1947–58	1953–58
Gross national product implicit price deflator	33.5	31.9	11.9	11.3	4.8	5.0
Personal consumption expenditures implicit price deflator	26.8	26.0	8.4	8.2	3.0	2.4
Consumer Price Index	29.3	28.6	8.0	7.8	2.4	2.5
Wholesale price index, finished goods, all items	25.6	19.6	9.3	6.8	23.4	26.9

[1] Percentage change in price index if steel price change had been only equal to that of all other prices in the particular index except for wholesale price index of finished goods, where steel price change was assumed to be equal to that of general wholesale price index.

SOURCE: Estimated on the basis of data from Department of Commerce, Bureau of Labor Statistics and Annual Statistical Reports of the American Iron and Steel Institute by procedures discussed in text except for wholesale price index of finished goods which is taken from Otto Eckstein and Gary Fromm, "Steel and Post War Inflation," U.S. Congress, Joint Economic Committee, Study Paper No. 2 (Washington: Government Printing Office, 1959.) The precise percentage changes were calculated on the basis of the data in the latter source rather than depending on the approximation percentage changes given therein.

[9] Eckstein and Fromm, op. cit., Table 3, p. 12.

to a change in the price of steel value added. It has been shown previously that only the latter should be considered as attributable to the steel industry *per se*.[10] If one takes the statement made by them that one-third of the price increase of steel is due to the rise in the costs of items purchased from other industries, and applies it as a reduction factor, the 23 percent figure for 1947–58 becomes 15 percent.

During the 1947–58 period, the prices of new business capital facilities rose substantially more than the prices of the products and services shown in table 1. From 1947 to 1958, the new nonresidential construction deflator rose 56 percent while the producers' durable equipment deflator rose 55 percent. The question arises as to what extent steel price increases influenced such price increases and how important they were, in turn, in raising final product prices. It is clear that a rise in the prices of capital facilities will filter through the business capital stock as it is replaced and expanded, thus eventually leading to a rise in the book value of such assets. If business firms in the long run must maintain a certain rate of return on capital, expressed in terms of its historical cost, to provide an incentive for further investment, then final product prices might be expected to increase *pari passu*, with the rise in the book value of capital assets.

We have attempted to make a very crude estimate of the effect of steel price changes on final product prices via their impact on the book value of capital facilities. Because of the distributive lag with which book values adjust to a change in the prices of new capital facilities, our methodology was somewhat different than that used above. The hypothetical question posed was: If steel prices changed by a specified amount, how much would overall final product prices change in the *long run*, other prices remaining unchanged? The notion involved is essentially that the prices of capital facilities rise and then stabilize at a new level and that the book value of the business capital stock adjusts with a long lag. When the book value of the capital stock is in full equilibrium with the prices of new capital facilities, how much higher is the final product price level? Obviously this hypothetical question cannot be answered except in a very approximate way on the basis of data drawn from real world processes.

The details of the methodology employed are presented in the technical appendix. Essentially the procedure depends upon estimates of

---

[10] This aspect of the method was no doubt tied up with the desire of Eckstein and Fromm to use the 1947 inverse matrix elements in their computations, where steel prices are an endogenous variable, thus avoiding the computation of a new inverse matrix as a solution of a new linear simultaneous equation system with steel prices considered as an exogenous variable.

six parameters: The weight of steel in producers' durable equipment and nonresidential construction, the weight of each in the business capital stock, the capital intensity per unit of output, the gross rate of return on capital in terms of its book value, and the weight of gross profits or returns per unit of output in the GNP. On the basis of this analysis, the tentative conclusion is that even a 100 percent rise in steel prices, as we have witnessed in the 1947–59 period, would lead to less than a 1 percent rise in the final product price level in the long run. It should be understood that this refers only to the effects of steel prices via capital facilities and gross profits in the long run and does not include the short run effects shown in table 1.

The above estimates of the effect of steel prices on various price indexes are made under rather limiting assumptions. Those appearing in table 1 assume a simple pass-through of the rise in the price of steel value added. Thus, price-cost relations at all production stages above the steel industry are assumed to be of such a nature that profits per unit of output remain constant. No consideration is given to the markup taken on cost at various stages of production and how it will be influenced by the conditions of demand for various products as well as for the Nation's overall output. If markups, feedbacks, and some of the other inflationary mechanisms mentioned previously have been operative, the price of value added both above and below the steel industry will have been substantially increased as a result and this will tend to make ex post estimates of the effect of steel prices smaller than they really are. The very interrelationships of value added at various stages of production will make it impossible to assess the ex ante impact of steel prices from post mortems of processes on the basis of ex post data.

Response to Changes in Steel Prices

Some impression of the impact of a rise in steel prices on overall prices may be gained by an examination of how steel-using product prices have behaved in relation to increases in steel prices during the postwar period. Table 2 gives a listing of steel-using products which are selected for study here. These items were chosen from the wholesale price index by stage of processing, namely, for durable manufacturing, components for manufacturing, and materials and components for construction. The wholesale price indexes of steel-using products and finished steel products are plotted monthly for the period 1947–60 on semi-log scales in a series of charts so that percentage changes over time can be roughly compared.

One aspect of price behavior which is of importance is the timing, between changes in the price of steel and that of steel-using products. A high temporal correlation of price changes may reflect two largely different price policies: First, where steel costs represent a very large proportion of total costs of a product, and where demand conditions are favorable, the price may be increased almost immediately or with a short lag following the rise in steel prices. Second, where steel costs are a much smaller proportion of total costs, it may be expedient for a business firm to accumulate various cost increases over a period of time and where demand conditions are not adverse, to adjust prices when steel prices rise.

TABLE 2.—*The response of steel-using product prices to increases in steel prices under varying demand conditions*

Wholesale price index items	Steel content [1]	Percent change 1953-54 recession [3]		Percent change 1957-58 recession [3]		Price change coefficient 1953-54 recession [4]		Price change coefficient 1957-58 recession [4]	
		Contraction	Expansion	Contraction	Expansion	Contraction	Expansion	Contraction	Expansion
Windows, steel, residential..	A	3.6	3.6	4.6	0.4	1.0	1.3	1.1	0.1
Bolts, nuts, screws, and rivets	A	4.6	1.8	5.5	-4.2	1.4	.6	1.3	-1.5
Metal containers	B	2.7	1.1	2.1	-1.8	.8	.4	.5	-.6
Hardware	B	1.8	3.0	.2	2.1	.5	1.1	.1	.8
Boilers, tanks, and sheet metal products	B	-2.6	.7	.8	.5	-.8	.3	.2	.2
Plow, moldboard, tractor drawn	B	4.8	3.8	9.4	2.5	1.4	1.4	2.2	.8
Harrow, disc	B	.6	-.1	2.7	5.5	.2	0	.6	2.0
Industrial fittings	C	9.5	1.1	.5	.2	2.8	.4	.1	.1
Industrial valves	C	1.0	5.1	-2.4	16.5	.3	1.8	-.6	5.9
Agricultural machinery and equipment	D	-.2	-.7	4.7	3.5	-.1	-.3	1.1	1.2
Construction equipment and machinery	D	1.6	2.4	4.9	4.0	.5	.9	1.2	1.4
Farm and garden tractors	D	-1.4	-2.3	4.7	4.5	-.4	-.8	1.1	1.6
Agricultural machinery, excluding tractors	D	.5	.6	4.7	4.4	.2	.2	1.1	1.6
Power cranes, draglines, and shovels	D	1.4	4.0	2.3	3.6	.4	1.4	.6	1.3
Tractors, other than farm	D	3.5	1.6	6.6	4.0	1.0	.6	1.6	1.4
Metalworking presses	D	0	8.5	-1.7	3.0	0	3.0	-.4	1.1
Other metalworking machinery	D	3.6	4.8	2.9	-.2	1.0	1.7	.7	-.1
Pumps, compressors, and equipment	D	1.2	2.3	4.8	6.0	.4	.8	1.1	2.1
Elevators and escalators	D	1.2	1.3	-.1	.7	.4	.5	0	.3
Industrial furnaces and ovens	D	4.5	-7.3	8.0	4.7	1.3	-2.6	1.9	1.7
Industrial material handling equipment	D	4.1	3.4	3.3	1.8	1.2	1.2	.8	.6
Mechanical power transmission equipment	D	4.0	3.5	2.1	2.2	1.2	1.3	.5	.8
Fans and blowers, except portable	D	6.5	-.1	2.4	1.1	1.9	0	.6	.4
Industrial scales	D	8.1	.7	2.5	9.9	2.4	.3	.6	3.4
Internal combustion engines	D	1.9	-.5	2.8	.4	.6	-.2	.7	.1
Motors, generators, and motor generator sets	D	-.8	-2.3	3.0	0	-.2	-.8	.7	0
Passenger cars	D	.7	2.6	2.7	3.1	.2	.9	.6	1.1
Motortrucks	D	-1.1	3.7	4.5	2.9	-.3	1.3	1.1	1.0
Household appliances	D	1.6	-3.1	.1	-8.5	.5	-1.1	0	-3.0
Lawn mowers	D	.7	-.4	1.6	-3.8	.2	-.1	.4	-1.4

[1] A—75 percent or more; B—50-74 percent; C—25-49 percent; D—below 25 percent.
[2] Contraction, June 1953 to June 1954; expansion, June 1954 to June 1955.
[3] Contraction, June 1957 to April 1958; expansion, April 1958 to July 1959.
[4] Ratio of percentage change of item to that of finished steel products.

SOURCE: Bureau of Labor Statistics for data underlying calculations and estimates of steel content.

Table 2 classifies the steel-using products on the basis of the value of their steel content to total value into four groups: A—75 percent or more, B—50 to 74 percent, C—25 to 49 percent, and D—below 25 percent. This indicated steel content of the various items in the Wholesale Price Index represents the judgment of commodity specialists in the BLS based upon their general knowledge of the products and industry. Since it is not based upon cost studies, it must be considered only a rough ranking.

An examination of table 2 shows quite a variation in the temporal correlation of price changes with those of steel prices. If one focuses attention primarily on the period since 1954, the following items seem to exhibit a significant correlation: (1) bolts, nuts, screws, and rivets, (2) harrow, disc, (3) agricultural machinery and equipment, (4) construction equipment and machinery, (5) fans and blowers, except portable, and (6) passenger cars. Other products show price changes that are much less systematically related over time to changes in steel prices. It will be noted that these items cover the entire spectrum of product steel content so that presumably the related timing of price changes is not necessarily due to the importance of steel as an element of cost. Thus such behavior must be dependent in a number of instances upon the second type of price policy mentioned above.

It might be expected that demand conditions would play a significant role in the extent to which the prices of steel-using products are increased following a rise in steel prices. To test roughly the influence of demand, we have made an analysis of the response of steel-using product prices to changes in steel prices during the business recessions of 1953–54 and 1957–58 and the recoveries therefrom. These two periods were divided into contraction and expansion phases and the percentage change in the prices of the steel-using products computed. While the peak and trough months were initially identified on the basis of the National Bureau of Economic Research's dating of turning points, it was necessary to make some adjustments in these dates in order to compute the price change from the month before a major steel price change to the month before the succeeding major steel price change. The phases established were: For the 1953–54 recession, contraction, June 1953 to June 1954, expansion June 1954 to June 1955. For the 1957–58 recession, contraction, June 1957 to April 1958, expansion, April 1958 to July 1959. The calculated percentage changes in the prices of the selected items in the WPI for each designated phase are presented in table 2. The last two columns express the percentage change so computed as a ratio of the percentage change in the price of finished steel products for the same time periods. This is designated in the table as the "price change coefficient."

Particular interest attaches to the steel-using products which have price changes that appear to be closely timed with changes in steel prices. Of the six such products, two do not conform to our general expectations in either of the cyclical test periods. In the case of bolts, nuts, screws, and rivets, the price change coefficient is higher during the contraction than during the expansion of the 1953–54 period; while for the 1957–58 period, the price coefficient is positive for the contraction and negative for the expansion. Again, in the case of fans and blowers, the price change coefficient is higher in contraction than in expansion in both cyclical periods. The remaining products do tend to exhibit higher price change coefficients for the expansion than for the contractions. Thus the evidence pertaining to the important items construction equipment and machinery and passenger cars suggests that their price behavior is influenced by demand conditions. However, in the case of disc harrows and agricultural machinery and equipment generally, their price behavior conforms to our expectations only in the most recent recession and recovery period. This is probably because the demand for these products is related significantly to farm income rather than to the aggregate demand for the Nation's output as a whole or associated variables. Net farm income was declining throughout both the contraction and subsequent expansion in the 1953–54 recession. Consequently, the demand for these products was influenced adversely even during the expansion following the 1953–54 recession. This seems to have been particularly true in the case of farm and garden tractors. Consequently the results obtained in this instance seem dependent upon the fact that our methodology is not appropriate where variations in the demand for the product follow a course substantially different from that of aggregate demand.

An analysis of the average price change coefficient for all the items in the two cyclical periods by phase shows somewhat diverse behavior. For the 1953–54 recession, the average price change coefficient is 0.7 for the contraction and 0.6 for the expansion if products relating to the agricultural sector are excluded—just the converse of our expectations. For the 1957–58 recession, the average price change coefficient is 0.7 for the contraction and 0.8 for the expansion, which is in keeping with our expectations.

Again, for the 1953–54 recession, 54 percent of the items, excluding those related to the agricultural sector, had a price change coefficient which was negative for the contraction and positive for the expansion or of greater positive value for the expansion than for the contraction period. Taking the 1957–58 recession, 48 percent of the items had a price change coefficient which was negative for the contraction and positive for the expansion or of greater positive value for the expansion than for the contraction period.

Although the above evidence does not lead to any general conclusions as to the influence of demand conditions on the response of steel-using product prices to an increase in steel prices, it does suggest that demand conditions may exert an influence on specific products or groups of products. Thus, in accordance with the results shown in table 2, demand conditions seem to be particularly important in the case of equipment and machinery used by the agricultural sector, construction machinery and equipment, passenger cars, and various other capital facilities items.[11] These results probably reflect the fact that in the period since 1953, changes in the composition of aggregate demand for the Nation's output have been very important in overall price behavior. While aggregate demand seldom seems to have been excessive during this period, demand pressures were evident in specific sectors of the economy. The economy rolled from a consumption boom centered largely in automobile expenditures in the 1954 upswing into an investment boom centered primarily in plant and equipment expenditures. The price behavior reflected in the items studied here seems to be roughly consistent with these developments in specific final demands. Finally, it may also be noted that the findings are consistent with respect to the weak markets experienced in the household appliances field.

Our methodology, of course, does not make it possible to isolate the "net effect" of a change in steel prices on the prices of steel-using products under varying conditions of demand. The price change coefficients for a particular cyclical phase are the resultant of changes in the prices of other inputs besides steel and in productivity which are associated with the movements of demand. There is no assurance that these latter variables will move in a consistent way with demand in other time periods of comparable cyclical position. Furthermore, our attempt to partial out the influence of demand conditions by its very nature can be only moderately successful. The demand for various products is not related to aggregate demand in the same way. It is for this reason that we have attempted to draw attention to certain specific products where the final demand profile departed substantially from that of aggregate demand. Finally, the effect of possible variations in attributes of the market structure and in the degree of excess plant capacity in different product areas on price policies has not been separated out.

---

[11] Items apart from those related to the agricultural sector that have price change coefficients in both periods that are consistent with the demand influence hypothesis are hardware, industrial valves, construction equipment and machinery, power cranes, draglines and shovels, metalworking presses, pumps, compressors, and equipment, elevators and escalators, and passenger cars.

IV. Conclusions

The exploratory analysis undertaken in this study suggests that the independent influence of steel prices on inflation has been modest in the postwar period. However, the quantitative estimates of the effect of steel prices increases on various price indexes, with the exception of the WPI are probably somewhat on the low side. This is true because the methodology used assumes a simple pass-through of steel price increases and also does not allow for secondary repercussions.

Our empirical analysis involving the results of market forces leads to the presumption that prices are sensitive to demand conditions in the case of a number of specific steel-using products. The mark-up taken on cost does seem to be related to demand conditions. While aggregate demand has not been excessive for any sustained period since 1953, the economy has undergone great surges in demand which were concentrated on final products requiring a substantial overall steel input. The price behavior of steel-using industries seems to have been dominated more by these circumstances than by the rise in steel prices per se. As a result of the momentum developed in the price structure and because of the short duration and mildness of recent recessions, there was a tendency for steel-using industries to show price increases even during declines in demand. Moreover, such conditions tended to preclude the likelihood of offsetting downward price movements elsewhere in other sectors of the price structure. This suggests that public policy should be directed toward a more balanced structure of demand as well as toward an adequate overall demand for the Nation's output. These are matters that call for extended study if we are to avoid inflationary tendencies in the future.

Part V

THE ROLE OF GOVERNMENT

CHAPTER 12

INSTANCES OF GOVERNMENT INTERVENTION

In the years since the organization of the basic steel industry, the Federal Government has intervened or played some role in a majority of the negotiations between the parties. The forms of Government intervention have varied widely. One of the commonest has been through executive and legislative pressure on steel prices, thereby affecting the wage-fringe settlement. At various times this pressure has taken the form of control of both wages and prices, control of prices only, investigations and studies of industry pricing-practice by two branches of the Federal Government, or merely statements concerning inflation and desirable collective bargaining settlements designed to influence public opinion and thereby the ultimate settlement. The importance of this type of intervention and its impact on collective bargaining has been discussed in chapter 7.

This chapter will summarize the types of direct Government intervention that have been used to prevent a steel strike or halt one already in existence. Over the years the methods used have included almost every one of the techniques commonly applied by Government for this purpose. These include mediation, both through the regular procedures of the Federal Mediation and Conciliation Service and less formalized mediation at the highest levels of Government; fact-finding, with and without recommendations; a form of arbitration; seizure; and injunction. Some have been used only once, others repeatedly. Some have been used alone; some in combination. Some have the purpose of providing a settlement for the parties, others to provide a framework upon which the parties can then negotiate a settlement. Seizure and injunction have the primary purpose of delaying or temporarily halting a strike in hope that the parties themselves will find a means of settlement during the period of delay. Mediation ordinarily serves as an aid to the collective bargaining process, but under some circumstances can become a pressure device of great effectiveness.

The following paragraphs will summarize the types of intervention and the years in which each was used in steel. An evaluation of this record will be made in the next chapter.

Arbitration

Compulsory arbitration is commonly considered one of the most extreme forms of Government intervention. Voluntary arbitration, on the other hand, is often recommended as an alternative to a strike. World War II provided the special circumstances in which a form of arbitration combining elements of both voluntarism and compulsion became the device for settling many labor-management disputes, including those in basic steel.

To effectuate wartime controls and to implement labor's "no strike" pledge it became necessary to provide some device for settling conflicts over the terms of labor agreements. The National War Labor Board was created to fulfill this dispute-settlement function, and in time came to set and administer wage stabilization policy as well. Parties who were unable otherwise to reach agreement came before the tripartite Board, presented their case, and received a decision which for all practical purposes was an arbitration award.

In 1942 the Little Steel companies were unable to reach agreement with the United Steelworkers of America on terms of their initial agreement and three issues were submitted to the WLB. The Board's award on wages became known as the "Little Steel" formula, which, by limiting wage increases to existing wage and cost-of-living relationships, established a basic policy for wage increases for all industry in the war years. The award was also used as the basis for a later decision involving the renegotiation of the agreement between U.S. Steel and the Steelworkers.

Once again, in 1944, the basic steel industry dispute was certified to the WLB when the parties were unable to reach agreement. The award that the WLB made in 1945 became their agreement. Although both industry and union from time to time expressed dissatisfaction with WLB decisions, for the most part the industrial relations scene in steel was peaceful throughout the war period.

Mediation

There is no record that U.S. Conciliation Service personnel ever participated in basic steel negotiations. In the late fall of 1945, Secretary of Labor Lewis Schwellenbach proffered the services of a special mediator from the New York State Board of Mediation to the parties rather than a mediator from his own Department. The offer was rejected by the industry.

The Conciliation Service became the independent Federal Mediation and Conciliation Service [FMCS] in 1947, but there was no need for its services in the steel negotiations of 1947 or 1948. In 1949 regular Federal mediation services played a role in steel bargaining. In that year, and again in 1952, FMCS Director Cyrus Ching, along with two of his subordinates, held mediation conferences in Washington and New York. In the 1949 negotiations the Service directed public attention toward its meetings with U.S. Steel while private meetings between Bethlehem Steel and the union provided the basis for the settlement of the crucial pension issue. In 1952, a number of joint mediation conferences were held, but because of the existence of the Wage Stabilization Board mediation did not play a significant role in the settlement.

In 1956, and again in 1959, FMCS Director Joseph Finnegan and several of his mediators held numerous meetings with the parties after the strikes had begun. Although settlements were not made in FMCS conferences, the efforts of the Service helped to keep negotiations in progress and were a significant part of the total Government mediatory effort in those years.

Mediation undertaken by persons outside the Conciliation Service or the FMCS has often played an important role in steel settlements, particularly in the postwar years. In 1946 the Chairman of the fact-finding board, Nathan Feinsinger, acted as a go-between for the parties, the White House, and the Office of War Mobilization and Reconversion. Meetings were held at the White House in which Presidential Assistant John Steelman and President Truman acted as mediators. The final settlement resulted from the conclusion of an agreement between the Government and the industry over prices, and the industry and the union over wages.

In 1952 Feinsinger again acted as a special mediator at the request of Steelman. When his efforts failed to avert a strike, Steelman himself held joint conferences at the White House. President Truman also participated by talking to the parties, and the final settlement was made between Murray and Fairless along with Steelman at the White House.

No mediation was necessary in the negotiations of 1953 and 1954, and the 1-day work-stoppage in 1955 was over before the FMCS could enter the dispute. In 1956, however, the efforts of high Government officials encouraged the parties to negotiate a settlement. After the strike had been in existence for nearly a month Secretary of Labor James Mitchell and Secretary of Treasury George Humphrey both became involved in the dispute. They intervened in the hope of avoiding the necessity for appointment of a non-Taft-Hartley fact-finding board with power to recommend a settlement. They were able to arrange for meetings which developed constructively, in contrast with the earlier failure of the parties to find any substantial area of agreement. A new industry offer quickly resulted in a negotiated settlement.

The 1959 settlement came about in a way similar to that of 1956, but with mediation by various Government officials playing an even more crucial role. At the same time that the FMCS was holding conferences, Secretary of Labor Mitchell and Vice President Nixon began holding private mediation conferences. The industry was convinced by Vice President Nixon that it should change its position, and as a consequence Secretary Mitchell was able to mediate effectively. Once again mediation, accompanied in this case by the threat of resumption of the strike and the accompanying possibility of congressional action, brought about a settlement.

Factfinding

The device of "factfinding" boards has often been adopted in response to a public demand that "something be done" about a given industrial dispute. The factfinding process itself can be used in various ways and for various purposes. In some cases it is used largely for the purpose of effecting delay of a strike. It may be a substitute for mediation, or, more often, a supplement to mediation. Factfinding may represent the final effort of Government to settle a dispute or may simply set the stage for even more vigorous intervention. It has been used in all of these ways in basic steel disputes.

During the Little Steel strike in 1937, Secretary of Labor Frances Perkins appointed a board that was to have the dual purpose of factfinding and mediation. When the company representatives refused to meet with the union, with or without the services of the board, the mediation function was doomed. The board then fell back on factfinding and as a result of its findings recommended that the companies make a written agreement with the SWOC. The companies rejected the proposal and attacked the board as biased, after which the board gave up its efforts.

Although factfinding as a process played an important part in the deliberations of the War Labor Board, the next use of factfinding in steel as a device for ending disputes occurred prior to the strike of 1946. The board, appointed by President Truman, was 1 of a series of 11 that were created during 1945 and 1946 in an effort to do something about the wave of disputes and strikes that occurred shortly after the war. The steel board, in actual fact, never held hearings in the dispute because the parties expressed a preference for further joint bargaining. The settlement which followed the strike was based upon a slight modification by the President of a factfinding recommendation made by another board appointed in the General Motors dispute.

Factfinding was again used in the 1949 steel dispute and became a source of major controversy. By this time the machinery of the Taft-Hartley Act for dealing with emergency disputes had been enacted. This machinery called for factfinding without power of recommendation as a part of the procedure. President Truman, however, decided to bypass these statutory provisions and appoint an *ad hoc* factfinding board that would have the power to make recommendations. Initially the industry balked at acceptance of a non-Taft-Hartley board, and even after it agreed to the procedure continued to protest the appointment before the board itself. The board's report was attacked by the industry on the basis that it recommend noncontributory pensions and insurance. It is generally conceded, however, that the industry's willingness to take the strike which followed was due not only to its objection to the recommendations themselves, but also in part to the feeling that the Administration had favored the union in the timing and type of board that was appointed.

In the steel dispute of 1952 the factfinding role was undertaken by the Wage Stabilization Board established during the Korean War. A special panel of the Board took 2 months to hear the positions of the parties and to submit its findings as to the issues in dispute. The Board itself then made recommendations in a procedure similar to that employed by the War Labor Board. In this case, the industry refused to accept the recommendations of the Board, and a strike later occurred. It should be noted that the WSB had power only to make "recommendations" while the WLB had issued "orders," that there was no "no-strike" pledge by labor during the Korean War, and that the public acceptance of controls was much weaker during that period than during World War II.

Two different kinds of factfinding were used during the 1959 strike. Shortly after the strike began, Secretary Mitchell announced that the Department of Labor was preparing background statistics bearing on the economic questions surrounding the dispute. The report was issued in August 1959, and was intended primarily to inform the public. It dealt with such areas as wages, productivity, prices, and profits, but did not draw conclusions.

Later in the 1959 dispute the national emergency provisions of the Taft-Hartley Act were applied to a steel strike for the first time. Factfinding is a part of these procedures, but the law prohibits the board of inquiry from making recommendations. After the strike had been in progress for nearly 90 days President Eisenhower appointed a board of inquiry, the first step of the statutory procedure. The board not only held hearings to determine the issues in dispute but mediated as well. These efforts were unsuccessful, and the board's Initial Report summarized and attempted some evaluation of the major areas in dispute between the parties. The board's Final Report, issued 60 days later, was made public just as the settlement was being announced, and played no part in it.

Seizure

In 1952, following the failure of the parties to agree upon the WSB recommendations as the basis for a negotiated settlement, President Truman ordered the seizure of the steel mills. He based the action upon his "inherent" powers as President. The Secretary of Commerce took symbolic possession of the mills and ordered management to perform its usual duties. The union immediately called off a strike which had barely begun.

It is possible that a negotiated settlement would have been reached during the seizure period, under the Government's threat to put the WSB wage recommendations into effect, had not the Supreme Court prohibited the making of changes while it took the industry's challenge of the seizure under advisement. The interest of the parties then turned to the Constitutional argument before the Supreme Court. When the Court held that the seizure in the circumstances of the dispute violated the Constitution, the President immediately ordered that the mills be returned to their owners. A strike lasting about 2 months followed.

Injunction

In 1959 an injunction was first used in a basic steel dispute. Following the Initial Report of the Taft-Hartley board of inquiry in 1959, President Eisenhower directed the Attorney General to seek an injunction against the strike. This action was in conformity with the national emergency dispute provisions of Title II of the Taft-Hartley Act. The union contested the application of these provisions to the dispute on the basis that the strike did not imperil the national health and safety, and that the provisions were unconstitutional. These issues were carried to the Supreme Court, which ruled against the union. Thirty days after the President had initiated the national emergency procedures the strike was finally discontinued.

The dispute was settled during the period of the injunction. The economic consequences of a recurrence of the strike, the apparent heavy defeat which the industry would have suffered if its "final offer" had gone to its employees for a vote, and the threat of congressional action created mounting pressure sufficient to force a compromise settlement.

Summary

The following list recapitulates the various forms of Government intervention into the collective bargaining relationship between the basic steel industry and the Steel Worker's Organizing Committee and its successor, the United Steelworkers of America. The dates following each type represent years in which intervention took place in a contract negotiation or wage reopening.

Wage and Price Control—1942, 1944, 1946, 1952.

Governmental Pressure Upon the Wage-Price Relationship—1941, 1948, 1950, 1956 and 1959.

Arbitration—1942, 1944.

Mediation by Federal Mediation and Conciliation Service Officials—1949, 1952, 1956, 1959.

Mediation by Other Government Officials—1946, 1952, 1956, 1959.

Fact-Finding With Recommendations—1937, 1946, 1949, 1952.

Fact-Finding Without Recommendations—1959.

Seizure—1952.

Injunction—1959.

It should be recognized that this list appears to magnify the total amount of intervention, in that several different types of intervention frequently occur in one negotiation year. Nevertheless, of the 16 different years in which steel negotiations have been undertaken, the only years not included in one or more of the above are the original U.S. Steel-SWOC agreement of 1937 and the negotiations of 1947, 1953, 1954, and 1955.

CHAPTER 13

AN EVALUATION OF INTERVENTION

In a free economic society it is *a priori* desirable that Government avoid intervention in labor-management disputes. The policy of the United States, as stated by the Congress in the Wagner Act and often reaffirmed in subsequent legislation, is that first reliance in the settlement of all labor-management disputes should be placed on the parties themselves through collective bargaining. It is a corollary of this basic policy that Government intervention in disputes tends to corrode collective bargaining. The reason for this is simply that intervention usually has the effect of postponing the economic pressures that are the ultimate incentive to the settlement of all major disputes between labor and management.

Early intervention to avoid a work stoppage often turns the parties away from face-to-face bargaining at what is normally the most fruitful time for settlement in any negotiation. Moreover, it causes them to modify their appraisal of issues in the light of what Government may be expected to do. If Government provides the parties with an alternative road to settlement, experience demonstrates that the parties will almost inevitably turn to the alternative rather than settle themselves. Even if the Government delays intervention in the hope that economic pressures will force a settlement, experience again demonstrates that the stoppage will often be prolonged until the Government is forced to act. This is particularly the case if the parties have some reason to believe that the Government will sooner or later move to halt the stoppage. As a general rule, therefore, the less ready the Government is to intervene the more likely that the parties will find their own solution through collective bargaining.

Despite these important considerations of timing and ultimate effect that militate against intervention, the Federal Government has repeatedly intervened in labor-management disputes. The reasons for intervention are equally clear. The history of Federal intervention makes it apparent that the reason above all others that has caused the President to exert his influence in labor disputes has been the pressure of public opinion. The American public has come to consider the President as guardian of the peace, and, rightly or wrongly, that this role includes the obligation to protect it from harmful results of industrial warfare as much as from any other misfortune affecting the welfare of the Nation. Regardless of how little encouragement may be received from the parties to an industrial dispute of national proportions, public opinion virtually forces the President to take notice of the dispute and some action in regard to it. While Executive discretion in labor-management disputes has been guided and limited to a degree by the Congress, fundamental responsibility in this area still falls on the President, or those whom he delegates to speak for him.

In any important labor dispute the pressures for intervention often begin to develop before a strike occurs. Strike threats alarm suppliers, customers, and all others who rely directly or indirectly on the product or services that may be curtailed. The actual detriment to the public welfare that could result from a strike might be insignificant compared with that which is feared, but a judgment to this effect, however valid, does not help to stem mounting public pressure.

Soon after a major strike begins, the pressures for intervention ordinarily increase. Some shortages of a commodity begin to appear even when most users have stockpiled substantial inventories. Unemployment in the industry itself and layoffs in supplier and user industries begin to cause hardships on individual workers and their families, with an adverse affect on the local economies. In some disputes, the exigencies of national defense make it incumbent upon the Government to protect its own sources of supply. Thus, the pressures favoring intervention are great in many disputes. In the case of basic steel strikes, despite many considerations counseling nonintervention, the pressures for intervention have always proved irresistible.

Three objectives underlie Government intervention in steel collective bargaining: (1) to postpone or stop a strike to prevent a threatened national emergency, (2) to aid in the process of bargaining and facilitate a settlement, and (3) to encourage terms of settlement believed to be more in accord with the public interest than a privately negotiated settlement. The complications introduced into collective bargaining by governmental attempts to influence or control price determination are treated in chapter 7. The impact of strikes on the economy and on defense production have been discussed in chapter 3. The economic significance of wage settlements and price adjustments has been analyzed in chapters 9, 10, and 11.

As a result of various combinations of the objectives listed above, intervention designed to prevent, delay, or end steel strikes has always occurred. This history has been detailed in appendix A and summarized in chapter 12. The forms of intervention have been various, comprising practically all of the devices commonly advocated for use in emergency disputes. The results have varied widely. The following sections evaluate each of these general approaches with reference to past steel experience and their potential usefulness should similar disputes occur in the future.

Arbitration

Arbitration is probably the most common publicly suggested solution for every major labor-management dispute that occurs in this Nation. The attraction of this idea is based on the assumption that relations between labor and management are analogous to the relations between individuals in our society. The argument runs that since individual quarrels within our society that have repercussions upon the society itself are normally settled by judicial process without recourse to personal conflict, why cannot the parties agree upon or the Government require the same solution of labor-management conflict? The argument is bolstered by the fact that within the past 20 years arbitration has been extensively adopted by labor and management as the sound way to settle disputes arising under the terms of existing agreements. Despite the acceptability of grievance arbitration and the superficial attractiveness of the arguments for arbitration of new contract terms, unions and managements ordinarily have been reluctant to delegate to arbitrators the power to determine the central provisions of the labor agreement.

This is certainly true of steel, which, like many major industries, had experience with a form of arbitration during World War II. In the crisis of those times it was possible for labor and management to agree that there should be no strikes or lockouts, that all disputes should be settled by peaceful means, and that a National War Labor Board (WLB) should be established to settle disputes if the parties failed to agree. The WLB was established, and in practice the device that it used to settle disputes was arbitration. In effect, labor and management voluntarily agreed upon compulsory arbitration of unresolved disputes for the duration of the war.

The 1942 WLB award to the steel industry and the Steelworkers granted a wage increase, maintenance of membership, and checkoff of union dues. The wage increase at U.S. Steel was made retroactive to the date of the Little Steel award, based upon a WLB finding that there had been a longtime industry practice of making wage adjustments effective on a common date.

At Christmas time in 1943 a 2-day partial work-stoppage occurred over the basis of submission of the next dispute to the WLB. This was the only steel dispute that approached industrywide proportions during the war, and was quickly settled when the President requested that all issues in dispute go to the WLB. In 1945 the WLB refused a union demand for a wage increase, but awarded improved vacation entitlement, severance pay, shift differentials, and approved guidelines for the elimination of intraplant wage inequities which could cost as much as 5 cents an hour.

Probably the most controversial of these awards was that of maintenance of membership. Under wartime circumstances that necessitated continuous production the industry acquiesced to the award, but it continued to resent this modification of the "open shop" policy that it had maintained for many years. It felt that the union had used the times and the Government to reach an objective that it could never have gained through collective bargaining, or even strikes.

Although the WLB had good reason for awarding the form of union security that it did, it must undoubtedly have been aware that when an "outsider" changes the basic structure of the relationship between two parties resentments are almost certain to arise.

It is, in fact, the fear of arbitration awards of this sort, that run counter to the longrun objectives or principles of one or the other of the parties, and the fear of economic decisions by those who have no responsibility for the consequences, that makes labor and management extremely reluctant to accept arbitration as a means of resolving disputes over the terms of new contracts. It is true that if the parties voluntarily accepted arbitration they could retain control of the issues that would be arbitrated. Similarly, they would have the opportunity to select an arbitrator in whom they both had confidence. While the parties might not be willing to have their whole contract subject to arbitration, specific issues might very well be judged to be arbitrable when they were precisely defined and were submitted to a mutually acceptable arbitrator.

In fact, as alternative to Government intervention, voluntary arbitration has much to commend it. It is a way of preserving the collective bargaining process by keeping control of basic decisions close to the parties. It is surely the best way of foreclosing Government intervention. Nevertheless, because of the extreme difficulty of establishing meaningful and agreed-upon arbitration criteria for economic and other contract issues, and because of the strong tradition favoring free collective bargaining that has grown in this Nation, it appears unlikely that the parties will voluntarily embrace arbitration as a peacetime alternative to the privilege of resorting to economic force.

Why not then use the power of Government to insist upon the arbitration of critical labor-management disputes? The immediate answer to this question is that resort to compulsory arbitration raises difficulties as great as those it purports to settle.

The fundamental handicap of compulsory arbitration is that it operates without either standards or consent. In the absence of participation in determining their own economic future, the parties will demand to know the basis for the decision. Unfortunately, there are few, if any, generally accepted standards which both labor and management will accept in setting wages and working conditions. In the area of wages alone there are over a half-dozen criteria that can be and have been used in determining rates and most of these are very general and controversial in application. The great advantage of free collective bargaining is that the economic decisions involved in a settlement are self-justifying, at least so far as the parties are concerned. Compulsory arbitration lacks this essential element.

It is sometimes said that the very existence of compulsory arbitration will encourage parties to make their own settlements through collective bargaining. This argument appears plausible. Experience with compulsory arbitration, in several American States and in Australia and New Zealand, points in exactly the opposite direction, however. Compulsory arbitration corrodes free collective bargaining. In almost every jurisdiction where it has been made mandatory the experience has been that the parties prepare for annual arbitration rather than annual negotiation.

One of the commonest charges against compulsory arbitration is that it is an almost sure road to even more extensive regulation of the economy. It is argued that those whose wages and working conditions are imposed by law will inevitably demand that the same controls be extended to prices, profits, and other areas of the economy. Interestingly enough, the experience with this in jurisdictions where compulsory arbitration has been tried, although not conclusive, suggests that this fear may be overstated. Nonetheless, it is a recurring threat.

One of the chief factors overlooked by proponents of compulsory arbitration legislation is that strikes do not disappear after the enactment of such legislation. All authorities agree that strikes have continued to occur in every jurisdiction in which it has ever been tried. A more pertinent question, therefore, is not whether compulsory arbitration will eliminate strikes, but whether it will improve the present record. On this question the authorities differ. Some feel that the experience has been better after the law was enacted, some that the strike record continues about as before, and in several cases that the legislation has been a contributory cause to strikes that might not otherwise have occurred. Moreover, all who have studied the problem agree that one of the great problems of compulsory arbitration is the question of enforcement. Both penal and monetary penalties for violation of orders have been enacted, but no jurisdiction has found it practically or politically expedient to enforce either. The universal experience, both in the United States and abroad, is that it is difficult if not impossible to enforce the award if one or the other of the parties chooses not to accept it.

In summary, arbitration of steel disputes worked reasonably well during World War II because the parties had no real alternative and it was operating within a frame of reference of general controls. Unless a time of national crisis should recur there seems no present likelihood that they will voluntarily embrace arbitration as an alternative to a strike. On the other hand, it appears undesirable for Government to force the steel industry and the union to accept arbitration of disputes over contract terms. Ultimately, of course, the public might decide that mandatory arbitration was preferable to recurring lengthy steel strikes. If this occurs it seems obvious that many problems would remain, some of which are as potentially disturbing as the strikes themselves.

Mediation

Experience has repeatedly shown that skillful mediation can be a useful and important adjunct to viable collective bargaining. The justification for mediation as a formalized Government activity is that the consequences of labor-management disagreements can be adverse to the general public as well as to the parties. In a sense, then, when the mediator comes to the bargaining table he represents the public interest in a peaceful settlement. Mediation is an aid or catalyst rather than a substitute for collective bargaining. In many negotiations there comes a time when the force of reasonableness begins to fade and the amicability of the relationship is endangered. At this point the real issues become apparent, the parties begin to threaten or defy each other, and relative economic strength begins to become the decisive factor.

The essential function of a mediator in such a dispute is to keep the parties in purposeful discussion with each other. Vindictiveness and obstinacy, bitterness and blocked communications are his principal problems, for they stand in the way of composing differences through reasoning. An antagonistic, unreasoning attitude of either party will undermine the entire bargaining process. A fixed position announced early in the discussions has a similar effect. Everything the mediator does is directed toward preventing or removing these obstacles to voluntary peaceful settlements. His effectiveness depends mainly upon the confidence he can inspire and on certain qualities he possesses. Among these are his ability intuitively to know what will arouse favorable response and to know when to make his moves and suggestions. He must be able to anticipate unfavorable responses and reactions and to help temper them so as not to divide the parties further in their search for areas of agreement.

This does not mean that the mediator's efforts are invariably successful. It is obvious that as long as the agreement-making process remains voluntary there will always be situations when strikes will occur, and occasionally be of extended duration. Unfortunately, the larger the industry and the more significant its dispute, the more likely that the normal processes of mediation will be ineffective. There are a number of reasons for this. Bargainers in critical industries are usually aware of the issues at stake and the ramifications of decisions they make. A substantial degree of rationality is normally already present in their negotiations. Additionally, negotiators in major industries are aware of the public interest in a peaceful settlement of their disputes and are not likely to be influenced by a mediator's repetition of these considerations. More sophisticated negotiators are in less need of the suggestions of alternatives and compromises that are the daily coin of the experienced mediator. Finally, experience in some major industries during recent decades has shown that intervention at the highest levels of Government can readily be obtained.

Most of these factors operate in the case of steel. Mediators of the pre-1947 U.S. Conciliation Service never participated in steel negotiations. Directors of the successor agency, the Federal Mediation and Conciliation Service [FMCS], have held meetings in four steel disputes. In none of these, however, have FMCS officials held joint meetings of the parties prior to the outbreak of a strike. The reason for this seems to be that the steel companies and the Steelworkers union feel that there is nothing that professional mediators can do for them that they cannot do themselves. Therefore, they discourage or refuse proffers of aid. Mediation is a voluntary process that works best when the parties desire it, so the FMCS does not ordinarily force mediation upon unwilling parties. Finally, then, in many negotiating years it becomes apparent that the parties have been unable peacefully to resolve their disagreement. By this time the best opportunity for mediation has passed, for all experience demonstrates that mediation is far more likely to be effective just before, rather than just after, a strike begins. In the case of steel this has meant that normal mediation has had little chance.

As previously noted, however, in 4 strike years, 1949, 1952, 1956, and 1959, two different Directors of the FMCS along with several of their most skilled subordinates held joint mediation conferences with the parties after a strike had begun. In no case were settlements made during their conferences, at times because the pressures upon the parties were not great enough to condition a settlement, or at other times because the parties also had available mediation by Cabinet members, Presidential assistants, the Vice President, and the President himself. Under such circumstances the parties have demonstrated a human preference for giving their attention and confidences to officials with highest prestige, thus giving professional mediators little chance. Even when the Director of the FMCS flew directly from Cabinet meetings to the negotiations, or was given the public support of the President, FMCS effectiveness was diminished by the availability of ranking officials. This history has been so consistent, and has so conditioned the parties, that the Government will have to make a definite effort if it is to establish its professional mediators in future steel negotiations.

Mediation has nonetheless been an important factor in a number of steel settlements. It is not an esoteric device. When used by officials of high rank it is occasionally more effective than when used by professionals. This is due to the addition of another factor. In the past, at least, these officials have made, or the parties have inferred, threats of unpleasant consequencies if they failed to agree. At various times in steel negotiations Presidents, or those who spoke for them, recommended settlements to the industry or the union and by implication threatened the industry with seizure or the union with injunction if settlement was not reached quickly. On other occasions the industry felt threatened with a factfinding board that might make recommendations adverse to the industry's position, or by the sanction of potentially adverse congressional action. It is true that these intervenors often used the techniques of conciliation and suggestions for compromise that are a part of normal mediation. It is also true that even these efforts were normally most successful when economic pressures were forcing the parties to consider changes in position in any event. Nevertheless, mediation of this type, "mediation with a club," is a resource that is unavailable to most peacemakers.

It has been suggested that this type of mediation is an illegitimate device, in that its reality is compulsion behind a facade of voluntarism. Free collective bargaining is not being served, it is argued, when governmental power is used to force bargainers to change their positions, to make offers and accept proposals that are contrary to what the parties privately judge to be their own best interests. The argument seems plausible, particularly when experience would indicate that the usual effect of Government tactics has been to bring pressure upon the industry to do something that the union had hitherto been unable or not permitted to force it to do.

The criticisms of these tactics must be considered in the light of the alternatives. If the emergency is real then Government is forced to take some steps to meet the problem. Under our system of free collective bargaining mediation is assumed to be the preferred means by which Government expresses the public's interest in the peaceful settlement of disputes. Even when supplemented by pressure tactics mediation would appear preferable to some more coercive device. Regardless of the pressure, in the last analysis the parties are free to resist and take their chances on what might come. The choice between present unpleasantness and future uncertainty may not be a desirable one, but it is still voluntary. Mediation preserves the element of voluntarism to a greater degree than any other means of intervention. While it can never be relied on to prevent or end all work stoppages it should nonetheless continue to be given first choice when opportunities for its use arise.

Factfinding

Factfinding is one of the commonest devices that have been used by Government in critical labor-management disputes. This is due to its extreme flexibility and the way in which it combines with other devices as well as its intrinsic merits.

Initially, factfinding ordinarily is used to delay a strike. This delay can often be accomplished by means of a request from the President, or other high Government official, that the parties voluntarily defer economic action while an inquiry into the facts of the dispute takes place. If the parties do not agree voluntarily, delay could be obtained by means of injunction of the parties or seizure of the industry, depending upon existing legislation and the circumstances of the dispute.

There is also great flexibility in the way in which factfinding can operate. Those who find the facts can be asked merely to report them, either privately or publicly, or they can be asked to make public or private recommendations for settlement of the dispute. Finally, the appointment of a factfinding board often gives another opportunity for mediation, with a new setting and even additional mediators.

The compulsory devices for obtaining delay that are often combined with factfinding—injunction and seizure—will be treated separately. This section will discuss the record of factfinding in steel and evaluate factfinding itself as a device for dispute settlement.

It is popularly assumed that factfinding boards can be extremely helpful both to the parties to a labor-management dispute and to the public as well. The premise is that knowledge of the facts—all the facts—will serve to provide the public with an understanding of the dispute, and hopefully, to dissipate the conflict between the parties. The theory of factfinding is that labor disputes relate to discoverable social and economic facts, and that men of good will can easily assess and evaluate such facts. It further assumes that men will not differ over facts once they are made apparent. Finally, it assumes that certain conclusions flow from the nature of the facts themselves which will tend to create agreement between the parties.

Another set of premises about factfinding goes to the relation of public opinion to labor disputes. The theory of factfinding assumes that public opinion is decisively molded by the findings of boards, and that public opinion in turn has important impact upon the parties, forcing them to settle their dispute.

The experience with factfinding in steel, as in labor disputes generally, indicates that these assumptions are largely exaggerated and unrealistic.

The first two factfinding boards appointed in basic steel disputes did not function normally. The board appointed in the 1937 Little Steel dispute was given the joint function of factfinding and mediation, but was unable to accomplish either when the companies refused to meet jointly with the union or to sign written contracts of any sort. The board recommended that the companies make a written agreement with the SWOC, but they refused, and went ahead to win the strike. In this dispute the board's recommendation engendered neither agreement nor apparent public pressure against the companies involved.

On the last day of 1945, President Truman appointed a factfinding board to inquire into a dispute between U.S. Steel and the Steelworkers. This board never met because the parties requested that they be allowed to continue private negotiations. The chairman of the board later functioned as a mediator in the ensuing strike, and the board's report, which came out after the strike was settled, merely seconded President Truman's previous recommendation of 18½ cents.

Factfinding was given its first real test in steel in the 1949 dispute. President Truman elected to bypass the Taft-Hartley procedures, and appointed an *ad hoc* board with power to make recommendations. The industry vigorously protested the President's action at the time of appointment of the board, but finally agreed to the procedure. Even so, the industry continued to protest the appointment of the board before the board itself, and continually maintained the position that it would not be bound by the board's recommendations.

The board, composed of prominent authorities in the field of industrial relations, held detailed hearings that took over a month to complete. When the report and recommendations were made public, they were given substantial praise by almost all commentators and cautious initial approval of both industry and union. Suddenly, the industry reacted with a concentrated attack upon the noncontributory feature of the board's pension and insurance recommendations, an issue which had hitherto seemed of minor importance. The parties bickered for several weeks on the issue of whether the recommendations were the occasion for renewed bargaining or were merely to be written into the contract, and a strike ensued. The strike was settled in the general outline of the board's recommendations, but only after considerable negotiating had resulted in some modifications.

In some respects, the experience with factfinding in 1952 was similar. Factfinding took place within the Wage Stabilization Board created during the Korean War. Once again lengthy and detailed hearings were held which resulted in a long report of the facts of some 60 issues in dispute. This report was submitted to the tripartite Wage Stabilization Board itself, which then negotiated a set of recommendations which were for the most part within the general area of wage stabilization policy. The industry once again rejected the proposals. The rejection was due to the unwillingness of the industry to accept substantial wage and fringe increases, in part because the industry was to be limited to the price increases that the Government was willing to grant under existing price stabilization policy. A further objection was the board recommendation that the parties negotiate a union shop. The strike which eventually occurred was fundamentally over this issue of union security, although the union regarded a substantial part of the economic package as still in dispute during the strike.

In the 1959 strike two different types of factfinding were employed. Secretary of Labor James P. Mitchell's publication of background statistics relating to steel wages, productivity, prices, and profits was the first. It deliberately drew no conclusions, leaving the responsibility for settlement upon the parties. Its purpose was to inform the public and, by taking this limited type of action, temporarily to reduce public pressure for more direct and coercive intervention into the dispute.

The second use of factfinding in 1959 was a part of the normal Taft-Hartley national emergency procedure. The factfinding board held hearings to delineate the issues in dispute and also attempted to mediate a settlement. When this effort failed the board then submitted its report to the President, stating that the major issues were those of economics and work rules, and detailing the major features of each of these areas of dispute. The report itself, as distinct from the hearings, received little publicity other than that connected with its role as another hurdle cleared on the road to injunction. Sixty days later, as required by the statute, the board submitted its final report, which detailed the efforts made toward settlement, and the positions of the parties. It was issued the day settlement was announced.

The history of factfinding experience in steel is related in detail in appendix A. Even the foregoing summary analysis of steel experience permits certain generalizations about factfinding.

Factfinding has neither prevented strikes nor resulted in the settlement of existing strikes. In the 1949 dispute the appointment of the board itself became a major point of controversy and indirectly, at least, contributed to the conflict. A strike occurred after factfinding in 1952 as well. Reports of basic statistics or the facts in dispute did little to settle the strike of 1959.

In terms of dispute settlement it seems clear that factfinding without recommendations has little to recommend it. A statement of the facts of a dispute adds little to public understanding. The national wire services give rather extensive coverage to critical disputes. A report that does not contain recommendations provides nothing new for the public beyond a recapitulation and summary of the basic essentials of the dispute—in short, no news at all. What is newsworthy is precisely what such a report fails to provide; a judgment of an expert and impartial board as to the merits of the case. Without new information the public is largely uninterested. Consequently, the thought that reports of facts alone will mobilize public opinion and thus bring pressure upon the parties to modify their position is illusory.

What then of factfinding that includes recommendations? A recommendation does capture headlines, and at least initiates the mobilization of public opinion. But even if it is assumed that the public in general believes that the parties should settle upon the recommendations, there remains a substantial question as to effect of this opinion upon the parties. Those who have opposed the making of recommendations by factfinding boards have done so because they feared that this would take on the character of compulsory arbitration. This fear appears to have been exaggerated. Steel labor and management have frequently resisted the pressures supposedly resulting from the recommendations. In some cases their countervailing public relations campaigns have been at least as effective in creating public opposition to the recommendations as is the generation of opinion favoring the recommendations. Even where the parties have eventually made a settlement that followed the broad outline of the recommendations, bargaining resulted in considerable modification before they became mutually acceptable.

There is, however, a potential difficulty with factfinding recommendations. Under certain circumstances they can intensify a dispute. The party favored by the recommendations often comes to feel that it has a "right" to it, and therefore is extremely reluctant to accept anything short of the full recommendation. The party opposing the recommendation faces public defeat if it yields. Positions thus generated are strongly held and publicly defended. Thus an unusually severe issue can be created through the injection of the recommendation.

Factfinding with or without recommendation, standing alone, has minimal merits. In the special case where parties genuinely and voluntarily welcome recommendations, factfinding can approximate voluntary arbitration, in that these parties will be apt to accept the recommendations of the board as a basis for settlement. There is the additional possibility that the parties may be persuaded to accept recommendations as a basis for compromise, although, as previously noted, such recommendations are perhaps equally likely to intensify the dispute.

Factfinding nevertheless provides a means to delay to temporarily halt a strike, whether the delay be secured through voluntary means or through compulsion. The time gained then gives a new opportunity for the parties to reassess their positions and for mediation. The scene is different, additional or new mediators may be made available, and the circumstances surrounding the dispute may change. Mediation coupled with factfinding without recommendations under Taft-Hartley has been successful in a number of industries in recent years. The point which deserves emphasis is that factfinding works to resolve a dispute only when it is a vehicle for, or supplemented by, effective mediation.

Seizure

Seizure is a device to gain time. Its purpose is to enforce delay of a stoppage while operations continue and to provide additional time for renewed effort to settle the dispute. Seizure itself does nothing to remedy the underlying problems; these remain to be dealt with. Experience has demonstrated the practical usefulness of occasional seizures, particularly in wartime, as one device that Government can use when faced with a critical labor dispute. Unfortunately, experience has also demonstrated that it has a number of pitfalls.

Seizure, whether viewed as a political, legal, or administrative concept is extremely unclear. The legal basis for seizure, the terms under which men are to work, the extent of managerial control that will be preempted by the Government, disposition of profits and losses, the terms under which the enterprise is to be returned to its normal owners—all these are but a few of the perplexing problems involved in the practice of seizure.

The theory behind seizure is simple and plausible. A strike represents a group unwillingness of employees to work at terms offered by the employer. The assumption behind seizure is that these same employees will be willing to work for the Government in a temporary emergency on terms on which they would not work for their private employer. The "imagery" of seizure then is that Government agents occupy the enterprise and take command of it. The reality is far different. In practice the procedure has been for Government to delegate to the regular management the authority to operate the plant, and to call back the regular work force. The amount of supervision exercised has varied, but has almost always been minimal. Under these circumstances, "seizure" is a fiction which requires, and ordinarily receives, the cooperation of labor and management.

Management is only nominally displaced in most seizures. Despite this, seizure is potentially damaging to the enterprise and apparently to the self-esteem and traditions of managers. Thus, seizure is generally regarded as a device distasteful to management. Given a choice of seizure or injunction as the means of securing delay of a strike, labor will prefer seizure and management will prefer injunction. In fact, however, seizure can be made equally distasteful to both parties, or unequally distasteful to one or the other if Government deems that the circumstances do not warrant equal treatment and is willing to undertake a substantial degree of intervention. Much hinges on the exact procedure employed and the commitment made to each of the parties.

For example, in most seizures the industry continues to produce for private customers as well as for the Government, and is permitted to retain all of its profits. If Government were to retain the profits achieved during its period of nominal or actual operation, management would obviously be strongly impelled to settle with the union on almost any terms. This approach creates some constitutional difficulties, but these might not be insurmountable.

Another possibility in a seizure is that Government may refuse to make any new agreement with the union, or alternatively, that it might put into effect new terms and conditions of employment during its period of operation. Either action sets a precedent the parties would find hard to ignore. The first of these approaches would be distasteful to the union, the latter to the management, and therefore could be used to force changes in position. This kind of pressure too, however, has inherent constitutional difficulties.

The basic steel industry has been seized once—in 1952. Following the failure of the industry and the Steelworkers to agree upon WSB recommendations, or to negotiate their own agreement, the Nation was faced with an industrywide steel strike during a time of war. A few hours before the strike was to begin, President Truman decided to bypass the national emergency machinery of the Taft-Hartley Act and to seize the industry. The seizure was nominal, as usual, and the employees remained at work. The industry immediately challenged the President's action in the Federal courts.

While a district court action enjoining the seizure was under appeal, and a month after the seizure had gone into effect, the President announced to the parties that unless the dispute was settled within 2 days he would order changes in working conditions in the steel mills. Presumably, he would have ordered the recommendations of the WSB put into effect. The practical effect of such an action would have been precedent-setting, forcing the industry almost of necessity to grant identical benefits in order to reach a settlement with the union. Under this threat bargaining was resumed. The parties apparently were close to agreement when the Supreme Court refused to allow the Government the right to make the threatened changes. Negotiations once again broke down, but the incident illustrates how seizure can be used as a pressure device upon the parties.

A majority of the U.S. Supreme Court later found that in the circumstances of this dispute the seizure was unconstitutional. Although it is difficult to find a clear majority holding, since all members of the majority wrote concurring opinions, it is clear that a seizure authorized by Congress would have been constitutional. Thus, seizure if authorized by Congress, remains available as a device which Government might use in meeting critical disputes.

Nevertheless, the hazards of seizure should not be overlooked. The very act of seizing is likely to set in motion a chain of consequences disruptive to the collective bargaining relationship and prejudicial to the role of Government as an impartial intervenor. After seizure the Government is placed in a position where it is impelled either to assume the burden of bargaining with the union or of continuing conditions of employment the workers found sufficiently onerous to lead them to go on strike. In the position of operator, the Government can hardly avoid consideration of the equities of the wage and work relationship. Yet, for the Government to make what are, in effect, permanent decisions for the parties in these areas involves some basic inconsistencies with our national economic system and traditions. It represents a degree of Government intervention not casually to be undertaken.

Another problem with seizure is that most students of its use conclude that it is a wasting asset. If it were to be used commonly, the parties might refuse to cooperate on the present basis of fictitious Government operation. Furthermore, repeated experience with it would result in the development of legal principles that would dissipate the uncertainties and peculiar risks that are now involved for both parties.

The chief value of seizure is as an available alternative, or in conjunction with other measures, where it emphasizes to both parties the public need for continued operation and yet where it is difficult for them to calculate its hazards. It is in no sense a device that can be frequently used in emergency disputes in steel or any other industry.

Injunction

Injunction, like seizure, is a device to delay or end a work-stoppage in order to gain time for renewed efforts to settle a dispute. In itself it contributes nothing to settlement, for it rarely "cools-off" the parties, usually reduces the pressure for settlement during most of its duration, and cannot ultimately even be depended upon to stop all strikes.

The theory of enforcing delay of a work-stoppage is that during the waiting period the parties will cool-off and reassess their positions. Experience demonstrates that this assumption is in most cases fallacious. Employees whose demands are subject to enforced delay are as likely to become warmer as cooler over the controversy. Nor are the experienced negotiators who usually bargain in major industries normally given to sudden and uncontrollable bursts of anger. The positions of the parties are ordinarily the product of calculation, and a burst of anger would more often be a part of their strategy than a reflection of heat that would cool.

There can be occasions, however, when delay of a strike is helpful to the parties. Bargainers sometimes overstep their positions. Unions and employers negotiate through representatives who are not always in full control of the situation in which they find themselves. Sometimes they become prisoners of their own tactics and strategy. In such situations the parties may be secretly relieved when it is suggested by Government that they not strike when they were in fact reluctant to do so.

Such advantage of a delay period, however, is lessened by use of injunction to enforce delay. The injunction, in the eyes of labor, is a device of attack upon it and a symbol of former oppression. "Injunction" is a word and an event which creates a deep emotional reaction on the part of labor groups and hardly improves the atmosphere for negotiation.

Negotiations during the greater part of most injunction periods are usually fruitless in any event. An injunction frees both parties from the threat or the reality of a work-stoppage and at the same time removes all economic pressure for a settlement. The usual experience is that negotiating sessions during an injunction period are little more than the reiteration of disagreement until such time as the parties are once again faced with the threat of a stoppage. Then they develop a renewed enthusiasm for bargaining and the search for agreement.

This was the experience when the Steelworkers were enjoined from continuing a strike in 1959. The President initiated the Taft-Hartley national emergency procedures after the strike had lasted for almost 3 months. A board of inquiry was appointed, made an effort to settle the dispute through mediation, and when this failed then filed its report of the facts of the dispute. The report, in accordance with the law, contained no recommendations for settlement. The Attorney General then requested and obtained an injunction against continuance of the strike. The injunction was not made effective pending appeal to the Supreme Court. In a per curiam opinion the Court held 8 to 1 that the injunction was appropriate in this case and constitutional. The strike, 116 days after it began, was enjoined and workers returned to their jobs.

Intensive mediation efforts were resumed by the FMCS, but these did not even result in new proposals. With the prospect of 80-days of continued operations ahead, neither party was under any pressure to modify its position. For nearly 6 weeks the parties remained deadlocked, and even moved farther apart at one point during this period. Then the passage of time once again forced the parties to face the possibility of the strike's recurrence with attendant economic hardships. This fact probably brought equal pressure to bear upon each of the parties. The industry was subject to two additional pressures. The Taft-Hartley ballot among employees on the employer's "last offer" was soon to be taken. It had become increasingly evident that the offer would be overwhelmingly rejected, giving the union a powerful new weapon against the industry's offer. In addition, recurrence of the strike would force the submission of the whole dispute to Congress, with prospects that appeared unpleasing from the industry's point of view. The operation of all of these factors forced changes in bargaining position and a mediated settlement became possible during the injunction period.

Interestingly, experience such as this with the Taft-Hartley emergency provisions in various industries has been fairly common. Despite the union objections to injunction as a device for obtaining delay, in a majority of the national emergency disputes where it has been used it has been possible later to settle the dispute without occurrence or recurrence of a stoppage. In many of these the settlement was not made during the injunction period but immediately thereafter. Continuous negotiation just prior to and immediately following the lapse of the injunction has been very fruitful. In some cases, during the first 5 years of experience with the Taft-Hartley provisions a strike occurred and ran its course after the injunction had ended, but the history of experience in recent years has been one of success from the point of view of preventing or ending critical strikes. The reasons for the parties' ability to settle their disputes in these cases have been various, and probably does not bear close relationship to the worth of the procedures themselves. Nevertheless, in the light of this experience, injunction is not a device that can be immediately rejected in critical disputes.

An injunction seems to be a sufficiently flexible device to be used at a single plant or group of plants within one industry. For example, if it were deemed possible to satisfy defense requirements by operating some plants while others remained on strike, if partial operation could not be achieved voluntarily the Taft-Hartley injunction could meet this objective.

Some labor disputes and strikes arise over atypical conditions beyond the control of the parties to resolve. In such cases, or the one noted earlier where the negotiators themselves might be privately relieved to be enjoined from striking, use of the injunction device might be considered desirable. Alternatively, the danger of injunction as a mandatory device for enforcing delay is that it often irritates more than it reduces tensions, and that its use reduces pressure for immediate settlement. Whether its use would be beneficial in a particular situation is a decision that could only be made in individual cases.

In any event, it is important to remember that the injunction does not contribute directly to the settlement of a dispute. It simply provides additional time for renewed efforts at settlement. What matters is the determination and skill of the parties and of Government representatives involved in the continuing task of searching for agreement. Where there is a good faith effort to reach settlement, but more time is needed, or where the negotiators must be removed from the pressure of those whom they represent, an injunction can occasionally be a useful device.

Arsenal of Weapons

One of the commonest approaches to the problem of critical workstoppages that has been advocated in recent years is the so-called "choice of procedures" or "arsenal of weapons." In brief, this approach would make available to the President, in the alternative or in combination, practically all of the devices that might be used by Government to cope with threatened or actual stoppages adversely affecting the public interest. Among these would be mediation, factfinding with or without recommendations, cooling-off periods of various length enforced by injunction, seizure, retroactive pay orders, last-offer ballots, compulsory arbitration, and any of various devices that particular proponents favor.

The theory behind such an arsenal of alternatives is twofold: first, to give the Government greater flexibility of approach, and second, to place the parties in a position of uncertainty and thus encourage them to settle themselves for fear of what the Government might do.

Underlying the first of these basic reasons, that of flexibility, is the reality that labor-management disputes are so complex that there is no single remedy to cure them. Furthermore, Government has more than one major interest in regard to them. If the function of Government in the area of critical disputes is simply to stop them there would be no reason for a variety of approaches: an injunction is ordinarily adequate. If, at the other extreme, Government is concerned primarily with the terms of settlement, then some form of compulsory arbitration is the only answer. The answer is, of course, that Government is interested in far more than in merely stopping strikes or in setting the terms of agreements; the Government's function is rather to implement the settlement of disputes through the collective bargaining process. It is the realization of the necessity of trying to make collective bargaining work even in crises that justifies the necessity for flexibility.

There are basic differences in the character, structure, economic circumstances, and organization of almost all of our major industries and unions. Even within each one the interrelationship of these factors can change from negotiation to negotiation. The forces that will exert pressure toward settlement in collective bargaining conferences in 1 year or upon one industry or union may be totally ineffective on another. The case for the flexible approach is that collective bargaining can be made to work in crisis situations only if whatever governmental intervention is necessary is geared to the variability of collective bargaining.

The second argument for the "arsenal of weapons" approach, that of uncertainty, is in part based upon the observable fact that when the approach that the Government must take is fixed, this will become part of the calculations, tactics, and expectations of the parties. In concrete terms, this means that a party that feels that it has something to gain from a specific procedure may devise its strategy in order to put pressure on the Government to resort to the procedure. Thus, the very existence of the procedures may encourage intervention and reduce the possibility that the settlement will be made in collective bargaining without intervention. But if the parties cannot be sure as to the approach that Government will take, and furthermore, if the Government can tailor its intervention to put greater pressure on the most intransigent or unreasonable party, then there is every incentive for both parties to avoid intervention by making their own settlement.

The arsenal of weapons approach, when written into a statute, might not satisfy the public desire for certainty. People generally assume that the law offers answers, even in areas which permit of few specific answers. From the point of view of politics, it is significant that there is broad public acceptance of the Taft-Hartley procedures as the answer to national emergency strikes, even though the procedures, however effective, provide no certain answers or solutions. To replace the existing procedures with ones even more unspecific which propose a variable answer depending upon variable circumstances may not interest the public or its representatives.

The procedures that would become part of the arsenal of weapons approach are largely those that have been discussed previously in this chapter. With the exception of "last-offer" ballots all have been used in one steel dispute or another. Insofar as this particular device—the last-offer ballot—is concerned, most industrial relations experts agree that it is of dubious utility. It is conceptually elusive, for in the course of negotiations many offers, firm and conditional, are made. It is sometimes difficult to ascertain which is the last offer upon which employees should vote. Furthermore, the making of a last offer for balloting purposes presents a barrier to all purposeful negotiations until the ballot can be held. Experience demonstrates that the employer's offer will be overwhelmingly rejected in the vast majority of cases, and thus only furnish the union with another bargaining point. The votes are not in reality on the issues involved but votes of confidence in the union leadership. The device irritates the union by implying that the leadership is not responsive to the wishes of the membership and not democratic in its procedures. For all of these reasons, last-offer ballots do not appear to be a generally effective device for settling labor-management disputes.

Aside from the weakness or strength of particular alternatives, however, there are overall problems with the arsenal of weapons approach.

There is a general fear that it would vest in the Executive department that kind of discretion in the exercise of power which permits of misuse. Although this danger might be mitigated by distributing parcels of the power among various agencies, or by including participation of "public" representatives, experience with charges and countercharges of misuse of power and favoritism by Government in past steel negotiations would make it appear that this is not a fear that can be lightly discarded. Moreover, even if there is no objective basis for the fears and charges, the experience in steel further demonstrates that the attitudes created by this type of controversy are real and have an extremely harmful impact on the possibility of a peaceful settlement.

Finally, there is considerable reason for conjecture as to whether the basic values of the arsenal of weapons approach may not be over-stated: (1) there is the question whether the very availability of mechanisms for intervention may not encourage formal intervention and frustrate bargaining; (2) in most disputes the realistic alternatives are few, and (3) management executives and union leaders, knowing the convictions and attitudes of the Chief Executive toward a dispute, are likely to surmise the form of his action. Thus, the achieved benefits of flexibility and uncertainty are not likely to be nearly so great as many expect. Moreover, the arsenal of weapons, like so many other approaches, is essentially procedural in nature and provides no real answer to the fundamental economic problems that are the heart of most disputes. The problem is not to stop strikes, but to settle disputes. The essence of effective assistance in settling disputes has normally turned on some form of mediation. Under these circumstances the problem posed is whether greater latitude in the mechanism of intervention will on balance facilitate or complicate the mediation process.

Part VI

APPENDIXES

Appendix A

PROFILES OF NEGOTIATIONS IN BASIC STEEL: 1937–59

THE 1937 U.S. STEEL-SWOC INITIAL CONTRACT NEGOTIATION

Unionization in the basic steel industry was effected by a centrally-directed, well-financed, and sustained campaign. In June 1936, John L. Lewis, president of the United Mine Workers and then president of the CIO, appointed a Steel Workers Organizing Committee (SWOC), composed of nine representatives of four unions and headed by Philip Murray, then vice president of the UMW. David McDonald, Murray's assistant, was made secretary-treasurer of the committee. The traditional steel union, the Amalgamated Association of Iron, Steel and Tin Workers, had never been a strong organization. It had drifted into moribundity, making only desultory attempts at organizing the industry. Under pressure from the CIO the Amalgamated in effect ceded jurisdiction to the SWOC, retaining only its existing contracts, members, and the right to issue charters to new locals organized by the SWOC.

In planning its campaign the SWOC faced an industry with approximately 480,000 employees, one with a long reputation as a stronghold of the open shop and of hostility to outside unionism. By far the largest concern in the industry was the United States Steel Corp., with 222,000 employees and about 38 percent of the Nation's ingot capacity. This corporation, composed of a number of semiautonomous operating divisions, was and is commonly called "Big Steel." Next in order were Bethlehem Steel, with 80,000 employees and 13 percent of capacity; Republic Steel, with 49,000 employees and 8 percent of capacity; and Jones and Laughlin, with 29,000 employees and 5 percent of capacity. The remaining major firms in so-called "Little Steel" were Youngstown Sheet and Tube and National Steel.

The SWOC had been well-prepared, however, and in its first 3 months established 35 subregional offices, with 158 full-time and 80 part-time employees. The largest proportion of these were full-time organizers drawn from the UMW and a few other unions. Funds were provided largely by the Mine Workers.

The first point of attack by the SWOC was the so-called company unions. During and after World War I a number of steel companies had introduced employee representation plans into their plants—U.S. Steel as late as 1933. Even before the advent of the SWOC, considerable restlessness and growing intractability manifested itself within these organizations. The SWOC capitalized on this by enlisting the support of key members of the plans and then by pushing grievances and wage and hour demands relentlessly. If these efforts were successful, the SWOC took the credit; if not, it denounced the weakness of the ERP's. The focal point of the SWOC attack was in the newer and more independent plans of U.S. Steel and the company found itself increasingly beleaguered and on the defensive with its own employees. Both the SWOC and the ERP's demanded a $5 a day common labor rate, 10 cents an hour increase for all others and a basic 40-hour week. By January 1937 the SWOC had filed charges with the National Labor Relations Board against U.S. Steel, charging unlawful company domination of the employee representa-

231

tion plan. Additionally, the SWOC was undoubtedly making headway in enrolling U.S. Steel employees. But this kind of organizing progress was slow and strikes were dangerous. No more than a small group of people in the industry and union were prepared for the sudden peaceful capitulation of U.S. Steel.

Some reasons for the decision of the corporation to recognize the SWOC, thus reversing long-established policies, as well as the best-available history of the negotiation leading up to the actual agreement, were cited by Myron C. Taylor, Chairman of U.S. Steel's board of directors, as follows:

> It seemed to us that the situation was one in which our principles of representation exactly applied and that the grave danger was in allowing events to proceed to a point where the ordinary rules of reason would not govern. I felt that it was my duty as a trustee for our stockholders and as a citizen to make any honorable settlement that would ensure a continuance of work, wages, and profits. I discovered that Mr. Lewis was similarly minded and we had an informal preliminary talk. We had the background of the captive coal mine agreements which preserved the principle of representatives in connection with union contracts. They had worked very well. . . .
>
> The first talk with Mr. Lewis was on January 9th, 1937, in Washington, D.C. We went into the subject rather thoroughly, but on broad lines. At once on my return ot New York, I discussed the whole situation with the available directors, and their unanimous opinion was that I should go ahead with the conversations to the end of reaching an agreement. Mr. Lewis and I continued our conversations on January 13th, but did not reach any conclusion that would conform with our policy.
>
> On the 18th of February, in a meeting of the chief officers of our subsidiaries, I discussed the principles involved and asked each of those present whether, if the occasion arose, he would negotiate with the SWOC, and they all answered in the affirmative. I also asked them whether, if an agreement were then reached, they would sign a contract in accord with the practice established with the employee representation groups in the steel plants in November 1936. This they also answered in the affirmative.
>
> Mr. Lewis was then in New York and expressed the desire further to explore matters with me, but we had no further meetings until February 25th, when at my house in New York, our conversations were resumed on the basis of this formula which, for the first time, I showed to him:
>
> "The Company recognizes the right of its employees to bargain collectively through representatives freely chosen by them without dictation, coercion, or intimidation in any form or from any source. It will negotiate and contract with the representatives of any group of its employees so chosen and with any organization as the representative of its members, subject to the recognition of the principle that the right to work is not dependent on membership or nonmembership in any organization and subject to the right of any employee freely to bargain in such manner and through such representatives, if any, as he chooses."
>
> For a time the negotiations seemed to be off, but on Sunday morning, February 28th, Mr. Lewis and Mr. Murray came to my house with Mr. Moses and, after a short talk, Messrs. Lewis and Murray accepted the formula in principle. [1]

The memorandum which was signed for the Carnegie-Illinois Steel Corp., a subsidiary of U.S. Steel, on March 2, 1937, contained the following details:

1. Recognition of the SWOC as bargaining agent for its members, while the SWOC agreed not to intimidate or coerce nonunion employees into membership.
2. Wage increase of 10 cents per hour for all employees and a $5 minimum daily wage, with some exceptions.
3. An 8-hour day and 40-hour week, with time and one-half over 8 hours in a day or 40 hours in a week.

---

[1] Myron C. Taylor, *Ten Years of Steel* (United States Steel Corp., 11938) pp. 40–42. This appendix is based upon interviews, official documents, and private and published materials. Documentation is limited to direct quotations.

This agreement, giving the SWOC recognition and its basic economic demands, was supplemented on March 17 by a series of collective bargaining agreements covering the operating subsidiaries of U.S. Steel. They contained the following sections, in addition to those listed above:

4. Statement of intent of the contracting parties, application of the agreement and definition of "employee."
5. One week's paid vacation after 5 years' service. Rate of pay based on average hourly earnings for the two pay periods immediately preceding the vacation period.
6. In cases of promotion or increase or decrease of forces, where (a) knowledge, training, skill, ability and efficiency; (b) physical fitness; (c) family status; and (d) place of residence are relatively equal, length of continuous service shall govern.
7. Five-step grievance procedure ending in arbitration, and definition of plant grievance committee.
8. Management rights clause.
9. Special time limits regarding discharge grievances, and provision for reinstatement with back pay.
10. Safety and health, obligating the company to make "reasonable" provisions, provide safety apparel, and provide heating and ventilation systems.
11. Inequalities in wage rates to be settled at local plant by mutual agreement.
12. Specification of date and place for 1938 negotiations.
13. No regular work except in continuous process operations on July 4th, Labor Day, and Christmas.
14. Contract to terminate on February 28, 1938.

Most of these contract provisions, such as those relating to vacations, seniority, safety, and holidays merely stated practice that had existed prior to the agreement.

The public impact of the announcement of agreement was great. True, the General Motors Corp. had recognized the United Automobile Workers a week earlier but this had followed a long and bitter sit-down strike, and intervention by both Federal and State Governments. Here, on the contrary, voluntary agreement was reached with perhaps the most significant corporation in the Nation, without Government intervention or industrial strife. It is difficult to overestimate the significance of the U.S. Steel-SWOC agreement, for not only did it practically ensure the existence of independent unionism in basic steel, it also proved of great psychological assistance in the CIO drive to organize other mass-production industries.

Exactly why U.S. Steel chose to recognize the SWOC can never be surely known without full access to company executive memoranda and minutes. The reasons that have been attributed are numerous, and all may have been motivating factors.[2] Among them, without an attempt to ascribe priorities, are the following:

1. Myron Taylor had not been a lifelong steel man, and was thus less imbued with the old traditions of antiunionism. His primary concern was with corporate stability and increased earnings, objectives that are normally incompatible with labor strife. Additionally, he was closely advised by Thomas Moses, who through his coal connections had had contracts and a good relationship with the Mine Workers and Lewis for some years.

[2] Among those who have studied this problem are Walter Galenson, *The CIO Challenge to the AFL*, Harvard University Press, 1960, pp. 93–95; Byron L. Perry, *Steel Management and the Acceptance of Unionism*, unpublished M.A. thesis, University of Illinois, 1957; and Frederick H. Harbison, "Steel" in *How Collective Bargaining Works*, Twentieth Century Fund, 1942, pp. 523–4.

2. For the first time since 1930, U.S. Steel was earning substantial profits. Demand for steel products was up substantially and production was over 80 percent of capacity. In February 1937, prospects for continuation of this boom seemed promising. The corporation was certainly desirous of avoiding a strike, which would have interrupted these favorable business developments. Additionally, substantial foreign armaments orders were pending, and it was rumoied that the British were asking for a guarantee of uninterrupted production before letting contracts.

3. The SWOC had largely infiltrated or disrupted U.S. Steel's employee representation plans, particularly at Carnegie-Illinois. The point had been reached where they were causing more friction and trouble than they were worth to the corporation and, in any event, no longer represented a defense against outside unions.

4. The costs of a strike would be substantial, while the chance of defeating the SWOC was incalculable. Although it is quite possible that U.S. Steel could have won a strike, there is little doubt that the SWOC had sufficient strength to close many of the plants for a substantial period. The example of a successful 6-week strike against General Motors could not have been lost on the corporation.

5. Current governmental developments encouraged the union. The re-election of President Roosevelt in November 1936 was widely hailed as a victory for trade unionism. Both the NLRB and the LaFollette Committee in the United States Senate were holding hearings on U.S. Steel's activities in the labor relations field, the results of which threatened adversely. The Pennsylvania State administration was prounion, and the value of a friendly State administration to the union had already been demonstrated in the General Motors strikes.

6. U.S. Steel was able to make a contract that did not appear burdensome. The 10 percent wage increase appeared necessary in any event, since Little Steel appeared ready to grant it in an effort to avoid unionization. The principal provision of the contract was on the company's terms: that representation would be for members only. The remainder of the provisions largely stated existing practice.

The CIO, the SWOC, and Lewis himself were jubilant over the agreement. But the reaction of the remaining steel companies was quite different. Twice during February their leaders had met wtih Taylor, and each time they had disagreed, the Little Steel leaders feeling that the employees could be bought off with a wage increase. When Taylor granted the CIO the wage increase and recognition, they were horrified and bitter. Although they almost immediately followed the wage and hour changes contained in the U.S. Steel agreement, it soon became clear that they did not also plan to recognize the SWOC.

FURTHER SWOC SUCCESSES

For 3 months after the signing of the U.S. Steel agreements the unionization drive in the steel industry moved ahead rapidly. By May 1, the SWOC claimed nearly 300,000 members, 600 lodges, and 88 signed agreements in various steel and allied fabricating companies. The Supreme Court, by declaring the Wagner Act constitutional, had sounded the death-knell of most employee representation plans in the industry, but despite this fact, none of the large independent companies with the exception of Wheeling Steel had signed contracts.

In May, attention focused on the Jones and Laughlin Steel Corp. In negotiations with the SWOC that company had offered to sign a contract like that of Carnegie-Illinois, provided management retained the right to make similar contracts with other groups of employees. The union rejected this proposal, following which the company agreed to grant the SWOC exclusive bargaining status if a majority favored the SWOC in an NLRB election. In a period of controversy which followed, local unions effectively closed down the company's plants for 36 hours. Under this pressure the company signed a preliminary agreement, and in the NLRB election which followed the SWOC gained a 2 to 1 victory. The company then signed an agreement recognizing the SWOC as the exclusive bargaining agent for its employees.

Several smaller companies, among which were Pittsburgh Steel and Sharon Steel, followed the lead of Jones and Laughlin and signed exclusive representation agreements. Crucible Steel, a major producer that had also been involved in NLRB proceedings, at this time voluntarily signed an agreement for "members only." Early in June 1937 the SWOC announced that it had contracts with 142 firms and a membership of 375,000.

THE ORGANIZATION OF LITTLE STEEL

The principal basic steel companies that were determined to resist the SWOC in 1937 were American Rolling Mill, National, Bethlehem, Inland, Republic, and Youngstown Sheet and Tube. This group of companies employed about 186,000 workers.

Although for the most part complying with the standards of wages and working conditions set forth in the Carnegie-Illinois control, the so-called Little Steel companies were unwilling to make an agreement with the SWOC, either oral or written. After a month in which these companies either refused to negotiate, or in which meetings proved unavailing, the SWOC set a strike deadline in those companies where it felt strongest. On May 26, 1937, stoppages began at Inland, Republic, and Youngstown Sheet and Tube. On June 11, a strike began at the Johnstown plant of Bethlehem.

Why did the Little Steel companies decide to fight the SWOC despite U.S. Steel's example? Were not the same economic and political considerations involved? The answer to these questions appears to be threefold. First, at the beginning of May 1937, a sharp decline began in the volume of new business in the steel industry. Although there was no immediate decline in production, the business outlook was somewhat less favorable than it had been at the beginning of the year when the U.S. Steel negotiations took place. Current economic conditions no longer favored the SWOC. Second, the men who led the secondary steel companies, Tom Girdler, Eugene Grace, and Frank Purnell, among others, did not share Myron Taylor's attitude toward unions and John L. Lewis. Principled opposition and personal animus against trade unions and all that they represent appear to have been a major factor in their determination to fight.[3] Last, they must have felt that there was a good chance to defeat the SWOC. The organizing campaign had made less headway in their areas, their few remaining ERP's seemed loyal, and the employees of these companies had less of a tradition of unionism. In summary, ideological convictions reinforced a belief that the cost of a strike would be less than the benefits of future nonunionization.

The Little Steel strikes were among the most bitter and violent in the history of the United States. The industrial warfare, which lasted for over a month, was characterized by violence on the part of strikers, plant guards, and citizens vigilante committees; outrages by local and special police that resulted in bloodshed and death; back-to-work movements inspired by the companies; and suppression of civil rights.[4]

---

[3] Tom M. Girdler, *Boot Straps* (New York: 1943), pp. 226, 317.

[4] U.S. Senate, 74th–77th Congress, various sessions, *Violations of Free Speech and the Rights of Labor, 1938–41*. These reports contain thousands of pages of testimony concerning steel labor policies and events of the Little Steel strike.

During the course of the 1937 strike, mediation efforts were made by the Governors of Ohio, Pennsylvania, and Indiana, and by the Federal Government. On June 17, the Secretary of Labor appointed a Federal steel mediation board, composed of Charles P. Taft, Lloyd K. Garrison, and Edward F. McGrady, to attempt to find a formula for settlement. The board was immediately rebuffed when the companies refused to delay reopening the struck plants for back-to-work movements during the mediation sessions. Later, appearing before the board, the heads of the four companies stated that they would make neither written nor oral agreements with the SWOC, and they refused to meet with the CIO leadership to discuss the matter. The board finally proposed that the companies make and sign an agreement with the SWOC, to become effective only if the SWOC won an NLRB election.[5] Although the SWOC was apparently willing to negotiate on this basis, the companies rejected the proposal and attacked the board as biased in favor of written agreements. The board gave up its efforts on June 24.

The strikes were finally broken during the first 2 weeks in July. In some areas this was accomplished by the imposition of martial law and the intervention of the National Guard which gave the protection necessary for successful back-to-work movements. The only course then left open to the SWOC was to press unfair labor practice charges with the NLRB against the Little Steel companies.

Some of the reasons why the strikes failed can easily be assumed. First, the SWOC tactically undertook more than it could handle. Calling simultaneous strikes on such a broad front called for more experienced personnel, staff, and money than was available. Second, the SWOC was still weak internally. While the workers who supported it were full of the enthusiasm engendered by earlier CIO successes, they were inexperienced in strikes and new to solidarity. As the strikes lengthened and pressures on them increased, many undoubtedly weakened. Third, the strikes came during an economic downturn, making it easier for the companies to close the mills. Finally, the SWOC apparently underestimated the companies' influence and control in the communities where their mills were located.

The strikes were costly to both sides. One student has concluded that Republic Steel lost $8 million in anticipated net income alone, while Inland and Youngstown suffered losses nearly as serious. Only Bethlehem, with a shorter and far less effective strike, fared comparatively well in relation to 1937 anticipated income.[6] The SWOC, on the other hand, had by the end of the Little Steel strikes, spent an amount approaching a million dollars. Costs of the strikes did not end in 1937. As a consequence of the NLRB proceedings noted earlier, Republic was eventually forced to reinstate workers who had been discriminated against with back pay amounting to $2 million, while Youngstown Sheet and Tube incurred a cost of $170,000 for similar reasons. Some years later Republic paid $350,000 to settle liabilities incurred in civil suits brought on behalf of strikers who had been killed or injured.

Organizational efforts in Little Steel remained practically at a standstill for nearly 2 years until, in August 1939, a drive patterned on the 1937 campaign was undertaken at Bethlehem. Results were negligible. The drive was again renewed in the fall of 1940. By this time the outbreak of the war in Europe and American rearmament resulted in a sharp improvement in employment,

---

[5] *Report of the Federal Steel Mediation Board to Secretary of Labor Frances Perkins, July 2, 1937.*

[6] Galenson, op. cit., p. 108.

making it possible for the SWOC to move ahead. During 1940 and 1941 several short but effective strikes over Bethlehem's alleged refusal to discuss grievances, and the results of NLRB-conducted elections, testified to the growing strength of the union. By the middle of 1941 the SWOC had won representation elections at all major Bethlehem plants. Probably influenced by these results, the remaining three holdout members of Little Steel, Republic, Youngstown Sheet and Tube, and the Great Lakes division of National agreed to NLRB-conducted crosschecks of SWOC membership cards against their payrolls. At all three companies the SWOC had well over 50 percent membership and thus became the exclusive bargaining representative of the employees at all major mills except the Weirton division of National and American Rolling Mill. For practical purposes the Little Steel battle was finally over. Four years after they had decisively defeated the SWOC, officials of the Little Steel companies sat down with union representatives to negotiate an initial contract.

THE 1938 U.S. STEEL-SWOC CONTRACT NEGOTIATIONS

To return temporarily to the 1937–38 period, perhaps an even greater blow to the SWOC than its initial defeat by Little Steel was the economic recession that developed during the last half of 1937. Steel production dropped sharply during the last quarter, so that December output was 70 percent below August, payrolls were cut almost in half and employment fell rapidly. Twenty-eight percent of steelworkers were laid off and only 15 percent were working full time. Steel mills were operating at 25 percent of capacity. Widespread unemployment discouraged new memberships, and dues payments from old members dwindled. Throughout this period the SWOC could do little more than bolster existing lodges, set up unemployment and relief committees, and attempt to enforce contract seniority provisions concerning layoff and recall. Organizational efforts were limited to small steel companies and fabricators.

Perhaps the union's greatest achievement during the period was the preservation of existing wage rates. The maintenance of unionization in the industry hinged on the negotiations for a new contract with U.S. Steel in February 1938, when the original 1937 agreements were to expire. SWOC leaders proposed liberalization of vacations and recognition of dues committeemen as the basis for a further 1-year contract. U.S. Steel countered with a demand for a general wage reduction, which the SWOC refused. Company spokesmen then offered to extend existing contracts indefinitely, with a proviso that either party might give the other 10 days' notice of a desire to change the agreement, and upon failure to agree to changes within 20 days, the 1937 agreements would terminate. This type of terminal "escape clause" was necessary, the company stated, in order to meet changing economic conditions necessitating wage reductions or in the event that Little Steel cut wages. It has been stated that additional private conversations between Lewis and Taylor resulted in this company proposal rather than a flat termination, as many in the industry had expected.[7] Since the offer gave the SWOC a breathing spell at a time when it badly needed one, the SWOC accepted. The only other change made in the 1937 agreement was a clarification to the effect that grievances over alleged wage rate inequities were not subject to arbitration.[8]

---

[7] Galenson, op. cit., p. 112.

[8] When attacked in the 1940 wage-policy meeting for making an unwarranted concession to the companies on this point, since many locals had hoped to raise individual rates through grievance arbitration, Philip Murray defended the clarification on the basis that the companies could not now lower individual wage rates without the union's consent. *Proceedings*, Wage and Policy Convention, SWOC, 1940, pp. 218–219.

Most of the independent basic steel companies and the steel fabricating companies with which SWOC had contracts followed the lead of U.S. Steel and extended their contracts even though the SWOC did not attempt to open them. One significant exception was Crucible Steel, which terminated its agreement. Contractual relationships were not resumed with Crucible until 1940. During this depression period the SWOC was particularly insistent upon strict contract compliance by local unions in order to give no justification for contract terminations.

In the late spring and again in the late fall of 1938 U.S. Steel informally asked SWOC to take wage cuts because of competition and impending price cuts. The SWOC refused, criticized price cutting, and hinted that wage cuts would result in a strike. Steel prices were reduced in the summer of 1938 and wage talks continued. At one time during this period U.S. Steel was thought to be ready to invoke the termination clause of the agreement. By the spring of 1939, however, business had so far revived that wage cuts were no longer a serious issue. The SWOC had forestalled general wage reductions during a severe business recession.

THE 1941 U.S. STEEL-SWOC CONTRACT NEGOTIATIONS

In the late fall of 1940 the SWOC decided to seek from U.S. Steel its first substantial contract improvements since the original contract of 1937. The timing was obvious, since for the first time in its dealings with U.S. Steel the union was in a position to exert considerable economic power. The industry was producing at over 95 percent of ingot capacity owing to domestic rearmament and sales to European nations at war. Additionally, managerial and technological advances had enabled the industry to absorb the effects of wage increases granted in earlier years.

Wage rates had increased nearly 25 percent since 1936. Yet in 1940 the industry produced 10 percent more steel than it had in the earlier year, with a 7 percent decrease in man-hours worked and a 3 percent reduction in total payroll. Prices, meanwhile, had fluctuated within a narrow range, remaining constant for all practical purposes owing both to economic and political pressures. Profits in 1940 had been substantial.

From the union's point of view, improvements needed in the 1937 contract were several, and resulted in the following demands:

1. Exclusive bargaining status and dues checkoff.
2. Improvements and extension of the grievance machinery.
3. Adjustment of individual and group wage rates by means of a joint commission to study rate inequities.
4. Substantial improvements in the seniority system.
5. New procedure for calculation of the workweek for payment of overtime.
6. Provision for leaves of absence for union business.

In addition to modifying the contract, the union further proposed:

7. A 10 cents an hour wage increase.
8. Liberalized vacations with pay.
9. Protection for job rights of employees in military service.

These demands, in effect terminating the contract, were presented to U.S. Steel on March 1, 1941, along with a proposal that iron-ore miners be included in the negotiations. Philip Murray remained president of the SWOC and chief negotiator for the union. Murray had, by this time, publicly broken with John L. Lewis and had also assumed the presidency of the CIO. Unlike Lewis, he had supported President Roosevelt's reelection in 1940, and was able to meet privately with the President in the midst of negotiations and announce, almost from the steps of the White House, "that wage increases can be granted out of profits without in any way calling for price increases on the finished product." [9]

U.S. Steel was under new leadership by 1941. Benjamin Fairless had become president of the corporation; and J. L. Perry, president of Carnegie-Illinois, was the corporation's spokesman in negotiations. Under their leadership, the company rejected most of the union's initial demands and countered the wage proposal with an offer of 2½ cents, tied, however, to production so that if production dropped below 85 percent of capacity, the company could withdraw the increase. Negotiations continued throughout March and beyond the expiration date into April. Extension of negotiations beyond the March 31 termination date was arranged after Murray and Fairless met separately at the White House with John R. Steelman and President Roosevelt. While progress was made on contract changes, wages continued to be the stumbling block. Apparently, however, the union was fully prepared to take several cents an hour less than its original demand of 10 cents. On April 5, Murray set a strike deadline for April 8 unless the union's demands were met. Although no price controls were in effect at the time the company announced: "The company has insisted it cannot increase wages without increasing the price of steel. The Government has firmly refused to sanction any such price advances." [10]

Suddenly, on April 8, E. T. Weir announced a 10-cent-an-hour increase for his employees at Weirton Steel. Weir dealt with an independent union, and his motives have been assumed to stem from a desire to undermine the SWOC. When the Ford Motor Co. recognized the CIO Automobile Workers and granted them 10 cents an hour during the same week there was apparently little for U.S. Steel to do but accept these wage settlements as a pattern. Philip Murray some years later told a confidante that Thomas W. Lamont, then head of J. P. Morgan and Co. and a director of U.S. Steel, had asked to meet with Murray in New York and that in the course of this conversation Lamont offered Murray a 10-cent settlement on behalf of U.S. Steel. In any event, on April 14, U.S. Steel granted a 10-cent-an-hour general wage increase, to be effective April 1, and substantial additional contract improvements. These consisted of the following:

1. One week's vacation after 3 years' service, 2 weeks' vacation after 15 years. Detailed specification of purpose and method of operation of vacation program.
2. Time and one-half for all days worked in excess of 5 within the workweek.
3. Two hours' call-in time, with 4 hours' pay guaranteed if work actually begun.
4. Various minor changes in seniority clause tending to reduce management discretion, and procedure for calculating length of continuous service.
5. Extensive revision and specification of the grievance procedure, particularly to set forth time limits at various steps.
6. Specification of procedures for rate establishment and adjustment, largely spelling out procedures developed under 1937 agreement.
7. Employees not on continuous processes, required to work on existing 3 holidays, to receive time and one-half.
8. Contract to be reopenable upon 10 days' notice by either party.

As in the past, all other major basic steel producers followed U.S. Steel's economic lead, granting an equivalent wage increase to their employees.

[9] *New York Times,* Mar. 6, 1941.
[10] *New York Times,* Apr. 6, 1941.

Although it is true that the SWOC gained nothing on its demand for exclusive bargaining status and dues checkoff, in all other respects the 1941 settlement was a significant achievement. Not only was the union fortunate enough to obtain its full economic demands, but the basic contract which resulted began to take on substantially the appearance of a modern labor agreement in detail and specificity. While no doubt leaving much to be desired from a union point of view, it was still a major advance from the two-page memorandum of understanding of 1937.

Three days after the settlement was announced, on April 17, the Office of Price Administration issued an order providing for the freezing of steel prices. If the company had intended to raise prices, and there was considerable indication that it had, it was now too late.[11] Steel prices were held at first-quarter-1941 levels, and were to remain there practically without change for the next 4 years.

1942 CONTRACT NEGOTIATIONS—THE NATIONAL WAR LABOR BOARD AND THE "LITTLE STEEL" FORMULA

Contrary to the usual sequence, it was the Little Steel companies that led throughout basic steel negotiations in 1942. Following the NLRB elections in 1941 in which the SWOC had gained bargaining rights in the Little Steel plants, negotiation of initial contracts had begun in September 1941. The negotiations, conducted separately with Inland Steel, Youngstown Sheet and Tube, Bethlehem Steel, and Republic Steel proved to be long and arduous. Initially, the union demanded wage increases sufficient to bring the wage levels of these companies up to the levels prevailing in union plants, exclusive representation, and other contract conditions similar to those in the U.S. Steel agreements. In one respect the proposals went beyond U.S. Steel: the union demanded the union shop and checkoff.

Negotiations continued throughout the fall of 1941, were recessed during December, and began again on January 16, 1942. Deadlock occurred with each of the four companies during the first week in February, and the cases were certified to the National War Labor Board. At this point a regression is necessary to place these developments in the context of the times.

American involvement in World War II came gradually between September 1939 and December 1941. During this period, the so-called defense period, critically needed production was recurrently delayed by work stoppages. The Government decided to meet these crises by the establishment of a National Defense Mediation Board (NDBM) in the spring of 1941. The President called upon labor and management in defense plants to settle their disputes without work stoppages and provided a tripartite board to assist them to reach this goal. Voluntary techniques were relied upon, and the Board had only the authority to mediate individual disputes and issue public recommendations.

For 8 months this essentially voluntary approach succeeded. In the 118 cases in which the Board was involved, work stoppages were infrequent and total time lost owing to strikes in Board cases was small. In only three unsettled cases

---

[11] On Apr. 12, Leon Henderson had taken office as Federal Price Administrator and immediately announced that he did not think a steel price increase would be justified even if the CIO gained its full 10 cents demand. (New York Times, Apr. 13, 1941.) The industry's bitterness over the freeze was summed up by one spokesman: "How can the industry be expected to increase wages 50 percent as it has since 1929 and then be permitted to have an increase of but 2 percent in the average steel prices in the same period?" (New York Times, Apr. 17, 1941.) Although the merits of the argument were debatable, there is no doubt that the industry felt it had been severely treated.

did the President deem it necessary to resort to compulsion and seize the plants in order to restore production.[12] By late fall of 1941, however, the board foundered and broke up on the reef of union security. The key case, the "captive mines" case, indirectly involved U.S. Steel and the Little Steel negotiations as well, and is therefore an important element in the background of their 1942 negotiations.

The United Mine Workers demanded that the union shop clause already included in their basic Appalachian agreement be accepted by the employers in the captive mines (mines owned by basic steel producers). The steel companies refused to go beyond the open shop clause contained in the previous agreement, and the NDMB was unable to bring them to agreement. The implications of the dispute were clear. The Mine Workers argued, and unions in general felt that without strong union security, in the absence of the right to strike, organization would be substantially slowed and that many established unions might even disintegrate. Union security seemed to the unions to be only minimum protection against loss of the gains made since 1935. Management representatives, on the other hand, felt that the unions were trying to gain through Government action something that they had been unable to win in collective bargaining, and that the union shop gave unions the monopolistic power to dictate the condition of labor. In the captive mines case, therefore, the employers were concerned not only with future effect upon the mines involved, but also with the possible effect upon the steel agreements wherein they were successfully resisting a similar demand. Unable to solve this conflict through procedural recommendations, the public members finally elected to vote with the employer members against the union shop, whereupon the CIO members announced their resignation. After that time, the future effectiveness of the Board was doubtful.[13] The Japanese attack on Pearl Harbor provided the Government with an opportunity and simultaneously created the necessity for finding a new device to handle critical labor disputes.

On December 17, 1941, President Roosevelt convened a conference of 24 leading labor and management representatives, placing upon them the task of finding a method of preventing interruption in production resulting from labor disputes during the war. The parties promptly agreed upon a simple formula: (1) No strikes or lockouts, (2) all disputes to be settled by peaceful means, and (3) the President should set up a War Labor Board to handle disputes. The labor and management representatives then deadlocked for 5 days on a management proposal that the new Board should have no authority to change existing union security provisions. President Roosevelt solved the conflict by simply passing it on to the proposed new National War Labor Board (WLB), established a few weeks later. This, then, was a portion of the history of conflict over the union security issue that, among other issues, faced the new WLB when the Little Steel disputes were certified to it on February 12, 1942.

---

[12] For details and evaluation of the Board's work, see U.S. Department of Labor, *Report of the National Defense Mediation Board*, BLS Bulletin No. 714, 1942; and U.S. Department of Labor, *Problems and Policies of Dispute Settlement and Wage Stabilization During World War II*, BLS Bull. No. 1009, 1950, pp. 32–45.

[13] The settlement of the captive mines dispute is instructive. After the Board's decision, the coal strike was resumed on Nov. 17. It was called off on Nov. 24, after the parties agreed that the dispute should be settled by an arbitration board consisting of John L. Lewis, Benjamin Fairless, and John R. Steelman. (On Nov. 20, President Roosevelt had publicly stated that the Government would not order the union shop. Steelman resigned as Director of the U.S. Conciliation Service while serving on the Board). On Dec. 7, 1941 (Pearl Harbor Day), the union shop was awarded to the Mine Workers by a two to one decision, Fairless dissenting.

Of equal national importance by this time was the issue of wage stabilization, for the union presented the Board with a list of proposals headed by a demand for a $1 a day wage increase. The decision on the steel cases was to be of major importance to the national war economy, to wage stabilization, and to the new disputes prevention machinery. The actual union proposals before the WLB were these:

1. A 12½ cents an hour general wage increase.
2. Daily minimum wage guarantee.
3. Union shop.
4. Checkoff.
5. Industrywide common agreements.
6. Elimination of geographical wage differentials.
7. Vacation and holiday improvement.
8. Seniority changes.
9. Union participation in administration of wage incentive system.

These proposals were presented to the Board on Feb. 25, 1942, and Chairman William H. Davis promptly appointed a special three-man factfinding panel composed of Arthur Meyer, Cyrus Ching, and Richard Frankensteen to investigate the facts and report to the Board. The hearings before the panel lasted for nearly 3 months, and 2 more months passed before the Board was ready to make its directive. The factfinding panel had reported to the Board that real weekly earnings of steelworkers had declined 13.3 percent since the last pay increase, that traditional earnings differentials favoring steelworkers against other wage earners in durable goods manufacturing had declined, and that the companies' ability to pay the wage increase requested by the union was excellent. The panel also favored the union shop and checkoff.

On July 16, 1942, the WLB gave its award, including the famous "Little Steel" formula. The Board granted the United Steelworkers of America (the name given to the union that grew out of the SWOC, created at a constitutional convention in 1942) a 15 percent wage increase over January 1941 levels, which, when allowance was made for the 10 cent increase granted in April 1941, and coupled with other inequity considerations, totaled 5½ cents an hour. The formula was based on limiting steel's wage increase to general patterns of wage and cost-of-living increases that had taken place during 1941 and the early spring of 1942. In addition to the wage increase, the Steelworkers won maintenance of membership and checkoff of dues. Employer representatives of course dissented vigorously from this portion of the award, as did the Little Steel companies in public statements. In any event, in the first weeks of August 1942, the four Little Steel companies that had been involved in the 1937 strike entered into written agreements with the union. The agreements embodied the WLB award, and in other respects were similar to the U.S. Steel agreement.

Meanwhile, the SWOC had turned to the NLRB in an effort to gain exclusive bargaining status form U.S. Steel, hitherto denied by the company in collective bargaining. In March 1942, it filed election petitions in all U.S. Steel subsidiaries. The union won about 90 percent of the votes at these elections and was granted exclusive bargaining rights.

As soon as the Little Steel award was made by the WLB, the union filed in regard to U.S. Steel, and on August 26, 1942, a decision virtually identical with that in Little Steel was made for Big Steel. Actually, the primary point of controversy with U.S. Steel was over effective dates of wage increases, since the union had delayed reopening the agreements. The Board ordered the same effective date as in Little Steel, reasoning that the company must have expected to follow the tradition of uniform and simultaneous adjustments that had grown up in the industry. The Board concluded: "The evidence presented in both this case and in the Little Steel case has left no doubt in the minds of the Board that a policy of industrywide wage uniformity is a well-established characteristic of the basic steel industry. This policy of industrywide wage uniformity is so well established that it has been the practice of the companies in the past to make wage adjustments retroactive to a common date." [14] In summary, so far as U.S. Steel's contract with the Steelworkers was concerned, the 1942 settlement was as follows:

National War Labor Board Decisions, August 26, 1942:

1. Wage increase of 5½ cents an hour, effective February 15, 1942.
2. Minimum daily wage guarantee.
3. Maintenance of membership.
4. Checkoff of union dues.

National Labor Relations Board Certification, September 5, 1942:

5. Exclusive bargaining status.

In addition, the parties agreed to:

6. Time and one-half for sixth day of work in a holiday week.
7. Time and one-half for all work on sixth and seventh day of any 7 consecutive days during which the first 5 were worked.
8. Vacation pay in lieu of time off at management discretion, and other vacation clarifications.
9. Establishment of a joint commission on wage rate inequities.
10. Reemployed veterans to be credited with unbroken seniority.
11. Contract reopenable upon 10 days' notice by either party.

The accomplishment of written agreements, maintenance of membership and exclusive bargaining status with both Big and Little Steel meant that the Steelworkers were secure for the immediate future. With the important assistance and support of the Federal Government, the union had in 6 years forced the powerful steel industry totally to revise its labor policy.

NATIONAL WAR LABOR BOARD AND BASIC STEEL, 1943–1945

In the fall of 1943 the leaders of American labor decided to press for a breakthrough in the Little Steel formula. In November, the CIO convention resolved upon the elimination of the formula and, in conformity with this resolution, on December 2, 1943, the Steelworkers Wage Policy Committee approved a 22-point program of demands for changes in existing steel contracts. Leading the list was a demand for a 17 cents an hour general wage increase, admittedly not in keeping with national wage stabilization policy.

Most of the contracts in the industry were terminable on short notice, and beginning on December 4, 1943, the Steelworkers served notices reopening all of its agreements, including those in basic steel. Additionally, before demands had been submitted to any of the companies, the union, on December 7, 1943, petitioned the War Labor Board, asking that it order the steel companies to sign contract extensions providing that any agreed-upon or subsequently ordered wage increases should be made retroactive to the termination date of the contracts. After a public hearing on December 21, the Board refused to grant the union's petition, and both labor and management representatives joined to reject a compromise offered by the public members.

---

[14] War Labor Reports, Vol. 2, p. 453H.

This precipitated a strike in the steel industry. As union contracts expired on December 24 and 25, the employees left their jobs, and within 3 days 135,000 workers in 10 States were idle. Basic steel production dropped to its lowest point since the beginning of World War II. On December 26, President Roosevelt telegraphed the union and some of the companies insisting upon a return to work but implying that any wage adjustments would be retroactive. He emphasized, however, that wage adjustments must conform to existing wage stabilization policies. On December 28, the striking employees returned to work and negotiations then began, although it was obvious to all involved that there was no likelihood of mutual agreement.

After less than 2 weeks of negotiations, U.S. Steel, on January 17, requested the Secretary of Labor to certify the dispute to the WLB, and on February 2, the Board took jurisdiction over cases involving approximately 500 Steelworker contracts, 86 of which were later included in a decision concerning the basic steel industry. The most significant of the 24 demands made by the union are summarized:

1. A 17 cent hourly wage increase.
2. Establishment of a joint industry fund for steelworkers in the Armed Forces.
3. Severance pay plan: 4 weeks, 1st through 3d year, 8 weeks thereafter.
4. Vacation improvement: 1 week 1st through 3d year, 2 weeks thereafter.
5. Sick leave plan: 7 days 1st through 3d year, 14 days thereafter.
6. Shift differentials of 5 and 10 cents.
7. Six paid holidays.
8. Elimination of geographical differentials.
9. A guaranteed annual wage plan.
10. A company-paid group insurance plan.
11. Numerous proposals on rate establishment and wage rate adjustment.
12. Changes in grievance procedure.
13. Changes in seniority provisions, based on length of continuous service.

The only management proposal, made by a few companies, was for elimination of maintenance of membership and checkoff.

The WLB set up a special panel to hear evidence in the case and joined all basic steel companies into one hearing. The significant response to this was coordination of the companies' presentation by the Steel Case Research Committee. It was an obvious answer to a specific need. In the absence of any arrangement for a cooperative presentation of their case, the 86 companies would have made a flood of repetitive individual arguments, or alternatively, been left to an unbecoming silent reliance on U.S. Steel. The Research Committee provided a vehicle for parceling out the industry presentation without restraining any company from making argument on individual points of distinction.

The drawback to this approach was that it might look like industrywide bargaining. Industrywide bargaining had been one of the earliest objectives of the SWOC which because of obvious circumstances had been forgone in place of agreements with individual companies. Industrywide agreements had been requested in the 1942 negotiations but had been denied by the WLB. The Research Committee was therefore careful to disavow any such intent or willingness to now bargain as a group. In his opening statement Committee Chairman John A. Stephens, who was also vice president of industrial relations for U.S. Steel, stated:

[T]he Steel Case Research Committee is not here as the representative of any company. It is an implement of coordination . . . It is not an industrywide presentation; it is a presentation prepared through the cooperation of attorneys for a number of companies in this case.[15]

Hearings before the WLB dragged on for many months, and not until November 25, 1944, did the Board make its award. It was understood by the parties, the Government, and the public that the case was a national test of the wage stabilization policy. The policy was held firm and a general wage increase was denied. The Board also rejected the demand for the elimination of geographical differentials and for equal pay for equal work throughout the industry. However, total take-home pay was increased by provision for shift differentials, by liberalized vacation pay, and by provision for as much as 5 cents an hour for elimination of intraplant wage rate inequities. (The whole wage rate inequities program resulting from this award is separately covered in the section which follows.) In summary, the Board made the following changes in the parties' contracts:

1. No general wage increase, although the subject was to be open for reconsideration in the event of a change in national wage stabilization policy.
2. No award of a guaranteed annual wage, but a recommendation that the President appoint a commission to undertake a national study.
3. One week's vacation after 1 year's service, and 2 after 5.
4. Severance pay principle approved, but referred to the parties for negotiation.
5. Shift differentials of 4 and 6 cents.
6. Establishment of guideposts as to scope, cost, and method to aid parties in negotiating adjustments to eliminate intraplant wage rate inequities, average cost per company not to exceed 5 cents.
7. Modified standard provision for maintenance of membership and check-off.
8. Adjustments with regard to vacations, shift differentials, and wage rate inequities to be applied retroactively to termination dates of the agreements.

In addition, with regard to the U.S. Steel contract, the parties agreed to:

9. A modified grievance procedure, with a tripartite Board of Conciliation and Arbitration as the final step.
10. Changes in seniority clause.

There were the usual dissents to the Board's opinion, the industry members dissenting as to the increased fringe benefits, the continuance of maintenance of membership, and retroactivity, while two of the labor members dissented as to the denial of sick leave, group insurance, and other matters. The Board made no award on the question of length of agreement, leaving this to the parties. The union requested a 2-year agreement with the right to reopen on wages upon 30-days' notice, while the companies requested a fully closed 2-year agreement. The parties failed to agree, and once again went back to the Board. On February 27, 1945, the Board awarded a fixed term agreement instead of the 10-day reopening that had long been common in the industry. The contracts were to terminate on October 15, 1946, with the proviso that in the event of a change in National wage stabilization policy permitting adjustments in wage rate structure, either party might reopen on wages. With the end of World War II, it was this contingency that became operative.

During the period 1943–45, the steel companies continued to insist that they were entitled to price relief if the union breached the wage line. The final settlement ordered by the WLB cost a small amount for the shift and vacation

---

[15] National War Labor Board, Case No. 111–6230–D, Statement of John A. Stephens, Apr. 25, 1944.

fringes, plus the contingent liability of 5 cents for inequity negotiations. Despite this increase, the whole price problem became involved in a three-cornered fight between WLB, OPA, and the Director of Economic Stabilization. OPA officials felt that high operating levels, standardization of production, and other economies offset increased costs. Not until 1945 did OPA finally allow any minor price adjustments and these averaged less than $1 per ton for pig iron and a few other products. The end result was that steel prices remained almost constant during the war period, while the industry's profit margins per sales dollar declined from their 1940 high all during this period. In part this was due to excess profit taxes but, in any event, the industry felt that it was never given adequate consideration in securing compensation for increased costs during World War II.

WAGE RATE EQUALIZATION; 1944–1947

When the first agreement was negotiated between U.S. Steel and the SWOC in 1937, Section 11 provided that all alleged inequalities in wage rates could be adjusted at the local plant level on a mutually satisfactory basis. This did not appear to be the solution, for the problem continued to plague the parties. By 1941 it was estimated that wage rates grievances comprised two-thirds of all grievances, as well as contributing to most slowdowns and wildcat strikes.[16] In their 1941 contract the parties substantially extended this section of the agreement, yet did not materially solve their problem.

In the contract signed in September 1942, U.S. Steel and the union provided for a joint commission to seek agreement on some method of creating an orderly wage structure. The commission was to determine a formula for determining and eliminating inequalities, yet the formula was not to result in any "substantial increase in the company's total payroll cost or prejudice to the company's competitive position." After 6 months of negotiations the effort failed. The corporation sought negotiations on the basis of its own job evaluation manual, which the union refused to consider. The union counterproposed the creation of an $8-million fund to correct inequities, an amount which the company felt was too great. The deadlock persisted and the commission was disbanded. Processing of individual wage rate grievances, which had been suspended during the life of the commission, was then resumed, their volume growing to almost overwhelming proportions.

Finally, in 1944, the WLB gave the parties direction toward a successful overall wage reclassification. During negotiation of the 1944 agreement the Steelworkers had proposed "equal pay for similar work throughout the industry." The companies objected to interplant or intercompany equalization, but U.S. Steel counterproposed an intraplant program. The WLB directive on this disputed issue provided for negotiations between each company and union for the elimination of intraplant inequities with the objective of an orderly and stabilized rate structure. The Board rejected elimination of geographical or interplant differentials, although the parties could take account of the latter in their negotiations. The Board stipulated that maximum costs under the program should not exceed an average of 5 cents per employee per hour worked.

---

[16] Jack Stieber, *The Steel Industry Wage Structure*, Harvard University Press; 1959, pp. 4–5. This book, along with two studies by Robert Tilove, *Collective Bargaining in the Steel Industry*, monograph, (University of Pennsylvania Press: 1948), and "The Wage Rationalization Program in United States Steel", *Monthly Labor Review*, pp. 967–82 (June 1947), are more detailed analyses of the wage equalization program.

The Board sought to facilitate negotiations by setting out basic steps: (1) Job description; (2) job ranking; (3) reduction of job classifications; (4) wage rate establishment; and (5) maintenance of out-of-line rates of incumbents outside of the permanent wage structure. As a second safeguard against deadlock, the Board provided that unresolved disputes were to be decided by a tripartite arbitration commission. The Steel Commission was therefore established on March 31, 1945, and was later continued after the WLB was abolished.

U.S. Steel took the leadership in the negotiation of the wage inequity program and began meeting with the union in the spring of 1945. Cooperation with other steel companies, however, was very close. More than a year before, as early as the end of 1943, twelve of the major steel companies had created an agency for cooperative study of the problem of wage inequities. Management, in general, was firmly committed to an industrial engineering evaluation approach to the problem. The industry agency, officially known as the Cooperative Wage Survey (CWS), had by the end of 1944 developed a basis for determining wage rate inequities and a tentative procedure for reclassification. After the WLB decision in 1944, the 12 member companies of the CWS invited the other 74 companies involved in the Board decision to join them. Many companies were initially reluctant to do so, since cooperation obviously implied, in the long run, equalization of rates with the larger and often higher-paying producers without regard to product or area. However, either because the companies reasoned that in the end they would have to do what U.S. Steel did and wanted some say in their future, or because of a genuine desire to eliminate wage rates from competition and end wage rate grievances, by 1947 the CWS comprised 51 companies employing 85 percent of all employees involved in the 1944 steel case. In summary, when U.S. Steel, opening inequity negotiations in 1945, proposed to the union the adoption of a complete plan of job classification, it was no longer U.S. Steel's own plan but the one which the CWS had developed. The company's negotiating committee was headed by R. Conrad Cooper, assistant vice-president, industrial relations, who had also been executive director of the CWS.

The chairman of the union's U.S. Steel inequity committee was Elmer E. Maloy, chairman of the union's contract department. Since Murray, Lee Pressman (the union counsel), and other Steelworker leaders apparently shared some of the traditional trade union distrust of job evaluation, the fact of union cooperation in the joint program and the success of the inequity negotiations has been largely attributed to Maloy and the confidence Murray had in him.[17] From the outset, U.S. Steel sought the union's complete participation in the program, and it is significant that it accepted this role. The reasons for this were various, but among them were the very seriousness and magnitude of the inequities problem, requiring a thorough rational overall solution, and the tradition of strongly centralized international leadership within the Steelworkers, which made it possible to overrule or ignore local pressures and objections to job evaluation. Overriding all may have been the lure of 5 cents for many employees. Underlying all of these factors must have been an atmosphere of mutual relations which give the union confidence in its future and in continued friendly working relations with U.S. Steel. It is significant that inequities negotiations continued even during the strike in 1946. If the union had felt that the corporation was challenging its continued strength or existence during the strike this would not have been possible. Finally, the economic background of the negotiations was one of prosperity and rising prices, which gave the companies ample margin with which to negotiate.

---

[17] Stieber, op. cit., pp. 22, 42–45.

On both sides of the table negotiations were conducted by high-caliber, high-ranking personnel with authority to make tentative commitments that carried through, as well as freedom to devote practically full time to the negotiations. The final result was a series of five written agreements, each representing a successive stage of the classification program.

The first formal agreement, signed in October 1945, covered the form of job descriptions, the procedure for review and approval, the classification manual, and principles governing the purposes of standard hourly rates. In their second agreement the parties treated the special problem of repair and maintenance jobs. By their third agreement, of May 1946, U.S. Steel undertook to spend 3⅝ cents per man-hour in each subsidiary company for the elimination of inequities. In other words, the size of the fund would determine the wage scales to be fixed, the objective being the equalization of wage scales as nearly as possible within each geographical district. When the negotiations finally came to setting the wage scales, however, they found that adherence to the 3⅝ cents formula would leave a variety of rates within geographical districts. In an agreement of January 1947, U.S. Steel chose uniformity at greater cost. The new total was 5.2 cents an hour, although retroactivity was limited to the 3⅝ cents figure. Finally, the result of all of these agreements was included in the master contract agreement negotiated on April 22, 1947.

By far the largest part of the industry followed U.S. Steel in adopting the same manual of classification, the same principles of application, and the same wage scales. The plan now covers approximately 90 percent of the industry's production and maintenance employees. Approximately 180,000 jobs have been described and classified in 450 basic steel plants.

Any final appraisal would also be incomplete without some recognition of the part played by Government. When one reviews the wide gulf between the positions of the parties in the 1944 steel case, the success of the War Labor Board decision appears all the more remarkable. The decision seems to have been just what was needed to break the parties away from crystalized positions and started on renewed bargaining. Additionally, the Steel Commission that the Board created appears to have been a significant backstop to the negotiations. While both the parties and the commissioners were careful that the Commission should not become a permanent board of arbitration for all disputed issues, nonetheless its very existence may have spurred the parties to find their own ways for resolution of deadlock. The most detailed study of the inequities agreements found that ". . . not one steel executive interviewed in the course of this study believed that the inequities agreements could have been successfully concluded in the absence of the War Labor Board directive order." Stieber concludes that: "The conclusion of the inequities agreements on the basis of the War Labor Board's directive order is an illustration of Government intervention at its best." [18]

Four developments occurred in subsequent years that are worthy of passing note. First, negotiations on technical and clerical jobs took place subsequent to the 1947 agreement. While the union and U.S. Steel originally agreed upon combining these salaried employees into the hourly pay scale, the union later had to withdraw the proposal. Despite the fact that it would have substantially increased take-home pay, intense resistance from salaried employees to being grouped with hourly employees made the plan politically impossible. The parties in 1950 made a salary rate inequities agreement, providing for only 16 job classes (as opposed to 32 in the hourly agreement) and different base

---

[18] Stieber, *op. cit.,* p. 70.

amounts. Second, continuing problems over jobs claimed to have been improperly classified led to a strike at the Tennessee Coal and Iron Division of U.S. Steel. As a result of the settlement, hundreds of jobs were reclassified and many discriminatory practices were eliminated. Third, as a part of their 1952 master contract agreement the parties agreed to negotiate for the purpose of developing a mutually satisfactory manual which would comprehend and bring together all applicable provisions of prior agreements. On January 1, 1953, such a manual was made effective. It contains descriptions and classifications of 2,345 benchmark and specimen jobs. The benchmark jobs and the principles and procedures used in classifying such jobs form the basic structure of this manual. In essence they, as distinct from the so-called specimen jobs, had previously provided a negotiated set of uniform procedures for application to jobs throughout the industry. Fourth, the 1956 agreements between the Steelworkers and most steel companies called for joint committees "to review the manual and job classifications with a view to achieving maximum understanding between the parties." Because of the vagueness of this language or perhaps for other reasons, no significant modifications in the manual or in existing classifications have been made, although at some U.S. Steel plants general reviews have been undertaken. In all reality, the basic job evaluation program negotiated between U.S. Steel and the Steelworkers has not been changed in any major respect since its introduction in 1947. It is now one of the subjects under consideration by the Human Relations Research Committee set up under the 1960 agreements.

1946 STEEL WAGE REOPENING

During the last year of World War II, Government officials responsible for the economic stabilization program generally assumed that the war in the Pacific would last at least a year beyond that in Europe. This premise assumed there would be time for gradual decontrol of wages and prices and for a transition from the no-strike pledge and War Labor Board procedures to customary collective bargaining. Thus, the sudden end of the war meant that between Tuesday evening, August 14, 1945, when the surrender of Japan was announced, and Friday morning, August 17, when the country returned to work after a 2-day holiday, a transition stabilization program had to be formulated and announced. The result was that the transition program that had been tentatively evolved for introduction over a year's period was placed into immediate effect.

On August 16, President Truman issued a statement on economic reconversion and labor policies. In it he announced that a conference of labor and management would be called "for the purpose of working out by agreement means to minimize the interruption of production by labor disputes in the reconversion period." He cited the wartime no-strike pledge and stated that a new industry-labor agreement was "imperatively needed." Until the conference was completed and a new plan worked out important disputes that could not be settled by collective bargaining would continue to be handled by the War Labor Board. Wage adjustments that affected prices would continue to be subject to stabilization control but "with the ending of war production, however, there is no longer any threat of an inflationary bidding up of wage rates by competition in a labor market." Therefore, the President authorized the WLB to permit voluntary wage increases that would not be used as a basis for seeking price increases.

Philip Murray, president of the CIO and of the Steelworkers, immediately announced that although he was planning to cooperate with the President's program, he expected that the CIO unions would now avail themselves of the clauses in their contracts permitting wage reopenings if the Government's wage policy changed. Interestingly enough, Murray did not advocate an immediate return to free and uncontrolled collective bargaining and strikes, but was apparently contemplating some kind of temporarily continuing board and machinery to minimize and arbitrate disputes. He asked for "universal restoration of collective bargaining throughout American industry, with proper incorporation of machinery for settlement of disputes." He urged that "labor and management accept the War Labor Board as the adjudicator for a while." [19] This point of view was contrary to that of the AFL and railroad unions which wished, during the reconversion period, to end immediately the operations of the WLB and substitute no Government machinery other than Federal conciliation. Differences developed between the Board and Secretary of Labor Lewis Schwellenbach, under whose jurisdiction the Board had been placed, and the Board gave up its jurisdiction over disputes soon after.

On September 11, after an all day meeting of the union's 240-member Wage and Policy Committee, it was decided to reopen all Steelworker contracts, approximately 1,100 in all, and ask for a $2 a day wage increase. Despite the fact that many unions were asking for a percentage increase, Murray defended the $2 across-the-board request on the basis that it would "achieve a more equitable distribution of the increase among workers." Actually, a fighting campaign for a substantial general wage increase was politically necessary for most unions at the time. Workers were restive after many years of continuous production and many grievances had been allowed to pile up. Leadership was anxious to recoup any prestige lost through wartime cooperation with management and return to traditional union leadership roles. Moreover, both officers and members felt that higher wages could be secured, for, in general, profits before taxes were high and the carry-forward and carry-back provisions of the corporate tax laws, enacted to ease the transition from war to peace, provided abundant union campaign material. Finally, unions correctly anticipated that the end of the war would mean a reduction in the workweek and a decline in take-home pay. Substantial increases were felt to be the answer to this genuine problem.

However, management, too, had problems during the reconversion period. The business community was equally restive after the wartime years of production, priority, manpower, price and wage regulations, and urged the fastest possible removal of Government controls. Productivity had in many cases dropped below prewar standards and the first concern of production men was to restore efficiency and readjust to peacetime conditions. Most importantly, there were many complaints about price control. Many enterprises felt they were entitled to higher profit ratios, especially where margins had been cut into by rising costs during the war. Management believed that readjustments in productivity, clarification of demand conditions, and changes in pricing standards should take place before wages should be considered. Most importantly, if any wage-rate changes should be made, these should be reflected immediately in price adjustments.

So far as the U.S. Steel was concerned, Benjamin Fairless made the latter point most forcibly in his immediate comments on the union's proposal. He told reporters: "It is time to put the record straight: No matter how much United States Steel may believe in high wages, wages cannot be increased in

[19] New York Times, Aug. 17, 1945, p. 1.

the steel industry at this time unless prices are materially increased. * * * Price increases for steel products are absolutely necessary now and have been for some time, to take care of wage and other costs increased already. * * * If Government policy involves wage increases, it must involve the responsibility for necessary increases in prices. * * * There is no sense of shadow-boxing about this matter. Recent Executive orders provide that wages cannot be raised voluntarily if the increased cost would result in a price increase. * * * To hold out through extensive bargaining any hope to employees and to the public that this important wage issue can be settled between the union and ourselves under existing Government controls would not be honest." [20]

In effect, Fairless was saying that the wage offer which management believed they could make within the price stabilization program was inadequate to satisfy the minimum demands of the unions. The problem was not unique to steel by any means; identical difficulties faced negotiators in contemporary bargaining in automobiles, meatpacking, nonferrous metals, electrical manufacturing, lumber, and oil.

As it finally developed, the Government was unable to keep wage and price determination separate. As a consequence, three-way simultaneous bargaining developed in which the unions bargained with management and the Government for wage settlements, and the companies bargained with the Government for price adjustments. The failure of the President's labor-management conference to agree upon alternative procedures to replace the WLB forced Government to improvise as each serious dispute came up. In the technique that was generally used the wage settlement process was split into two steps, with a Government factfinding board (or in the case of basic steel, the President) making recommendations, and a second stage in which union and management bargained over the recommendation. The wartime procedures under which wages were settled first and then prices fixed according to established standards had to be abandoned. The wave of strikes, which reached the highest peak in the Nation's history in January and February 1946, was as much the result of the breakdown of price negotiations as of the failure of collective bargaining. The 1946 negotiations in steel typify this pattern.

The Steelworkers $2-a-day demand was presented to U.S. Steel at the first collective bargaining conference of the parties on October 11, 1945. Murray told the company that this proposal was not subject to "dickering or compromise" and suggested that an early "yes" or "no" answer would be appropriate.

On October 23, U.S. Steel replied by letter, stating: "existing ceiling prices for steel products, together with wage stabilization policy, do not enable us to grant a wage increase at this time." At the same time the company suggested that an expected Presidential statement on wage and price policy might clarify the situation.

On October 29, 1945, the union filed an application for a Government-conducted strike vote in accordance with Section 8 of the War Labor Disputes (Smith-Connally) Act. The application covered 1,100 contracts in basic steel, processing and fabricating companies, iron-ore companies and others. When this vote was held a month later the vote was 411,401 favoring a strike and 83,859 against.

On October 30, President Truman addressed the Nation on wage-price policy. He advocated substantially higher wages for American workers but stated that prices must be held stable. He said that deflation was just as dangerous as inflation: "Wage increases are therefore imperative," but "we must above all

[20] *New York Times,* Sept. 15, 1945, p. 2.

else hold the line on prices." He expressed the opinion that "there is room in the existing price structure for business as a whole to grant increases in wage rates" and rejected specifically the idea that both wages and prices should be increased. He also rejected the idea that "the Government should step in and decide who is to increase wages and by exactly how much" and instead urged a return to free collective bargaining. The speech met with cold rejection from management spokesmen and criticism from the unions because it failed to specify the amount of wage increase appropriate.

On November 3, Secretary of Labor Schwellenbach requested the parties to resume negotiations under the auspices of a special conciliator, Arthur Meyer of the New York State Mediation Board. The union accepted, but U.S. Steel declined. It stated that collective bargaining seemed "futile" until the OPA granted price increases approximating $7.00 a ton to compensate for "past heavy increases in costs," and an additional guarantee that "prices will also be increased so as simultaneously to compensate for any wage increases which may result from the union's present wage demand."

On November 9, the Secretary of Labor again requested the parties to resume negotiations, stating that "that there has yet been no collective bargaining." Secretary of Commerce Wallace announced that "industry in general can raise wages 10 percent without increasing prices."

On November 22, Fairless told the Nation: "Once the OPA is out of the way and we can arrive at a fair price for our product I am certain that labor and management can get together on a fair wage."

On November 23, the OPA stated that it "finds no cause at this time for a general increase in steel prices."

On December 3, President Truman asked Congress for a law patterned after the Railway Labor Act to curb strikes in all major industries; and announced that he was appointing a factfinding board in the steel dispute. Management was cautiously approving, but Murray assailed the President, and said that the proposal "can be but the first step for ever more savage legislative repression." He accused the administration of yielding "in abject cowardice" to industry's refusal to bargain. In later comment on this he added, "unlike the union in the General Motors case the steel union . . . has not coupled its demand for wage increases with a flat demand that present basic steel prices be maintained." The Steelworkers, unlike the Auto Workers, consistently held that price was no concern of theirs. No wage bargaining took place, however, and on December 11 the union set January 14, 1946, as a strike deadline.

On December 31, 1945, the President appointed a factfinding board in the dispute between the steel-producing subsidiaries of U.S. Steel and the United Steelworkers of America. The Members of the Board were Nathan P. Feinsinger, chairman, an attorney and former WLB public member, Roger I. McDonough, associate justice of the Supreme Court of Utah, and James M. Douglas, chief justice of the Supreme Court of Missouri. Simultaneous with the appointment of the Board, the President indicated he would request the OPA "to review the price ceiling structure on steel products with a view to determining by not later than February 1, 1946, whether any wage increases would be proper." The Board was instructed to report February 10 so that it might have the benefit of the OPA report.

The Board never held hearings in the 1946 dispute. Before it could familiarize itself with the dispute the parties were requested by the President to resume collective bargaining and thenceforth the Board functioned in what was termed an "advisory" capacity to the President.

The sequence of events during the next 3 weeks is illustrative of the sort of three-way negotiations that befogged collective bargaining in 1946. On January 9 "a responsible officer of the Government" telephoned Fairless and asked whether a $4 a ton price increase would enable the company to offer a wage increase.[21] The Administration's dilemma was either to accept a steel strike, followed by strikes in other industries, or to allow a further breach in the stabilization program. Apparently John W. Snyder, Chief of the Office of War Mobilization and Reconversion, decided to accept the second alternative, overrule OPA and Chester Bowles (who had insisted that a $2.50 price increase was all that should be allowed), and try and trade prices for settlements. Although the company rejected the price offer as insufficient it did accept it as a signal for the resumption of collective bargaining with the union.

In meetings in New York on January 10, U.S. Steel made its first wage offer of 12½ cents, at which point Murray reduced the union's demand from 25 cents to 20 cents. On January 11, U.S. Steel raised its offer to 15 cents. Again, according to Fairless, "this new offer was made after I was informed from Washington by a high Government official that the Government was willing to sanction some price increase over the promised $4 a ton if the labor dispute could be settled."

On that same day the factfinding board in the General Motors dispute made a recommendation of a 19½-cent wage increase. Murray immediately adopted the figure and remained adamant upon it with the consequence that negotiations were broken off. President Truman then obtained a promise of a 1-week extension of the strike deadline, to January 21, and requested further collective bargaining at the White House. In the first of these meetings, on January 12, Murray is said to have proposed that if the companies would accept the 19½-cent figure the union would reduce to 3 cents the 5-cent figure proposed by the War Labor Board in 1945 for the settlement of wage inequities. U.S. Steel took this proposal up with other steel companies, but it was rejected. On January 17, Murray and Fairless met twice with President Truman who personally acted as a mediator, but when they failed to agree he announced that he would make a public recommendation the following day. On January 18 the President proposed an 18½ cent settlement retroactive to January 1. Steelman suggested this figure to the President, both because he believed that this was the highest Fairless would go, and because it was necessary to modify the GM recommendation in some way, hoping to end the auto strike. Murray agreed after Feinsinger is said to have appealed to his patriotism, although this was 1 cent less than the General Motors recommendation, but on the following day after industry consultation the company rejected the proposal. Murray appeared incensed and criticized the industry harshly for rejecting the President's recommendation.

At midnight January 21 a complete strike began involving both basic steel and steel fabricators with whom the Steelworkers had contracts.[22] Approximately 750,000 workers went on strike. Only one basic steel plant continued in

---

[21] Benjamin Fairless, radio address, Jan. 23, 1946.

[22] This was the only time in the history of the basic steel-Steelworker relationship that all fabricators were struck along with the basic segment of the industry. Interviews are conflicting as to the reason why it was done, but, in general, it appears that Murray was determined to set a national pattern of 18½ cents and ordered the fabricator strike in order to illustrate his firmness. In addition, fabricator employees were subject to the same postwar economic uncertainties as were employees in basic steel. Then too, at this time, unlike the case in later years most fabricator contracts expired at the same time as the basic steel agreements, and the WLB doctrine on retroactivity had died with it.

operation, the Fontana, Calif. plant of Henry J. Kaiser, who signed with the union for 18½ cents at a meeting at the White House the day after the strike began.

The bloody battles which had marked steel strikes less than 10 years earlier, however, were not found in the month-long test of strength. Only words were hurled back and forth. Always before, a major steel strike had involved a fight against the existence of the union with an attempt being made to keep the plants open. This meant strikebreakers and open war. By 1946 the industry had apparently realized that the union was a permanent institution and that the relationship would continue after the strike was over. This brought a peacefulness hitherto generally lacking in basic steel strikes.

In the weeks that followed it was evident that lack of a price formula continued as the stumbling block. On January 28, Ford settled for 18 cents and Chrysler for 18½ cents. On January 30, U.S. Steel announced that a price increase of $6.25 a ton was necessary to pay for an 18½ cent wage increase. This was immediately denied by Government officials, who nevertheless must have realized it was now their move. By February 6, union and U.S. Steel officials began to meet secretly, and by February 10 it was common gossip in the newspapers that the 18½ cent wage increase had been agreed to. Only price remained an issue. Finally, on Saturday, February 15 the break came. OWMR Chief Snyder met with the companies and then announced a $5 a ton price increase. Company and union settled their sole remaining difference, retroactivity, by splitting the difference. Half of the increase, 9¼ cents, became effective on January 1, 1946, and the other 9¼ cents was effective upon return to work. The mills began to reopen on Monday, February 17, and within 4 days most basic producers were operating again. However, some fabricators were struck for as much as 2 months longer over local issues.

Both parties could claim a victory, at least privately. The union gained a "substantial" increase, and the companies had forced the Government to reformulate stabilization policy. Under the new policy resulting from the strike settlement, all first-round wage increases were given regional approval, and were then considered in fixing new price ceilings. The settlement was a retreat to higher wage and price ground and partly because of this, the whole stabilization program was to prove untenable in a few more months.

1947 BASIC STEEL CONTRACT NEGOTIATIONS

As a part of the settlement of the 1946 strike in basic steel, the master contracts had been extended to February 15, 1947. Looking forward to this date, on the previous December 18, the Steelworkers' Wage and Policy Committee completed formulation of a substantial program of proposals for economic benefits and contract revision. The major items were:

1. General wage increase.
2. Reduction in geographical differentials.
3. Changes in overtime computation.
4. Improved reporting allowance.
5. Severance pay.
6. Improvement in vacations and premium rates for work on holidays.
7. Guaranteed annual wage.
8. Changes in seniority.
9. Social insurance program.
10. Union shop.
11. Changes in grievance procedure.
12. Changes in job scheduling and safety provisions.
13. Time and one-half for Saturday work; double time for Sunday work.
14. Protection against modification of local plant work rule agreements.

It was significant that no specific size of wage increase was mentioned, other than "substantial." Repeatedly during the ensuing months, steel company representatives and newspaper reporters as well pressed Murray for a specific figure, and their questions were as often evaded. Murray, in his role as president of the CIO, was leading a fight for a national CIO wage policy in the second round of postwar increases, and the answer to the question "how much" was not to be determined for many months.

As was traditional, U.S. Steel was scheduled to begin negotiations first, early in January. These were postponed by mutual agreement but without explanation; the union's proposals were therefore first presented to the Jones and Laughlin and Bethlehem companies. On January 25, the reason for the postponement became clear when U.S. Steel and the union jointly announced the settlement of the cost package of the inequities negotiation. As was described earlier, this 5.2 cents settlement involved somewhat greater cost than had been called for under the War Labor Board's original order, and the timing of the announcement is therefore noteworthy. It was not done so far in advance of expiration that it could not have been delayed for inclusion by the company as part of the renegotiation package. On the other hand, it was not done so close to contract renewal that the union could claim it as part of the next round pattern. This would appear to represent an effort at good faith by both parties, or the desire to keep the inequities settlement out of the give and take of negotiations insofar as possible. Whatever the motives, the announcement seems to have brought a general aura of good feeling to the 1947 U.S. Steel negotiations. After their first joint meeting at the end of January, U.S. Steel and the Steel-workers agreed to extend the contract until April 30 to allow time for "good faith negotiations." This move was promptly followed by all other important basic steel producers, and was hailed by Government officials as the beginning of a new era of peaceful steel negotiations.

In reality, a general feeling that a peaceful settlement of the 1947 negotiations was likely had been suggested by almost all commentators as early as January. The reasons given were various: the parties had had a strike the previous year and did not appear anxious for another; that while the general economy was in an uncertain state with recession appearing imminent to many, demand for steel was at an alltime high with a substantial gray market existing for many types and sizes, thus influencing the companies to maintain maximum production at any reasonable price; that the end of price controls meant that Government would not "interfere" with collective bargaining; and perhaps more important, that public opinion was aroused over recurrent major work stoppage and other aspects of the labor field thus impelling unions in general and Murray and the Steelworkers in particular to do nothing further to arouse the Congress during the hearings on proposed revisions in labor legislation.

For the next 2 months negotiations between the parties continued on a regular basis with little publicity. It was rumored that most of the discussions were on nonwage items, with the chief stumbling blocks concerning incentives, work rules and inequities; the companies' insistence that they be given relief from portal-to-portal pay litigation; and the union shop demand countered by proposals from most companies that maintenance of membership be circumscribed or even deleted. Jockeying on the size of the eventual cost package also continued. A special report by Robert R. Nathan made for the Steelworkers stated that the steel companies could raise wages 25.3 cents an hour without increasing prices or reducing profits. When this was coupled with the Automobile Workers' concurrent demand for 23½ cents the result was a common assumption that this was the area of union desire. This was countered by the companies' oft-repeated statements that cost increases would necessitate price increases. Finally a wage settlement pattern began to emerge. Following a meeting of the presidents of major CIO unions called by Murray early in April, the Rubber Workers accepted a settlement of 11½ cents in wages and 3½ cents in fringes. Two weeks later, in mid-April, the United Electrical, Radio and Machine Workers, one of the CIO Big Three, accepted a similar settlement from General Motors and from Westinghouse. Although the UAW bitterly characterized this settlement as a "sellout," the pattern had been formed.

U.S. Steel negotiations came to a head on April 18–20. After a private meeting with John A. Stephens on April 17, Philip Murray scheduled a meeting of the union's Wage and Policy Committee for the 20th. Beginning on the 18th, a company subcommittee composed of Stephens, R. Conrad Cooper, his assistant, and Leroy Lewis, a U.S. Steel Attorney, met for 2 days with a union subcommittee of Murray, David MacDonald, and Lee Pressman, the union's attorney. By the morning of April 21 a press conference was called to announce the settlement of the basic agreement under which the parties were to live for the next 5 years.

The economic package settlement negotiated was worth slightly over 15 cents an hour. The major features, to be effective the previous April 1, were:

    1. A 12½ cents wage increase to all employees, including those with redcircled out-of-line differentials. This represented a company accommodation to pressures on the union from member's dissatisfied with the new standard hourly scales negotiated 2 months previously.
    2. One-half cent increase in job class increments, from 3½ to 4 cents, thus solving the problem of maintaining the integrity of the job classification structure by giving increasing amounts to employees in higher skilled classifications. Employees receiving out-of-line differentials did not receive benefits from this increase, however, which tended to reduce or eliminate differentials. Incentive workers received this increase on their guaranteed rates.
    3. Three cents an hour reduction in the southern differential.
    4. Elimination of the 2½ cents differential at the Duluth plant of American Steel and Wire.
    5. Three weeks' vacation to employees with 25 years' service.
    6. In final conformity with the 1944 WLB decision, and effective on April 22, 1947, severance pay to employees separated because of permanent discontinuance of plant or department. The terms were 4 weeks' pay after 3 years' service, 6 weeks' after 5 years', 7 weeks' after 7, and 8 weeks' after 10.

Contract changes in other areas were of equal or greater significance. Among those were:

    7. Substantial revision of the seniority clause, providing that where ability and fitness were relatively equal, seniority to control in promotion, layoffs, and rehiring. A joint study of seniority problems was agreed upon.
    8. Extension and substantial revision of the safety clause, entitling an employee to refuse to work on a job considered unsafe by the employee,[23] or to file an immediate third-step grievance. Joint safety committees on a local basis were also created.
    9. The tripartite arbitration board was retained as the final step in the grievance procedure, but was relieved of the duty to attempt mediation before arbitration. The grievance procedure was closed to claims of wage rate inequities, except those based on improper classification or failure of management to develop a new description for a changed job.
    10. No provision was made for a guaranteed annual wage or an insurance program but in a separate letter the company agreed to a joint study of a

---

[23] This privilege is considered "dangerous" by a number of other major producers who have never agreed to go this far. Their contracts substitute an immediate grievance for private judgment.

comprehensive social insurance program to be concluded by November 1947. The new plan was to be put into effect as soon as agreed upon.

11. By supplemental agreement, the company was not to be liable for portal-to-portal pay claims except to the extent that such payments were being made under existing practices. The union agreed not to process or support existing or future claims.

12. Various provisions were made for modifying incentive plans and installation of new plans, and the joint wage rate inequity negotiating committee was directed to continue the task of developing the principles for determining a fair day's work.

13. The existence of local working conditions was recognized and the protection of these and the method for changing them was agreed upon.

14. A rather long clause setting forth the purpose and intent of the parties was agreed upon, including their attitudes toward each other and their mutual desire for fairness and understanding. To effectuate these desires, hopes, or expectations the parties agreed to meet quarterly to discuss the administration of the contract.

15. The contract was extended until April 30, 1949. Either party was given the right to reopen on wage rates on April 1, 1948, but without the right to strike in the event of failure to agree.

No changes were made in the union security sections of the contract, which continued as maintenance of membership with a 15-day escape clause. In comment on this, Benjamin Fairless stated: "We continue opposed to compulsory or restrictive forms of membership and in our judgment this matter represents a major problem for [national] policy determination." [24]

The Steelworkers turned immediately to the remainder of the industry upon completion of U.S. Steel negotiations, with their prime objectives a comparable 15-cent package and equalization with U.S. Steel rates. Negotiations at Bethlehem had been broken off on April 15, but on April 22 a resumption of negotiations led to a settlement in a few days. By and large the rest of the industry followed quickly, although some paid substantially more than 15 cents. Companies that had low rates compared with U.S. Steel were forced to equalize and for some the 1947 settlement was close to 20 cents. Allegheny Ludlum Steel Corp. granted a fully paid comprehensive social insurance program instead of the promise of a study. By the end of April all but one of the major Steelworker agreements in basic steel were signed. Inland, which apparently felt it had been suffering unduly from "quickie" work stoppages, offered the standard economic package but in return demanded contract language giving increased protection against wildcat strikes. The union rejected the company's proposed language and on May 1, 14,000 employees went on strike. The strike was settled a week later with the company gaining a substantial part of its proposal, primarily requiring affirmative action by union officials against acts in violation of the contract, and eliminating negotiations during illegal stoppages.

The union hailed the 1947 basic steel agreements as a triumph of collective bargaining. In commenting about them at a later date, Murray said:

> There was absolutely no participation by Government in any phase of the negotiations. This is conclusive proof that men of good will can reach a settlement of grave industrial relations problems on their own volition when they make up their minds to do so. We believe our 1947 negotiations provided an example for industry, labor, and Government to follow. [25]

U.S. Steel was also proud of its labor relations record during 1947 [26] but continued to be involved with the Government in controversy over its pricing

[24] *New York Times,* Apr. 22, 1947, p. 4. The policy determination referred to was the then-current Congressional debate on what later became the Taft-Hartley Act.

[25] Proceedings of the Fourth Constitutional Convention of the United Steelworkers of America, May 11, 1948, p. 27.

[26] 46th Annual Report, U.S. Steel Corp., pp. 13–14.

policies. President Truman had publicly asked for price reductions to avoid a recession, and immediately upon completion of negotiations Fairless announced that although no reductions were possible, the company hoped to be able to offset new wage costs through a high level of operations. On July 20 four Little Steel firms announced increases averaging $5 a ton, attributing increased Steelworker and Mine Worker wage costs, increased railroad rates, and scrap prices as their reason. U.S. Steel followed the increase on July 30. This was the first general increase since December of 1946, when prices had gone up $2.50 a ton. Actually, the increased list prices did not in many cases meet the going gray market prices for certain types of steel. Prices on individual products and semifinished steel continued to inch upward during the rest of 1947, often initiated by other producers and matched by Big Steel. A special study by the President's Council of Economic Advisors characterizing steel price increases as the prime cause of inflation, an attack by the Federal Trade Commission on the basing point method of pricing and selling products, and a futile year-end attempt by the President to gain authority from Congress for reimposition of wage and price controls did nothing to halt the general upward price trend.

In general summary, 1947 represents the first high water mark in the relations between the basic steel companies and the United Steelworkers. The completion of the basic wage inequities agreement, the comprehensive yet peaceful renegotiation of basic labor agreements without Government intervention, the frequent reliance on joint labor-management committees to solve many continuing problems existing under the contract, and the effort to place in the contract a philosophy of peaceful relations implemented by regular top-level meetings; all of these were symptomatic of joint hope for continuing improvement in the future of the relationship.

1948 STEEL WAGE REOPENING

Inflation continued during 1948. The formalized three-sided wage-price drama that had been a significant part of postwar collective bargaining in steel therefore also continued. The roles, the players, and the finale remained about the same; the scenario was somewhat different. During this negotiation year the Steelworkers had a wage reopener but no right to strike. They were therefore compelled to follow the bargaining lead of other unions, particularly the Auto Workers.

The first act was laid in the early spring. On January 18, 1948, U.S. Steel announced price increases averaging $5 a ton on semifinished steel, and its lead was followed within 3 weeks by all other major producers. The price increase was the third since the last wage increase had been negotiated 10 months previously and came shortly before negotiations were to begin again. Net profits for 1947 had been the greatest in the industry's history, although profits as a percent of sales had been exceeded in a few previous years in the industry's history. Steel was still in short supply, demand was strong, and gray market operators were obtaining prices substantially above list price. Despite this latter fact, the increases brought immediate protests from the President and from Congressmen of both parties.

President Truman ordered investigations by the Departments of Justice and Commerce and a study by the Council of Economic Advisors of the steel price situation. Justice sent agents of the FBI to the offices of 16 steel companies about possible antitrust violations, but later announced it had found no evidence of collusion. In its report to the President, the Council of Economic Advisors stated :

> It is futile for the steel industry to call for restraint in the matter of wage negotiations at the same time that it is itself raising prices. * * * All those who occupy strategic positions in the setting of prices * * * must recognize the public interest in their private economic decisions in a way the steel industry has not shown in this instance.[27]

On March 2, 1948, Benjamin Fairless was called to testify before the Joint Committee on the Economic Report by Senator Taft, the Committee's chairman. Fairless protested "widespread misrepresentations" about the semifinished steel price increase, and contended that the products on which prices had been raised had been selling at a loss. Senator Taft criticized Fairless sharply and deemed this defense irrelevant, since overall profits were so favorable, and suggested that increases should at least have been offset by compensating reductions on profitable products.[28] When asked by the Senator if the increases would not make the coming wage negotiations more difficult, Fairless replied, " I hope not. Steel prices can always be reduced, you know." [29] At the conclusion of the hearings, although the industry refused to concede that the increases were unnecessary, Fairless did admit that they had made a mistake in the political "visibility" of the increases. It was not a mistake the industry was likely to make again. In the future, as in the past, major general price increases were announced following wage increases.

On April 1, 1948, the Steelworkers presented 6,000 steel manufacturing and fabricating companies with a demand for a "substantial" wage increase. This demand had been agreed upon by a union's Wage Policy Committee in February, but as early as February 16, Murray said publicly that the union would observe its contracts and would not strike to enforce the demand.

Stephens of U.S. Steel and Murray held their first meeting on April 5, in the course of which Murray indicated that the union would be willing to accept a comprehensive social insurance and pension plan in lieu of the greater part of the "substantial" wage increase. The company asked for an adjournment, and meetings were not resumed for 10 days.

Collective bargaining conferences were held sporadically from April 14 through April 22, at which time negotiations came to a halt. U.S. Steel announced to the union and to the public that it was going to take a major step in the fight against inflation by refusing a wage increase and simultaneously cutting steel prices on various products from $1 to $5 a ton, resulting in a total reduction of $25 million in steel costs annually. Fairless said that this was the equivalent of a "5 percent pay increase" to U.S. Steel's employees and benefited the rest of the Nation as well.

The Steelworkers were unconvinced. Murray assailed the company with charges during the next several weeks. They had "bargained in bad faith," and had attempted to justify it by a "picayune price cut averaging $1.24 a ton." He charged U.S. Steel with using "a moderate wage increase in 1947 as an excuse to raise prices three times since then," and that these price cuts "didn't begin to match the raises." They were "so paltry as to have no effect on the cost of

---

[27] Report of the Council of Economic Advisors to the President, Mar. 15, 1948.

[28] U.S. Congress, Hearings before the Joint Committee on the Economic Report, *Increases in Steel Prices,* 80th Cong., 2d sess. (Washington : Government Printing Office, 1948), p. 15.

[29] Idem, p. 16.

living;" consequently, this was "no attack on prices but merely shadow boxing for public opinion." [30]

Most of the remaining major steel producers immediately announced similar price reductions, but all producers, whether or not they cut prices, followed U.S. Steel's lead in refusing wage increases. Despite these rebuffs the union's Wage Policy Committee and the union convention reaffirmed their belief in the sanctity of contractual commitments, noting that they would continue to negotiate with U.S. Steel by means of subcommittees appointed to study social insurance. Negotiations were also to continue in other industries where the union had contracts.

Meanwhile, national attention turned to automobile negotiations which had been underway since March, with a May 12 termination date at Chrysler and a scheduled termination of May 28 at General Motors. When the rejection of wage increases in steel was announced, the UAW publicized its intention not to let developments in steel inhibit its own drive for wage increases. The UAW also pointedly differentiated between itself and the Steelworkers, who could not strike. Chrysler had refused to make a wage offer; it too said that it was fighting inflation. Finally, in the last week of negotiations, Chrysler offered a 6 cent increase and the UAW moved from its original proposal of 30 cents to 18½ cents, but the parties were unable to come closer together and on May 12 Chrysler workers went on strike.

Negotiations between the UAW and General Motors continued. On May 21 the company made its first proposal on wages. After 4 days of intensive bargaining the company's proposal became the basis for one of the most significant wage settlements ever made in this country. The wage formula had four major parts which (1) sought to close the gap that had developed since 1940 between living costs and wages; (2) established an "escalator" by which wages would be adjusted up or down each quarter at a rate of 1 cent in hourly wage rates for each 1.14 points change in the BLS Consumer Price Index; (3) limited downward adjustment to a maximum of 5 cents an hour; and (4) advanced hourly wage rates by 3 cents each year, to improve employees' standard of living in line with anticipated advances in national productivity. Application of this formula yielded an 11 cent hourly increase to General Motors employees in 1948.

The G.M. settlement was to become highly influential in negotiations in other industries in future years; in 1948 it simply "broke the dam" that had held back wage increases in large sectors of the economy. On May 28, 1948, Chrysler settled the strike at its plants by a flat 13 cents an hour wage increase plus escalation. During June many other industries followed the general patterns. The can industry settled with the Steelworkers for a 10 cent increase. The rubber industry settled for 11 cents. Electrical equipment manufacturers who, like steel, had earlier refused to grant any increase, granted an 8 percent increase, or approximately 11 cents. Perhaps most important in its relationship to steel, the Mine Workers negotiated an increase of 12½ cents plus increased health and welfare benefits throughout the coal industry.

The steel industry could no longer maintain its position in the face of these increases and the fact that the Consumer Price Index had advanced more than 4 percent since the last steel wage increase and nearly 2½ percent in the few months since it had refused an increase. At the end of June, Alan Wood Steel and several smaller basic steel producers announced 10-cent wage increases. Wierton Steel, never loath to accept comparison with the rest of the industry in

---

[30] The quotations are from the *New York Times* in the 2 weeks after April 23.

employee relations, announced that it was granting a "substantial" increase, later specified to be 14 cents.

On June 28, 1948, John Stephens told Murray privately that it had become "clear that [U.S. Steel's] effort to help at wage and price stabilization had failed and that, accordingly, to keep faith, we would extend a wage increase to the steelworkers." [81] Stephens also offered to allow up to 4 cents of any increase negotiated to be applied to social insurance. On July 8, Stephens offered Murray a 12½ cents average increase in return for an extension of the basic agreement until 1950. Murray rejected this because it would not allow him to negotiate on insurance and pensions for 2 more years, and because the company's insurance proposal was objectionable in that it was both contributory and inadequate.

In subsequent meetings with David McDonald and Arthur Goldberg, the union's attorney, Stephens expressed a willingness to consider asking his associates if they would increase their offer to 13½ cents, and to reopen on wages only in 1949. On July 13, Murray told Stephens the company could do as it pleased about wages, but that he would not recommend or accept any settlement that put off social security for 2 years. Two days later Stephens proposed to Murray that the 1949 reopening involve both wages and insurance, but not pensions, and warned Murray that the company would take a strike in 1949 rather than agree to pensions before it was ready to do so. Later that day, according to Stephens' memoranda of telephone conversations, Murray agreed to accept a 13 cent average increase, and a 1949 reopening on wages and social insurance. The narrative of the 1948 negotiations given to the factfinding board in 1949 makes it clear that the companies would have been willing to go to a 13½ cent average increase, but Murray preferred 13 cents and a social insurance reopener. These agreements were consummated on July 16, by supplemental agreement to the 1947 agreement. The details of the supplement were as follows:

1. A 9½ cent general wage increase plus ½ cent increase in the increments between job classes, the total increase averaging 13 cents.

2. The total adjustment for each job class was added to earnings of workers covered by incentive plans in effect prior to April 22, 1947.

3. Provision for maintenance of membership and checkoff after April 1949.

4. Master contract extended to April 30, 1950, with a reopener 60 days prior to July 16, 1949 on (a) rates of pay, and (b) life, accident, health, medical and hospital insurance benefits.

By the end of July all other major steel producers followed Big Steel's lead and granted similar wage increases.

On July 20, U.S. Steel raised its prices. The increases averaged 9.6 percent, or over $10 a ton. They were promptly matched by all other producers. This action by the industry produced vigorous protests from some Congressmen, but no Presidential or congressional investigations. As the final curtain fell on the 1948 steel negotiations it was at last clear, if it had not always been, that completion of wage negotiations with the union did much to obscure the "political visibility" of subsequent price increases.

1949 BASIC STEEL REOPENING

On May 16, 1949, the Steelworkers notified the basic steel companies under contract with it of its desire to negotiate for changes in wage rates, as well as for life, accident, health, medical and hospital insurance benefits. These were

---

[81] Proceedings, U.S Steel Industry Board, Aug. 11, 1949, Vol. 7, p. 914. The following description of 1948 negotiations is taken from John Stephens' testimony before the Board, pp. 903–935.

of course the subjects listed for reopening in the 1948 supplemental agreement. Additionally, a separate letter transmitted to each company the union's desire to negotiate also on the subject of pensions.[32]

The steel industry in the spring and early summer of 1949 experienced the first slackening of demand in almost 10 years. Although the industry had operated at over 100 percent of capacity in the first quarter of 1949, in the second quarter it had operated at about 85 percent of capacity, and by July, was under 80 percent. Profits in 1948 had been the highest in history, but 1949 projections showed profits off as much as 25 percent in some companies. Minor price cuts on some items had been listed during the spring. The Nation as a whole was experiencing some recession and employment figures dropped sharply during the first two quarters of 1949. The Consumer Price Index showed a modest decline, close to 2 percent, in the first half of the year. For the first time since 1941, steel negotiations were not taking place against a background of full employment, rising prices and a full backlog of orders within the industry.

Intermittent negotiations with U.S. Steel and other companies continued from June 15 to July 7. The union pressed its three demands, for wages, social insurance, and pensions without providing the companies with precise language or monetary proposals. In response, all the companies rejected the proposal for wage increases because of economic conditions, but some made offers or indicated a willingness to make offers on social insurance. With the sole exception of Inland Steel, all companies maintained that pensions were not a bargainable subject at all. Neither side moved from these original positions.

The next development is recounted by Cyrus S. Ching, who was then director of the Federal Mediation and Conciliation Service:

> With the situation hopelessly deadlocked, I called both sides to Washington for a 3-day round of mediation conferences. It was impossible to get either party to move from its position. Finally, I went to President Truman, explained the situation, and told him that I felt it would be necessary to have some kind of Presidential action in the dispute. It was my opinion that the best way to cope with the controversy was to appoint a factfinding panel to study the case and make recommendations for a fair and equitable settlement. I was convinced then, and still am, that such a course of action was the soundest way to handle that particular situation.
>
> The White House was reluctant to get into the case, but after some discussions, the President was persuaded to name a factfinding board in the steel dispute. I had talked with the late Philip Murray and he gave me his word that, if a factfinding board were appointed, he would postpone strike action until the panel's findings were received and sufficient time had elapsed for negotiations to be resumed on the basis of the board's recommendations.[33]

The dilemma in which the Ching request placed the White House is highlighted by reference to the political situation of the time. High on the agenda of the 81st Congress, which had been meeting all through the spring of 1949, was revision of the Taft-Hartley Act with particular emphasis on proposed changes in the national emergency provisions. For months, administration spokesmen in the House and Senate had belabored the existing provisions as cumbersome, inflexible, and inadequate and had fought for the administration's

---

[32] None of these pension letters mentioned the contract. Therefore, it is a legitimate inference that at this time the union believed that its right to bargain was not given by the contract but only by the Labor Management Relations Act, 1947 as interpreted in the matter of Inland Steel Company, 77 N.L.R.B. 1 (1948). The union later argued that both contract and statute permitted it to bargain on pensions.

[33] *Review and Reflection,* Forbes, 1953, pp. 73–4.

alternative—a system of voluntary delay and factfinding with recommendations. The debate in committees and on the floor of both houses had gone on for months, concerned with the proper way of handling emergency disputes, the role and powers of the President, and the relative efficacy of factfinding, seizure, and injunction. Finally, on June 30, hardly 2 weeks previous to the Ching request, the administration had been defeated. The Taft-Hartley provisions remained the statutorily prescribed method of handling critical labor-management disputes.

Thus the breakdown in steel negotiations posed difficult alternatives. If the Taft-Hartley provisions were to be used it would be construed as an admission that their proponents had been right all along and that the provisions were needed to stave off impending strikes. Their use would mean the issuance of an injunction against Philip Murray, generally considered a cooperative union leader, and certainly a strong administration supporter. The provisions did not allow recommendations, which administration leaders (and also Senator Taft by this time) considered generally desirable. Finally, to use the procedures required a Presidential determination that a steel work stoppage at that time would be a "national emergency," and there was doubt in many minds about this. On the other hand, if the President was going to intervene, refusal to use Taft-Hartley machinery would fly directly in the face of the decision resulting from the previous months of debate.

President Truman rejected what he felt to be an erroneous congressional decision, and set up a Steel Industry Board which was to function in the way the administration had proposed to Congress. In the telegram which went to the parties on July 12, 1949, the President requested continuance of operations under the old contract for 60 days while a factfinding board was "to investigate and to inquire into the issues in dispute" and to prepare a public report, including its "recommendations as to fair and equitable terms of settlement."

The union accepted the following day. The companies, however, raised many objections, and initially refused to accept the President's request. Benjamin Fairless of U.S. Steel replied to the President:

> We are unwilling to go outside the [Taft-Hartley Act] as you propose, and accept a board with power to make recommendations to the parties as to terms of settlement. * * * In our opinion the question of whether this Nation is to have a fourth round of wage increases or other increased labor costs at this time should not be determined on the basis of the recommendations of such a board as you propose.[34]

Other companies publicly accused President Truman of "making a deal" or of "paying-off" Philip Murray for election support the previous year.

By July 15, however, all major companies, including U.S. Steel as one of the last, had agreed to the President's request. Almost all conditioned their acceptance by the declaration that they would not consider themselves bound by Board recommendations. On that day the Board was formally established with Carroll R. Daugherty, chairman, and Samuel I. Rosenman and David L. Cole, as members.

Board proceedings began on July 26 and lasted for over a month. Hearings were held in the U.S. Court House in New York and were conducted in a judicial manner. An official transcript was taken which eventually filled 20 thick volumes. In addition the parties submitted extensive histories of bargaining relationships, volumes of economic data, and legal briefs and rebuttal. In the words of the executive secretary of the Board:

---

[34] *New York Times,* July 13, 1949, p. 1.

The hearings were an astonishing collection of data—of many kinds of "facts." They told, first and foremost, a tragic story of confused and complicated personal relationships among the key bargainers. Promises, reservations to commitments, explicit and implied commitments—all were tangled together in a web of confusion which overlaid the memories of the parties, and either baffled them or gave them a sure conviction that their opponent must be a dishonest rogue.[35]

The 1949 Steel Industry Board generally behaved as if it were a judicial or arbitration agency, only in the last day of hearings making an attempt at mediation. By this time the public hearings had exhausted the parties and deepened their animosities; the effort to discover true positions was unavailing. The Board was left to guess about the parties' probable reaction to its recommendations. The following sections summarize the major areas of controversy in the dispute, the positions of the parties, and the comments and recommendations contained in the Board's Report, submitted to the President on September 10, 1949.[36]

Collective Bargaining in Basic Steel

Murray initially charged that the companies had failed to bargain:

At the very outset of negotiations, the various companies, through their representatives, expressed their prior determination to deny the Union's demands. The final turndown by the companies is only a reiteration of the decision arrived at before the commencement of negotiations.

In reply, the companies stressed the implications of "pattern bargaining" implemented by the "monopoly power" of "industrywide unions." They also stressed the impact of interunion rivalry.

In addition, counsel for smaller companies urged that the Board not establish one settlement or pattern upon all companies, many of which were in different product and declining markets, different competitive situations, and even unprofitable.

In reply, the union charged the companies with responsibility for the pattern bargaining they were now deploring. By taking uniform positions in collective bargaining, by insisting they wait until a pattern was set before even being willing to negotiate, and by always insisting upon identical settlements, they had made "individual company bargaining meaningless."

The Board concluded that individual plant bargaining had become stifled in basic steel, regardless of whose fault it was.

An agreement is first reached by the union with the United States Steel Corp. or with that corporation and a selected few of the other industry leaders and is then accepted by all other managements.

While the Board felt there was merit in the complaints of some companies that their individual problems did not get consideration under this system, it concluded:

If a different concept of collective bargaining from that heretofore held is needed, then a study leading to a reappraisal and a redefinition of the terms should be made by the appropriate body, which we think is the Congress itself. We should certainly not undertake to do this * * *

---

[35] Harold L. Enarson, *Fact-Finding as a Technique for Settlement of National Emergency Labor Disputes*, unpublished doctoral dissertation, American University, 1951, p. 207.

[36] Quotations in the following sections are from *Report of Proceedings before the Steel Industry Board*, July 26–Aug. 29, 1949, New York, 20 volumes; and *Report to the President of the United States on the Labor Dispute in the Basic Steel Industry*, Sept. 10, 1949.

Government Intervention in Steel Negotiations

The companies maintained their opposition to Presidential intervention before the Board itself. A. B. Homer, president of Bethlehem, refused a request from Judge Rosenman for an apology, and insisted on maintaining that the Board was "designed merely as a vehicle for forcing upon us important concessions to the unions."

Clarence Randall, president of Inland, was even more forceful:

> When the President announced the formation of this board he was in fact announcing an industrial revolution in America * * * Through this means, whether he knew it or not, he has proclaimed that wages shall be fixed by the Government. * * * [I]f this strategy works this time, collective bargaining will never come back. The precedent here attempted, reflecting the similar attempt made in 1946, would commit us to boards and Government wage-fixing forever.
>
> And no thoughtful person should be deceived by the naive suggestion that your findings are to be recommendations only. The moment your announcement is made every power of the Government will be brought to bear to compel both sides to accept your conclusions. * * *

Randall concluded by charging, "Through political alliance with the Government [Mr. Murray] possesses the power to induce the President of the United States to take extra-legal action at his request."

Murray indignantly replied that "the attack" was "plainly designed to intimidate the board" and Randall's charges that the board undermined collective bargaining were "sheer and utter nonsense." The implication "of a 'political alliance' is an insult both to the high office and the person of the President. * * * My first knowledge of the appointment of this board came in the wire which I received from the President on the same day that similar wires were received by the companies."

The Board calmly set forth its findings on this point as follows:

> We think in many ways factfinding boards promote and supplement rather than hinder collective bargaining * * *
>
> First, they serve generally to postpone a strike date, and this provides a cooling-off period. A "cooling-off period" imposed by injunction has not been found to create the atmosphere for reaching settlement by bargaining; *voluntary* bargaining and *compulsion* are inherently contradictory.
>
> Second, they provide, often for the first time, an opportunity to the parties to hear from each other, in the course of their presentations to the board, a calm, reasoned recital of the merits which are claimed for their respective positions.
>
> Third, for the first time in the process, they provide an opportunity for the public at large to become informed on the issues of the case. * * *
>
> After all voluntary efforts have failed, including the inability to agree on arbitration, no machinery more effective than factfinding boards with power to recommend has as yet been suggested.

Wages

In thousands of pages of argument and economic data the Steelworkers made three basic arguments for a wage increase: (1) employees' right to, and need for, increased rates and take home pay; (2) the ability of the industry to pay increases, based on profits, prices, worker productivity, and low break-even points; and (3) the benefit increased worker purchasing power would have upon the economy.

In as many thousands of pages the companies replied: (1) the Steelworkers were among the top 10 percent of American workers in earnings and real income; (2) the industry's ability to pay for increased labor costs was vastly overrated by the union, whose figures were usually erroneous or misleading; and (3) wage increases would be inflationary or would create greater unemployment.

The Board rejected the union's arguments—the decision reminiscent of the Scotch verdict "not proven:"

> The union has not * * * succeeded in proving its contention that productivity has risen 49.5 percent since 1939. * * *
>
> There are no inequities of Steelworkers at present which require redress through a general wage-rate increase. * * *
>
> The cost of living has remained stable within the last year, in fact it has slowly declined * * * Therefore there is no inequity in respect to other income-receiving groups in the general economy. * * *
>
> [T]here is a probability that a wage-rate increase in steel would be urged as a pattern to be followed in other industries; this in turn might well cause price dislocations, with adverse effects on the general economy and on the steel industry itself * * *

The Board's recommendation on wages was bsaed on then-current economic conditions. It went on to state that the expected modernization and expansion in the industry would substantially lower costs and increase profits. The Board felt that these savings should be passed on to the consumer in the form of lower prices.

> And if this does not happen, and if business conditions continue to be generally favorable, there would appear to be justification for the union to renew its demand for larger participation in the industry's income.

Social Insurance

The arguments of the parties upon insurance and pensions were integrated in many ways with their arguments on wage increases. The union stressed need and ability of the companies to provide the benefits. It also maintained that they should be provided for by the companies on a noncontributory basis as a normal cost of doing business. The union felt a 6.27 cents an hour contribution by the company would cover the benefits stipulated.

The companies on the whole agreed on the desirability of social insurance benefits covering illness and accidents and medical and hospital care. They stated that most companies had such programs already in effect and were willing to discuss increasing their contributions to them. However, they pointed out that the union underestimated costs of the benefits demanded, and they insisted that the join contribution principle be maintained to preserve the individual's right to spend or save as he saw fit.

The Board judged the last company point to be one of no great significance, judging by the slightness of testimony concerning it, and had no great difficulty with its decision on insurance:

> * * * Social insurance and pensions should be considered a part of normal business costs to take care of temporary and permanent depreciation in the human "machine," in much the same way as provision is made for depreciation and insurance of plant and machinery. * * *
>
> It is recommended as fair and equitable under all the circumstances, that a social insurance plan be incorporated into the collective-bargaining agreements of the industry. The details and specific benefits of the plans should be determined through collective bargaining between each company and the union. The plans should be paid for by the employers without contribution by the employees; but should be limited in net cost to a maximum of about $80 per year per employee, or 4 cents an hour, on a basis of a 2,000-hour work year.

Pensions

From the beginning of the 1949 negotiations one of the major stumbling blocks had been whether pensions were "bargainable." The unions insisted they were under a loose interpretation of "wages" in the contract reopening, and in any event by the law of the Inland Steel case. The union requested pensions of $125 a month, exclusive of social security, which it estimated would cost 11.23 cents an hour. The companies stood firmly on the contract clause which limited reopening to wage changes and insurance.

The Board concluded that under the contract pensions were not bargainable in 1949. However, as it construed the law, pensions were bargainable because of the continuing obligation to bargain on subjects not covered by the contract, the history of the contract's reopening clause notwithstanding.

It is recommended as fair and equitable under all the circumstances that pension plans be established in this industry, with the cost to be borne by the employers without contribution from the employees.

Pensions should be limited in net cost to a maximum of about $120 per employee per year, or 6 cents per hour. * * * this will provide, when added to average social security benefits, about $100 per month on retirement at age 65 * * *

Recognizing that installation of a pension program was a complicated matter, the Board suggested a joint study of pensions be undertaken, with the results to be made available for bargaining the following spring.

Throughout its hearings the Board had been troubled by the fact that it was not dealing with a single dispute but with related disputes between 1 union and over 50 companies. It concluded its recommendations with the suggestion that although its wage recommendations applied throughout the industry, the pension and insurance recommendations presumably would apply only to the 19 leading basic steel manufacturers.

Both parties were apparently surprised by the Board's recommendations to the extent that the initial reactions of both, as reported in statements to the press, had to be reversed within the day. The union had expected some sort of general wage increase and its reaction was one of disappointment. However, the next day the union stated that it accepted the recommendations and asked that the companies meet with them to write contracts based upon the Board's guidelines. The companies, on the other hand, were apparently pleasantly surprised that the Board had rejected the union's demands for increased wages and initial, although unofficial, statements reflected this pleasure. The general public reaction was favorable, and many previously hostile press commentators reversed themselves and showered the Board with praise.

Suddenly the climate changed again. Almost overnight the leading steel companies began to cry in unison that the principle of noncontributory social benefits was un-American and contrary to the most cherished ideals of self-reliance and personal initiative. On September 14, the day following a special meeting of his board of directors, Fairless stated:

The most important issue raised by the report of the Presidential Steel Board is whether such a Board, possessing no statutory authority, power or responsibility, is to be permitted by public opinion or otherwise to impose upon American industry for all time a noncontributory system of social security, with the entire cost borne by the employer.[37]

There followed 2 weeks of sparring between the union and U.S. Steel, with negotiations conducted as much in the newspapers as in bargaining sessions.

---

[37] *New York Times*, Sept. 15, 1949, p. 1.

The union demanded simply that a contract be written embodying the Board's recommendations. The companies admitted that the Board's recommendations would be useful as a basis for renewed bargaining, but would not accept them as an arbitration award. Neither gave in the slightest on the issue of contribution vs. noncontribution.[38]

The union set a strike deadline for September 25 but this was postponed until October 1 at the request of President Truman. In final negotiations held by the Federal Mediation and Conciliation Service, U.S. Steel modified its previous position to the extent that it accepted the "10 cent package," i.e. 6 cents for pensions and 4 cents for insurance, but insisted that employees had to make an additional contribution in each area. The union persisted in its demand that the Board's recommendations be accepted completely, including noncontribution. Each party thus became a prisoner of its own strategy and "principles." On September 30, U.S. Steel, still protesting the union's use of the recommendations as "equivalent to compulsory arbitration," announced its refusal "to bow to such an ultimatum," and the strike began.

Almost one-half million employees of 37 basic steel companies, as well as employees of some steel fabricators, left their jobs. Just as in 1946, the strike was peaceful, with the plants closed in good order and maintenance men left behind in special cases. No attempt to operate plants or break the strike was made. No high degree of emotionalism was engendered by the issues; nevertheless the workers solidly supported the union and Murray.

After the strike had been in progress for 10 days, FMCS Director Ching again began holding meetings, particularly with U.S. Steel, the traditional industry leader. The mediators hoped that the Ford Motor Co. settlement might influence U.S. Steel. On September 29, on the eve of the steel strike, Ford and the UAW had reached agreement on insurance and $100 a month pensions. However, U.S. Steel continued inflexible.

Attention was then directed to Bethlehem Steel. In Ching's words:

* * * Insofar as Bethlehem was concerned, this highly controversial issue [contributory pensions] was not nearly so important because the firm had had a noncontributory plan in effect since 1923. Bethlehem's philosophy was that a pension plan constituted an inactive payroll. While the employee was working he was on the active payroll of the company; when the employee reached retirement age, he was transferred to the inactive payroll.
The job, then, was to get Bethlehem and the union together. I talked with Eugene Grace, chairman of the board of directors of Bethlehem, and J. M. Larkin, vice president of the company, and both said the company was willing to meet with Mr. Murray. The union president also consented to the conference. Everything was all set. It was apparent, however, in view of the public hue and cry over the steel shutdown, that the talks stood a lot better chance of success if they could be held without publicity. A meeting was arranged quietly at the Drake Hotel. Only representatives of the union and the company were present. The session was not very fruitful and both sides so advised me. I kept closely in touch with the parties, and persuaded them to try again, and another meeting was held 4 days later. It was at-

[38] Enarson says that the Board was surprised when the issued of contribution became paramount since they had never regarded is as significant. He further suggests that had they realized how deep the companies' feeling was on this issue they might have been able to tailor their recommendations to settle the dispute. Enarson, op. cit., p. 216, n. 1. If, as appears more likely, however, the companies' real issue of "principle" was as much opposition to nonstatutory factfinding boards as it was contribution, then hardly any recommendation would have been acceptable. Cf. Robert C. Spencer, Bargaining with the Government, unpublished doctoral dissertation, University of Chicago (1955), p. 118. In any event, the issue had cost, as well as moral, implications in this as well as future negotiations.

tended only by Mr. Murray; Arthur Goldberg, CIO general counsel, one of Murray's most trusted advisers and a steadying influence in the big labor union; Mr. Larkin of Bethlehem; and J. H. Morse, Bethlehem's counsel.[39]

Although nothing was accomplished with U.S. Steel, the meetings at the Drake were successful. On October 31, Murray was able to announce that "a company other than U.S. Steel has taken on itself the responsibility of leadership in setting a pattern for the industry." The settlement, a partial victory for the union, called for noncontributory pensions but contributory insurance. In summary, the agreement included:

1. Pension plan effective March 1, 1950, stipulated a $100 minimum, including social security, for employees with 25 years' service, at age 65. Actual pension to be based upon a 1 percent formula.
2. Insurance plan effective February 1, 1950. Maximum cost 5 cents, half to be paid by employer. Life insurance, range $2,000 to $4,500, reduced to $1,250 upon retirement after age 65 and continued at no cost to employee; accident and sickness, $26 per week to 26 weeks; 70-day Blue Cross hospital plan.
3. Establishment of a permanent Pension and Insurance Committee.
4. Pension and insurance agreements effective until October 31, 1954.
5. Master contract extended to 1952 with a wage reopener on December 31, 1950.

The Bethlehem settlement set a pattern for the industry. Within hours after it was announced U.S. Steel asked the union for a resumption of negotiations. However, the Little Steel companies were the next to sign; Jones and Laughlin on November 8, then Republic and Youngstown. U.S. Steel finally signed on November 11. All major producers signed programs largely identical with Bethlehem's except Inland Steel, which retained its old contributory plan with increased benefits or the new noncontributory plan on an employee's option basis.

On December 16, 1949, a month after negotiations were completed, U.S. Steel announced a general price increase of about $4 a ton, which was immediately followed by other producers. Congressmen again responded with criticism of the industry's action and for the second time within 11 months the Joint Committee on the Economic Report began hearings on steel price increases. When the report was made the Committee concluded: "The recent increase in steel prices was not only untimely but unwarranted and may set off a substantial downturn in business activity late this year."[40] These forebodings were not to be realized; the outbreak of war in Korea made inflation the threat once again.

THE 1950 STEEL WAGE REOPENING

The United Steelworkers of America requested on September 21, 1950, in a letter to some 1,400 steelmaking and fabricating companies, that their contracts be reopened. By this time the Korean War, which had begun on June 25, 1950, had resulted in shortages of steel, an urgent need for labor in several fields, scare buying by businesses and consumers, and an inflationary spiral which had caused a sizable rise in the Consumer Price Index. The Congress had passed the Defense Production Act of 1950 and the President signed it on September 8. By Executive order the following day the President announced that the Economic Stabilization Agency would be established with two subsidiary agen-

[39] Ching, op. cit., pp. 74–5.
[40] U.S. Congress, Joint Committee on the Economic Report, December 1949 Steel Price Increases, S. Rept. 1371, 81st Cong., 2d Session (1950), p. 23.

cies—a Wage Stabilization Board and an Office of Price Stabilization. In his radio address, the President also urged business and labor that they voluntarily seek to hold prices and wages down.

The Murray letter to the industry requested that talks be begun October 9, some 3 weeks in advance of the earliest date provided for in the 1949 contract. He stated that this was based on (1) the need of the steelworkers; (2) a manpower shortage that would be felt in the next several months; and (3) the problem of maintaining the supply of steel at the highest possible level. In addition, the union undoubtedly was concerned about the possibility of a wage freeze by the end of the year.

The industry response to the Murray letter of September 21 was favorable. Some 41 companies agreed to meet on October 9. United States Steel responded favorably, also, but could not meet on October 9. U.S. Steel and the Steelworkers met on October 16, from which time on the principal negotiations took place between the two. Talks with the remaining companies were largely suspended pending the outcome of the U.S. Steel negotiations. After the October 16 meeting, when the union's basic proposal was presented, the negotiators recessed until October 27 to afford U.S. Steel time to study the proposal.

On the whole, the union was in a superb bargaining position. There was widespread concern in the industry and among the fabricators about a possible labor shortage. Demand for steel was such that a gray market had developed; fabricators were resigned to increased prices, which they felt would still be below the gray market prices. The steel industry had been producing at over 100 percent of capacity for some time. In addition, steel profits were excellent, in some cases at alltime highs.

In a speech on November 16, 1950, Fairless intimated that the Steelworkers would receive a fifth round wage increase, and that despite pressure from Washington this would be reflected in increased steel price, which he believed would be only slightly inflationary. He cited wage increases in other industries as pointing the way, and he added that if the union demand could be brought in line with the general pattern of fifth round wage increase a satisfactory agreement could easily be worked out. He also declared that a 15-cent an hour increase, coupled with other higher costs to steel, would add about another $10 a ton to the cost of producing steel.[41]

During most of this period Government stabilization influence was minimal. The 10- to 12-week period from early September until the end of November 1950, when Communist Chinese forces began their successful attack on the UN troops in North Korea, was one of "suspended animation" insofar as economic stabilization activities were concerned. The military picture looked optimistic; panic buying was at an end. Public attention was directed to the congressional election campaign then underway. In general, the view that wage and price controls were perhaps unnecessary extended throughout the administration. Main reliance was placed on voluntary restraint; inflation, it was hoped, could be contained by use of credit controls and increased taxation.

The establishment of the Government machinery under the Defense Production Act proceeded slowly. Wage Stabilization Director Cyrus Ching was appointed on October 10, 1950; the full membership of the Board was not announced until November 24, only 2 days prior to the announcement of the new steel contract. Alan Valentine was named to be the Administrator of the Economic Stabilization Agency (ESA) on October 7, but Michael DiSalle was not appointed as Director of Price Stabilization until December 1. Accordingly,

---

[41] *New York Times*, Nov. 17, 1950, pp. 1, 23.

the only Agency that could have influenced steel prices was ESA itself, and during most of this period that Agency was largely a paper organization. Valentine's position, which he publicly stated, was that voluntary restraints were adequate under the then-current circumstances.

Despite the inchoate state of the ESA organization, during the latter part of October and November there were several discussions in ESA about prospective wage and price increases in steel. This apparently was common knowledge to the steel industry. Moreover, Stuart Symington, who at that time was the head of the National Security Resources Board, warned businesses that if they raised prices the Government might force them to cancel such increases at a later date.[42]

By the end of the third week in November, the negotiators were about ready to settle. The final problem, which was of course not a part of collective bargaining but had impact upon the industry's position, was whether there would be an increase in steel prices. Talks had taken place between Fairless and Valentine; it was reported that President Truman had also been consulted. It seems clear that Government officials tacitly approved a price increase prior to completion of negotiations. An industry leader later said that while the wage negotiations were not specifically tailored to the amount of price increase that the Government would approve, certainly the industry's bargaining posture would have been far different if there had not been a clear indication that some increase in prices would be approved.

An agreement was reached on November 29, and was signed on November 30. The agreement became effective the next day, and included the following terms:

(1) A basic wage increase of 12½ cents per hour.
(2) A ½ cent increase in the increments between job classes.
(3) A 4½ cent reduction in geographical differentials.
(4) The contract expiration date of December 31, 1951, remained unchanged.

Murray estimated the total hourly wage increase to be 18 cents an hour, while Fairless estimated it at 20 cents. The other steel companies quickly negotiated agreements on the same terms.

On November 30, 1950, U.S. Steel announced price increases in steel prices from $3 to $13 per ton effective December 1. These averaged $5.58 per ton, or a 5½ percent increase. All other companies immediately followed suit.

The price increases in steel caused an unfavorable reaction in the Congress, and ESA Administrator Valentine was called by a Senate committee to answer questions on December 4. He stated "that nobody in Government approved" either wage or price increases, and added, that insofar as he knew no one in the Government had. He refused to answer whether the Government was consulted prior to the increases, however, but offered to talk further on the subject in closed session.[43] There was no further action in regard to the steel price increase, but events in December further illuminate the price developments.

Early in December, Valentine requested the automobile industry not to carry out their announced intention to increase the prices of passenger automobiles. He continued to urge in private talks with the auto industry that it voluntarily withdraw its announced increases, but without success. Following the announcement by President Truman on December 16, 1950, of a state of national emergency, ESA issued a regulation to the effect that prices were to be rolled back to those existing on December 1, 1950. The steel price increase, having been made effective on November 30, was thus exempted.

---

[42] *Wall Street Journal,* Nov. 3, 1950, p. 1.
[43] *Wall Street Journal,* Dec. 5, 1950, p. 4.

1952 BASIC STEEL NEGOTIATIONS

In an era generally dominated by insecurity, 1952 v as especially notable for frustration and bitterness in the United States. The Korean War was entering its third year and the end seemed not yet in sight. Truce negotiations at Pan-munjon had been conducted fruitlessly for a year, amidst alarming reports of Communist troop buildups and recurrent threats that Russia was ready to begin World War III. The limited war continued to unsettle the economy, producing mounting inflation, only slightly contained by wage and price controls.

Domestically, bitter debates, charges and countercharges on issues of loyalty and security were at their peak as the final year of President Truman's administration ran its course. Congress was in the firm control of a Republican-Southern Democratic coalition which rejected more of the administration's domestic legislative proposals than ever before. Meanwhile, Republicans, determined to end the Democrats' 20-year hold on the White House, pushed steaming investigations of alleged corruption, tax favoritism, and influence peddling while seizing upon every new issue that could be turned to election year advantage.

To add to these tensions, 1952 was a year of widespread labor unrest. The strike record was the worst since 1946. Three and a half million workers left their jobs in industries such as coal, construction, maritime, petroleum refining and telegraphy. In culmination, the longest strike in the history of the Steel-worker's union to that time took place in basic steel, the most important and strategic of American heavy industries.

Almost all negotiations in basic industries can be variously viewed as studies in politics, economics, history, Government, sociology, or law. In the light of the national pressures existing on all parties, it is hardly surprising that the 1952 steel negotiations were perhaps the most complex and many-faceted in labor-management history.[44] Necessarily it must be viewed in sections, of which the first is the background of wage and price stabilization that existed at the time.

Economic Stabilization During Korea

On July 19, 1950, only a few weeks after the Korean War broke out, President Truman had called upon Congress for an Act giving him a full range of production and credit controls. The Defense Production Act of 1950, which became law in September (but which would be subject to yearly renewal) not only gave the President what he asked but additional broad power to control prices and wages. However, Congress stipulated that Presidential control over prices and wages be exercised through a single Executive Agency.

To meet this requirement President Truman established the Economic Stabilization Agency (ESA) under the direction of Alan Valentine, who set up a tripartite Wage Stabilization Board (WSB). During the late months of 1950 neither ESA nor WSB attempted more than planning and persuasion, since it looked as if the emergency would soon be over.

At the end of November 1950, China entered the Korean War, and for a time it appeared that the Soviet Union would follow. Estimates of military

---

[44] At least four substantial studies of the 1952 steel negotiations have been written: Grant McConnell, "The Steel Seizure of 1952," Inter-University Case Program, University of Alabama Press, 1960; Harold L. Enarson, "The Politics of an Emergency Dispute," in *Emergency Disputes and National Policy*, Bernstein, Enarson and Fleming, editors, Harper and Bros., 1955; Alan F. Westin, *The Anatomy of a Constitutional Law Case*, Macmillian, 1958; and "The Steel Industry: The 1952 Negotiations" in Benjamin M. Selekman, Sylvia K. Selekman and Stephen H. Fuller, *Problems in Labor Relations*, 2d ed. McGraw-Hill, 1958. In addition the dispute generated at least a dozen articles in learned journals and law reviews.

need for men and materiel soared and scare buying swept the country. The administration decided that direct controls over wages and prices were needed immediately, as well as a distinguished overall mobilization director. This position was given to Charles E. Wilson, President of General Electric Co., who became Director of Defense Mobilization, with responsibility for the ESA, which had in turn two nominally subordinate operations, the WSB and the newly created Office of Price Stabilization (OPS).

The parallel and independent existence of the WSB and the OPS in the closely related areas of wage and price was to prove a primary source of difficulty in the steel crisis of 1952. The OPS Administrator determined prices by formulas so the executive branch found it difficult to bargain in the price area. On the other hand, the tripartite representative character of the WSB necessarily implied some degree of bargaining in the wage field. Since in the long run one cannot raise wages indefinitely without affecting prices except where the rate of increase in productivity is unusually high, the administration appeared to have placed itself in the very divided position the Congress had sought to avoid. However, a divided system had worked in World War II and had the approbation of most industrial relations experts, so it appeared reasonable to try it again.

In early January 1951, Wilson ordered immediate imposition of wage and price controls and on January 25, Eric Johnston, the new ESA Director, delegated appropriate power to the WSB and the OPS. Throughout February, WSB worked to create a formula to permit wage increases in situations of inequity caused by the January wage freeze. On February 16, WSB issued Regulation 6, which allowed wage and fringe increases only up to 10 percent of rates in effect on January 15, 1950. The labor members of WSB who had fought for 12 percent and who were in any event dissatisfied with what they felt were inequities in the stabilization program, resigned en masse, as did labor representatives associated with seven other Government agencies.

The mass resignations created a stabilization crisis that proved difficult to compromise. A means had to be found to bring labor members back to the stabilization agencies, particularly WSB, without alienating industry members. Perhaps the chief point of controversy in the following weeks was whether any special machinery should be established for settlement of labor disputes affecting mobilization and defense. The argument of those who opposed special machinery, industry spokesmen for the most part, was that the Taft-Hartley national emergency machinery was still effective, and that in any event mixing disputes machinery with wage stabilization would impair stabilization in that it would mix economic and noneconomic issues. Behind this latter argument was the recurrent fear, expressed by industry and reflected in congressional debate, that a disputes board might again order union security provisions objectionable to industry.

The opposing view shared by the administration was that disputes must be handled on a case by case basis, and that settlement chances would be hopelessly crippled if it could not handle all important issues in a dispute. Those who argued this way pointed out that labor disputes cover both economic and noneconomic issues, and their settlement requires a realistic acceptance of this fact. They felt further that the vague language of Title V of the Defense Production Act of 1950 authorized disputes settlement functions within WSB.

Finally, after weeks of meetings between Government, industry, and labor officials, a decision was approved by the newly created National Advisory Board on Mobilization Policy. The WSB was reconstituted on April 21, again tripartite, but with 18 members instead of 9. Additionally, it was given jurisdiction over disputes threatening interruption of national defense work either upon joint submission by the parties or referral by the President. In the latter case, the Board was to investigate and report directly to the President with recommendations. No action was to be taken incompatible with the Taft-Hartley Act, and recommendations were to be binding only upon prior agreement of the parties.

The process of resolving this crisis had been essentially one of bargaining with top representatives of labor and management. The solution, which largely mollified labor's leadership, still left industry representatives with a sense of injury. Their feelings were made known in the subsequent controversy over renewal of the Defense Production Act during the summer of 1951.

Hearings on renewal were held by the labor committees of both House and Senate, and involved essentially the same issues that had been in controversy at the time of reconstitution of the WSB. The congressional proposals that were of most concern to the administration were the so-called Lucas Committee amendments, reported from the House labor committee, but supported by Senator Taft as well. These were threefold: (a) to change the tripartite character of the WSB to a board of public members only; (b) to limit its function solely to that of making recommendations to the ESA director; and (c) to eliminate its disputes function, returning to mediation and Taft-Hartley as the sole method of resolving disputes. These proposals were eventually defeated and the Defense Production Act reenacted largely in its original form.

The few months following were relatively peaceful on the domestic stabilization front, but all those concerned with the stabilization program were aware that a major struggle was ahead in steel. Evidence of impending trouble began to accumulate in October 1951. Various steelworker locals began to pass resolutions calling for "substantial" wage increases. Simultaneously it was rumored that the industry would demand price increases to offset generally rising costs, plus additional amounts to compensate for any wage increase. The battle with the Government had begun.

Free Collective Bargaining

At the end of October 1951, with the industry operating at 104 percent of capacity, letters giving notice of contract cancellation went out to all the steel companies. The steel industry had rebounded sharply from the 1949 recession and output and profits were at historic peaks. From the union's point of view this was fortunate, for this was to be the first opportunity for general contract revision since 1947.

In the second week in November the Steelworkers' Wage Policy Committee approved 22 demands, the chief ones being:

1. A substantial wage increase.
2. Elimination of all geographic differentials.
3. Increase in shift differentials.
4. Time and one-half for Saturday, double-time for Sunday.
5. Eight holidays, double-time if worked.
6. Two weeks' vacation after 2 years' service, 3 after 5, 4 after 15.
7. Guaranteed annual wage after 3 years' service.
8. Full union shop and checkoff.
9. Limitations of subcontracting.
10. Modification of contract provisions concerning seniority, grievance procedure, local work practices, job eligibility and scheduling, pensions, insurance, discrimination, and safety.
11. Companywide agreements with uniform expiration dates.

In the face of these proposals, Bethlehem Steel announced it would have "no offer to make," and Fairless stated publicly that the wage issue "probably cannot be determined by collective bargaining and will apparently have to be decided finally in Washington." [45]

Contract negotiations with U.S. Steel began on November 26, and the first 4 days were concerned with the presentation of union demands. The company too had proposals:

1. Company to have complete freedom to rearrange duties and assign the work, and to establish, change, or terminate jobs.
2. Incentive rates to be established by company on the basis of a centralized manual of engineering.

Murray said these would turn the clock back to the 19th century, and waited in vain for an economic counterproposal. A few more days of perfunctory meetings, a recess, and the "negotiations" were "deadlocked," with the contract expiring on December 31.

Cyrus Ching called in the parties on December 20:

As director of the Federal Mediation Service, I had been in touch with the parties for several months before the expiration of the contract, and finally called the negotiators to Washington in an effort to break the impasse. The industry took the position that the noneconomic issues, of which the union shop demand was a big one, must be settled before they would talk about money. The union * * * said money matters should be dealt with first. The steel companies, saying the Government would set the final terms anyway, * * * made no offer. Neither side would move from its position, and there was no room for mediation. [46]

However, the companies were bargaining—but with the Government, not the union. To the industry an agreement with the Government on price relief was a precondition of a wage offer. The Government felt that tying price increases to wage increases would destroy stabilization, and in any event, there was no one since Agency in a position to make this kind of deal. After a meeting with Fairless, Roger Putnam, the new ESA Administrator, announced the steel companies were "bargaining with their own money." The company replied that it would defend stabilization, and would forego price increases if the union would forego wage increases. Philip Murray termed this "callous" and the union's Wage Policy Committee voted a strike on December 31.

To the administration it was unthinkable that a strike should occur. The old objections to Taft-Hartley still existed, but the alternative for which the administration had fought was at hand. In the words of former President Truman:

* * * The Taft-Hartley Act had been designed for peacetime labor problems. The Wage Stabilization Board, however, had been established especially for defense labor disputes and had been reaffirmed by Congress in this function within the year. The kind of situation we were facing caused me to turn to the Wage Stabilization Board. [47]

At this point, however, Taft-Hartley was apparently not unthinkable to the President. Murray had arranged for his Wage Policy Committee to commit him to strike on December 31, thus insuring a stoppage until the decision could be reversed at a special union convention called for January 3, 1952. Upon hearing that Murray would not guarantee continuous work if the dispute were sent to

[45] *New York Times*, Nov. 16, 1951, p. 17.
[46] Cyrus S. Ching, *Review and Reflection*, Forbes, 1953, p. 99.
[47] Harry S. Truman, *Years of Trial and Hope*, Doubleday, 1956, II, p. 467.

WSB, the President ordered his staff to "draw up the Taft-Hartley papers." [48] Murray was advised of this and arranged to have his hands untied.

On Christmas eve 1951, the President called on both sides to accept certification of the dispute to the WSB for its study and recommendation. The companies accepted immediately; the union accepted on December 27.

The crisis was postponed. The union convention authorized a 45-day strike postponement and work continued. Excitement over the dispute subsided as the parties turned to making a major presentation of their case to the Government.

Wage Stabilization Board

The Wage Board set up a special panel of six members headed by Harry Shulman to hear the presentation of the parties. The industry once again set up a "coordinating committee" representing 35 companies to present its case, but the presentations of both sides nevertheless took 1 month. Not until March 13 did the panel submit to the WSB its 66 page report which merely summarized without recommendation the proposals, arguments, and counterarguments of each on 23 different issues.

Now bargaining began within the WSB, but time was short and pressures were again building up. OPS was leaking stories that price increases of $2 to $3 a ton were available under current regulations, but the steel industry ignored this tentative offer. The union had twice given extensions of the strike deadline at the request of WSB Chairman Nathan Feisinger, but was keeping on the pressure with an ever-greater show of reluctance to any additional delay. The industry had meanwhile undertaken a massive campaign in press, radio, and television to demonstrate that the union was once again using Government to try to force the "un-American" union shop upon them. The administration suddenly began to wonder what was going to be in the WSB decision and what would happen if a settlement were not produced.

In the midst of all of this the public members of the WSB took the initiative in meeting with industry and union representatives to find an area of unanimous recommendation, or, failing this, at least a majority recommendation. On March 18, the employer members of the board suggested a 13.7 cent package of 9 cents an hour and fringe benefits. This proved too low for union acceptance. The following day Feinsinger proposed to the employer representatives a 17.6 cent package for 1 year, composed of 12½ cents wages and various fringes. This was too high for industry acceptance. The nub of the board's difficulty with the economic package recommendation revolved around the problem of the annual improvement factor of 4 cents, called for in the auto agreements. In cases coming voluntarily before the board, there had been approval of a 12½ cent package composed of 8½ cents for cost-of-living and 4 cents for the improvement factor. The board had never made a recommendation of such a settlement, however, and if it were to recommend 12½ cents in the steel case, this figure, which had been the maximum, would become the new minimum for which all unions would strive. Therefore, the industry proposal which did not include the improvement factor was unacceptable to the union. The Feinsinger proposal, which did include it, was not acceptable to the industry members.

The public members encountered similar rebuffs on the crucial union shop issue. They proposed to both sides that the issue be returned to the parties for further bargaining, but in event of failure to agree, to be brought back to the

---

[48] Enarson, *op. cit.*, p. 54, n. 13.

WSB. This proposal was rejected by the union representatives because it did not contain a strong enough recommendation favoring the union shop, and by the industry representatives because it implied that the Board might later award the union shop if the parties failed to negotiate it.

At this point some of the public members suggested that it would be appropriate to issue a separate public-member report advocating a middle-ground settlement, allowing industry and labor representatives to dissent if they cared to. Chairman Feinsinger rejected this approach, insisting that the obligation to try to find a solution for the dispute required the public members to at least find an acceptable majority solution and, hopefully, that public pressure would force the dissenting third party to go along.

It appeared that industry's position was the more rigid; even that the industry representatives would dissent to almost any recommendations regardless of what they might be. Therefore, the public members turned to bargaining with labor for a majority recommendation. After two days and nights of intense negotiations a public-labor majority recommendation of wage and fringe benefits, plus the union shop, was submitted to the public. In essence, the public members justified the recommendations on the basis that it was about like the 1951 auto settlement, composed of cost-of-living, plus one annual improvement factor, and with the addition of one more annual improvement factor for the extra 6 months of an 18-month agreement. The only new costly fringe involved was that of time and one-quarter for Sunday work. In detail, the recommendations were:

1. An 18-month agreement, expiring June 30, 1953.
2. A 12½ cent increase, retroactive to expiration date, 2½ cents after 6 months, 2½ cents after 12 months.
3. A 5 cent reduction in southern differentials.
4. Six paid holidays, double time if worked.
5. Shift differentials increased to 6 cents and 9 cents.
6. Sunday premium of one and one-quarter time.
7. Three weeks' vacation after 15 years' service.
8. Union shop, details to be negotiated by the parties.
9. Joint committee to study GAW.
10. Penalties for sporadic rescheduling.
11. Companies to provide union with accurate seniority lists.
12. Incentive pay inequities returned to parties for further negotiation, with guidelines set forth.

Proposals on a number of issues were withdrawn: reporting allowance, subcontracting, local working conditions, job structure, and management rights. Although the public members of the WSB felt that the companies were serious about their proposals, especially in regard to local working practices, Shulman had advised that it was not a critical issue in which the Government should be involved, so no attempt was even made to suggest an approach the parties might take to solving such problems.

Industry members dissented bitterly from the recommendations, and a nine-page commentary and explanation by Chairman Feinsinger did not help to counteract their criticism. The Nation's press, following the industry member's claim in their dissent, immediately characterized it as a "26-cent package," largely ignoring the fact that it was to run half again as long as the standard 1-year agreement. Twenty-six cents looked high, and the immediate public reaction was critical. The union accepted the recommendations immediately; the industry as promptly rejected.

The Crisis in Stabilization

Spokesmen for the steel industry immediately announced that the recommendations would cost 28.8 cents an hour, and if they were met would require a price increase of $12 a ton. The union's Wage Policy Committee voted to resume negotiations, but that if no agreement on the recommendation was reached by April 4, to give a 96-hour strike notice. On March 21, the six largest companies met with the union in New York, but the meeting was fruitless.

Defense Mobilizer Wilson, after meeting with the steel companies, met with President Truman in Key West, and returned to Washington with what he felt was authority to offer the steel industry whatever price increase was necessary to settle the dispute. An incautious Wilson statement critical of the WSB recommendation angered Murray, who refused to meet with Wilson. ESA Director Putnam and OPS Director Ellis Arnall both apparently refused to allow Wilson to jeopardize price stabilization without their public protest. After a series of meetings with all concerned, including another with the President in which Wilson felt his approach had been repudiated, Wilson resigned, stating that the Government's wage-price policies were inequitable and that "I cannot accept public responsibility for major stabilization actions which I cannot control."

From the administration's point of view, it had been a choice between supporting Wilson or losing control of price stabilization and the Wage Stabilization Board. After further analysis, the WSB proposals did not look too high, particularly in light of what were felt to be exorbitant industry price demands. The loss of Wilson, although serious from a public relations point of view, was less serious than the alternatives. In any event, he had not found the solution for the crisis.

John R. Steelman, a former Director of the Conciliation Service, and currently the Assistant to the President, was named to replace Wilson as Director of Mobilization, and promptly acted in the steel crisis. He named Feinsinger as special mediator, and meetings were resumed. On April 3, the major steel producers made their first offer, 5 months after negotiations had begun. The making of the offer was presumably influenced by the fact that OPS Director Arnall, after meetings with Steelman and Fairless, had made a new "best offer" to the companies on price—$4.50 a ton, or about a dollar less than Wilson had had in mind. The industry offer to the union was a 14½-cent 1-year package—9 cents retroactive to March 1, and fringes as in the WSB recommendations, but no Sunday premium. The offer further included additional 2½ cent increases in July and January, but no union shop. Murray insisted upon the full WSB recommendation, including the union shop, and Feinsinger's efforts on April 4 to bring the parties closer together were unavailing.[49]

Seizure

At this point the White House, faced with the possibility of a steel strike, had the following alternatives open to it should the threat become real:

1. *The Taft-Hartley Act.* The use of the national emergency provisions offered the easy way out in terms of public and congressional opinion. On the other hand, the appointment of a factfinding board seemed inappropriate, and would surely destroy any remaining hope of a negotiated settlement. Its use seemed unfair in that the injunction was largely directed at the union, no longer considered by the President to be the recalcitrant party, and because the union had already voluntarily delayed beyond the 80 days

[49] According to contemporary observers, mediation of this dispute was unusually difficult. The industry was not anxious to settle and told the mediators this. On the union side, Murray was ill, uncooperative, and unusually adamant.

of delay the injunction would have provided. Moreover, using the provisions now would discredit the WSB, and raise the possibility that no union would in the future take its disputes to the Board.

2. *Seizure under Section 18 of the Selective Service Act.* Under this Act the President was empowered to place orders with plants producing articles for the Armed Forces; failure to fill the order was ground for seizure. Application of this Act did not eem appropriate when what was deemed needed was not individual products but the whole output of the industry, only a small part of which was direct defense needs. The Defense Department felt unable to specify its needs, and time to draw up the necessary orders was lacking before the April 8 deadline.

3. *Seizure under the "inherent powers" of the President.* This alternative would keep the mills operating, since it was assumed that Murray would cooperate. On the other hand there were constitutional problems, although the Justice Department felt these could be overcome. Certainly, too, a substantial group in Congress would object. However, this approach seemed to be the best choice.

The President, therefore, ordered seizure papers drawn up, while news of this was leaked out in the hope that it might encourage voluntary settlement. Up to the last few hours it was hoped that Feinsinger could produce a settlement. On the last day for negotiations he again met with the parties. Stephens indicated that U.S. Steel would raise its offer to 12½ cents, plus 5½ cents for fringes, but no Sunday premium, no union shop, and no subsequent wage increases. Stephens and Murray met personally later in the day, but at the end Murray said: "The strike order stands."

By the time Feinsinger reported failure to the White House it was late afternoon of April 8, steel furnaces were being banked, and the men would leave the mills at midnight. President Truman held a last minute conference of the Defense Mobilization Board, all of whose members warned of the disastrous consequences of a strike. In the President's words:

All of this presented a very serious picture. The Congress was debating and doing a lot of talking about the steel crisis, and I would have welcomed any practical solution from it. But discussion was not enough. I had to act to prevent the stoppage of steel production, which would imperil the Nation * * *. I could see no alternative but to order the seizure of the steel mills by the Government.[50]

At 10:30 p.m. that evening the President spoke to the Nation and announced that he was directing the Secretary of Commerce to take over the steel mills at midnight. The President's speech was harsh, and laid almost the entire blame for the impasse upon the industry. He defended the fairness of the WSB recommendations, and accused the industry of trying to obtain preferential price treatment at a time when, even if they absorbed the entire cost of the WSB recommendations, they would be left with profits of $17 to $18 a ton. However, he did not mention the union shop and neglected to say that these were profits before taxes, points that were not overlooked in a scathing radio rebuttal by Clarence Randall, president of Inland Steel, the following evening.

In response to the President's announcement Secretary of Commerce Charles Sawyer wired the companies that he was taking possession and ordered them to perform their "usual functions and duties." Murray immediately called off the strike, the furnaces were reheated and production was resumed.

The following morning, April 9, several companies filed motions in Federal District Court, Washington, D.C., for a temporary restraining order against the seizure as an unlawful act. On the next day Judge Alexander Holtzoff denied the application on the basis that he did not believe he should enjoin the Presi-

[50] Truman, op. cit., p. 470.

dent or his agent where the plaintiffs had adequate remedies by way of action for damages. The companies then went ahead with their motion for a preliminary injunction before Judge David Pine, also of the Federal District Court in Washington, D.C. This motion was set for trial on April 24. An important constitutional argument was slowly building.

Meanwhile, on April 10, Steelman brought the companies and union together in Washington for further bargaining. Steelman now attempted mediation personally, but without success. Fairless again conferred with Arnall, but no settlement was announced. Negotiations continued for several more days until Steelman announced they were being temporarily abandoned. The union's Wage Policy Committee met and passed a resolution requesting the Government to institute the WSB recommendations and noted that the steelworkers' patience was "not inexhaustible." Congress authorized four different hearings to investigate the seizure, and the general tenor of congressional statement was hostile to the President's action. On April 18, Secretary Sawyer announced that if agreement was not soon reached the Government would grant the recommended wage increase, whereupon the steel companies amended their injunction petition to request injunction against any changes in wages and working conditions.

In hearings before Judge Pine on April 24 and 25, the administration finally lost the battle for public support. Under probing from the Court, counsel for the Government made the oral claim that the power of the President to meet emergencies was unlimited by law or the Constitution. This statement was greeted by a storm of congressional and newspaper criticism, which subsequent disclaimers by the White House and the Justice Department never were able to quell. The administration, already defending its refusal to use Taft-Hartley, now had another rearguard action to fight.

On April 29, Judge Pine ruled the seizure illegal, maintaining that the results of any strike would be "less injurious to the public than the injury which would flow from a timorous judicial recognition that there is some basis for a claim to unlimited and unrestrained executive power."[51] In less than an hour after Pine's decision steelworkers began to walk off their jobs as Murray ordered the strike to begin.

The Government at this time still considered a strike unthinkable. A hasty decision was made to appeal Judge Pine's decision to the Supreme Court and request Murray to call off the strike while the appeal was pending. The Court of Appeals granted a stay of Pine's order, refusing to attach a freeze on wages requested by the steel companies. Thus, seizure was maintained during the appeal to the Supreme Court, and made possible a successful appeal to the union to return to work. On May 2, the strike was called off.

On May 3, one more attempt to settle the dispute was made. The President called the parties to the White House and told the negotiators that unless the dispute was settled by Monday, May 5, he would order changes in the terms and conditions of steel employment. Presumably he would have instituted the WSB recommendations. Under this threat bargaining was resumed. Stephens and Murray began to meet separately and quietly, and all observers were optimistic. Suddenly, on May 4, at 5:00 p.m. word was received that the Supreme Court had granted certiorari, but had forbidden the Government to change employment conditions. All pressure for settlement evaporated. The negotiations broke off amid angry charges and countercharges, and nothing constructive in the way

---

[51] *Youngstown Sheet and Tube Corp.* v. *Sawyer*, 103 F. Supp. 569 (D.C.D.C. 1952).

of negotiation was accomplished during the month the Supreme Court had the case under advisement.

Extensive oral argument was conducted before the Supreme Court on May 12 and 13, and on June 2 the Court's decision was handed down. The President's seizure of the steel mills was unconstitutional.[52]

Strike

At 2:00 p.m., June 2, Murray called the steelworkers out on strike. Barely 2 hours after the Supreme Court's decision, the men began to leave the mills and within 24 hours 560,000 workers in basic steel and iron-ore mines were idle. The unthinkable strike had occurred and no one seemed to have immediate plans for ending it.

With the constitutional question answered, however, the dispute was once again a problem in industrial relations. The President had immediately ordered the steel mills returned to their owners. He also sent another message to the Congress, reporting his action and suggesting that the Congress might accept the Court's suggestion that it take some action. Congress did not act. The President could still use Taft-Hartley if he chose. On June 11, the Senate formally recommended that he do so.

Bargaining between the parties again seemed possible, despite the strike. Steelman once more called the parties to the White House, and negotiations on June 5–9 made some progress. On June 8, the industry was ready to make a new offer. It included a 16-cent wage increase and 5 cents in fringes for a 2-year contract with a wage reopener in the second year. More importantly perhaps, the companies indicated some flexibility on the union shop. It was indicated they might do something in the second year, or that they might allow the union to solicit members at the time of hiring of new employees. A tentative settlement was even reached on price. The industry indicated that $4.50 a ton might be satisfactory if the Government would add the amount of a recent freight increase, or another 70 cents a ton. Steelman indicated this was reasonable, and settlement seemed very close.

Murray, however, rejected the company offer on union solicitation of new hires. After a 24-hour hiatus during which Fairless urged Steelman to keep the meetings going, the company negotiators suddenly back-tracked on the hint that something could be done on the union shop later during the life of the agreement. Industry principals had decided to hold firm against any union shop concession. The negotiations collapsed and the strike dragged on.

Although it is common among most students of the 1952 steel dispute to characterize it as an industry strike against Government price policy, and to deprecate the industry's position on the union shop as a public relations smoke screen, these events show that the strike itself was purely a labor-management conflict over union security with some few economic items still in dispute. The industry proposal of June 8, to which all parties gave tentative assent at the White House in early June, and the price commitment of $5.20 a ton, were almost identical with the settlement that came 6 weeks later.[53] Whether the industry's willingness

---

[52] *Youngstown Sheet and Tube Corp.* v. *Sawyer,* 343 U.S. 579 (1952). Justice Black spoke for the Court, but each of the six members of the majority felt the question presented in the case was important enough to file separate concurring opinions. Chief Justice Vinson and two other members of the Court dissented.

[53] John Stephens made this explicit in testimony before the Congress a year later. U.S. Senate, Hearings before the Committee on Labor and Public Welfare, "Proposed Revisions of the Labor Management Relations Act of 1947," 83d Cong., 1st sess. (1953), p. 855.

to take the strike on the union shop issue resulted from a long-maintained philosophical objection, or whether they had become imprisoned by their own intensive public relations campaign on the issue is an open question. In any event, an important contributory factor to the strike must undoubtedly have been the emotional attitudes engendered by 6 months of intense struggle. Bitterness and frustration arising out of personal conflict between the bargainers and constant entanglement with the Government certainly affected the parties. While such subjective influences cannot be measured in precise terms, they are often as important as "real" issues.

One of the reasons why negotiations were permitted to break off without a settlement in sight and why President Truman resisted repeated congressional and editorial pressure for the use of a Taft-Hartley injunction was that the strike had few immediate visible effects. Upon resumption of the strike in June, the National Production Authority gave defense orders top priority in nonstruck plants. The NPA also allocated all shipments of finished steel at the mills to defense needs during the weeks of strike. Union and management cooperated fully in shipping finished steel, but no system of mill reopening was ever agreed upon or put into effect, despite many meetings between industry, union, and NPA officials.

Not until June 20 were full joint efforts at negotiations renewed. During the previous week the union had reached a tentative settlement with Bethlehem Steel on the union security issue. The so-called Bethlehem formula would require new employees to make application for membership and authorize dues deductions, but the applications could be revoked by notice to the company and union within 20 days. However, some other major companies rejected the Bethlehem formula and, since all were negotiating together, it was rejected. One of the minor producers, Pittsburgh Steel, signed an agreement based on the formula, but no major producer deviated from the industry policy.

Off-the-record meetings in late June and early July produced nothing. The union refused to consider anything less than the Bethlehem formula: the companies met privately and decided against further concessions. Negotiations were again broken off and the strike dragged on. President Truman commented tersely on the situation in his press conference:

> I understand that a good many of the steel companies are ready to settle with the union on all the issues. I also understand that these companies are being prevented from settling because pressure is being put on them by other steel companies. This appears to me to be a conspiracy against the public interest and not a labor dispute * * *.[54]

The union filed formal charges under the Taft-Hartley Act against U. S. Steel, Bethlehem, Jones and Laughlin, Republic, Youngstown, and Inland charging a conspiracy among them to prevent each other or any other company from making a separate settlement. The union also attempted to get the Justice Department to institute antitrust actions against the steel companies. Nothing came of either effort.

On July 10, the negotiators met in Pittsburgh. Concurrent meetings between industry officials and Steelman nailed down what had been certain for weeks— a $5.20 a ton price increase could be had whenever a new labor agreement was signed. It seemed as if agreement was certain, when on the 14th the negotiations were again broken off.

The parties met again on July 20, at Steelman's request. On July 21 the unions Wage Policy Committee met, and for the first time in the history of

---

[54] New York Times, July 4, 1952, p. 1.

the relationship industry representatives accepted a routine invitation to attend the meeting and present their case to the delegates. Stephens, Ben Moreell of Jones and Laughlin, and John M. Larkin and John Morse of Bethlehem, attended the meeting. Before they spoke, Murray summarized the issues remaining in dispute as (1) union shop, (2) management's insistence upon contract changes allowing greater authority over crew sizes, and (3) iron mine wage rates. The company representatives expressed surprise that the union shop was such an issue with the delegates, emphasized that little remained to be worked out, and said that the union had gained a "hell of a victory" in concessions already made by management. After the company representatives had made their presentations, and had sat down to applause, Murray asked the delegates whether they wanted to modify their earlier resolution calling for the full WSB proposals. The answer was shouted back, "No!"

Once again an impasse, although the margin between the parties was minute. Suddenly, Secretary of Defense Lovett gave all concerned a strong push. On July 23d he called a press conference and announced that he had kept silent until he could document the fact that the national defense program faced catastrophe because of a shortage of steel. After 51 days the mobilization program was coming to a complete halt.

Settlement

Lovett's strongly worded statement precipitated renewed action. Telegrams went out to the parties asking them to meet at the White House on July 24. That morning the President met briefly with Fairless and Murray and told them that the stoppage must be ended, and ended that day.

Within a few hours Fairless and Murray reached agreement. The cost-package was about the same as the one that had been available for over a month, and the union shop issue was settled with an agreement roughly similar to the Bethlehem formula. The agreement specified that a new employee must apply for union membership to take effect within 30 days, unless revoked by the applicant in the last 15 days of the 30-day period following employment. All union members were given the right to drop membership within the last 15 days of the contract. The company had maintained the principle of voluntary union membership; yet for practical purposes the union had the benefit of virtually complete membership in the plants.

Other major items in the U.S. Steel settlement package, in summary, were:

1. A 12½ cent general wage increase, plus one-half cent increase in increments between job classes, the total averaging 16 cents, effective March 1, 1952.
2. A 5 cent reduction in southern differential, effective July 25, 1952.
3. Six paid holidays, double-time if worked, effective August 15, 1952.
4. Three weeks' vacation after 15 years' service, effective January 1, 1952.
5. Grievance arbitration board changed to single-member and function limited solely to arbitration.
6. Modified maintenance of membership as described above.
7. Procedure established for setting up interim and modified incentives.
8. Procedure established for adjusting incentives installed between 1947 and 1952.
9. When completed, the job description and classification manual to be made a part of the contract.
10. Company to furnish union with up-to-date seniority lists every 6 months.
11. A 2-year contract to run to June 30, 1954, reopenable by either party on June 30, 1953, on the subject of wage adjustments only, with a right to strike or lockout in the event of failure to agree.

At 4:45 p.m. July 24, the President announced to reporters that agreement had been reached. Then, suddenly, the end of the strike was delayed. Fairless and Murray had not, as part of their understanding, reached full agreement on iron-ore mine wages. By the time Murray returned from the White House to his office, it was realized that there was still no settlement acceptable to workers on the Mesabi range.

During steel strikes in previous years iron-ore workers had continued at work at the behest of the union's International. As a consequence, when a basic steel strike was settled, iron-ore miners had slight economic strength remaining and had been forced to accept what they felt to be inferior settlements. In 1952 the miners had refused to stay at work building up a stockpile during the strike. This time the miners were determined to obtain a settlement while they still had economic strength.

The strike continued for 2 more days. Finally, the miners obtained what they felt was a satisfactory comparability on wages and fringes. On July 26, both steelworkers and miners started back to work. The strike, originally considered unthinkable during a time of heavy wartime demand and international crisis, had lasted 59 days.

Regardless of what the gains or losses of the parties may have been, the large objectives of Government policy were lost. From an initial position that a strike could not be endured, the position shifted to acceptance of what was then the longest strike in steel history. Economic stabilization also suffered, both from the effects of a large wage increase as well as a substantial price increase. In the longrun the disputes powers of the WSB were lost as well, for Congress refused to reenact them. Last, but certainly not least, the Administration lost the fight for public support. Through refusal to use Taft-Hartley, the President became convicted in the public's eyes of reaching for unchecked power—although in reality the Government actually had insufficient influence to accomplish any one of its major objectives.

1953 BASIC STEEL WAGE REOPENING

The 1952 CIO convention was scheduled for November in Los Angeles. While en route, Philip Murray, whose health had not been good for several years, died suddenly. Murray's death left vacant both the presidencies of the CIO and of the United Steelworkers of America. After a bitter convention battle, Walter Reuther was elected president of the CIO. David J. McDonald, secretary-treasurer of the Steelworkers, was named acting president of the union by its executive board pending the regular election scheduled in February 1953. While Murray had never made real plans for the Steelworker succession, and had actually moved to reduce McDonald's powers somewhat in previous years, it was still generally accepted that McDonald was the heir apparent.

In February 1953, McDonald was elected to a full 4-year term as president. He was 50 years old and had been in association with Murray for 30 years. He had been Murray's personal secretary in the United Mine Workers, had been appointed secretary-treasurer of the SWOC at its inception, and in 1942 had been elected to the same position in the Steelworkers union. McDonald had a flair for public speaking and a broad international union background. However, he had no substantial experience as a worker either in the mines or mills. Without Murray's firm base of personal loyalty from the average steelworker, there was considerable speculation early in 1953 where McDonald could lead the Steelworkers union as cohesively or effectively in future negotiations as it had been in the past.

The 1952 contracts between the Steelworkers and the major steel companies were reopenable on or before May 1, 1953, "with respect to a general and uniform change in wage rates" only, with the right to strike or lockout if no agreement was reached by June 30, 1953. The master agreement would not terminate until June 1954.

The union's Wage Policy Committee met at the end of April 1953, and agreed to place three requests upon the companies.

1. General wage increase, amount unspecified.
2. Elimination of all geographical differentials.
3. Joint studies of guaranteed annual wage (GAW), pensions, and insurance.

So far as business conditions were concerned, it seemed an excellent time for the union to negotiate for an increase. The national economy was booming and demand for steel was at peak levels. Production was running at 95–100 percent of capacity and future orders were strong and well distributed. Many companies were operating behind schedules on current orders and had future books filled for 4 to 6 months. Although all steel indicators, including profits, had been down in 1952 owing to the strike, 1953 promised to be an extremely good year.

Negotiations opened on May 14, with U.S. Steel and Youngstown Sheet and Tube, and were followed within a few days by negotiations with other major companies. Early in the talks McDonald admitted in the U.S. Steel negotiations that the union could not strike to enforce the demands for joint studies. At this point the companies agreed to listen sympathetically to union proposals for the study of pensions and insurance, but not of GAW. Early in June agreement on this problem was reached. U.S. Steel and a number of other companies agreed by separate letter that the joint committee on insurance and pensions, established by the 1949 agreement, would meet regularly during the next year to analyze a large number of specified problems. The committee would not negotiate or bargain on these problems, but would be ready with the facts and recommendations in time for the 1954 negotiation.

As steel negotiations proceeded, the companies made public statements that no wage increase was justified, citing the fact the CPI had remained almost stable since the last increase. Despite these statements, McDonald remained calm and made no strike threats.

On May 22, an announcement was made that vitiated the steel industry's "no increase" position. General Motors had acceded to the UAW's "living document" approach, and reached agreement with the union on wage and fringe changes that would substantially improve a contract that still had 2 years to run. Ford followed in a few days with even more substantial improvements. From this time on, it was apparent that the Steelworkers would get something, the question being the size of the wage increase and the amount and timing of the price increase to follow.

To the surprise of most observers, the settlement of U.S. Steel came on June 12, almost 3 weeks before the deadline. Negotiations had brought on an argument between the company and the union as to the price of the automobile settlement. U.S. Steel had said it was worth no more than 6½ cents an hour, the union had argued it would cost the automobile manufacturers 9.6 cents. As a consequence of this difference, the Steelworkers asked a 10 cent across the board increase; U.S. Steel offered 5 cents on base rates.

On June 12, the union's district directors waited in one hotel in Pittsburgh while U.S. Steel representatives met at another. The company indicated they had a new offer to make, but were reluctant to believe that the union would accept a final offer so early. McDonald was reported as convincing Stephens that he would "sell" any "reasonable" offer to the Wage Policy Committee, and after 12 hours of shuttling back and forth between the hotels the negotiation was over. The settlement was announced as:

1. A 8½ cents general wage increase, effective June 12, three weeks before expiration.
2. Reduction of the southern differential in two steps, 2½ cents effective January 1, 1954 and 2½ cents effective July 1, 1954.
3. Elimination of some geographic differentials; most effective immediately; a few in 6 months.

Most other major producers announced an 8½ cent settlement the same day. Other companies with geographic differentials, primarily Republic, agreed to reduce or eliminate them. By June 19, all major contracts in basic steel were signed. Even before all contracts were signed U.S. Steel, followed by the rest of the industry, announced price increases averaging $4 a ton. Neither congressional leaders nor spokesmen for the new administration in Washington offered comment on the increases.

Immediately after the U.S. Steel settlement, McDonald and Stephens had high praise for each other, using such phrases as "statesmanlike conduct" and "honorable compromise." In addition, Clifford Hood, the president of U.S. Steel, who had earlier said that no increase was appropriate, said that the company had reversed itself because of a desire to have the workers feel they were fairly treated, and "patterns set in other industries." [55] However, at least two other company motives can be fairly assumed. First, the brisk state of the steel market made it easy to increase prices and pass any cost increases on to steel users. Second, the industry apparently wanted to get off to a good start with McDonald. A quietly negotiated reasonable settlement would convince him that the industry did not intend to use the death of Murray or the end of Democratic rule in Washington as a pretext for undermining the union or forcing it to strike to make reasonable collective bargaining gains.

One other factor operative in the relations between U.S. Steel and the Steelworkers at the time was the attitude of the leadership of the corporation itself. Early in 1953, Benjamin Fairless, who had been president of U.S. Steel since 1938, had become chairman of the board of directors and the chief executive officer of U.S. Steel. Fairless had never been fundamentally hostile to the union and apparently felt fewer compunctions about making concessions to the union as the price of peace than some of his predecessors. John Stephens, long-time vice president of U.S. Steel for industrial relations, had developed a good personal relationship with Murray and later with McDonald, and fitted in well with Fairless' apparent intentions toward the union.

As evidence of Fairless' attitude, a byproduct of the 1952 strike settlement had been that Murray and Fairless would make a joint tour of U.S. Steel plants. The stated purpose of the trips was to give both men the opoprtunity to observe, firsthand, union-management relations at the local plant level and also lead to a better understanding by local union and management officials of each others' problems. Murray died before any visits were made, but McDonald and Fairless agreed to carry out the plan. The visits were made during November and December 1953 and January 1954, arousing favorable newspaper publicity and editorial comment. What they may have done for the longrun relations between U.S. Steel and the Steelworkers is not readily apparent; at least they were

---

[55] *New York Times*, June 13, 1953, pp. 1, 34.

symptomatic of a desire for a better working and collective bargaining relationship. The 1953–54 period probably represents the second high-water mark in peaceful labor relations in the steel industry. The desire of each party for harmony was similar to the 1947 period, and again made steel collective bargaining a fruitful and comparatively peaceful process.

1954 BASIC STEEL CONTRACT NEGOTIATION

It was commonly thought that the 1954 negotiations in steel would be both significant and difficult. For the first time since 1949 negotiations were to take place against a background of recession. The whole contract was open for negotiation, and in addition, the 1949 pension and welfare agreements, which originally had been scheduled to expire in October of 1954, had, as a stipulation of the 1953 settlement, been made a part of the 1954 contract renegotiation. The guaranteed annual wage, talked about for years in labor-management circles, was felt to be a serious issue with the Steelworkers. Finally, this was to be David McDonald's first full contract renegotiation, and there was speculation over whether he could repeat his 1953 achievement of making substantial gains without an overt strike threat.

The first move in the 1954 negotiations came 9 months before the contract was to expire, in October 1953. An unusual wage-policy meeting was held, dubbed "Operation Sound-off" by the union, in which the leadership was to hear the desires of the rank-and-file for changes in the contract. In his remarks to the delegates McDonald stated that pensions, insurance, and the GAW were to be the major demands. However, McDonald described his attitude as "flexible." [56] The union's general counsel, Arthur Goldberg, also spoke, and stressed that gains would probably not be as large as some present would like. Even as this meeting was going on, the economic indicators for the steel industry, which had looked so promising a few months before, began to turn down.

By January 1954, operations were down to 75 percent of capacity, compared with the previous year's average of 95 percent. Average weekly hours and manhours worked were down over 15 percent from the previous fall.

Later, in the spring, it was estimated that 190,000 steelworkers were on layoff, and another quarter–million were on short work-weeks. Profits were down as well. First quarter sales in 1954 were off substantially and before-tax profits were down 35 percent from the same period in the previous year.

When the union's Wage Policy Committee met again, in May, to prepare demands, the economic picture for the industry was one of low-level operations, reduced profits, and substantial unemployment. Nevertheless, the demands were substantial, as follows:

1. General wage increase.
2. Elimination of all geographical differentials.
3. Two additional paid holidays.
4. Reporting pay increased from 4 to 8 hours.
5. Improved vacations.
6. Union shop.
7. Higher shift premiums.
8. Improved pensions.
9. Insurance change from contributory to noncontributory, and improve life, sickness, accident, hospital and surgical benefits.
10. A guaranteed wage plan, providing 80 percent of take-home pay for 52 weeks, funded by a 4 percent payroll contribution.
11. Changes in contract provisions covering incentives, overtime, seniority, job classification manual, subcontracting, severance pay, safety, and local working conditions.

---

[56] New York Times, Oct. 23, 1953, p. 12.

In announcing these proposals, McDonald cautioned against interpreting the June 30 contract expiration date as a strike deadline. In fact, there was little indication that a strike was anticipated by either side as the first negotiating meeting with U.S. Steel was scheduled for May 18, 1954. It was generally assumed by observers that the aftereffects of the 1952 strike, the market condition of the industry, the pattern set the previous year by the auto industry, and a still-continuing desire of the steel industry to build a friendly relationship with McDonald were all factors that would operate to create an amicable and reasonable settlement. The fact that Benjamin Fairless attended the first negotiating session, the first time a chairman of the board of U.S. Steel had ever done so, was taken as indication that the industry wished to build bargaining harmony by capitalizing on whatever good will had been created by the Fairless-McDonald tours of the previous year.

As has become traditional in steel collective bargaining, the first meeting was ritualistic in nature. It was attended by over 100 people and lasted only 2 hours. After initial statements from both sides emphasizing their desire for a quick peaceful agreement, the union presented its already widely publicized demands, made brief supporting statements, and the meeting was adjourned. On the following day the company asked a few brief questions and the meeting was adjourned for several weeks in order that the company might study the union's proposals. Meanwhile, negotiations with all other major producers were begun, demands were presented, and then, as usual, postponed pending developments in U.3. Steel negotiations.

When meetings with U.S. Steel were resumed during the first week in June, the union expanded upon its earlier arguments in support of its demands. It argued that shorter workweeks and elimination of overtime had reduced weekly earnings of steelworkers below amounts necessary to maintain an adequate standard of living. Productivity had expanded faster than real average hourly earnings, according to the union's figures, so that the steel companies still had enormous capacity to absorb a wage increase despite recent declines in profits. Wage increases in steel had lagged behind those in other industries in recent years, and wage increases were needed to maintain consumer purchasing power.

U.S. Steel replied that with the industry operating at about 70 percent of capacity, efforts should be directed at returning laid-off employees to their jobs and getting the industry back on a 40-hour week. This could not be accomplished by increasing wage costs which would dampen expansion of industry activity. In regard to the level of wage increases granted in previous years, the steel industry felt that it compared favorably with many other industries, and, in the past 4 years, had granted greater increases in wages than auto, rubber, or meatpacking industries. In light of recent declines in the CPI, the company did not accept the union's purchasing power arguments.

In reply to the union's arguments for a guaranteed wage, the company maintained that stabilization of employment was beyond the control of any one company or the industry itself because of wide fluctuations in consumer demand. For this reason unemployment should continue to be the proper concern of Government through the Federal-State unemployment compensation systems.

Despite the company's position against increased labor costs, it conceded that improvements in benefit levels for pensions and insurance were in order. The joint union-industry study of pensions and insurance undertaken during the previous year had showed that rising insurance costs had eaten up sizable reserves accumulated during the first year or so of operation. Increased costs, primarily for life insurance and hospitalization, had dropped retained reserves below the required $4 million, so that U.S. Steel had instituted an increased deduction from employees of 50 cents a month for dependent surgical coverage. Republic and Jones and Laughlin had increased employee deductions considerably more than this. In addition, insurance benefit levels were somewhat below the average of 40 other companies studied. U.S. Steel insisted, however, that despite any benefit adjustments agreed upon, the program's cost must be shared equally between the company and the employees.

In regard to pensions, the joint study had shown three major things. The industry had had an unusually high percentage of disability retirements, probably due to a rather advanced age of the work force.[57] Second owing to increases in social security voted by Congress, the cost to the steel industry for pension contributions had dropped substantially in recent years. Last, the level of pension benefits provided by the steel industry was substantially below that provided by 24 other companies studied. For these reasons U.S. Steel was prepared to offer the steelworkers improvement in the benefit levels for normal and disability retirements. However, the company maintained its position that the social security offset should be retained.

McDonald scheduled a meeting of the Wage Policy Committee for June 22, 1954. Just prior to this meeting U.S. Steel made a package offer of a 2½ cent wage increase, a minimum pension raise from $100 to $130 a month, still offset by social security, and an increase in the insurance program from 5 cents to 9 cents an hour. The insurance program was still to be contributory, however, and the increased employee contribution would just match the 2 cent wage increase offered.

McDonald, who up to this time had put his reliance on the olive branch in hope that the company would do well by him, suddenly changed his tactics. In a fighting speech to the Wage Policy Committee he accused Big Steel executives of trying to bring back the dog-eat-dog days. He inveighed against "vultures" who sought to get ahead in the corporation by showing how tough they could be toward the union, and accused them of trying to push the union into a strike. However, he specifically exempted Fairless from his charges. The Wage Policy Committee rejected the company offer and voted to go on strike on July 1, if agreement was not reached by that date.

This reversal of previous peaceful attitudes, the militancy of McDonald's speech, and the strike vote apparently came as a surprise to observers and, according to published reports, to the rank and file as well. It had always been Murray's practice to prepare carefully for a strike and build up strike sentiment for months in advance. This was McDonald's first strike threat since he had become president of the union, and it came largely without warning. It was difficult to tell whether the sudden reversal to a tougher attitude was merely a bargaining device or a portent of real trouble looming. Regardless of their surprise, it appeared that employees were ready to go on strike. The Federal Mediation and Conciliation Service, asked if it planned to intervene, officially responded that the situation was unlike 1952, and that it had not even assigned a mediator to the case.

In any event, the sudden bitter tone did not signal the end of negotiations. Stephens and McDonald continued to meet and another Wage Policy meeting

[57] During the first 3 years of the plan's operation, almost 20 percent of employees retired had done so for disability. This compared, for example, with the Ford Motor Co.-UAW pension plan, which for the similar period had experienced disability retirements of 8.5 percent. Case material of the Harvard Graduate School of Business Administration, mimeograph, 1955, p. 18.

was scheduled for June 29. Presumably company officials were aware that the auto industry had settled for 5 cents in wages, health and welfare, and pension improvement. On June 30, settlement was announced following this pattern. In detail, the settlement was as follows:

1. A 5 cents general wage increase, effective July 1, 1954.
2. Total insurance cost increased from 5 cents to 9 cents, one-half to be paid by company, and company to pay full costs of administration. Life insurance increased by $1,000 to new range of $3,000 to $5,500. Accident and sickness increased $14 to $40 a week. Hospitalization entitlement increased by 50 days to 120 days. The earlier 50 cents a month increase to employees for dependent surgical benefits now to be paid by the plan. The agreement to run to October 31, 1956.
3. Primary pension benefit raised from $100 per month, including social security to $140 including social security, but maximum entitlement qualification raised from 25 to 30 years. Minimum pension for permanent incapacity raised from $50 to $75 per month. Company pension benefit not to be reduced by future changes in social security. This agreement to run to October 31, 1957.
4. New system and standards established for description and classification of new or changed jobs.
5. Change in procedure for adjustment of old incentives.
6. Clarification of seniority units.
7. Master contract to run until June 30, 1956, with a wage reopener on May 1, 1955, with the right to strike failing agreement by June 30, 1955.

By June 30, the union announced that it had signed similar agreements with other steel companies representing 90 percent of basic steel production. These were substantially the same as the U.S. Steel agreement, although variations in pension costs raised the cost to some companies somewhat. One interesting variation occurred at Bethlehem Steel, where the parties agreed to resume negotiations on July 7 on seniority, grievance procedure, and other issues, but in the event of failure to agree, the old contract language would remain and there would be no strike. On July 1, U.S. Steel and the union announced that they would resume quarterly meetings to discuss problems unrelated to wages or current grievances. Primary subjects listed for discussion were methods of cutting production costs, improving productive efficiency, and providing greater work security.

The final development in the 1954 negotiation concerned prices. On July 1, U.S. Steel, followed by all other major producers, announced increases ranging from $3 to $4 a ton.

McDonald said of the settlement:

> This has been another historic agreement. I think we can both be proud of what has been accomplished. The press has told the world of our conferences which opened and have been conducted on a harmonious note.[58]

The total package was approximately 9 cents, perhaps a cent higher or lower in a few companies, depending on pension costs and funding. This was approximately ½ cent more than the industry had given the previous year when business and profits had been better. It also gave the Steelworkers the 5 cent wage increase and fringe benefits the Auto Workers had previously received. If anything, the Steelworkers had a somewhat better pension plan than the UAW at this time.

On the other hand, the insurance program was still contributory. While employer contributions went up 2 cents, to 4½ cents an hour, so did the employee contribution, which reduced the wage increase to 3 cents net. Pensions

---

[58] *Steel Labor*, July 1954, p. 1.

were improved to $140 a month, slightly higher than the UAW pension plan, but unlike the UAW plan the service requirement to receive the $140 pension was 30 years, rather than 25.

Finally, the guaranteed annual wage was given up by the union. While it is doubtful that the union ever intended, or realistically ever could have struck to obtain the GAW, the terms of the settlement precluded the union from bargaining about it for 2 more years. The UAW master agreement would be open in 1955, and it seemed likely that they would bargain for and perhaps obtain the GAW before the Steelworkers. The fact that this was allowed to happen can be attributed to the economic conditions of 1954. The size of the economic settlement the companies actually gave, in spite of the recession, can be attributed to a continued desire in the industry to have peace with the union. In total, the agreement must have looked fairly satisfactory to both sides.

1955 BASIC STEEL WAGE REOPENING

The contracts between the United Steelworkers of America and all major steel producers were opened by the union on April 27, 1955, for negotiations "with respect to hourly rates of pay to be effective after June 30, 1955." The union's Wage Policy Committee met early in May and ratified demands for the usual "substantial wage increase," and also signified the intention of negotiating GAW plans wherever and whenever contracts were properly open on the subject.

Of considerably greater significance was the announcement by McDonald at the meeting that all negotiations in 1955 would be conducted in Pittsburgh, and that he would serve as chairman of all negotiating committees with the Big Six industry producers. Always in the past each major producer had carried on negotiations, whether genuine or pro forma, with a local committee usually headed by a district director. McDonald's move toward centralization and consolidation of negotiating authority, long a union desire, was generally interpreted as a device to strengthen his own position vis-a-vis that of several of the district directors. Then too, the new arrangement would allow the international officers to exercise closer supervision over major negotiations and insure greater uniformity of contractual provisions. This did not explain, however, why the industry, which throughout its history had adamantly insisted upon maintaining at least the fiction of individual company bargaining, had agreed to this new approach. The answer seems simply to have been that U.S. Steel was anxious to move in the direction of making public the real nature of industry decisionmaking in collective bargaining.

For many years U.S. Steel officials had followed the practice of meeting with executives of other steel corporations before and during negotiations to counsel and receive advice on bargaining strategy and tactics. This practice had its origin in the fact that it was confronted by one union, making almost uniform demands upon each company. It had been advanced by the necessity of making consolidated presentations before the War Labor Board in World War II, the factfinding boards in 1946 and 1949, and the Wage Stabilization Board in 1952. By the middle 1950's, it had become common practice for a committee representing other producers to wait close at hand while U.S. Steel conducted its negotiations, and for the committee or the company presidents they represented to expect to play a joint part in decisionmaking. U.S. Steel was in effect obligated to bargain for the whole industry, with all of the difficulties attendant upon multiemployer bargaining, while the facade of individual bargaining required it to accept any public and congressional obloquy resulting from collective decisions. Thus, McDonald's step toward making more public the realty of industrywide bargaining was thoroughly acceptable to U.S. Steel. In brief, this is the background of the decision to modify previous practices, which then developed into joint and simultaneous individual bargaining in 1956 and industrywide bargaining by the so-called Big 12 in 1959.[59]

The first negotiating meeting was held with U.S. Steel on June 7, 1955. Three developments of the previous months seemed certain to have an impact upon the results. In January, U.S. Steel had announced a 2 for 1 stock split and its first dividend increase in 4 years, raising its dividend rate from 75 cents to $1 a share. Secondly, while 1954 production and profits had been down from previous years because of national recession, 1955 gave strong promise of being steel's best year in history. New output peaks had followed month after month during the spring. By the time negotiations opened, the industry was producing at 97 percent of capacity.

The third happening which seemed certain to have an effect upon steel bargaining came just 1 day before negotiations began. The United Automobile Workers and the Ford Motor Co. announced agreement on a new 3 year agreement. The settlement was sizable: changes in the cost-of-living escalator formula; a 2½ percent increase in the annual improvement factor with a minimum of 6 cents; liberalized vacations, holidays, pensions, and insurance; additional wage increases to skilled crafts; and, perhaps most significant, a supplementary unemployment benefits plan funded by a 5 cent an hour company contribution. The package was estimated at 20 cents, and there was every indication that General Motors would meet and perhaps even improve on this settlement in a few days. Steel industry negotiators, with only wages open, were faced with a difficult pattern.

One further industry development is worth noting, although its impact on negotiations is difficult to assess. On May 2, Benjamin Fairless retired as chairman of U.S. Steel's Board of Directors. He was succeeded by Roger M. Blough, who had been vice chairman and a member of the finance committee. Blough, who had also functioned as chief counsel for the corporation, had in this latter capacity been involved in many past labor negotiations and had considerable familiarity with labor-management problems in steel.

In the negotiation session on June 7, the union pointed to the corporation's record first quarter profits and reduced total labor costs as justification for substantial wage and employee benefit increases without any necessity for increased prices. The union further specified its idea of improvements: 16 cent wage increase, 5 cents for supplemental unemployment benefits, and improved pension and welfare benefits to match or improve on the Auto Workers recent gains. The company replied that it was there to negotiate on "wages only" whereupon McDonald warned that he was not talking about "nickels and dimes." After 2 days, negotiations were recessed, as were those with all other major producers.

Talks were resumed on June 20. U.S. Steel maintained that profits, rather than being too high, were hardly adequate to provide the funds necessary to finance modernization and expansion. However, by June 23 Stephens announced to the union's top officials that after consultation with the other five of the Big Six producers, Bethlehem, Republic, Jones and Laughlin, Inland, and Youngstown, the industry was prepared to make a wage offer substantially better than the wage improvement in the auto contracts. They would grant a general in-

---

[59] Further and somewhat different analysis of this history may be found in Jack Stieber, "Company Cooperation in Basic Steel Bargaining," *Monthly Labor Review*, p. 586 (June 1960). Chapter 6 of this Report analyzes this history in greater detail.

crease of 6½ cents, plus a half cent increase in the increments between labor grades, or a total package slightly in excess of 10 cents. The company contended the offer was a full cent above the auto increase and should provide a basis for settlement.

McDonald quickly rejected the offer, characterizing it as only half of what the auto industry had given. Private meetings between Stephens and McDonald over the weekend of June 25 appeared to bring settlement no closer. The union then notified all local unions in the steel industry that a strike impended.

On June 27, Inland Steel made a wage offer totaling 10½ cents, which was also rejected by the union as being fundamentally the same as the offer of the rest of the industry. Inland then asked if the union was going to honor Inland's unique contract requirement of 120 hours' strike notice. McDonald replied indirectly, saying; "I believe there is still time to write out an equitable settlement" and that the union was not "strike happy." Inland was running at 107 percent of capacity, and decided not to begin closing its mills.

During most of June 28 and 29, the chief negotiators appeared to be more concerned with press releases and television appearances than in trying to bring about a settlement. In large newspaper advertisements and later before television cameras, McDonald stated that the companies were solely responsive for the crisis. He argued that only 2 out of every 5 steelworkers earned the $4,200 annually necessary for a modest living, that individual worker productivity had increased substantially, and that profits were up 60 percent and dividends 33 percent while the companies proposed to increase wages only 4½ percent. President Hood of U.S. Steel replied that the company's offer was "fair and equitable" and that the union was responsible for forcing an unnecessary strike upon the industry and the Nation. McDonald replied that time was short and urged Hood as well as all other top industry officials to take part in negotiations. This suggestion was rejected by the company presidents, and Stephens reiterated his conviction that renewed efforts could result in a settlement. Meanwhile, plans for closing the mills went forward, the furnaces were cooled, and food and cots were brought into the mills for supervisors and technicians who would stay in during a strike.

Late on June 29, the negotiations were resumed. John Stephens and Heath Larry of U.S. Steel met with McDonald and Arthur Goldberg. Stephens intimated that the industry would move to 12½ cents (which it had long considered its final settlement figure) if the union would drop below 16 cents in wages plus SUB. McDonald replied that he would accept the industry's 10 cent offer provided the company would agree to supplement it with a 5 cent contribution to an SUB fund. This proposal was tempting to some in the industry, who foresaw that with the automobile capitulation steel would eventually be forced to concede on SUB. The union proposal was rejected, however, for the reason that in the light of previous history the principle of holding the union to the exact terms of its reopening was too important to sacrifice. After this refusal, the meetings again were adjourned.

When they were resumed on June 30, rumors began to circulate that a settlement was imminent. During that same evening Stephens increased the company offer to 13½ cents, whereupon the union made its first proposal on wages only—18 cents. By midnight the union had come down to its final figure of 15 cents and Stephens had agreed to go to industry representatives and try to get that amount.

Although McDonald had not requested strike sanction from the Wage Policy Committee, in many parts of the country steelworkers left their jobs at midnight. Many other mills had been closed and furnaces cooled in anticipation of a strike. In total, nearly 400,000 workers were idle.

After 3 a.m. on July 1, Stephens reported no agreement, and suggested an adjournment until 9:30 a.m. in the morning. When the four negotiators met in the morning, the industry had agreed to the union's terms. Within 20 minutes the settlement was submitted to the union's Wage Policy Committee and ratified. At 11:00 a.m., after the shortest major work-stoppage in the history of the industry, the settlement was announced: a basic increase of 11½ cents and a half cent increase in the increments between classifications. This averaged 15.2 cents over the industry, in a year when autos had increased wages only 8½ to 9 cents. By July 3, all employees had returned to their jobs and full production was immediately resumed.

The day after the settlement, U.S. Steel announced a $7.50 per ton price increase. All other steel producers followed suit.

1956 BASIC STEEL CONTRACT NEGOTIATIONS

The year 1955 saw the heaviest production and greatest profits in the history of the steel industry. Output per man-hour, total hours worked, and average hourly earnings had also reached new highs. Although 1956 was not quite this fruitful for the industry and those working in it, the first 6 months' experience gave no reason for despair. Production had been running at approximately 90 percent of capacity, down only 3 percent from the previous year's average. Company profits and employee earnings seemed on the way to surpass the previous year.

An unusual amount of prenegotiation squabbling between companies and union seemed to darken this picture, however. In its annual report published in March 1956, U.S. Steel laid the blame for continuing national inflation and higher prices on two institutions. The one was the Federal Government's "full employment" policy and inflation of the money supply. The other was:

> [T]he institution of industrywide labor unions, headed by leaders who, with power to bring about industrywide strikes, seek always to outdo each other in elevating employment costs in their respective industry.[60]

McDonald promptly characterized this as a gratuitous insult. He publicly denied that the gains made by the workers had caused inflation, for, he said, their gains had been far more than offset by their increased productivity. He, in turn, accused the corporation of repeatedly making increased profits by raising prices immediately following wage increases, during times when actual wage costs per ton of steel had continued to fall.[61]

Roger Blough in turn told stockholders that the union was now readying wage demands, "which, if granted even in part, would—in the absence of a compensating price increase—seriously reduce our present profit level and compound the financial problems we must face in the future."[62]

Near the end of April the union informed the companies that it desired to terminate its existing contracts on June 30. This was routine. It was somewhat surprising when the major companies uniformly, and for the first time in many years, informed the union that they too intended to terminate the contracts on June 30. Although this move did not mean too much at the time, it was perhaps symptomatic of changed attitudes to come.

[60] Fifty-Fourth Annual Report, United States Steel Corp. (1956), p. 27.
[61] New York Times, Mar. 23, 1956, p. 43.
[62] New York Times, May 8, 1956, p. 43.

On May 16, the Steelworkers' Wage Policy Committee met to complete formulation of demands, which had earlier been summarized at a second "Operation Sound-off" as: wages, SUB, premium pay for weekend work, and improved insurance coverage.

On May 24, some indication was given as to the industry's thinking. Joseph L. Block, president of Inland Steel, told the Iron and Steel Institute that a long-term contract was the only way to avoid either an industrywide strike or more inflation. He added that steel, like other industries, should be able to negotiate stability for a period of years, and still be fair to both industry and the worker.

It appears that the industry had a number of reasons for preferring a longer-term contract:

1. Annual negotiations, with the extreme difficulty of first trying to obtain a consensus within the industry, and then agreement with the union, were very taxing of time and energy of top executives.

2. The industry had underway a substantial program of long-range capital investment and desired to avoid strikes as well as wide fluctuation of production and prices while the program was being effectuated.

3. It was already clear that the union proposals would be substantial and costly: the only way to approach them was on a piecemeal basis over a period of years.

Pursuant to this objective John Stephens had initiated a number of talks with David McDonald to sound out whether the union would modify its traditional pattern of biennial contracts with annual wage reopenings. McDonald was sympathetic; there were many precedents for longer-term closed agreements and they had received the approbation of many in the industrial relations field. Although there had been discussion of a 5-year agreement, no specific commitments were made.

With these developments behind them, the parties to all of the Big Six major agreements opened negotiations in Pittsburgh on May 28 and 29, 1956. While, as noted earlier, the industry had been expecting a package of proposals with a high price tag, the actual proposals contained even more in the way of fringe items than had been expected. The union demanded:

1. A substantial wage increase, exact amount unspecified.
2. Time and one-half for Saturday work, double-time for Sunday.
3. An SUB plan of 52 weeks of partial pay for laid-off workers.
4. Union shop.
5. One week's vacation after 1 year's service, 2 after 2, 3 after 5 and 4 after 15.
6. Shift differentials of 5 and 10 percent.
7. Two additional paid holidays.
8. Industry to pay all welfare and insurance benefits.
9. Expanded life insurance, sickness benefits, and welfare program.
10. Elimination of geographical differentials, and increase in reporting and jury pay.

McDonald told each company that he would set a specific wage figure later in the negotiations, that he desired an SUB Plan similar to that negotiated with the major can companies the previous fall, and that the union was particularly insistent upon its demand for premium pay for weekend work. After the union's demands were set out a 10-day recess in the negotiations was jointly agreed upon.

When negotiations were resumed, two changes in arrangements had been made. First, the conferences were now to be held at New York rather than Pittsburgh, the parties jointly explaining that they desired to be removed from "local pressures." Second, bargaining for the industry was to be conducted by a four-man committee from three companies. These were: Stephens; R. Heath Larry, counsel for U.S. Steel; Tom Patton, vice president of Republic Steel; and John Morse, counsel for Bethlehem Steel. The union, too, was to be represented by a four-man committee: McDonald, Goldberg, vice president Howard Hague and secretary-treasurer I. W. Abel. While Stephens stated for the record that the industry representatives were negotiating separately but concurrently, all concerned must have understood that they were effectively representing the entire industry.

After conversations on June 6 and 7, the meetings were again adjourned until June 13, when the industry had its package counterproposal ready. This was a closed 5-year agreement with periodic improvements in wage and fringe benefits, as follows:

1. *Wages*. Effective July 1, 1956, all rates to be increased by 6 cents an hour and the increments between job classes to be increased by 0.2 cent. Identical increases to be made effective on July 1, 1957, 1958, 1959, and 1960.

2. *SUB*. Effective July 1, 1956, establish an SUB plan providing 65 percent of after-tax take-home pay for 52 weeks to laid-off employees with 3 years' seniority. Funded by a 5-cent employer contribution.

3. *Premiums*. Effective July 1, 1958, increase shift premiums to 7 cents for afternoon and 10 cents for night shifts. Effective July 1, 1960, increase afternoon shift to 8 cents and night shift to 12 cents.
Effective July 1, 1959, establish a 10-cent premium for Sunday shifts.
Effective July 1, 1960, increase Sunday premium to 12 cents.

4. *Holidays*. Effective July 1, 1957, add a seventh paid holiday.

5. *Jury Pay*. Effective July 1, 1959, pay for time lost on jury duty.

6. *Insurance*. Effective November 1, 1956, make improvement in existing insurance program.

7. *Pensions*. Effective November 1, 1957, improve minimum benefits by increasing the monthly multiplier factor from $2.25 to $2.50.

8. *Term of Agreement*. Five years, without reopening, to expire June 30, 1961.

This package was valued at 65 cents an hour by the steel companies, who insisted that no individual parts of the whole were negotiable.

On June 15, McDonald announced that the package had been submitted to the Wage Policy Committee and had been rejected for five reasons: (1) The wage proposals were "picayune;" (2) the Sunday premium proposal was "inadequate;" (3) the SUB proposal provided no system for alternate payments in States which prohibited simultaneous public and private payments to laid-off employees; (4) no proposal for protection of purchasing power during the life of the agreement; and (5) no union shop proposal. McDonald said that the proposal was worth no more than 45 cents, when he characterized an offering too little over too long a time.

Item 4 in the Wage Policy Committee's objections represented a change from long-standing Steelworker policy. Protection of purchasing power implied wage escalation based upon changes in the cost of living, an idea that had not been traditional in steel unionism for over 20 years. The union had always previously insisted upon annual wage reopenings to protect employees from inflation. Nevertheless, the industry must have anticipated the union's modification of position, for on the following day the industry increased its offer to include a cost-of-living escalator.

Despite this change in the offer, negotiations were soon at an impasse. On June 18 the Wage Policy Committee authorized a strike on June 30, failing agreement by that time. The union gave up its efforts at talks with the Big Three and instituted individual talks with a number of major companies. When these resulted in identical offers from each of the twelve majors, talks were again resumed, on June 20, with the Big Three negotiators, who announced that they also were speaking for Jones and Laughlin, Youngstown Sheet and Tube, Inland, Armco, Great Lakes, Wheeling, Pittsburgh, Allegheny-Ludlum, and Colorado Fuel and Iron.

Progress was slow to negligible. Officially, the industry was unwilling to modify its proposal on a 5-year agreement. However, the union was told it would have to lower its demands before the industry could make a proposal based on 3 years. This the union was unwilling to do. Pricing the industry's proposal out at about 10 cents a year for 5 years, the union wanted this much or more over a 3-year period. Then too, the union felt the industry had placed them in an untenable position by making a fairly substantial offer, publicizing it directly to the employees, and then refusing to move from it. Arthur Goldberg put this feeling in words when he told the industry and reporters: "We want more Fairlessness and less Boulwarism." [63]

As a consequence of these rigid positions, the parties once again turned to fighting their case in the public communications media. The union placed full-page advertisements in many newspapers, which were replied to in industry advertisements. Television appearances and press conferences were resorted to by both sides. Recognizing that trouble was brewing, the Secretary of Labor announced that the administration had no plans to use Taft-Hartley, but that the services of the Federal Mediation and Conciliation Service were available. The parties did not appear anxious to avail themselves of this offer, and the Service did not intervene in the dispute.

Finally, on June 27, the industry modified its proposal slightly. By means of a letter, the Big 12 informed the union that it would reduce its proposed length of contract by 8 months, so that the new proposal would expire on October 31, 1960. The industry went on to say that it would propose to reduce benefits proportionately, although how this was to be done was unspecified. Presumably, if the union had shown some interest, it could have had the original 5-year benefits on a 4-year and 4-months' contract. In this letter the industry further suggested that the union agree to give 72 hours' prior written notice of intent to strike, and that negotiations continue after June 30.

The union rejected both proposals. The contract term offer was rejected out-of-hand as being inadequate to meet the union's objectives in any substantial way. In regard to continuing work after June 30, the union proposed a 15-day extension of the contract with any benefits negotiated to be retroactive to July 1. The industry refused to obligate itself to retroactivity, and began to bank the furnaces.

On June 28 McDonald proposed that the top industry executives leave their "ivory towers" and come to the bargaining table. Ten of the 12 companies replied, stating that no useful purpose would be served by this. On June 29 Stephens said that the industry was willing to meet, but McDonald replied that unless the industry had some new proposal there was no reason for a meeting. Despite this, off-the-record informal talks continued until early evening of June 30 when they were finally broken off. At midnight approximately one-half million workers were officially on strike.

Aside from their official statements, each party had an unofficial reason for believing that the strike could not be avoided. The union was convinced that Fairless' retirement had put a new "get tough" group in command of the industry's labor policy, and that John Stephens was no longer allowed to negotiate in the "old" manner. As a consequence, despite McDonald's number of

---

[63] *New York Times,* June 19, 1956, p. 16.

years of fairly soft answers, his public utterances in 1956 were more bellicose than Murray's had generally been.

The industry, on the other hand, was dismayed at the size of the package the union wanted after what it felt to be its generous 1955 settlement, and was particularly opposed to the thought of substantial weekend premiums, long an anathema to continuous-process industries. Then too, the industry was afraid that the union and the employees had been misled by the 1-day stoppage in 1955 into thinking that the industry could easily be caved-in by pressure. It was determined not to allow this belief to grow, first, by negotiating hard, and second, if pushed to a strike, to have it last long enough to demonstrate the industry's ability and willingness to fight.

As a consequence of these attitudes, within 2 days of the strike's beginning, stories began appearing in the newspapers that the strike would not be settled until the Government intervened. The Government's first response was through the Federal Mediation and Conciliation Service. Director Finnegan held separate talks with both parties on July 5 and 6, and called joint negotiations in Pittsburgh on July 12 and 13, but without success. Finnegan attended a Cabinet meeting on July 18 and then flew directly to Pittsburgh to warn the parties in joint meeting that President Eisenhower was concerned and would take some action if settlement was not soon reached. Despite these efforts, nothing of great significance was accomplished in mediation sessions.

By this time the effects of the strike were beginning to be felt in some areas of the economy. Secondary unemployment was growing, and shortages of construction steel were threatening to halt some job site work. Some specialty steels were in short supply soon after the strike began. On the other hand, the automobile industry had enough steel in inventory to finish up what had been a rather slow production year.

The net effect was sufficient to cause the administration considerable concern. Cold war tensions and hot war threats were heavy enough to make any slowdown in defense production a source of worry. Domestically, political observers feared that a strike going into the late summer and early fall might cause enough interruption in the flow of business to affect the Presidential election in November. In combination, these pressures were sufficient to force the administration to consider modifying its hands-off position. But the question of the form of increased intervention created a dilemma.

A Taft-Hartley injunction, if upheld by the courts, would reopen the mills until after the election. The basic problem, however, would still remain to be solved at that time. Another factor that militated against the use of injunction was that it would anger the union movement. Alternatively, to institute a non-Taft-Hartley factfinding board would run counter to the Republican Party's long-time criticism of previous Democratic administration's bypassing of Taft-Hartley. To avoid these alternatives, some Cabinet officers intervened at the same time that Federal Mediation conferences were going on.

Secretary of Labor James Mitchell had maintained close contact with the union during the negotiation, and was familiar with its desire for certain benefits, based on a 3-year contract. The Secretary met privately on July 12 with Presidents Hood, Homer, and White, of U.S. Steel, Bethlehem, and Republic, respectively, assessing the situation as he saw it and clarifying for them the union's point of view. Secretary Mitchell also had some part in making arrangements for the meetings of the parties that later resulted in a settlement, but he did not participate in them.

Secretary of the Treasury Humphrey, a former coal-steel executive, also talked to industry leaders. He is understood to have pointed out to President White of Republic Steel that in the event of a continued stalemate in negotiations the Government might find it necessary to appoint a non-Taft-Hartley fact-finding board with power to recommend settlement. He suggested that if the industry wished to avoid this they might consider modifying their position.

Under these circumstances, U.S. Steel recommended settlement to the other members of the Big Three rather than accept the risks of uncertainty as to what might be recommended by a factfinding board. John Stephens, who had hitherto been restricted by overall policy in his freedom to negotiate or even to talk privately to McDonald during the 1956 bargaining, was instructed by President Hood of U.S. Steel to go ahead and make the best deal that he could.

Stephens requested a private meeting with McDonald. In a few hours of face-to-face talks between the two men a tentative understanding was reached. Joint Big Three meetings were scheduled for Tuesday, July 24 in New York. By July 27 a memorandum of understanding was signed by all of the Big 12 companies and ratified by the Wage Policy Committee.

The settlement was as follows:

1. *Wages.* Effective July 27, 1956, all rates to be increased by 7½ cents an hour and the increment between job classes to be increased by 0.3 cent. Effective July 1, 1958, and again in 1959 wage increases of 7 cents and 0.2 cent increases in the increments were to become effective.

Wages to be ecalated semiannually, at the rate of 1 cent for each alternative 0.4 and 0.5 change in the BLS Consumer Price Index, above a level of 116.2.

Job classes 1 and 2 were combined, thus revising the industry's minimum rate.

2. *SUB.* A 52-week SUB plan, applicable to employees with 2 years' seniority. A combination of SUB and severance pay was also agreed upon.

3. *Premiums.* Effective July 1, 1958, increase premium to 8 cents on the afternoon shift and 12 cents on the evening shift.

Effective September 1, 1956, a premium of 10 percent to be paid for Sunday work.

Effective July 1, 1957, a Sunday premium of 20 percent and a holiday premium of 10 percent.

Effective July 1, 1958, the Sunday and holiday premiums to be raised to 25 percent.

4. *Holidays.* One additional holiday, as originally proposed by the industry. Good Friday was later selected as the day.

5. *Jury Pay.* Effective August 3, 1956, pay for time lost on jury service.

6. *Insurance.* Various improvements in benefits.

7. *Pensions.* Various improvements in benefits.

8. *Vacation.* Effective January 1, 1958, one-half week of additional vacation pay for employees in the 3–5, 10–15, and over 25 year brackets.

9. *Union Security.* A modified union shop.

10. *Joint Committees.* To review job classification and incentive systems.

11. *Term of Agreement.* Three years, without reopening, to expire June 30, 1959.

As can be seen by reference to their original proposal made in June (p. 296, *supra*), the industry settled by paying approximately as much for a 3-year contract as it had offered for 5. It also granted Sunday premiums, something which it had always adamantly opposed. Interestingly, if no longer significantly, the steel industry, which had taken one major strike and endless disputes over union security, quietly and almost without protest granted a modified union shop. The industry's chief victory was the avoidance of annual negotiations for the next 2 years, allowing it to go ahead with its expansion and modernization program without fear of industrial warfare.

The union characterized the settlement as its greatest victory in its history, pointing to a total package in excess of 45 cents over 3 years, nearly 20 cents of which came in the first year. Neither party made much of the escalation feature of the agreement, yet it was to cost the industry a total of 17 cents an hour over the next 3 years, almost as much as the specified wage increases.

One of the conditions in the July 27 memorandum of understanding was that each company was still to negotiate the language of its individual agreement. Immediately after the signing, all companies began individual company negotiations in the effort to get back into production as soon as possible. In many instances difficult problems had to be settled before the strike was ended.

On August 6, U.S. Steel announced that after consideration of steel making costs, including the initial costs of the new labor agreement, it was raising prices an average of $8.50 per ton. The rest of the industry promptly followed. During the 3 years of the 1956 agreement, total hourly employment costs in the industry increased nearly 30 percent. Productivity increases only partially offset these increased costs. Prices were raised approximately $21 per ton. Inflation, its causes and effects, was a continuing source of conflict and controversy between the Government, the steel industry, and the Steelworkers union in the years to come.

1959 BASIC STEEL CONTRACT NEGOTIATION

The 1959 renegotiation of basic steel contracts was not accomplished until after the largest single strike in United States history had occurred. The strike directly involved more than 500,000 workers and, although figures on secondary unemployment in industries dependent on steel operations are uncertain, by its end probably idled an additional quarter-million workers. The direct stoppage resulted in 42 million man-days of idleness, a volume exceeded by the total for all work stoppages in only 3 years in the Nation's history. The strike brought on public concern over the problem of "national emergencies" perhaps unequaled since 1946, and raised questions about the labor-management relationship in steel that were in part responsible for the initiation of this study.

Introduction

The 1959 steel negotiations began in an atmosphere of concern over unemployment, employment costs, competition, and inflation. The union was deeply concerned over the effects of short-range economic layoffs and long-range drop in employment resulting from technological change. During the 1958 recession, employment had dropped 25 percent from what it had been a little over a year previously, and while by spring of 1959 it had picked up substantially, total employment of production workers was still 10 percent less than it had been when the 1956 contract was signed. Perhaps more significantly, total production worker employment in the spring of 1959 was only 1 percent higher than similar employment 12 years earlier, although production had increased by 50 percent in those years. In these circumstances, the union felt that increased economic benefits for employees were appropriate. Certainly the general economic picture did not preclude substantial concessions, for production was high, and first-quarter steel earnings were in many cases the highest in history. Although much of this could be attributed to inventory building in fear of a strike, it was nonetheless a factor in the calculations and expectations of the union.

The industry, on the other hand, was deeply concerned over the increase in employment costs that had occurred as a result of the 1956 agreement, increasing competition from other materials and foreign steel producers, and once again with mounting public and governmental concern over steel prices and general inflation. Under the 1956 agreement, employment costs had increased 25 cents an hour each year, or nearly 8 percent a year. Steel average hourly earnings, $3.08 in 1959, were 86 cents higher than the all-manufacturing average, and 38 cents higher than auto earnings with which they had been on a par a few years previously, even though it was true that most of these differentials had resulted from increased incentive earnings. Additionally, the industry could demonstrate that output per man-hour had not gone up as fast in steel as it had in many other industries. As for profits, the industry felt the total dollar figures were misleading; as a percentage of stockholders' equity they were if anything slightly less than the all-manufacturing average. In essence, both sides were deeply convinced of the reality of their own problems and could bring supporting data to buttress their positions.

Public concern over steel wages and prices was evidenced by two statements concerning the coming steel negotiations by President Eisenhower at March press conferences. At one he said: "I have always urged that wage increases should be measured by increase of productivity, and I think there would be no inflationary effect if they were measured by that criterion." Subsequently he remarked that the measure of statesmanship in steel negotiations was that they should result in no price increase. The industry felt it was getting the worst of this, for they felt these statements implied that the union should have some wage increases while the companies should have no price increase. However, the President had the same view as the industry about the necessity for controlling increased costs and inflation. The Senate antitrust subcommittee also became a forum for debate on the causes of inflation. Hearings on a bill concerning "administered prices," while not resulting in legislation, gave both industry and union a sounding board for their respective opinions on costs, prices, and inflation.

Both parties early began the battle for favorable public opinion. The union placed 25 advertisements in 40 papers, the companies placed 20 advertisements in over 400 papers. In addition, the American Iron and Steel Institute stepped up the campaign against cost-push inflation that it had begun shortly after the conclusion of the 1956 negotiation. The public relations campaign was intense even before the union announced its demands.

On April 10, the Big 12 steel companies sent a letter to the union proposing that wages and benefits be extended without change for another year, because of inflation's dangers, the high level of existing wages and benefits, and low productivity. Additionally, they proposed that cost-of-living escalation be discontinued as inflation-engendering. McDonald replied that the union too was concerned about inflation. He proposed, therefore, that there be an agreement that steel prices should not be raised during the life of the new agreement. Wage negotiations, McDonald continued, would then take place in the light of protecting real wages, reflecting increased output per manhour, and protecting stockholders' return of equity. The industry officially replied that the price proposal was illegal and the remainder of the union proposal wholly unacceptable. Conflicting public statements continued throughout April and into May.

Pre-strike Negotiations

By 1959 the steel industry had, for practical purposes, embraced industrywide bargaining. A committee of 12, mostly vice presidents of the 12 largest producers, was to consult on negotiations and report to the company presidents. The actual negotiating team was composed of R. Conrad Cooper and Heath

Larry of U.S. Steel; H. C. Lumb, counsel for Republic Steel; and John H. Morse, counsel for Bethlehem Steel. Cooper was the chief industry spokesman, replacing John Stephens who had retired in 1958. The union bargaining team was to be the same as in 1956: McDonald, Goldberg, Hague and Abel.

The union's Wage Policy Committee met on April 30 and approved a substantial list of demands, the major ones of which were:

1. A substantial wage increase.
2. Continuation of cost-of-living escalation.
3. Improvement in Sunday premium and establishment of a Saturday premium.
4. Improvement in holiday premium and number of paid holidays.
5. Improved vacation benefits, including 3 months' vacation with pay every 5 years.
6. SUB improvement, including increase in contribution.
7. Improved pensions, including benefit level, liberalized vesting, and lump sum payment at time of retirement.
8. Noncontributory social insurance with improved benefit periods and amounts.
9. Improved reporting pay, shift premiums, and severance allowance.
10. Agency shop in States outlawing the union shop.
11. Limits on subcontracting.
12. Changes in grievance procedure, seniority, safety and health, military service, work schedules, and hours of work.

On May 5, negotiations began between the union and the individual companies. A week later, with nothing accomplished, negotiations were undertaken with the four-man teams. On June 10, the industry made public its first proposal involving contractual changes. It offered to make a "modest" wage improvement and some improvements in fringe benefits, but in return it demanded contract changes in eight areas: (1) Local working conditions, (2) wildcat strikes, (3) incentives, (4) work scheduling, (5) vacations, (6) duplication of benefits, (7) seniority, and (8) clarification of contract language. McDonald replied that the union did not propose to repeal its agreement or to become a company union. Negotiations were then recessed and the Wage Policy Committee empowered its officers to call a strike.

In the third week in June the union proposed a 7 cent per hour general wage increase, 0.2 cents per hour increase between job classes, and major and costly improvements in a sizable number of frinze benefits. On June 24, the industry proposed an indefinite postponement of the strike (scheduled for July 1) with continuation of existing agreements except for wage escalation, and without retroactivity. The union agreed to an extension to July 15, and after some discussion and a Presidential request to each party for an extension, the terms were that the contract was to be extended in its entirety, but without retroactivity. A week's bargaining under the extension accomplished nothing except continued production.

On July 7, Vice President Nixon met in Pittsburgh with both industry and union leaders, amid reports that the union would not agree to a further extension. The Nixon talks did not help in the search for agreement. The industry proposals for contract changes had become a major stumbling block. As a condition of any settlements, the union insisted that the industry drop its demands, although the union was willing to accept committees to study the issues. By July 12, talks were at a breaking point on three of the industry proposals relating to local working conditions, wildcat strikes, and proposals relating to increased efficiency.

When the union refused to concede more on these issues than that a study group be set up that would report before the next negotiation, the industry returned to its earlier proposal of a straight 1-year contract extension, or an indefinite extension cancellable on 5-days' notice. The union rejected both, as it did a further plea from President Eisenhower for continued negotiations.

The Strike

At 12:01 a.m. July 15, a basic steel strike began. The stoppage directly involved 519,000 workers, and approximately 87 percent of the Nation's rated steel capacity. Layoffs immediately followed in railroads, barge and truck lines, and in coal mines.

Joseph Finnegan, Director of the FMCS, who had hitherto maintained only informal telephone and personal contact with the negotiations, on July 15 arrived in New York for separate talks with the parties. His conclusion afterward was that the dispute was not going to be capable of easy or early solution. President Eisenhower told a press conference that he did not intend to appoint a factfinding board (as the union had requested) or apply for a Taft-Hartley injunction.

For the next 10 weeks the parties sparred with each other, and with the Government. A series of Federal mediation conferences failed to develop new proposals. Secretary of Labor Mitchell undertook to coordinate Government activities regarding the strike and reports to the President on the strike's effect, and volunteered the Department's services to find facts concerning the steel industry. When this factfinding report came out,[44] both parties found support for their positions in the facts that were presented. For one period of 3 weeks neither McDonald nor Goldberg would participate in the negotiations because heads of companies refused to participate. From September 10 through 23, separate company subcommittee meetings were undertaken, but without result. Secondary unemployment resulting from the strike began to grow during September. Many bills were proposed in Congress suggesting various methods of settling the strike, but no action was taken on them. At the end of September the parties met separately with the President. McDonald met privately with Roger Blough, Chairman of the Board of U.S. Steel.

Perhaps as a result of these meetings, the parties exchanged new offers, but without substantially enlarging the area of agreement. The union's executive board rejected an industry offer on October 4 as being too small and continuing the objectionable proposals for contract changes. Talks between Blough and McDonald, and between Secretary Mitchell and both parties resulted in no changes. As he had warned the parties he would, the president on October 9 appointed a Taft-Hartley Board of Inquiry to inquire into and report on the issues in dispute.

Board of Inquiry and Injunction

The Board of Inquiry appointed by the President was composed of George W. Taylor, University of Pennsylvania, chairman; Paul N. Lehoczky, Ohio State University; and John A. Perkins, University of Delaware. The Board made no findings on whether the national health and safety was imperiled by the strike as this finding was made by the President when he appointed the Board. Instead the Board made an attempt to delineate the issues clearly and a mediation effort.

In joint negotiations held by the Board of Inquiry, further new offers were exchanged. The industry improved its offer to what it stated to be a 31-cent

[44] U.S. Department of Labor, *Background Statistics Bearing on the Steel Dispute*, Bull. No. S-1 (August 1959). Additional supplementary tables were included when the bulletin was reissued in October 1959.

package for 3 years and set aside preconditions on contract changes, suddenly offering instead to arbitrate the working conditions issue. Union leaders, apparently surprised by the unexpected offer to arbitrate, rejected it. The union valued this industry offer at 24½ cents over the 3 years, and counterproposed a 2-year package based on fringe improvements the first year and wage increases the second that it valued at 20 cents and the industry at 32. The differences in valuation, a bone of contention throughout the negotiations, resulted from differences over whether a price should be placed on cost-of-living proposals, differences over the amounts that indirect effects would increase total employment costs, and in evaluation of pension and insurance costs. The union also proposed the establishment of a nine-member tripartite committee to recommend a long range formula for the equitable sharing of the fruits of the industry's economic progress. The industry rejected this union offer. Kaiser Steel, the smallest of the Big 12, undertook private negotiations looking toward an independent settlement based on the union proposal. Other offers were exchanged by the union and the remainder of the industry group on October 15 and 17, but these still left the parties apart.

After its mediation efforts failed, the Board of Inquiry submitted its report,[65] concluding that "work rules" and the economic package were the major issues, and that there were no significant areas of agreement between the parties.

The President instructed the Attorney General to seek an injunction to end the 97-day-old strike.

The Government petitioned the District Court for the western district of Pennsylvania in Pittsburgh to issue an injunction requiring the reopening of the mills, basing its request on the importance of steel to the economy, low levels of steel supplies, shortages of steel adversely affecting missile and weapons programs, and unemployment. The union contested the application on the ground that the strike did not imperil the national health and safety in the sense intended by the statute, and that the statute was unconstitutional. The District Judge found for the Government, but a stay of the order was granted while the union appealed to the Court of Appeals. The appellate ruling came down a week later: a 2–1 decision upholding the District ruling. Issuance of the injunction was again stayed, pending appeal to the Supreme Court.

Meanwhile, on October 26, Kaiser Steel made an independent settlement with the union, a 20-month contract based roughly on the terms proposed by the union before the Board of Inquiry. The remainder of the industry, with several minor exceptions, showed no inclination to follow Kaiser's lead, declaring that its settlement failed to eliminate wasteful work practices.

On November 7, a week after it had held its hearings, the Supreme Court upheld the injunction that had originally been issued on October 21.[66] Almost immediately McDonald ordered all striking steelworkers to return to their jobs. After 116 days the strike was ended, at least temporarily.

---

[65] Report to the President by the Board of Inquiry appointed by Executive Order 10843, "The 1959 Labor Dispute in the Steel Industry," Oct. 19, 1959.

[66] *United Steelworkers of America* v. *United States,* 361 U.S. 39 (1959). In an unsigned opinion, eight members of the court held that the national emergency provisions were constitutional and did not place a nonjudicial function on the courts. The Court did not go into the question of whether the strike imperiled the national health, finding that it did imperil the national safety by stopping or slowing defense production. The court did not feel that the Government was obligated by the statute to erect a plan of partial operation of the industry in order to satisfy specific defense needs.

Justice Douglas was the sole dissenter, stating that there was not a clear showing of peril to the national health and safety, and recommended that the case be returned to the appeals court for specific findings on this issue, and findings on exactly what plants would have to be reopened in order to satisfy defense needs.

Once again the Federal Mediation and Conciliation Service began holding joint conferences, while at the same time the Steelworkers' Wage Policy Committee voted unanimously to renew the strike if settlement was not reached before the injunction was to expire on January 26.

On November 15, the industry improved slightly its previous 3-year offer made before the Board of Inquiry, proposing some additional pension benefits, which the industry estimated improved its offer from a 2.6 percent to a 2.7 percent increase in annual employment costs. According to industry estimates, this was the maximum increase that could be assimilated by productivity increases, and thus noninflationary. The union rejected the offer as being no significant change. A few weeks later the industry announced that this was its "final offer" that would be submitted to employees in the Taft-Hartley ballot.

Once again negotiations came practically to a standstill while the union turned to negotiating agreements on extended contracts in the aluminum and can industries. Both of these negotiations were completed early in December, resulting in 3-year agreements with a total package cost approximating 35 cents. The steel companies estimated that these settlements, if applied to them, would cost approximately 55 cents an hour.

By early December, pressure was beginning to mount on the steel industry. Production was back up to over 90 percent of capacity, but the dispute was no nearer settlement. The union, which had successfully aroused great militancy among employees in opposition to industry proposals for contract changes, showed every intention of striking again after the injunction period. The economic losses that would be attendant upon a recurrence of the strike brought great pressure upon both parties to modify their position. Many industry leaders felt by this time that in proposing to change contractual working conditions they had given the union the best issue it could have found on which to take the strike. Continued insistence on the changes practically ensured that the employer's "last offer" would be overwhelmingly defeated in the coming balloting. Congressional opinion seemed to be such that a recurrence of the strike would bring some sort of action: uncertainty as to the form it might take encouraged both parties to attempt to avoid it. Finally, the surrounding settlements at Kaiser and Detroit Steel, and in cans and aluminum, while not forming any sort of binding pattern for the steel industry, did indicate the size of economic package the union would accept and tended to throw some doubt on the industry's position that the union was completely unreasonable in its proposals.

On December 4, President Eisenhower told a nationwide television audience that he would like to see the dispute settled while he was away on a forthcoming worldwide tour. In response to all these factors, pressures for settlement began to build once again. FMCS Director Finnegan began holding daily mediation conferences. Vice President Nixon began holding small joint meetings at his home, and these continued off-and-on throughout the month. In addition to the Vice President, the usual participants were Blough, McDonald, Goldberg and Secretary of Labor Mitchell. Secretary Mitchell publicly proposed three alternatives to the parties: (1) They could ask a board to make recommendations; (2) they could ask Finnegan to make a recommendation; or (3) they could seek voluntary arbitration. The industry rejected all of these alternatives on the basis that third-party intervention could only result in proposals that had already been rejected by the union, or proposals "that would clearly be inflationary."

Settlement

Despite the surface impasse that appeared at this time, demonstrated by hostile press releases, unfruitful mediation, and pending litigation over retro-activity and a cost-of-living increase of 4 cents due under the old contract in January, an area of possible compromise was beginning to emerge. While the industry had always maintained that it would make no offer exceeding 2.7 per-cent of employment costs over each year of a 3-year contract, or 30.6 cents total, Roger Blough finally conceded to Vice President Nixon and Secretary Mitchell that U.S. Steel would consider going as high as 35 cents, and the Gov-ernment officials estimated that there was still some room to move above this. The union, on the other hand, was insisting upon a package which, when com-puted by the industry, totaled 44.8 cents for 3 years. Mitchell told the union that the settlement would have to be under 40 cents and, with McDonald's approval, Mitchell and Goldberg then worked out a tentative settlement based on using a previously agreed-upon maximum of 6 cents in potential cost-of-living increases for offsetting any increased insurance costs. This brought the total value of the tentative package, under the industry's system of evaluation, to 39 cents. Another part of this agreement was that the work-rules issue would become the subject of a joint study.

This formula was produced on December 28 and approved by the union and U.S. Steel. Some in the industry still balked, however, and on December 29 and 30 Vice President Nixon maintained contact with industry leaders, out-lining possible events if the impasse were allowed to continued. He is under-stood to have told them that congressional opinion would be anti-industry and that the administration would be unable to protect them against hostile legis-lation. On January 2, Mitchell informed other top Government officials that the details had been practically worked out and approved by the industry and union. All negotiations were completed in a 24-hour session on January 3d, and settle-ment was announced by Secretary Mitchell the morning of the 4th.[67] It con-sisted of the following terms:

1. Effective December 1, 1960, a 7 cents an hour general wage increase and an increase of 0.2 cents between job class increments.
Effective October 1, 1961, a 7 cents an hour general wage increase and a 0.1 cents increase between increments.
2. Effective January 1, 1960, insurance program to be noncontributory and benefits improved.
3. Effective January 1, 1960, improvements in the pension program.
4. Cost-of-living escalation maintained, but adjustments limited to two, limited to 3 cents on December 1, 1960 and 6 cents (less December 1, 1960 ad-justment, if any) on October 1, 1961, further limited by offset related to increase in insurance costs, if any.
5. SUB plan maintained, with restoration of 2 cents contingent liability.
6. Agency shop in States that had made the union shop illegal.
7. Establishment of a joint Human Relations Research Committee to study various problems relating to wages, benefits, classifications, incentives, seniority and medical care.
8. Liberalization of seniority retention in cases of layoff or physical disability.
9. Local working conditions problems to be studied by a tripartite com-mittee, to report to parties by November 30, 1960.
10. Contract to terminate on June 30, 1962.

---

[67] On December 28 the Board of Inquiry met to make its final report, which was sub-mitted following the settlement.

The settlement was announced in the newspapers as a 39 or 41 cent package, depending upon whether the reports included the restored 2 cent liability for SUB. This looked large, and most comment was critical. It was variously described as a defeat for the industry, a capitulation to the union that was bound to give new impetus to inflation, and an industrial Munich. Unsupported charges were made that the industry had agreed to withhold price increases until after the Presidential elections. It was also described as a settlement forced upon the industry by politically motivated Government officials.

In sober retrospect the settlement was quite otherwise. The direct wage costs were considerably less than reported—about 34 cents. The settlement represented a 3.7 percent annual increase in total employment costs, as compared with an 8 percent annual increase under the 1956 agreement and only about 1 percent higher than the offer the industry had made before the Board of Inquiry. It compared favorably with other settlements made by the Steelworkers: the Kaiser settlement represented a 5 percent annual increase in employment costs, and the can and aluminum settlements about 4.7 percent. The employees got no wage increase the first year, although the industry agreement to pay the full cost of insurance coverage represented an immediate increase in take-home pay. The union gave up 4 cents in escalation to which it would have been entitled under the expired agreement and coupled continued escalation with the possibility that the insurance program would eat up some of any future escalation increases. Perhaps the greatest defeat suffered by the industry was that it received no assured changes in local working conditions or in added protection against wildcat strikes. These issues may remain as future sources of conflict. The defeat suffered by all concerned—industry, union and public—is that it might have been possible to make the same settlement in July as was finally made in January.

Appendix B

STRIKES AND INDUSTRIAL RELATIONS IN THE STEEL INDUSTRIES OF SELECTED COUNTRIES [1]

This paper summarizes the findings and conclusions of a larger detailed and documented report which was one of several background studies commissioned by the Department of Labor in connection with its steel study. The questions with which this background report dealt were directly related to only one of the two basic issues under consideration—industrial conflict and the role of Government. Essentially the purposes of the background study were these:

(1) To summarize the record of industrial peace or conflict in the steel industries of several countries: The United Kingdom, Sweden, West Germany, Australia, Japan, Canada, France, Belgium, and Luxembourg.

(2) To outline those features of the respective national industrial relations systems (e.g., provisions for compulsory conciliation or arbitration) or of the structure and organization of the steel industries per se (e.g., special bargaining arrangements, nationalization, codetermination) which affect methods of dispute settlement and proneness to industrial peace or conflict.

(3) To assess the relevance of this survey for American experience and to note any relevant "lessons from abroad" for public policy consideration concerning "Government and collective bargaining in steel."

Preliminary Caveats

1. International comparisons of strike data are fraught with pitfalls. These are particularly vexing in industry comparisons where adjustments must be made for varying definitions of the industry and of "numbers employed" in the industry.

2. Available information on strike and industrial relations experience in the various iron and steel industries was plentiful and reliable for some countries but only sparse and conjectural for others. Labor attachés helped fill some of the gaps in available published sources, but many remained.

These technical disparities and substantive gaps necessarily imply that the data summarizing strike experience are "best estimates" rather than precisely definitive and that interpretations (which are necessarily personal, in the first place) are subject to such minor modifications or qualifications as may be required by existent but currently unavailable detail concerning the industrial relations systems of the steel industries surveyed. Neither caveat, however, seems to me to destroy the general validity of the substantive findings concerning strike experience or the warrant for the general interpretive conclusions made.

Strike Experience

In general, strike activity in the iron and steel industries of the nine countries surveyed appears to have been very low or nonexistent in six countries and

---

[1] Prepared by Abraham J. Siegel of the Massachusetts Institute of Technology.

moderate in the other three during the periods covered by the survey. In no country was steel a "problem" industry in industrial relations.[2]

(1) *United Kingdom.* The steel industry in Great Britain is relatively strike-free. For the pre-1949 period when annual strike statistics were reported only by seven very broad industrial groupings, there are a number of reiterated qualitative testaments to industrial peace in British iron and steel. From 1949 on, when strike data are available for narrow industrial groupings, we have the quantitative evidence of moderate employee involvement and duration of strikes when they do occur but we find that the annual employee loss ratio for the 1949–58 period was on the average about a quarter of a day per worker—a very nominal loss ratio in relation to the same ratio in other British industries and elsewhere.

(2) *Sweden.* Strike experience in the iron and steel industry in Sweden is easily summarized. There have been no strikes in the Swedish steel industry for the past 30 years. This is still a remarkable record despite the fact that for the country as a whole strike activity has been very low since the 1930's.

(3) *West Germany.* There have been virtually no strikes (in the statistically reportable category) in the West German steel industry since World War II. There are records of a few wildcat and very brief (1 to 2 hours) stoppages but since none of these lasted at least 1 day or involved the loss of more than 100 man-days, they were not officially recorded as "strikes." Once again, for the country as a whole, the level of post-World War II strike activity has been very low. The postwar record in steel, however, stands in remarkable contrast with the pre-Nazi strike experience in iron and steel. For the 1925–32 period, the annual average of working days lost in steel strikes exceeded 1¼ million and these accounted, on the average, for more than 17 percent of the total man-days lost in stoppages in all industry annually. Although all industries experienced fewer strikes in the postwar period, it is apparent that the decrease was much more marked in the iron and steel industry.

(4) *Luxembourg.* The history of industrial relations in the Luxembourg steel industry has been one of almost unbroken peace for the past 40 years. With the exception of several wildcat strikes of short duration and affecting only small numbers of workers, there have been no strikes since the early 1920's. In the past decade only one serious threat to this record of labor peace occurred but last-minute mutual agreement to accept arbitration averted a strike in 1959.

(5) *Belgium.* Strike data for Belgian steel are available only from 1957 on. Prior to 1957, steel strikes were included in the broader industrial grouping of metal fabrication. Qualitative comments, however, suggest that there have been very few strikes in the postwar period and that those which did occur were, for the most part, "sympathy" strikes in which steelworkers joined in demonstrations of trade union solidarity in concert with workers in the entire metalworking industry.

---

[2] Periods covered varied among countries according to availability of published information concerning strike experience. The rank designation of "low," "moderate," or "high" was necessarily arbitrary, but the detailed report includes a discussion of the basis for such ranking. Wherever possible, the performance of the steel industry was ranked in a variety of comparable dimensions of strike activity (e.g., average duration, union membership and employee involvement ratios, union membership and employee loss ratios, average magnitude, etc.) in relation to the performance of other industries and/or the performance of "all industries" in the country. In addition, consideration was given to the relation of the strike experience of the steel industry in country X to the aggregate experience in the steel industries of all countries.

(6) *Japan.* In general, strike experience in the Japanese iron and steel industry does not appear to deviate too far from the average experience of aggregate Japanese strike activity. The general pattern is one of high worker participation and brief duration of stoppages. For the postwar period, the the average duration of steel disputes has been somewhat lower than the already low average duration of all disputes (3.9 days as against 5.2 days). The average size of each dispute was about 2,500 employees, and the average number of working days lost annually per employee was 1.9. Such strikes as do occur are not only brief but orderly, usually involve only one shop or department in a plant at a time, rarely shut down a blast furnace, and are generally conducted by local union officers with a prior agreement with management about the timing, limits, and methods of the strike.

(7) *Australia.* There are no precise data available on strike experience in the Australian iron and steel industry. Steel disputes are included in the broader metal trades and engineering industrial category. Other information, however, indicates that the Australian steel industry has been generally free from lengthy and total shutdowns. The only prolonged stoppage in the industry since World War II was a 13-week strike in 1945. Also, the steel industry shares two aspects characteristic of Australian industrial disputes taken as a whole: relatively high frequency of disputes and a markedly low average duration of stoppages. Coal mining and stevedoring have accounted for a major portion of total strike activity in Australia. The metal trades and engineering group has generally ranked third in incidence of disputes, but this is undoubtedly a higher ranking than would be attained by the steel industry alone. All in all, the steel industry's record does not distinguish itself sharply from the experience of industry as a whole when the coal mining and stevedoring industries are excluded.

(8) *France.* Once again, there are no precise data on strike experience in the French iron and steel industry. Figures are available only for metal production as a whole. There is no information to suggest that steel is either a "problem" industry or one which ranks inordinately "low" in strike activity. We do know that strikes are usually of relatively brief duration.

(9) *Canada.* Of all the countries surveyed, strike experience in the Canadian iron and steel industry appears to rank highest. During the 1947–58 period, strikes in the ferrous metal products industry entailed an average annual loss of over 5 days per employee. The average duration of disputes in this period was almost 14 days. The ferrous metal products industry during this period accounted (on the average) for almost 15 percent of the total number of strikes occurring each year and for more than 13 percent of man-days lost annually in work stoppages. There were sporadic strikes in the basic steel industry during the initial organizational years when the Steel Workers Organizing Committee (SWOC) began its efforts to unionize Canadian steelworkers. During World War II, the steelworkers did not pledge a no-strike policy and managed to improve wage rates despite wartime wage controls and to secure industry-wide uniformity in base rates. This was accomplished through the use of the strike. The Government, anxious to restore production of vitally needed steel, in each case virtually compelled reluctant employers to grant concessions to the SWOC. The largest of these wartime disputes occurred after several smaller ones had been evaded and after union recognition had been ceded. In January 1943, after extended negotiations, intervention of Government conciliation boards, the appointment of a special commission, and so on, the steelworkers at Dosco and Algoma struck to obtain improvements in wages and other

conditions (recognition was not an issue here). The dispute was ended only after a Memorandum of Understanding between union and Government was concluded in late January 1943. In July 1946, an industry shutdown occurred despite the proclamation of a temporary Government controllership over the industry and the provision in P.C. 2901 (which established the controllership) of severe penalties for failure to report to work without just cause. The strike lasted from July 14 to early October and the Government made no effort to impose the penalties under P.C. 2901. After the bitter 1946 strike, there was no resort to strike action over the negotiation of new agreements nor was there resort to the conciliation board step of the two-stage conciliation procedure between 1947 and 1953. Negotiations in 1954 were markedly different from those in previous postwar years. Adverse economic conditions hardened the companies' bargaining stance and the parties came closer to an industrywide strike than at any time since 1946. The face-saving concessions recommended by conciliation boards and agreed to by the companies and the union barely averted another industrywide stoppage. A series of wildcat stoppages at Algoma erupted in mid-1955. In the 1958 Canadian steel negotiations, a 12-week strike occurred at Stelco, the "giant" of the industry. The settlement at Algoma, which normally had waited upon the Stelco settlement as a pattern for its own, averted an even broader stoppage and served as the basis for an eventual settlement at Stelco.

Bargaining and Dispute Settlement Procedures

1. In a comparative study where findings are uniform, the stimulus to ferret for generally prevailing explanations is almost compulsive and occasionally rewarding. In an earlier interindustry comparison of strike experience in 11 countries, for example, it was found that the coal-mining and longshoring industries tended to rank consistently high in proneness to strike. It seemed plausible in that international comparison to suggest a general explanatory hypothesis that related two aspects of the industrial environment of these industries to the prevailing high levels of strike activity in the coal-mining and longshoring industrial sectors.[3]

There have been a number of "rough and ready" hypotheses tossed off from time to time relating certain aspects of the industrial environment in the iron and steel industry to presumed consequences concerning industrial peace or conflict results. It has been suggested, for example, that the technology of the industry attracts necessarily "tough" workers and that this, combined with a traditionally hard-bitten, individualistic employer attitude, tends to foster combative industrial relations. On the other hand, we have encountered, perhaps more frequently, another general hypothesis relating the industrial organization of the steel industry to industrial relations results. Steel, it has been suggested, is a "big" industry, at best oligopolistic and at worst monopolistic, which tends to be confronted eventually by an equally "big" industrywide union. The tendency read into this juxtaposition is one of tacit collusion whereby both parties "get theirs" at the expense of the public and evolve, via this "mutuality," an accommodative rapport which results in industrial peace.

The findings of this comparative study support neither of these (nor any other) simple hypotheses as generally valid and prevailing explanations for industrial peace or conflict results in the iron and steel industry. They may be

---

[3] See Clark Kerr and Abraham Siegel, "The Interindustry Propensity to Strike—An International Comparison," in A. Kornhauser, R. Dubin, A. M. Ross, editors, *Industrial Conflict*, New York, McGraw-Hill Book Co., 1954, pp. 189–212.

valid at one time or place, but no generally valid explanation for the pattern of strike activity revealed in this international comparison (where the steel industries ranked "low" in strike experience in six countries, "moderate" in three, and in the United States would rank between "moderate" and "high") emerges from the study. There simply does not appear (as there did in the case of the coal-mining and longshoring industries) to be any inherent characteristic of the industrial environment in iron and steel fabrication which tends to override the effects of differences in national industrial relations systems, industrial collective bargaining history and machinery, or cultural contexts, and which bids fair to predominate in the shaping of employee-employer relations in the industry, whatever its industrial location. The basic environment involving the relationships of workers, work process, and employers in the production of steel does not per se lead toward industrial peace or industrial conflict. In short, the explanations for the historical experience in steel appear to be at best partial and are frequently combined with unique causal factors. Both the partially transferable and the unique factors appear to lie outside the characteristics of the industrial environment imposed by the technology of steel production.

2. If we are deterred from proposing general cross-cut and all-encompassing valid explanations, we may yet legitimately attempt to seek out partial explanations for the generally modest level of strike activity revealed by the study. Unfortunately, this is neither simple nor sure, for we are confronted by an almost bewildering array of bargaining and dispute settlement relationships involving varying roles for Government in the iron and steel industries of each of the countries surveyed.

(a) In Britain, we find a history of early accommodation between employer and worker organizations in steel and a long-standing record of mutual acceptance which dates from 1867. Each of the parties is strong and effective; in relation to each other they are fairly evenly matched, and in relation to the constituent memberships organizational leadership exercises effective control and discipline. We find an industrial bargaining machinery established in a hierarchy of levels. Industrywide negotiations deal with broadly applicable issues such as hours, holidays, cost of living bonuses, and minimum rates for laborers; districtwide and regional bargaining encompasses relevant district issues; and bargaining at the plant level supplements these agreements and incorporates the settling of individual rates, extras, plant work rules, and so on. There is a well-established dispute-settlement machinery whereby most disputes have been peacefully resolved by the parties, locally. There is also provision in some sections of the industry for an informal method of arbitration by a neutral committee consisting of two representatives of employers and two of workers chosen from employers and workers not directly concerned in the dispute. Those few disputes not settled locally have moved up for resolution in joint conferences at the district or national level and if necessary, to private arbitration. Union leaders and employers have both agreed that a strike is a sign of failure. There have been close formal and informal relationships at all levels of the organizations. Both sides accept the fact that negotiations, while in progress, should be confidential and private to the parties concerned and statements should be made jointly to the press at the conclusion of negotiations. The role of Government in the dispute-settlement machinery has been the model of voluntarism, and only in one instance has the Government intervened via a court of inquiry to inquire into the facts of a dispute and to issue a nonbinding report. The industry went from private ownership to nationalized ownership and back to private ownership with some general Government supervision of pricing policies, etc., all without affecting the industrial relations arrangements or experience in the industry.

(b) *In Sweden,* there is a similar history of generally accommodative relationships between worker and employer associations in steel which date from the first decade of the century, and we find a long and uninterrupted period of mutual acceptance. Again each of the parties is strong and effective. The bargaining machinery is such that industrywide bargaining takes place within the framework of general nationwide limits negotiated between the central employer and worker organizations, the *Svenska Arbetsgivaeforeningen* (SAF) and the *Landsorganisationen i Sverige* (LO). In addition, there are advisory "enterprise councils." Dispute-settlement machinery has functioned extremely well. The role of Government in dispute-settlement involves compulsory arbitration of disputes arising out of contract interpretation. Labor courts decide such disputes where no private machinery has been established by the parties for their resolution. Few disputes in steel ever get to the labor courts. In disputes over new contract terms, the Government's role is limited to mediation. Ownership in the industry is, for the most part, private, but a portion of the industry is Government-owned. No differences either in industrial relations procedure or practice arise out of this ownership pattern.

(c) *In Germany,* a complex web of collective bargaining was reestablished after more than a decade of disuse, but political bargaining plays a significant role in the German industrial relations system. Strong employer associations bargain with less strong national unions and negotiate very general contractual terms on an industrywide level. At the plant level, the works councils (not part of the trade union machinery) negotiate supplementary agreements with individual employers and administer all agreements. Out of this combination of processes a number of general and specialized contracts emerge. The wide disparity between actual earnings and benefits and the level of wages scheduled in collective agreements negotiated between employer associations and the trade union (I.G. Metall) is an increasing concern of the union. The union has been promoting in recent years a new approach in collective bargaining which is aimed at increasing union (as opposed to works council or unilateral employer decision) participation in wage determination at the plant level and designed to reduce this gap—all in the hope of bolstering union appeal for workers and arresting membership stagnation of recent years. This development runs counter to the continuing internal union appeals for more centralized federation authority and coordination of wage policies between the 16 national unions which comprise the federation. The Government offers voluntary conciliation and arbitration services via labor courts but in the "codetermined" steel industry, few disputes have gotten to the labor courts. The strong paternalist heritage and the newly found status and machinery via codetermination in the steel industry plus the general disinclination (and inability?) of the postwar German worker to strike and the great emphasis on reconstruction have reduced industrial conflict in the German steel industry to virtually zero in marked contrast with the strike record in steel prior to World War II.

(d) *In Luxembourg,* we find a long record of labor peace in a virtual "one-industry" economy, with more than half its 45,000 industrial workers employed in the iron and steel industry. The industry is almost entirely an export industry, is highly efficient and pays the highest steel wages in continental Europe.

Workers have had few economic incentives for striking and the psychological rapport between labor and management seems high. Although there are three competing unions, rivalry is confined to the recruiting of members and to political differences. In negotiating with management, a united front is always maintained (unlike the French situation). Industrial relations in the steel industry operate to a large extent in an atmosphere of free bargaining which is characterized by a sense of responsibility (in view of the vital dependence of the economy upon steel) without any direct involvement of Government legislation or agencies. Only when free collective bargaining fails to produce agreement does the Government (in the form of the National Conciliation Office) enter the picture as mediator. Recommendations for settlement, however, are not binding, although in instances where the Conciliation Office has intervened it has proved very effective in developing compromises and agreements. In practice, the great majority of settlements are reached in private negotiation stages by management and union representatives and only infrequently does a dispute reach the conciliation stage (unlike the Canadian experience).

(e) *In Belgium,* industrial relations in the steel industry since World War II have generally been considered as good. Like the Luxembourg industry, it came out of the war intact and has been prosperous. There are two major unions in the industry, the Socialist and the Catholic metalworkers' unions. In the Belgian steel industry, grievances are first considered at the plant level by joint labor-management committees. If they are not settled there, they are taken to the industry's *Commission Paritaire,* or joint committee, on which sit representatives of labor and management who endeavor to work out agreements and avert strike action. This joint committee arrangement whereby employers and workers themselves, in effect, act as conciliators, dates from 1919 in the metalworking industry and by the Decree of July 27, 1946, was officially established as a procedural arrangement for various branches of industry. The national industry joint committees are composed of representatives of employers and workers who are appointed by the Government from lists of candidates submitted by the organizations qualified to represent the employers and workers. In the case of national strike threats, where this conciliation machinery has broken down, the Prime Minister generally calls for at least one more effort, usually naming the Minister of Labor as his representative in conciliation. Apart from these arrangements, Belgium has no other conciliation and no arbitration machinery, for steel or any other industry.

(f) *In Japan,* collective bargaining is a postwar phenomenon and bargaining has been confined, for the most part, to the single enterprise. The paternalist heritage dies hard and the revived employer associations are strong. In steel, there is no industrywide bargaining. Within the enterprise, bargaining tends to be centralized, terms negotiated are vague and skimpy, and worker-management councils established outside the purview of the trade union machinery duplicate some of these loose negotiations. There are no formal grievance procedures in most Japanese steel companies. If the grievances cannot be worked out in the shop, they become the subject of top-level negotiations. These frequently take the form of "consultation" between top management and top local union leaders. Steel is no "pattern setter" in Japan; rather, the determination of wage and bonus levels in the industry tend to be influenced by Government scales. There is almost no private arbitration resorted to and disputes tend to be resolved by the parties and occasionally via the intervention (frequently unofficial) of the Labor Relations Commissions. Government legislation provides for a large number of standards and terms and conditions of employment which, in the United States, are for the most part bargainable issues.

In these moderate strike experience countries, we again find a variety of industrial bargaining machinery, dispute-settlement arrangements, and varying degrees and methods of Government intervention.

(g) In Australia, we find bargaining between well-organized parties and a State-imposed system of compulsory conciliation and arbitration. There is one major steel-producing company; on the employee side we find about 60 percent of the manual workers covered by the Federation of Ironworkers and skilled maintenance workers covered by some 16 other unions. Suspicions of the political motivation of some of the craft unions and skepticism about the possibility of winning any major concessions through the use of the strike weapon have effectively limited industrywide solidarity among unions. The steel industry seems content to avoid any major concessions in direct negotiations and to turn over responsibility for the determination of wages and conditions to the Industrial Commission. The tribunals have generally been reluctant to introduce radical changes in the existing structure of wages and conditions, and this has led unions to turn to legislation as a means of securing major improvements. Despite the fact that in theory the arbitration system is intended as a substitute for the employment of direct economic pressure, it is difficult to estimate to what extent, if any, it has reduced overall loss to the community as a result of strikes. Perhaps the safest generalization is that under arbitration there are fewer protracted industrywide strikes and more disputes leading to work stoppages than might otherwise be the case.

(h) In France, we find strong employer associations, weak and divided unions, area-wide bargaining which generally settles little, and supplementary plant-level negotiations which may or may not involve effective collective bargaining. The State sets the "minimum vital" and many other "rules" governing working conditions, provides for compulsory conciliation of disputes, mediation, and voluntary arbitration. Conciliation or mediation has been used very little in the French steel industry, however. Day-to-day relations at the plant level operate within the framework of the legislation dealing with the *Comité d'Entreprise* and the *Delegué de Personnel.* Although steel production is one of the major industries in the private sector, Government has been able nevertheless to exert a certain amount of influence over wage and other labor policies because many steel companies (particularly in eastern France) received important financial assistance from the Government during their post-World War II modernization and expansion programs.

(i) In Canada, with bargaining machinery most similar to the American, there is the distinctive two-stage compulsory conciliation arrangement provided by Federal and Provincial legislation.

Some Modest Conclusions

Despite this variegated industrial relations experience underlying the generally modest level of industrial strike experience, there are a few tentative, general conclusions that appear most relevant for American experience.

(1) The role of Government (either in ownership or in dispute settlement) in no instance of low strike activity (Britain, Sweden, Belgium, Germany, Japan, and Luxembourg) appears to be the critical or principal determinant of industrial peace in the industry. In Australia and in Canada, where some form of compulsory governmental dispute-settlement machinery is involved, the collective

bargaining process reflects this in the generally more intractable and extreme positions initially adopted by the parties as they look toward the eventuality of dispute settlement by Government tribunal. Revision in the Government's role in dispute settlement in American steel industrial relations is likely therefore to assume a tactical rather than a strategic role in affecting industrial peace or conflict results, and considerations of this factor are inextricably bound up with a congeries of additional considerations concerning the "actors" and their own attitudes and machinery.

(2) In those countries in which collective bargaining, rather than bargaining via the legislature, is the predominant mode of rule-setting in industrial relations, the parties in steel have accepted and respected each other's survival and sovereignty. In Britain or in Sweden or in Australia, the question of complete employer acceptance of trade unionism has been buried for a long, long time. Bakke's assertions in *Mutual Survival*, the principal conclusion of the Final Report of the National Planning Association's *Causes of Industrial Peace* series, and the countless other reiterations of the same theme—i.e., that a necessary, if not sufficient, condition for industrial peace in collective bargaining situations is genuine and unquestioned mutual acceptance—still appear to be relevant in considering variations in bargaining experience.

(3) Finally, it is interesting to note that the bargaining machinery in steel in several of the low strike experience countries minimizes the potential for conflict growing out of all-encompassing top-side negotiations. The "hierarchy" of bargaining levels involving the coordination of national or industrywide, district or regional, and local terms and conditions of employment tends to reserve for each bargaining layer those issues about which the bargaining parties are best equipped to negotiate. The apparent prerequisites for such split-level bargaining involve either strong unions with effective internal discipline and coordinated bargaining with equally effective employer associations and individual employers, or splintered and relatively ineffectual local bargaining units which tend generally to be dominated by strong employers and employer groups. There is little doubt that although in both instances the arrangements are conducive to "peace," the substantive achievements made via bargaining may vary markedly. Yet, in light of the 1959 American experience with the work rules issue, the practices of the British bargaining machinery, for example, with respect to relegation of issues to the proper working level of familiarity in the bargaining hierarchy, are certainly worth more than a casual glance.